www.wadsworth.com

www.wadsworth.com is the World Wide Web site for Wadsworth and is your direct source to dozens of online resources.

At *www.wadsworth.com* you can find out about supplements, demonstration software, and student resources. You can also send email to many of our authors and preview new publications and exciting new technologies.

www.wadsworth.com
Changing the way the world learns®

CONFLICT AND COOPERATION
Evolving Theories of International Relations

Second Edition

Marc A. Genest
University of Rhode Island
Visiting Professor, Naval War College

THOMSON
WADSWORTH

Australia • Canada • Mexico • Singapore • Spain
United Kingdom • United States

THOMSON

™

WADSWORTH

Political Science Editor: *David Tatom*
Assistant Editors: *Heather Hogan/Rebecca Green*
Editorial Assistant: *Reena Thomas*
Technology Project Manager: *Melinda Newfarmer*
Marketing Manager: *Janise A. Fry*
Marketing Assistant: *Mary Ho*
Advertising Project Manager: *Nathaniel Bergson-Michelson*
Project Manager, Editorial Production: *Emily Smith*
Print/Media Buyer: *Rebecca Cross*
Permissions Editor: *Elizabeth Zuber*

Production Service: *Lachina Publishing Services*
Copy Editor: *Lachina Publishing Services*
Illustrator: *Lachina Publishing Services*
Compositor: *Lachina Publishing Services*
Cover Designer: *Sue Hart*
Cover Image: *The Studio Dog/Getty Images*
Text and Cover Printer: *Webcom*

Printed in Canada

2 3 4 5 6 7   07 06 05 04

For more information about our products, contact us at:
Thomson Learning Academic Resource Center
1-800-423-0563

For permission to use material from this text,
contact us by:
Phone: 1-800-730-2214 **Fax:** 1-800-730-2215
Web: http://www.thomsonrights.com

Library of Congress Control Number: 2003110883

ISBN 0-534-50690-9

Wadsworth/Thomson Learning
10 Davis Drive
Belmont, CA 94002-3098
USA

Asia
Thomson Learning
5 Shenton Way #01-01
UIC Building
Singapore 068808

Australia/New Zealand
Thomson Learning
102 Dodds Street
Southbank, Victoria 3006
Australia

Canada
Nelson
1120 Birchmount Road
Toronto, Ontario M1K 5G4
Canada

Europe/Middle East/Africa
Thomson Learning
High Holborn House
50/51 Bedford Row
London WC1R 4LR
United Kingdom

Latin America
Thomson Learning
Seneca, 53
Colonia Polanco
11560 Mexico D.F.
Mexico

Spain/Portugal
Paraninfo
Calle/Magallanes, 25
28015 Madrid, Spain

TABLE OF CONTENTS

System Level
International Relations Theories

State-Level International Relations Theories

Chapter Ten
PEACE STUDIES THEORY   547

PREFACE

There is an ancient Chinese curse that condemns an individual to "live in interesting times." The past several years since the first edition of this book was published certainly qualify as interesting. The panoply of opportunities posed by rapid globalization and emerging markets, the tragic events of September 11, 2001, and the 2003 war with Iraq all demonstrate that global politics continues and will continue to present us with unexpected challenges and prospects.

Taken together, these astonishing events provide us with an important opportunity from which to step back and reexamine our study of world politics. Perhaps no other period in time so clearly epitomizes the title of (and need for) this book, *Conflict and Cooperation: Evolving Theories of International Relations.* Our past and present are full of vivid accounts of war and conflict. Yet we sometimes forget that our history has been equally characterized by cooperation between people and states. Just as these relationships evolve, so too must our theories about the world, how it operates, and our place within it.

This constantly shifting and complex international environment is demanding for scholar and student alike. With this in mind, the second edition of this text has attempted to place contemporary events such as September 11, the invasion of Afghanistan, and U.S. intervention in Iraq into a broader theoretical framework. Consequently, among the seventeen new articles in this edition, seven readings were specifically selected to offer a sampling of responses to these dramatic events by noted scholars and practioners each of whom represent the major paradigms presented in this book. For example, the reading by Henry Kissinger, in chapter one, offers a realist response to the events of September 11. He places great emphasis on using U.S. allies to assist in managing the threat posed by global terrorism. In contrast, the selection by Noam Chomsky from chapter 4—Class System Theory—explains the events of September 11 as arising from a backlash against U.S. global hegemony. In chapter 5 the article by Saba Gul Khattak, presents a feminist perspective which focuses on the U.S. bombing of Afghanistan and its impact on Afghan women, while Benjamin Barber offers a civilizationist interpretation of recent events in his article in chapter 6. All of these new articles offer unique perspectives of current events and allow the reader to understand how various theories can be used to place contemporary events in a wider theoretical perspective.

The overall purpose of this book is to present and discuss classic offerings in international relations theory as well as contemporary selections that propose new ways of interpreting human behavior. This type of theorizing is part of a long-standing tradition in history—attempting to answer the question, "Why do people (and, hence, states) act the way they do?" In answering that question, theories of international relations provide frameworks that enable scholars and statesmen to describe, analyze, and predict the behavior of states. The ultimate purpose of such theories is to help formulate effective policies.

The difference between this book of readings and others that focus on international relations theory lies in both its organization and user friendliness. These two characteristics are actually linked. First, the organization is based on three traditional levels of analysis: system, state, and individual, and because many other main textbooks and curricula are structured according to levels of analysis, this reader serves as a *practical* complement. Also, this reader serves as an important *theoretical* complement because the levels are valuable conceptual tools that provide explanations and points of focus; thus, the structure of this book helps to simplify and organize our thinking about complex international phenomena.

The most important difference between this book of readings and others is its user friendliness. Because the intent is to provide a survey of some important classical and contemporary contributions to international relations theories, the level of reading is somewhat sophisticated. But, rather than omitting challenging articles, a number of pedagogical tools have been provided to assist the student in the learning process.

First, the introduction to the book discusses the nature of international relations theory, theory formulation, and the levels of analysis; this discussion sets the stage for the entire volume. Second, each of the three parts of the book opens with an overview of the given level of analysis and of the general characteristics of the theories falling within that level. Third, a box, which summarizes the core components of each theory, is placed at the beginning of each chapter. This box promotes quick understanding of, as well as comparisons among, theories. Fourth, each chapter contains a substantial introduction, which is central to the pedagogical emphasis of this book. These introductions discuss the development, characteristics, and strengths and weaknesses of each theory; in addition, they discuss the readings, their individual themes, and their contributions to the theories. Fifth, each reading is accompanied by a headnote that provides a brief description of the reading and a biography of the author. Sixth, two questions at the end of each reading may be used for class discussion or writing assignments. Last, key terms are noted in bold type throughout the chapter introductions and are listed, with their definitions, at the end of each chapter's introduction.

This reader is divided into three parts: system, state, and individual levels of analysis, and including the introductory chapter, it has 10 chapters and 44 readings. Of these readings, 18 readings were eliminated from the first edition while 17 articles were added to reflect the evolving nature of IR theory. Part I covers the System Level of Analysis. Chapter 2 on Realist Theory presents classic as well as neoclassic realism, and includes, among others, such thinkers as Thucydides, Machiavelli, Morgenthau, and Waltz. Chapter 3 on Liberal Theory presents the institutional and economic branches of Liberalism. Such writers as Grotius and Wilson, show how international institutions and law have a vital role in affecting the behavior of states, and Nye and Keohane discuss the growing influence of economic interdependence and nonstate actors in fostering cooperation and in guiding world economic policy. Chapter 4 on Class System Theory includes articles on Marxism, imperialism, dependency, and the roots and implications of the collapse of the former Soviet Union. Selections are from such writers as Marx, Wallerstein, and Halliday. Chapter 5 on Postmodernism covers the newest system-level paradigm of international relations. This chapter introduces readers to the Constructivist and Feminist branches of Postmodernism. Scholars such as Lapid and Wendt discuss the importance of ideas and culture in shaping our understanding of global affairs. The postmodernist chapter also includes Feminist Theory in International Relations and provides excerpts from pioneering efforts to reinterpret the nature of world politics; these show how and to what effect feminist perspectives and women have been excluded from international affairs. The Tickner and Keohane articles may be of particular interest because they engage in a debate over the relative merits and contributions of Feminist IR theory.

The State Level of Analysis is the subject of Part II. Chapter 6 on Political Cultural Theory first focuses on regimes and their influence in determining a country's domestic and foreign policy behavior; of note is Fukuyama's end of history thesis. The chapter then focuses on the civilizationists' arguments, as expressed by Huntington, which emphasize the impact of culture (e.g., ethnicity, race, religion, language, and traditions) in shaping the nature of a country and its policies. Chapter 7 on Decision-Making Process Theory shifts to a discussion of how the nuts and bolts of state governance affect a country's behavior. Finally, the influence of bureaucracies and policymaking structures are discussed by such authors as Snyder, Sapin, Bruck, and Allison.

Part III of the text concentrates on the Individual Level of Analysis. Chapter 8 on Human Nature Theory includes classic works on the basic nature of mankind and on how this nature affects our relations with one another; selections are from Aristotle, Hobbes, and Freud. Chapter 9 on Cognitive Theory presents readings on the interaction between nature and nurture. Lasswell and Hermann discuss the effects of personality traits on foreign policy and Jervis analyzes the role of shared perceptions. Chapter 10 on Peace Studies Theory also offers a new approach to the study of international relations; it embraces sociological analysis, Gandhian nonviolence, and epistemology. Crews and Stein separately discuss the goals of peace studies and the varied approaches it employs.

It is vital in our changing environment to acquaint new students of international relations with contemporary approaches in world affairs. This collection of readings is one of the few comprehensive sources that offers selections on such important post-Cold War theories as political culture (regimist and civilizationist), postmodernism, and peace studies. With current shifts in international politics resulting from the increasing pressures of economic and social globalization, new theories of international affairs now have more opportunity to be considered in the academic and policymaking communities.

ACKNOWLEDGMENTS

I would like to thank the following reviewers for their valuable suggestions: Ralph G. Carter, Texas Christian University; Larry Elowitz, Georgia College; Howard P. Lehman, University of Utah; Joseph Lepgold, Georgetown University; Susan Stoudinger Northcutt, University of South Florida-Tampa; Henry A. Shockley, Boston University; Randolph M. Siverson, University of California-Davis; Donald A. Sylvan, Ohio State University-Columbus; Mary Ann Tetreault, Old Dominion University; Paul A. Tharp, University of Oklahoma; Herbert K. Tillema, University of Missouri-Columbia; (second edition) Timothy J. White, Xavier University; Jeff Corntassel, Department of Political Science, Virginia Tech; Stephen Twing, Assistant Professor, Political Science, Frostburg State University; Juliet Johnson, Stanford University; Diddy M. Hitchins, PhD., University of Alaska-Anchorage.

I owe special thanks to Kailash Mohaptra and Christopher Lamonica, Adjunct Professors at the University of Rhode Island. I also thank my colleague Art Stein from the University of Rhode Island for his insightful comments and contributions to Chapter 10. Over the course of this project, I have received wonderful support from my research assistant Todd Anderson, as well as from David Munoz-Storer, and Armando Heredia, all of whom performed above and beyond my expectations. Thanks also go to Jeffrey Hamill and Paul Paliotta for their help with the second edition of this text.

I am sincerely grateful to the University of Rhode Island, its Political Science Department, and its students for providing an academic environment that is conducive to both scholarship and teaching. Also, much of the work done on the second edition of this book was completed during my time as a visiting professor in the Strategy and Policy Department at the United States Naval War College. I wish to specifically thank Thomas Nichols, the chairman of the Strategy and Policy department at the War College for his support and encouragement of this project.

From the beginning to the end of this project, the staff of Harcourt Brace and Wadsworth have been a pleasure to work with. I would like to thank David Tatom, Acquisitions Editor, for his faith in the viability of this project. A special thanks goes to Fritz Schanz who played the dual role of Developmental Editor and diplomat as he managed to convince me that deadlines are flexible, but not imaginary. I also thank Barbara Moreland and Emily Smith, Project Editors, for efficiently managing editorial and production responsibilities. Heather Hogan, Wadsworth's Assistant Editor for the second edition of this book was also wonderful to work with and deserves high praise for her work on this project.

Finally, I would like to thank my beautiful and talented wife Pauline Genest for her love, support, editorial assistance and most importantly, for being the best mom in the world to our two children Nathaniel and Caroline.

CONFLICT AND COOPERATION

Evolving Theories of International Relations

Second Edition

Chapter 1

INTRODUCTION

WHAT IS INTERNATIONAL RELATIONS THEORY?

More than ever, our lives are shaped by the world in which we live and the people, or groups of people, that surround us. We have formed boundaries, cultures, and communities that define what we call nations. The relationship of nations and their behavior toward one another—international relations—is what makes up our human history.

Scholars throughout history have studied the human condition—assessing, evaluating, and even predicting patterns of behavior—using and developing various theories. A **theory** is a proposition, or set of propositions, that tries to analyze, explain or predict something. An **international relations theory,** then, is defined as a set of principles and guidelines used to analyze both world events and relations between states. International relations scholars often interchange various terms with theory, such as *paradigm, model, image,* or *perspective.* Whatever the words, the important thing to remember is that theories help to assess past and present conditions and, in turn, provide a reasonable basis for predicting future trends.

The development of international relations theory could be compared to a laboratory experiment. Scientists use their knowledge of specific elements and their properties to predict how they might behave in various combinations and under specific conditions, as well as to produce a certain reaction or outcome. Theories about international relations are formed in a similar way. In this case, though, the laboratory is the international system as a whole, and we must speculate about the behavior of the states and individuals within it.

Theories of international relations can be grouped into two broad categories: explanatory theories and prescriptive theories. As the name implies, **explanatory theories** try to explain events and circumstances. They are based on description and evaluation of past events, conditions, and patterns of behavior. Scholars form a theory based on how nations have acted and interacted in the past in order to predict what their future behavior may be. For example, many theorists have studied past wars, trying to find certain patterns of behavior that may tell them why war is such a perennial problem in international relations. One popular international relations theory, realism, can be considered an explanatory theory.

Prescriptive theories, also referred to as normative theories, do not discount the value of historical experience but also incorporate moral principles and the setting of goals. A **prescriptive theory** is a set of principles or guidelines that contain overt value judgments about how the world ought to be rather than how the world actually is. Prescriptive theory often involves the development of standards or principles for the conduct of international relations. Based on both past and contemporary conditions and patterns, theories prescribe or suggest a particular course of action, policy, or doctrine. This prescription is designed to improve and enhance relations between states within the international system. Peace studies is an example of this category of prescriptive theories. Many theories, such as liberalism, class system theory, and postmodernism, actually cross over, incorporating both the explanatory and prescriptive methods.

Finally, it is important to note that a theory may be correct, incorrect, or even partially correct. In the end, it is up to individual students to decide for themselves which theory or theories provide the most accurate and useful guidelines for understanding the course of global politics.

How Is International Relations Theory Formed?

We have discussed what international relations theory is; now let us address the question of how it is formed. In developing a theory of international relations, social scientists and scholars of world affairs consider a number of factors. They do not simply look at distinct, isolated events that have occurred over the course of history. They also examine the various elements that acted as the driving force of the crises. These elements provide important clues in discovering how a crisis originated. The nature of the states and system when not in crisis can serve as a starting point for the investigation. That is, the specific details of a crisis lose their meaning if we do not know what led up to the event and what happened afterwards.

Scholars begin with what is called a **hypothesis.** A hypothesis is essentially an educated guess or proposition about how or why something—an event or specific set of conditions—occurred. A hypothesis must, however, have a certain degree of probability; if one does not believe something to be possible, there is no point in determining its likelihood.

The hypothesis is then put to the test using certain methods. The methodology commonly employed in the development of international relations theory consists of several components, used either singly or in combination: analysis of historical events, conditions, or progressions; reasoned deduction based on the facts or evidence; and assessment of quantitative data.

By using these techniques, scholars and students of international relations come up with theories about the behavior and interaction of states. These theories might be explained through case studies. A **case study** uses a specific event, set of circumstances, or period of time to introduce and/or exemplify the key concepts of a given theory. A **concept** is an idea, thought, or notion derived from the theory.

There can be no absolutes in theorizing about international relations, particularly given the vaguaries and random actions that can, and do, occur in human interaction. Unlike many stable, constant elements of a laboratory experiment— whether solids, gases, or liquids—the world is an ever-changing environment. A theory of international relations may well be relevant and applicable during a specific period of history with a specific set of circumstances. New theories, however, must be periodically adapted and applied to our changing environment. Quite apart from simply invalidating the "old" theory, this continuous theoretical growth instead speaks to the exciting, even limitless, possibilities for examining, evaluating, and developing international relations theory.

LEVELS OF ANALYSIS: A METHOD FOR STUDYING INTERNATIONAL RELATIONS THEORY

One apparently lasting methodology for studying international relations theory is what is known as the levels of analysis. Developed originally in the 1950s by Kenneth Waltz, **levels of analysis** is exactly what it says—a method for examining international relations theory based on three different "units of measure," in purely scientific terms, or "levels." These levels are—from broad to narrow in scope— system level, state level, and individual level. That is, each theory or set of theories associated with a given level emphasizes the characteristics, conditions, and confines of that particular level in understanding and explaining world events and relations between states.[1]

Different levels focus on different questions. The system level of analysis looks at the international environment and how that shapes the pattern of interaction between countries. At the system level of analysis, questions center on how the distribution of military and economic power among states affects the course of international relations and how the global political environment affects the behavior of states. The second level, the state level of analysis, examines how states make foreign policy. This level asks two fundamental questions: First, are some types of governments more prone to war than others?

Second, does the competition for influence over policy making between interest groups and within bureaucracies have a significant impact on a state's foreign policy? Finally, individual-level analyses center on whether and how the characteristics, values, and perspectives of individual leaders affect their foreign policy decisions.

The levels of analysis concept is a tool to assist us in our examination of international relations. It helps us understand that international politics is the result of numerous sources. Each level features a different view of the event or events we are examining. It is like taking a picture from different distances. The system-level approach will give you a sense of the broad features of the environment and provide the widest perspective, but will give very little detail of the individual parts. The state level can be compared to a photograph taken from several steps closer.

---

[1] Some works on international relations theory have identified as many as six levels of analysis: individual, roles, government, society, international relations, and the world system. See Bruce Russet and Harvey Starr's *World Politics: The Menu for Choice,* 4th edition (New York: W.H. Freeman and Company, 1992), pp. 11–17. For this textbook, Kenneth Waltz's original three levels provide students with a clearer, more basic framework for studying international relations theory.

We can now distinguish the objects in the photograph, though specific details remain unclear. The individual level provides the closest look at our subject, offering terrific detail but eliminating the perspective provided by the broader views. Like the different photographs, all three levels of analysis have unique value. Together they provide the most accurate and complete understanding of international relations.

For an international relations example, we see that the origins of the Cold War cannot be analyzed properly without the proper context—the role of certain key individual leaders, the types of countries involved, and the way the structure of the international system shaped or constrained the behavior of the United States and the Soviet Union. This provides perspective on the causes and ramifications of the event itself.

At the beginning of the Cold War, many countries were still suffering from the effects of World War II. Great Britain was weak from the effort of defeating Nazi Germany, and all three of the traditional European powers—Great Britain, France, and Germany—were trying to rebuild from the rubble of countless battles and bombings. Indeed, after the United States dropped the first two atomic bombs on Japan in 1945, all of the former Axis powers (Germany, Italy, and Japan) who had initiated World War II had been defeated.

Only two nations at this time were strong enough to take leading roles on the international stage: the United States and the Soviet Union. But the styles of government in these two states were at opposite ends of the political spectrum and were not at all compatible. In the democratic United States, individual rights were and are valued and protected. Checks and balances within the government and on the government ensure these individual freedoms, yet provide a structure for national self-determination. Reliance on capitalist economic principles with free trade and open markets both helps to support American-style democracy and is supported by the democratic process.

The communist government of the Soviet Union emphasized collective rights over individual rights and freedoms. Power flowed from the center of the political structure and was dictatorial in nature, particularly under the rule of Joseph Stalin in the early Cold War years. Along with this centralized political authority came centralized economic planning. That is, the government owns the "means of production"—from factories and farms to tools and other equipment. Essentially, everyone in the Soviet Union was an employee of the state, and private ownership was kept to a bare minimum.

So, in the broadest sense, we see that the world was in a very delicate position at the beginning of the Cold War. The traditional European powers of Great Britain, France, and Germany were recovering from the damage of World War II. Only the United States and the Soviet Union were powerful enough to influence world politics. The problem lay in the extreme differences of the two nations. Each state wanted to channel the course of international politics in its own direction and rebuild the world in its own image. For the Soviet Union, that image was communist. For the United States, the image was democratic capitalism. These differences and the power vacuum created by the weakness of the other states in the international system contributed to the competition and confrontation of the United States and Soviet Union.

In addition to the weakness of the system and the confrontational relationship between the two countries, we might also take a step closer and speculate about the psychological motivations of individual leaders. With Joseph Stalin as head of the Soviet Union during this period, his need for absolute authority, as well as his insecurities and ruthlessness, shaped both his decisions and Soviet foreign policy. These tendencies, combined with Stalin's documented fear of the West, compounded—and was compounded by—the shaky condition of the international system and the inevitable friction between the two competing political-economic systems.

On the American side, the fact that Harry Truman quite suddenly became president of the United States upon the death of Franklin Roosevelt made him feel somewhat anxious about the need to appear decisive and in control. His state of mind with respect to the Soviet Union is best described in his own words: "If the Soviets do not wish to join us, they could go to Hell." This attitude may have exacerbated hostility between the two nations and made cooperation much less likely in the post–World War II environment.

Let us now reexamine our example on the origins of the Cold War within the levels of analysis framework. On a system level, the United States and the Soviet Union were the two most powerful states left standing in the post-war world. The global situation was in turmoil. Formerly strong nations were helpless in the wake of a massive war effort.

So, we have two strong powers dominating the international system. Looking at the situation from a state-level perspective, conflict between the democratic United States and the communist Soviet Union is not surprising. The countries had radically different political and economic structures with neither, at that point, willing to compromise.

Finally, on an individual level, there was a serious mistrust on the part of both President Truman and Soviet leader Stalin. There was an almost cyclical reinforcement between these different levels of analysis and interaction. Competition between the United States and the Soviet Union was natural because of their differences. This competition reinforced those differences and fed the fears and wariness of the individual leaders.

Overall, we see that there are points to be made at each level of analysis with respect to this example. Let us now examine the specifics of each level—system, state, and individual—and the theories of international relations that go along with them.

System Level

Beginning with the broadest method, the theories associated with **system-level analysis**—realist, liberal, class system, and, to a lesser extent, postmodernism—all tend to suggest that relations between states can be explained by factors that influence the system as a whole and by the characteristics and proclivities of the system itself. Allocation of power among states or groups of states, economic interdependence, and distribution of wealth are some of the general factors used in system-level analysis. The dynamic created both within and by the system then shapes the relations of states and individuals.

For example, one type of system-level theory is known as the realist school of thought. Realist theory emphasizes that the distribution of power in the international system shapes the behavior of the states within it. Some realists focus on the structure of the international system and the fact that there is no international authority to achieve and maintain global peace and stability among nations. Realists call this condition—the absence of an overarching government in the system—anarchy. States, then, are forced to be self-reliant and use their own power—or establish a mutually beneficial alliance structure with other states—to preserve their independence. Power—its uneven distribution in the system and the quest of states for it—shapes the behavior of nations and alliances.

The first scholar to remark on the importance of power and shifts in power was the Greek historian Thucydides, in 461 B.C. Using the rivalry between the city-states of Athens and Sparta as his case study, Thucydides found not only that uneven rates of development and levels of power create tension between nations but that generally "strong states do what they have the power to do and weak states accept what they must." And with no international government in place to preserve law and order, as well as the rights of the weak, it is understandable that power—its acquisition and preservation—becomes an important commodity.

If the realists are generally pessimistic in their view of power and the anarchic nature of the international system, a second group of theorists, whom we shall call the liberals, take a somewhat brighter view. Though liberals, like realists, accept that the world is anarchic, they also suggest that this condition is not static and the system can be changed. Liberals base this assumption on the notion that even in the absence of an overarching government in the international system, a harmony of interests does exist among nations. This implies that the incentive to cooperate with one another is stronger than the incentive for conflict. Creating international organizations and international law can build on these bonds and further promote good relations between states.

Liberals who advocate this kind of institutional approach—that is, the creation of international political organizations and international law—are known as liberal institutionalists (sometimes referred to as idealists). Proponents of this theory are looking to establish an international society in which hostility and mistrust no longer characterize relations among states. Selfishness is replaced by mutual respect and understanding.

Despite their faith in the ability of these organizations and the rule of law to help avoid conflict, liberal institutionalists acknowledge that some friction within the system is inevitable. At these times, states can come together under what they call collective security. The term *collective security* suggests that if all states agree to join together to defend the independence of every state in the international community, then their collective ability to rebuff the aggression of a single state is greatly enhanced. Similar to the old adage about safety in numbers, collective security provides for the safety and security of its members.

According to liberal institutionalists, cooperation and collective security can be established through the use of international organizations. Thus liberal institutionalists are proponents of international organizations such as the United Nations which focus on enhancing cooperation and stability. These organizations are designed to preserve and enforce specific rules and norms in global politics. Economic liberals, on the other hand, emphasize the importance of other transnational actors, such as multinational corporations (MNCs). MNCs build bonds between nations based on economics and trade. Economic liberals contend that by expanding international economic ties, all nations will have a stake in preserving peace and promoting stability. In short, while the institutional and economic branches of liberalism emphasize different mechanisms and actors, they both focus on the common goal of building international cooperation.

The third theory in our presentation of system-level analyses is based primarily on an economic foundation. Class system theory suggests that the distribution of wealth within the international system shapes the system itself. Among class system theorists, it is generally accepted that this shape is capitalist. In the world capitalist system, wealthy people and wealthy countries mold global affairs to their own benefit. This perpetuates a cycle of dependency among poor and weak states.

Karl Marx and V. I. Lenin were perhaps the best known advocates of this theory. They contended that this exploitation crossed state boundaries and would eventually unite the working class, or proletariat, in an international revolution against imperialist domination. Conflict, then, occurs primarily on an economic basis— the global exploitation of the poor by the wealthy and by the imperialist force of capitalism.

The final system-level theory is labeled postmodernism. This paradigm includes a rather diverse array of theories that have certain key assumptions in common. Postmodernism focuses primarily on the importance of ideas and culture in shaping our understanding of international politics. Postmodernists argue that traditional theories of international relations are inherently subjective and merely reflect the biases and motivations of the people who created the theories in the first place. Many postmodernists argue that it is impossible to construct an objective or unbiased theory of international relations and therefore focus on how our understanding of international relations is shaped by our beliefs and social identities.

State Level

State-level analysis brings the examination of relations between states and the formulation of international relations theory a step closer. State level emphasizes the nature and characteristics of individual states in evaluating the dynamics of global politics and the international system. As we see in our example on the origins of the Cold War, the fundamental differences between communist states and capitalist democracies can be a source of tension.

Both of the two major state-level theories that we will discuss in this book— political regime theory and decision-making process theory—emphasize the domestic factors of nations in their international behavior. These factors include the type of government and how it operates, level of citizen participation, sense of popular well-being, and adaptability of the state to both internal and external pressures and changes.

KEY CONCEPTS

Case study   uses a specific event, set of circumstances, or period of time to introduce and/or exemplify the key concepts of a given theory.

Concept   is an idea, thought, or notion derived from a theory.

Explanatory theories   try to explain events and circumstances. They are based on description and evaluation of past events, conditions, and patterns of behavior. Scholars form a theory based on how nations have acted and interacted in the past in order to predict what their future behavior might be.

Hypothesis   is essentially an educated guess or proposition about how or why something—an event or specific set of conditions—occurred. A hypothesis must, however, have a certain degree of probability.

Individual-level analysis   is an approach to understanding international relations that focuses on the role and impact of particular individuals, or looks for explanations based on "human nature," or common characteristics of all individuals.

International relations theory   is a set of principles and guidelines used to analyze both world events and relations between states. Such theories help to assess past and present conditions and, in turn, provide a reasonable basis for predicting future trends.

Levels of analysis   is a method for examining international relations theory based on three different perspectives or levels. These levels are, from broad to narrow in scope, system level, state level, and individual level.

(continued)

Important

In political regime theory, the central question is whether the type of government of a nation has an impact on that nation's foreign policy. More specifically, we might ask, are authoritarian regimes more prone to conflict or war than democracies?

Francis Fukuyama argues that different types of governments do behave differently and that democracies are, indeed, less likely to go to war than authoritarian or totalitarian regimes. He generally attributes this to the fact that the political ideals forming the basis of democracies incorporate a great respect for human rights, the value of international law, and the resolution of conflict through negotiation. Since democratic leaders must answer to a popular mandate, the foreign policy of democratic countries conforms to these principles as closely as possible.

(continued from previous page)

Each theory or set of theories associated with a given level emphasizes the characteristics, conditions, and confines of that particular level in understanding and explaining world events and relations between states.

Prescriptive theory is a set of principles and guidelines that contain overt value judgments about how the world ought to be rather than how the world actually is. Prescriptive theory often involves the development of standards or principles for the conduct of international relations. Based on both past and contemporary conditions and patterns, these theories prescribe or suggest a particular course of action, policy, or doctrine. This prescription is designed to improve and enhance relations between states within the international system.

State-level analysis is an analytical approach to international relations that focuses on the domestic or internal causes of state actions. State-level theories attempt to explain international relations by emphasizing the internal workings of the state itself.

System-level analysis attempts to explain international relations by focusing on the manner in which the structure of the international system (global distribution of resources among states) shapes or constrains the actions of states. System-level theories contend that relations between states can be explained by factors that influence the system as a whole and by the characteristics and proclivities of the system itself.

Theory is a proposition or set of propositions that tries to analyze, explain, or predict something.

The other state-level theory presented, decision-making process theory, emphasizes not the type of government but the characteristics of the bureaucratic machine itself. That is, how do governments make foreign policy and how does that, in turn, affect foreign policy?

Process theorists contend that decisions are quite often the result of compromise between competing factions or groups within the government bureaucracy. An example might be the influence of the U.S. military-industrial complex on companies that specialize in manufacturing military hardware and the influence branches of the military have over the country's defense and foreign policy. The role of these factions in the government and the competition between them are important contributing factors to the politics of the state.

Individual Level

The third and final level of analysis takes a look at the role of the individual in society. **Individual level** approaches to understanding international politics emphasize the common characteristics of all individuals, often referred to as "human nature," or they look for explanations based on the impact that particular individuals have on the foreign policy of a given state.

Individual-level explanations examine the human actor in several different ways. The first approach looks at the base characteristics of human nature in general. According to Thomas Hobbes, it is the nature of the individual, which is naturally insecure and aggressive, that shapes, defines, and characterizes society and government. The second analyzes the motives, principles, and preconceptions of individuals. Thomas Carlyle once said, "The history of the world is but the biography of great men." This notion suggests that the perceptions, misperceptions, and behavior of individual leaders can have a dramatic impact on the actions of a state. These actions then create ripples through the international system as a whole.

Using these guidelines, this study will examine the individual level of international-relations analysis in terms of three theoretical treatments: human nature, the nature of the individual, and the mitigation of human aggression. The articles in this section offer a range of viewpoints. From pessimists, such as Thomas Hobbes, one is left with the impression that people are by nature aggressive and driven in a quest for power. Only strong governments, Hobbes suggests, can mitigate these tendencies and preserve domestic and international stability.

An alternate approach addresses the ability of a single leader or personality to shape the actions of a nation. In so doing, that individual is able to alter the course of political interaction on a global scale. The rise and fall of Adolf Hitler is one of the most vivid contemporary examples of such a leader, but he is certainly not alone. From George Washington to Ronald Reagan, from Lenin to Mikhail Gorbachev, individuals have made, and no doubt will continue to make, their marks on the international system.

Finally, an optimistic perspective of the individual is set forth in the last section. As part of the relatively new field of peace studies, Arthur Stein characterizes humans as potentially "good" and capable of positively transforming individuals, societies, and the world in general. The theory of peace studies more broadly focuses on building harmonious relations among individuals and states. It asserts that if certain prescriptions are followed, a more peaceful and stable world may be created. Individual enlightenment, accordingly, is the key.

It is important to understand that Waltz's three levels of analysis for international relations theory differ not in their coverage but in their emphasis. No single level by itself can provide a complete explanation of events and changes in world politics. Each level organizes the facts in its own particular fashion, and each level focuses on different facts. Only by examining what scholars and proponents of all three levels have said about individuals and their societies as well as the global environment can we hope to create a more complete picture of our world and our future.

The second reading in this chapter, by Stephen Walt, presents a very insightful evaluation of the strengths and weaknesses of the four predominant system-level paradigms of international relations theory. It is important for readers to note that in some cases, the names of the theories differ from those used in this text. For example, Walt uses the term "radical theory" to describe what this book refers to as class system theory (Chapter 4). There are two explanations for this confusion. The first is that international relations scholars are stubborn academics and cannot seem to agree on a common label for the different paradigms. The second and more profound reason is that international relations theory is a dynamic field of study. Scholars constantly devise new theories, and even the traditional theories continue to evolve and adjust to fill in theoretical gaps or respond to changes in global affairs. To limit the confusion, each chapter begins by identifying the alternative labels for every paradigm that is covered in this text.

One final note: The articles in this book have been organized by level of analysis—system, state, and individual, in that order. This methodology is an analytical tool used to clarify and order our exploration of the different dimensions of international relations theory. However, students should be aware that many of the theorists presented in this volume incorporate some of the basic assumptions of more than one level of analysis. For example, Hans Morganthau, a realist, is categorized as a system-level theorist even though he had strong views about human nature (individual level) and the role of governments (state level) in shaping foreign policy. His overall emphasis, though, was primarily directed at the behavior of states as shaped by the international system. So again, it is a matter of emphasis rather than exclusivity that allows us to categorize theories according to the three levels of analysis.

1.   Man, the State and War

Kenneth N. Waltz

In this selection, Kenneth N. Waltz identifies three alternative "images," or "levels of analysis," that can be used to explain the causes of war: individual, state, and international systems. Waltz concludes that although the immediate causes of war are found in the individual and state levels, the permissive cause of war is the anarchic nature of the international system. This excerpt is from *Man, the State and War* (1959).

Kenneth N. Waltz is Ford Professor of Political Science at the University of California, Berkeley. His other books include *Foreign Policy and Democratic Politics: The American and British Experience* (1967, reissued 1992), *Theory of International Politics* (1979), and numerous essays.

INTRODUCTION

Asking who won a given war, someone has said, is like asking who won the San Francisco earthquake. That in wars there is no victory but only varying degrees of defeat is a proposition that has gained increasing acceptance in the twentieth century. But are wars also akin to earthquakes in being natural occurrences whose control or elimination is beyond the wit of man? Few would admit that they are, yet attempts to eliminate war, however nobly inspired and assiduously pursued, have brought little more than fleeting moments of peace among states. There is an apparent disproportion between effort and product, between desire and result. The peace wish, we are told, runs strong and deep among the Russian people; and we are convinced that the same can be said of Americans. From these statements there is some comfort to be derived, but in the light of history and of current events as well it is difficult to believe that the wish will father the condition desired.

Social scientists, realizing from their studies how firmly the present is tied to the past and how intimately the parts of a system depend upon each other, are inclined to be conservative in estimating the possibilities of achieving a radically better world. If one asks whether we can now have peace where in the past there has been war, the answers are most often pessimistic. Perhaps this is the wrong question. And indeed the answers will be somewhat less discouraging if instead the following questions are put: Are there ways of decreasing the incidence of war, of increasing the chances of peace? Can we have peace more often in the future than in the past?

Peace is one among a number of ends simultaneously entertained. The means by which peace can be sought are many. The end is pursued and the means are applied under varying conditions. Even though one may find it hard to believe that there are ways to peace not yet tried by statesmen or advocated by publicists, the very complexity of the problem suggests the possibility of combining activities in different ways in the hope that some combination will lead us closer to the goal. Is one then led to conclude that the wisdom of the states-man lies in trying first one policy and then another, in doing what the moment seems to require? An affirmative reply would suggest that the hope for improve-ment lies in policy divorced from analy-sis, in action removed from thought. Yet each attempt to alleviate a condition im-plies some idea of its causes: to explain how peace can be more readily achieved requires an understanding of the causes of war. It is such an understanding that we shall seek in the following pages.

THE FIRST IMAGE: INTERNATIONAL CONFLICT AND HUMAN BEHAVIOR

There is deceit and cunning and from these wars arise.

—CONFUCIUS

According to the first image of interna-tional relations, the focus of the impor-tant causes of war is found in the nature and behavior of man. Wars result from selfishness, from misdirected aggressive impulses, from stupidity. Other causes are secondary and have to be interpreted in the light of these factors. If these are the primary causes of war, then the elim-ination of war must come through uplift-ing and enlightening men or securing their psychic-social readjustment. This estimate of causes and cures has been dominant in the writings of many seri-ous students of human affairs from Con-fucius to present-day pacifists. It is the leitmotif of many modern behavioral sci-entists as well.

Prescriptions associated with first-image analyses need not be identical in content, as a few examples will indicate. Henry Wadsworth Longfellow, moved to poetic expression by a visit to the arse-nal at Springfield, set down the follow-ing thoughts:

> Were half the power that fills the world
>   with terror,
> Were half the wealth bestowed on camps
>   and courts,
> Given to redeem the human mind from
>   error,
> There were no need of arsenals or forts.

Implicit in these lines is the idea that the people will insist that the right policies be adopted if only they know what the right policies are. Their instincts are good, though their present gullibility may prompt them to follow false leaders. By attributing present difficulties to a defect in knowledge, education becomes the remedy for war. The idea is wide-spread. Beverly Nichols, a pacifist writing in the 1930s, thought that if Norman Angell "could be made educational dictator of the world, war would vanish like the morning mist, in a single generation."[1] In 1920, a conference of Friends, unwilling to rely upon intellectual development alone, called upon the people of the world to replace self-seeking with the spirit of sacrifice, cooperation, and trust.[2] Bertrand Russell, at about the same time and in much the same vein, saw a decline in the possessive instincts as a prerequi-site to peace.[3] By others, increasing the chances of peace has been said to require not so much a change in "instincts" as a channeling of energies that are presently expended in the destructive folly of war. If there were something that men would rather do than fight, they would cease to fight altogether. Aristophanes saw the point. If the women of Athens would deny themselves to husbands and lovers, their men would have to choose between the pleasures of the couch and the exhil-arating experiences of the battlefield. Aris-tophanes thought he knew the men, and women, of Athens well enough to make the outcome a foregone conclusion. William James was in the same tradition. War, in his view, is rooted in man's bellicose nature, which is the product of centuries-old tradition. His nature cannot be changed or his drives suppressed, but they can be diverted. As alternatives to military service James suggests drafting the youth of the world to mine coal and man ships, to build skyscrapers and roads, to wash dishes and clothes. While his estimate of what diversions would be sufficient is at once less realistic and more seriously intended than that of Aristophanes, his remedy is clearly the same in type.[4]

The prescriptions vary, but common to them all is the thought that in order to achieve a more peaceful world men must be changed, whether in their moral-intellectual outlook or in their psychic-social behavior. One may, however, agree with the first-image analysis of causes without admitting the possibility of practicable prescriptions for their removal. Among those who accept a first-image explanation of war there are both optimists and pessimists, those who think the possibilities of progress so great that wars will end before the next generation is dead and those who think that wars will continue to occur though by them we may all die.

THE SECOND IMAGE: INTERNATIONAL CONFLICT AND THE INTERNAL STRUCTURE OF STATES

However conceived in an image of the world, foreign policy is a phase of domestic policy, an inescapable phase.

—CHARLES BEARD,
A Foreign Policy For America

The first image did not exclude the influence of the state, but the role of the state was introduced as a consideration less important than, and to be explained in terms of, human behavior. According to the first image, to say that the state acts is to speak metonymically. We say that the state acts when we mean that the people in it act, just as we say that the pot boils when we mean that the water in it boils. The preceding [section] concentrated on the contents rather than the container; the present [section] alters the balance of emphasis in favor of the latter. To continue the figure: Water running out of a faucet is chemically the same as water in a container, but once the water is in a container, it can be made to "behave" in different ways. It can be turned into steam and used to power an engine, or, if the water is sealed in and heated to extreme temperatures, it can become the instrument of a destructive explosion. Wars would not exist were human nature not what it is, but neither would Sunday schools and brothels, philanthropic organizations and criminal gangs. Since everything is related to human nature, to explain anything one must consider more than human nature. The events to be explained are so many and so varied that human nature cannot possibly be the single determinant.

The attempt to explain everything by psychology meant, in the end, that psychology succeeded in explaining nothing. And adding sociology to the analysis simply substitutes the error of sociologism for the error of psychologism. Where Spinoza, for example, erred by leaving out of his personal estimate of cause all reference to the causal role of social structures, sociologists have, in approaching the problem of war and peace, often erred in omitting all reference to the political framework within which individual and social actions occur. The conclusion is obvious: to understand war and peace political analysis must be used to supplement and order the findings of psychology and sociology. What kind of political analysis is needed? For possible explanations of the occurrence or nonoccurrence of war, one can look to international politics (since war occurs among states), or one can look to the states themselves (since it is in the name of the state that the fighting is actually done). The former approach is postponed [until the next section] according to the second image, the internal organization of states is the key to understanding war and peace.

One explanation of the second-image type is illustrated as follows. War most often promotes the internal unity of each state involved. The state plagued by internal strife may then, instead of waiting for the accidental attack, seek the war that will bring internal peace. Bodin saw this clearly, for he concludes that "the best way of preserving a state, and guaranteeing it against sedition, rebellion, and civil war is to keep the subjects in amity one with another, and to this end, to find an enemy against whom they can make common cause." And he saw historical evidence that the principle had been applied, especially by the Romans, who "could find no better antidote to civil war, nor one more certain in its effects, than to oppose an enemy to the citizens."[5] Secretary of State William Henry Seward followed this reasoning when, in order to promote unity within the country, he urged upon Lincoln a vigorous foreign policy, which included the possibility of declaring war on Spain and France.[6] Mikhail Skobelev, an influential Russian military officer of the third quarter of the nineteenth century, varied the theme but slightly when he argued that the Russian monarchy was doomed unless it could produce major military successes abroad.[7]

The use of internal defects to explain those external acts of the state that bring war can take many forms. Such explanation may be related to a type of government that is thought to be generically bad. For example, it is often thought that the deprivations imposed by despots upon their subjects produce tensions that may find expression in foreign adventure. Or the explanation may be given in terms of defects in a government not itself considered bad. Thus it has been argued that the restrictions placed upon a government in order to protect the prescribed rights of its citizens act as impediments to the making and executing of foreign policy. These restrictions, laudable in original purpose, may have the unfortunate effect of making difficult or impossible the effective action of that government for the maintenance of peace in the world.[8] And, as a final example, explanation may be made in terms of geographic or economic deprivation or in terms of deprivations too vaguely defined to be labeled at all. Thus a nation may argue that it has not attained its "natural" frontiers, that such frontiers are necessary to its security, that war to extend the state to its deserved compass is justified or even necessary.[9] The possible variations on this theme have been made familiar by the "have-not" arguments so popular in this century. Such arguments have been used both to explain why "deprived" countries undertake war and to urge the satiated to make the compensatory adjustments thought necessary if peace is to be perpetuated.[10]

The examples just given illustrate in abundant variety one part of the second image, the idea that defects in states cause wars among them. But in just what ways should the structure of states be changed? What definition of the "good" state is to serve as a standard? Among those who have taken this approach to international relations there is a great variety of definitions. Karl Marx defines "good" in terms of ownership of the means of production; Immanuel Kant in terms of abstract principles of right; Woodrow Wilson in terms of national self-determination and modern democratic organization. Though each definition singles out different items as crucial, all are united in asserting that if, and only if, substantially all states reform will world peace result. That is, the reform prescribed is considered the sufficient basis for world peace. This, of course, does not exhaust the subject. Marx, for example, believed that states would disappear shortly after they became socialist. The problem of war, if war is defined as violent conflict among states, would then no longer exist. Kant believed that republican states would voluntarily agree to be governed in their dealings by a code of law drawn up by the states themselves. Wilson urged a variety of requisites to peace, such as improved international understanding, collective security and disarmament, a world confederation of states. But history proved to Wilson that one cannot expect the steadfast cooperation of undemocratic states in any such program for peace.

For each of these men, the reform of states in the ways prescribed is taken to be the *sine qua non* of world peace. The examples given could be multiplied. Classical economists as well as socialists, aristocrats and monarchists as well as democrats, empiricists and realists as well as transcendental idealists— all can furnish examples of men who have believed that peace can be had only if a given pattern of internal organization becomes widespread. Is it that democracies spell peace, but we have had wars because there have never been enough democracies of the right kind? Or that the socialist form of government contains within it the guarantee of peace, but so far there have never been any true socialist governments?[11] If either question were answered in the affirmative, then one would have to assess the merits of different prescriptions and try to decide just which one, or which combination, contains the elusive secret formula for peace. The import of our criticism, however, is that no prescription for international relations written entirely in terms of the second image can be valid, that the approach itself is faulty. Our criticisms of the liberals apply to all theories that would rely on the generalization of one pattern of state and society to bring peace to the world.

Bad states lead to war. As previously said, there is a large and important sense in which this is true. The obverse of this statement, that good states mean peace in the world, is an extremely doubtful proposition. The difficulty, endemic with the second image of international relations, is the same in kind as the difficulty encountered in the first image. There the statement that men make the societies, including the international society, in which they live was criticized not simply as being wrong but as being incomplete. One must add that the societies they live in make men. And it is the same in international relations. The actions of states, or, more accurately, of men acting for states, make up the substance of international relations. But the international political environment has much to do with the ways in which states behave. The influence to be assigned to the internal structure of states in attempting to solve the war-peace equation cannot be determined until the significance of the international environment has been reconsidered.

THE THIRD IMAGE: INTERNATIONAL CONFLICT AND INTERNATIONAL ANARCHY

For what can be done against force without force?

—CICERO, *The Letters to His Friends*

With many sovereign states, with no system of law enforceable among them, with each state judging its grievances and ambitions according to the dictates of its own reason or desire—conflict, sometimes leading to war, is bound to occur. To achieve a favorable outcome from such conflict a state has to rely on its own devices, the relative efficiency of which must be its constant concern. This, the idea of the third image, is to be examined [here]. It is not an esoteric idea; it is not a new idea. Thucydides implied it when he wrote that it was "the growth of the Athenian power, which terrified the Lacedaemonians and forced them into war."[12] John Adams implied it when he wrote to the citizens of Petersburg, Virginia, that "a war with France, if just and necessary, might wean us from fond and blind affections, which no Nation ought ever to feel towards another, as our experience in more than one instance abundantly testifies."[13] There is an obvious relation between the concern over relative power position expressed by Thucydides and the admonition of John Adams that love affairs between states are inappropriate and dangerous. This relation is made explicit in Frederick Dunn's statement that "so long as the notion of self-help persists, the aim of maintaining the power position of the nation is paramount to all other considerations."[14]

In anarchy there is no automatic harmony. The three preceding statements reflect this fact. A state will use force to attain its goals if, after assessing the prospects for success, it values those goals more than it values the pleasures of peace. Because each state is the final judge of its own cause, any state may at any time use force to implement its policies. Because any state may at any time use force, all states must constantly be ready either to counter force with force or to pay the cost of weakness. The requirements of state action are, in this view, imposed by the circumstances in which all states exist.

In a manner of speaking, all three images are a part of nature. So fundamental are man, the state, and the state system in any attempt to understand international relations that seldom does an analyst, however wedded to one image, entirely overlook the other two. Still, emphasis on one image may distort one's interpretation of the others. It is, for example, not uncommon to find those inclined to see the world in terms of either the first or the second image countering the oft-made argument that arms breed not war but security, and possibly even peace, by pointing out that the argument is a compound of dishonest myth, to cover the interests of politicians, armament makers, and others, and honest illusion entertained by patriots sincerely interested in the safety of their states. To dispel the illusion, Cobden, to recall one of the many who have argued this way, once pointed out that doubling armaments, if everyone does it, makes no state more secure and, similarly, that none would be endangered if all military establishments were simultaneously reduced by, say, 50 percent.[15] Putting aside the thought that the arithmetic is not necessarily an accurate reflection of what the situation would be, this argument illustrates a supposedly practical application of the first and second images. Whether by educating citizens and leaders of the separate states or by improving the organization of each of them, a condition is sought in which the lesson here adumbrated becomes the basis for the policies of states. The result?—disarmament, and thus economy, together with peace, and thus security, for all states. If some states display a willingness to pare down their military establishments, other states will be able to pursue similar policies. In emphasizing the interdependence of the policies of all states, the argument pays heed to the third image. The optimism is, however, the result of ignoring some inherent difficulties. [Here Waltz takes up Rousseau's view of man in the early state of nature. —Ed.]

In the early state of nature, men were sufficiently dispersed to make any pattern of cooperation unnecessary. But finally the combination of increased numbers and the usual natural hazards posed, in a variety of situations, the proposition: cooperate or die. Rousseau illustrates the line of reasoning with the simplest example. The example is worth reproducing, for it is the point of departure for the establishment of government and contains the basis for his explanation of conflict in international relations as well. Assume that five men who have acquired a rudimentary ability to speak and to understand each other happen to come together at a time when all of them suffer from hunger. The hunger of each will be satisfied by the fifth part of a stag, so they "agree" to cooperate in a project to trap one. But also the hunger of any one of them will be satisfied by a hare, so, as a hare comes within reach, one of them grabs

it. The defector obtains the means of satisfying his hunger but in doing so permits the stag to escape. His immediate interest prevails over consideration for his fellows.[16]

The story is simple; the implications are tremendous. In cooperative action, even where all agree on the goal and have an equal interest in the project, one cannot rely on others. Spinoza linked conflict causally to man's imperfect reason. Montesquieu and Rousseau counter Spinoza's analysis with the proposition that the sources of conflict are not so much in the minds of men as they are in the nature of social activity. The difficulty is to some extent verbal. Rousseau grants that if we knew how to receive the true justice that comes from God, "we should need neither government nor laws."[17] This corresponds to Spinoza's proposition that "men in so far as they live in obedience to reason, necessarily live always in harmony one with another."[18] The idea is a truism. If men were perfect, their perfection would be reflected in all of their calculations and actions. Each could rely on the behavior of others, and all decisions would be made on principles that would preserve a true harmony of interests. Spinoza emphasizes not the difficulties inherent in mediating conflicting interests but the defectiveness of man's reason that prevents their consistently making decisions that would be in the interest of each and for the good of all. Rousseau faces the same problem. He imagines how men must have behaved as they began to depend on one another to meet their daily needs. As long as each provided for his own wants, there could be no conflict; whenever the combination of natural obstacles and growth in population made cooperation necessary, conflict arose. Thus in the stag-hunt example, the tension between one man's immediate interest and the general interest of the group is resolved by the unilateral action of the one man. To the extent that he was motivated by a feeling of hunger, his act is one of passion. Reason would have told him that his long-run interest depends on establishing, through experience, the conviction that cooperative action will benefit all of the participants. But reason also tells him that if he forgoes the hare, the man next to him might leave his post to chase it, leaving the first man with nothing but food for thought on the folly of being loyal.

The problem is now posed in more significant terms. If harmony is to exist in anarchy, not only must I be perfectly rational but I must be able to assume that everyone else is too. Otherwise there is no basis for rational calculation. To allow in my calculation for the irrational acts of others can lead to no determinate solutions, but to attempt to act on a rational calculation without making such an allowance may lead to my own undoing. The latter argument is reflected in Rousseau's comments on the proposition that "a people of true Christians would form the most perfect society imaginable." In the first place he points out that such a society "would not be a society of men." Moreover, he says, "For the state to be peaceable and for harmony to be maintained, *all* the citizens *without exception* would have to be [equally] good Christians; if by ill hap there should be a single self-seeker or hypocrite . . . he would certainly get the better of his pious compatriots."[19]

If we define cooperative action as rational and any deviation from it irrational, we must agree with Spinoza that conflict results from the irrationality of men. But if we examine the require-

ments of rational action, we find that even in an example as simple as the stag hunt we have to assume that the reason of each leads to an identical definition of interest, that each will draw the same conclusion as to the methods appropriate to meet the original situation, that all will agree instantly on the action required by any chance incidents that raise the question of altering the original plan, and that each can rely completely on the steadfastness of purpose of all the others. Perfectly rational action requires not only the perception that our welfare is tied up with the welfare of others but also a perfect appraisal of details so that we can answer the question: Just *how* in each situation is it tied up with everyone else's? Rousseau agrees with Spinoza in refusing to label the act of the rabbit-snatcher either good or bad; unlike Spinoza, he also refuses to label it either rational or irrational. He has noticed that the difficulty is not only in the actors but also in the situations they face. While by no means ignoring the part that avarice and ambition play in the birth and growth of conflict,[20] Rousseau's analysis makes clear the extent to which conflict appears inevitably in the social affairs of men.

In short, the proposition that irrationality is the cause of all the world's troubles, in the sense that a world of perfectly rational men would know no disagreements and no conflicts, is, as Rousseau implies, as true as it is irrelevant. Since the world cannot be defined in terms of perfection, the very real problem of how to achieve an approximation to harmony in cooperative and competitive activity is always with us and, lacking the possibility of perfection, it is a problem that cannot be solved simply by changing men. Rousseau's conclusion, which is also the heart of his theory of international relations, is accurately though somewhat abstractly summarized in the following statement: That among particularities accidents will occur is not accidental but necessary.[21] And this, in turn, is simply another way of saying that in anarchy there is no automatic harmony.

If anarchy is the problem, then there are only two possible solutions: (1) to impose an effective control on the separate and imperfect states; (2) to remove states from the sphere of the accidental, that is, to define the good state as so perfect that it will no longer be particular. Kant tried to compromise by making states good enough to obey a set of laws to which they have volunteered their assent. Rousseau, whom on this point Kant failed to follow, emphasizes the particular nature of even the good state and, in so doing, makes apparent the futility of the solution Kant suggests.[22] He also makes possible a theory of international relations that in general terms explains the behavior of all states, whether good or bad.[23]

In the stag-hunt example, the will of the rabbit-snatcher was rational and predictable from his own point of view. From the point of view of the rest of the group, it was arbitrary and capricious. So of any individual state, a will perfectly good for itself may provoke the violent resistance of other states.[24] The application of Rousseau's theory to international politics is stated with eloquence and clarity in his commentaries on Saint-Pierre and in a short work entitled *The State of War.* His application bears out the preceding analysis. The states of Europe, he writes, "touch each other at so many points that no one of them can move without giving a jar to all the rest; their variances are all the more deadly, as their ties are more closely woven." They "must inevitably fall into quarrels and dissensions at the first changes that come about." And if we ask why they must "inevitably" clash, Rousseau answers: Because their union is "formed and maintained by nothing better than chance." The nations of Europe are willful units in close juxtaposition with rules neither clear nor enforceable to guide them. The public law of Europe is but "a mass of contradictory rules which nothing but the right of the stronger can reduce to order: so that in the absence of any sure clue to guide her, reason is bound, in every case of doubt, to obey the promptings of self-interest—which in itself would make war inevitable, even if all parties desired to be just." In this condition, it is foolhardy to expect automatic harmony of interest and automatic agreement and acquiescence in rights and duties. In a real sense there is a "union of the nations of Europe," but "the imperfections of this association make the state of those who belong to it worse than it would be if they formed no community at all."[25]

The argument is clear. For individuals the bloodiest stage of history was the period just prior to the establishment of society. At that point they had lost the virtues of the savage without having acquired those of the citizen. The late stage of the state of nature is necessarily a state of war. The nations of Europe are precisely in that stage.[26]

What then is cause: the capricious acts of the separate states or the system within which they exist? Rousseau emphasizes the latter:

> Every one can see that what unites any form of society is community of interests, and what disintegrates [it] is their conflict; that either tendency may be changed or modified by a thousand accidents; and therefore that, as soon as a society is founded,

some coercive power must be provided to co-ordinate the actions of its members and give to their common interests and mutual obligations that firmness and consistency which they could never acquire of themselves.[27]

But to emphasize the importance of political structure is not to say that the acts that bring about conflict and lead to the use of force are of no importance. It is the specific acts that are the immediate causes of war,[28] the general structure that permits them to exist and wreak their disasters. To eliminate every vestige of selfishness, perversity, and stupidity in nations would serve to establish perpetual peace, but to try directly to eliminate all the immediate causes of war without altering the structure of the "union of Europe" is utopian.

What alteration of structure is required? The idea that a voluntary federation, such as Kant later proposed, could keep peace among states, Rousseau rejects emphatically. Instead, he says, the remedy for war among states "is to be found only in such a form of federal Government as shall unite nations by bonds similar to those which already unite their individual members, and place the one no less than the other under the authority of the Law."[29] Kant made similar statements only to amend them out of existence once he came to consider the reality of such a federation. Rousseau does not modify his principle, as is made clear in the following quotation, every point of which is a contradiction of Kant's program for the pacific federation:

> The Federation [that is to replace the "free and voluntary association which now unites the States of Europe"] must embrace all the important Powers in its membership; it must have a Legislative Body, with powers to pass laws and ordinances binding upon all its members; it must have a coercive force capable of compelling every State to obey its common resolves whether in the way of command or of prohibition; finally, t must be strong and firm enough to make it impossible for any member to withdraw at his own pleasure the moment he conceives his private interest to clash with that of the whole body.[30]

It is easy to poke holes in the solution offered by Rousseau. The most vulnerable point is revealed by the questions: How could the federation enforce its law on the states that comprise it without waging war against them? and How likely is it that the effective force will always be on the side of the federation? To answer these questions Rousseau argues that the states of Europe are in a condition of balance sufficiently fine to prevent any one state or combination of states from prevailing over the others. For this reason, the necessary margin of force will always rest with the federation itself. The best critical consideration of the inherent weakness of a federation of states in which the law of the federation has to be enforced on the states who are its members is contained in the *Federalist Papers*. The arguments are convincing, but they need not be reviewed here. The practical weakness of Rousseau's recommended solution does not obscure the merit of his theoretical analysis of war as a consequence of international anarchy.

CONCLUSION

The third image, like the first two, leads directly to a utopian prescription. In each image a cause is identified in terms of which all others are to be understood. The force of the logical relation between the third image and the world-government prescription is great enough to cause some to argue not only the merits of world government but also the ease with which it can be realized.[31] It is of course true that with world government there would no longer be international wars, though with an ineffective world government there would no doubt be civil wars. It is likewise true, reverting to the first two images, that without the imperfections of the separate states there would not be wars, just as it is true that a society of perfectly rational beings, or of perfect Christians, would never know violent conflict. These statements are, unfortunately, as trivial as they are true. They have the unchallengeable quality of airtight tautologies: perfectly good states or men will not do bad things; within an effective organization highly damaging deviant behavior is not permitted. The near perfection required by concentration upon a single cause accounts for a number of otherwise puzzling facts: the pessimism of St. Augustine, the failure of the behavioral scientists as prescribers for peace, the reliance of many liberals on the forces of history to produce a result not conceivably to be produced by the consciously directed efforts of men, the tendency of socialists to identify a corrupting element every time harmony in socialist action fails to appear. It also helps to explain the often rapid alternation of hope and despair among those who most fully adopt a single-cause approach to this or to almost any other problem. The belief that to make the world better requires changing the factors that operate within a precisely defined realm leads to despair whenever it becomes apparent that changes there, if possible at all, will come slowly and with insufficient force. One is constantly defeated by the double problem of demonstrating how the "necessary changes" can

be produced and of substantiating the assertion that the changes described as necessary would be sufficient to accomplish the object in view.

The contrary assertion, that all causes may be interrelated, is an argument against assuming that there is a single cause that can be isolated by analysis and eliminated or controlled by wisely constructed policy. It is also an argument against working with one or several hypotheses without bearing in mind the interrelation of all causes. The prescriptions directly derived from a single image are incomplete because they are based upon partial analyses. The partial quality of each image sets up a tension that drives one toward inclusion of the others. With the first image the direction of change, representing Locke's perspective as against Plato's, is from men to societies and states. The second image catches up both elements. Men make states, *and* states make men; but this is still a limited view. One is led to a search for the more inclusive nexus of causes, for states are shaped by the international environment as are men by both the national and international environments. Most of those whom we have considered in preceding [sections] have not written entirely in terms of one image. That we have thus far been dealing with the consequences arising from differing degrees of emphasis accounts for the complexity of preceding [sections] but now makes somewhat easier the task of suggesting how the images can be interrelated without distorting any one of them.

The First and Second Images in Relation to the Third

It may be true that the Soviet Union poses the greatest threat of war at the present time. It is not true that were the Soviet

Union to disappear the remaining states could easily live at peace. We have known wars for centuries; the Soviet Union has existed only for decades. But some states, and perhaps some forms of the state, are more peacefully inclined than others. Would not the multiplication of peacefully inclined states at least warrant the hope that the period between major wars might be extended? By emphasizing the relevance of the framework of action, the third image makes clear the misleading quality of such partial analyses and of the hopes that are often based upon them. The act that by individual moral standards would be applauded may, when performed by a state, be an invitation to the war we seek to avoid. The third image, taken not as a theory of world government but as a theory of the conditioning effects of the state system itself, alerts us to the fact that so far as increasing the chances of peace is concerned there is no such thing as an act good in itself. The pacification of the Hukbalahaps was a clear and direct contribution to the peace and order of the Philippine state. In international politics a partial "solution," such as one major country becoming pacifistic, might be a real contribution to world peace; but it might as easily hasten the coming of another major war.

The third image, as reflected in the writings of Rousseau, is based on an analysis of the consequences arising from the framework of state action. Rousseau's explanation of the origin of war among states is, in broad outline, the final one so long as we operate within a nation-state system. It is a final explanation because it does not hinge on accidental causes—irrationalities in men, defects in states—but upon his theory of the framework within which *any* accident can bring about a war. That state A wants certain things that it can get only by war does not explain war. Such a desire may

or may not lead to war. My wanting a million dollars does not cause me to rob a bank, but if it were easier to rob banks, such desires would lead to much more bank robbing. This does not alter the fact that some people will and some will not attempt to rob banks no matter what the law enforcement situation is. We still have to look to motivation and circumstance in order to explain individual acts. Nevertheless one can predict that, other things being equal, a weakening of law enforcement agencies will lead to an increase in crime. From this point of view it is social structure—institutionalized restraints and institutionalized methods of altering and adjusting interests—that counts. And it counts in a way different from the ways usually associated with the word "cause." What causes a man to rob a bank are such things as the desire for money, a disrespect for social properties, a certain boldness. But if obstacles to the operation of these causes are built sufficiently high, nine out of ten would-be bank robbers will live their lives peacefully plying their legitimate trades. If the framework is to be called cause at all, it had best be specified that it is a permissive or underlying cause of war.

Applied to international politics this becomes, in words previously used to summarize Rousseau, the proposition that wars occur because there is nothing to prevent them. Rousseau's analysis explains the recurrence of war without explaining any given war. He tells us that war may at any moment occur, and he tells us why this is so. But the structure of the state system does not directly cause state A to attack state B. Whether or not that attack occurs will depend on a number of special circumstances—location, size, power, interest, type of government, past history and tradition—each of which will influence the actions of both states. If they fight against each other it will be for reasons especially defined for the occasion by each of them. These special reasons become the immediate, or efficient, causes of war. These immediate causes of war are contained in the first and second images. States are motivated to attack each other and to defend themselves by the reason and/or passion of the comparatively few who make policies for states and of the many more who influence the few. Some states, by virtue of their internal conditions, are both more proficient in war and more inclined to put their proficiency to the test. Variations in the factors included in the first and second images are important, indeed crucial, in the making and breaking of periods of peace—the immediate causes of every war must be either the acts of individuals or the acts of states.

If every war is preceded by acts that we can identify (or at least try to identify) as cause, then why can we not eliminate wars by modifying individual or state behavior? This is the line of thinking followed by those who say: To end war, improve men; or: To end war, improve states. But in such prescriptions the role of the international environment is easily distorted. How can some of the acting units improve while others continue to follow their old and often predatory ways? The simplistic assumption of many liberals, that history moves relentlessly toward the millennium, is refuted if the international environment makes it difficult almost to the point of impossibility for states to behave in ways that are progressively more moral. Two points are omitted from the prescriptions we considered under the first and second images: (1) If an effect is produced by two or more causes, the effect is not permanently eliminated by removing one of them. If wars occur because men are less than perfectly rational and because states are less than perfectly formed, to improve only states may do little to decrease the number and intensity of wars. The error here is in identifying one cause where two or more may operate. (2) An endeavor launched against one cause to the neglect of others may make the situation worse instead of better. Thus, as the Western democracies became more inclined to peace, Hitler became more belligerent. The increased propensity to peace of some participants in international politics may increase, rather than decrease, the likelihood of war. This illustrates the role of the permissive cause, the international environment. If there were but two loci of cause involved, men and states, we could be sure that the appearance of more peacefully inclined states would, at worst, not damage the cause of world peace. Whether or not a remedy proposed is truly a remedy or actually worse than none at all depends, however, on the content and timing of the acts of all states. This is made clear in the third image.

War may result because state A has something that state B wants. The efficient cause of the war is the desire of state B; the permissive cause is the fact that there is nothing to prevent state B from undertaking the risks of war. In a different circumstance, the interrelation of efficient and permissive causes becomes still closer. State A may fear that if it does not cut state B down a peg now, it may be unable to do so ten years from now. State A becomes the aggressor in the present because it fears what state B may be able to do in the future. The efficient cause of such a war is derived from the cause that we have labeled permissive. In the first case, conflicts arise from disputes born of specific issues. In an age of hydrogen bombs, no single issue may be worth the risk of full-scale war. Settlement, even on bad grounds, is preferable to self-destruction. The use of reason would seem to require the adoption of a doctrine of "non-recourse to force." One whose reason leads him down this path is following the trail blazed by Cobden when in 1849 he pointed out "that it is almost impossible, on looking back for the last hundred years, to tell precisely what any war was about," and thus implied that Englishmen should never have become involved in them.[32] He is falling into the trap that ensnared A. A. Milne when he explained the First World War as a war in which ten million men died because Austria-Hungary sought, unsuccessfully, to avenge the death of one archduke.[33] He is succumbing to the illusion of Sir Edward Grey, who, in the memoirs he wrote some thirty years ago, hoped that the horrors of the First World War would make it possible for nations "to find at least one common ground on which they should come together in confident understanding: an agreement that, in the disputes between them, war must be ruled out as a means of settlement that entails ruin."[34]

It is true that the immediate causes of many wars are trivial. If we focus upon them, the failure to agree to settlement without force appears to be the ultimate folly. But it is not often true that the immediate causes provide sufficient explanation for the wars that have occurred. And if it is not simply particular disputes that produce wars, rational settlement of them cannot eliminate war. For, as Winston Churchill has written, "small matters are only the symptoms of the dangerous disease, and are only important for that reason. Behind them lie the interests, the passions and the destiny of mighty races of men; and long antagonisms express themselves in trifles."[35] Nevertheless Churchill may be justified in hoping that the fear induced by a "balance of terror" will produce a temporary truce. Advancing technology makes war more horrible and presumably increases the desire for peace; the very rapidity of the advance makes for uncertainty in everyone's military planning and destroys the possibility of an accurate estimate of the likely opposing forces. Fear and permanent peace are more difficult to equate. Each major advance in the technology of war has found its prophet ready to proclaim that war is no longer possible: Alfred Nobel and dynamite, for example, or Benjamin Franklin and the lighter-than-air balloon. There may well have been a prophet to proclaim the end of tribal warfare when the spear was invented and another to make a similar prediction when poison was first added to its tip. Unfortunately, these prophets have all been false. The development of atomic and hydrogen weapons may nurture the peace wish of some, the war sentiment of others. In the United States and elsewhere after the Second World War, a muted theme of foreign-policy debate was the necessity of preventive war—drop the bomb quickly before the likely opponent in a future war has time to make one of his own. Even with two or more states equipped with similar weapon systems, a momentary shift in the balance of terror, giving a decisive military advantage temporarily to one state, may tempt it to seize the moment in order to escape from fear. And the temptation would be proportionate to the fear itself. Finally, mutual fear of big weapons may produce, instead of peace, a spate of smaller wars.

The fear of modern weapons, of the danger of destroying the civilizations of the world, is not sufficient to establish the conditions of peace identified in our discussions of the three images of international relations. One can equate fear with world peace only if the peace wish exists in all states and is uniformly expressed in their policies. But peace is the primary goal of few men or states. If it were the primary goal of even a single state, that state could have peace at any time—simply by surrendering. But, as John Foster Dulles so often warned, "Peace can be a cover whereby evil men perpetrate diabolical wrongs."[36] The issue in a given dispute may not be: Who shall gain from it? It may instead be: Who shall dominate the world? In such circumstances, the best course of even reasonable men is difficult to define; their ability always to contrive solutions without force, impossible to assume. If solutions in terms of none of the three images is presently—if ever—possible, then reason can work only within the framework that is suggested by viewing the first and second images in the perspective of the third, a perspective well and simply set forth in the *Federalist Papers,* especially in those written by Hamilton and Jay.

What would happen, Jay asks, if the thirteen states, instead of combining as one state, should form themselves into several confederations? He answers:

> Instead of their being "joined in affection" and free from all apprehension of different "interests," envy and jealousy would soon extinguish confidence and affection, and the partial interests of each confederation, instead of the general interests of all America, would be the only objects of their policy and pursuits. Hence, like most *bordering*

nations, they would always be either involved in disputes and war, or live in the constant apprehension of them.[37]

International anarchy, Jay is here saying, is the explanation for international war. But not international anarchy alone. Hamilton adds that to presume a lack of hostile motives among states is to forget that men are "ambitious, vindictive, and rapacious." A monarchical state may go to war because the vanity of its king leads him to seek glory in military victory; a republic may go to war because of the folly of its assembly or because of its commercial interests. That the king may be vain, the assembly foolish, or the commercial interests irreconcilable: none of these is inevitable. However, so many and so varied are the causes of war among states that "to look for a continuation of harmony between a number of independent, unconnected sovereigns in the same neighborhood, would be to disregard the uniform course of human events, and to set at defiance the accumulated experience of the ages."[38]

Jay and Hamilton found in the history of the Western state system confirmation for the conclusion that among separate sovereign states there is constant possibility of war. The third image gives a theoretical basis for the same conclusion. It reveals why, in the absence of tremendous changes in the factors included in the first and second images, war will be perpetually associated with the existence of separate sovereign states. The obvious conclusion of a third-image analysis is that world government is the remedy for world war. The remedy, though it may be unassailable in logic, is unattainable in practice. The third image may provide a utopian approach to world politics. It may also provide a realistic approach, and one that avoids the tendency of some realists to attribute the necessary amorality, or even immorality, of world politics to the inherently bad character of man. If everyone's strategy depends upon everyone else's, then the Hitlers determine in part the action, or better, reaction, of those whose ends are worthy and whose means are fastidious. No matter how good their intentions, policy makers must bear in mind the implications of the third image, which can be stated in summary form as follows: Each state pursues its own interests, however defined, in ways it judges best. Force is a means of achieving the external ends of states because there exists no consistent, reliable process of reconciling the conflicts of interest that inevitably arise among similar units in a condition of anarchy. A foreign policy based on this image of international relations is neither moral nor immoral, but embodies merely a reasoned response to the world about us. The third image describes the framework of world politics, but without the first and second images there can be no knowledge of the forces that determine policy; the first and second images describe the forces in world politics, but without the third image it is impossible to assess their importance or predict their results.

NOTES

1. Beverly Nichols, *Cry Havoc!* (New York: Doubleday, Doran & Co., 1933), p. 164.
2. Margaret E. Hirst, *The Quakers in Peace and War* (London: Swarthmore Press, 1923), pp. 521–25.
3. Bertrand Russell, *Political Ideals* (New York: Century Co., 1971), p. 42. In one way or another the thought recurs in Lord Russell's many writings on international relations.
4. William James, "The Moral Equivalent of War," in *Memories and Studies* (New York: Longmans, Green and Co., 1912), pp. 262–72, 290.
5. Jean Bodin, *Six Books of the Commonwealth,* abridged and trans. M. J. Tooley (Oxford: Basil Blackwell, n.d.), p. 168.
6. "Some Thoughts for the President's Consideration," Apr. 1, 1861, in *Documents of American History,* ed. Henry Steele Commager, 3d ed. (New York: F. S. Crofts & Co., 1946), p. 392.
7. Hans Herzfeld, "Bismarck und die Skobelewespisode," *Historische Zeitschrift* 142 (1930): 279–302.
8. Cf. Robert E. Sherwood, *Roosevelt and Hopkins* (New York: Harper and Brothers, 1948), pp. 67–68, 102, 126, 133–36, 272, and esp. 931; and Secretary of State Hay's statement in Henry Adams, *The Education of Henry Adams* (New York: Book League of America, 1928), p. 374. Note that in this case the fault is one that is thought to decrease the ability of a country to implement a peaceful policy. In the other examples, the defect is thought to increase the propensity of a country to go to war.
9. Cf. Bertrand Russell, who in 1917 wrote: "There can be no good international system until the boundaries of states coincide as nearly as possible with the boundaries of nations" (*Political Ideals,* p. 146).
10. Frank H. Simonds and Brooks Emery, *The Great Powers in World Politics* (New York: American Book Co., 1939), passim; W. S. Thompson, *Danger Spots in World Population* (New York: Alfred A. Knopf, 1930), esp. the Preface and chaps. 1 and 13.
11. Cf. Vladimir Dedijer, "Albania, Soviet Pawn," *Foreign Affairs* 30 (1951): 104: socialism, but not Soviet Union state capitalism, means peace.
12. Thucydides, *History of the Peloponnesian War,* trans. B. Jowett, 2d ed. (London: Oxford University Press, 1900), bk. 1, par. 23.
13. John Adams to the citizens of the town of Petersburg, Virginia, June 6, 1798, reprinted in the program for the visit of

William Howard Taft, Petersburg, May 19, 1909.

14. Frederick S. Dunn, *Peaceful Change* (New York: Council on Foreign Relations, 1937), p. 13.

15. Richard Cobden, esp. *Speeches on Peace, Financial Reform, Colonial Reform and Other Subjects Delivered during 1849* (London: James Gilbert, n.d.), p. 135.

16. Jean Jaques Rousseau, *The Social Contract and Discourses,* trans. G. D. H. Cole, Everyman's Library Edition (New York: E.P. Dutton and Co., 1950); esp. *Inequality,* pp. 234 ff.

17. Ibid., p. 34.

18. Benedict de Spinoza, *The Chief Works of Benedict de Spinoza,* trans. R. H. M. Elwes, 2 vols. (New York: Dover Publications, 1951), *Ethics,* pt. 4, prop. 35, proof.

19. Rousseau, *Social Contract and Discourses,* pp. 135–36 (bk. 4, chap. 8), italics added. The word "equally" is necessary for an accurate rendering of the French text but does not appear in the translation cited.

20. Jean Jacques Rousseau, *A Lasting Peace through the Federation of Europe and the State of War,* trans. C. E. Vaughan (London: Constable and Co., 1917), p. 72.

21. This parallels Hegel's formulation: "It is to what is by nature accidental that accidents happen, and the fate whereby they happen is thus a necessity" [G. W. F.] Hegel, *Philosophy of Right,* trans. T. M. Knox (Oxford: Clarendon Press, 1942), sec. 324.

22. Kant is more willing to admit the force of this criticism than is generally realized.

23. This is not, of course, to say that no differences in state behavior follow from the different constitutions and situations of states. This point raises the question of the relation of the third image to the second, which will be discussed below.

24. Rousseau, *Social Contract and Discourses,* pp. 290–91.

25. Rousseau, *A Lasting Peace,* pp. 46–48, 58–59.

26. Ibid., pp. 38, 46–47. On p. 121, Rousseau distinguishes between the "state of war," which always exists among states, and war proper, which manifests itself in the settled intention to destroy the enemy state.

27. Ibid., p. 49.

28. In ibid., p. 69, Rousseau presents his exhaustive list of such causes.

29. Ibid., pp. 38–39.

30. Ibid., pp. 59–60.

31. Cf. Karl Popper, *The Open Society and Its Enemies* (Princeton: Princeton University Press, 1950), pp. 158–59; and William Esslinger, *Politics and Science* (New York: Philosophical Library, 1955), passim.

32. Richard Cobden, *Speeches on Questions of Public Policy,* 2 vols., ed. John Bright and James E. Thorold Rogers (London: Macmillan & Co., 1870), 2: 165.

33. A. A. Milne, *Peace and War* (New York: E. P. Dutton & Co., 1934), p. 11.

34. Edward Grey, *Twenty-Five Years,* 2 vols. (New York: Frederick A. Stokes Co., 1925), 2: 285.

35. Winston Churchill, *The World Crisis, 1911-1914,* 4 vols. (New York: Charles Scribner's Sons, 1923–29), 1: 52.

36. "Excerpts from Dulles Address on Peace," Washington, D.C., Apr. 11, 1955, in *New York Times,* Apr. 12, 1955, p. 6.

37. Alexander Hamilton, John Jay, and James Madison, *The Federalist* (New York: Modern Library, 1941), pp. 23–24 (no. 5).

38. Ibid., pp. 27–28 (no. 6); cf. p. 18 (no. 4, Jay) and pp. 34–40 (no. 7, Hamilton).

QUESTIONS

1. Which image do you think offers the best explanation for war and why?

2. Why does Waltz distinguish between the "immediate" causes of war and the "permissive" causes of war?

2.   International Relations: One World, Many Theories

Stephen M. Walt

In this article Stephen M. Walt offers a summary and a critical evaluation of the major system-level theories of international relations. The author concludes that realism remains the most useful and persuasive theory for understanding international relations.

Stephen M. Walt is a professor of political science and master of the social science collegiate division at the University of Chicago. He is also a member of the editorial board of *Foreign Policy* magazine.

Why should policymakers and practitioners care about the scholarly study of international affairs? Those who conduct foreign policy often dismiss academic theorists (frequently, one must admit, with good reason), but there is an inescapable link between the abstract world of theory and the real world of policy. We need theories to make sense of the blizzard of information that bombards us daily. Even policymakers who are contemptuous of "theory" must rely on their own (often unstated) ideas about how the world works in order to decide what to do. It is hard to make good policy if one's basic organizing principles are flawed, just as it is hard to construct good theories without knowing a lot about the real world. Everyone uses theories—whether he or she knows it or not—and disagreements about policy usually rest on more fundamental disagreements about the basic forces that shape international outcomes.

Take, for example, the current debate on how to respond to China. From one perspective, China's ascent is the latest example of the tendency for rising powers to alter the global balance of power in potentially dangerous ways, especially as their growing influence makes them more ambitious. From another perspective, the key to China's future conduct is whether its behavior will be modified by its integration into world markets and by the (inevitable?) spread of democratic principles. From yet another viewpoint, relations between China and the rest of the world will be shaped by issues of culture and identity: Will China see itself (and be seen by others) as a normal member of the world community or a singular society that deserves special treatment?

In the same way, the debate over NATO expansion looks different depending on which theory one employs. From a "realist" perspective, NATO expansion is an effort to extend Western influence—well beyond the traditional sphere of U.S. vital interests—during a period of Russian weakness and is likely to provoke a harsh response from Moscow. From a liberal perspective, however, expansion will reinforce the nascent democracies of Central Europe and extend NATO's conflict-management mechanisms to a potentially turbulent region. A third view might stress the value of incorporating the Czech Republic, Hungary, and Poland within the Western security community, whose members share a common identity that has made war largely unthinkable.

No single approach can capture all the complexity of contemporary world politics. Therefore, we are better off with a diverse array of competing ideas rather than a single theoretical orthodoxy. Competition between theories helps reveal their strengths and weaknesses and spurs subsequent refinements, while revealing flaws in conventional wisdom. Although we should take care to emphasize inventiveness over invective, we should welcome and encourage the heterogeneity of contemporary scholarship.

WHERE ARE WE COMING FROM?

The study of international affairs is best understood as a protracted competition between the realist, liberal, and radical traditions. Realism emphasizes the enduring propensity for conflict between states; liberalism identifies several ways to mitigate these conflictive tendencies; and the radical tradition describes how the entire system of state relations might be transformed. The boundaries between these traditions are somewhat fuzzy and a number of important works do not fit neatly into any of them, but debates within and among them have largely defined the discipline.

Realism

Realism was the dominant theoretical tradition throughout the Cold War. It depicts international affairs as a struggle for power among self-interested states and is generally pessimistic about the prospects for eliminating conflict and war. Realism dominated in the Cold War years because it provided simple but powerful explanations for war, alliances, imperialism, obstacles to cooperation, and other international phenomena, and because its emphasis on competition was consistent with the central features of the American-Soviet rivalry.

Realism is not a single theory, of course, and realist thought evolved considerably throughout the Cold War. "Classical" realists such as Hans Morgenthau and Reinhold Niebuhr believed that states, like human beings, had an innate desire to dominate others, which led them to fight wars. Morgenthau also stressed the virtues of the classical, multipolar, balance-of-power system and saw the bipolar rivalry between the United States and the Soviet Union as especially dangerous.

By contrast, the "neorealist" theory advanced by Kenneth Waltz ignored human nature and focused on the effects of the international system. For Waltz, the international system consisted of a number of great powers, each seeking to survive. Because the system is anarchic (i.e., there is no central authority to protect states from one another), each state has to survive on its own. Waltz argued that this condition would lead weaker states to balance against, rather than bandwagon with, more powerful rivals. And contrary to Morgenthau, he claimed that bipolarity was more stable than multipolarity.

An important refinement to realism was the addition of offense-defense theory, as laid out by Robert Jervis, George Quester, and Stephen Van Evera. These scholars argued that war was more likely when states could conquer each other easily. When defense was easier than offense, however, security was more plentiful, incentives to expand declined, and cooperation could blossom. And if defense had the advantage, and states could distinguish between offensive and defensive weapons, then states could acquire the means to defend themselves without threatening others, thereby dampening the effects of anarchy.

For these "defensive" realists, states merely sought to survive and great powers could guarantee their security by forming balancing alliances and choosing defensive military postures (such as retaliatory nuclear forces). Not surprisingly, Waltz and most other neorealists believed that the United States was extremely secure for most of the Cold War. Their principle fear was that it might squander its favorable position by adopting an overly aggressive foreign policy. Thus, by the end of the Cold War, realism had moved away from Morgenthau's dark brooding about human nature and taken on a slightly more optimistic tone.

Liberalism

The principal challenge to realism came from a broad family of liberal theories. One strand of liberal thought argued that economic interdependence would discourage states from using force against each other because warfare would threaten each side's prosperity. A second strand, often associated with President Woodrow Wilson, saw the spread of democracy as the key to world peace, based on the claim that democratic states were inherently more peaceful than authoritarian states. A third, more recent theory argued that international institutions such as the International Energy Agency and the International Monetary Fund could help overcome selfish state behavior, mainly by encouraging states to forego immediate gains for the greater benefits of enduring cooperation.

Although some liberals flirted with the idea that new transnational actors, especially the multinational corporation, were gradually encroaching on the power of states, liberalism generally saw states as the central players in international affairs. All liberal theories implied that cooperation was more pervasive than even the defensive version of realism allowed, but each view offered a different recipe for promoting it.

Radical Approaches

Until the 1980s, marxism was the main alternative to the mainstream realist and liberal traditions. Where realism and liberalism took the state system for granted, marxism offered both a different explanation for international conflict and a blueprint for fundamentally transforming the existing international order.

Orthodox marxist theory saw capitalism as the central cause of international conflict. Capitalist states battled each other as a consequence of their incessant struggle for profits and battled socialist states because they saw in them the seeds of their own destruction. Neomarxist "dependency" theory, by contrast, focused on relations between advanced capitalist powers and less developed states and argued that the former—aided by an unholy alliance with the ruling classes of the developing world—had grown rich by exploiting the latter. The solution was to overthrow these parasitic elites and install a revolutionary government committed to autonomous development.

Both of these theories were largely discredited before the Cold War even ended. The extensive history of economic and military cooperation among the advanced industrial powers showed that capitalism did not inevitably lead to conflict. The bitter schisms that divided the communist world showed that socialism did not always promote harmony. Dependency theory suffered similar empirical setbacks as it became increasingly clear that, first, active participation in the world economy was a better route to prosperity than autonomous socialist development; and, second, many developing countries proved themselves quite capable of bargaining successfully with multinational corporations and other capitalist institutions.

As marxism succumbed to its various failings, its mantle was assumed by a group of theorists who borrowed heavily from the wave of postmodern writings in literary criticism and social theory. This "deconstructionist" approach was openly skeptical of the effort to devise general or universal theories such as realism or liberalism. Indeed, its proponents emphasized the importance of language and discourse in shaping social outcomes. However, because these scholars focused initially on criticizing the mainstream paradigms but did not offer positive alternatives to them, they remained a self-consciously dissident minority for most of the 1980s.

Domestic Politics

Not all Cold War scholarship on international affairs fit neatly into the realist, liberal, or marxist paradigms. In particular, a number of important works focused on the characteristics of states, governmental organizations, or individual leaders. The democratic strand of liberal theory fits under this heading, as do the efforts of scholars such as Graham Allison and John Steinbruner to use organization theory and bureaucratic politics to explain foreign policy behavior, and those of Jervis, Irving Janis, and others, which applied social and cognitive psychology. For the most part, these ef-

forts did not seek to provide a general theory of international behavior but to identify other factors that might lead states to behave contrary to the predictions of the realist or liberal approaches. Thus, much of this literature should be regarded as a complement to the three main paradigms rather than as a rival approach for analysis of the international system as a whole.

NEW WRINKLES IN OLD PARADIGMS

Scholarship on international affairs has diversified significantly since the end of the Cold War. Non-American voices are more prominent, a wider range of methods and theories are seen as legitimate, and new issues such as ethnic conflict, the environment, and the future of the state have been placed on the agenda of scholars everywhere.

Yet the sense of deja vu is equally striking. Instead of resolving the struggle between competing theoretical traditions, the end of the Cold War has merely launched a new series of debates. Ironically, even as many societies embrace similar ideals of democracy, free markets, and human rights, the scholars who study these developments are more divided than ever.

Realism Redux

Although the end of the Cold War led a few writers to declare that realism was destined for the academic scrapheap, rumors of its demise have been largely exaggerated.

A recent contribution of realist theory is its attention to the problem of relative and absolute gains. Responding to the institutionalists' claim that international institutions would enable states to forego short-term advantages for the sake of greater long-term gains, realists such as Joseph Grieco and Stephen Krasner point out that anarchy forces states to worry about both the absolute gains from cooperation and the way that gains are distributed among participants. The logic is straightforward: If one state reaps larger gains than its partners, it will gradually become stronger, and its partners will eventually become more vulnerable.

Realists have also been quick to explore a variety of new issues. Barry Posen offers a realist explanation for ethnic conflict, noting that the breakup of multiethnic states could place rival ethnic groups in an anarchic setting, thereby triggering intense fears and tempting each group to use force to improve its relative position. This problem would be particularly severe when each group's territory contained enclaves inhabited by their ethnic rivals—as in the former Yugoslavia—because each side would be tempted to "cleanse" (preemptively) these alien minorities and expand to incorporate any others from their ethnic group that lay outside their borders. Realists have also cautioned that NATO, absent a clear enemy, would likely face increasing strains and that expanding its presence eastward would jeopardize relations with Russia. Finally, scholars such as Michael Mastanduno have argued that U.S. foreign policy is generally consistent with realist principles, insofar as its actions are still designed to preserve U.S. predominance and to shape a postwar order that advances American interests.

The most interesting conceptual development within the realist paradigm has been the emerging split between the "defensive" and "offensive" strands of thought. Defensive realists such as Waltz,

Van Evera, and Jack Snyder assumed that states had little intrinsic interest in military conquest and argued that the costs of expansion generally outweighed the benefits. Accordingly, they maintained that great power wars occurred largely because domestic groups fostered exaggerated perceptions of threat and an excessive faith in the efficacy of military force.

This view is now being challenged along several fronts. First, as Randall Schweller notes, the neorealist assumption that states merely seek to survive "stacked the deck" in favor of the status quo because it precluded the threat of predatory revisionist states—nations such as Adolf Hitler's Germany or Napoleon Bonaparte's France that "value what they covet far more than what they possess" and are willing to risk annihilation to achieve their aims. Second, Peter Liberman, in his book *Does Conquest Pay?,* uses a number of historical cases— such as the Nazi occupation of Western Europe and Soviet hegemony over Eastern Europe—to show that the benefits of conquest often exceed the costs, thereby casting doubt on the claim that military expansion is no longer cost-effective. Third, offensive realists such as Eric Labs, John Mearsheimer, and Fareed Zakaria argue that anarchy encourages all states to try to maximize their relative strength simply because no state can ever be sure when a truly revisionist power might emerge.

These differences help explain why realists disagree over issues such as the future of Europe. For defensive realists such as Van Evera, war is rarely profitable and usually results from militarism, hypernationalism, or some other distorting domestic factor. Because Van Evera believes such forces are largely absent in post-Cold War Europe, he concludes that the region is "primed for peace." By contrast, Mearsheimer and other offensive realists believe that anarchy forces great powers to compete irrespective of their internal characteristics and that security competition will return to Europe as soon as the U.S. pacifier is withdrawn.

New Life for Liberalism

The defeat of communism sparked a round of self-congratulation in the West, best exemplified by Francis Fukuyama's infamous claim that humankind had now reached the "end of history." History has paid little attention to this boast, but the triumph of the West did give a notable boost to all three strands of liberal thought.

By far the most interesting and important development has been the lively debate on the "democratic peace." Although the most recent phase of this debate had begun even before the Soviet Union collapsed, it became more influential as the number of democracies began to increase and as evidence of this relationship began to accumulate.

Democratic peace theory is a refinement of the earlier claim that democracies were inherently more peaceful than autocratic states. It rests on the belief that although democracies seem to fight wars as often as other states, they rarely, if ever, fight one another. Scholars such as Michael Doyle, James Lee Ray, and Bruce Russett have offered a number of explanations for this tendency, the most popular being that democracies embrace norms of compromise that bar the use of force against groups espousing similar principles. It is hard to think of a more influential, recent academic debate, insofar as the belief that "democracies don't fight each other" has been an important justification for the Clinton administration's efforts to enlarge the sphere of democratic rule.

It is therefore ironic that faith in the "democratic peace" became the basis for U.S. policy just as additional research was beginning to identify several qualifiers to this theory. First, Snyder and Edward Mansfield pointed out that states may be more prone to war when they are in the midst of a democratic transition, which implies that efforts to export democracy might actually make things worse. Second, critics such as Joanne Gowa and David Spiro have argued that the apparent absence of war between democracies is due to the way that democracy has been defined and to the relative dearth of democratic states (especially before 1945). In addition, Christopher Layne has pointed out that when democracies have come close to war in the past their decision to remain at peace ultimately had little do with their shared democratic character. Third, clear-cut evidence that democracies do not fight each other is confined to the post-1945 era, and, as Gowa has emphasized, the absence of conflict in this period may be due more to their common interest in containing the Soviet Union than to shared democratic principles.

Liberal institutionalists likewise have continued to adapt their own theories. On the one hand, the core claims of institutionalist theory have become more modest over time. Institutions are now said to facilitate cooperation when it is in each state's interest to do so, but it is widely agreed that they cannot force states to behave in ways that are contrary to the states' own selfish interests. [For further discussion please see Robert Keohane's article, "Cooperation and International Regimes," page 163.—ED.] On the other hand, institutionalists such as John Duffield and Robert McCalla have extended the theory into new substantive areas, most notably the study of NATO. For these scholars, NATO's highly institutionalized character helps explain why it has been able to survive and adapt, despite the disappearance of its main adversary.

The economic strand of liberal theory is still influential as well. In particular, a number of scholars have recently suggested that the "globalization" of world markets, the rise of transnational networks and nongovernmental organizations, and the rapid spread of global communications technology are undermining the power of states and shifting attention away from military security toward economics and social welfare. The details are novel but the basic logic is familiar: As societies around the globe become enmeshed in a web of economic and social connections, the costs of disrupting these ties will effectively preclude unilateral state actions, especially the use of force.

This perspective implies that war will remain a remote possibility among the advanced industrial democracies. It also suggests that bringing China and Russia into the relentless embrace of world capitalism is the best way to promote both prosperity and peace, particularly if this process creates a strong middle class in these states and reinforces pressures to democratize. Get these societies hooked on prosperity and competition will be confined to the economic realm.

This view has been challenged by scholars who argue that the actual scope of "globalization" is modest and that these various transactions still take place in environments that are shaped and regulated by states. Nonetheless, the belief that economic forces are superseding traditional great power politics enjoys widespread acceptance among scholars, pundits, and policymakers, and the role of the state is likely to be an important topic for future academic inquiry.

Constructivist Theories

Whereas realism and liberalism tend to focus on material factors such as power or trade, constructivist approaches emphasize the impact of ideas. Instead of taking the state for granted and assuming that it simply seeks to survive, constructivists regard the interests and identities of states as a highly malleable product of specific historical processes. They pay close attention to the prevailing discourse(s) in society because discourse reflects and shapes beliefs and interests, and establishes accepted norms of behavior. Consequently, constructivism is especially attentive to the sources of change, and this approach has largely replaced marxism as the preeminent radical perspective on international affairs.

The end of the Cold War played an important role in legitimating constructivist theories because realism and liberalism both failed to anticipate this event and had some trouble explaining it. Constructivists had an explanation: Specifically, former president Mikhail Gorbachev revolutionized Soviet foreign policy because he embraced new ideas such as "common security."

Moreover, given that we live in an era where old norms are being challenged, once clear boundaries are dissolving, and issues of identity are becoming more salient, it is hardly surprising that scholars have been drawn to approaches that place these issues front and center. From a constructivist perspective, in fact, the central issue in the post-Cold War world is how different groups conceive their identities and interests. Although power is not irrelevant, constructivism emphasizes how ideas and identities are created, how they evolve, and how they shape the way states understand and respond to their situation. Therefore, it matters whether Europeans define themselves primarily in national or continental terms; whether Germany and Japan redefine their pasts in ways that encourage their adopting more active international roles; and whether the United States embraces or rejects its identity as "global policeman."

Constructivist theories are quite diverse and do not offer a unified set of predictions on any of these issues. At a purely conceptual level, Alexander Wendt has argued that the realist conception of anarchy does not adequately explain why conflict occurs between states. The real issue is how anarchy is understood—in Wendt's words, "Anarchy is what states make of it." Another strand of constructivist theory has focused on the future of the territorial state, suggesting that transnational communication and shared civic values are undermining traditional national loyalties and creating radically new forms of political association. Other constructivists focus on the role of norms, arguing that international law and other normative principles have eroded earlier notions of sovereignty and altered the legitimate purposes for which state power may be employed. The common theme in each of these strands is the capacity of discourse to shape how political actors define themselves and their interests, and thus modify their behavior.

Domestic Politics Reconsidered

As in the Cold War, scholars continue to explore the impact of domestic politics on the behavior of states. Domestic politics are obviously central to the debate on the democratic peace, and scholars such as Snyder, Jeffrey Frieden, and Helen Milner have examined how domestic interest groups can distort the formation of state preferences and lead to suboptimal international behavior. George Downs, David Rocke, and others have also explored how domestic institutions can help states deal with the perennial problem of uncertainty, while students of psychology have applied prospect theory and other new tools to explain why decision makers fail to act in a rational fashion. [For further discussion about foreign policy decision making, please see "Explaining Foreign Policy Behavior Using the Personal Characteristics of Political Leaders" by Margaret Hermann and Joe Hagan, beginning on page 516. —ED.]

The past decade has also witnessed an explosion of interest in the concept of culture, a development that overlaps with the constructivist emphasis on the importance of ideas and norms. Thus, Thomas Berger and Peter Katzenstein have used cultural variables to explain why Germany and Japan have thus far eschewed more self-reliant military policies; Elizabeth Kier has offered a cultural interpretation of British and French military doctrines in the interwar period; and Iain Johnston has traced continuities in Chinese foreign policy to a deeply rooted form of "cultural realism." Samuel Huntington's dire warnings about an imminent "clash of civilizations" are symptomatic of this trend as well, insofar as his argument rests on the claim that broad cultural affinities are now supplanting national loyalties. Though these and other works define culture in widely varying ways and have yet to provide a full explanation of how it works or how enduring its effects might be, cultural perspectives have been very much in vogue during the past five years. This trend is partly a reflection of the broader interest in cultural issues in the academic world (and within the public debate as well) and partly a response to the upsurge in ethnic, nationalist, and cultural conflicts since the demise of the Soviet Union.

TOMORROW'S CONCEPTUAL TOOLBOX

While these debates reflect the diversity of contemporary scholarship on international affairs, there are also obvious signs of convergence. Most realists recognize that nationalism, militarism, ethnicity, and other domestic factors are important; liberals acknowledge that power is central to international behavior; and some constructivists admit that ideas will have greater impact when backed by powerful states and reinforced by enduring material forces. The boundaries of each paradigm are somewhat permeable, and there is ample opportunity for intellectual arbitrage.

Which of these broad perspectives sheds the most light on contemporary international affairs, and which should policymakers keep most firmly in mind when charting our course into the next century? Although many academics (and more than a few policymakers) are loathe to admit it, realism remains the most compelling general framework for understanding international relations. States continue to pay close attention to the balance of power and to worry about the possibility of major conflict. Among other things, this enduring preoccupation with power and security explains why many Asians and Europeans are now eager to preserve—and possibly expand—the U.S. military presence in their

regions. As Czech president Vaclav Havel has warned, if NATO fails to expand, "we might be heading for a new global catastrophe . . . [which] could cost us all much more than the two world wars." These are not the words of a man who believes that great power rivalry has been banished forever.

As for the United States, the past decade has shown how much it likes being "number one" and how determined it is to remain in a predominant position. The United States has taken advantage of its current superiority to impose its preferences wherever possible, even at the risk of irritating many of its long-standing allies. It has forced a series of one-sided arms control agreements on Russia, dominated the problematic peace effort in Bosnia, taken steps to expand NATO into Russia's backyard, and become increasingly concerned about the rising power of China. It has called repeatedly for greater reliance on multilateralism and a larger role for international institutions, but has treated agencies such as the United Nations and the World Trade Organization with disdain whenever their actions did not conform to U.S. interests. It refused to join the rest of the world in outlawing the production of landmines and was politely uncooperative at the Kyoto environmental summit. Although U.S. leaders are adept at cloaking their actions in the lofty rhetoric of "world order," naked self-interest lies behind most of them. Thus, the end of the Cold War did not bring the end of power politics, and realism is likely to remain the single most useful instrument in our intellectual toolbox.

Yet realism does not explain everything, and a wise leader would also keep insights from the rival paradigms in mind. Liberal theories identify the instruments that states can use to achieve shared interests, highlight the powerful economic forces with which states and societies must now contend, and help us understand why states may differ in their basic preferences. Paradoxically, because U.S. protection reduces the danger of regional rivalries and reinforces the "liberal peace" that emerged after 1945, these factors may become relatively more important, as long as the United States continues to provide security and stability in many parts of the world.

Meanwhile, constructivist theories are best suited to the analysis of how identities and interests can change over time, thereby producing subtle shifts in the behavior of states and occasionally triggering far-reaching but unexpected shifts in international affairs. It matters if political identity in Europe continues to shift from the nation-state to more local regions or to a broader sense of European identity, just as it matters if nationalism is gradually supplanted by the sort of "civilizational" affinities emphasized by Huntington. Realism has little to say about these prospects, and policymakers could be blind-sided by change if they ignore these possibilities entirely.

In short, each of these competing perspectives captures important aspects of world politics. Our understanding would be impoverished were our thinking confined to only one of them. The "compleat diplomat" of the future should remain cognizant of realism's emphasis on the inescapable role of power, keep liberalism's awareness of domestic forces in mind, and occasionally reflect on constructivism's vision of change.

QUESTIONS

1. Why does Walt conclude that "realism remains the most compelling general framework for understanding international relations?"

2. Why does Walt believe that constructivist theories best explain change in world affairs?

System Level International Relations Theories

In the preceding section, we introduced the levels of analysis methodology used in the study of international relations theory. In this section, as well as the sections that follow, we will take a closer look at each of these levels and provide some of the classic readings from the available literature.

We focus here on theories from the system level of analysis. System-level theorists assume that international relations is best understood by taking a broad, global perspective. They look at the nature of the system as a whole and at how states behave within that system. The system, then, sets the standard; it conditions and constrains the behavior of those who operate within it.

We present four major system-level theories in this section: realism, liberalism, class system, and postmodernism. Since each of these theories is discussed in detail in the following chapters, here we will merely summarize how they characterize the international system and the role of states and other major actors in that system.

Realist theory focuses on power. It looks at how the distribution of power, quest for power, and ability to preserve power within the system supercede other goals and dictate the behavior of states and organizations. Some realists argue that this situation is the result of the structure of the international system in which there are no overarching authorities to maintain order on a global scale. States arm themselves and form strategic military alliances for security and self-preservation. This sense of "everyone for him- or herself" tends to strengthen a system dominated by the drive for upward mobility in a hierarchy of power.

Our second theory, liberalism, does not dispute that the international system lacks a global authority to instill order and regulate the behavior of states. Liberals, though, argue that this does not necessarily have to be the case. There are a number of instances in which states have positive incentives to cooperate with one another—trade and other economic partnerships or environmental and conservation efforts, for example. Another aspect of liberal theory points out that international organizations, such as the United Nations, do exist to help bring order to the global community and could be strengthened and expanded.

The third system-level theory is what we have termed class system theory. As the name implies, this theory focuses on the distribution of wealth throughout the world and how that distribution—usually uneven—creates economic classes of people that transcend state boundaries. Essentially, the world is segregated by economics into "haves" and "have-nots." Under such conditions the wealthy classes in different countries have more in common with one another than with the poorer classes of their own nation. They also have a substantial stake in preserving the existing system. Conflict occurs along economic class lines on a global basis, cutting across state boundaries, as the poorer classes revolt against economic imperialism.

The final system-level theory falls under the label of postmodernism. Postmodernism encompasses a rather broad array of perspectives that are united by the contention that reality is shaped by perceptions. The postmodernist emphasis on the subjectivity of ideas, theories, and even social science methodology provides a highly useful counterweight to mainstream perspectives of international relations theory. The constructivist branch of postmodernism focuses on the identities and perceptions of elites and states and the ways in which these preferences are socially constructed. The feminist branch asserts that gender is the key to understanding world politics. Feminist postmodernists focus on the social construction of gender roles and its impact on the structure of society and international relations.

These theories all provide unique perspectives on the system and the behavior of states within it.

In the coming chapters, we will discuss the readings, highlight important terms and concepts, and look at some of the strengths and weaknesses of each paradigm. An effective theory of international relations—whether system, state, or individual level—provides not only a frame of reference for looking at past events but also a method for analyzing current conditions and making projections about our future.

Chapter 2

REALIST THEORY

COMPONENTS OF REALIST THEORY

Focus of Analysis ········▶	• Struggle for power among states in an anarchic international system
Major Actors ········▶	• States
Behavior of States ········▶	• Rational, unitary actors
Goals of States ········▶	• Enhance power and security
View of Human Nature ········▶	• Pessimistic
Condition of International System ········▶	• Anarchic Self-help system
Key Concepts ········▶	• Security dilemma; Balance of power; Power politics; Anarchy; Self-help system; Rational actor; Hegemon; Neo-realism

INTRODUCTION

Realism is the oldest theory for understanding and explaining international politics. The roots of this school of thought extend back nearly 2,500 years. The fundamental principles and implications of realism can be found in the writings of the ancient Greek historian Thucydides and the Italian Renaissance political philosopher Niccolo Machiavelli. Many contemporary scholars, including Hans Morgenthau, Edward Hallett Carr, and Kenneth Waltz, have further explored and developed realist principles.

Indeed, the realist school of thought so dominated the study of international politics in the post–World War II era that it became the theoretical basis for U.S. foreign policy during the Cold War. The list of practitioners includes some of the most influential people in the American foreign policy establishment. George Kennan, U.S. envoy to the Soviet Union during World War II and chief architect of the Containment Doctrine, used the realist balance-of-power concept in constructing the American policy to contain Soviet influence in the Cold War years. American presidents Harry Truman, Dwight Eisenhower, and Richard Nixon and Secretaries of State John Foster Dulles and Henry Kissinger relied to a significant extent on realist principles in shaping their foreign policy decisions.

Many scholars argue that realism's influence on political leaders is evidence of the strength and utility of its principles. They contend that leaders rely on realist theory because it presents a "realistic" view of international relations and focuses on how the world *is* rather than how it *ought* to be. They believe that a careful and objective assessment of world history is important because the fundamental characteristics and behavior of countries have remained essentially unchanged. Thus, realist scholars attempt to discern patterns of behavior among states in the past and then use these observations to analyze and predict the behavior and actions of nations in contemporary international politics.

For realists, power is the key factor in understanding international relations. Global politics is considered a contest for power among states. A state's power is measured primarily in terms of its military capabilities. International diplomacy is based on **power politics,** in which force or the threat of force is the primary method states use to further their interests. According to realists, international relations is a struggle for power and security among competing states. It is the responsibility of each nation-state to provide for its own defense and security. Thus, states are compelled to base foreign policy decisions on considerations of power and security, rather than morality or ideals.

CLASSICAL REALISM

In his work *The History of the Peloponnesian War,* the Greek scholar and historian Thucydides was one of the first to distinguish these realist principles. He used the war between the city-states of Athens and Sparta as a case study for his analysis. Thucydides described the underlying cause of war between Athens and Sparta in clear terms: "What made war inevitable was the growth of Athenian power and the fear which this caused in Sparta." Sparta was wary of the innovative and dynamic nature of Athenian society, which was growing and modernizing both economically and militarily. The Spartans perceived a shift in the balance of power between the two states. The **balance of power** principle contends that if two or more states, or coalitions of states, maintain an even distribution of power, neither side can be confident of victory should conflict arise. Under such conditions, we would presume that states are reluctant to initiate or pursue a military resolution to their differences with other states. In this way, balance and stability in the system are preserved.

Returning to Thucydides' example, Sparta began to strengthen its position militarily in response to the vitality of Athens. The Athenians then grew fearful of their rival's arms build-up and responded in a similar fashion. War between Athens and

Sparta erupted shortly thereafter. Thucydides recorded and analyzed these events to provide a background on the nature of war for future historians and scholars.

One of those who followed was the Italian philosopher Niccolo Machiavelli. Machiavelli is considered the first modern political theorist because, in traditional realist fashion, he sought to describe politics as it is, not as it ought to be. In his book *The Prince,* Machiavelli sought to separate politics from ethics because he wished to provide a practical and objective account of the political process.

In addition, Machiavelli made two other notable contributions to realism. First, his view that humans are "wicked" became one of the central tenets of classical realism. In *The Prince,* Machiavelli wrote that the "gulf between how one should live and how one does live is so wide that a man who neglects what is done for what should be done learns the way to self-destruction rather than self-preservation." Second, this pessimistic assessment of human nature led Machiavelli to emphasize the importance of military power and national security. The survival of the state, as represented figuratively by the prince, is the most important goal in politics. Machiavelli argued that "it is unreasonable to expect that an armed man should obey one who is not or that an unarmed man should remain safe and secure when his servants are armed." Certainly, this statement demonstrates his conviction that those who hold the reins of power must be prepared to contend with threats to their rule. That is, leaders who neglect national security not only do so at their own peril but also jeopardize the security of the state as a whole.

In his book *Politics Among Nations,* Hans Morganthau used the principles of classical realism to both analyze and shape geopolitics of 1948. In doing so, Morgenthau created a more scientific approach to the study and practice of foreign affairs in our contemporary age.

Morgenthau, like Machiavelli, maintained that insecurity, aggression, and war are recurring themes of international politics and that these themes are ultimately rooted in human nature. Morgenthau, again like his realist predecessors, recognized that on a fundamental level, conflict was driven not by political or ideological differences as much as by human desire to dominate other humans. He suggested that "statesmen think and act in terms of power."[1] One common characteristic of all states, Morgenthau assumed, was their tendency to behave as rational actors. According to the **rational actor** assumption, states pursue prudent goals that are within their power (capability) to achieve. Likewise, a state's foreign policy is based on prudent calculations of national interest.

Morgenthau's prescription for a "rational theory of international politics" was based on the notion of "interest defined as power." That is, in a system consisting of individual states or blocs of states struggling for power, Morgenthau suggested that the "ever present threat of large-scale violence" had in the past, and could in the future, be contained by pursuing a balance-of-power strategy. As discussed earlier, this strategy contends that if two or more coalitions of states maintain a roughly equal distribution of power, no single state can be confident in its ability to win a

---

[1] Hans J. Morgenthau, *Politics Among Nations* (New York: McGraw-Hill, 1993), p. 5.

war. Consequently, all states would be reluctant to initiate conflict, and balance, order, and peace would, in theory, be preserved.

The selection by George Kennan provides an excellent example of the application of realist principles to the formulation of American foreign policy. In 1946, Kennan, an American diplomat then serving in Moscow, sent his now-famous "long telegram" to Washington. The telegram was a detailed assessment of the sources of Soviet conduct. One year later, using the pseudonym of X, Kennan's argument was published in the highly respected journal *Foreign Affairs*. His ideas provided the intellectual and geopolitical foundation for the United States postwar policy of "containment," aimed at curbing Soviet expansionism. Kennan's analysis and policy recommendations relied upon the realist concepts of both power politics and balance of power.

NEO-REALISM

Some contemporary proponents of realist theory, known as neo-realists, suggest that it is not just the uneven development or distribution of power among states—like that between Athens and Sparta—that leads to conflict. **Neo-realism** differs from classical realism on one basic point: Neo-realists believe that the struggle for power is the result of the structure of the international system as a whole rather than a fundament of human nature. Specifically, the problem is found in the anarchic nature of the international system. The term **anarchy** refers to the lack of a central authority or government to enforce law and order between states and throughout the globe.

Kenneth Waltz, founder of neo-realist theory, suggests that this lack of central authority is key to understanding the international system and international relations theory. According to Waltz, states are compelled to base their foreign policy on national security considerations because they are ultimately responsible for their own survival. Since there is no overarching world government to enforce peace, states exist in a **self-help system.** Like the call on a sinking ship, the anarchic nature of the international system leaves "every state for itself."

This type of self-help situation leads to a security dilemma. A **security dilemma** is the result of fear, insecurity, and lack of trust among states living in an anarchic international system. States arm themselves in order to pursue the rational goal of self-preservation. But by arming themselves, more fear and insecurity is created among other states. These states, in turn, also increase their armaments. Even though a state may be arming itself for purely defensive purposes, this process makes all states within the system less secure and fuels an arms race. We see that each state may be acting rationally on an individual basis, but, collectively, their actions lead to unintended consequences. At the very least, these consequences can include an expensive and wasteful arms race, and, in the end, such actions can even lead to war.

Many of the assumptions of neo-realism outlined above can be found in Kenneth Waltz's piece, in which he discusses the relevance of structural realism in the post–Cold War era. Waltz defends the key concepts of structural realism and argues that the demise of the Cold War has not changed the essential behavior of states. Waltz analyzes alternative explanations for the transformation of international politics including the spread of democracy, interdependence, and the role of international institutions and finds that all three lack the insights and explanatory power of structural realism.

The excerpt from Robert Gilpin's book *War and Change in World Politics* highlights the realist principle of hegemony. A **hegemon** is a preponderant power that dominates other states within its sphere of influence. Gilpin discusses the realist view of how change occurs in international politics and identifies a pattern by which hegemonic states both rise and fall from power. Gilpin distinguishes three structural causes of a decline in power. First is the economic and military burdens of maintaining dominance over other states. Second, hegemons tend to gradually lose their economic and military vitality because domestic consumption rises as the public enjoys the benefits of world preeminence. Third, the inevitable spread of technology tends to weaken a hegemon's economic and military advantages over its competitors. In the end, the hegemon's weakness is increasingly evident and it becomes vulnerable to challenges from potential rivals.

In the final reading, former Secretary of State Henry Kissinger presents a realist interpretation of the global war on terrorism. The author discusses the impact of the events of September 11, 2001, on the course and conduct of American foreign policy. He argues for a strong response to the events of September 11 because the "whole structure of the security of the post-war world will disintegrate" if the United States fails to respond to an attack on its own territory. Finally, Dr. Kissinger offers some insights into how the war on terrorism is likely to affect U.S. relations with its traditional European allies as well as with Russia, China, and South Asia.

A CRITIQUE OF REALIST THEORY

As we have discussed, classical realism and the more contemporary neo-realism offer important and unique insights into the essential characteristics of international relations. Like any theory of international relations, however, the realist paradigm has both strengths and weaknesses. From a practical standpoint, realist theory offers a set of simple, straightforward principles that have guided political leaders in their decision making for many years. These pragmatic guidelines strip away moral and idealistic notions of how states *should* act or how international dialogue is to be conducted. Rather, the focus is on how nations actually *do* behave within the international system, both individually and collectively.

Realism also has some valid strengths from a historical, scholarly standpoint. From the ancient Greek historian Thucydides to contemporary scholars like Hans Morgenthau and Kenneth Waltz, there is certainly a wide body of historical evidence to support the realists' supposition that states are locked in a struggle for power that can, and often does, lead to war.

Realists contend, as well, that history tends to favor their approach to international relations theory. The conflict between Athens and Sparta, the conditions that led to the Cold War, and even the U.S. war with Iraq in 2003 all serve as case studies and provide data to support an argument for realism.

That so much of history can be used to support the realist perspective and that so many leaders and policymakers have relied on realist principles are valid, if somewhat self-serving, testaments to the strength of the theory. We must also acknowledge, however, some problems in applying realism to conditions in our world today. As we shall see in the next chapter, liberal theorists argue that realism places too great an emphasis on conflict while underestimating the role of international institutions in promoting cooperation. The nature of international competition has changed, and war is no longer considered a natural extension of politics among major powers. Perhaps most dramatically, nuclear weapons have made the pursuit of power using war or armed conflict dangerous and costly. It is fairly safe to assume that war between two nuclear powers would be unwinnable.

Aside from the devastating consequences, the use of force—under most conditions—is less acceptable in today's increasingly interdependent world. In its emphasis on conflict, realist theory tends to ignore the current expansion of cooperation between states. Further, the international conditions that allow for, indeed even promote, cooperation between nations challenge the neo-realist notion of anarchy. Certain generally accepted rules and norms—as well as the institutions that establish and uphold them—play an important role in facilitating and promoting an appropriate climate for cooperation. Anarchy, even anarchy ordered by a specific power structure as neo-realists describe, does not offer an adequate explanation for the kind of cooperation and transnational linkages so common in our contemporary world.

With this idea of extended cooperation, we can see some other weaknesses of realist theory. States are no longer the only important actors on the international stage. International organizations, like the United Nations, and nongovernmental organizations, such as multinational corporations and environmental organizations, perform important functions in maintaining stability and expanding cooperation worldwide.

Another problem confronting realism is the increasing relevance of substate actors such as terrorists. Realists contend that states are the primary actors on the international stage and that all other identities are less important to our understanding of global affairs. Surely the events of September 11 and the current global war on terrorism highlight the significant security threat posed by global terrorist networks like Al Qaeda.

And we must question, too, whether states, particularly under these more complex global conditions, can be considered truly unitary actors in the realist sense. Can a nation be viewed monolithically, able to make coherent decisions based strictly on considerations of the national interest? The politics of a state, both internal and external, are more likely a messy business, full of compromise and competing interests. That the actions of a state reflect rational, consistent cost-benefit calculations based purely on self-interest, as realist theory suggests, is, at the very least, difficult to prove.

One final weakness in the case for realism is the theory's inability to account for peaceful change. According to realists, change in the international system can only come about from, and is often the catalyst for, war. In the wake of the Cold War and peaceful dissolution of the Soviet Union, we might say that realism is left holding the theoretical bag on the phenomenon of peaceful change.

KEY CONCEPTS

Anarchy   refers to the lack of a central authority or government to enforce law and order between states and throughout the globe.

Balance of power   is a policy aimed at maintaining the international status quo. According to this theory, peace and stability are best preserved when power is distributed among five or more states and no single state has a preponderance of military power.

Hegemon   A state with overwhelming military, economic, and political power that has the ability to maintain its dominant position in the international system.

Neo-realism   is a variant of realism that contends that the struggle for power among states is the result of the anarchic structure of the international system as a whole, rather than a fundament of human nature.

Power politics   are policies in which force, or the threat of force, is the primary method used to further a state's interests. According to realists, international relations is a struggle for power and security among competing states.

Rational actor   refers to the realist assumption that states generally pursue attainable, prudent goals that are commensurate with their power (capability) to achieve.

Security dilemma   is the result of fear, insecurity, and lack of trust among states living in an anarchic international system. States arm themselves in order to pursue the rational goal of self-preservation. But by arming themselves, more fear and insecurity is created among other states. These states, in turn, also increase their armaments. Even though a state may be arming itself for purely defensive purposes, this process makes all states within the system less secure and fuels an arms race.

Self-help system   is the neo-realist concept that, in an anarchic international system where there is no overarching global authority (like a world government) to enforce peace and stability, each state is responsible for its own survival and cannot rely on the help of other states.

Twenty-first century society is more and more characterized by the spread of consumerism and the free exchange of ideas and technology, by expanded economic and political ties, and by growth through cooperation and conflict resolution through peaceful means. Without some sort of modification, proponents of realist theory might be put in a difficult position if these trends continue well into the next decade.

In response, realists would question whether the international politics of today are, indeed, so different from the past. The latest war with Iraq certainly demonstrates that war between nations is not an obsolete concept. Moreover, the continuing tension between India and Pakistan offers almost daily reminders of the realist principles of power politics and the utility of nuclear deterrence. Finally, the contemporary tragedies in Bosnia, Somalia, and Rwanda, to name just a few examples, provide ample evidence that violence and conflict are still very much a part of our world.

3. The History of the Peloponnesian War

Thucydides

In this famous excerpt, known as the Melian Dialogue, Thucydides describes the conference between Athenian diplomats and Melian officials in which the Athenians are attempting to persuade the Melians to join the war against Sparta. This discussion contains some of the most important elements of the realist view of the relationship between strong and weak states. While the Melians rely on moral arguments, the Athenians, representing the more powerful state, warn the Melians that the "strong do what they have the power to do and the weak accept what they have to accept." In the end, the Melian plea for fair play and justice fails, and all the men of Melos are killed and the women and children are enslaved. This selection is from *History of the Peloponnesian War.*

Thucydides (460–400 B.C.) was an Athenian historian and is credited with being the founder of international relations theory. He is also one of the first scholars to be identified with the realist tradition.

Thucydides the Athenian wrote the history of the war fought between Athens and Sparta, beginning the account at the very outbreak of the war, in the belief that it was going to be a great war and more worth writing about than any of those which had taken place in the past. My belief was based on the fact that the two sides were at the very height of their power and preparedness, and I saw, too, that the rest of the Hellenic world was committed to one side or the other; even those who were not immediately engaged were deliberating on the courses which they were to take later. This was the greatest disturbance in the history of the Hellenes, affecting also a large part of the non-Hellenic world, and indeed, I might almost say, the whole of mankind. For though I have found it impossible, because of its remoteness in time, to acquire a really precise knowledge of the distant past or even of the history preceding our own period, yet, after looking back into it as far as I can, all the evidence leads me to conclude that these periods were not great periods either in warfare or in anything else.

. . . So for a long time the state of affairs everywhere in Hellas was such that nothing very remarkable could be done by any combination of powers and that even the individual cities were lacking in enterprise.

Finally, however, the Spartans put down tyranny in the rest of Greece, most of which had been governed by tyrants for much longer than Athens. From the time when the Dorians first settled in Sparta there had been a particularly long period of political disunity; yet the Spartan constitution goes back to a very early date, and the country has never been ruled by tyrants. For rather more than 400 years, dating from the end of the late war, they have had the same system of government, and this has been not only a source of internal strength, but has enabled them to intervene in the affairs of other states.

Reprinted by permission of Penguin Books, Viking Penguin, Inc.

Not many years after the end of tyrannies in Hellas the battle of Marathon was fought between the Persians and the Athenians. Ten years later the foreign enemy returned with his vast armada for the conquest of Hellas, and at this moment of peril the Spartans, since they were the leading power, were in command of the allied Hellenic forces. In face of the invasion the Athenians decided to abandon their city; they broke up their homes, took to their ships, and became a people of sailors. It was by a common effort that the foreign invasion was repelled; but not long afterwards the Hellenes—both those who had fought in the war together and those who later revolted from the King of Persia—split into two divisions, one group following Athens and the other Sparta. These were clearly the two most powerful states, one being supreme on land, the other on the sea. For a short time the war-time alliance held together, but it was not long before quarrels took place and Athens and Sparta, each with her own allies, were at war with each other, while among the rest of the Hellenes states that had their own differences now joined one or other of the two sides. So from the end of the Persian War till the beginning of the Peloponnesian War, though there were some intervals of peace, on the whole these two Powers were either fighting with each other or putting down revolts among their allies. They were consequently in a high state of military preparedness and had gained their military experience in the hard school of danger.

The Spartans did not make their allies pay tribute, but saw to it that they were governed by oligarchies who would work in the Spartan interest. Athens, on the other hand, had in the course of time taken over the fleets of her allies (except for those of Chios and Lesbos) and had made them pay contributions of money instead. Thus the forces available to Athens alone for this war were greater than the combined forces had ever been when the alliance was still intact.

In investigating past history, and in forming the conclusions which I have formed, it must be admitted that one cannot rely on every detail which has come down to us by way of tradition. People are inclined to accept all stories of ancient times in an uncritical way—even when these stories concern their own native countries. Most people in Athens, for instance, are under the impression that Hipparchus, who was killed by Harmodius and Aristogiton, was tyrant at the time, not realizing that it was Hippias who was the eldest and the chief of the sons of Pisistratus, and that Hipparchus and Thessalus were his younger brothers. What happened was this: on the very day that had been fixed for their attempt, indeed at the very last moment, Harmodius and Aristogiton had reason to believe that Hippias had been informed of the plot by some of the conspirators. Believing him to have been forewarned, they kept away from him, but, as they wanted to perform some daring exploit before they were arrested themselves, they killed Hipparchus when they found him by the Leocorium organizing the Panathenaic procession.

The rest of the Hellenes, too, make many incorrect assumptions not only about the dimly remembered past, but also about contemporary history. For instance, there is a general belief that the kings of Sparta are each entitled to two votes, whereas in fact they have only one; and it is believed, too, that the Spartans have a company of troops called "Pitanate." Such a company has never existed.

Most people, in fact, will not take trouble in finding out the truth, but are much more inclined to accept the first story they hear.

However, I do not think that one will be far wrong in accepting the conclusions I have reached from the evidence which I have put forward. It is better evidence than that of the poets, who exaggerate the importance of their themes, or of the prose chroniclers, who are less interested in telling the truth than in catching the attention of their public, whose authorities cannot be checked, and whose subject-matter, owing to the passage of time, is mostly lost in the unreliable streams of mythology. We may claim instead to have used only the plainest evidence and to have reached conclusions which are reasonably accurate, considering that we have been dealing with ancient history. As for this present war, even though people are apt to think that the war in which they are fighting is the greatest of all wars and, when it is over, to relapse again into their admiration of the past, nevertheless, if one looks at the facts themselves, one will see that this was the greatest war of all.

In this history I have made use of set speeches some of which were delivered just before and others during the war. I have found it difficult to remember the precise words used in the speeches which I listened to myself and my various informants have experienced the same difficulty; so my method has been, while keeping as closely as possible to the general sense of the words that were actually used, to make the speakers say what, in my opinion, was called for by each situation.

And with regard to my factual reporting of the events of the war I have made it a principle not to write down the first story that came my way, and not even to be guided by my own general impressions; either I was present myself at the events which I have described or else I heard of them from eye-witnesses whose reports I have checked with as much thoroughness as possible. Not that even so the truth was easy to discover: different eye-witnesses give different accounts of the same events, speaking out of partiality for one side or the other or else from imperfect memories. And it may well be that my history will seem less easy to read because of the absence in it of a romantic element. It will be enough for me, however, if these words of mine are judged useful by those who want to understand clearly the events which happened in the past and which (human nature being what it is) will, at some time or other and in much the same ways, be repeated in the future. My work is not a piece of writing designed to meet the taste of an immediate public, but was done to last for ever.

The greatest war in the past was the Persian War; yet in this war the decision was reached quickly as a result of two naval battles and two battles on land. The Peloponnesian War, on the other hand, not only lasted for a long time, but throughout its course brought with it unprecedented suffering for Hellas. Never before had so many cities been captured and then devastated, whether by foreign armies or by the Hellenic powers themselves (some of these cities, after capture, were resettled with new inhabitants); never had there been so many exiles; never such loss of life—both in the actual warfare and in internal revolutions. Old stories of past prodigies, which had not found much confirmation in recent experience, now became credible. Wide areas, for instance, were affected by violent earthquakes; there were more frequent eclipses of the sun than had ever been recorded before; in various parts of the country there were extensive droughts followed by famine; and there was the plague which did more harm and destroyed more life than almost any other single factor. All these calamities fell together upon the Hellenes after the outbreak of war.

War began when the Athenians and the Peloponnesians broke the Thirty Years Truce which had been made after the capture of Euboea. As to the reasons why they broke the truce, I propose first to give an account of the causes of complaint which they had against each other and of the specific instances where their interests clashed: this is in order that there should be no doubt in anyone's mind about what led to this great war falling upon the Hellenes. But the real reason for the war is, in my opinion, most likely to be disguised by such an argument. What made war inevitable was the growth of Athenian power and the fear which this caused in Sparta. As for the reasons for breaking the truce and declaring war which were openly expressed by each side, they are as follows. . . .

THE MELIAN DIALOGUE

Next summer Alcibiades sailed to Argos with twenty ships and seized 300 Argive citizens who were still suspected of being pro-Spartan. These were put by the Athenians into the nearby islands under Athenian control.

The Athenians also made an expedition against the island of Melos. They had thirty of their own ships, six from Chios, and two from Lesbos; 1,200 hoplites, 300 archers, and twenty mounted archers, all from Athens; and about 1,500 hoplites from the allies and the islanders.

The Melians are a colony from Sparta. They had refused to join the Athenian empire like the other islanders, and at first had remained neutral without helping either side; but afterwards, when the Athenians had brought force to bear on them by laying waste their land, they had become open enemies of Athens.

Now the generals Cleomedes, the son of Lycomedes, and Tisias, the son of Tisimachus, encamped with the above force in Melian territory and, before doing any harm to the land, first of all sent representatives to negotiate. The Melians did not invite these representatives to speak before the people, but asked them to make the statement for which they had come in front of the governing body and the few. The Athenian representatives then spoke as follows:

"So we are not to speak before the people, no doubt in case the mass of the people should hear once and for all and without interruption an argument from us which is both persuasive and incontrovertible, and should so be led astray. This, we realize, is your motive in bringing us here to speak before the few. Now suppose that you who sit here should make assurance doubly sure. Suppose that you, too, should refrain from dealing with every point in detail in a set speech, and should instead interrupt us whenever we say something controversial and deal with that before going on to the next point? Tell us first whether you approve of this suggestion of ours."

The Council of the Melians replied as follows:

"No one can object to each of us putting forward our own views in a calm atmosphere. That is perfectly reasonable. What is scarcely consistent with such a proposal is the present threat, indeed the certainty, of your making war on us. We see that you have come prepared to judge the argument yourselves, and that the likely end of it all will be either war, if we prove that we are in the right, and so refuse to surrender, or else slavery."

Athenians: If you are going to spend the time in enumerating your suspicions about the future, or if you have met here for any other reason except to look the facts in the face and on the basis of these facts to consider how you can save your city from destruction, there is no point in our going on with this discussion. If, however, you will do as we suggest, then we will speak on.

Melians: It is natural and understandable that people who are placed as we are should have recourse to all kinds of arguments and different points of view. However, you are right in saying that we are met together here to discuss the safety of our country and, if you will have it so, the discussion shall proceed on the lines that you have laid down.

Athenians: Then we on our side will use no fine phrases saying, for example, that we have a right to our empire because we defeated the Persians, or that we have come against you now because of the injuries you have done us—a great mass of words that nobody would believe. And we ask you on your side not to imagine that you will influence us by saying that you, though a colony of Sparta, have not joined Sparta in the war, or that you have never done us any harm. Instead we recommend that you should try to get what it is possible for you to get, taking into consideration what we both really do think; since you know as well as we do that, when these matters are discussed by practical people, the standard of justice depends on the equality of power to compel and that in fact the strong do what they have the power to do and the weak accept what they have to accept.

Melians: Then in our view (since you force us to leave justice out of account and to confine ourselves to self-interest)—in our view it is at any rate useful that you should not destroy a principle that is to the general good of all men—namely, that in the case of all who fall into danger there should be such a thing as fair play and just dealing, and that such people should be allowed to use and to profit by arguments that fall short of a mathematical accuracy. And this is a principle which affects you as much as anybody, since your own fall would be visited by the most terrible vengeance and would be an example to the world.

Athenians: As for us, even assuming that our empire does come to an end, we are not despondent about what would happen next. One is not so much frightened of being conquered by a power which rules over others, as Sparta does (not that we are concerned with Sparta now), as of what would happen if a ruling power is attacked and defeated by its own subjects. So far as this point is concerned, you can leave it to us to face the risks involved. What we shall do now is to show you that it is for the good of our own empire that we are here and that it is for the preservation of your city that we shall say what we are going to say. We do not want any trouble in bringing you into our empire, and we want you to be spared for the good both of yourselves and of ourselves.

Melians: And how could it be just as good for us to be the slaves as for you to be the masters?

Athenians: You, by giving in, would save yourselves from disaster; we, by not destroying you, would be able to profit from you.

Melians: So you would not agree to our being neutral, friends instead of enemies, but allies of neither side?

Athenians: No, because it is not so much your hostility that injures us; it is rather the case that, if we were on friendly terms with you, our subjects would regard that as a sign of weakness in us, whereas your hatred is evidence of our power.

Melians: Is that your subjects' idea of fair play—that no distinction should be made between people who are quite unconnected with you and people who are mostly your own colonists or else rebels whom you have conquered?

Athenians: So far as right and wrong are concerned they think that there is no difference between the two, that those who still preserve their independence do so because they are strong, and that if we fail to attack them it is because we are afraid. So that by conquering you we shall increase not only the size but the security of our empire. We rule the sea and you are islanders, and weaker islanders too than the others; it is therefore particularly important that you should not escape.

Melians: But do you think there is no security for you in what we suggest? For here again, since you will not let us mention justice, but tell us to give in to your interests, we, too, must tell you what our interests are and, if yours and ours happen to coincide, we must try to persuade you of the fact. Is it not certain that you will make enemies of all states who are at present neutral, when they see what is happening here and naturally conclude that in course of time you will attack them too? Does not this mean that you are strengthening the enemies you have already and are forcing others to become your enemies even against their intentions and their inclinations?

Athenians: As a matter of fact we are not so much frightened of states on the continent. They have their liberty, and this means that it will be a long time before they begin to take precautions against us. We are more concerned about islanders like yourselves, who are still unsubdued, or subjects who have already become embittered by the constraint which our empire imposes on them. These are the people who are most likely to act in a reckless manner and to bring themselves and us, too, into the most obvious danger.

Melians: Then surely, if such hazards are taken by you to keep your empire and by your subjects to escape from it, we who are still free would show ourselves great cowards and weaklings if we failed to face everything that comes rather than submit to slavery.

Athenians: No, not if you are sensible. This is no fair fight, with honour on one side and shame on the other. It is rather a question of saving your lives and not resisting those who are far too strong for you.

Melians: Yet we know that in war fortune sometimes makes the odds more level than could be expected from the difference in numbers of the two sides. And if we surrender, then all our hope is lost at once, whereas, so long as we remain in action, there is still a hope that we may yet stand upright.

Athenians: Hope, that comforter in danger! If one already has solid advantages to fall back upon, one can indulge in hope. It may do harm, but will not destroy one. But hope is by nature an expensive commodity, and those who are risking their all on one cast find out what it means only when they are already ruined; it never fails them in the period when such a knowledge would enable them to take precautions. Do not let this happen to you, you who are weak and whose fate depends on a single movement of the scale. And do not be like those people who, as so commonly happens, miss the chance of saving themselves in a human and practical way, and, when every clear and distinct hope has left them in their adversity, turn to what is blind and vague, to prophecies and oracles and such things which by encouraging hope lead men to ruin.

Melians: It is difficult, and you may be sure that we know it, for us to oppose your power and fortune, unless the terms be equal. Nevertheless we trust that the gods will give us fortune as good as yours, because we are standing for what is right against what is wrong; and as for what we lack in power, we trust that it will be made up for by our alliance with the Spartans, who are bound, if for no other reason, then for honour's sake, and because we are their kinsmen, to come to our help. Our confidence, therefore, is not so entirely irrational as you think.

Athenians: So far as the favour of the gods is concerned, we think we have as much right to that as you have. Our aims and our actions are perfectly consistent with the beliefs men hold about the gods and with the principles which govern their own conduct. Our opinion of the gods and our knowledge of men lead us to conclude that it is a general and necessary law of nature to rule whatever one can. This is not a law that we made ourselves, nor were we the first to act upon it when it was made. We found it already in existence, and we shall leave it to exist for ever among those who come after us. We are merely acting in accordance with it, and we know that you or anybody else with the same power

as ours would be acting in precisely the same way. And therefore, so far as the gods are concerned, we see no good reason why we should fear to be at a disadvantage. But with regard to your views about Sparta and your confidence that she, out of a sense of honour, will come to your aid, we must say that we congratulate you on your simplicity but do not envy you your folly. In matters that concern themselves or their own constitution the Spartans are quite remarkably good; as for their relations with others, that is a long story, but it can be expressed shortly and clearly by saying that of all people we know the Spartans are most conspicuous for believing that what they like doing is honourable and what suits their interests is just. And this kind of attitude is not going to be of much help to you in your absurd quest for safety at the moment.

Melians: But this is the very point where we can feel most sure. Their own self-interest will make them refuse to betray their own colonists, the Melians, for that would mean losing the confidence of their friends among the Hellenes and doing good to their enemies.

Athenians: You seem to forget that if one follows one's self-interest one wants to be safe, whereas the path of justice and honour involves one in danger. And, where danger is concerned, the Spartans are not, as a rule, very venturesome.

Melians: But we think that they would even endanger themselves for our sake and count the risk more worth taking than in the case of others, because we are so close to the Peloponnese that they could operate more easily, and because they can depend on us more than on others, since we are of the same race and share the same feelings.

Athenians: Goodwill shown by the party that is asking for help does not mean security for the prospective ally. What is looked for is a positive preponderance of power in action. And the Spartans pay attention to this point even more than others do. Certainly they distrust their own native resources so much that when they attack a neighbour they bring a great army of allies with them. It is hardly likely therefore that, while we are in control of the sea, they will cross over to an island.

Melians: But they still might send others. The Cretan sea is a wide one, and it is harder for those who control it to intercept others than for those who want to slip through to do so safely. And even if they were to fail in this, they would turn against your own land and against those of your allies left unvisited by Brasidas. So, instead of troubling about a country which has nothing to do with you, you will find trouble nearer home, among your allies, and in your own country.

Athenians: It is a possibility, something that has in fact happened before. It may happen in your case, but you are well aware that the Athenians have never yet relinquished a single siege operation through fear of others. But we are somewhat shocked to find that, though you announced your intention of discussing how you could preserve yourselves, in all this talk you have said absolutely nothing which could justify a man in thinking that he could be preserved. Your chief points are concerned with what you hope may happen in the future, while your actual resources are too scanty to give you a chance of survival against the forces that are opposed to you at this moment. You will therefore be showing an extraordinary lack of common sense if, after you have asked us to retire from this meeting, you still fail to reach a conclusion wiser than anything you have

mentioned so far. Do not be led astray by a false sense of honour—a thing which often brings men to ruin when they are faced with an obvious danger that somehow affects their pride. For in many cases men have still been able to see the dangers ahead of them, but this thing called dishonour, this word, by its own force of seduction, has drawn them into a state where they have surrendered to an idea, while in fact they have fallen voluntarily into irrevocable disaster, in dishonour that is all the more dishonourable because it has come to them from their own folly rather than their misfortune. You, if you take the right view, will be careful to avoid this. You will see that there is nothing disgraceful in giving way to the greatest city in Hellas when she is offering you such reasonable terms—alliance on a tribute-paying basis and liberty to enjoy your own property. And, when you are allowed to choose between war and safety, you will not be so insensitively arrogant as to make the wrong choice. This is the safe rule—to stand up to one's equals, to behave with deference towards one's superiors, and to treat one's inferiors with moderation. Think it over again, then, when we have withdrawn from the meeting, and let this be a point that constantly recurs to your minds—that you are discussing the fate of your country, that you have only one country, and that its future for good or ill depends on this one single decision which you are going to make.

The Athenians then withdrew from the discussion. The Melians, left to themselves, reached a conclusion which was much the same as they had indicated in their previous replies. Their answer was as follows:

"Our decision, Athenians, is just the same as it was at first. We are not prepared to give up in a short moment the liberty which our city has enjoyed from its foundation for 700 years. We put our trust in the fortune that the gods will send and which has saved us up to now, and in the help of men—that is, of the Spartans; and so we shall try to save ourselves. But we invite you to allow us to be friends of yours and enemies to neither side, to make a treaty which shall be agreeable to both you and us, and so to leave our country."

The Melians made this reply, and the Athenians, just as they were breaking off the discussion, said:

"Well, at any rate, judging from this decision of yours, you seem to us quite unique in your ability to consider the future as something more certain than what is before your eyes, and to see uncertainties as realities, simply because you would like them to be so. As you have staked most on and trusted most in Spartans, luck, and hopes, so in all these you will find yourselves most completely deluded."

The Athenian representatives then went back to the army, and the Athenian generals, finding that the Melians would not submit, immediately commenced hostilities and built a wall completely round the city of Melos, dividing the work out among the various states. Later they left behind a garrison of some of their own and some allied troops to blockade the place by land and sea, and with the greater part of their army returned home. The force left behind stayed on and continued with the siege.

About the same time the Argives invaded Phliasia and were ambushed by the Phliasians and the exiles from Argos, losing about eighty men.

Then, too, the Athenians at Pylos captured a great quantity of plunder from Spartan territory. Not even after this did the Spartans renounce the treaty and make war, but they issued a proclamation saying that any of their people who wished to do so were free to make raids on the Athenians. The Corinthians also made some attacks on the Athenians because of private quarrels of their own, but the rest of the Peloponnesians stayed quiet.

Meanwhile the Melians made a night attack and captured the part of the Athenian lines opposite the market-place. They killed some of the troops, and then, after bringing in corn and everything else useful that they could lay their hands on, retired again and made no further move, while the Athenians took measures to make their blockade more efficient in future. So the summer came to an end.

In the following winter the Spartans planned to invade the territory of Argos, but when the sacrifices for crossing the frontier turned out unfavourably, they gave up the expedition. The fact that they had intended to invade made the Argives suspect certain people in their city, some of whom they arrested, though others succeeded in escaping.

About this same time the Melians again captured another part of the Athenian lines where there were only a few of the garrison on guard. As a result of this, another force came out afterwards from Athens under the command of Philocrates, the son of Demeas. Siege operations were now carried on vigorously and, as there was also some treachery from inside, the Melians surrendered unconditionally to the Athenians, who put to death all the men of military age whom they took, and sold the women and children as slaves. Melos itself they took over for themselves, sending out later a colony of 500 men.

QUESTIONS

1. What are the main points the Melians make to the Athenians in the dialogue?

2. Do you agree with the maxim that, in international politics, the "strong do what they have the power to do and the weak accept what they have to accept"?

---

4.   The Prince

Niccolo Machiavelli

In this excerpt, Niccolo Machiavelli offers his recommendations on how a ruler should lead a nation. Relying on historical observation, Machiavelli suggests that a leader must, at times, take measures that might otherwise be considered unacceptable to preserve the security of the state. For Machiavelli, the successful ruler makes the security and power of the state superior to all considerations of morality and ethics. This selection is from his classic work *The Prince* (1513).

Niccolo Machiavelli (1469–1527) was influenced by many ancient Greek and Roman works in writing *The Prince.* Machiavelli's sixteenth-century Italy was divided among several city-states—similar to Thucydides' Greece. Machiavelli served as a civil servant and diplomat until the Republic of Florence was defeated in 1512. Forced from public life, Machiavelli devoted himself to writing andcompleted *The Prince* (1513), *Discourses on the First Decade of Livy* (1514), and *The History of Florence* (1525).

THE THINGS FOR WHICH MEN, AND ESPECIALLY PRINCES, ARE PRAISED OR BLAMED

It now remains for us to see how a prince must govern his conduct towards his subjects or his friends. I know that this has often been written about before, and so I hope it will not be thought presumptuous for me to do so, as, especially in discussing this subject, I draw up an original set of rules. But since my intention is to say something that will prove of practical use to the inquirer, I have thought it proper to represent things as they are in real truth, rather than as they are imagined. Many have dreamed up republics and principalities which have never in truth been known to exist; the gulf between how one should live and how one does live is so wide that a man who neglects what is actually done for what should be done learns the way to self-destruction rather than self-preservation. The fact is that a man who wants to act virtuously in every way necessarily comes to grief among so many who are not virtuous. Therefore if a prince wants to maintain his rule he must learn how not to be virtuous, and to make use of this or not according to need.

So leaving aside imaginary things, and referring only to those which truly exist, I say that whenever men are discussed (and especially princes, who are more exposed to view), they are noted for various qualities which earn them either praise or condemnation. Some, for example, are held to be generous, and others miserly (I use the Tuscan word rather than the word avaricious: we call a man who is mean with what he possesses, miserly, and a man who wants to plunder others, avaricious).[1] Some are held to be benefactors, others are called grasping; some cruel, some compassionate; one man faithless, another faithful; one man effeminate and cowardly, another fierce and courageous; one man courteous, another proud; one man lascivious, another pure; one guileless, another crafty; one stubborn, another flexible; one grave, another frivolous; one religious, another sceptical; and so forth. I know everyone will agree that it would be most laudable if a prince possessed all the qualities deemed to be good among those I have enumerated. But, because of conditions in the world, princes cannot have those qualities, or observe them completely. So a prince has of necessity to be so prudent that he knows how to escape the evil reputation attached to those vices which could lose him his state, and how to avoid those vices which are not so dangerous, if he possibly can; but, if he cannot, he need not worry so much about the latter. And then, he must not flinch from being blamed for vices which are necessary for safeguarding the state. This is because, taking everything into account, he will find that some of the things that appear to be virtues will, if

he practises them, ruin him, and some of the things that appear to be vices will bring him security and prosperity.

GENEROSITY AND PARSIMONY

So, starting with the first of the qualities I enumerated above, I say it would be splendid if one had a reputation for generosity; nonetheless if you do in fact earn a reputation for generosity you will come to grief. This is because if your generosity is good and sincere it may pass unnoticed and it will not save you from being reproached for its opposite. If you want to acquire a reputation for generosity, therefore, you have to be ostentatiously lavish; and a prince acting in that fashion will soon squander all his resources, only to be forced in the end, if he wants to maintain his reputation, to lay excessive burdens on the people, to impose extortionate taxes, and to do everything else he can to raise money. This will start to make his subjects hate him, and, since he will have impoverished himself, he will be generally despised. As a result, because of this generosity of his, having injured many and rewarded few, he will be vulnerable to the first minor setback, and the first real danger he encounters will bring him to grief. When he realizes this and tries to retrace his path he will immediately be reputed a miser.

So as a prince cannot practise the virtue of generosity in such a way that he is noted for it, except to his cost, he should if he is prudent not mind being called a miser. In time he will be recognized as being essentially a generous man, seeing that because of his parsimony his existing revenues are enough for him, he can defend himself against an aggressor, and he can embark on enterprises without burdening the people.

So he proves himself generous to all those from whom he takes nothing, and they are innumerable, and miserly towards all those to whom he gives nothing, and they are few. In our own times great things have been accomplished only by those who have been held miserly, and the others have met disaster. Pope Julius II made use of a reputation for generosity to win the papacy but subsequently he made no effort to maintain this reputation, because he wanted to be able to finance his wars. The present king of France has been able to wage so many wars without taxing his subjects excessively only because his long-standing parsimony enabled him to meet the additional expenses involved. Were the present king of Spain renowned for his generosity he would not have started and successfully concluded so many enterprises.

So a prince must think little of it, if he incurs the name of miser, so as not to rob his subjects, to be able to defend himself, not to become poor and despicable, not to be forced to grow rapacious. Miserliness is one of those vices which sustain his rule. Someone may object: Caesar came to power by virtue of his generosity, and many others, because they practised and were known for their generosity, have risen to the very highest positions. My answer to this is as follows. Either you are already a prince, or you are on the way to becoming one. In the first case, your generosity will be to your cost; in the second, it is certainly necessary to have a reputation for generosity. Caesar was one of those who wanted to establish his own rule over Rome; but if, after he had established it, he had remained alive and not moderated his expenditure he would have fallen from power.

Again, someone may retort: there have been many princes who have won great successes with their armies, and who have had the reputation of being extremely generous. My reply to this is: the prince gives away what is his own or his subjects', or else what belongs to others. In the first case he should be frugal; in the second, he should indulge his generosity to the full. The prince who campaigns with his armies, who lives by pillaging, sacking, and extortion, disposes of what belongs to aliens; and he must be open-handed, otherwise the soldiers would refuse to follow him. And you can be more liberal with what does not belong to you or your subjects, as Caesar, Cyrus, and Alexander were. Giving away what belongs to strangers in no way affects your standing at home; rather it increases it. You hurt yourself only when you give away what is your own. There is nothing so self-defeating as generosity: in the act of practising it, you lose the ability to do so, and you become either poor and despised or, seeking to escape poverty, rapacious and hated. A prince must try to avoid, above all else, being despised and hated; and generosity results in your being both. Therefore it is wiser to incur the reputation of being a miser, which invites ignominy but not hatred, than to be forced by seeking a name for generosity to incur a reputation for rapacity, which brings you hatred as well as ignominy.

CRUELTY AND COMPASSION; AND WHETHER IT IS BETTER TO BE LOVED THAN FEARED, OR THE REVERSE

Taking others of the qualities I enumerated above, I say that a prince must want to have a reputation for compassion rather than for cruelty: nonetheless, he must be careful that he does not make bad use of compassion. Cesare Borgia was accounted cruel; nevertheless, this cruelty of his reformed the Romagna, brought it unity, and restored order and obedience. On reflection, it will be seen that there was more compassion in Cesare than in the Florentine people, who, to escape being called cruel, allowed Pistoia to be devastated.[2] So a prince must not worry if he incurs reproach for his cruelty so long as he keeps his subjects united and loyal. By making an example or two he will prove more compassionate than those who, being too compassionate, allow disorders which lead to murder and rapine. These nearly always harm the whole community, whereas executions ordered by a prince only affect individuals. A new prince, of all rulers, finds it impossible to avoid a reputation for cruelty, because of the abundant dangers inherent in a newly won state. Vergil, through the mouth of Dido, says:

Res dura, et regni novitas me talia cogunt moliri, et late finis custode tueri.[3]

Nonetheless, a prince must be slow to take action, and must watch that he does not come to be afraid of his own shadow; his behaviour must be tempered by humanity and prudence so that overconfidence does not make him rash or excessive distrust make him unbearable.

From this arises the following question: whether it is better to be loved than feared, or the reverse. The answer is that one would like to be both the one and the other; but because it is difficult to combine them, it is far better to be feared than loved if you cannot be both. One can make this generalization about men: they are ungrateful, fickle, liars, and deceivers, they shun danger and are greedy for profit; while you treat them well, they are yours. They would shed their blood for you, risk their property, their lives, their children, so long, as I said above, as danger is remote; but when you are in danger they turn against you. Any prince who has come to depend entirely on promises and has taken no other precautions ensures his own ruin; friendship which is bought with money and not with greatness and nobility of mind is paid for, but it does not last and it yields nothing. Men worry less about doing an injury to one who makes himself loved than to one who makes himself feared. The bond of love is one which men, wretched creatures that they are, break when it is to their advantage to do so; but fear is strengthened by a dread of punishment which is always effective.

The prince must nonetheless make himself feared in such a way that, if he is not loved, at least he escapes being hated. For fear is quite compatible with an absence of hatred; and the prince can always avoid hatred if he abstains from the property of his subjects and citizens and from their women. If, even so, it proves necessary to execute someone, this is to be done only when there is proper justification and manifest reason for it. But above all a prince must abstain from the property of others; because men sooner forget the death of their father than the loss of their patrimony. It is always possible to find pretexts for confiscating someone's property; and a prince who starts to live by rapine always finds pretexts for seizing what belongs to others. On the other hand, pretexts for executing someone are harder to find and they are less easily sustained.

However, when a prince is campaigning with his soldiers and is in command of a large army then he need not worry about having a reputation for cruelty; because, without such a reputation, no army was ever kept united and disciplined. Among the admirable achievements of Hannibal is included this: that although he led a huge army, made up of countless different races, on foreign campaigns, there was never any dissension, either among the troops themselves or against their leader, whether things were going well or badly. For this, his inhuman cruelty was wholly responsible. It was this, along with his countless other qualities, which made him feared and respected by his soldiers. If it had not been for his cruelty, his other qualities would not have been enough. The historians, having given little thought to this, on the one hand admire what Hannibal achieved, and on the other condemn what made his achievements possible.

That his other qualities would not have been enough by themselves can be proved by looking at Scipio, a man unique in his own time and through all recorded history. His armies mutinied against him in Spain, and the only reason for this was his excessive leniency, which allowed his soldiers more licence than was good for military discipline. Fabius Maximus reproached him for this in the Senate and called him a corrupter of the Roman legions. Again, when the Locri were plundered by one of Scipio's officers, he neither gave them satisfaction nor punished his officer's insubordina-

tion; and this was all because of his having too lenient a nature. By way of excuse for him some senators argued that many men were better at not making mistakes themselves than at correcting them in others. But in time Scipio's lenient nature would have spoilt his fame and glory had he continued to indulge it during his command; when he lived under orders from the Senate, however, this fatal characteristic of his was not only concealed but even brought him glory.

So, on this question of being loved or feared, I conclude that since some men love as they please but fear when the prince pleases, a wise prince should rely on what he controls, not on what he cannot control. He must only endeavour, as I said, to escape being hated.

NOTES

1. The two words Machiavelli uses are *misero* and *avaro*.
2. Pistoia, a subject-city of Florence, forcibly restored order when conflict broke out between two rival factions in 1501–02. Machiavelli was concerned with this business at first hand.
3. "Harsh necessity, and the newness of my kingdom, force me to do such things and to guard my frontiers everywhere." *Aeneid* i, 563.

QUESTIONS

1. Why does Machiavelli propose that it is better for a leader to be feared rather than liked?

2. Can Machiavelli's Prince be considered a tyrant? Why or why not?

5. Politics Among Nations

Hans J. Morgenthau

In this reading Hans J. Morgenthau, one of the great contemporary scholars of realist theory, argues that politics are "governed by objective laws" and that it is possible to develop a "rational theory that reflects . . . these objective laws." Morgenthau's key points are that international politics is a struggle for power among states with competing interests and that states define their interest in terms of power. This selection is from *Politics Among Nations: The Struggle for Power and Peace* (1978).

Hans J. Morgenthau (1904–1980) practiced and taught law in Frankfurt, Germany. He left to teach at the University of Geneva a year before Adolf Hitler came to power. From there, he went to Madrid and then to the United States, in 1937. Morgenthau taught first at Brooklyn College and the University of Kansas City before being appointed to the University of Chicago in 1943. Morgenthau's other works include *In Defense of the National Interest* (1951), *The Purpose of American Politics* (1960), *Politics in the Twentieth Century* (1962), *A New Foreign Policy for the United States* (1969), and *Science: Servant Or Master?* (1972).

ON THE SIX PRINCIPLES OF POLITICAL REALISM

1. Political realism believes that politics, like society in general, is governed by objective laws that have their roots in human nature. In order to improve society it is first necessary to understand the laws by which society lives. The operation of these laws being impervious to our preferences, men will challenge them only at the risk of failure.

Realism, believing as it does in the objectivity of the laws of politics, must also believe in the possibility of developing a rational theory that reflects, however imperfectly and one-sidedly, these objective laws. It believes also, then, in the possibility of distinguishing in politics between truth and opinion—between what is true objectively and rationally, supported by evidence and illuminated by reason, and what is only a subjective judgment, divorced from the facts as they are and informed by prejudice and wishful thinking.

Human nature, in which the laws of politics have their roots, has not changed since the classical philosophies of China, India, and Greece endeavored to discover these laws. Hence, novelty is not necessarily a virtue in political theory, nor is old age a defect. The fact that a theory of politics, if there be such a theory, has never been heard of before tends to create a presumption against, rather than in favor of, its soundness. Conversely, the fact that a theory of politics was developed hundreds or even thousands of years ago—as was the theory of the balance of power—does not create a presumption that it must be outmoded and obsolete. A theory of politics must be subjected to the dual test of reason and experience. To dismiss such a theory because it had its flowering in centuries past is to present not a rational argument but a modernistic prejudice that takes for granted the superiority of the present over the past. To dispose of the revival of such a theory as a "fashion" or "fad" is tantamount to assuming that in matters political we can have opinions but no truths.

For realism, theory consists in ascertaining facts and giving them meaning through reason. It assumes that the character of a foreign policy can be ascertained only through the examination of the political acts performed and of the foreseeable consequences of these acts. Thus we can find out what statesmen have actually done, and from the foreseeable consequences of their acts we can surmise what their objectives might have been.

Yet examination of the facts is not enough. To give meaning to the factual raw material of foreign policy, we must approach political reality with a kind of rational outline, a map that suggests to us the possible meanings of foreign policy. In other words, we put ourselves in the position of a statesman who must meet a certain problem of foreign policy under certain circumstances, and we ask ourselves what the rational alternatives are from which a statesman may choose who must meet this problem under these circumstances (presuming always that he acts in a rational manner), and which of these rational alternatives this particular statesman, acting under these circumstances, is likely to choose. It is the testing of this rational hypothesis against the actual facts and their consequences that gives theoretical meaning to the facts of international politics.

2. The main signpost that helps political realism to find its way through the landscape of international politics is the concept of interest defined in terms of power. This concept provides the link between reason trying to understand international politics and the facts to be understood. It sets politics as an autonomous sphere of action and understanding apart from other spheres, such as economics (understood in terms of interest defined as wealth), ethics, aesthetics, or religion. Without such a concept a theory of politics, international or domestic, would be altogether impossible, for without it we could not distinguish between political and nonpolitical facts, nor could we bring at least a measure of systemic order to the political sphere.

We assume that statesmen think and act in terms of interest defined as power, and the evidence of history bears that assumption out. That assumption allows us to retrace and anticipate, as it were, the steps a statesman—past, present, or future—has taken or will take on the political scene. We look over his shoulder when he writes his dispatches; we listen in on his conversation with other statesmen; we read and anticipate his very thoughts. Thinking in terms of interest defined as power, we think as he does, and as disinterested observers we understand his thoughts and actions perhaps better than he, the actor on the political scene, does himself.

The concept of interest defined as power imposes intellectual discipline upon the observer, infuses rational order into the subject matter of politics, and thus makes the theoretical understanding of politics possible. On the side of the actor, it provides for rational discipline in action and creates that astounding continuity in foreign policy which makes American, British, or Russian foreign policy appear as an intelligible, rational continuum, by and large consistent within itself, regardless of the different motives, preferences, and intellectual and moral qualities of successive statesmen. A realist theory of international politics, then, will guard against two popular fallacies: the concern with motives and the concern with ideological preferences.

To search for the clue to foreign policy exclusively in the motives of statesmen is both futile and deceptive. It is futile because motives are the most illusive of psychological data, distorted as they are, frequently beyond recognition, by the interests and emotions of actor and observer alike. Do we really know what our own motives are? And what do we know of the motives of others?

Yet even if we had access to the real motives of statesmen, that knowledge would help us little in understanding foreign policies, and might well lead us astray. It is true that the knowledge of the statesman's motives may give us one among many clues as to what the direction of his foreign policy might be. It cannot give us, however, the one clue by which to predict his foreign policies. History shows no exact and necessary correlation between the quality of motives and the quality of foreign policy. This is true in both moral and political terms.

We cannot conclude from the good intentions of a statesman that his foreign policies will be either morally praiseworthy or politically successful. Judging his motives, we can say that he will not intentionally pursue policies that are morally wrong, but we can say nothing about the probability of their success. If we want to know the moral and political qualities of his actions, we must know them, not his motives. How often have statesmen been motivated by the desire to improve the world, and ended by making it worse? And how often have they sought one goal, and ended by achieving something they neither expected nor desired?

Neville Chamberlain's politics of appeasement were, as far as we can judge, inspired by good motives; he was probably less motivated by considerations of personal power than were many other British prime ministers, and he sought to preserve peace and to assure the happiness of all concerned. Yet his policies helped to make the Second World War inevitable, and to bring untold miseries to millions of people. Sir Winston Churchill's motives, on the other hand, were much less universal in scope and much more narrowly directed toward personal and national power, yet the foreign policies that sprang from these inferior motives were certainly superior in moral and political quality to those pursued by his predecessor. Judged by his motives, Robespierre was one of the most virtuous men who ever lived. Yet it was the utopian radicalism of that very virtue that made him kill those less virtuous than himself, brought him to the scaffold, and destroyed the revolution of which he was a leader.

Good motives give assurance against deliberately bad policies; they do not guarantee the moral goodness and political success of the policies they inspire. What is important to know, if one wants to understand foreign policy, is not primarily the motives of a statesman, but his intellectual ability to comprehend the essentials of foreign policy, as well as his political ability to translate what he has comprehended into successful political action. It follows that while ethics in the abstract judges the moral qualities of motives, political theory must judge the political qualities of intellect, will, and action.

A realist theory of international politics will also avoid the other popular fallacy of equating the foreign policies of a statesman with his philosophic or political sympathies, and of deducing the former from the latter. Statesmen, especially under contemporary conditions, may well make a habit of presenting their foreign policies in terms of their philosophic and political sympathies in order to gain popular support for them. Yet they will distinguish with Lincoln between their "*official* duty," which is to think and act in terms of the national interest, and their "*personal* wish," which is to see their own moral values and political principles realized throughout the world. Political realism does not require, nor does it condone, indifference to political ideals and moral principles, but it requires indeed a sharp distinction between the desirable and the possible—between what is desirable everywhere and at all times and what is possible under the concrete circumstances of time and place.

It stands to reason that not all foreign policies have always followed so rational, objective, and unemotional a course. The contingent elements of personality, prejudice, and subjective preference, and of all the weaknesses of intellect and will which flesh is heir to, are bound to deflect foreign policies from their rational course. Especially where foreign policy is conducted under the conditions of democratic control, the need to marshal popular emotions to the support of foreign policy cannot fail to impair the rationality of foreign policy itself. Yet a theory of foreign policy which aims at rationality must for the time being, as it were, abstract from these irrational elements and seek to paint a picture of foreign policy which presents the rational essence to be found in experience, without the contingent deviations from rationality which are also found in experience.

Deviations from rationality which are not the result of the personal whim or the personal psychopathology of the policy maker may appear contingent only from the vantage point of rationality, but may themselves be elements in a coherent system of irrationality. The possibility of constructing, as it were, a counter-theory of irrational politics is worth exploring.

When one reflects upon the development of American thinking on foreign policy, one is struck by the persistence of mistaken attitudes that have survived—under whatever guises—both intellectual argument and political experience. Once that wonder, in true Aristotelian fashion, has been transformed into the quest for rational understanding, the quest yields a conclusion both comforting and disturbing: we are here in the presence of intellectual defects shared by all of us in different ways and degrees. Together they provide the outline of a kind of pathology of international politics. When the human mind approaches reality with the purpose of taking action, of which the political encounter is one of the outstanding instances, it is often led astray by any of four common mental phenomena: residues of formerly adequate modes of thought and action now rendered obsolete by a new social reality; demonological interpretations of reality which substitute a fictitious reality—peopled by evil persons rather than seemingly intractable issues—for the actual one; refusal to come to terms with a threatening state of affairs by denying it through illusory verbalization; reliance upon the infinite malleability of a seemingly obstreperous reality.

Man responds to social situations with repetitive patterns. The same situation, recognized in its identity with previous situations, evokes the same response. The mind, as it were, holds in readiness a number of patterns appropriate for different situations; it then requires only the identification of a particular case to apply to it the preformed pattern appropriate to it. Thus the human mind follows the principle of economy of effort, obviating an examination *de novo* of each individual situation and the pattern of thought and action appropriate to it. Yet when matters are subject to dynamic change, traditional patterns are no longer appropriate: they must be replaced by new ones reflecting such change. Otherwise a gap will open between traditional patterns and new realities, and thought and action will be misguided.

On the international plane it is no exaggeration to say that the very structure of international relations—as reflected in political institutions, diplomatic procedures, and legal arrangements—has tended to become at variance with, and in large measure irrelevant to, the reality of international politics. While the former assumes the "sovereign equality" of all nations, the latter is dominated by an extreme inequality of nations, two of which are called super-powers because they hold in their hands the unprecedented power of total destruction, and many of which are called "ministates" because their power is minuscule even compared with that of the traditional nation states. It is this contrast and incompatibility between the reality of international politics and the concepts, institutions, and procedures designed to make intelligible and control the former, which has caused, at least below the great-power level, the unmanageability of international relations which borders on anarchy. International terrorism and the different government reactions to it, the involvement of foreign governments in the Lebanese civil war, the military operations of the United States in Southeast Asia, and the military intervention of the Soviet Union in Eastern Europe cannot be explained or justified by reference to traditional concepts, institutions, and procedures.

All these situations have one characteristic in common. The modern fact of interdependence requires a political order which takes that fact into account, while in reality the legal and institutional superstructure, harking back to the nineteenth century, assumes the existence of a multiplicity of self-sufficient, impenetrable, sovereign nation states. These residues of an obsolescent legal and institutional order not only stand in the way of a rational transformation of international relations in light of the inequality of power and the interdependence of interests, but they also render precarious, if not impossible, more rational policies within the defective framework of such a system.

It is a characteristic of primitive thinking to personalize social problems. That tendency is particularly strong when the problem appears not to be susceptible to rational understanding and successful manipulation. When a particular person or group of persons is identified with the recalcitrant difficulty, that may seem to render the problem both intellectually accessible and susceptible of solution. Thus belief in Satan as the source of evil makes us "understand" the nature of evil by focusing the search for its origin and control upon a particular person whose physical existence we assume. The complexity of political conflict precludes such simple solutions. Natural catastrophes will not be prevented by burning witches; the threat of a powerful Germany to establish hegemony over Europe will not be averted by getting rid of a succession of German leaders. But by identifying the issue with certain persons over whom we have—or hope to have—control, we reduce the problem, both intellectually and pragmatically, to manageable proportions. Once we have identified certain individuals and groups of individuals as the source of evil, we appear to have understood the causal nexus that leads from the individuals to the social problem; that apparent understanding suggests the apparent solution: Eliminate the individuals "responsible" for it, and you have solved the problem.

Superstition still holds sway over our relations within society. The demonological pattern of thought and action has now been transferred to other fields of human action closed to the kind of rational enquiry and action that have driven superstition from our relations with nature. As William Graham Sumner put it, "The amount of superstition is not much changed, but it now attaches to politics, not to religion."[1] The numerous failures of the United States to recognize and respond to the polycentric nature of Communism is a prime example of this defect. The corollary of this indiscriminate opposition to Communism is the indiscriminate support of governments and movements that profess and practice anti-Communism. American policies in Asia and Latin America have derived from this simplistic position. The Vietnam War and our inability to come to terms with mainland China find here their rationale. So do the theory and practice of counterinsurgency, including large-scale assassinations under the Phoenix program in Vietnam and the actual or attempted assassinations of individual statesmen. Signs of a similar approach have been evident more recently in Central America.

The demonological approach to foreign policy strengthens another pathological tendency, which is the refusal to acknowledge and cope effectively with a threatening reality. The demonological approach has shifted our attention and concern towards the adherents of Communism—individuals at home and abroad, political movements, foreign governments—and away from the real threat: the power of states, Communist or not. McCarthyism not only provided the most pervasive American example of the demonological approach but was also one of the most extreme examples of this kind of misjudgment: it substituted the largely illusory threat of domestic subversion for the real threat of Russian power.

Finally, it is part of this approach to politics to believe that no problems—however hopeless they may appear—are really insoluble, given well-meaning, well-financed, and competent efforts. I have tried elsewhere to lay bare the intellectual and historical roots of this belief,[2] here I limit myself to pointing out its persistent strength despite much experience to the contrary, such as the Vietnam War and the general decline of American power. This preference for economic solutions to political and military problems is powerfully reinforced by the interests of potential recipients of economic support, who prefer the obviously profitable transfer of economic advantages to painful and risky diplomatic bargaining.

The difference between international politics as it actually is and a rational theory derived from it is like the difference between a photograph and a painted portrait. The photograph shows everything that can be seen by the naked eye; the painted portrait does not show everything that can be seen by the naked eye, but it shows, or at least seeks to show, one thing that the naked eye cannot see: the human essence of the person portrayed.

Political realism contains not only a theoretical but also a normative element. It knows that political reality is replete with contingencies and systemic irrationalities and points to the typical influences they exert upon foreign policy. Yet it shares with all social theory the need, for the sake of theoretical understanding, to stress the rational elements of political reality; for it is these rational elements that make reality intelligible for theory. Political realism presents the theoretical construct of a rational foreign policy which experience can never completely achieve.

At the same time political realism considers a rational foreign policy to be good foreign policy; for only a rational foreign policy minimizes risks and maximizes benefits and, hence, complies both with the moral precept of prudence and the political requirement of success. Political realism wants the photographic picture of the political world to resemble as much as possible its painted portrait. Aware of the inevitable gap between good—that is, rational—foreign policy and foreign policy as it actually is, political realism maintains not only that theory must focus upon the rational elements of political reality, but also that foreign policy ought to be rational in view of its own moral and practical purposes.

Hence, it is no argument against the theory here presented that actual foreign policy does not or cannot live up to it. That argument misunderstands the intention of this book, which is to present not an indiscriminate description of political reality, but a rational theory of international politics. Far from being invalidated by the fact that, for instance,

a perfect balance of power policy will scarcely be found in reality, it assumes that reality, being deficient in this respect, must be understood and evaluated as an approximation to an ideal system of balance of power.

3. Realism assumes that its key concept of interest defined as power is an objective category which is universally valid, but it does not endow that concept with a meaning that is fixed once and for all. The idea of interest is indeed of the essence of politics and is unaffected by the circumstances of time and place. Thucydides' statement, born of the experiences of ancient Greece, that "identity of interests is the surest of bonds whether between states or individuals" was taken up in the nineteenth century by Lord Salisbury's remark that "the only bond of union that endures" among nations is "the absence of all clashing interests." It was erected into a general principle of government by George Washington:

A small knowledge of human nature
will convince us, that, with far the
greatest part of mankind, interest
is the governing principle; and that
almost every man is more or less,
under its influence. Motives of public
virtue may for a time, or in particular
instances, actuate men to the observance
of a conduct purely disinterested; but
they are not of themselves sufficient
to produce persevering conformity to
the refined dictates and obligations of
social duty. Few men are capable of
making a continual sacrifice of all
views of private interest, or advantage,
to the common good. It is vain to
exclaim against the depravity of human
nature on this account; the fact is so,
the experience of every age and nation
has proved it and we must in a great
measure, change the constitution

of man, before we can make it otherwise. No institution, not built on the presumptive truth of these maxims can succeed.[3]

It was echoed and enlarged upon in our century by Max Weber's observation:

Interests (material and ideal), not ideas, dominate directly the actions of men. Yet the "images of the world" created by these ideas have very often served as switches determining the tracks on which the dynamism of interests kept actions moving.[4]

Yet the kind of interest determining political action in a particular period of history depends upon the political and cultural context within which foreign policy is formulated. The goals that might be pursued by nations in their foreign policy can run the whole gamut of objectives any nation has ever pursued or might possibly pursue.

The same observations apply to the concept of power. Its content and the manner of its use are determined by the political and cultural environment. Power may comprise anything that establishes and maintains the control of man over man. Thus power covers all social relationships which serve that end, from physical violence to the most subtle psychological ties by which one mind controls another. Power covers the domination of man by man, both when it is disciplined by moral ends and controlled by constitutional safeguards, as in Western democracies, and when it is that untamed and barbaric force which finds its laws in nothing but its own strength and its sole justification in its aggrandizement.

Political realism does not assume that the contemporary conditions under which foreign policy operates, with their

extreme instability and the ever present threat of large-scale violence, cannot be changed. The balance of power, for instance, is indeed a perennial element of all pluralistic societies, as the authors of *The Federalist* papers well knew; yet it is capable of operating, as it does in the United States, under the conditions of relative stability and peaceful conflict. If the factors that have given rise to these conditions can be duplicated on the international scene, similar conditions of stability and peace will then prevail there, as they have over long stretches of history among certain nations.

What is true of the general character of international relations is also true of the nation state as the ultimate point of reference of contemporary foreign policy. While the realist indeed believes that interest is the perennial standard by which political action must be judged and directed, the contemporary connection between interest and the nation state is a product of history, and is therefore bound to disappear in the course of history. Nothing in the realist position militates against the assumption that the present division of the political world into nation states will be replaced by larger units of a quite different character, more in keeping with the technical potentialities and the moral requirements of the contemporary world.

The realist parts company with other schools of thought before the all-important question of how the contemporary world is to be transformed. The realist is persuaded that this transformation can be achieved only through the workmanlike manipulation of the perennial forces that have shaped the past as they will the future. The realist cannot be persuaded that we can bring about that transformation by confronting a political reality that has its own laws with an abstract ideal that refuses to take those laws into account.

4. Political realism is aware of the moral significance of political action. It is also aware of the ineluctable tension between the moral command and the requirements of successful political action. And it is unwilling to gloss over and obliterate that tension and thus to obfuscate both the moral and the political issue by making it appear as though the stark facts of politics were morally more satisfying than they actually are, and the moral law less exacting that it actually is.

Realism maintains that universal moral principles cannot be applied to the actions of states in their abstract universal formulation, but that they must be filtered through the concrete circumstances of time and place. The individual may say for himself: "*Fiat justitia, pereat mundus* (Let justice be done, even if the world perish)," but the state has no right to say so in the name of those who are in its care. Both individual and state must judge political action by universal moral principles, such as that of liberty. Yet while the individual has a moral right to sacrifice himself in defense of such a moral principle, the state has no right to let its moral disapprobation of the infringement of liberty get in the way of successful political action, itself inspired by the moral principle of national survival. There can be no political morality without prudence; that is, without consideration of the political consequences of seemingly moral action. Realism, then, considers prudence—the weighing of the consequences of alternative political actions—to be the supreme virtue in politics. Ethics in the abstract judges action by its conformity with the moral law; political ethics judges action by its political consequences. Classical and medieval philosophy knew this, and so did Lincoln when he said:

I do the very best I know how, the very best I can, and I mean to keep doing so until the end. If the end brings me out all right, what is said against me won't amount to anything. If the end brings me out wrong, ten angels swearing I was right would make no difference.

5. Political realism refuses to identify the moral aspirations of a particular nation with the moral laws that govern the universe. As it distinguishes between truth and opinion, so it distinguishes between truth and idolatry. All nations are tempted—and few have been able to resist the temptation for long—to clothe their own particular aspirations and actions in the moral purposes of the universe. To know that nations are subject to the moral law is one thing, while to pretend to know with certainty what is good and evil in the relations among nations is quite another. There is a world of difference between the belief that all nations stand under the judgment of God, inscrutable to the human mind, and the blasphemous conviction that God is always on one's side and that what one wills oneself cannot fail to be willed by God also.

The lighthearted equation between a particular nationalism and the counsels of Providence is morally indefensible, for it is that very sin of pride against which the Greek tragedians and the Biblical prophets have warned rulers and ruled. That equation is also politically pernicious, for it is liable to engender the distortion in judgment which, in the blindness of crusading frenzy, destroys nations and civilizations—in the name of moral principle, ideal, or God himself.

On the other hand, it is exactly the concept of interest defined in terms of power that saves us from both that moral excess and that political folly. For if we look at all nations, our own included, as political entities pursuing their respective interests defined in terms of power, we are able to do justice to all of them. And we are able to do justice to all of them in a dual sense: We are able to judge other nations as we judge our own and, having judged them in this fashion, we are then capable of pursuing policies that respect the interests of other nations, while protecting and promoting those of our own. Moderation in policy cannot fail to reflect the moderation of moral judgment.

6. The difference, then, between political realism and other schools of thought is real, and it is profound. However much of the theory of political realism may have been misunderstood and misinterpreted, there is no gainsaying its distinctive intellectual and moral attitude to matters political.

Intellectually, the political realist maintains the autonomy of the political sphere, as the economist, the lawyer, the moralist maintain theirs. He thinks in terms of interest defined as power, as the economist thinks in terms of interest defined as wealth; the lawyer, of the conformity of action with legal rules; the moralist, of the conformity of action with moral principles. The economist asks: "How does this policy affect the wealth of society, or a segment of it?" The lawyer asks: "Is this policy in accord with the rules of law?" The moralist asks: "Is this policy in accord with moral principles?" And the political realist asks: "How does this policy affect the power of the nation?" (Or of the federal gov-

ernment, of Congress, of the party, of agriculture, as the case may be.)

The political realist is not unaware of the existence and relevance of standards of thought other than political ones. As political realist, he cannot but subordinate these other standards to those of politics. And he parts company with other schools when they impose standards of thought appropriate to other spheres upon the political sphere. It is here that political realism takes issue with the "legalistic-moralistic approach" to international politics. That this issue is not, as has been contended, a mere figment of the imagination, but goes to the very core of the controversy, can be shown from many historical examples. Three will suffice to make the point.[5]

In 1939 the Soviet Union attacked Finland. This action confronted France and Great Britain with two issues, one legal, the other political. Did that action violate the Covenant of the League of Nations and, if it did, what countermeasures should France and Great Britain take? The legal question could easily be answered in the affirmative, for obviously the Soviet Union had done what was prohibited by the Covenant. The answer to the political question depends, first, upon the manner in which the Russian action affected the interests of France and Great Britain; second, upon the existing distribution of power between France and Great Britain, on the one hand, and the Soviet Union and other potentially hostile nations, especially Germany, on the other; and, third, upon the influence that the countermeasures were likely to have upon the interests of France and Great Britain and the future distribution of power. France and Great Britain, as the leading members of the League of Nations, saw to it that the Soviet Union was expelled from the

League, and they were prevented from joining Finland in the war against the Soviet Union only by Sweden's refusal to allow their troops to pass through Swedish territory on their way to Finland. If this refusal by Sweden had not saved them, France and Great Britain would shortly have found themselves at war with the Soviet Union and Germany at the same time.

The policy of France and Great Britain was a classic example of legalism in that they allowed the answer to the legal question, legitimate within its sphere, to determine their political actions. Instead of asking both questions, that of law and that of power, they asked only the question of law; and the answer they received could have no bearing on the issue that their very existence might have depended upon.

The second example illustrates the "moralistic approach" to international politics. It concerns the international status of the Communist government of China. The rise of that government confronted the Western world with two issues, one moral, the other political. Were the nature and policies of that government in accord with the moral principles of the Western world? Should the Western world deal with such a government? The answer to the first question could not fail to be in the negative. Yet it did not follow with necessity that the answer to the second question should also be in the negative. The standard of thought applied to the first—the moral—question was simply to test the nature and the policies of the Communist government of China by the principles of Western morality. On the other hand, the second—the political—question had to be subjected to the complicated test of the interests involved and the power available on either side, and of the bearing of

one or the other course of action upon these interests and power. The application of this test could well have led to the conclusion that it would be wiser not to deal with the Communist government of China. To arrive at this conclusion by neglecting this test altogether and answering the political question in terms of the moral issue was indeed a classic example of the "moralistic approach" to international politics.

The third case illustrates strikingly the contrast between realism and the legalistic-moralistic approach to foreign policy. Great Britain, as one of the guarantors of the neutrality of Belgium, went to war with Germany in August 1914 because Germany had violated the neutrality of Belgium. The British action could be justified either in realistic or legalistic-moralistic terms. That is to say, one could argue realistically that for centuries it had been axiomatic for British foreign policy to prevent the control of the Low Countries by a hostile power. It was then not so much the violation of Belgium's neutrality per se as the hostile intentions of the violator which provided the rationale for British intervention. If the violator had been another nation but Germany, Great Britain might well have refrained from intervening. This is the position taken by Sir Edward Grey, British Foreign Secretary during that period. Under Secretary for Foreign Affairs Hardinge remarked to him in 1908: "If France violated Belgian neutrality in a war against Germany, it is doubtful whether England or Russia would move a finger to maintain Belgian neutrality, while if the neutrality of Belgium was violated by Germany, it is probable that the converse would be the case." Whereupon Sir Edward Grey replied: "This is to the point." Yet one could also take the legalistic and moralistic position that the violation of

Belgium's neutrality per se, because of its legal and moral defects and regardless of the interests at stake and of the identity of the violator, justified British and, for that matter, American intervention. This was the position which Theodore Roosevelt took in his letter to Sir Edward Grey of January 22, 1915:

> To me the crux of the situation has been Belgium. If England or France had acted toward Belgium as Germany has acted I should have opposed them, exactly as I now oppose Germany. I have emphatically approved your action as a model for what should be done by those who believe that treaties should be observed in good faith and that there is such a thing as international morality. I take this position as an American who is no more an Englishman than he is a German, who endeavors loyally to serve the interests of his own country, but who also endeavors to do what he can for justice and decency as regards mankind at large, and who therefore feels obliged to judge all other nations by their conduct on any given occasion.

This realist defense of the autonomy of the political sphere against its subversion by other modes of thought does not imply disregard for the existence and importance of these other modes of thought. It rather implies that each should be assigned its proper sphere and function. Political realism is based upon a pluralistic conception of human nature. Real man is a composite of "economic man," "political man," "moral man," "religious man," etc. A man who was nothing but "political man" would be a beast, for he would be completely lacking in moral restraints. A man who was nothing but "moral man" would be a fool, for he would be completely lacking in pru-

dence. A man who was nothing but "religious man" would be a saint, for he would be completely lacking in worldly desires.

Recognizing that these different facets of human nature exist, political realism also recognizes that in order to understand one of them one has to deal with it on its own terms. That is to say, if I want to understand "religious man," I must for the time being abstract from the other aspects of human nature and deal with its religious aspect as if it were the only one. Furthermore, I must apply to the religious sphere the standards of thought appropriate to it, always remaining aware of the existence of other standards and their actual influence upon the religious qualities of man. What is true of this facet of human nature is true of all the others. No modern economist, for instance would conceive of his science and its relations to other sciences of man in any other way. It is exactly through such a process of emancipation from other standards of thought, and the development of one appropriate to its subject matter, that economics has developed as an autonomous theory of the economic activities of man. To contribute to a similar development in the field of politics is indeed the purpose of political realism.

It is in the nature of things that a theory of politics which is based upon such principles will not meet with unanimous approval—nor does, for that matter, such a foreign policy. For theory and policy alike run counter to two trends in our culture which are not able to reconcile themselves to the assumptions and results of a rational, objective theory of politics. One of these trends disparages the role of power in society on grounds that stem from the experience and philosophy of the nineteenth century. . . . The other trend, opposed to the realist theory and practice of politics, stems from the very relationship that exists, and must exist, between the human mind and the political sphere. . . . The human mind in its day-by-day operations cannot bear to look the truth of politics straight in the face. It must disguise, distort, belittle, and embellish the truth—the more so, the more the individual is actively involved in the processes of politics, and particularly in those of international politics. For only by deceiving himself about the nature of politics and the role he plays on the political scene is man able to live contentedly as a political animal with himself and his fellow men.

Thus it is inevitable that a theory which tries to understand international politics as it actually is and as it ought to be in view of its intrinsic nature, rather than as people would like to see it, must overcome a psychological resistance that most other branches of learning need not face. A book devoted to the theoretical understanding of international politics therefore requires a special explanation and justification.

NOTES

1. "Mores of the Present and Future," in *War and Other Essays* (New Haven: Yale University Press, 1911), p. 159.
2. *Scientific Man versus Power Politics* (Chicago: University of Chicago Press, 1946).
3. *The Writings of George Washington,* edited by John C. Fitzpatrick (Washington: United States Printing Office, 1931–44), Vol. X, p. 363.
4. Marianne Weber, *Max Weber* (Tuebingen: J. C. B. Mohr, 1926), pp. 347–8. See also Max Weber, *Gesammelte Aufsätze zur Religionssoziologie* (Tuebingen: J. C. B. Mohr, 1920), p. 252.
5. See the other examples discussed in Hans J. Morgenthau, "Another 'Great Debate': The National Interest of the United States," *The American Political Science Review,* Vol. XLVI (December 1952), pp. 979 ff. See also Hans J. Morgenthau, *Politics in the 20th Century,* Vol. 1, *The Decline of Democratic Politics* (Chicago: University of Chicago Press, 1962), pp. 79 ff; and abridged edition (Chicago: University of Chicago Press, 1971), pp. 204 ff.

QUESTIONS

1. What does Morgenthau mean by the phrase "international politics is the concept of interest defined in terms of power"?

2. Compare and contrast Morgenthau's view of the role of ethics in international politics with that of Machiavelli. What are the similarities and differences between the two theorists?

6.   The Sources of Soviet Conduct

George Kennan

In his famous "X" article, George Kennan lays out the framework for the policy of containment—a strategy adopted by the United States in the aftermath of World War II to prevent the spread of Soviet communism. Kennan points out the weaknesses of the Soviet Union's political and economic infrastructure, recommending that the United States contain Soviet military, political, and moral influence worldwide. This selection is from the journal *Foreign Affairs* (1946).

George Kennan, professor emeritus of the School of Historical Studies at the Institute for Advanced Study in Princeton, New Jersey, has also written *Realities of American Foreign Policy 1900–1950* (1951), *Russia, The Atom and The West* (1958), and *On Dealing With the Communist World* (1964), in addition to many contributions to journals of international affairs. Kennan also served as the U.S. ambassador to Yugoslavia from 1961 to 1963.

The political personality of Soviet power as we know it today is the product of ideology and circumstances: ideology inherited by the present Soviet leaders from the movement in which they had their political origin, and circumstances of the power which they now have exercised for nearly three decades in Russia. There can be few tasks of psychological analysis more difficult than to try to trace the interaction of these two forces and the relative role of each in the determination of official Soviet conduct. Yet the attempt must be made if that conduct is to be understood and effectively countered.

It is difficult to summarize the set of ideological concepts with which the Soviet leaders came into power. Marxian ideology, in its Russian-Communist projection, has always been in process of subtle evolution. The materials on which it bases itself are extensive and complex. But the outstanding features of Communist thought as it existed in 1916 may perhaps be summarized as follows:

(a) that the central factor in the life of man, the factor which determines the character of public life and the "physiognomy of society," is the system by which material goods are produced and exchanged; (b) that the capitalist system of production is a nefarious one which inevitably leads to the exploitation of the working class by the capital-owning class and is incapable of developing adequately the economic resources of society or of distributing fairly the material goods produced by human labor; (c) that capitalism contains the seeds of its own destruction and must, in view of the inability of the capital-owning class to adjust itself to economic change, result eventually and inescapably in a revolutionary transfer of power to the working class; and (d) that imperialism, the final phase of capitalism, leads directly to war and revolution.

The rest may be outlined in Lenin's own words: "Unevenness of economic and political development is the inflexible law of capitalism. It follows from

From *Foreign Affairs Review,* pp. 556–582, Index Volume 25, Nos. 1–4, 1946.

this that the victory of Socialism may come originally in a few capitalist countries or even in a single capitalist country. The victorious proletariat of that country, having expropriated the capitalists and having organized Socialist production at home, would rise against the remaining capitalist world, drawing to itself in the process the oppressed classes of other countries."[1] It must be noted that there was no assumption that capitalism would perish without proletarian revolution. A final push was needed from a revolutionary proletariat movement in order to tip over the tottering structure. But it was regarded as inevitable that sooner or later that push be given.

For 50 years prior to the outbreak of the Revolution, this pattern of thought had exercised great fascination for the members of the Russian revolutionary movement. Frustrated, discontented, hopeless of finding self-expression—or too impatient to seek it—in the confining limits of the Tsarist political system, yet lacking wide popular support for their choice of bloody revolution as a means of social betterment, these revolutionists found in Marxist theory a highly convenient rationalization for their own instinctive desires. It afforded pseudo-scientific justification for their impatience, for their categoric denial of all value in the Tsarist system, for their yearning for power and revenge and for their inclination to cut corners in the pursuit of it. It is therefore no wonder that they had come to believe implicitly in the truth and soundness of the Marxian-Leninist teachings, so congenial to their own impulses and emotions. Their sincerity need not be impugned. This is a phenomenon as old as human nature itself. It has never been more aptly described than by Edward Gibbon, who wrote in *The Decline and Fall of the Roman Empire:* "From enthusiasm to imposture the step is perilous and slippery; the demon of Socrates affords a memorable instance how a wise man may deceive himself, how a good man may deceive others, how the conscience may slumber in a mixed and middle state between self-illusion and voluntary fraud." And it was with this set of conceptions that the members of the Bolshevik Party entered into power.

Now it must be noted that through all the years of preparation for revolution, the attention of these men, as indeed of Marx himself, had been centered less on the future form which Socialism[2] would take than on the necessary overthrow of rival power which, in their view, had to precede the introduction of Socialism. Their views, therefore, on the positive program to be put into effect, once power was attained, were for the most part nebulous, visionary and impractical. Beyond the nationalization of industry and the expropriation of large private capital holdings there was no agreed program. The treatment of the peasantry, which according to the Marxist formulation was not of the proletariat, had always been a vague spot in the pattern of Communist thought; and it remained an object of controversy and vacillation for the first ten years of Communist power.

The circumstances of the immediate post-revolution period—the existence in Russia of civil war and foreign intervention, together with the obvious fact that the Communists represented only a tiny minority of the Russian people—made the establishment of dictatorial power a necessity. The experiment with "war Communism" and the abrupt attempt to eliminate private production and trade had unfortunate economic consequences and caused further bitterness against the new revolutionary régime. While the temporary relaxation of the effort to communize Russia, represented by the New Economic Policy, alleviated some of this economic distress and thereby served its purpose, it also made it evident that the "capitalistic sector of society" was still prepared to profit at once from any relaxation of governmental pressure, and would, if permitted to continue to exist, always constitute a powerful opposing element to the Soviet régime and a serious rival for influence in the country. Somewhat the same situation prevailed with respect to the individual peasant who, in his own small way, was also a private producer.

Lenin, had he lived, might have proved a great enough man to reconcile these conflicting forces to the ultimate benefit of Russian society, though this is questionable. But be that as it may, Stalin, and those whom he led in the struggle for succession to Lenin's position of leadership, were not the men to tolerate rival political forces in the sphere of power which they coveted. Their sense of insecurity was too great. Their particular brand of fanaticism, unmodified by any of the Anglo-Saxon traditions of compromise, was too fierce and too jealous to envisage any permanent sharing of power. From the Russian-Asiatic world out of which they had emerged they carried with them a skepticism as to the possibilities of permanent and peaceful coexistence of rival forces. Easily persuaded of their own doctrinaire "rightness," they insisted on the submission or destruction of all competing power. Outside of the Communist Party, Russian society was to have no rigidity. There were to be no forms of collective human activity or association which would not be dominated by the Party.

No other force in Russian society was to be permitted to achieve vitality or integrity. Only the Party was to have structure. All else was to be an amorphous mass.

And within the Party the same principle was to apply. The mass of Party members might go through the motions of election, deliberation, decision and action; but in these motions they were to be animated not by their own individual wills but by the awesome breath of the Party leadership and the overbrooding presence of "the word."

Let it be stressed again that subjectively these men probably did not seek absolutism for its own sake. They doubtless believed—and found it easy to believe—that they alone knew what was good for society and that they would accomplish that good once their power was secure and unchallengeable. But in seeking that security of their own rule they were prepared to recognize no restrictions, either of God or man, on the character of their methods. And until such time as that security might be achieved, they placed far down on their scale of operational priorities the comforts and happiness of the peoples entrusted to their care.

Now the outstanding circumstance concerning the Soviet régime is that down to the present day this process of political consolidation has never been completed and the men in the Kremlin have continued to be predominantly absorbed with the struggle to secure and make absolute the power which they seized in November 1917. They have endeavored to secure it primarily against forces at home, within Soviet society itself. But they have also endeavored to secure it against the outside world. For ideology, as we have seen, taught them that the outside world was hostile and that it was their duty eventually to overthrow the political forces beyond their borders. The powerful hands of Russian history and tradition reached up to sustain them in this feeling. Finally, their own aggressive intransigence with respect to the outside world began to find its own reaction; and they were soon forced, to use another Gibbonesque phrase, "to chastise the contumacy" which they themselves had provoked. It is an undeniable privilege of every man to prove himself right in the thesis that the world is his enemy; for if he reiterates it frequently enough and makes it the background of his conduct he is bound eventually to be right.

Now it lies in the nature of the mental world of the Soviet leaders, as well as in the character of their ideology, that no opposition to them can be officially recognized as having any merit or justification whatsoever. Such opposition can flow, in theory, only from the hostile and incorrigible forces of dying capitalism. As long as remnants of capitalism were officially recognized as existing in Russia, it was possible to place on them, as an internal element, part of the blame for the maintenance of a dictatorial form of society. But as these remnants were liquidated, little by little, this justification fell away; and when it was indicated officially that they had been finally destroyed, it disappeared altogether. And this fact created one of the most basic of the compulsions which came to act upon the Soviet régime: since capitalism no longer existed in Russia and since it could not be admitted that there could be serious or widespread opposition to the Kremlin springing spontaneously from the liberated masses under its authority, it became necessary to justify the retention of the dictatorship by stressing the menace of capitalism abroad.

This began at an early date. In 1924 Stalin specifically defended the retention of the "organs of suppression," meaning, among others, the army and the secret police, on the ground that "as long as there is a capitalist encirclement there will be danger of intervention with all the consequences that flow from that danger." In accordance with that theory, and from that time on, all internal opposition forces in Russia have consistently been portrayed as the agents of foreign forces of reaction antagonistic to Soviet power.

By the same token, tremendous emphasis has been placed on the original Communist thesis of a basic antagonism between the capitalist and Socialist worlds. It is clear, from many indications, that this emphasis is not founded in reality. The real facts concerning it have been confused by the existence abroad of genuine resentment provoked by Soviet philosophy and tactics and occasionally by the existence of great centers of military power, notably the Nazi régime in Germany and the Japanese Government of the late 1930s, which did indeed have aggressive designs against the Soviet Union. But there is ample evidence that the stress laid in Moscow on the menace confronting Soviet society from the world outside its borders is founded not in the realities of foreign antagonism but in the necessity of explaining away the maintenance of dictatorial authority at home.

Now the maintenance of this pattern of Soviet power, namely, the pursuit of unlimited authority domestically, accompanied by the cultivation of the semimyth of implacable foreign hostility, has gone far to shape the actual machinery of Soviet power as we know it today. Internal organs of administration which did not serve this purpose withered on the vine. Organs which did serve this purpose became vastly swollen. The security of Soviet power came to rest on the iron discipline of the Party, on the severity and ubiquity of the secret police, and on the uncompromising economic monopolism of the state. The "organs of suppression," in which the Soviet leaders had sought security from rival forces, became in large measure the masters of those whom they were designed to serve. Today the major part of the structure of Soviet power is committed to the perfection of the dictatorship and to the maintenance of the concept of Russia as in a state of siege, with the enemy lowering beyond the walls. And the millions of human beings who form that part of the structure of power must defend at all costs this concept of Russia's position, for without it they are themselves superfluous.

As things stand today, the rulers can no longer dream of parting with these organs of suppression. The quest for absolute power, pursued now for nearly three decades with a ruthlessness unparalleled (in scope at least) in modern times, has again produced internally, as it did externally, its own reaction. The excesses of the police apparatus have fanned the potential opposition to the régime into something far greater and more dangerous than it could have been before those excesses began.

But least of all can the rulers dispense with the fiction by which the maintenance of dictatorial power has been defended. For this fiction has been canonized in Soviet philosophy by the excesses already committed in its name; and it is now anchored in the Soviet

structure of thought by bonds far greater than those of mere ideology.

II

So much for the historical background. What does it spell in terms of the political personality of Soviet power as we know it today?

Of the original ideology, nothing has been officially junked. Belief is maintained in the basic badness of capitalism, in the inevitability of its destruction, in the obligation of the proletariat to assist in that destruction and to take power into its own hands. But stress has come to be laid primarily on those concepts which relate most specifically to the Soviet régime itself: to its position as the sole truly Socialist régime in a dark and misguided world, and to the relationships of power within it.

The first of these concepts is that of the innate antagonism between capitalism and Socialism. We have seen how deeply that concept has become imbedded in foundations of Soviet power. It has profound implications for Russia's conduct as a member of international society. It means that there can never be on Moscow's side any sincere assumption of a community of aims between the Soviet Union and powers which are regarded as capitalist. It must invariably be assumed in Moscow that the aims of the capitalist world are antagonistic to the Soviet régime, and therefore to the interests of the peoples it controls. If the Soviet Government occasionally sets its signature to documents which would indicate the contrary, this is to be regarded as a tactical manoeuvre permissible in dealing with the enemy (who is without honor) and should be taken in the spirit of *caveat emptor.* Basically, the antagonism remains. It is postulated. And from it flow many of the phenomena which we find disturbing in the Kremlin's conduct of foreign policy: the secretiveness, the lack of frankness, the duplicity, the wary suspiciousness, and the basic unfriendliness of purpose. These phenomena are there to stay, for the foreseeable future. There can be variations of degree and of emphasis. When there is something the Russians want from us, one or the other of these features of their policy may be thrust temporarily into the background; and when that happens there will always be Americans who will leap forward with gleeful announcements that "the Russians have changed," and some who will even try to take credit for having brought about such "changes." But we should not be misled by tactical manoeuvres. These characteristics of Soviet policy, like the postulate from which they flow, are basic to the internal nature of Soviet power, and will be with us, whether in the foreground or the background, until the internal nature of Soviet power is changed.

This means that we are going to continue for a long time to find the Russians difficult to deal with. It does not mean that they should be considered as embarked upon a do-or-die program to overthrow our society by a given date. The theory of the inevitability of the eventual fall of capitalism has the fortunate connotation that there is no hurry about it. The forces of progress can take their time in preparing the final *coup de grâce*. Meanwhile, what is vital is that the "Socialist fatherland"—that oasis of power which has been already won for Socialism in the person of the Soviet Union—should be cherished and defended by all good Communists at home and abroad, its fortunes promoted, its enemies badgered and confounded. The promotion of premature, "adventuristic" revolutionary projects abroad which might embarrass Soviet power in any way would be an inexcusable, even a counter-revolutionary act. The cause of Socialism is the support and promotion of Soviet power, as defined in Moscow.

This brings us to the second of the concepts important to contemporary Soviet outlook. That is the infallibility of the Kremlin. The Soviet concept of power, which permits no focal points of organization outside the Party itself, requires that the Party leadership remain in theory the sole repository of truth. For if truth were to be found elsewhere, there would be justification for its expression in organized activity. But it is precisely that which the Kremlin cannot and will not permit.

The leadership of the Communist Party is therefore always right, and has been always right ever since in 1929 Stalin formalized his personal power by announcing that decisions of the Politburo were being taken unanimously.

On the principle of infallibility there rests the iron discipline of the Communist Party. In fact, the two concepts are mutually self-supporting. Perfect discipline requires recognition of infallibility. Infallibility requires the observance of discipline. And the two together go far to determine the behaviorism of the entire Soviet apparatus of power. But their effect cannot be understood unless a third factor be taken into account: namely, the fact that the leadership is at liberty to put forward for tactical purposes any particular thesis which it finds useful to the cause at any particular moment and to require the faithful and unquestioning acceptance of that thesis by the members of the movement as a whole. This means that truth is not a constant but is actually created, for all intents and purposes, by the Soviet leaders themselves. It may vary from week to week, from month to month. It is nothing absolute and immutable—nothing which flows from objective reality. It is only the most recent manifestation of the wisdom of those in whom the ultimate wisdom is supposed to reside, because they represent the logic of history. The accumulative effect of these factors is to give to the whole subordinate apparatus of Soviet power an unshakeable stubbornness and steadfastness in its orientation. This orientation can be changed at will by the Kremlin but by no other power. Once a given party line has been laid down on a given issue of current policy, the whole Soviet governmental machine, including the mechanism of diplomacy, moves inexorably along the prescribed path, like a persistent toy automobile wound up and headed in a given direction, stopping only when it meets with some unanswerable force. The individuals who are the components of this machine are unamenable to argument or reason which comes to them from outside sources. Their whole training has taught them to mistrust and discount the glib persuasiveness of the outside world. Like the white dog before the phonograph, they hear only the "master's voice." And if they are to be called off from the purposes last dictated to them, it is the master who must call them off. Thus the foreign representative cannot hope that his words will make any impression on them. The most that he can hope is that they will be transmitted to those at the top, who are capable of changing the party line. But even those are not likely to be swayed by any normal logic in the words of the bourgeois representative. Since there can be no appeal to common purposes, there can be no appeal to common mental approaches. For this reason, facts speak louder than words to the ears of the Kremlin; and words carry the greatest weight when they have the ring of reflecting, or being backed up by, facts of unchallengeable validity.

But we have seen that the Kremlin is under no ideological compulsion to accomplish its purposes in a hurry. Like the Church, it is dealing in ideological concepts which are of long-term validity, and it can afford to be patient. It has no right to risk the existing achievements of the revolution for the sake of vain baubles of the future. The very teachings of Lenin himself require great caution and flexibility in the pursuit of Communist purposes. Again, these precepts are fortified by the lessons of Russian history: of centuries of obscure battles between nomadic forces over the stretches of a vast unfortified plain. Here caution, circumspection, flexibility and deception are the valuable qualities; and their value finds natural appreciation in the Russian or the oriental mind. Thus the Kremlin has no compunction about retreating in the face of superior force. And being under the compulsion of no timetable, it does not get panicky under the necessity for such retreat. Its political action is a fluid stream which moves constantly, wherever it is permitted to move, toward a given goal. Its main concern is to make sure that it has filled every nook and cranny available to it in the basin of world power. But if it finds unassailable barriers in its path, it accepts these philosophically and accommodates itself to them. The main thing is that there should always be pressure, unceasing constant pressure, toward the desired goal. There is no trace of any feeling in Soviet psychology that that goal must be reached at any given time.

These considerations make Soviet diplomacy at once easier and more difficult to deal with than the diplomacy of individual aggressive leaders like Napoleon and Hitler. On the one hand it is more sensitive to contrary force, more ready to yield on individual sectors of the diplomatic front when that force is felt to be too strong, and thus more rational in the logic and rhetoric of power. On the other hand it cannot be easily defeated or discouraged by a single victory on the part of its opponents. And the patient persistence by which it is animated means that it can be effectively countered not by sporadic acts which represent the momentary whims of democratic opinion but only by intelligent long-range policies on the part of Russia's adversaries—policies no less steady in their purpose, and no less variegated and resourceful in their application, than those of the Soviet Union itself.

In these circumstances it is clear that the main element of any United States policy toward the Soviet Union must be that of a long-term, patient but firm and vigilant containment of Russian expansive tendencies. It is important to note, however, that such a policy has nothing to do with outward histrionics: with threats or blustering or superfluous gestures of outward "toughness." While the Kremlin is basically flexible in its reaction to political realities, it is by no means unamenable to considerations of prestige. Like almost any other government, it can be placed by tactless and threatening gestures in a position where it cannot afford to yield even though this might be dictated by its sense of real-

ism. The Russian leaders are keen judges of human psychology, and as such they are highly conscious that loss of temper and of self-control is never a source of strength in political affairs. They are quick to exploit such evidences of weakness. For these reasons, it is a *sine qua non* of successful dealing with Russia that the foreign government in question should remain at all times cool and collected and that its demands on Russian policy should be put forward in such a manner as to leave the way open for a compliance not too detrimental to Russian prestige.

III

In the light of the above, it will be clearly seen that the Soviet pressure against the free institutions of the western world is something that can be contained by the adroit and vigilant application of counter-force at a series of constantly shifting geographical and political points, corresponding to the shifts and manoeuvres of Soviet policy, but which cannot be charmed or talked out of existence. The Russians look forward to a duel of infinite duration, and they see that already they have scored great successes. It must be borne in mind that there was a time when the Communist Party represented far more of a minority in the sphere of Russian national life than Soviet power today represents in the world community.

But if ideology convinces the rulers of Russia that truth is on their side and that they can therefore afford to wait, those of us on whom that ideology has no claim are free to examine objectively the validity of that premise. The Soviet thesis not only implies complete lack of control by the west over its own economic destiny, it likewise assumes

Russian unity, discipline and patience over an infinite period. Let us bring this apocalyptic vision down to earth, and suppose that the western world finds the strength and resourcefulness to contain Soviet power over a period of ten to fifteen years. What does that spell for Russia itself?

The Soviet leaders, taking advantage of the contributions of modern technique to the arts of despotism, have solved the question of obedience within the confines of their power. Few challenge their authority; and even those who do are unable to make that challenge valid as against the organs of suppression of the state.

The Kremlin has also proved able to accomplish its purpose of building up in Russia, regardless of the interests of the inhabitants, an industrial foundation of heavy metallurgy, which is, to be sure, not yet complete but which is nevertheless continuing to grow and is approaching those of the other major industrial countries. All of this, however, both the maintenance of internal political security and the building of heavy industry, has been carried out at a terrible cost in human life and in human hopes and energies. It has necessitated the use of forced labor on a scale unprecedented in modern times under conditions of peace. It has involved the neglect or abuse of other phases of Soviet economic life, particularly agriculture, consumers' goods production, housing and transportation.

To all that, the war has added its tremendous toll of destruction, death and human exhaustion. In consequence of this, we have in Russia today a population which is physically and spiritually tired. The mass of the people are disillusioned, skeptical and no longer as accessible as they once were to the magical attraction which Soviet power still radiates to its followers abroad. The avidity with which people seized upon the slight respite accorded to the Church for tactical reasons during the war was eloquent testimony to the fact that their capacity for faith and devotion found little expression in the purposes of the régime.

In these circumstances, there are limits to the physical and nervous strength of people themselves. These limits are absolute ones, and are binding even for the cruelest dictatorship, because beyond them people cannot be driven. The forced labor camps and the other agencies of constraint provide temporary means of compelling people to work longer hours than their own volition or mere economic pressure would dictate; but if people survive them at all they become old before their time and must be considered as human casualties to the demands of dictatorship. In either case their best powers are no longer available to society and can no longer be enlisted in the service of the state.

Here only the younger generation can help. The younger generation, despite all vicissitudes and sufferings, is numerous and vigorous; and the Russians are a talented people. But it still remains to be seen what will be the effects on mature performance of the abnormal emotional strains of childhood which Soviet dictatorship created and which were enormously increased by the war. Such things as normal security and placidity of home environment have practically ceased to exist in the Soviet Union outside of the most remote farms and villages. And observers are not yet sure whether that is not going to leave its mark on the over-all capacity of the generation now coming into maturity.

In addition to this, we have the fact that Soviet economic development, while it can list certain formidable achievements, has been precariously spotty and uneven. Russian Communists who speak of the "uneven development of capitalism" should blush at the contemplation of their own national economy. Here certain branches of economic life, such as the metallurgical and machine industries, have been pushed out of all proportion to other sectors of economy. Here is a nation striving to become in a short period one of the great industrial nations of the world while it still has no highway network worthy of the name and only a relatively primitive network of railways. Much has been done to increase efficiency of labor and to teach primitive peasants something about the operation of machines. But maintenance is still a crying deficiency of all Soviet economy. Construction is hasty and poor in quality. Depreciation must be enormous. And in vast sectors of economic life it has not yet been possible to instill into labor anything like that general culture of production and technical self-respect which characterizes the skilled worker of the west.

It is difficult to see how these deficiencies can be corrected at an early date by a tired and dispirited population working largely under the shadow of fear and compulsion. And as long as they are not overcome, Russia will remain economically a vulnerable, and in a certain sense an impotent, nation, capable of exporting its enthusiasms and of radiating the strange charm of its primitive political vitality but unable to back up those articles of export by the real evidences of material power and prosperity.

Meanwhile, a great uncertainty hangs over the political life of the Soviet Union. That is the uncertainty involved in the transfer of power from one individual or group of individuals to others.

This is, of course, outstandingly the problem of the personal position of Stalin. We must remember that his succession to Lenin's pinnacle of preëminence in the Communist movement was the only such transfer of individual authority which the Soviet Union has experienced. That transfer took 12 years to consolidate. It cost the lives of millions of people and shook the state to its foundations. The attendant tremors were felt all through the international revolutionary movement, to the disadvantage of the Kremlin itself.

It is always possible that another transfer of preëminent power may take place quietly and inconspicuously, with no repercussions anywhere. But again, it is possible that the questions involved may unleash, to use some of Lenin's words, one of those "incredibly swift transitions" from "delicate deceit" to "wild violence" which characterize Russian history, and may shake Soviet power to its foundations.

But this is not only a question of Stalin himself. There has been, since 1938, a dangerous congealment of political life in the higher circles of Soviet power. The All-Union Congress of Soviets, in theory the supreme body of the Party, is supposed to meet not less often than once in three years. It will soon be eight full years since its last meeting. During this period membership in the Party has numerically doubled. Party mortality during the war was enormous; and today well over half of the Party members are persons who have entered since the last Party congress was held. Meanwhile, the same small group of men has carried on at the top through an amazing series of national vicissitudes. Surely there is some reason why the experiences of the war brought basic political changes to every one of the great governments of the west. Surely the causes of that phenomenon are basic enough to be present somewhere in the obscurity of Soviet political life, as well. And yet no recognition has been given to these causes in Russia.

It must be surmised from this that even within so highly disciplined an organization as the Communist Party there must be a growing divergence in age, outlook and interest between the great mass of Party members, only so recently recruited into the movement, and the little self-perpetuating clique of men at the top, whom most of these Party members have never met, with whom they have never conversed, and with whom they can have no political intimacy.

Who can say whether, in these circumstances, the eventual rejuvenation of the higher spheres of authority (which can only be a matter of time) can take place smoothly and peacefully, or whether rivals in the quest for higher power will not eventually reach down into these politically immature and inexperienced masses in order to find support for their respective claims? If this were ever to happen, strange consequences could flow for the Communist Party: for the membership at large has been exercised only in the practices of iron discipline and obedience and not in the arts of compromise and accommodation. And if disunity were ever to seize and paralyze the Party, the chaos and weakness of Russian society would be revealed in forms beyond description. For we have seen that Soviet power is only a crust concealing an amorphous mass of human beings among whom no independent organizational structure is tolerated. In Russia there is not even such a thing as local government. The present generation of Russians have never known spontaneity of collec-

tive action. If, consequently, anything were ever to occur to disrupt the unity and efficacy of the Party as a political instrument, Soviet Russia might be changed overnight from one of the strongest to one of the weakest and most pitiable of national societies.

Thus the future of Soviet power may not be by any means as secure as Russian capacity for self-delusion would make it appear to the men in the Kremlin. That they can keep power themselves, they have demonstrated. That they can quietly and easily turn it over to others remains to be proved. Meanwhile, the hardships of their rule and the vicissitudes of international life have taken a heavy toll of the strength and hopes of the great people on whom their power rests. It is curious to note that the ideological power of Soviet authority is strongest today in areas beyond the frontiers of Russia, beyond the reach of its police power. This phenomenon brings to mind a comparison used by Thomas Mann in his great novel *Buddenbrooks*. Observing that human institutions often show the greatest outward brilliance at a moment when inner decay is in reality farthest advanced, he compared the Buddenbrook family, in the days of its greatest glamour, to one of those stars whose light shines most brightly on this world when in reality it has long since ceased to exist. And who can say with assurance that the strong light still cast by the Kremlin on the dissatisfied peoples of the western world is not the powerful afterglow of a constellation which is in actuality on the wane? This cannot be proved. And it cannot be disproved. But the possibility remains (and in the opinion of this writer it is a strong one) that Soviet power, like the capitalist world of its conception, bears within it the seeds of its own decay, and that the sprouting of these seeds is well advanced.

IV

It is clear that the United States cannot expect in the foreseeable future to enjoy political intimacy with the Soviet régime. It must continue to regard the Soviet Union as a rival, not a partner, in the political arena. It must continue to expect that Soviet policies will reflect no abstract love of peace and stability, no real faith in the possibility of a permanent happy coexistence of the Socialist and capitalist worlds, but rather a cautious, persistent pressure toward the disruption and weakening of all rival influence and rival power.

Balanced against this are the facts that Russia, as opposed to the western world in general, is still by far the weaker party, that Soviet policy is highly flexible, and that Soviet society may well contain deficiencies which will eventually weaken its own total potential. This would of itself warrant the United States entering with reasonable confidence upon a policy of firm containment, designed to confront the Russians with unalterable counter-force at every point where they show signs of encroaching upon the interests of a peaceful and stable world.

But in actuality the possibilities for American policy are by no means limited to holding the line and hoping for the best. It is entirely possible for the United States to influence by its actions the internal developments, both within Russia and throughout the international Communist movement, by which Russian policy is largely determined. This is not only a question of the modest measure of informational activity which this government can conduct in the Soviet Union and elsewhere, although that, too,

is important. It is rather a question of the degree to which the United States can create among the peoples of the world generally the impression of a country which knows what it wants, which is coping successfully with the problems of its internal life and with the responsibilities of a World Power, and which has a spiritual vitality capable of holding its own among the major ideological currents of the time. To the extent that such an impression can be created and maintained, the aims of Russian Communism must appear sterile and quixotic, the hopes and enthusiasm of Moscow's supporters must wane, and added strain must be imposed on the Kremlin's foreign policies. For the palsied decrepitude of the capitalist world is the keystone of Communist philosophy. Even the failure of the United States to experience the early economic depression which the ravens of the Red Square have been predicting with such complacent confidence since hostilities ceased would have deep and important repercussions throughout the Communist world.

By the same token, exhibitions of indecision, disunity and internal disintegration within this country have an exhilarating effect on the whole Communist movement. At each evidence of these tendencies, a thrill of hope and excitement goes through the Communist world; a new jauntiness can be noted in the Moscow tread; new groups of foreign supporters climb on to what they can only view as the band wagon of international politics; and Russian pressure increases all along the line in international affairs.

It would be an exaggeration to say that American behavior unassisted and alone could exercise a power of life and death over the Communist movement and bring about the early fall of Soviet power in Russia. But the United States has it in its power to increase enormously the strains under which Soviet policy must operate, to force upon the Kremlin a far greater degree of moderation and circumspection than it has had to observe in recent years, and in this way to promote tendencies which must eventually find their outlet in either the break-up or the gradual mellowing of Soviet power. For no mystical, Messianic movement—and particularly not that of the Kremlin—can face frustration indefinitely without eventually adjusting itself in one way or another to the logic of that state of affairs.

Thus the decision will really fall in large measure in this country itself. The issue of Soviet-American relations is in essence a test of the over-all worth of the United States as a nation among nations. To avoid destruction the United States need only measure up to its own best traditions and prove itself worthy of preservation as a great nation.

Surely, there was never a fairer test of national quality than this. In the light of these circumstances, the thoughtful observer of Russian-American relations will find no cause for complaint in the Kremlin's challenge to American society. He will rather experience a certain gratitude to a Providence which, by providing the American people with this implacable challenge, has made their entire security as a nation dependent on their pulling themselves together and accepting the responsibilities of moral and political leadership that history plainly intended them to bear.

NOTES

1. "Concerning the Slogans of the United States of Europe," August 1915. Official Soviet edition of Lenin's works.
2. Here and elsewhere in this paper "Socialism" refers to Marxist or Leninist Communism, not to liberal Socialism of the Second International variety.

QUESTIONS

1. What weaknesses does Kennan associate with the Soviet Union?

2. Can the view presented in the "X" article be considered realist? Why or why not?

---

7.   War and Change in World Politics

Robert Gilpin

In this selection, Robert Gilpin uses realist assumptions to produce a cyclical theory of world politics. Using examples from the great empires of the past, Gilpin explains the long-term causes for the rise and decline of major powers. He identifies three key factors: burden of leadership, rising domestic consumption, and the diffu-

From *War and Change in World Politics,* pp. 1–15, 39–44. Reprinted with permission of Cambridge University Press.

sion of technology. These factors combine to weaken the great power, leaving it vulnerable to challenge by rival states. War establishes a new hierarchy, and a new cycle of "growth, expansion, and eventual decline" begins again.

Robert Gilpin is a Princeton University professor emeritus. He is the author of numerous books and articles. His latest work is *The Challenge of Global Capitalism: The World Economy in the 21st Century* (2000).

During the 1970s and early 1980s a series of dramatic events signaled that international relations were undergoing a significant upheaval. Long-established and seemingly stable sets of relationships and understandings were summarily cast aside. Political leaders, academic observers, and the celebrated "man in the street" were suddenly conscious of the fact that the energy crisis, dramatic events in the Middle East, and tensions in the Communist world were novel developments of a qualitatively different order from those of the preceding decade. These developments and many others in the political, economic, and military realms signaled far-reaching shifts in the international distribution of power, an unleashing of new sociopolitical forces, and the global realignment of diplomatic relations. Above all, these events and developments revealed that the relatively stable international system that the world had known since the end of World War II was entering a period of uncertain political changes.

Ours is not the first age in which a sudden concatenation of dramatic events has revealed underlying shifts in military power, economic interest, and political alignments. In the twentieth century, developments of comparable magnitude had already taken place in the decades preceding World War I and World War II. This awareness of the dangers inherent in periods of political instability and rapid change causes profound unease and apprehension. The fear grows that events may get out of hand and the world may once again plunge itself into a global conflagration. Scholars, journalists, and others turn to history for guidance, asking if the current pattern of events resembles the pattern of 1914 and 1939.[1]

These contemporary developments and their dangerous implications raise a number of questions regarding war and change in international relations: How and under what circumstances does change take place at the level of international relations? What are the roles of political, economic, and technological developments in producing change in international systems? Wherein lies the danger of intense military conflict during periods of rapid economic and political upheaval? And, most important of all, are answers that are derived from examination of the past valid for the contemporary world? In other words, to what extent have social, economic, and technological developments such as increasing economic interdependence of nations and the advent of nuclear weapons changed the role of war in the process of international political change? Is there any reason to hope that political change may be more benign in the future than it has been in the past?

The purpose of this book is to explore these issues. In this endeavor we shall seek to develop an understanding of international political change more systematic than the understanding that currently exists. We do not pretend to develop a general theory of international relations that will provide an overarching explanatory statement. Instead, we attempt to provide a framework for thinking about the problem of war and change in world politics. This intellectual framework is intended to be an analytical device that will help to order and explain human experience. It does not constitute a rigorous scientific explanation of political change. The ideas on international political change presented are generalizations based on observations of historical experience rather than a set of hypotheses that have been tested scientifically by historical evidence; they are proposed as a plausible account of how international political change occurs.[2]

To this end we isolate and analyze the more obvious regularities and patterns associated with changes in international systems. However, we make no claim to have discovered the "laws of change" that determine when political change will occur or what course it will take.[3] On the contrary, the position taken here is that major political changes are the consequences of the conjuncture of unique and unpredictable sets of developments. However, the claim is made that it is possible to identify recurrent patterns, common elements, and general tendencies in the major turning points in international history. As the distinguished economist W. Arthur Lewis put it, "The process of social change is much the same today as it was 2,000 years ago . . . We can tell how change will occur if it occurs; what we cannot foresee is what change is going to occur."[4]

The conception of political change presented in this book, like almost all social science, is not predictive. Even economics is predictive only within a narrow range of issues.[5]

Most of the alleged theories in the field of political science and in the subfield of international relations are in fact analytical, descriptive constructs; they provide at best a conceptual framework and a set of questions that help us to analyze and explain a type of phenomenon.[6] Thus, Kenneth Waltz, in his stimulating book *Man, the State and War,* provided an explanation of war in general terms, but not the means for predicting any particular war.[7] In similar fashion, this study seeks to explain in general terms the nature of international political change.

The need for a better understanding of political change, especially international political change, was well set forth by Wilbert Moore in the latest edition of the *International Encyclopedia of the Social Sciences:* "Paradoxically, as the rate of social change has accelerated in the real world of experience, the scientific disciplines dealing with man's actions and products have tended to emphasize orderly interdependence and static continuity."[8]

Moore's judgment concerning the inadequate treatment of political change by social scientists is borne out by analyses of international-relations textbooks and theoretical works. Although there are some recent outstanding exceptions,[9] few of these books have addressed the problem of political change in systematic fashion. As David Easton rightly commented, "students of political life have . . . been prone to forget that the really crucial problems of social research are concerned with the patterns of change."[10]

It is worth noting, as Joseph Schumpeter pointed out, that the natural development of any science is from static analysis to dynamic analysis.[11] Static theory is simpler, and its propositions are easier to prove. Unfortunately, until the statics of a field of inquiry are sufficiently well-developed and one has a good grasp of repetitive processes and recurrent phenomena, it is difficult if not impossible to proceed to the study of dynamics. From this perspective, systematic study of international relations is a young field, and much of what passes for dynamics is in reality an effort to understand the statics of interactions of particular international systems: diplomatic bargaining, alliance behavior, crisis management, etc. The question whether or not our current understanding of these static aspects is sufficiently well advanced to aid in the development of a dynamic theory poses a serious challenge to the present enterprise.

A second factor that helps to explain the apparent neglect, until recent years, of the problem of political change is what K. J. Holsti called the decline of "grand theory."[12] The political realism of Hans Morgenthau, the systems theory of Morton Kaplan, and the neofunctionalism of Ernst Haas, as well as numerous other "grand theories," have one element in common: the search for a general theory of international politics. Each in its own way, with varying success, has sought, in the words of Morgenthau, "to reduce the facts of experience to mere specific instances of general propositions."[13] Yet none of these ambitious efforts to understand the issues (war, imperialism, and political change) has gained general acceptance. Instead, "the major preoccupations of theorists during the past decade have been to explore specific problems, to form hypotheses or generalizations explaining limited ranges of phenomena, and particularly, to obtain data to test those hypotheses."[14] In brief, the more

recent emphasis on so-called middle-range theory, though valuable in itself, has had the unfortunate consequence of diverting attention away from more general theoretical problems.[15]

A third reason for neglect of the study of political change is the Western bias in the study of international relations. For a profession whose intellectual commitment is the understanding of the interactions of societies, international relations as a discipline is remarkably parochial and ethnocentric. It is essentially a study of the Western state system, and a sizable fraction of the existing literature is devoted to developments since the end of World War II. Thus the profession has emphasized recent developments within that particular state system. Although there are exceptions, the practitioners of this discipline have not been forced to come to terms with the dynamics of this, or any other, state system."[16] As Martin Wight suggested, international relations lacks a tradition of political theorizing. In large measure, of course, this is because of the paucity of reliable secondary studies of non-Western systems.[17] This situation in itself is a formidable obstacle to the development of a theory of international political change.

A fourth reason for neglect of the theoretical problem of political change is the widespread conviction of the futility of the task. Prevalent among historians, this view is also held by many social scientists.[18] The search for "laws of change" is held to be useless because of the uniqueness and complexity of historical events. Thus the search for generalizations or patterns in human affairs is regarded as a hopeless enterprise. Such a position, if taken at face value, denies the very possibility of a science or history of society; yet one should note its admonitions that there are no immutable laws of change and that although repetitive patterns may exist, social change is ultimately contingent on unique sets of historical events.

Finally, the development of a theory of political change has been inhibited by ideology and emotion. In part this is due to a conservative bias in Western social science. Most academic social scientists have a preference for stability or at least a preference for stability or at least a preference for orderly change. The idea of radical changes that threaten accepted values and interests is not an appealing one. This issue is especially acute for the theorist of international political change, who must confront directly the fundamental problem of international relations: war. The inhibiting effect of this dreadful issue has been well put by John Burton in a sweeping indictment of contemporary international-relations scholarship:

> The chief failure of orthodoxy has been in relation to change. The outstanding feature of reality is the dynamic nature of International Relations. No general theory is appropriate which cannot take into consideration the rapidly changing technological, social and political environment in which nations are required to live in peace one with the other. But the only device of fundamental change which is possible in the context of power politics is that of war, for which reason war is recognized as a legitimate instrument of national policy. It is not surprising that International Relations has tended to be discussed in static terms, and that stability has tended to be interpreted in terms of the maintenance of the *status quo*. A dynamic approach to International Relations would immediately confront the analyst with

> no alternative but to acknowledge war as the only available mechanism for change.[19]

Burton's challenge to orthodox theory of international relations goes to the heart of the present study. In recent years theorists of international relations have tended to stress the moderating and stabilizing influences of contemporary developments on the behavior of states, especially the increasing economic interdependence among nations and the destructiveness of modern weapons. These important developments have encouraged many individuals to believe that peaceful evolution has replaced military conflict as the principal means of adjusting relations among nation-states in the contemporary world. This assumption has been accompanied by a belief that economic and welfare goals have triumphed over the traditional power and security objectives of states. Thus, many believe that the opportunity for peaceful economic intercourse and the constraints imposed by modern destructive warfare have served to decrease the probability of a major war.

In the present study we take a very different stance, a stance based on the assumption that the fundamental nature of international relations has not changed over the millennia. International relations continue to be a recurring struggle for wealth and power among independent actors in a state of anarchy. The classic history of Thucydides is as meaningful a guide to the behavior of states today as when it was written in the fifth century B.C. Yet important changes have taken place. One of the subthemes . . . , in fact, is that modern statecraft and premodern statecraft differ in significant respects, a situation first appreciated by Montesquieu, Edward Gibbon, and other earlier writers on the subject. Nevertheless, we contend that the fundamentals have not been altered. For this reason, the insights of earlier writers and historical experience are considered relevant to an understanding of the ways in which international systems function and change in the contemporary era.

Thus although there is obviously an important element of truth in the belief that contemporary economic and technological development have altered relations among states, events in Asia, Africa, and the Middle East in the 1970s and early 1980s force us once again to acknowledge the continuing unsolved problem of war and the role of war in the process of international political change. Even more than in the past, in the last decades of the twentieth century we need to understand the relationship of war and change in the international system. Only in this way can we hope to fashion a more peaceful alternative. As E. H. Carr reminded us, this is the basic task of the study of international relations: "To establish methods of peaceful change is . . . the fundamental problem of international morality and of international politics."[20] But if peace were the ultimate goal of statecraft, then the solution to the problem of peaceful change would be easy. Peace may always be had by surrender to the aggressor state. The real task for the peaceful state is to seek a peace that protects and guarantees its vital interests and its concept of international morality.

THE NATURE OF INTERNATIONAL POLITICAL CHANGE

An international system is established for the same reason that any social or political system is created; actors enter social relations and create social structures in order to advance particular sets of political, economic, or other types of interests. Because the interests of some of the actors may conflict with those of other actors, the particular interests that are most favored by these social arrangements tend to reflect the relative powers of the actors involved. That is, although social systems impose restraints on the behavior of all actors, the behaviors rewarded and punished by the system will coincide, at least initially, with the interests of the most powerful members of the social system. Over time, however, the interests of individual actors and the balance of power among the actors do change as a result of economic, technological, and other developments. As a consequence, those actors who benefit most from a change in the social system and who gain the power to effect such change will seek to alter the system in ways that favor their interests. The resulting changed system will reflect the new distribution of power and the interests of its new dominant members. Thus, a precondition for political change lies in a disjuncture between the existing social system and the redistribution of power toward those actors who would benefit most from a change in the system.

This conception of political change is based on the notion that the purpose or social function of any social system, including the international system, may be defined in terms of the benefits that various members derived from its operation.[21]

As in the case with domestic society, the nature of the international system determines whose interest are being served by the functioning of the system. Changes in the system imply changes in the distribution of benefits provided to and costs imposed on individual members of the system. Thus the study of international political change must focus on the international system and especially on the efforts of political actors to change the international system in order to advance their own interests. Whether these interests are security, economic gain or ideological goals, the achievement of state objectives is dependent on the nature of the international system (i.e., the governance of the system, the rules of the system, the recognition of rights, etc.). As is the case in any social or political system, the process of international political change ultimately reflects the efforts of individuals or groups to transform institutions and systems in order to advance their interests. Because these interests and the powers of groups (or states) change, in time the political system will be changed in ways that will reflect these underlying shifts in interest and power. The elaboration of this approach for the understanding of international polit-ical change is the purpose of the subsequent discussion.

A FRAMEWORK FOR UNDERSTANDING INTERNATIONAL POLITICAL CHANGE

The conceptualization of international political change to be presented [here] rests on a set of assumptions regarding the behavior of states:

1. An international system is stable (i.e., in a state of equilibrium) if no state believes it profitable to attempt to change the system.

2. A state will attempt to change the international system if the expected benefits exceed the expected costs (i.e., if there is an expected net gain).

3. A state will seek to change the international system through territorial, political, and economic expansion until the marginal costs of further change are equal to or greater than the marginal benefits.

4. Once an equilibrium between the costs and benefits of further change and expansion is reached, the tendency is for the economic costs of maintaining the status quo to rise faster than the economic capacity to support the status quo.

5. If the disequilibrium in the international system is not resolved, then the system will be changed, and a new equilibrium reflecting the redistribution of power will be established.

Obviously these assumptions are abstractions from a highly complex political reality. They do not describe the actual decision processes of statesmen, but as in the case of economic theory, actors are assumed to behave as if they were guided by such a set of cost/benefit calculations. Moreover, these assumptions are not mutually exclusive; they do overlap. Assumptions 2 and 4 are mirror images of one another, assumption 2 referring to a revisionist state and assumption 4 referring to a status quo state.

On the basis of these assumptions, the conceptualization of international political change to be presented here seeks to comprehend a continuing historical process. Because history has no starts and stops, one must break into the flow of history at a particular point. The following analysis of political change begins with an international system in a state of equilibrium as shown in Figure 1. An international system is in a state of equilibrium if the more powerful states in the system are satisfied with the existing ter-

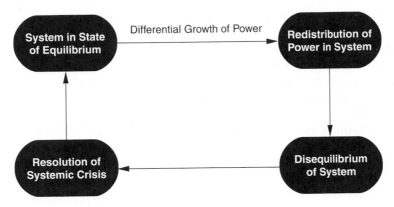

FIGURE 1 *Diagram of International Political Change*

ritorial political, and economic arrangements. Although minor changes and adjustments may take place, an equilibrium condition is one in which no powerful state (or group) believes that a change in the system would yield additional benefits commensurate with the anticipated costs of bringing about a change in the system.[22] Although every state and group in the system could benefit from particular types of change, the costs involved will discourage attempts to seek a change in system. As one writer has put it, "a power equilibrium represents a stable political configuration provided there are no changes or returns to conquest."[23] Under these conditions, where no one has an incentive to change the system, the status quo may be said to be stable.

In the more traditional language of international relations, the international status quo is held to be a legitimate one, at least by the major states in the system. The meaning of legitimacy was defined by Henry Kissinger as follows:

> [Legitimacy] implies the acceptance of the framework of the international order by all major powers, at least to the extent that no state is so dissatisfied that, like Germany after the Treaty of Versailles, it expresses its dissatisfaction in a revolutionary foreign policy. A legitimate order does not make conflicts impossible, but it limits their scope. Wars may occur, but they will be fought in *the name of* the existing structure and the peace which follows will be justified as a better expression of the "legitimate," general consensus. Diplomacy in the classic sense, the adjustment of differences through negotiations, is possible only in "legitimate international orders."[24]

What this quotation suggests is that an international system or order exists in a condition of homeostatic or dynamic equilibrium. Like any other system, it is not completely at rest; changes at the level of interstate interactions are constantly taking place. In general, however, the conflicts, alliances, and diplomatic interactions among the actors in the system tend to preserve the defining characteristics of the system. Thus, as Kissinger demonstrated, the legitimate order or equilibrium created by the Congress of Vienna (1814) survived limited conflicts and diplomatic maneuvering until it finally collapsed in response to the profound economic, technological, and political upheavals of the latter part of the nineteenth century. This issue of legitimacy will be discussed later.

In every international system there are continual occurrences of political, economic, and technological changes that promise gains or threaten losses for one or another actor. In most cases these potential gains and losses are minor, and only incremental adjustments are necessary in order to take account of them. Such changes take place within the existing international system, producing a condition of homeostatic equilibrium. The relative stability of the system is, in fact, largely determined by its capacity to adjust to the demands of actors affected by changing political and environmental conditions. In every system, therefore, a process of disequilibrium and adjustment is constantly taking place. In the absence of large potential net benefits from change, the system continues to remain in a state of equilibrium.

If the interests and relative powers of the principal states in an international system remained constant over time, or if power relations changed in such a way as to maintain the same relative distribution of power, the system would continue indefinitely in a state of equilibrium. However, both domestic and international developments undermine the stability of the status quo. For example, shifts in domestic coalitions may necessitate redefinition of the "national interest." However, the most destabilizing factor is the tendency in an international system for the powers of member states to change at different rates because of political, economic, and technological developments. In time, the differential growth in power of the various states in the system causes a fundamental redistribution of power in the system.

The concept of power is one of the most troublesome in the field of international relations and, more generally, political science. Many weighty books have analyzed and elaborated the concept. In this book, power refers simply to the military, economic, and technological capabilities of states. This definition obviously leaves out important and intangible elements that affect the outcomes of political actions, such as public morale, qualities of leadership, and situational factors. It also excludes what E. H. Carr called "power over opinion."[25] These psychological and frequently incalculable aspects of power and international relations are more closely associated with the concept of prestige. . . .

As a consequence of the changing interests of individual states, and especially because of the differential growth in power among states, the international system moves from a condition of equilibrium to one of disequilibrium. Disequilibrium is a situation in which economic, political, and technological development have increased considerably the potential benefits or decreased the potential costs to one or more states of seeking to change the international system. Forestalling one's losses or increasing one's gains becomes an incentive for one or more states to attempt to change the system. Thus there develops a disjuncture between the existing international system and the potential gains to particular states from a change in the international system.

The elements of this systemic disequilibrium are twofold. First, military, technological, or other changes have increased the benefits of territorial conquest or the benefits of changing the international system in other ways. Second, the differential growth in power among the states in the system has altered the cost of changing the system. This transformation of the benefits and/or

Table I Mechanisms of Control (Components of System)

Government[a]	Dominance of great power[b]
Authority	Hierarchy of prestige
Property rights	Division of territory
Law	Rules of the system
Domestic economy	International economy

[a] Based on distribution of power among domestic groups, coalitions, classes, etc.
[b] Based on distribution of power among states in the system

the costs of changing the system produces an incongruity or disjuncture among the components of the system (Table 1). On the one hand, the hierarchy of prestige, the division of territory, the international division of labor, and the rules of the system remain basically unchanged; they continue to reflect primarily the interests of the existing dominant powers and the relative power distribution that prevailed at the time of the last systemic change. On the other hand, the international distribution of power has undergone a radical transformation that has weakened the foundations of the existing system. It is this disjuncture between the several components of the system and its implications for relative gains and losses among the various states in the system that cause international political change.

This disjuncture within the existing international system involving the potential benefits and losses to particular powerful actors from a change in the system leads to a crisis in the international system. Although resolution of a crisis through peaceful adjustment of the systemic disequilibrium is possible, the principal mechanism of change throughout history has been war, or what we shall call hegemonic war (i.e., a war that determines which state or states will be dominant and will govern the system). The peace settlement following such a hegemonic struggle re-orders the political, territorial, and other bases of the system. Thus the cycle of change is completed in that hegemonic war and the peace settlement create a new status quo and equilibrium reflecting the redistribution of power in the system and the other components of the system.

NOTES

1. Miles Kahler, "Rumors of War: The 1914 Analogy," *Foreign Affairs* 58 (1979-80), pp. 374-396.
2. However, in principle, these ideas are translatable into specific testable hypotheses. At least we would argue that this is possible for a substantial fraction of them. The carrying out of this task, or part of it, would require another volume.
3. The term "law" . . . is to be interpreted as a general tendency that may be counteracted by other developments. This conception of law is taken from Jean Baechler, *Les Origines du Capitalisme* (Paris: Editions Gallimard; 1971). English edition (Oxford: Basil Blackwell, 1975), p. 52.
4. W. Arthur Lewis, *The Theory of Economic Growth* (New York: Harper & Row, 1970), pp. 17-18.
5. F. S. C. Northrop, *The, Logic of the Sciences and the Humanities* (New York: Macmillan, 1947), pp. 243-45.
6. Stanley Hoffmann (ed.), *Contemporary Theory in International Relations* (Englewood Cliffs, N.J.: Prentice Hall, 1960), p. 40.
7. Kenneth N. Waltz, *Man, the State and War* (New York: Columbia University Press, 1959), p. 232.

8. Wilbert E. Moore, "Social Change" in *International Encyclopedia of the Social Sciences,* vol. 14, ed. by David Sils (New York: Crowell Collier and Macmillan, 1968), p. 365.

9. Nazli Choucri and Robert C. North, *Nations in Conflict* (San Francisco: W. H. Freeman, 1975); Robert O. Keohane and Joseph S. Nye, *Power and Independence* (Boston: Little, Brown, 1977); Kenneth N. Waltz, *Theory of International Politics* (Reading, MA: Addison-Wesley, 1979).

10. David Easton, *The Political System* (New York: Alfred A. Knopf, 1953), p. 42. It is symptomatic of this continued general neglect that the *Handbook of Political Science* does not contain a section devoted to The problem of political change. Nor does the entry "political change" appear in its cumulative index. See Fred 1. Greenstein and Nelson W. Polsby, eds. *Handbook of Political Science* (Reading, Mass.: Addison-Wesley, 1975).

11. Joseph Schumpeter, *History of Economic Analysis* (New York: Oxford University Press, 1954), p. 964.

12. K. J. Holsti, "Retreat from Utopia," *Canadian Journal of Political Science,* Vol. 4 (1971), pp. 165–177.

13. *Ibid,* p. 167.

14. *Ibid,* p. 171.

15. Several important books have recently indicated revival of interest in general theory. See Choucri and North, *Nations in Conflict;* Hedley Bull, *The Anarchical, Society* (New York Columbia University Press, 1977); Keohane and Nye, *Power and Interdependence;* Stanley Hoffmann, *Primacy or World Order* (New York: McGraw-Hill, 1978); Ralph Pettman, *State and Class* (London: Croom Helm, 1979); Kenneth N. Waltz, *Theory of International Politics* (Reading, Mass.: Addison-Wesley, 1979). Marxist scholars, of course, never lost interest in "grand theory."

16. Three recent exceptions are Evan Luard, *Types of International Society* (New York: Free Press, 1976); Robert G. Wesson, *The Imperial Order* (Berkeley: University of California Press, 1967); Martin Wight, *Systems of States,* ed. Hedley Bull (Leicester, England: Leicester University Press, 1977).

17. Martin Wight, "Why Is There No International Theory?" in Herbert Butterfield and Martin Wight (eds.), *Diplomatic Investigations* (London: George Allen and Unwin, 1966), pp. 17–34.

18. Albert O. Hirschman, "The Search for Paradigms as a Hindrance to Understanding," *World Politics,* Vol. 22 (1970), pp. 329–43.

19. John Burton, *International Relations: A General Theory* (Cambridge, MA: Cambridge University Press, 1965), pp. 71–72.

20. E. H. Carr, *The Twenty Years' Crisis* (London: Macmillan, 1951).

21. John Harsanyi, "Rational-Choice Models of Political Behavior vs. Functionalist and Conformist Theories," *World Politics,* Vol. 21 (1969), pp. 513–38.

22. R. L. Curry Jr. and L. L. Wade, *A Theory of Political Exchange* (Englewood Cliffs, N.J.: Prentice Hall, 1968), p. 49; and Lance E. Davis and Douglass C. North, *Institutional Change and American Economic Growth* (Cambridge England: Cambridge University Press, 1971), p.40.

23. Trout Rader, *The Economics of Feudalism* (New York: Gordon and Breach, 1971), p. 50.

24. Henry A. Kissinger, *A World Restored* (Boston: Houghton Mifflin, 1967), pp. 1–2.

25. Carr, *Twenty Years' Crisis*, p. 132.

QUESTIONS

1. Is Robert Gilpin's theory of hegemonic rise and decline useful in explaining the end of the Cold War?

2. What does the author mean by the phrase "diffusion of technology?"

8.   Structural Realism After the Cold War

Kenneth N. Waltz

In this article, Kenneth N. Waltz argues that structural realism is still applicable to the post–Cold War era. The collapse of the Soviet Union and the end of the Cold War has transformed the structure of the international system from bipolar to unipolar, but it has not changed the essential nature of international politics. This selection is from *International Security* (2000).

Kenneth N. Waltz, former Ford Professor of Political Science at the University of California, Berkeley, is a research associate of the Institute of War and Peace Studies and adjunct professor at Columbia University. He has authored many books, including *Foreign Policy and Democratic Politics: The American and British Experience* (1967, reprinted in 1992) and *Theory of International Politics* (1979), as well as numerous essays.

Some students of international politics believe that realism is obsolete.[1] They argue that, although realism's concepts of anarchy, self-help, and power balancing may have been appropriate to a bygone era, they have been displaced by changed conditions and eclipsed by better ideas. New times call for new thinking. Changing conditions require revised theories or entirely different ones.

True, if the conditions that a theory contemplated have changed, the theory no longer applies. But what sorts of changes would alter the international political system so profoundly that old ways of thinking would no longer be relevant? Changes *of* the system would do it; changes *in* the system would not. Within-system changes take place all the time, some important, some not. Big changes in the means of transportation, communication, and war fighting, for example, strongly affect how states and other agents interact. Such changes occur at the unit level. In modern history, or perhaps in all of history, the introduction of nuclear weaponry was the great-

est of such changes. Yet in the nuclear era, international politics remains a self-help arena. Nuclear weapons decisively change how some states provide for their own and possibly for others' security; but nuclear weapons have not altered the anarchic structure of the international political system.

Changes in the structure of the system are distinct from changes at the unit level. Thus, changes in polarity also affect how states provide for their security. Significant changes take place when the number of great powers reduces to two or one. With more than two, states rely for their security both on their own internal efforts and on alliances they may make with others. Competition in multipolar systems is more complicated than competition in bipolar ones because uncertainties about the comparative capabilities of states multiply as numbers grow, and because estimates of the cohesiveness and strength of coalitions are hard to make.

Both changes of weaponry and changes of polarity were big ones with

From *International Security*, 25:1 (Summer 2000), pp. 5–41. © 2000 by the President and Fellows of Harvard College and the Massachusetts Institute of Technology.

ramifications that spread through the system, yet they did not transform it. If the system were transformed, international politics would no longer be international politics, and the past would no longer serve as a guide to the future. We would begin to call international politics by another name, as some do. The terms "world politics" or "global politics," for example, suggest that politics among self-interested states concerned with their security has been replaced by some other kind of politics or perhaps by no politics at all.

What changes, one may wonder, would turn international politics into something distinctly different? The answer commonly given is that international politics is being transformed and realism is being rendered obsolete as democracy extends its sway, as interdependence tightens its grip, and as institutions smooth the way to peace. I consider these points in successive sections. A fourth section explains why realist theory retains its explanatory power after the Cold War.

DEMOCRACY AND PEACE

The end of the Cold War coincided with what many took to be a new democratic wave. The trend toward democracy combined with Michael Doyle's rediscovery of the peaceful behavior of liberal democratic states *inter se* contributes strongly to the belief that war is obsolescent, if not obsolete, among the advanced industrial states of the world.[2]

The democratic peace thesis holds that democracies do not fight democracies. Notice that I say "thesis," not "theory." The belief that democracies constitute a zone of peace rests on a perceived high correlation between governmental form and international outcome. Francis Fuku-

yama thinks that the correlation is perfect: Never once has a democracy fought another democracy. Jack Levy says that it is "the closest thing we have to an empirical law in the study of international relations."[3] But, if it is true that democracies rest reliably at peace among themselves, we have not a theory but a purported fact begging for an explanation, as facts do. The explanation given generally runs this way: Democracies of the right kind (i.e., liberal ones) are peaceful in relation to one another. This was Immanuel Kant's point. The term he used was *Rechtsstaat,* or republic, and his definition of a republic was so restrictive that it was hard to believe that even one of them could come into existence, let alone two or more.[4] And if they did, who can say that they would continue to be of the right sort or continue to be democracies at all? The short and sad life of the Weimar Republic is a reminder. And how does one define what the right sort of democracy is? Some American scholars thought that Wilhelmine Germany was the very model of a modern democratic state with a wide suffrage, honest elections, a legislature that controlled the purse, competitive parties, a free press, and a highly competent bureaucracy.[5] But in the French, British, and American view after August of 1914, Germany turned out not to be a democracy of the right kind. John Owen tried to finesse the problem of definition by arguing that democracies that perceive one another to be liberal democracies will not fight.[6] That rather gives the game away. Liberal democracies have at times prepared for wars against other liberal democracies and have sometimes come close to fighting them. Christopher Layne shows that some wars between democracies were averted not because of the reluctance of democracies to fight each other but for fear of a third party—a good realist reason. How, for example, could Britain and France fight each other over Fashoda in 1898 when Germany lurked in the background? In emphasizing the international political reasons for democracies not fighting each other, Layne gets to the heart of the matter.[7] Conformity of countries to a prescribed political form may eliminate some of the causes of war; it cannot eliminate all of them. The democratic peace thesis will hold only if all of the causes of war lie inside of states.

The Causes of War

To explain war is easier than to understand the conditions of peace. If one asks what may cause war, the simple answer is "anything." That is Kant's answer: The natural state is the state of war. Under the conditions of international politics, war recurs; the sure way to abolish war, then, is to abolish international politics.

Over the centuries, liberals have shown a strong desire to get the politics out of politics. The ideal of nineteenth-century liberals was the police state, that is, the state that would confine its activities to catching criminals and enforcing contracts. The ideal of the laissez-faire state finds many counterparts among students of international politics with their yen to get the power out of power politics, the national out of international politics, the dependence out of interdependence, the relative out of relative gains, the politics out of international politics, and the structure out of structural theory.

Proponents of the democratic peace thesis write as though the spread of democracy will negate the effects of anarchy. No causes of conflict and war will any longer be found at the structural level. Francis Fukuyama finds it "perfectly possible to imagine anarchic state systems that are nonetheless peaceful." He sees no reason to associate anarchy with war. Bruce Russett believes that, with enough democracies in the world, it "may be possible in part to supersede the 'realist' principles (anarchy, the security dilemma of states) that have dominated practice . . . since at least the seventeenth century."[8] Thus the structure is removed from structural theory. Democratic states would be so confident of the peace-preserving effects of democracy that they would no longer fear that another state, so long as it remained democratic, would do it wrong. The guarantee of the state's proper external behavior would derive from its admirable internal qualities. . . .

Democracies may live at peace with democracies, but even if all states became democratic, the structure of international politics would remain anarchic. The structure of international politics is not transformed by changes internal to states, however widespread the changes may be. In the absence of an external authority a state cannot be sure that today's friend will not be tomorrow's enemy. Indeed, democracies have at times behaved as though today's democracy is today's enemy and a present threat to them. . . . In the latter half of the nineteenth century, as the United States and Britain became more democratic, bitterness grew between them, and the possibility of war was at times seriously entertained on both sides of the Atlantic. France and Britain were among the principal adversaries in the great power politics of the nineteenth century, as they were earlier. Their becoming democracies did not change their behavior toward each other. In 1914, democratic England

and France fought democratic Germany, and doubts about the latter's democratic standing merely illustrate the problem of definition. Indeed, the democratic pluralism of Germany was an underlying cause of the war. In response to domestic interests, Germany followed policies bound to frighten both Britain and Russia. And today if a war that a few have feared were fought by the United States and Japan, many Americans would say that Japan was not a democracy after all, but merely a one-party state.

What can we conclude? Democracies rarely fight democracies, we might say, and then add as a word of essential caution that the internal excellence of states is a brittle basis of peace.

Democratic Wars

Democracies coexist with undemocratic states. Although democracies seldom fight democracies, they do, as Michael Doyle has noted, fight at least their share of wars against others.[16] Citizens of democratic states tend to think of their countries as good, aside from what they do, simply because they are democratic. Thus former Secretary of State Warren Christopher claimed that "democratic nations rarely start wars or threaten their neighbors."[17] One might suggest that he try his proposition out in Central or South America. Citizens of democratic states also tend to think of undemocratic states as bad, aside from what they do, simply because they are undemocratic. Democracies promote war because they at times decide that the way to preserve peace is to defeat nondemocratic states and make them democratic. . . .

That peace may prevail among democratic states is a comforting thought. The obverse of the proposition—that democracy may promote war against undemocratic states—is disturbing. If the latter holds, we cannot even say for sure that the spread of democracy will bring a net decrease in the amount of war in the world. . . .

If the world is now safe for democracy, one has to wonder whether democracy is safe for the world. When democracy is ascendant, a condition that in the twentieth century attended the winning of hot wars and cold ones, the interventionist spirit flourishes. The effect is heightened when one democratic state becomes dominant, as the United States is now. Peace is the noblest cause of war. If the conditions of peace are lacking, then the country with a capability of creating them may be tempted to do so, whether or not by force. The end is noble, but as a matter of *right*, Kant insists, no state can intervene in the internal arrangements of another. As a matter of *fact*, one may notice that intervention, even for worthy ends, often brings more harm than good. The vice to which great powers easily succumb in a multipolar world is inattention; in a bipolar world, overreaction; in a unipolar world, overextention.

Peace is maintained by a delicate balance of internal and external restraints. States having a surplus of power are tempted to use it, and weaker states fear their doing so. The laws of voluntary federations, to use Kant's language, are disregarded at the whim of the stronger, as the United States demonstrated a decade ago by mining Nicaraguan waters and by invading Panama. In both cases, the United States blatantly violated international law. In the first, it denied the jurisdiction of the International Court of Justice, which it had previously accepted. In the second, it flaunted the law embodied in the Charter of the Organization of American States, of which it was a principal sponsor.

If the democratic peace thesis is right, structural realist theory is wrong. One may believe, with Kant, that republics are by and large good states *and* that unbalanced power is a danger no matter who wields it. Inside of, as well as outside of, the circle of democratic states, peace depends on a precarious balance of forces. The causes of war lie not simply in states or in the state system; they are found in both. Kant understood this. Devotees of the democratic peace thesis overlook it.

THE WEAK EFFECTS OF INTERDEPENDENCE

If not democracy alone, may not the spread of democracy combined with the tightening of national interdependence fulfill the prescription for peace offered by nineteenth-century liberals and so often repeated today?[24] To the supposedly peaceful inclination of democracies, interdependence adds the propulsive power of the profit motive. Democratic states may increasingly devote themselves to the pursuit of peace and profits. The trading state is replacing the political-military state, and the power of the market now rivals or surpasses the power of the state, or so some believe. . . .[25]

That interdependence promotes war as well as peace has been said often enough. What requires emphasis is that, either way, among the forces that shape international politics, interdependence is a weak one. . . .

The uneven effects of interdependence, with some parties to it gaining more, others gaining less, are obscured by the substitution of Robert Keohane's and Joseph Nye's term "asymmetric interdependence" for relations of dependence and independence among states.[30] Relatively independent states are in a stronger position than relatively dependent ones. If I depend more on you than you depend on me, you have more ways of influencing me and affecting my fate than I have of affecting yours. Interdependence suggests a condition of roughly equal dependence of parties on one another. Omitting the word "dependence" blunts the inequalities that mark the relations of states and makes them all seem to be on the same footing. Much of international, as of national, politics is about inequalities. Separating one "issue area" from others and emphasizing that weak states have advantages in some of them reduces the sense of inequality. Emphasizing the low fungibility of power furthers the effect. If power is not very fungible, weak states may have decisive advantages on some issues. Again, the effects of inequality are blunted. But power, not very fungible for weak states, is very fungible for strong ones. The history of American foreign policy since World War II is replete with examples of how the United States used its superior economic capability to promote its political and security interests. . . .[31]

The history of the past two centuries has been one of central governments acquiring more and more power. Alexis de Tocqueville observed during his visit to the United States in 1831 that "the Federal Government scarcely ever interferes in any but foreign affairs; and the governments of the states in reality direct society in America."[35] After World War II, governments in Western Europe disposed of about a quarter of their peoples' income. The proportion now is more than half. At a time when Americans, Britons, Russians, and Chinese were decrying the control of the state over their lives, it was puzzling to be told that states were losing control over their external affairs. Losing control, one wonders, as compared to when? Weak states have lost some of their influence and control over external matters, but strong states have not lost theirs. The patterns are hardly new ones. In the eighteenth and nineteenth centuries, the strongest state with the longest reach intervened all over the globe and built history's most extensive empire. In the twentieth century, the strongest state with the longest reach repeated Britain's interventionist behavior and, since the end of the Cold War, on an ever widening scale, without building an empire. The absence of empire hardly means, however, that the extent of America's influence and control over the actions of others is of lesser moment. The withering away of the power of the state, whether internally or externally, is more of a wish and an illusion than a reality in most of the world.

Under the Pax Britannica, the interdependence of states became unusually close, which to many portended a peaceful and prosperous future. Instead, a prolonged period of war, autarky, and more war followed. The international economic system, constructed under American auspices after World War II and later amended to suit its purposes, may last longer, but then again it may not. The character of international politics changes as national interdependence tightens or loosens. Yet even as relations vary, states have to take care of themselves as best they can in an anarchic environment. Internationally, the twentieth century for the most part was an unhappy one. In its last quarter, the clouds lifted a little, but twenty-five years is a slight base on which to ground optimistic conclusions. Not only are the effects of close inter-

dependence problematic, but so also is its durability.

THE LIMITED ROLE OF INTERNATIONAL INSTITUTIONS

One of the charges hurled at realist theory is that it depreciates the importance of institutions. The charge is justified, and the strange case of NATO's (the North Atlantic Treaty Organization's) outliving its purpose shows why realists believe that international institutions are shaped and limited by the states that found and sustain them and have little independent effect. Liberal institutionalists paid scant attention to organizations designed to buttress the security of states until, contrary to expectations inferred from realist theories, NATO not only survived the end of the Cold War but went on to add new members and to promise to embrace still more. Far from invalidating realist theory or casting doubt on it, however, the recent history of NATO illustrates the subordination of international institutions to national purposes. . . .

Using the example of NATO to reflect on the relevance of realism after the Cold War leads to some important conclusions. The winner of the Cold War and the sole remaining great power has behaved as unchecked powers have usually done. In the absence of counterweights, a country's internal impulses prevail, whether fueled by liberal or by other urges. The error of realist predictions that the end of the Cold War would mean the end of NATO arose not from a failure of realist theory to comprehend international politics, but from an underestimation of America's folly. The survival and expansion of NATO illustrate not the defects but the limitations of structural explanations. Structures shape and shove; they do not determine the actions of states. A state that is stronger than any other can decide for itself whether to conform its policies to structural pressures and whether to avail itself of the opportunities that structural change offers, with little fear of adverse affects in the short run.

Do liberal institutionalists provide better leverage for explaining NATO's survival and expansion? According to Keohane and Martin, realists insist "that institutions have only marginal effects."[51] On the contrary, realists have noticed that whether institutions have strong or weak effects depends on what states intend. Strong states use institutions, as they interpret laws, in ways that suit them. Thus Susan Strange, in pondering the state's retreat, observes that "international organization is above all a tool of national government, an instrument for the pursuit of national interest by other means."[52]

Interestingly, Keohane and Martin, in their effort to refute Mearsheimer's trenchant criticism of institutional theory, in effect agree with him. Having claimed that his realism is "not well specified," they note that "institutional theory conceptualizes institutions both as independent and dependent variables."[53] Dependent on what?—on "the realities of power and interest." Institutions, it turns out, "make a significant difference in conjunction with power realities."[54] Yes! Liberal institutionalism, as Mearsheimer says, "is no longer a clear alternative to realism, but has, in fact, been swallowed up by it."[55] Indeed, it never was an alternative to realism. Institutionalist theory, as Keohane has stressed, has as its core structural realism, which Keohane and Nye sought "to broaden."[56] The institutional approach starts with structural theory, applies it to the origins and operations of institutions, and unsurprisingly ends with realist conclusions.

Alliances illustrate the weaknesses of institutionalism with special clarity. Institutional theory attributes to institutions causal effects that mostly originate within states. The case of NATO nicely illustrates this shortcoming. Keohane has remarked that "alliances are institutions, and both their durability and strength . . . may depend in part on their institutional characteristics."[57] In part, I suppose, but one must wonder in how large a part. The Triple Alliance and the Triple Entente were quite durable. They lasted not because of alliance institutions, there hardly being any, but because the core members of each alliance looked outward and saw a pressing threat to their security. Previous alliances did not lack institutions because states had failed to figure out how to construct bureaucracies. Previous alliances lacked institutions because in the absence of a hegemonic leader, balancing continued within as well as across alliances. NATO lasted as a military alliance as long as the Soviet Union appeared to be a direct threat to its members. It survives and expands now not because of its institutions but mainly because the United States wants it to.

NATO's survival also exposes an interesting aspect of balance-of-power theory, Robert Art has argued forcefully that without NATO and without American troops in Europe, European states will lapse into a "security competition" among themselves.[58] As he emphasizes, this is a realist expectation. In his view, preserving NATO, and maintaining America's leading role in it, are required in order to prevent a security competition that would promote conflict within, and impair the institutions of, the European Union. NATO now is an anomaly; the dampening of intra-alliance tension is the main task left, and it is a task not for the alliance but for its leader. The secondary task of an alliance, intra-alliance management, continues to be performed by the United States even though the primary task, defense against an external enemy, has disappeared. The point is worth pondering, but I need to say here only that it further illustrates the dependence of international institutions on national decisions. Balancing among states is not inevitable. As in Europe, a hegemonic power may suppress it. As a high-level European diplomat put it, "it is not acceptable that the lead nation be European. A European power broker is a hegemonic power. We can agree on U.S. leadership, but not on one of our own."[59] Accepting the leadership of a hegemonic power prevents a balance of power from emerging in Europe, and better the hegemonic power should be at a distance than next door.

Keohane believes that "avoiding military conflict in Europe after the Cold War depends greatly on whether the next decade is characterized by a continuous pattern of institutionalized cooperation."[60] If one accepts the conclusion, the question remains: What or who sustains the "pattern of institutionalized cooperation"? Realists know the answer. . . .

BALANCING POWER: NOT TODAY BUT TOMORROW

With so many of the expectations that realist theory gives rise to confirmed by what happened at and after the end of the Cold War, one may wonder why realism is in bad repute.[65] A key proposition derived from realist theory is that international politics reflects the distribution of national capabilities, a proposition daily borne out. Another key proposition is that the balancing of power by some states against others recurs. Realist

theory predicts that balances disrupted will one day be restored. A limitation of the theory, a limitation common to social science theories, is that it cannot say when. William Wohlforth argues that though restoration will take place, it will be a long time coming.[66] Of necessity, realist theory is better at saying what will happen than in saying when it will happen. Theory cannot say when "tomorrow" will come because international political theory deals with the pressures of structure on states and not with how states will respond to the pressures. The latter is a task for theories about how national governments respond to pressures on them and take advantage of opportunities that may be present. One does, however, observe balancing tendencies already taking place.

Upon the demise of the Soviet Union, the international political system became unipolar. In the light of structural theory, unipolarity appears as the least durable of international configurations. This is so for two main reasons. One is that dominant powers take on too many tasks beyond their own borders, thus weakening themselves in the long run. Ted Robert Gurr, after examining 336 polities, reached the same conclusion that Robert Wesson had reached earlier: "Imperial decay is . . . primarily a result of the misuse of power which follows inevitably from its concentration."[67] The other reason for the short duration of unipolarity is that even if a dominant power behaves with moderation, restraint, and forbearance, weaker states will worry about its future behavior. America's founding fathers warned against the perils of power in the absence of checks and balances. Is unbalanced power less of a danger in international than in national politics?

Throughout the Cold War, what the United States and the Soviet Union did, and how they interacted, were dominant factors in international politics. The two countries, however, constrained each other. Now the United States is alone in the world. As nature abhors a vacuum, so international politics abhors unbalanced power. Faced with unbalanced power, some states try to increase their own strength or they ally with others to bring the international distribution of power into balance. The reactions of other states to the drive for dominance of Charles V, Hapsburg ruler of Spain, of Louis XIV and Napoleon I of France, of Wilhelm II and Adolph Hitler of Germany, illustrate the point.

The Behavior of Dominant Powers

Will the preponderant power of the United States elicit similar reactions? Unbalanced power, whoever wields it, is a potential danger to others. The powerful state may, and the United States does, think of itself as acting for the sake of peace, justice, and well-being in the world. These terms, however, are defined to the liking of the powerful, which may conflict with the preferences and interests of others. In international politics, overwhelming power repels and leads others to try to balance against it. With benign intent, the United States has behaved and, until its power is brought into balance, will continue to behave in ways that sometimes frighten others . . . .

The absence of serious threats to American security gives the United States wide latitude in making foreign policy choices. A dominant power acts internationally only when the spirit moves it. One example is enough to show this.

When Yugoslavia's collapse was followed by genocidal war in successor states, the United States failed to respond until Senator Robert Dole moved to make Bosnia's peril an issue in the forthcoming presidential election; and it acted not for the sake of its own security but to maintain its leadership position in Europe. American policy was generated not by external security interests, but by internal political pressure and national ambition.

Aside from specific threats it may pose, unbalanced power leaves weaker states feeling uneasy and gives them reason to strengthen their positions. The United States has a long history of intervening in weak states, often with the intention of bringing democracy to them. American behavior over the past century in Central America provides little evidence of self-restraint in the absence of countervailing power. Contemplating the history of the United States and measuring its capabilities, other countries may well wish for ways to fend off its benign ministrations. Concentrated power invites distrust because it is so easily misused. To understand why some states want to bring power into a semblance of balance is easy, but with power so sharply skewed, what country or group of countries has the material capability and the political will to bring the "unipolar moment" to an end?

Balancing Power in a Unipolar World

The expectation that following victory in a great war a new balance of power will form is firmly grounded in both history and theory. The last four grand coalitions (two against Napoleon and one in each of the world wars of the twentieth century) collapsed once victory was achieved. Victories in major wars leave the balance of power badly skewed. The winning side emerges as a dominant coalition. The international equilibrium is broken; theory leads one to expect its restoration.

Clearly something has changed. Some believe that the United States is so nice that, despite the dangers of unbalanced power, others do not feel the fear that would spur them to action. Michael Mastanduno, among others, believes this to be so, although he ends his article with the thought that "eventually, power will check power."[69] Others believe that the leaders of states have learned that playing the game of power politics is costly and unnecessary. In fact, the explanation for sluggish balancing is a simple one. In the aftermath of earlier great wars, the materials for constructing a new balance were readily at hand. Previous wars left a sufficient number of great powers standing to permit a new balance to be rather easily constructed. Theory enables one to say that a new balance of power will form but not to say how long it will take. National and international conditions determine that. Those who refer to the unipolar moment are right. In our perspective, the new balance is emerging slowly; in historical perspectives, it will come in the blink of an eye.

I ended a 1993 article this way: "One may hope that America's internal preoccupations will produce not an isolationist policy, which has become impossible, but a forbearance that will give other countries at long last the chance to deal with their own problems and make their own mistakes. But I would not bet on it."[70] I should think that few would do so now. Charles Kegley has said, sensibly, that if the world becomes multipolar once again, realists will be vindicated.[71] Seldom do signs of vindication appear so promptly.

The candidates for becoming the next great powers, and thus restoring a balance, are the European Union or Germany leading a coalition, China, Japan, and in a more distant future, Russia. The countries of the European Union have been remarkably successful in integrating their national economies. The achievement of a large measure of economic integration without a corresponding political unity is an accomplishment without historical precedent. On questions of foreign and military policy, however, the European Union can act only with the consent of its members, making bold or risky action impossible. The European Union has all the tools—population, resources, technology, and military capabilities—but lacks the organizational ability and the collective will to use them. As Jacques Delors said when he was president of the European Commission: "It will be for the European Council, consisting of heads of state and government . . . , to agree on the essential interests they share and which they will agree to defend and promote together."[72] Policies that must be arrived at by consensus can be carried out only when they are fairly inconsequential. Inaction as Yugoslavia sank into chaos and war signaled that Europe will not act to stop wars even among near neighbors. Western Europe was unable to make its own foreign and military policies when it was an organization of six or nine states living in fear of the Soviet Union. With less pressure and more members, it has even less hope of doing so now. Only when the United States decides on a policy have European countries been able to follow it. . . .

International Structure and National Responses

Throughout modern history, international politics centered on Europe. Two world wars ended Europe's dominance. Whether Europe will somehow, someday emerge as a great power is a matter for speculation. In the meantime, the all-but-inevitable movement from unipolarity to multipolarity is taking place not in Europe but in Asia. The internal development and the external reaction of China and Japan are steadily raising both countries to the great power level.[74] China will emerge as a great power even without trying very hard so long as it remains politically united and competent. Strategically, China can easily raise its nuclear forces to a level of parity with the United States if it has not already done so.[75] China has five to seven intercontinental missiles (DF-5s) able to hit almost any American target and a dozen or more missiles able to reach the west coast of the United States (DF-4s).[76] Liquid fueled, immobile missiles are vulnerable, but would the United States risk the destruction of, say, Seattle, San Francisco, and San Diego if China happens to have a few more DF-4s than the United States thinks or if it should fail to destroy all of them on the ground? Deterrence is much easier to contrive than most Americans have surmised. Economically, China's growth rate, given its present stage of economic development, can be sustained at 7 to 9 percent for another decade or more. Even during Asia's near economic collapse of the 1990s, China's growth rate remained approximately in that range. A growth rate of 7 to 9 percent doubles a country's economy every ten to eight years.

Unlike China, Japan is obviously reluctant to assume the mantle of a great power. Its reluctance, however, is steadily though slowly waning. Economically, Japan's power has grown and spread remarkably. The growth of a country's economic capability to the great power level places it at the center of regional and global affairs. It widens the range of a state's interests and increases their importance. The high volume of a country's external business thrusts it ever more deeply into world affairs. In a self-help system, the possession of most but not all of the capabilities of a great power leaves a state vulnerable to others that have the instruments that the lesser state lacks. Even though one may believe that fears of nuclear blackmail are misplaced, one must wonder whether Japan will remain immune to them. . . .

America's policy of containing China by keeping 100,000 troops in East Asia and by providing security guarantees to Japan and South Korea is intended to keep a new balance of power from forming in Asia. By continuing to keep 100,000 troops in Western Europe, where no military threat is in sight, and by extending NATO eastward, the United States pursues the same goal in Europe. The American aspiration to freeze historical development by working to keep the world unipolar is doomed. In the not very long run, the task will exceed America's economic, military, demographic, and political resources; and the very effort to maintain a hegemonic position is the surest way to undermine it. The effort to maintain dominance stimulates some countries to work to overcome it. As theory shows and history confirms, that is how balances of power are made. Multipolarity is developing before our eyes. Moreover, it is emerging in accordance with the balancing imperative.

American leaders seem to believe that America's preeminent position will last indefinitely. The United States would then remain the dominant power without rivals rising to challenge it—a position without precedent in modern history. Balancing, of course, is not universal and omnipresent. A dominant power may suppress balancing as the United States has done in Europe. Whether or not balancing takes place also depends on the decisions of governments. Stephanie Neuman's book, *International Relations Theory and the Third World,* abounds in examples of states that failed to mind their own security interests through internal efforts or external arrangements, and as one would expect, suffered invasion, loss of autonomy, and dismemberment.[87] States are free to disregard the imperatives of power, but they must expect to pay a price for doing so. Moreover, relatively weak and divided states may find it impossible to concert their efforts to counter a hegemonic state despite ample provocation. This has long been the condition of the Western Hemisphere.

In the Cold War, the United States won a telling victory. Victory in war, however, often brings lasting enmities. Magnanimity in victory is rare. Winners of wars, facing few impediments to the exercise of their wills, often act in ways that create future enemies. Thus Germany, by taking Alsace and most of Lorraine from France in 1871, earned its lasting enmity; and the Allies' harsh treatment of Germany after World War I produced a similar effect. In contrast, Bismarck persuaded the kaiser not to march his armies along the road to Vienna after the great victory at Königgrätz in 1866. In the Treaty of Prague, Prussia took no Austrian territory. Thus Austria, having

become Austria-Hungary, was available as an alliance partner for Germany in 1879. Rather than learning from history, the United States is repeating past errors by extending its influence over what used to be the province of the vanquished.[88] This alienates Russia and nudges it toward China instead of drawing it toward Europe and the United States. Despite much talk about the "globalization" of international politics, American political leaders to a dismaying extent think of East *or* West rather than of their interaction. With a history of conflict along a 2,600 mile border, with ethnic minorities sprawling across it, with a mineral-rich and sparsely populated Siberia facing China's teeming millions, Russia and China will find it difficult to cooperate effectively, but the United States is doing its best to help them do so. Indeed, the United States has provided the key to Russian–Chinese relations over the past half century Feeling American antagonism and fearing American power, China drew close to Russia after World War II and remained so until the United States seemed less, and the Soviet Union more, of a threat to China. The relatively harmonious relations the United States and China enjoyed during the 1970s began to sour in the late 1980s when Russian power visibly declined and American hegemony became imminent. To alienate Russia by expanding NATO, and to alienate China by lecturing its leaders on how to rule their country, are policies that only an overwhelmingly powerful country could afford, and only a foolish one be tempted, to follow. The United States cannot prevent a new balance of power from forming. It can hasten its coming as it has been earnestly doing.

In this section, the discussion of balancing has been more empirical and speculative than theoretical. I therefore end with some reflections on balancing theory. Structural theory, and the theory of balance of power that follows from it, do not lead one to expect that states will always or even usually engage in balancing behavior. Balancing is a strategy for survival, a way of attempting to maintain a state's autonomous way of life. To argue that bandwagoning represents a behavior more common to states than balancing has become a bit of a fad. Whether states bandwagon more often than they balance is an interesting question. To believe that an affirmative answer would refute balance-of-power theory is, however, to misinterpret the theory and to commit what one might call "the numerical fallacy"—to draw a qualitative conclusion from a quantitative result. States try various strategies for survival. Balancing is one of them; bandwagoning is another. The latter may sometimes seem a less demanding and a more rewarding strategy than balancing, requiring less effort and extracting lower costs while promising concrete rewards. Amid the uncertainties of international politics and the shifting pressures of domestic politics, states have to make perilous choices. They may hope to avoid war by appeasing adversaries, a weak form of bandwagoning, rather than by rearming and realigning to thwart them. Moreover, many states have insufficient resources for balancing and little room for maneuver. They have to jump on the wagon only later to wish they could fall off.

Balancing theory does not predict uniformity of behavior but rather the strong tendency of major states in the system, or in regional subsystems, to resort to balancing when they have to. That states try different strategies of survival is hardly surprising. The recurrent emergence of balancing behavior, and the appearance of the patterns the behavior produces, should all the more be seen as impressive evidence supporting the theory.

CONCLUSION

Every time peace breaks out, people pop up to proclaim that realism is dead. That is another way of saying that international politics has been transformed. The world, however, has not been transformed; the structure of international politics has simply been remade by the disappearance of the Soviet Union, and for a time we will live with unipolarity. Moreover, international politics was not remade by the forces and factors that some believe are creating a new world order. Those who set the Soviet Union on the path of reform were old Soviet apparatchiks trying to right the Soviet economy in order to preserve its position in the world. The revolution in Soviet affairs and the end of the Cold War were not brought by democracy, interdependence, or international institutions. Instead the Cold War ended exactly as structural realism led one to expect. As I wrote some years ago, the Cold War "is firmly rooted in the structure of postwar international politics and will last as long as that structure endures."[89] So it did, and the Cold War ended only when the bipolar structure of the world disappeared.

Structural change affects the behavior of states and the outcomes their interactions produce. It does not break the essential continuity of international politics. The transformation of international politics alone could do that. Transformation, however, awaits the day when the international system is no longer populated by states that have to help themselves. If the day were here, one would be able to say who could be relied on to help the disadvantaged or endangered. Instead, the ominous shadow of the future continues to cast its pall over interacting states. States' perennial uncertainty about their fates presses governments to prefer relative over absolute gains. Without the shadow, the leaders of states would no longer have to ask themselves how they will get along tomorrow as well as today. States could combine their efforts cheerfully and work to maximize collective gain without worrying about how each might fare in comparison to others.

Occasionally, one finds the statement that governments in their natural, anarchic condition act myopically—that is, on calculations of immediate interest—while hoping that the future will take care of itself. Realists are said to suffer from this optical defect.[90] Political leaders may be astigmatic, but responsible ones who behave realistically do not suffer from myopia. Robert Axelrod and Robert Keohane believe that World War I might have been averted if certain states had been able to see how long the future's shadow was.[91] Yet, as their own discussion shows, the future was what the major states were obsessively worried about. The war was prompted less by considerations of present security and more by worries about how the balance might change later. The problems of governments do not arise from their short time horizons. They see the long shadow of the future, but they have trouble reading its contours, perhaps because they try to look too far ahead and see imaginary dangers. In 1914, Germany feared Russia's rapid industrial and population growth. France and Britain suffered from the same fear about Germany, and in addition Britain worried about the rapid growth of Germany's navy. In an important sense, World War I was a preventive war all around. Future fears dominated hopes for short-term gains. States do not live in the happiest of conditions that Horace in one of his odes imagined for man:

> Happy the man, and happy he alone, who can say,
>
> Tomorrow do thy worst, for I have lived today.[92]

Robert Axelrod has shown that the "tit-for-tat" tactic, and no other, maximizes collective gain over time. The one condition for success is that the game be played under the shadow of the future.[93] Because states coexist in a self-help system, they may, however, have to concern themselves not with maximizing collective gain but with lessening, preserving, or widening the gap in welfare and strength between themselves and others. The contours of the future's shadow look different in hierarchic and anarchic systems. The shadow may facilitate cooperation in the former; it works against it in the latter. Worries about the future do not make cooperation and institution building among nations impossible; they do strongly condition their operation and limit their accomplishment. Liberal institutionalists were right to start their investigations with structural realism. Until and unless a transformation occurs, it remains the basic theory of international politics.

NOTES

1. For example, Richard Ned Lebow, "The Long Peace, the End of the Cold War, and the Failure of Realism," *International*

Organization, Vol. 48, No. 2 (Spring 1994), pp. 249-277; Jeffrey W. Legro and Andrew Moravcsik, "Is Anybody Still a Realist?" *International Security,* Vol. 24, No. 2 (Fall 1999), pp. 5-55; Bruce Russett, *Grasping the Democratic Peace: Principles for a Post-Cold War Peace* (Princeton, N.J.: Princeton University Press, 1993); Paul Schroeder, "Historical Reality vs. Neorealist Theory," *International Security,* Vol. 19, No. 1 (Summer 1994), pp. 108-148; and John A. Vasquez, "The Realist Paradigm and Degenerative vs. Progressive Research Programs: An Appraisal of Neotraditional Research on Waltz's Balancing Proposition," *American Political Science Review,* Vol. 91, No. 4 (December 1997), pp. 899-912.

2. Michael W. Doyle, "Kant, Liberal Legacies, and Foreign Affairs, Parts 1 and 2," *Philosophy and Public Affairs,* Vol. 12, Nos. 3 and 4 (Summer and Fall 1983); and Doyle, "Kant: Liberalism and World Politics," *American Political Science Review,* Vol. 80, No. 4 (December 1986), pp. 1151-1169.

3. Francis Fukuyama, "Liberal Democracy as a Global Phenomenon," *Political Science and Politics,* Vol. 24, No. 4 (1991), p. 662. Jack S. Levy, "Domestic Politics and War," in Robert I. Rotberg and Theodore K. Rabb, eds., *The Origin and Prevention of Major Wars* (Cambridge: Cambridge University Press, 1989), p. 88.

4. Kenneth N. Waltz, "Kant, Liberalism, and War," *American Political Science Review,* Vol. 56, No. 2 (June 1962). Subsequent Kant references are found in this work.

5. Ido Oren, "The Subjectivity of the 'Democratic' Peace: Changing U.S. Perceptions of Imperial Germany," *International Security,* Vol. 20, No. 2 (Fall 1995), pp. 157ff.; Christopher Layne, in the second half of Layne and Sean M. Lynn-Jones, *Should America Spread Democracy? A Debate* (Cambridge, Mass.: MIT Press, forthcoming), argues convincingly that Germany's democratic control of foreign and military policy was no weaker than France's or Britain's.

6. John M. Owen, "How Liberalism Produces Democratic Peace," *International Security,* Vol. 19, No. 2 (Fall 1994), pp. 87-125. Cf. his *Liberal Peace, Liberal War: American Politics and International Security* (Ithaca, N.Y: Cornell University Press, 1997).

7. Christopher Layne, "Kant or Cant: The Myth of the Democratic Peace," *International Security,* Vol. 19, No. 2 (Fall 1994), pp. 5-49.

8. Francis Fukuyama, *The End of History and the Last Man* (New York: Free Press, 1992), pp. 254-256. Russett, *Grasping the Democratic Peace,* p. 24.

16. Doyle, "Kant, Liberal Legacies, and Foreign Affairs, Part 2," p. 337.

17. Warren Christopher, "The U.S.-Japan Relationship: The Responsibility to Change," address to the Japan Association of Corporate Executives, Tokyo, Japan, March 11, 1994 (U.S. Department of State, Bureau of Public Affairs, Office of Public Communication), p. 3.

24. Strongly affirmative answers are given by John R. Oneal and Bruce Russett, "Assessing the Liberal Peace with Alternative Specifications: Trade Still Reduces Conflict," *Journal of Peace Research,* Vol. 36, No. 4 (July 1999), pp. 423-442; and Russett, Oneal, and David R. Davis, "The Third Leg of the Kantian Tripod for Peace: International Organizations and Militarized Disputes, 1950-85," *International Organization,* Vol. 52, No. 3 (Summer 1998), pp. 441-467.

25. Richard Rosecrance, *The Rise of the Trading State: Commerce and Coalitions in the Modern World* (New York: Basic Books, 1986); and at times Susan Strange, *The Retreat of the State: The Diffusion of Power in the World Economy* (New York: Cambridge University Press, 1996).

30. Robert O. Keohane and Joseph S. Nye, *Power and Interdependence,* 2d ed. (New York: HarperCollins, 1989).

31. Keohane and Nye are on both sides of the issue. See, for example, ibid., p. 28. Keohane emphasized that power is not very fungible in Keohane, ed., "Theory of

World Politics," *Neorealism and Its Critics* (New York: Columbia University Press, 1986); and see Kenneth N. Waltz, "Reflection on Theory of International Politics: A Response to My Critics," in ibid. Robert J. Art analyzes the fungibility of power in detail. See Art, "American Foreign Policy and the Fungibility of Force," *Security Studies,* Vol. 5, No. 4 (Summer 1996).

35. Alexis de Tocqueville, *Democracy in America,* ed. J.P. Mayer, trans. George Lawrence (New York: Harper Perennial, 1988), p. 446, n. 1.

51. Keohane and Martin, "The Promise of Institutionalist Theory," pp. 42, 46. [Robert O. Keohane and Lisa L. Martin, "The Promise of Institutionalist Theory," *International Security,* Vol. 20, No. 1 (Summer 1995), pp. 42, 46.]

52. Strange, *Retreat of the State,* p. xiv; and see pp. 192–193. Cf. Carr, *The Twenty Years' Crisis,* p. 107: "international government is, in effect, government by that state which supplies the power necessary for the purpose of governing."

53. Keohane and Martin, "The Promise of Institutionalist Theory," p. 46.

54. Ibid., p. 42.

55. Mearsheimer, "A Realist Reply," p. 85. [John J. Mearsheimer, "A Realist Reply," *International Security,* Vol. 20, No. 1 (Summer 1995), p. 85.]

56. Keohane and Nye, *Power and Interdependence,* p. 251; cf. Keohane, "Theory of World Politics," in Keohane, *Neorealism and its Critics,* p. 193, where he describes his approach as a "modified structural research program."

57. Robert O. Keohane, *International Institutions and State Power: Essays in International Relations Theory* (Boulder, Colo.: Westview, 1989), p. 15.

58. Robert J. Art, "Why Western Europe Needs the United States and NATO," *Political Science Quarterly,* Vol. 111, No. 1 (Spring 1996).

59. Quoted in ibid., p. 36.

60. Robert O. Keohane, "The Diplomacy of Structural Change: Multilateral Institutions and State Strategies," in Helga Haftendorn and Christian Tuschhoff, eds., *America and Europe in an Era of Change* (Boulder, Colo.: Westview, 1993), P. 53.

65. Robert Gilpin explains the oddity. See Gilpin, "No One Leaves a Political Realist," *Security Studies,* Vol. 5, No. 3 (Spring 1996). pp. 3–28.

66. William C. Wohlforth, "The Stability of a Unipolar World," *International Security,* Vol. 24, No. 1 (Summer 1999), pp. 5–41.

67. Quoted in Ted Robert Gurr, "Persistence and Change in Political Systems, 1800–1971," *American Political Science Review,* Vol. 68, No. 4 (December 1974), p. 1504, from Robert G. Wesson, *The Imperial Order* (Berkeley: University of California Press, 1967), unpaginated preface. Cf. Paul Kennedy, *The Rise and Fall of the Great Powers: Economic Change and Military Conflict from 1500 to 2000* (New York: Random House, 1987).

69. Michael Mastanduno, "Preserving the Unipolar Moment: Realist Theories and U.S. Grand Strategy after the Cold War," *International Security,* Vol. 21, No. 4 (Spring 1997), p. 88. See Josef Joffe's interesting analysis of America's role, "'Bismarck' or 'Britain'? Toward an American Grand Strategy after Bipolarity," *International Security,* Vol. 19, No. 4 (Spring 1995).

70. Waltz, "The Emerging Structure of International Politics," p. 79. [Kenneth N. Waltz, "The Emerging Structure of International Politics," *International Security,* Vol. 18, No. 2 (Fall 1993), p. 79.]

71. Charles W. Kegley, Jr., "The Neoidealist Moment in International Studies? Realist Myths and the New International Realities," *International Studies Quarterly,* Vol. 37, No. 2 (June 1993), p. 149.

72. Jacques Delors, "European Integration and Security," *Survival,* Vol. 33, No. 1 (March/April 1991), p. 106.

74. Statistics for China and Japan are adapted from Waltz, "The Emerging Structure of International Politics."

75. Nuclear parity is reached when countries have second-strike forces. It does not require quantitative or qualitative equality of forces. See Waltz, "Nuclear Myths and Political Realities," *American Political Science Review,* Vol. 84, No. 3 (September 1990).

76. David E. Sanger and Erik Eckholm, "Will Beijing's Nuclear Arsenal Stay Small or Will It Mushroom?" *New York Times,* March 15, 1999, p. Al.

87. Stephanie Neuman, ed., *International Relations Theory and the Third World* (New York: St. Martin's, 1998).

88. Tellingly, John Lewis Gaddis comments that he has never known a time when there was less support among historians for an announced policy. Gaddis, "History, Grand Strategy, and NATO Enlargement," *Survival,* Vol. 40, No. 1 (Spring 1998), p. 147.

89. Kenneth N. Waltz, "The Origins of War in Neorealist Theory," *Journal of Interdisciplinary History,* Vol. 18, No. 4 (Spring 1988), p. 628.

90. The point is made by Robert O. Keohane, *After Hegemony: Cooperation and Discord in the World Political Economy* (Princeton, N.J.: Princeton University Press, 1984), pp. 99, 103, 108.

91. Robert Axelrod and Robert O. Keohane, "Achieving Cooperation under Anarchy: Strategies and Institutions," in David Baldwin, ed., *Neorealism and Neoliberalism: The Contemporary Debate* (New York: Columbia University Press, 1993). For German leaders, they say, "the shadow of the future seemed so small" (p. 92). Robert Powell shows that "a longer shadow . . . leads to greater military allocations." See Powell, "Guns, Butter, and Anarchy," *American Political Science Review,* Vol. 87, No. 1 (March 1993), p. 116; see also p. 117 on the question of the compatibility of liberal institutionalism and structural realism.

92. My revision.

93. Robert Axelrod, *The Evolution of Cooperation* (New York: Basic Books, 1984).

QUESTIONS

1. Do you agree with Waltz's argument that a change in the structure of the international system from bipolarity to unipolarity does not mean that international politics has been transformed?

2. Are Waltz's views in this article consistent with his realist perspective in *Man, The State and War* (page 12)?

3. Do you think Waltz's structural realism provides an adequate explanation for the end of the Cold War and for the current state of international politics?

REALIST PERSPECTIVE OF SEPTEMBER 11

9.   Foreign Policy in the Age of Terrorism

Henry Kissinger

This selection is taken from a speech that Dr. Kissinger gave shortly after the terrorist attack on the World Trade Center on September 11, 2001. Kissinger discusses how the terrorist attack affected U.S. relations with Russia, China, and its NATO allies.

Henry Kissinger has served as National Security Adviser and as Secretary of State and has received the Nobel Peace Prize, the Presidential Medal of Freedom, and the Medal of Liberty, among other awards. Dr. Kissinger is a former professor at Harvard University and the author of many books and articles.

FOREIGN POLICY IN THE AGE OF TERRORISM

I want to talk to you about the foreign policy issues raised by the period of terrorism.

I want to make two points: the events of September 11th were a great tragedy—that can turn into an extraordinary opportunity if the changed circumstances for America, for Europe, for Russia, China and other parts of the world are properly understood.

For America it was a wake-up call against the background of a period of indolence and self-satisfaction. The illusion was that history was over, that foreign policy had become a version of economics or sociology, that there were no major political issues left was at an end. The illusion that we have an unlimited range of choice, or that we can choose among our options those which most flatter our preconceptions, has also been severely shaken. Much of the debate, at least as far as America is concerned, that has characterised our discussions since the Vietnam War—between power and morality, between national interests and idealism—is being subsumed and, at the moment, overshadowed by a situation in which it is clear that these are not the ultimate alternatives of foreign policy. Our alliances, our relations with Russia, China and South Asia can be looked at in a different context.

Any American concerned with foreign policy is bound to express his respect and appreciation for the conduct of British policy in this period. I belong to the generation that grew up in the context of a belief in the 'special relationship' between Britain and America. Some had begun, if not to dismiss it, to look at it from the perspective of a perhaps outdated sentimentality. But those of us who have observed not just the actions of the British Government, but the explanations which identified the British concerns so much with American concerns, have seen that there still is a very special attitude in the relationship between our two countries; and that this relationship should be preserved in the

From the Center for Policy Studies, Lecture at Rattenberg, October 31, 2001.

years ahead for the challenges that are clearly facing us. I know no other leaders that have so identified the experiences of New York and Washington with the attitudes of their own people as those of the British government.

Now when I speak of the conduct of the war against terrorism, I look at it as a common enterprise and not as an American projection of an American national view. And, indeed, in its deeper sense, it is a common enterprise not just for Britain and the United States but for all peoples concerned with world order. It is a war that has no front-lines. It is a war that had no issues on September 10th. Until then the American public would have been astonished to hear that there were fundamental differences between the United States and Islam, or that there was such a thing as a concept of a war of civilisations. For them, that was confined to academic treatises.

The American public still does not understand why, exactly, we were attacked nor what, precisely, it is that we are supposed to do. This is what has generated this extraordinary sense of defiant unity which I have never seen in America, not even after Pearl Harbour, to quite this emotional extent. That is why there has been no pressure on the American Government that it might be doing too much. If there is any psychological pressure, it will come from the opposite direction.

Now the shadowy nature of the challenge, the imprecision of the issues that have been rhetorically more aimed at our existence than at our policies in the early stages, nevertheless do not prevent some definition of what it is that needs to be done. It seems to me that the fundamental challenge of terrorism is that it exists in many cells all over the world,

but it cannot survive without some base and without some direction. If one reads of the structure of the various plots that one knows about, they all go back to a variety of base areas that provide organisation, recruitment, fund-raising and a sort of coherence. It is for this reason that the elimination of these base areas, or at any rate the suppression of them by the host governments, has to be the strategic objective of the common policy. President Bush, in his speech to the Congress, said:

> "From this day forward, any nation that continues to harbour or support terrorism will be regarded, by the United States, as a hostile regime."

If you look at the record of President Bush, you will see that he tends to mean what he says. So the war in Afghanistan must be seen as an attack on the most flagrant harbourer of terrorists and against the most symbolic representative of terrorism in the person of bin Laden.

I do not believe that the elimination of bin Laden will end the problem; nor do I believe that success in Afghanistan will, by itself, end the issue. What America is attempting to do, together with those members of the Coalition who in fact are doing something, is to demonstrate that safe havens cannot be tolerated if terrorism is to be ended. If America takes the lead it is, of course, in part because of the effect of the offence in attacking New York and Washington; but it is also, importantly, because for the entire post-war period the security of free peoples anywhere has depended upon America's willingness to defend them, whether that was always recognised or not. If America fails in its reaction to an attack on its own territory, the whole structure of the security of the post-war world will disintegrate—even for those people who are critical, or sometimes for domestic reasons pretend to be critical. That is the fundamental issue.

In Afghanistan we clearly cannot have as an objective the occupation of Afghanistan. Our goal needs to be to destroy the network of bin Laden and, by removing the Taleban from the government of Afghanistan, to make clear the penalties for tolerating and even encouraging this sort of activity. It also puts all of us under a certain amount of pressure, because the longer this part of the conflict continues, the longer the Taleban can remain standing, the more the war itself becomes the emphasis and the larger issue tends to be obscured. We also have to face the fact that at some point in this process, a surviving Taleban can become a symbol for the defiance of the Coalition and the American joint effort with its allies. When that point will be reached is not for me to say here, but it would be wrong to believe that there is an unlimited period of time and that one can afford too many experiments.

I do not believe that when those two objectives are reached—that is, the destruction of the Taleban and the destruction of the network—that American and allied military forces have the primary rôle to play in the so-called 'nation-building' of Afghanistan. The pacification of all of Afghanistan has eluded many previous countries that have attempted it and it is something that should be turned over to the United Nations—perhaps by the creation of some 'Contact Group' of neighbouring countries, together with those countries that participated in the conflict, and with generous economic assistance from the Western countries. But if the war as such for

us should end with the destruction of the Taleban and the destruction of the bin Laden network, then at that point the war against terrorism will confront the next challenge.

That challenge is: how does one deal with State-supported terrorism in the aftermath of Afghanistan? If we slacken in this effort, if we think that what I have defined as 'victory in Afghanistan' is the only purpose and is an adequate reaction to what happened on September 11th, we will find that terrorism will come back; it will engulf first the moderate States in the region, but blackmail many other countries—as we see now in the nature of the Coalition in many parts of the world. We will then face the question of what the Coalition is supposed to do; whether the Coalition is a convoy that sails at the rate of the slowest ship, or whether there is another way of interpreting it. The President and the Secretary of State have spoken of a Coalition in which every member does what it is most comfortable with doing. This is what might be called an 'à la carte' Coalition policy. It can be interpreted in two ways: that nations can do as little as they want, but also that those who wish to do more can join together in those actions and will continue to demand not much more than the condemnation of terrorism which characterises the contributions of so many members of the current Coalition.

In any event, at that point, there has to be some definition of what constitutes a terrorist organisation and of what represents State support of that organisation. What matters is what those members of the Coalition who are prepared to act will do in response. At some point this question will arise and will oblige countries which are now technically part of the Coalition to choose between whether they wish to remain in the Coalition or to engage in actions that support terrorism. This is one of the challenges for the next stage and I have every hope that we and our European allies and other countries—such as Russia, China and India—can stay together on the definition of aspects of these issues. In that case, I believe we shall also have support from some Middle Eastern countries.

It is often said that this is not simply a question of terrorism but that there are other issues which have caused terrorism and which must be eliminated in order to achieve what we have set out to do. To some extent this is true, but one should keep in mind at least three aspects. The first is that almost all of these issues have a longer time-frame for their solution than the immediate issue with which we are confronted. The second is to make sure the solution cannot be represented as a victory for the terrorists' measures—that is, that people cannot say they were the result of the attack on the United States. The third is to develop some idea of what it is that one is attempting to do.

This is not the occasion to discuss the issue of the future of Palestine, but it is important to keep in mind what it is for which one should ask. Almost everybody knows that in any negotiation what will be asked of Israel (and what often, or at least on occasion, what Israel has conceded) is some territorial change, some modification of settlement policy—and therefore some sacrifice. What is not so clear is what is being asked of the other side. The overwhelming concern, of not only Israelis but of many who have looked at the subject, is that for too many on the Arab side any negotiations are considered an intermediate process

to the total destruction of the Israeli State. Some definition of what constitutes Israeli legitimacy, and some definition of the content of security, must be supplied by the Arab side and not simply an unconditional demand for a negotiation whose content on one side is clear and on the other side is nebulous. The second issue has to do with the remedy of economic development as the solution for all problems. There is no doubt that many governments in the region are backward and have not fulfilled the aspirations of their populations. It is also true that if one looks at the economic development of these countries and compares that with the situation in the 1950s and with the situation today in, say, Korea and in many countries in the Middle East, there is no doubt that a country like Korea that has undertaken major reforms has made much more rapid progress—and this is not primarily due to the actions of foreigners.

The second challenge that we face in this respect is to know what it is we want. It is now very fashionable in our media to attack Saudi Arabia and Egypt and other countries for their attitude towards terrorism and related activities. It is true that in many countries in the Middle East there is a kind of tacit agreement between these 'cells' and the government in which the government tolerates these cells so long as they do not direct their actions against the countries in which they are located. It is also the case that an attempt to bring about in a very brief period of time the evolution that took centuries in the West is more likely to produce chaos than democracy. What the intermediate steps should be, and how one can have reforms such as those which brought Islamic Turkey to a democratic system, are matters on which Western thinking has been largely confined to domestic debates between those who are allegedly concerned primarily with expediency, and those who claim for themselves the mantle of abstract idealism and who forget that sometimes crusades can produce more suffering than incremental steps.

These are tall orders with which to deal in a relatively brief time. I began by saying that we started with a tragedy and we are winding up with what I believe to be an opportunity. This opportunity has this component. Before September 11th it was fashionable in some circles in America to speak of the end of history; it was certainly fashionable on the Continent to think that there was no longer the sort of danger that justified an Atlantic relationship. Indeed, it was commonplace to seek European identity in distinction from the United States and NATO ran the risk of becoming an institution that was used for 'liturgical' purposes and occasional meetings, but with less operational content. I think that on both sides of the Atlantic and, importantly so far as America is concerned, because of the attitude of this government here in Britain, there is now a much greater understanding of the continued importance of restoring the vitality of the Atlantic relationship.

Many of the issues that on September 10th absorbed us, like missile defence or the Kyoto protocol, will now be able to be dealt with in a quite different context. Missile defence will find a solution, so far as the overall global relationship is concerned, in the negotiations between President Bush and President Putin. The issue of the global significance of environmental and medical issues will have to be addressed when we

deal, as we must, with the question of biological warfare as it has emerged in recent weeks.

Whatever the causes of the particular incident in America, whatever its origins, the question of States developing these weapons cannot be left to the occurrence of an incident like the one on September 11th. This is an issue with which the Atlantic nations first, and then on a much broader basis other nations, must come to grips jointly. I am not talking simply of the traditional Atlantic relationship because we face, in relation to Russia, a situation that none of us has had to consider in the period since World War II. The attempt by Russia to enter the international system on the basis of borders that have not existed in Russia since Peter the Great is a new event for Europe, for America and for Russia. How to bring Russia into this system is a challenge with which all of us have to deal. Up to now there has been a temptation to believe that perhaps Europe should act as a mediator in this process between an excessively slow America and a Russia that needed psychological help. That is no longer the case. Indeed, any attempt by Europe or America to deal with this on a regional basis or on a national basis is likely to create temptations that it is in our interest to discourage in Russia. At the moment the opportunity for America to do this as a bilateral negotiation is quite considerable.

There are some people who argue that the way to deal with it is to respond to occasional Russian hints that they might join NATO; I believe this to be a great mistake. NATO is not an organisation for bringing Russia into the international system; the attempt to do so will only lead to confusion in NATO, to bureaucratisation of the process, and to weakening even the prospect of the ultimate reconciliation between Russia and the West. What Russia should be able to participate in is in the political and fundamental choices about the future of the issues raised by terrorism and the construction of the international system for which the opportunity exists.

To the many people who think that I read the debates of the Congress of Vienna by candlelight, let me say that there is indeed an analogy. At the end of the Napoleonic Wars there was a quadripartite alliance directed against the resurgence of French expansionism, but there was also a Concert of Powers in which France participated as an equal and full member. The quadripartite alliance was never invoked and the Concert of Europe operated very well—at least until Britain withdrew from it and therefore the necessary balance was no longer fully at hand. It seems to me that some kind of new relationship should be established, first within the Atlantic region and on the political side opened to Russia, in which in time NATO would play the rôle of the quadripartite alliance of the previous period. This is a great opportunity for the West and a great opportunity for Russia.

I have mentioned that the debates, at least in America, on many of the issues like missile defence and those generated by the Kyoto protocol, are coming to an end. So are those about China. The theories of some of those who attempt to slight China, to put China into the position vacated by the Soviet Union and to organise the international system as a kind of coalition against China, are also substantially superseded by the considerable cooperation that is now taking place on the issue of terrorism, and that will take place on the issue of trade and that can be expanded into other areas.

I mention these opportunities without doubting that there can be many challenges, and leaving out such phenomena such as the rôles of India and of South Asia, because my fundamental point is not to pretend that there exists a detailed answer to all these issues. It is rather this: we have been challenged by terrorism and this has given us an opportunity to rediscover fundamentals; it is therefore an occasion to think, not simply of how to overcome the immediate challenge, but of how to deal with the deeper issue of what a world order for the twenty-first century should look like.

When I was a young professor, in an indescribably long ago past, I once called on President Truman who had just left office. I asked him what he had done of which he was most proud and he said: 'I am most proud of the fact that we totally defeated our enemies and that then we brought them back to the community of nations as equals.' In a way, we now have the same opportunity as the leaders who created the post-war world between 1945 and 1950; but we have got to get the sequence straight; we have got to defeat the enemies, and then we shall be able to create a community of nations.

QUESTIONS

1. In what ways does Dr. Kissinger's assessment of U.S. policy in the war against terrorism reflect general realist principles? In what ways does it differ?

2. Why does Dr. Kissinger believe that Russia and China will join a U.S.-led coalition against terrorism? What factors might limit Russian and Chinese cooperation with the United States?

Chapter 3

LIBERAL THEORY

Focus of Analysis ....▶	• Enhancing global political and economic cooperation
Major Actors ....▶	• States • International organizations • Multinational corporations (MNCs) • Nongovernmental organizations (NGOs)
Behavior of States ....▶	• States not always rational actors • Compromise between various interests within the state
Goals of States ....▶	• Economic prosperity • International stability
View of Human Nature ....▶	• Optimistic
Condition of ** ....▶ **International System	• Anarchic • Possible to mitigate anarchy
Key Concepts ....▶	• Interdependence; International law; Collective security; Regime; Economic liberalism; Harmony of interests; Complex interdependence; Liberal institutionalism; Multinational corporations; Natural law

INTRODUCTION

The idea of promoting global order through expanded political and economic ties leads us to our next theory, liberalism. Liberals point out that realism fails to offer an adequate explanation for the order that we see within our presumably anarchic system. Advocates of liberalism argue that states cooperate as much as, if not more than, they compete. And this cooperation, they assert, is more consistent than the realists' fleeting convergence of national interest among limited numbers of states. Rather, states cooperate because it is in their common interest to do so, and prosperity and stability in the international system are the direct result of that cooperation.

In addition, liberals believe that states are not motivated solely by national interest defined in terms of power. Unlike realism, liberalism contends that international politics can no longer be divided into "high" and "low" politics. While the high politics of national security and military power remain important, liberals maintain that economic, social, and environmental issues—or low politics—have become priorities on the international agenda.

The establishment and success of international order, according to liberalism, depends largely on four major factors: the role of international institutions; international rules and norms for behavior of states; the increasing economic interdependence between nations; and technological advancement and the growth of global communication. Liberals acknowledge that international institutions, rules and norms, economic interdependence, and advances in global telecommunications can neither create nor enforce the type of stable international order that might be provided by a strong world government. These elements do, however, play an indispensable role in constraining, or regulating, the behavior of nation-states within the system as well as in shaping the international environment as a whole. The transnational linkages that these four factors represent build incentives for cooperation, enhance trust between nations, and promote negotiation rather than military confrontation as a means to resolve disputes between states.

INSTITUTIONAL LIBERALISM

At this point, we must distinguish between two branches of liberal theory. The first branch, which we shall call **liberal institutionalism** (also referred to as *idealism*), focuses on institutionalizing global cooperation. Liberal institutionalists call for the creation of a new global power structure, supported by a variety of international organizations. Advocates of this theory believe that global cooperation is founded upon three primary factors: enhancing the role and influence of international organizations, instituting collective security, and enforcing international law. All three of these factors might be viewed as prescriptions for how states should behave, with an ultimate goal of reforming the anarchy of the international system and forging a harmonious community of nations.

An early proponent of what we now call liberal institutionalism was the classical legal scholar Hugo Grotius. In his book *On the Law of War and Peace* (1625), Grotius contended that a fundamental "natural law" exists and that this natural law transcends the domestic law of states. **Natural law** is based on the belief that humans have basic, inalienable rights. These inalienable rights (essentially, rights to life and liberty) bind states together, forming an international "society of states" linked through certain rules and norms of conduct.

Grotius thought these universal rules of international behavior would determine relations between states within the system—even to the point of regulating the conduct of war. This concept would later form the basis for international law in the European state system. **International law** is the codification of rules that regulate the behavior of states and set limits upon what is permissible and what is not permissible. These rules are binding on states, as well as on other international actors.

Contemporary liberal institutionalism was also influenced by idealist scholars and political leaders who dominated the formulation and practice of international relations after World War I. The idealists believed that the relations between states in the international system needed to be fundamentally reformed to ensure that future wars might be avoided.

One notable idealist at that time was U.S. President Woodrow Wilson. He believed that the balance-of-power premise, so critical in realist theory, was unlikely to produce a stable international order. Instead, Wilson, like Grotius, wanted to build an international community of nations. This new community would follow international law as well as specific rules and norms of behavior and would be regulated by international institutions. The transnational linkages established by these international institutions, such as the League of Nations and, later, the United Nations, would presumably moderate—or, ideally, even eliminate—the need for power politics.

Acknowledging the need to temper such idealistic goals with the harsh realities of international politics, Wilson suggested that order within the community could be preserved through collective security. **Collective security** is a system in which states band together to safeguard the territorial independence and security of one another against aggression. That is, the use of force by a state or group of states would be curtailed by the strength of all states working through an international institution designed for that purpose. Collective security differs from balance-of-power politics in that it is directed not against a specific nation but against any state that threatens the status quo. Enforcing international law would then be a collective responsibility for the good of all states within the community.

Wilson, then, believed that order within the international system could be established through reform and the creation of effective international organizations capable of enforcing order and facilitating cooperation between states.

Another liberal institutionalist, Hedley Bull, interpreted the nature and course of international relations in a somewhat more practical manner. Bull focused on the tools and methods by which order already exists within the system. He suggested that while anarchy could not be abolished, the behavior of states in the international system could be constrained. According to Bull, diplomacy, balance-of-power politics, and alliances, as well as international law and institutions, all contribute to preserving order, enhancing cooperation, and promoting international ethical standards.

ECONOMIC LIBERALISM

The second branch of liberals emphasizes economic ties between nations as a basis for establishing and preserving order within the international system. Similar to institutional liberalism, **economic liberalism** (also referred to as the *interdependence model*) highlights the transnational ties or linkages between states. Economic liberals, however, identify the increasingly integrated nature of the global economy as a major force in promoting those linkages.

With this merging of international and domestic economic interests, states, according to economic liberals, have become increasingly interconnected or interdependent. Interdependence is a pivotal part of economic liberalism. **Interdependence** can be defined as the "mutual dependence" of nations within the international system and liberals argue that it is a defining characteristic of our contemporary world. Joseph Nye provides a good summary of the principal components of interdependence. Nye believes that the expansion of global trade and investment has blurred the distinction between domestic economies of individual states and of the international economy as a whole. The more states interact within the global marketplace, the more their prosperity depends on the political and economic cooperation of other states.

As in any interdependent relationship, however, we must acknowledge that some states are more vulnerable than others to the ups and downs of the global economy. That is, smaller, less developed nations can be more vulnerable in such a relationship than larger, more economically diverse countries. Although interdependence generally carries substantial economic benefits, the various levels of sensitivity between nations to downturns in the international economy can create both political and economic tension.

As a practical matter, we might suggest that interdependence is based on three general assumptions: First, states are not the only key actors in international relations. International institutions; nongovernmental organizations (NGOs), such as large multinational corporations (MNCs); economic cartels, such as OPEC; Greenpeace; or even large religious groups, such as the Catholic Church—all these actors take positions on the global stage. Second, the agenda of international relations is more complex and diverse than it was in the past. Issues such as trade, technology, and the environment can be as important as traditional national security concerns. Finally, military force plays less of a role in contemporary international politics. Economic interdependence, along with expanded political ties, have increased the value of cooperation and decreased the utility of force.

According to economic liberals, interdependence has transformed the nature of power in the international system. No international actor can meet its needs—whether those needs involve national security or economic prosperity—without the cooperation or participation of other states and nonstate actors. Power is no longer measured solely in terms of military strength. Influence is often the result of economic flexibility or technological innovation, and leadership involves negotiating expertise and economic coordination. Interdependence has dramatically increased the incentives for cooperation, not only among states but among all international actors.

Robert Keohane, in his book *After Hegemony,* argues that international cooperation is not restricted to formal international organizations like the United Nations. Instead, cooperation often results from the creation of international regimes. A **regime** is a set of accepted rules, norms, and procedures that regulates the behavior of states and other actors in a given issue area. A regime also encompasses the international institutions, NGOs, and treaties that enhance cooperation in that area. Issues such as trade, the environment, monetary relations, and so forth represent a host of different international concerns that might be targeted. Cooperation, then, according to Keohane, is based on a variety of regimes designed to meet the needs of specific issue areas.

Economic liberals tend to focus on international economic integration and the role of nongovernmental organizations as a means to enhance this cooperation. They argue that, with greater cooperation and integration, a state's economy is merely one piece of an increasingly integrated, world-economic whole. In this **complex interdependence,** we see "more actors, more issues, greater interactions, and less hierarchy in international politics."[1] Hence, though it is important to encourage economic growth of individual nations so that they, too, might have a stake in preserving and increasing interdependence, the capacity of a single state to have decisive control over the global economy is limited.

Within this interdependent economic system, the realist assumption that states are the primary actor in international relations is no longer the case in a strict sense. As we noted, economic liberals suggest that nonstate actors—nongovernmental organizations and multinational corporations—play a vital role in building and maintaining global interdependence. These organizations help to break down national boundaries and blend domestic and international political interests.

Multinational corporations are companies that have production facilities or branches in several countries. The influence of multinational corporations is twofold. First, MNCs expand and reinforce global economic and political linkages among people and groups across national borders. These organizations can have greater economic resources and international influence than many smaller or less developed nations. Companies conducting business across state boundaries also make states more interdependent and create a new context in which countries make decisions about one another.

One thing to keep in mind, however, is that these MNCs have their own agendas; their interests do not necessarily coincide with the interests of those states in which they conduct business. MNCs operate in the interests of their stockholders, and their goal is to maximize profits for those stockholders. For example, when General Motors decides to close a plant in Michigan and open a new plant in Mexico, the impact of this decision is felt by both nations. The United States must contend with increased unemployment, while Mexico gains job opportunities and tax revenue.

Though MNCs might operate to further their own agenda, their well-being is linked to that of the international community in a fundamental way, which leads to our second point. MNCs need a stable international environment—an environment

---

[1] Joseph S. Nye, Jr., "Understanding U.S. Strength," *Foreign Policy* 72 (Fall 1988), p. 108.

that facilitates trade, commerce, and international investment. Economic liberals suggest that in a self-reinforcing pattern, force plays a smaller role in international politics because states have formed closer economic, as well as political, linkages. These linkages—and the NGOs and MNCs that help to promote them—flourish only in a stable international environment. Consequently, all members of the community have a stake in preserving order to further their own interests.

Perhaps the best way to describe this process is as a harmony of interests among states. **Harmony of interests** is the belief that the interest of all states coincides with the interest of each state. This concept is generally accepted by both institutional and economic liberals and focuses on the mutual advantages of cooperation between nations. For institutional liberals, harmony of interests emphasizes that the security of all nations is enhanced by international cooperation. For economic liberals, that harmony of interests revolves around the growing economic interdependence of nations. For both branches of liberal theory, the utility of power and military force as instruments of foreign policy has been marginalized by greater linkages and expanded cooperation—political or economic—among all nations of the international system.

A Critique of Liberalism

Critics of liberalism—both institutional and economic—contend that the theory places too much emphasis on this harmony of interests. Cooperation between states, whether political, economic, or even military, is subject to a number of internal and external pressures, making success much more problematic than liberals might imply.

The critique of liberalism tends to focus on three broad issues: basic tendencies of human nature, national security interests, and economic cooperation. With respect to human nature, realist critics suggest that liberalism underestimates the conflictual aspects of state interests and that the benefits of cooperation can often be outweighed by fear and mistrust.

Though these feelings might be engendered by past experiences, liberalism also fails to take into account the powerful role of nationalism in world politics. Human history—both ancient and contemporary—is, quite literally, littered with examples in which religion or ethnicity formed the basis for conflict between nations. From the Crusades to more recent events in Iraq and Rwanda, human nature offers more complex questions than liberals are prepared to answer in this regard.

Compromise and settlements are often clouded by the unavoidable intrusion of human passions—complicating already volatile situations. In an unusual sense, the end of the Cold War actually signals the beginning of new, more complex conflicts, no longer frozen or confined by the two great ideological camps. Nuclear weapons may have deterred superpower confrontation, but conventional conflict between smaller states still occurs. Moreover, critics point to recent tensions between India and Pakistan as evidence that there is still a danger of conventional conflict escalating into a potential nuclear confrontation. Since the demise of the Cold War, states and even nonstate actors such as terrorist organizations now pursue their own narrow interests—often guided by ethnic or nationalist ideals. Liberalism fails to take these more unpredictable factors into account in its approach to international relations theory.

Critics of liberal institutionalism also argue that states cannot be expected to pursue collective gains on a consistent basis. Maintaining long-term or comprehensive cooperation between nations is more problematic than liberalism implies. States—like individuals—can be attracted by relative gains, settling for less gain but more control and self-reliance than the broader cooperation of liberalism necessitates. Also, the goals and priorities of states can change, making such an arrangement too confining or inappropriate under new or altered circumstances.

Realists tend to criticize liberals particularly with respect to our second issue—national security. The theme of national interest defined as self-interest (as opposed to liberalism's collective interest) is evident in many past and contemporary conflicts throughout the world.

Certainly the most glaring lapses in a collective security arrangement—and, indeed, in liberal theory generally—occurred prior to World War II when the League of Nations failed to either prevent or offset the rise of Hitler and Mussolini. Despite idealistic goals and cooperative intent of the League of Nations, fascism gained not only a toehold but a firm grip on Western Europe that only a prolonged and costly world war could break.

In addition, the direct intervention by the United States to relieve widespread starvation in Somalia is the exception, rather than the rule, in international politics. The prolonged bloodshed in Rwanda and the Congo and the failure of the Western powers to mobilize either sufficient political or military force to alleviate the situations illustrate the reluctance of states to extend themselves when vital interests are not at risk. This point is clear when we recall how quickly and effectively the international community responded in 1991 when Iraq threatened the vast oil reserves of Kuwait during the first Persian Gulf War. It seems, then, that collective security is problematic at best. Small countries with limited economic or geopolitical value to the major powers rely on collective security only at their own considerable peril.

Similarly, realists are also skeptical of the liberals' notion that "low politics" have become as important as these national security issues. Certainly, the world community has become more attuned to social, environmental, and economic issues. According to realists, however, national security and the well-being of the state remain top priorities for leaders in formulating and implementing foreign and domestic policy.

Realists point to a tendency among liberal theorists to cross the line between describing the interaction of states in the international system and attributing certain patterns of behavior to certain global conditions into a more prescriptive posture. That is, liberals actually become advocates of their own program for global interdependence, rather than maintaining theory positions as neutral observers and analysts of international relations.

In addition, liberalism's proposed economic interdependence is subject to criticism on several points. Realists argue that the economic integration of states ascribed by liberalism does not necessarily lead to greater cooperation. As we discussed earlier, realists are more skeptical about the long-term success of converging

KEY CONCEPTS

Collective security is a liberal institutionalist concept of a system of world order in which aggression against an individual state is considered aggression against all states and will be met by a collective response from all states within the system. Collective security differs from balance-of-power politics in that it is not directed against a specific nation but against any state that threatens the status quo.

Complex interdependence is an economic liberalist concept that assumes states are not the only important actors, social welfare issues share center stage with security issues on the global agenda, and cooperation is as dominant a characteristic of international politics as conflict.

Economic liberalism is a theory of international relations that highlights the economic transnational ties or linkages between states. Economic liberals identify the increasingly integrated nature of the global economy as a major force in international relations. According to economic liberals, with the merging of international and domestic economic interests, states have become increasingly interconnected or interdependent and less dependent on, or less willing to use, force or the threat of force to further their national interests.

Harmony of interests is a liberal concept stating that the interest of all states coincides with the interest of each state. This concept is generally accepted by both institutional and economic liberals and focuses on the mutual advantages of cooperation between nations. Harmony of interests implies that the incentive to cooperate with one another is stronger than the incentive for conflict.

Interdependence is an economic liberalist concept that focuses on the "mutual dependence" of nations in which two or more states are mutually

(continued)

state interests. Changing priorities or global conditions make the outlook for prolonged economic interdependence somewhat problematic.

Finally, proponents of class system theory, which will be discussed in greater detail in the next section, also question the assumption that interdependence facilitates greater cooperation among nations. In addition to being "Western-centric," they view interdependence as exploitative of, rather than beneficial to, less-developed countries. Indeed, interdependence affects countries differently. Developing nations, such as Haiti and Botswana, are more vulnerable to the economic shifts and cultural intrusion or imperialism associated with interdependence than richer, industrialized states like the United States.

(continued from previous page)

sensitive and vulnerable to each other's actions. Economic liberals argue that this is a defining characteristic of our contemporary world.

International law is the codification of rules that regulate the behavior of states and set limits upon what is permissible and what is not permissible. In theory, these rules are binding on states, as well as other international actors.

Liberal institutionalism is a theory of international relations that contends global cooperation is founded upon three primary factors: enhancing the role and influence of international organizations, instituting collective security, and enforcing international law. All three of these factors might be viewed as prescriptions for how states should behave, with an ultimate goal of reforming the anarchy of the international system and forging a harmonious community of nations.

Multinational corporations (MNCs) are companies that have production facilities or branches in several countries.

Natural law is a view that there is a system of rules and principles for the conduct of human affairs, founded on the belief that all people have basic, inalienable rights. In theory, these inalienable rights (essentially to life and liberty) supersede any mortal authority and cannot be legitimately denied by any government or society. Natural law is widely accepted as one of the philosophical foundations of international law.

Regime is a set of accepted rules, norms, and procedures that regulate the behavior of states and other actors in a given issue area. A regime also encompasses the international institutions, NGOs, and treaties that enhance cooperation in that area. Issues such as trade, the environment, monetary relations, and so forth represent a host of different international concerns that might be targeted. International cooperation is based on a variety of regimes designed to meet the needs of specific issue areas.

Liberals might respond to their critics by stating that their theory presents a systemic explanation that takes into account the changing nature of twenty-first-century international relations. The realist emphasis on military power and conflict and the class system focus on the exploitation of the poor by the rich are too simplistic and do not provide accurate explanations of international relations.

To the realist's critique, liberals would respond by saying that they do not reject many of the major tenets of realism; they simply use them as a foundation upon which to build new explanations for contemporary global politics. For example, liberals accept the realist notion of anarchy, but argue that the growth of international economic interdependence and the expanding roles of nonstate actors and international institutions have transformed world politics, making it less anarchic and more cooperative.

To the class system theorists, liberals would point out that they do take into account that less-developed countries (LDCs) are more vulnerable than advanced industrialized states. However, they reject the argument that the global economy is structured to oppress the LDCs. Liberals view international relations as much more complex and subtle. They contend that the ability of individual corporations or states to control the course of international relations is more limited than the class system theorists believe.

Overall, liberalism offers a fairly flexible and nuanced explanation for contemporary international relations. Like all theories of global politics, liberalism has gaps and weaknesses, but it does offer unique insights into the changing nature of our twenty-first-century world.

10. On the Law of War and Peace

Hugo Grotius

In this selection, Hugo Grotius posits that relations between states should be based on universal rules of international behavior—even to the point of regulating the conduct of war. This concept would later form the basis for international law in the European state system. This selection is from *The Rights of War and Peace* (1625).

Hugo Grotius (1583–1645), a Dutch philosopher, theologian, and jurist, is generally regarded as the founder of international law.

I.   The first and most necessary divisions of war are into one kind called private, another public, and another mixed. Now public war is carried on by the person holding the sovereign power. Private war is that which is carried on by private persons without authority from the state. A mixed war is that which is carried on, on one side by public authority, and on the other by private persons. But private war, from its greater antiquity, is the first subject for inquiry.

The proofs that have been already produced, to shew that to repel violence is not repugnant to natural law, afford a satisfactory reason to justify private war, as far as the law of nature is concerned. But perhaps it may be thought that since public tribunals have been erected, private redress of wrongs is not allowable. An objection which is very just. Yet although public trials and courts of justice are not institutions of nature, but erected by the invention of men, yet as it is much more conducive to the peace of society for a matter in dispute to be decided by a disinterested person, than by the partiality and prejudice of the party aggrieved, natural justice and reason will dictate the necessity and advantage of every one's submitting to the equitable decisions of public judges. Paulus, the Lawyer, observes that "what can be done by a magistrate with the authority of the state, should never be intrusted to individuals; as private redress would give rise to greater disturbance. And "the reason," says King Theodoric, "why laws were invented, was to prevent any one from using personal violence, for wherein would peace differ from all the confusion of war, if private disputes were terminated by force?" And the law calls it force for any man to seize what he thinks his due, without seeking a legal remedy.

II.   It is a matter beyond all doubt that the liberty of private redress, which once existed, was greatly abridged after courts of justice were established. Yet there may be cases, in which private redress must be allowed, as for instance, if the way to legal justice were not open. For when the law prohibits any one from redressing his own wrongs, it can only be understood to apply to circumstances where a legal remedy exists. Now the obstruction in the way to legal redress may be either temporary or absolute. Temporary, where it is impossible for the injured party to wait for a legal remedy, without imminent danger and even destruction. As for instance, if a man were attacked in the night, or in a secret place where no assistance could be procured. Absolute, either as the right, or the fact may require. Now there are many situations, where the right must cease from the impossibility of supporting it in a legal way, as in unoccupied places, on the seas, in a wilderness, or desert island, or any other place, where there is no civil government. All legal remedy too ceases by fact, when subjects will not submit to the judge, or if he refuses openly to take cognizance of matters in dispute. The assertion that all private war is not made repugnant to the law of nature by the erection of legal tribunals, may be understood from the law given to the Jews, wherein God thus speaks by the mouth of Moses, Exod. xxii. 2. "If a thief be found breaking up, that is, by night, and be smitten that he dies, there shall no blood be shed for him, but if the sun be risen upon him, there shall be blood shed for him." Now this law, making so accurate a distinction in the merits of the case, seems not only to imply impunity for killing any one, in self-defence, but to explain a natural right, founded not on any special divine command, but on the common principles of justice. From whence other nations have plainly followed the same rule. The passage of the twelve tables is well known, undoubtedly taken from the old Athenian Law, "If a thief commit a robbery in the night, and a man kill him, he is killed lawfully." Thus by the laws of all known and civilized nations, the person is judged innocent, who kills another, forcibly attempting or endangering his life; a conspiring and universal testimony, which proves that in justifiable homicide, there is nothing repugnant to the law of nature. . . .[1]

IV. Public war, according to the law of nations, is either SOLEMN, that is FORMAL, or LESS SOLEMN, that is INFORMAL. The name of lawful war is commonly given to what is here called formal, in the same sense in which a regular will is opposed to a codicil, or a lawful marriage to the cohabitation of slaves. This opposition by no means implies that it is not allowed to any man, if he pleases, to make a codicil, or to slaves to cohabit in matrimony, but only, that, by the civil law, FORMAL WILLS and SOLEMN MARRIAGES, were attended with peculiar privileges and effects. These observations were the more necessary; because many, from a misconception of the word just or lawful, think that all wars, to which those epithets do not apply, are condemned as unjust and unlawful. Now to give a war the formality required by the law of nations, two things are necessary. In the first place it must be made on both sides, by the sovereign power of the state, and in the next place it must be accompanied with certain formalities. Both of which are so essential that one is insufficient without the other.

Now a public war, LESS SOLEMN, may be made without those formalities, even against private persons, and by any magistrate whatever. And indeed, considering the thing without respect to the civil law, every magistrate, in case of resistance, seems to have a right to take up arms, to maintain his authority in the execution of his office; as well as to defend the people committed to his protection. But as a whole state is by war involved in danger, it is an established law in almost all nations that no war can be made but by the authority of the sovereign in each state. There is such a law as this in the last book of Plato ON LAWS. And by the Roman law, to make war, or levy troops without a commission from the Prince was high treason. According to the Cornelian law also, enacted by Lucius Cornelius Sylla, to do so without authority from the people amounted to the same crime. In the code of Justinian there is a constitution, made by Valentinian and Valens, that no one should bear arms without their knowledge and authority. Conformably to this rule, St. Augustin says, that as peace is most agreeable to the natural state of man, it is proper that Princes should have the sole authority to devise and execute the operations of war. Yet this general rule, like all others, in its application must always be limited by equity and discretion.

In certain cases this authority may be communicated to others. For it is a point settled beyond all doubt that subordinate magistrates may, by their officers, reduce a few disobedient and tumultuous persons to subjection, provided, that to do it, it requires not a force of such enormous magnitude as might endanger the state. Again, if the danger be so imminent as to allow of no time for an application to the sovereign executive power, here too the necessity is admitted as an exception to the general rule. Lucius Pinarius the Governor of Enna, a Sicilian garrison, presuming upon this right, upon receiving certain information that the inhabitants had formed a conspiracy to revolt to the Carthaginians, put them all to the sword, and by that means saved the place. Franciscus Victoria allows the inhabitants of a town to take up arms, even without such a case of necessity, to redress their own wrongs, which the Prince neglects to avenge, but such an opinion is justly rejected by others.

V. Whether the circumstances, under which subordinate magistrates are authorised to use military force, can properly be called public war or not, is a matter of dispute among legal writers, some affirming and others denying it. If indeed we call no other public war, but that which is made by magisterial authority, there is no doubt but that such suppressions of tumult are public wars, and those who in such cases resist the magistrate in the execution of his office, incur the guilt of rebellion against superiors. But if public war is taken in the higher sense of FORMAL war, as it undoubtedly often is; those are not public wars; because to entitle them to the full rights of such, the declaration of the sovereign power and other requisites are wanting. Nor do the loss of property and the military executions, to which the offenders are subject, at all affect the question.[2] For those casualties are not so peculiarly attached to formal war, as to be excluded from all other kinds. For it may happen, as in an extensive empire for instance, that persons in subordinate authority, may, when attacked, or threatened with attack, have powers granted to commence military operations. In which case the war must be supposed to commence by the authority of the sovereign power; as a person is considered to be the author of a measure which by virtue of his authority he empowers another to perform. The more doubtful point is, whether, where there is no such commission, a conjecture of what is the will of the sovereign power be sufficient. This seems not admissible. For it is not sufficient to consider, what we suppose would be the Sovereign's pleasure, if he were consulted; but what would be his actual will, in matters admitting of time for deliberation, even though he were not formally consulted; if a law was to be passed upon those matters. "For though UNDER SOME PARTICULAR CIRCUMSTANCES, it may be necessary to waive consulting the will of the sovereign, yet this would by no means authorise it as a GENERAL PRACTICE. For the safety of the state would be endangered, if subordinate powers should usurp the right of making war at their discretion." It was not without reason, that Cneus Manlius was accused by his Lieutenants of having made war upon the Galatians without authority from the Roman people. For though the Galatians had supplied Antiochus with troops, yet as peace had been made with him, it rested with the Roman people, and not with Manlius to determine in what manner the Galatians should be punished for assisting an enemy. Cato proposed that Julius Caesar should be delivered up to the Germans for having attacked them in violation of his promise, a proposal proceeding rather from the desire to be rid of a formidable rival, than from any principle of justice.

The case was thus; the Germans had assisted the Gauls, enemies of the Roman people, therefore they had no reason to complain of the injury done to them, if the war against the Gauls, in which they had made themselves a party concerned, was just. But Caesar ought to have contented himself with driving the Germans out of Gaul, the province assigned him, without pursuing them into their own country, especially as there was no farther danger to be apprehended from them; unless he had first consulted the Roman people. It was plain, then, the Germans had no right to demand the surrender of Caesar's person, though the Romans had a right to punish him for having exceeded his commission. On a similar occasion the Carthaginians answered the Romans; "It is not the subject of inquiry whether Hannibal has besieged Saguntum, by his own private or by public authority, but whether justly or unjustly. For with respect to one of our own subjects it is our business to inquire by what authority he has acted; but the matter of discussion with you is, whether he has broken any treaty." Cicero defends the conduct of Octavius and Decimus Brutus, who had taken up arms against Antony. But though it was evident that Antony deserved to be treated as an enemy, yet they ought to have waited for the determination of the Senate and people of Rome, whether it were for the public interest not to take notice of his conduct or to punish it, to agree to terms of peace with him, or to have recourse to arms. This would have been proper; for no one is obliged to exercise the right of punishing an enemy, if it is attended with probable danger.

But even if it had been judged expedient to declare Antony an enemy, the choice of the persons to conduct the war should have been left to the Senate and people of Rome. Thus when Cassius demanded assistance of the Rhodians, according to treaty, they answered they would send it, if the senate thought proper. This refutation of Cicero's opinion will serve, along with many other instances to be met with; as an admonition not to be carried away by the opinions of the most celebrated writers, particularly the most brilliant orators, who often speak to suit the circumstances of the moment. But all political investigation requires a cool and steady judgment, not to be biased by examples, which may rather be excused than vindicated.

Since then it has already been established that no war can lawfully be made but by the sovereign power of each state, in respect to all the questions connected with war, it will be necessary to examine what that sovereign power is, and who are the persons that hold it.

VI.   The moral power then of governing a state, which is called by Thucydides the civil power, is described as consisting of three parts which form the necessary substance of every state; and those are the right of making its own laws, executing them in its own manner, and appointing its own magistrates. Aristotle, in the fourth book of his Politics, comprises the sovereignty of a state in the exercise of the deliberative, executive, and judicial powers. To the deliberative branch he assigns the right of deciding upon peace or war, making or annulling treaties, and framing and passing new laws. To these he adds the power of inflicting death, banishment, and forfeiture, and of punishing also for public peculation. In the exercise of judicial power, he includes not only the punishment of crimes and misdemeanors, but the redress of civil injuries.[3] Dionysius of Halicarnassus, points out three distinguishing marks of sovereign power; and those are, the right of appointing magistrates, the right of enacting and repealing laws, and the right of making war and peace. To which, in another part, he adds the administration of justice, the supreme authority in matters of religion, and the right of calling general councils.

A true definition comprehends every possible branch of authority that can grow out of the possession and exercise of sovereign power. For the ruler of every state must exercise his authority either in person, or through the medium of others. His own personal acts must be either general or special. He may be said to do GENERAL acts in passing or repealing laws, respecting either temporal matters, or spiritual concerns, as far as the latter relate to the welfare of the state. The knowledge of these principles is called by Aristotle the masterpiece in the science of government.

The particular acts of the Sovereign are either directly of a public nature, or a private, but even the latter bear reference to his public capacity. Now the acts of the sovereign executive power of a directly public kind are the making of peace and war and treaties, and the imposition of taxes, and other similar exercises of authority over the persons and property of its subjects, which constitute the sovereignty of the state. Aristotle calls the knowledge of this practice political and deliberative science.

The private acts of the sovereign are those, in which by his authority, disputes between individuals are decided, as it is conducive to the peace of society that these should be settled. This is called by Aristotle the judicial power. Thus the acts of the sovereign are done in his name by his magistrates or other officers, among whom ambassadors are reckoned. And in the exercise of all those rights sovereign power consists.

VII. That power is called sovereign, whose actions are not subject to the controul of any other power, so as to be annulled at the pleasure of any other human will. The term ANY OTHER HUMAN WILL exempts the sovereign himself from this restriction, who may annul his own acts, as may also his successor, who enjoys the same right, having the same power and no other. We are to consider then what is the subject in which this sovereign power exists. Now the subject is in one respect common, and in another proper, as the body is the common subject of sight, the eye the proper, so the common subject of sovereign power is the state, which has already been said to be a perfect society of men.

NOTES

1. As the topics of the third section have been so fully stated in the second chapter, that section has been omitted, and the translation goes on from the second of the original to the fourth. (Translator)

2. In case of rebellion, the subjects taken in arms have no right to be treated as prisoners of war but are liable to punishment as criminals.
3. "Wrongs are divisible into two sorts or species, PRIVATE WRONGS, and PUBLIC WRONGS. The former are an infringement or privation of the private or civil rights belonging to individuals, considered as individuals, and are therefore frequently termed civil injuries; the latter are a breach and violation of public rights and duties which affect the whole community considered as a community, and are distinguished by the harsher appellation of crimes and misdemeanors."—Blackst. Com. b. iii. c. i.

QUESTIONS

1. According to Grotius, what is the difference between "private war" and "public war"?

2. How does Grotius define the concept of sovereignty?

11.   Fourteen Points

Woodrow Wilson

In this excerpt, President Woodrow Wilson proposes his Fourteen Points as part of a broader program to establish a new international order in the wake of World War I. These fourteen points were presented in response to news that several of the Allies had made secret treaties designed to divide the conquered nations for geopolitical and economic gain. Wilson's plan identified the need for "open covenants of peace, openly arrived at. . . ." In this text, Wilson introduces the concept of collective security. This speech was delivered before Congress on January 8, 1918.

In addition to serving as President of the United States, Woodrow Wilson (1856–1924) was a professor of political science and president of Princeton University. He first entered politics when he was elected governor of New Jersey in 1910. His works include *Congressional Government* and the five-volume *History of the American People.*

. . . We entered this war because violations of right had occurred which touched us to the quick and made the life of our own people impossible unless they were corrected and the world secured once for all against their recurrence. What we demand in this war, therefore, is nothing peculiar to our-

From *Speeches of the American Presidents,* pp. 394, 396–399. © 1988 H. W. Wilson Company, New York. Used by permission.

selves. It is that the world be made fit
and safe to live in; and particularly that it
be made safe for every peace-loving nation which, like our own, wishes to live
its own life, determine its own institutions, be assured of justice and fair dealing by the other peoples of the world as
against force and selfish aggression. All
the peoples of the world are in effect
partners in this interest, and for our own
part we see very clearly that unless justice be done to others it will not be
done to us. The program of the world's
peace, therefore, is our program; and
that program, the only possible program,
as we see it, is this:

I. Open covenants of peace, openly
arrived at, after which there shall be no
private international understandings of
any kind but diplomacy shall proceed always frankly and in the public view.

II. Absolute freedom of navigation
upon the seas, outside territorial waters,
alike in peace and in war, except as the
seas may be closed in whole or in part
by international action for the enforcement of international covenants.

III. The removal, so far as possible,
of all economic barriers and the establishment of an equality of trade conditions among all the nations consenting
to the peace and associating themselves
for its maintenance.

IV. Adequate guarantees given and
taken that national armaments will be reduced to the lowest point consistent with
domestic safety.

V. A free, open-minded, and absolutely impartial adjustment of all colonial
claims, based upon a strict observance
of the principle that in determining all
such questions of sovereignty the interests of the populations concerned must
have equal weight with the equitable
claims of the government whose title is
to be determined.

VI. The evacuation of all Russian
territory and such a settlement of all
questions affecting Russia as will secure
the best and freest coöperation of the
other nations of the world in obtaining
for her an unhampered and unembar-
rassed opportunity for the independent
determination of her own political development and national policy and assure her of a sincere welcome into the
society of free nations under institutions
of her own choosing; and, more than a
welcome, assistance also of every kind
that she may need and may herself desire. The treatment accorded Russia by
her sister nations in the months to come
will be the acid test of their good will,
of their comprehension of her need as
distinguished from their own interests,
and of intelligent and unselfish sympathy.

VII. Belgium, the whole world will
agree, must be evacuated and restored,
without any attempt to limit the sovereignty which she enjoys in common
with all other free nations. No other single act will serve as this will serve to restore confidence among the nations in
the laws which they have themselves set
and determined for the government of
their relations with one another. Without this healing act the whole structure
and validity of international law is forever impaired.

VIII. All French territory should be
freed and invaded portions restored, and
the wrong done to France by Prussia in
1871 in the matter of Alsace-Lorraine,
which has unsettled the peace of the
world for nearly fifty years, should be
righted, in order that peace may once
more be made secure in the interest of all.

IX. A readjustment of the frontiers
of Italy should be effected along clearly
recognizable lines of nationality.

X. The peoples of Austria-Hungary,
whose place among the nations we wish

to see safe-guarded and assured, should be accorded the freest opportunity of autonomous development.

XI. Rumania, Serbia, and Montenegro should be evacuated; occupied territories restored; Serbia accorded free and secure access to the sea; and the relations of the several Balkan states to one another determined by friendly counsel along historically established lines of allegiance and nationality; and international guarantees of the political and economic independence and territorial integrity of the several Balkan states should be entered into.

XII. The Turkish portions of the present Ottoman Empire should be assured a secure sovereignty, but the other nationalities which are now under Turkish rule should be assured an undoubted security of life and an absolutely unmolested opportunity of autonomous development, and the Dardanelles should be permanently opened as a free passage to the ships and commerce of all nations under international guarantees.

XIII. An independent Polish state should be erected which should include the territories inhabited by indisputably Polish populations, which should be assured a free and secure access to the sea, and whose political and economic independence and territorial integrity should be guaranteed by international covenant.

XIV. A general association of nations must be formed under specific covenants for the purpose of affording mutual guarantees of political independence and territorial integrity to great and small states alike.

In regard to these essential rectifications of wrong and assertions of right we feel ourselves to be intimate partners of all the governments and peoples associated together against the imperialists. We cannot be separated in interest or divided in purpose. We stand together until the end.

For such arrangements and covenants we are willing to fight and to continue to fight until they are achieved; but only because we wish the right to prevail and desire a just and stable peace such as can be secured only by removing the chief provocations to war, which this program does remove. We have no jealousy of German greatness, and there is nothing in this program that impairs it. We grudge her no achievement or distinction of learning or of pacific enterprise such as have made her record very bright and very enviable. We do not wish to injure her or to block in any way her legitimate influence or power. We do not wish to fight her either with arms or with hostile arrangements of trade if she is willing to associate herself with us and the other peace-loving nations of the world in covenants of justice and law and fair dealing. We wish her only to accept a place of equality among the peoples of the world—the new world in which we now live—instead of a place of mastery.

Neither do we presume to suggest to her any alteration or modification of her institutions. But it is necessary, we must frankly say, and necessary as a preliminary to any intelligent dealings with her on our part that we should know whom her spokesmen speak for when they speak to us, whether for the Reichstag majority or for the military party and the men whose creed is imperial domination.

We have spoken now, surely, in terms too concrete to admit of any further doubt or question. An evident principle runs through the whole program I have outlined. It is the principle of justice to all peoples and nationalities, and their right to live on equal terms of liberty and safety with one another, whether they be strong or weak. Unless this principle be made its foundation no part of the structure of international justice can stand. The people of the United States could act upon no other principle; and to the vindication of this principle they are ready to devote their lives, their honor, and everything that they possess. The moral climax of this the culminating and final war for human liberty has come, and they are ready to put their own strength, their own highest purpose, their own integrity and devotion to the test.

QUESTIONS

1. How does Wilson's view differ from the realist perspective?

2. If the Fourteen Points had been approved, could World War II have been prevented?

---

12.   The Anarchical Society

Hedley Bull

In this excerpt, Hedley Bull examines three traditions of thought in international relations: Hobbesian (realist), Kantian, and Grotian (this textbook places the latter two authors into the liberal school of thought). For his own part, Bull combines some of the concepts we have in realist theory, such as balance of power, with other internationalist notions about the effective use of generally accepted rules and norms. This selection is from *The Anarchical Society* (1977).

Hedley Bull (1932–1985) taught at the London School of Economics and the Australian National University. He was a leading authority on both arms control issues and problems of the Third World. Bull's other works include *The Control of the Arms Race* (1961) and contributions to various international studies journals.

DOES ORDER EXIST IN WORLD POLITICS?

We have now made it clear what is meant in this study by order in world politics. The question we must now ask is: does it exist?

Order in world politics may one day take the form of the maintenance of elementary goals of social life in a single world society or great society of all mankind. How far the system of states is giving place to such a society, and whether or not it is desirable that it should, are questions that will be considered later in this study. It could not be seriously argued, however, that the society of all mankind is already a going concern. In the present phase we are still accustomed to thinking of order in world politics as consisting of domestic order, or order within states, and international order, or order among them.

No one would deny that there exists within some states a high degree of domestic or municipal order. It is, however, often argued that international order does not exist, except as an aspiration, and that the history of international relations consists simply of disorder or strife. To many people the idea of international order suggests not anything that has occurred in the past, but simply a possible or desirable future state of international relations, about which we might speculate or which we might work to bring about. To those who take this view a study of international order suggests simply a design for a future world, in the tradition of Sully, Cruce, St. Pierre and other irenists or peace theorists.

This present study takes as its starting-point the proposition that, on the contrary, order is part of the historical record of international relations; and in particular, that modern states have formed, and continue to form, not only a system of states but also an international society. To establish this proposition I shall begin by showing first that there has always been present, throughout the history of the modern states system, an idea of international society, proclaimed by philosophers and publicists, and present in the rhetoric of the leaders of states. Second, I shall seek to show that this idea is reflected, at least in part, in international reality; that the idea of international society has important roots in actual international practice. Third, I shall set out the limitations of the idea of international society as a guide to the actual practice of states, the precarious and imperfect nature of the order to which it gives rise.

THE IDEA OF INTERNATIONAL SOCIETY

Throughout the history of the modern states system there have been three competing traditions of thought: the Hobbesian or realist tradition, which views international politics as a state of war; the Kantian or universalist tradition, which sees at work in international politics a potential community of mankind; and the Grotian or internationalist tradition, which views international politics as taking place within an international society. Here I shall state what is essential to the Grotian or internationalist idea of international society, and what divides it from the Hobbesian or realist tradition on the one hand, and from the Kantian or universalist tradition on the other. Each of these traditional patterns of thought embodies a description of the nature of international politics and a set of prescriptions about international conduct.

The Hobbesian tradition describes international relations as a state of war of all against all, an arena of struggle in which each state is pitted against every other. International relations, on the Hobbesian view, represent pure conflict between states and resemble a game that is wholly distributive or zero-sum: the interests of each state exclude the interests of any other. The particular international activity that, on the Hobbesian view, is most typical of international activity as a whole, or best provides the clue to it, is war itself. Thus peace, on the Hobbesian view, is a period of recuperation from the last war and preparation for the next.

The Hobbesian prescription for international conduct is that the state is free to pursue its goals in relation to other states without moral or legal restrictions of any kind. Ideas of morality and law, on this view, are valid only in the context of a society, but international life is beyond the bounds of any society. If any moral or legal goals are to be pursued in international politics, these can only be the moral or legal goals of the state itself. Either it is held (as by Machiavelli) that the state conducts foreign policy in a kind of moral and legal vacuum, or it is held (as by Hegel and his successors) that moral behaviour for the state in foreign policy lies in its own self-assertion. The only rules or principles which, for those in the Hobbesian tradition, may be said to limit or circumscribe the behaviour of states in their relations with one another are rules of prudence or expediency. Thus agreements may be kept if it is expedient to keep them, but may be broken if it is not.

The Kantian or universalist tradition, at the other extreme, takes the essential nature of international politics to lie not in conflict among states, as on the Hobbesian view, but in the transnational social bonds that link the individual human beings who are the subjects or citizens of states. The dominant theme of international relations, on the Kantian view, is only apparently the relationship among states, and is really the relationship among all men in the community of mankind—which exists potentially, even if it does not exist actually, and which when it comes into being will sweep the system of states into limbo.

Within the community of all mankind, on the universalist view, the interests of all men are one and the same; international politics, considered from this perspective, is not a purely distributive or zero-sum game, as the Hobbesians maintain, but a purely co-operative or non-zero-sum game. Conflicts of interest exist among the ruling cliques of states, but this is only at the superficial or transient level of the existing system of states; properly understood, the interests of all peoples are the same. The particular international activity which, on the Kantian view, most typifies international activity as a whole is the horizontal conflict of ideology that cuts across the boundaries of states and divides human society into two camps—the trustees of the immanent community of mankind and those who stand in its way, those who are of the true faith and the heretics, the liberators and the oppressed.

The Kantian or universalist view of international morality is that, in contrast to the Hobbesian conception, there are moral imperatives in the field of international relations limiting the action of states, but that these imperatives enjoin not coexistence and co-operation among states but rather the overthrow of the system of states and its replacement by a cosmopolitan society. The community of mankind, on the Kantian view, is not only the central reality in international politics, in the sense that the forces able to bring it into being are present; it is also the end or object of the highest moral endeavour. The rules that sustain coexistence and social intercourse among states should be ignored if the imperatives of this higher morality require it. Good faith with heretics has no meaning, except in terms of tactical convenience; between the elect and the damned, the liberators and the oppressed, the question of mutual acceptance of rights to sovereignty or independence does not arise.

What has been called the Grotian or internationalist tradition stands between the realist tradition and the universalist tradition. The Grotian tradition describes international politics in terms of a society of states or international society. As against the Hobbesian tradition, the Grotians contend that states are not engaged in simple struggle, like gladiators in an arena, but are limited in their conflicts with one another by common rules and institutions. But as against the Kantian or universalist perspective the Grotians accept the Hobbesian premise that sovereigns or states are the principal reality in international politics; the immediate members of international society are states rather than individual human beings. International politics, in the Grotian understanding, expresses neither complete conflict of interest between states nor complete identity of interest; it resembles a game that is partly distributive but also partly productive. The particular international activity which, on the Grotian view, best typifies international activity as a whole is neither war between states, nor horizontal conflict cutting across the boundaries of states, but trade—or, more generally, economic and social intercourse between one country and another.

The Grotian prescription for international conduct is that all states, in their dealings with one another, are bound by the rules and institutions of the society they form. As against the view of the Hobbesians, states in the Grotian view are bound not only by rules of prudence or expediency but also by imperatives of morality and law. But, as against the view of the universalists, what these imperatives enjoin is not the overthrow of the system of states and its replacement by a universal community of mankind, but rather acceptance of the requirements of coexistence and co-operation in a society of states.

Each of these traditions embodies a great variety of doctrines about international politics, among which there exists only a loose connection. In different periods each pattern of thought appears in a different idiom and in relation to different issues and preoccupations. This is not the place to explore further the connections and distinctions within each tradition. Here we have only to take account of the fact that the Grotian idea of international society has always been present in thought about the states system, and to indicate in broad terms the metamorphoses which, in the last three to four centuries, it has undergone. . . .

World International Society

In the twentieth century, as in the sixteenth and seventeenth centuries, the idea of international society has been on the defensive. On the one hand, the Hobbesian or realist interpretation of international politics has been fed by the two World Wars, and by the expansion of international society beyond its originally European confines. On the other hand, Kantian or universalist interpretations have been fed by a striving to transcend the states system so as to escape the conflict and disorder that have accompanied it in this century, and by the Russian and Chinese revolutions, which have given a new currency to doctrines of global transnational solidarity, both communist and anticommunist. Ideas of international society in the twentieth century may be said to be closer to those that were entertained in the early centuries of the states system than to those that prevailed in the eighteenth and nineteenth centuries.

In the twentieth century international society ceased to be regarded as specifically European and came to be considered as global or world wide. In the 1880s the Scottish natural lawyer James Lorimer expressed the orthodox doctrine of the time when he wrote that mankind was divided into civilised humanity, barbarous humanity and savage humanity. Civilised humanity comprised the nations of Europe and the Americas, which were entitled to full recognition as members of international society. Barbarous humanity comprised the independent states of Asia—Turkey, Persia, Siam, China and Japan—which were entitled to partial recognition. And savage humanity was the rest of mankind, which stood beyond the pale of the society of states, although it was entitled to 'natural or human recognition'. It is worth noting in passing that Lorimer's distinction is in fact the same one which is made by social scientists today when they distinguish between modern societies, traditional societies and primitive societies.

Today, when non-European states represent the great majority in international society and the United Nations is nearly universal in its membership, the doctrine that this society rests upon a specific culture or civilisation is generally rejected and even the echo of it that survives in the Statute of the International Court of Justice—which lists the law common to civilised states among the sources of international law it recognises—has become an embarrassment. It is important to bear in mind, however, that if contemporary international society does have any cultural basis, this is not any genuinely global culture, but is rather the culture of so-called 'modernity'. And if we ask what is modernity in culture, it is not clear how we answer this except by saying that it is the culture of the dominant Western powers. . . .

In the twentieth century, also, there has been a retreat from the confident assertions, made in the age of Vattel, that the members of international society were states and nations, towards the ambiguity and imprecision on this point that characterised the era of Grotius. The state as a bearer of rights and duties, legal and moral, in international society today is widely thought to be joined by international organisations, by non-state groups of various kinds operating across frontiers, and—as implied by the Nuremberg and Tokyo War Crimes Tribunals, and by the Universal Declaration of Human Rights—by individuals. There is no agreement as to the relative importance of these different kinds of legal and moral agents, or on any general scheme of rules that would relate them one to another, but Vattel's conception of a society simply of states has been under attack from many different directions.

In this century, also, the theory of international society has moved away from the emphasis of eighteenth- and nineteenth-century legal and historical positivism on existing practice as the source of norms about international conduct, in favour of a return to natural law principles or to some contemporary equivalent of them; in political as in legal analysis of international relations the idea of international society has been rested less on the evidence of cooperation in the actual behaviour of states than on principles purporting to show how they should behave, such as those proclaimed in the League Covenant, the Kellogg-Briand Pact or the Charter of the United Nations.

Going along with this there has been a reappearance of universalist or solidarist assumptions in the way the rules of coexistence are formulated. The idea that the means states use in war should be limited has been qualified by the re-appearance of the distinction between objectively just and unjust causes for which war is waged, as in the attempts to prohibit "aggressive" war. The idea that neutrals should behave impartially towards belligerent states has been qualified in the same way, as in the doctrine of 'collective security' embodied in the League of Nations Covenant and the United Nations Charter.

The twentieth-century emphasis upon ideas of a reformed or improved international society, as distinct from the elements of society in actual practice, has led to a treatment of the League of Nations, the United Nations and other general international organisations as the chief institutions of international society, to the neglect of those institutions whose role in the maintenance of international order is the central one. Thus there has developed the Wilsonian rejection of the balance of power, the denigration of diplomacy and the tendency to seek to replace it by international administration, and a return to the tendency that prevailed in the Grotian era to confuse international law with international morality or international improvement.

The Reality of International Society

But does this idea of international society conform to reality? Do the theories of philosophers, international lawyers and historians in the Grotian tradition reflect the thought of statesmen? If statesmen pay lip-service to international society and its rules, does this mean that the latter affect their decisions? If the idea of international society played some real part during periods of relative interna-

tional harmony, as in Europe for long stretches of the eighteenth and nineteenth centuries, was it not extinguished during the wars of religion, the wars of the French Revolution and Napoleon, and the World Wars of the present century? What meaning can it have, for example, to say that Hitler's Germany and Stalin's Russia, locked in a struggle to the death during the Second World War, regarded each other as bound by common rules and co-operated in the working of common institutions? If the Christian and, later, European international system that existed from the sixteenth century to the nineteenth was also an international society, were not the bonds of this society stretched and ultimately broken as the system expanded and became worldwide? Is not the international politics of the present time best viewed as an international system that is not an international society?

The Element of Society

My contention is that the element of a society has always been present, and remains present, in the modern international system, although only as one of the elements in it, whose survival is sometimes precarious. The modern international system in fact reflects all three of the elements singled out, respectively, by the Hobbesian, the Kantian and the Grotian traditions: the element of war and struggle for power among states, the element of transnational solidarity and conflict, cutting across the divisions among states, and the element of co-operation and regulated intercourse among states. In different historical phases of the states system, in different geographical theatres of its operation, and in the policies of different states and statesmen, one of these three elements may predominate over the others.

Thus one may say that in the trade and colonial wars fought in the late seventeenth and eighteenth centuries, chiefly by Holland, France and England, where the object was trading monopoly enforced by sea power and the political control of colonies, the element of a state of war was predominant. In the wars of religion that marked the first phase of the states system up till the Peace of Westphalia, in the European convulsion of the wars of the French Revolution and Napoleon, and in the ideological struggle of communist and anti-communist powers in our own times, the element of transnational solidarity and conflict has been uppermost—expressed not only in the revolutionist transnational solidarities of the Protestant parties, the democratic or republican forces favourable to the French Revolution, and the Communist Internationals, but also in the counter-revolutionist solidarities of the Society of Jesus, International Legitimism and Dullesian anti-communism. In nineteenth-century Europe, in the interval between the struggle of revolutionism and Legitimism that remained in the aftermath of the Napoleonic wars, and the re-emergence, late in the century, of the patterns of great power conflict that led to the First World War, one may say that the element of international society was predominant.

The element of international society has always been present in the modern international system because at no stage can it be said that the conception of the common interests of states, of common rules accepted and common institutions worked by them, has ceased to exert an influence. Most states at most times pay some respect to the basic rules of coexistence in international society, such as mutual respect for sovereignty, the rule that agreements should be kept, and rules limiting resort to violence. In the same way most states at most times take part in the working of common institutions: the forms and procedures of international law, the system of diplomatic representation, acceptance of the special position of great powers, and universal international organisations such as the functional organisations that grew up in the nineteenth century, the League of Nations and the United Nations.

The idea of "international society" has a basis in reality that is sometimes precarious but has at no stage disappeared. Great wars that engulf the states system as a whole strain the credibility of the idea, and cause thinkers and statesmen to turn to Hobbesian interpretations and solutions, but they are followed by periods of peace. Ideological conflicts in which states and factions within them are ranged on opposite sides sometimes lead to a denial of the idea of international society by both sides, and lend confirmation to Kantian interpretations, but they are followed by accommodations in which the idea reappears.

Even at the height of a great war or ideological conflict the idea of international society, while it may be denied by the pronouncements of the contending states—each side treating the other as outside the framework of any common society—does not disappear so much as go underground, where it continues to influence the practice of states. The Allied and Axis powers at the height of the Second World War did not accept each other as members of a common international society, and they did not co-operate with each other in the work-ing of common institutions. But one could not say that the idea of interna-tional society ceased to affect the prac-tice of international relations in that period. The Allied powers continued to respect the ordinary rules of interna-tional society in their relations among themselves and in their dealings with neutral countries; so did Germany, Italy and Japan. Within both groups of bel-ligerent powers there were persons and movements who sought out the basis of a negotiated peace. The Allied and Axis states each insisted that the others were bound as members of international soci-ety to observe the Geneva conventions concerning prisoners of war, and in the case of the Western allies and Germany, in respect of one another's prisoners, in large measure actually did observe these conventions.

Similarly, when the Cold War was being prosecuted most vigorously, the United States and the Soviet Union were inclined to speak of each other as here-tics or outcasts beyond the pale, rather than as member states of the same inter-national society. However, they did not even then break off diplomatic rela-tions, withdraw recognition of one an-other's sovereignty, repudiate the idea of a common international law or cause the break-up of the United Nations into rival organisations. In both the Western and communist blocs there were voices raised in favour of compromise, drawing attention to the common interests of the two sides in coexistence and restat-ing, in secular form, the principle *cuijus regio, eijus religio* that had provided a basis for accommodation in the wars of religion. Thus, even in periods when in-ternational politics is best described in terms of a Hobbesian state of war or a

Kantian condition of transnational soli-darity, the idea of international society has survived as an important part of reality, and its survival in these times of stress lays the foundation for the recon-struction of international society when war gives place to peace or ideological conflict to *detente*.

It may help to make clear the per-sistent reality of the element of interna-tional society if we contrast the rela-tions of states within that system with examples of relations between indepen-dent political communities in which the element of society is entirely absent. The relations of Chingis Khan's Mongol invaders, and the Asian and European peoples whom they subjugated, were not moderated by a belief on each side in common rules binding on both in their dealings with one another. Chingis Khan's conquests did have a basis in the moral ideas of the Mongols themselves: Chingis believed that he had the man-date of heaven to rule the world, that whatever peoples lay outside the *de facto* control of the Mongols were neverthe-less *de jure* subjects of the Mongol em-pire, and that peoples who failed to sub-mit to the Mongol court were therefore rebels against the divinely inspired or-der, against whom the waging of war was a right and a duty. But these ideas formed no part of the thinking of the peoples who were subjugated and in some cases annihilated by the Mongols.

When the Spanish Conquistadors confronted the Aztecs and the Incas, this similarly took place in the absence of any common notion of rules and insti-tutions. The Spaniards debated among themselves what duties they had to-wards the Indians—whether their right to invade derived from the claim of the Pope to *imperium mundi,* the duty of a

Christian prince to spread the faith, the failure of the Indians to extend rights of hospitality, and so on. But the rights which the Indians were acknowledged—by scholars such as Victoria—to have, were rights deriving from a system of rules recognised by the Spaniards; they did not derive from any system of rules acknowledged by the Indians also. The Spaniards and the Indians were able to recognise each other as human beings, to engage in negotiations and to conclude agreements. But these dealings took place in the absence of any common framework of rules and institutions.

The long history of relations between Europe and Islam provides a further illustration of this theme. As long as modern international society thought of itself as Christian or European, Islam in its successive embodiments was viewed as a barbarian power against which it was the duty of Christian princes to maintain a common front, even if they did not always do so in practice. Islamic thought reciprocated by dividing the world into *dar-al-Islam,* the region of submission to the will of God, and *dar-al-Harb,* the region of war which was yet to be converted. Coexistence with infidel states was possible; diplomatic exchanges, treaties and alliances could be and were concluded; and these relations were subject to rules—but only rules binding on Moslems. There was no conception of a common society in which Islamic and infidel states both had their place; the latter were regarded as having only a provisional existence, and coexistence with them as only a temporary phase in a process leading inexorably to their absorption.

It might be argued that while there is indeed a contrast between cases where a common idea of international society is shared by adversary communities, and cases where no such idea exists, this is of no practical consequence; the language of a common international society spoken by states in the modern international system is mere lip-service. Thus, as Grotius notes, for some states which claim that they have a just cause for going to war with one another, this just cause is often simply a pretext, their real motives being quite otherwise. Grotius distinguishes between causes of war that are 'justifiable', that is to say which are undertaken in the belief that there is a just cause, from causes of war that are merely 'persuasive', that is in which allegation of a just cause is simply a pretext.

The question, however, is whether an international system in which it is necessary to have a pretext for beginning a war is not radically different from one in which it is not. The state which at least alleges a just cause, even where belief in the existence of a just cause has played no part in its decision, offers less of a threat to international order than one which does not. The state which alleges a just cause, even one it does not itself believe in, is at least acknowledging that it owes other states an explanation of its conduct, in terms of rules that they accept. There are, of course, differences of opinion as to the interpretation of the rules and their application to concrete situations; but such rules are not infinitely malleable and do circumscribe the range of choice of states which seek to give pretexts in terms of them. The giving of a pretext, moreover, means that the violence which the offending state does to the structure of commonly accepted rules by going to war in disregard of them is less than it would otherwise be; to make war without any explanation, or with an explanation stated only in terms of the recalcitrant state's own beliefs—such as the Mongols' belief in the Mandate of Heaven, or the belief of the Conquistadors in the Pope's *imperium mundi*—is to hold all other states in contempt, and to place in jeopardy all the settled expectations that states have about one another's behavior.

Grotius recognises that while international society is threatened by states which wage war for merely "persuasive" causes, and not for "justifiable" ones, it is even more threatened by states which wage war without "persuasive" causes either; wars which lack causes of either sort he speaks of as "the wars of savages." Vattel speaks of those who wage war without pretext of any kind as 'monsters unworthy of the name of men', whom nations may unite to suppress.

The Anarchical Society

It is often maintained that the existence of international society is disproved by the fact of anarchy, in the sense of the absence of government or rule. It is obvious that sovereign states, unlike the individuals within them, are not subject to a common government, and that in this sense there is, in the phrase made famous by Goldsworthy Lowes Dickinson, an "international anarchy." A persistent theme in the modern discussion of international relations has been that, as a consequence of this anarchy, states do not form together any kind of society; and that if they were to do so it could only be by subordinating themselves to a common authority.

A chief intellectual support of this doctrine is what I have called the domestic analogy, the argument from the experience of individual men in domestic society to the experience of states, according to which states, like individuals, are capable of orderly social life only if, as in Hobbes's phrase, they stand in awe of a common power. In the case of Hobbes himself and his successors, the domestic analogy takes the form simply of the assertion that states or sovereign princes, like individual men who live without government, are in a state of nature which is a state of war. It is not the view of Hobbes, or other thinkers of his school, that a social contract of states that would bring international anarchy to an end either should or can take place. By contrast, in the thinking of those who look forward—or backward— to a universal or world government, the domestic analogy is taken further, to embrace not only the conception of a state of nature but also that of a social contract among states that will reproduce the conditions of order within the state on a universal scale.

There are three weaknesses in the argument that states do not form a society because they are in a condition of international anarchy. The first is that the modern international system does not entirely resemble a Hobbesian state of nature. Hobbes's account of relations between sovereign princes is a subordinate part of his explanation and justification of government among individual men. As evidence for his speculations as to how men would live were they to find themselves in a situation of anarchy, Hobbes mentions the experience of civil war, the life of certain American tribes and the facts of international relations:

> But though there had never been any time wherein particular men were in a condition of warre one against another; yet in all times Kings, and

Persons of Soveraigne authority, because of their Independency, are in continual jealousies, and in the state and posture of Gladiators; having their weapons pointing, and their eyes fixed on one another; that is, their Forts, Garrisons and Guns, upon the Frontiers of their Kingdomes; and continual Spyes upon their neighbours; which is a posture of warre.

In Hobbes's account the situation in which men live without a common power to keep them in awe has three principal characteristics. In this situation there can be no industry, agriculture, navigation, trade or other refinements of living because the strength and invention of men is absorbed in providing security against one another. There are no legal or moral rules: "The notions of Right and Wrong, Justice and Injustice have there no place. . . . It is consequent also to the same condition, that there can be no Propriety, no Dominion, no *Mine* and *Thine* distinct; but only that to be every mans, that he can get; and for so long as he can keep it." Finally, the state of nature is a state of war: war understood to consist "not in actual fighting; but in the known disposition thereto, during all the time there is no assurance to the contrary"; and to be "such a warre, as is of every man, against every man."

The first of these characteristics clearly does not obtain in international anarchy. The absence of a world government is no necessary bar to industry, trade and other refinements of living. States do not in fact so exhaust their strength and invention in providing security against one another that the lives of their inhabitants are solitary, poor, nasty, brutish and short; they do not as a rule invest resources in war and military preparations to such an extent that their economic fabric is ruined. On the contrary, the armed forces of states, by providing security against external attack and internal disorder, establish the conditions under which economic improvements may take place within their borders. The absence of a universal government has not been incompatible with international economic interdependence.

It is also clear that the second feature of Hobbes's state of nature, the absence in it of notions of right and wrong, including notions of property, does not apply to modern international relations. Within the system of states that grew up in Europe and spread around the world, notions of right and wrong in international behaviour have always held a central place.

Of the three principal features of Hobbes's state of nature the only one that might be held to apply to modern international relations is the third—the existence in it of a state of war, in the sense of a disposition on the part of every state to war with every other state. Sovereign states, even while they are at peace, nevertheless display a disposition to go to war with one another, inasmuch as they prepare for war and treat war as one of the options open to them.

The second weakness of the argument from international anarchy is that it is based on false premises about the conditions of order among individuals and groups other than the state. It is not, of course, the case that fear of a supreme government is the only source of order within a modern state: no account of the reasons why men are capable of orderly social coexistence within a modern state can be complete which does not give due weight to factors such as reciprocal interest, a sense of community or general will, and habit or inertia.

If, then, we are to compare international relations with an imagined, pre-contractual state of nature among individual men, we may well choose not Hobbes's description of that condition but Locke's. Locke's conception of the state of nature as a society without government does in fact provide us with a close analogy with the society of states. In modern international society, as in Locke's state of nature, there is no central authority able to interpret and enforce the law, and thus individual members of the society must themselves judge and enforce it. Because in such a society each member of it is a judge in his own cause, and because those who seek to enforce the law do not always prevail, justice in such a society is crude and uncertain. But there is nevertheless a great difference between such a rudimentary form of social life and none at all.

The third weakness of the argument from international anarchy is that it overlooks the limitations of the domestic analogy. States, after all, are very unlike human individuals. Even if it could be contended that government is a necessary condition of order among individual men, there are good reasons for holding that anarchy among states is tolerable to a degree to which among individuals it is not.

We have already noted that, unlike the individual in Hobbes's state of nature, the state does not find its energies so absorbed in the pursuit of security that the life of its members is that of mere brutes. Hobbes himself recognises this when, having observed that persons in sovereign authority are in "a posture of war," he goes on to say that "because they uphold thereby the industry of their subjects, there does not follow from it that misery which accompanies the liberty of particular men." The same sovereigns that find themselves in a state of nature in relation to one another have provided, within their territories, the conditions in which refinements of life can flourish.

Moreover, states are not vulnerable to violent attack to the same degree that individuals are. Spinoza, echoing Hobbes in his assertion that 'two states are in the same relation to one another as two men in the condition of nature,' goes on to add, 'with this exception, that a commonwealth can guard itself against being subjugated by another, as a man in the state of nature cannot do. For, of course, a man is overcome by sleep every day, is often afflicted by disease of body or mind, and is finally prostrated by old age; in addition, he is subject to troubles against which a commonwealth can make itself secure.' One human being in the state of nature cannot make himself secure against violent attack; and this attack carries with it the prospect of sudden death. Groups of human beings organised as states, however, may provide themselves with a means of defence that exists independently of the frailties of any one of them. And armed attack by one state upon another has not brought with it a prospect comparable to the killing of one individual by another. For one man's death may be brought about suddenly in a single act; and once it has occurred it cannot be undone. But war has only occasionally resulted in the physical extinction of the vanquished people.

In modern history it has been possible to take Clausewitz's view that "war is never absolute in its results," and that defeat in it may be "a passing evil which can be remedied." Moreover, war in the past, even if it could in principle lead to the physical extermination of one or both of the belligerent peoples, could not be thought capable of doing so at once in the course of a single act. Clausewitz, in holding that war does not consist of a single instantaneous blow, but always of a succession of separate actions, was drawing attention to something that in the past has always held true and has rendered violence among independent political communities different from violence between individual persons. It is only in the context of nuclear weapons and other recent military technology that it has become pertinent to ask whether war could not now both be "absolute in its results" and "take the form of a single, instantaneous blow," in Clausewitz's understanding of these terms; and whether, therefore, violence does not now confront the state with the same sort of prospect it has always held for the individual.

This difference, that states have been less vulnerable to violent attack by one another than individual men, is reinforced by a further one: that in so far as states have been vulnerable to physical attack, they have not been equally so. Hobbes builds his account of the state of nature on the proposition that 'Nature hath made men so equal, in the faculties of body and mind, [that] the weakest has strength enough to kill the strongest.' It is this equal vulnerability of every man to every other that, in Hobbes's view, renders the condition of anarchy intolerable. But in modern international society there has been a persistent distinction between great powers and small. Great powers have not been vulnerable to violent attack by small powers to the same extent that small powers have been vulnerable to attack by great ones. Once again it is only the spread of nuclear weapons to small states, and the

possibility of a world of many nuclear powers, that raises the question whether in international relations, also, a situation may come about in which 'the weakest has strength enough to kill the strongest.'

The argument, then, that because men cannot form a society without government, sovereign princes or states cannot, breaks down not only because some degree of order can in fact be achieved among individuals in the absence of government, but also because states are unlike individuals, and are more capable of forming an anarchical society. The domestic analogy is no more than an analogy; the fact that states form a society without government reflects features of their situation that are unique.

The Limitations of International Society

We have shown that the modern international system is also an international society, at least in the sense that international society has been one of the elements permanently at work in it; and that the existence of this international society is not as such disproved by the fact of international anarchy. It is important, however, to retain a sense of the limitations of the anarchical international society.

Because international society is no more than one of the basic elements at work in modern international politics, and is always in competition with the elements of a state of war and of transnational solidarity or conflict, it is always erroneous to interpret international events as if international society were the sole or the dominant element. This is the error committed by those who speak or write as if the Concert of Europe, the

League of Nations or the United Nations were the principal factors in international politics in their respective times; as if international law were to be assessed only in relation to the function it has of binding states together, and not also in relation to its function as an instrument of state interest and as a vehicle of transnational purposes; as if attempts to maintain a balance of power were to be interpreted only as endeavours to preserve the system of states, and not also as manoeuvres on the part of particular powers to gain ascendancy; as if great powers were to be viewed only as 'great responsibles' or 'great indispensables,' and not also as great predators; as if wars were to be construed only as attempts to violate the law or to uphold it, and not also simply as attempts to advance the interests of particular states or of transnational groups. The element of international society is real, but the elements of a state of war and of transnational loyalties and divisions are real also, and to reify the first element, or to speak as if it annulled the second and third, is an illusion.

Moreover, the fact that international society provides some element of order in international politics should not be taken as justifying an attitude of complacency about it, or as showing that the arguments of those who are dissatisfied with the order provided by international society are without foundation. The order provided within modern international society is precarious and imperfect. To show that modern international society has provided some degree of order is not to have shown that order in world politics could not be provided more effectively by structures of a quite different kind.

QUESTIONS

1. How does Bull explain the possibility that an international system governed by law has always existed?

2. Is such a world society sustainable under current conditions? Explain.

---

13.   Interdependence and Power

Joseph S. Nye Jr.

In this excerpt, Joseph S. Nye Jr. presents the primary concepts of interdependence using the oil crisis of 1973 as a case in point. He suggests that interdependence is not simply cooperation among nations but a relationship between states characterized by cooperation, dependence, and interaction in a number of different areas. States, as well as other transnational actors, are connected in a global network of

Excerpt pp. 160–170 from *Understanding International Conflicts,* Joseph S. Nye, Jr. © 1993 by Joseph S. Nye, Jr. Reprinted by permission of Addison-Wesley Educational Publishers, Inc.

cooperation and interdependence. This selection is from *Understanding International Conflicts: An Introduction to Theory* (1993).

Joseph S. Nye Jr. is a professor of international politics at Harvard University. His other works include *Nuclear Ethics* (1986) and *Understanding International Conflict* (1993).

Economic interdependence increased rapidly in the postwar period, but it was the 1973 oil crisis that brought economic conflict to center stage. Some people think that interdependence means peace and cooperation, but unfortunately it is not that simple. Conflict goes on, even in a world of interdependence. Because the coalitions are more complex and different forms of power are used, the conflicts are often like playing chess on several boards at the same time. Conflicts in the late twentieth century involve *both* guns and butter. China's Chairman Mao Tse-tung said that power grows out of the barrel of a gun. After the oil crisis of 1973, the world was reminded that power can also grow out of a barrel of oil. Some realists overreacted to the oil crisis of 1973, likening it to events in 1914 and 1939. Hans Morgenthau, a great thinker in the realist tradition, said that 1973 was historically unprecedented because it divorced military power from economic power based on raw materials.

The 1973 oil crisis presents an important question: Why did the most powerful countries in the world allow the transfer of hundreds of billions of dollars to weak states and not use force? Such an event would have been unthinkable in the eighteenth century. Or, in the nineteenth century, the rich countries would have used their superior military power, colonized the troublesome era, and settled the situation on their own terms. What changed in 1973? It was neither a new era of power based on

raw materials and cartels nor a total divorce of military and economic power. Rather, all these factors became intertwined in complex relationships. To understand the changes in world politics, we must consider how interdependence can be a source of power.

THE CONCEPT OF INTERDEPENDENCE

Interdependence is a fuzzy term used in a variety of conflicting ways like other political words such as nationalism or imperialism. Statesmen and analysts have different motives when they use political words. The statesman wants as many people marching behind his or her banner as possible. Political leaders blur meanings and try to create a connotation of a common good: "We are all in the same boat together, therefore we must cooperate, therefore follow me." The analyst, on the other hand, makes distinctions to understand the world better. She distinguishes questions of good and bad from more and less. The analyst may point out the boat we are all in may be heading for one person's port but not another's, or that one person is doing all the rowing while another steers or has a free ride. In other words, interdependence can be used both ideologically as well as analytically, and we should be aware of such different usage. As a political verb, interdependence is conjugated "I depend; you depend; we depend; they rule."

As an analytical word, interdependence refers to situations in which actors or events in different parts of a system affect each other. Simply put, interdependence means mutual dependence. Such a situation is neither good nor bad in itself, and there can be more or less of it. In personal relations, interdependence is summed up by the marriage vow in which each partner is interdependent with another "for richer, for poorer, for better, or for worse." And interdependence among nations sometimes means richer, sometimes poorer, sometimes for better, sometimes for worse. In the eighteenth century, Jean-Jacques Rousseau pointed out that along with interdependence comes friction and conflict. His "solution" was isolation and separation. But this is seldom possible in the modern world. When countries try isolation, like Albania or Myanmar (formerly Burma), it comes at enormous economic cost. It is not easy for nations to divorce the rest of the world.

Sources of Interdependence

Four distinctions illuminate the dimensions of interdependence: its sources, benefits, relative costs, and symmetry. Interdependence can originate in physical (i.e., in nature) or social (economic, political, or perceptual) phenomena. Both are usually present at the same time. The distinction helps to make clear the degree of choice in situations of reciprocal or mutual dependence.

Military interdependence is the mutual dependence that arises from military competition. There is a physical aspect in the weaponry, especially dramatic since the development of nuclear weapons and the resulting possibility of mutually assured destruction. However, there is also an important element of perception involved in interdependence, and a change in perception or policy can reduce the intensity of the military interdependence. Americans lost little sleep over the existence of British or French nuclear weapons because there was no perception that those weapons would ever land on American soil. Similarly, Westerners slept a bit easier in the late 1980s after Gorbachev announced his "new thinking" in Soviet foreign policy. It was not so much the number of Soviet weapons that made the difference, but the change in the perception of Soviet hostility or intent.

Generally speaking, economic interdependence is similar to military interdependence, in that it is the stuff of traditional international politics and has a high degree of social, especially perceptual, origin. Economic interdependence involves policy choices about values and costs. For example, in the early 1970s, there was concern the world's population was outstripping global food supplies. Many countries were buying American grain, which in turn drove up the price of food in American supermarkets. A loaf of bread cost more in the United States because the Indian monsoons failed and because the Soviet Union had mishandled its harvest. In 1973, the United States, in an effort to prevent price rises at home, decided to stop exporting soybeans to Japan. As a result, Japan invested in soybean production in Brazil. A few years later, when supply and demand were better equilibrated, U.S. farmers greatly regretted that embargo because the Japanese were buying their soybeans from a cheaper source in Brazil. Social choices as well as physical shortages affect economic interdependence in the long run. It is always worth considering the long-term perspective when making short-term choices.

Benefits of Interdependence

The benefits of interdependence are sometimes expressed as zero sum and non-zero sum. In a zero-sum situation, your loss is my gain and vice versa. In a positive-sum situation, we both gain; in a negative-sum situation, we both lose. Dividing a pie is zero sum, baking a larger pie is positive sum, and dropping it on the floor is negative sum. Both zero-sum and non-zero-sum aspects are present in mutual dependence.

Some liberal economists tend to think of interdependence only in terms of joint gain, that is, positive-sum situations in which everyone benefits and everyone is better off. Failure to pay attention to the inequality of benefits and the conflicts that arise over the distribution of relative gains causes such analysts to miss the political aspects of interdependence. It is true that both sides can gain from trade, for example, if Japan and Korea trade textiles and television sets, but how will the gains from trade be divided? Even if Japan and Korea are both better off, is Japan a lot better off and Korea only a little better off, or vice versa? The distribution of benefits—who gets how much of the joint gain—is a zero-sum situation in which one side's gain is the other's loss. The result is that there is almost always some political conflict in economic interdependence. Even when there is a larger pie, people can fight over who gets the biggest slices. Even if interdependent countries enjoy a joint gain, there may be conflict over who gets more or less of the joint gain.

Some political analysts make the mistake of thinking that as the world becomes more interdependent, cooperation will replace competition. Their reason is that interdependence creates joint benefits, and those joint benefits encourage cooperation. But economic interdependence can also be used as a weapon—witness the oil crisis of 1973. Indeed, economic interdependence is more effective than force in some cases because it may have more subtle gradations and fewer collateral costs. And in some circumstances, states are less interested in their absolute gain from interdependence than how the relatively greater gains of their rivals might be used to hurt them.

Even ecological interdependence can be used as a weapon, as it was in 1991 when Iraq set fire to Kuwait's oil fields, and released oil into the Persian Gulf. There can also be conflicts over global ecological issues. For example, if global warming occurs, who will win and who will lose? If the temperature of the earth rises on average two degrees centigrade, Maldive Islanders at sea level or Africans who live at the edge of the Sahara would suffer terribly if the islands were submerged or the desert moved southward. But some Siberians or Canadians might be better off. If so, will Siberians or Canadians pay to slow global warming?

Some analysts believe that traditional world politics was always zero sum. But that is misleading about the past. Traditional international politics could be positive sum, depending on the actors' intentions. It made a difference whether Bismarck or Hitler was in charge of Germany. If one party sought aggrandizement, as Hitler did, then indeed politics was zero sum—one side's gain was another's loss. But if all parties wanted stability, there could be joint gain in the balance of power. Conversely, the new politics of economic interdependence has competitive zero-sum aspects as well as cooperative positive-sum aspects.

In the politics of interdependence, the distinction about what is domestic and what is foreign becomes blurred. For example, the soybean situation mentioned earlier involved the domestic issue of controlling inflation at home, as well as American relations with Japan and Brazil. Or to take another example, after Iran's 1979 revolution curtailed oil production, the American government urged citizens to cut their energy consumption by driving 55 mph and turning down thermostats; was that a domestic or a foreign policy issue? Should the United States allow strip mining of coal if the coal is to be exported? Do those who import that coal pay the additional costs that accompany the destruction of the countryside in West Virginia? Interdependence thoroughly mixes domestic and foreign issues, which gives rise to much more complex coalitions, more intricate patterns of conflict, and a different way of distribution of benefits than in the past.

Interdependence also affects domestic politics in a different way. In 1890, a French politician concerned with relative gains needed a policy of holding Germany back. Today a policy of slowing economic growth in Germany is not good for France. Economic interdependence between France and Germany means that the best predictor of whether France is better off economically is when Germany is growing economically. Now it is in the self-interest of the French politicians that Germany do well economically. The classical balance-of-power theory which predicts that one country will act only to keep the other down lest the other gain preponderance does not fit well. In economic interdependence, states are interested in ab-

solute gains as well as gains relative to other states.

Costs of Interdependence

The costs of interdependence can involve short-run sensitivity or long-term vulnerability. *Sensitivity* refers to the amount and rapidity of the effects of dependence; that is, how quickly does change in one part of the system bring about change in another part? For example, in the 1970s, a rumor about a possible exchange rate change led to $2 billion flooding into Germany in one day. In 1987, the New York stock market crashed suddenly because of foreigners' anxieties about U.S. interest rates and what might happen to the price of bonds and stocks. It all happened very quickly; the market was very sensitive to the withdrawal of foreign funds.

A high level of sensitivity, however, is not the same as a high level of vulnerability. *Vulnerability* refers to the relative costs of changing the structure of a system of interdependence. It is the cost of escaping from the system or of changing the rules of the game. The less vulnerable of two countries is not necessarily the less sensitive, but rather the one that would incur lower costs from altering the situation. During the 1973 oil crisis, the United States depended on imported energy for only about 16 percent of its total energy uses. On the other hand, in 1973, Japan depended about 95 percent on imported energy. The United States was sensitive to the Arab oil boycott insofar as prices shot up in 1973, but it was not as vulnerable as Japan was.

Vulnerability involves degree. When the shah of Iran was overthrown in 1979, Iranian oil production was disrupted at a time when demand was high and markets were already tight. The loss of Iran's oil caused the total amount of oil on the world markets to drop by about 5 percent, but that led to a very large increase in oil prices. Markets were sensitive, and shortages of supply were rapidly transformed into higher prices. But Americans could save 5 percent of their energy use simply by turning down their thermostats and driving 55 mph. It appears that the United States was sensitive but not very vulnerable if it could avoid damage by such simple actions.

Vulnerability, however, depends on more than aggregate measures. It also depends on whether a society is capable of responding quickly to change. For example, the United States was less adept at responding to changes in the oil markets than Japan. Furthermore, private actors, large corporations, and speculators in the market may each look at a market situation and decide to hoard supplies because they think shortages are going to grow worse. Their actions will drive the price even higher, because it will make the shortages greater and put more demand on the market. Thus degrees of vulnerability are not quite so simple as they first look.

Vulnerability also depends on whether or not substitutes are available and whether there are diverse sources of supply. In 1970, Lester Brown of the World Watch Institute expressed alarm about the increasing dependence of the United States, and therefore its vulnerability, on imported raw materials. Of 13 basic industrial raw materials, the United States was dependent on imports for nearly 90 percent of aluminum, chromium, manganese, and nickel. By 1985, he predicted the United States would be dependent on imports in 10 of the basic 13. He felt this would lead to a dramatic increase in U.S. vulnerability as well as drastically increasing the strength of the less developed countries that produced those raw materials.

But in the 1980s, raw materials prices went down, not up. What happened to his prediction? In judging vulnerability, Brown failed to consider the alternative sources of raw materials and the diversity of sources of supply that prevented producers from jacking up prices artificially. Moreover, technology develops. Yesterday's waste may become a new resource. Companies now mine discarded tailings because new technology has made it possible to extract copper from ore that was considered depleted years ago. Today's reduced use of copper is also due to the introduction of fiber optic cables made from silicon whose basic origin is sand. Thus projections of U.S. vulnerability to shortages of raw materials went wrong because technology and alternatives were not adequately considered.

Symmetry of Interdependence

Symmetry refers to situations of relatively balanced versus unbalanced dependence. Being less dependent can be a source of power. If two parties are interdependent but one is less dependent than the other, the less dependent party has a source of power as long as both value the interdependent relationship. Manipulating the asymmetries of interdependence can be a source of power in international politics. Analysts who say that interdependence occurs only in situations of equal dependence, define away the most interesting political behavior. Such perfect symmetry is quite rare; so are cases of complete imbalance in which one side is totally dependent and the other is not dependent at all.

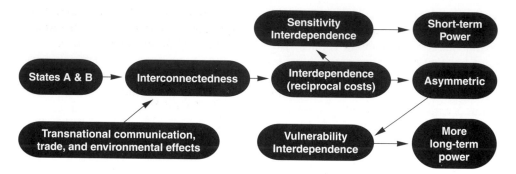

FIGURE 1 *The Dimensions of Interdependence*

Asymmetry is at the heart of the politics of interdependence. (See Figure 1.)

Asymmetry often varies according to different issues. In the 1980s, when the United States cut taxes and raised expenditures, it became dependent on imported Japanese capital to balance its federal government budget. Some argued that this gave Japan tremendous power over the United States. But the other side of the coin was that Japan would hurt itself as well as the United States if it stopped lending to the United States. In addition, Japanese investors who already had large stakes in the United States would have found their investments devalued by the damage done to the American economy if Japan suddenly stopped lending to the United States. Japan's economy was a little over half the size of the American economy, and that meant the Japanese needed the American market for their exports more than vice versa, although both needed each other and both benefited from the interdependence.

Moreover, security was often linked to other issues in the U.S.-Japan relationship. After World War II, Japan followed the policy of a trading state and did not develop a large military capability or gain nuclear weapons. It relied on the Ameri-can security guarantee to balance the power of the Soviet Union and China in the East Asian region. Thus when a dispute seemed to be developing between the United States and Japan over trade in 1990, the Japanese made concessions to prevent weakening the overall security relationship.

When there is asymmetry of interdependence in different issue areas, a state may try to link or unlink issues. If each issue could be thought of as a poker game, and all poker games were played simultaneously, one state might have most of the chips at one table and another state might have most of the chips at another table. Depending on a state's interests and position, it might want to keep the games separate or create linkages between the tables. Therefore, much of the politics of interdependence involves the creation or prevention of linkage. States want to manipulate interdependence in the areas where they are strong and avoid being manipulated in areas where they are relatively weak.

By setting agendas and defining issue areas, international institutions often set the rules for the trade-offs in interdependent relationships. States try to use international institutions to set the rules that affect the transfer of chips among tables. Ironically, international institutions can benefit the weaker players by keeping some of the issues where the poorer states are relatively better endowed separated from the military table where strong states dominate. The danger remains, however, that some players will be strong enough to overturn one or more of the tables. With separate institutions for money, shipping, pollution, and trade, if the militarily strong players are beaten too badly, there is a danger they may try to kick over the other tables. Yet when the United States and Europe were beaten at the oil table in 1973, they did not use their preponderant military force to kick over the oil table because, as we see later, a complex web of linkages held them back.

The largest state does not always win in the manipulation of economic interdependence. If a smaller or weaker state has a greater concern about an issue, it may do quite well. For instance, because the United States accounts for nearly three-quarters of Canada's foreign trade while Canada accounts for about one-quarter of the U.S. foreign trade, Canada is more dependent on the United States than vice versa. Nonetheless, Canada often prevailed in a number of disputes with the United States because Canada was willing to threaten retaliatory actions, such as tariffs and restrictions, that deterred the United States. The Canadians would have suffered much more than the United States if their actions had led to a full dispute, but Canada felt it was better to risk occasional retaliation than to agree to rules that would *always* make them lose. Deterrence via manipulation of economic interdependence is somewhat like nuclear deterrence, in that it rests on a capability for effective damage and credible intentions. Small states can often use their greater intensity and greater credibility to overcome their relative vulnerability in asymmetrical interdependence.

Leadership in the World Economy

By and large, the rules of international economy are set by the largest states. In the nineteenth century, Great Britain was the strongest of the major world economies. In the monetary area, the Bank of England adhered to the gold standard, which set a stable framework for world money. Britain also enforced freedom of the seas for navigation and commerce, and provided a large open market for world trade until 1932. After World War I, Britain was severely weakened by its fight against the kaiser's Germany. The United States became the world's largest economy, but it turned away from international affairs. The largest player in the world economy behaved as if it could still take a free ride rather than provide the leadership its size implied. Some economists believe that the Great Depression of the 1930s was aggravated by bad monetary policy and lack of American leadership. Britain was too weak to maintain an open international economy and the United States was not living up to its new responsibilities.

After World War II, the lessons of the 1930s were on the minds of American statesmen and they set up institutions to maintain an open, international economy. The International Monetary Fund (IMF) lends money, usually to developing countries, to help when they have difficulties with their balance of payments or with paying interest on their debts. The IMF generally conditions its loans on the recipient country reforming its economic policies, for example reducing budget deficits and price subsidies. The International Bank for Reconstruction and Development (the World Bank) lends money to poorer countries for development projects. (There are also regional development banks for Asia, Latin America, Africa, and Eastern Europe.) The General Agreement on Tariffs and Trade (GATT) established rules for liberal trade and has served as the locus for a series of rounds of multilateral negotiations that have lowered trade barriers. The Organization for Economic Cooperation and Development (OECD) serves as a forum for two dozen of the most developed countries to coordinate their international economic policies. Since the mid-1970s, the leaders of the seven largest economies that account for two-thirds of world production have met at annual summit conferences (the Group of Seven) to discuss conditions of the world economy. These institutions helped reinforce government policies that allow rapid growth of private transnational interactions. The result has been a rapid increase in economic interdependence. In most of the period after 1945, trade grew between 3 and 9 percent a year, faster even than the growth of world product. International trade, which represented 4 percent of the U.S. GNP in 1950, tripled to 13 percent of the U.S. GNP by 1990. Large multinational corporations with global strategies became more significant as international investments increased by nearly 10 percent per year.

Nonetheless, there are still problems in managing a transnational economy in a world of separate states. In the 1980s, the United States became a net debtor when it refused to tax itself to pay its bills at home and instead borrowed money from abroad. Some analysts believed that this was setting the scene for a repeat of the 1930s, that the United States would experience decline as Britain did, while Japan becomes the new world economic superpower. They feared the Japanese in the 1990s would have the same free-rider mentality that the Americans had in the 1930s, unwilling to open their markets or maintain international stability. But this need not be the case. The United States need not decline and turn inward. Much will depend on what happens in the relationships of the large economies and the willingness of their governments to cooperate to maintain stability in the international economic system. In any case, the international political and economic system is more complicated and complex. There will be more sectors, more states, more issues, and more private actors involved in the complexity of interdependent relationships.

Realism and Complex Interdependence

What would the world look like if the three key assumptions of realism were reversed? These assumptions are that states are the only significant actors, military force is the dominant instrument, and security is the dominant goal. Reversed, we postulate a different world politics: (1) states are not the only significant actors—transnational actors working across state boundaries are also major actors; (2) force is not the only significant instrument—economic manipulation and the use of international institutions is the dominant instrument; (3) security is not the dominant goal—welfare is the dominant goal. We can label this antirealist world *complex interdependence.* Social scientists call complex interdependence an "ideal type." It is an imaginary concept

FIGURE 2

that does not exist in the real world, but neither does realism perfectly fit the real world. Complex interdependence is a thought experiment that allows us to imagine a different type of world politics.

Both realism and complex interdependence are simple models or ideal types. The real world lies somewhere between the two. We can ask where certain country relationships fit on a spectrum between realism and complex interdependence. The Middle East is closer to the realist end of the spectrum, but relations between the United States and Canada or relations between France and Germany today come much closer to the complex interdependence end of the spectrum. Different politics and different forms of the struggle for power occur depending on where on the spectrum a particular relationship between a set of countries is located. In fact, countries can change their position on the spectrum. In the Cold War the U.S.-Soviet relationship was clearly near the realist end of the spectrum, but with Gorbachev's changes the Soviet-U.S. relationship moved closer to the center between realism and complex interdependence. (See Figure 2.)

QUESTIONS

1. Provide a detailed description of the benefits and costs of interdependence as defined by Nye.

2. Explain the role of the multinational corporation in Nye's thesis, beginning on page 154.

14.   Cooperation and International Regimes

Robert O. Keohane

In this selection, Robert Keohane examines the roles of harmony, cooperation, and discord in the international system and assesses their individual effects on the relationships of nation-states. In this selection, he argues that "cooperation is possible and that it is facilitated by international regimes." Keohane uses the example of trade relations to help explain the effect of interdependence, and how nations either cooperate or an atmosphere of discord is perpetuated. This selection is from his book *After Hegemony: Cooperation and Discord in the World Political Economy* (1984).

Robert Keohane is a professor of political science at Duke University. He is the author of many books, among which is *Power and Interdependence: World Politics in Transition.*

Hegemonic leadership can help to create a pattern of order. Cooperation is not antithetical to hegemony; on the contrary, hegemony depends on a certain kind of asymmetrical cooperation, which successful hegemons support and maintain. . . . Contemporary international economic regimes were constructed under the aegis of the United States after World War II. In accounting for the creation of international regimes, hegemony often plays an important role, even a crucial one.

Yet the relevance of hegemonic cooperation for the future is questionable. . . . The United States is less preponderant in material resources now than it was in the 1950s and early 1960s. Equally important, the United States is less willing than formerly to define its interests in terms complementary to those of Europe and Japan. The Europeans, in particular, are less inclined to defer to American initiatives, nor do they believe so strongly that they must do so in order to obtain essential military protection against the Soviet Union. Thus the subjective elements of American hegemony have been eroded as much as the tangible power resources upon which hegemonic systems rest. But neither the Europeans nor the Japanese are likely to have the capacity to become hegemonic powers themselves in the foreseeable future.[1]

This prospect raises the issue of cooperation "after hegemony." . . . It also leads back to a crucial tension between economics and politics: international coordination of policy seems highly beneficial in an interdependent world economy, but cooperation in world politics is particularly difficult. One way to relax this tension would be to deny the premise that international economic policy coordination is valuable by assuming that international markets will automatically yield optimal results (Corden, 1981). The decisive objection to this argument is that, in the absence of cooperation, governments will interfere in markets unilaterally in pursuit of what they regard as their own interests, whatever liberal economists may say. They will intervene in foreign exchange markets, impose various restrictions on imports, subsidize favored domestic industries, and set prices for commodities such as petroleum (Strange, 1979). Even if one accepted cooperation to maintain free markets, but no other form of policy coordination, the further objection could be raised that economic market failure would be likely to occur (Cooper, 1983, pp. 45–46). Suboptimal outcomes of transactions could result, for a variety of reasons including problems of collective action. It would take an ideological leap of faith to believe that free markets lead necessarily to optimal results.

Rejecting the illusion that cooperation is never valuable in the world political economy, we have to cope with the fact that it is very difficult to organize. One recourse would be to lapse into fatalism—

acceptance of destructive economic conflict as a result of political fragmentation. Although this is a logically tenable position for those who believe in the theory of hegemonic stability, even its most powerful theoretical advocate shies away from its bleak normative implications (Gilpin, 1981). A fatalistic view is not taken here. Without ignoring the difficulties that beset attempts to coordinate policy in the absence of hegemony, this [writer] contends that nonhegemonic cooperation is possible, and that it can be facilitated by international regimes.

In making this argument, I will draw a distinction between the creation of international regimes and their maintenance. . . . When shared interests are sufficiently important and other key conditions are met, cooperation can emerge and regimes can be created without hegemony. Yet this does not imply that regimes can be created easily, much less that contemporary international economic regimes actually came about in this way. . . . I argue that international regimes are easier to maintain than to create, and that recognition of this fact is crucial to understanding why they are valued by governments. Regimes may be maintained, and may continue to foster cooperation, even under conditions that would not be sufficiently benign to bring about their creation. Cooperation is possible after hegemony not only because shared interests can lead to the creation of regimes, but also because the conditions for maintaining existing international regimes are less demanding than those required for creating them. Although hegemony helps to explain the creation of contemporary international regimes, the decline of hegemony does not necessarily lead symmetrically to their decay.

This chapter analyzes the meaning of two key terms: "cooperation" and "international regimes." It distinguishes cooperation from harmony as well as from discord, and it argues for the value of the concept of international regimes as a way of understanding both cooperation and discord. Together the concepts of cooperation and international regimes help us clarify what we want to explain: how do patterns of rule-guided policy coordination emerge, maintain themselves, and decay in world politics?

HARMONY, COOPERATION, AND DISCORD

Cooperation must be distinguished from harmony. Harmony refers to a situation in which actors' policies (pursued in their own self-interest without regard for others) *automatically* facilitate the attainment of others' goals. The classic example of harmony is the hypothetical competitive-market world of the classical economists, in which the Invisible Hand ensures that the pursuit of self-interest by each contributes to the interest of all. In this idealized, unreal world, no one's actions damage anyone else; there are no "negative externalities," in the economists' jargon. Where harmony reigns, cooperation is unnecessary. It may even be injurious, if it means that certain individuals conspire to exploit others. Adam Smith, for one, was very critical of guilds and other conspiracies against freedom of trade (1776/1976). Cooperation and harmony are by no means identical and ought not to be confused with one another.

Cooperation requires that the actions of separate individuals or organizations—which are not in pre-existent harmony—be brought into conformity with one another through a process of negotiation, which is often referred to as "policy coordination." Charles E. Lindblom has defined policy coordination as follows (1965, p. 227):

> A set of decisions is coordinated if adjustments have been made in them, such that the adverse consequences of any one decision for other decisions are to a degree and in some frequency avoided, reduced, or counterbalanced or overweighed.

Cooperation occurs when actors adjust their behavior to the actual or anticipated preferences of others, through a process of policy coordination. To summarize more formally, *intergovernmental cooperation takes place when the policies actually followed by one government are regarded by its partners as facilitating realization of their own objectives, as the result of a process of policy coordination.*

With this definition in mind, we can differentiate among cooperation, harmony, and discord, as illustrated by Figure 1. First, we ask whether actors' policies automatically facilitate the attainment of others' goals. If so, there is harmony: no adjustments need to take place. Yet harmony is rare in world politics. Rousseau sought to account for this rarity when he declared that even two countries guided by the General Will in their internal affairs would come into conflict if they had extensive contact with one another, since the General Will of each would not be general for both. Each would have a partial, self-interested perspective on their mutual interactions. Even for Adam Smith, efforts to ensure state security took precedence over measures to increase national prosperity. In

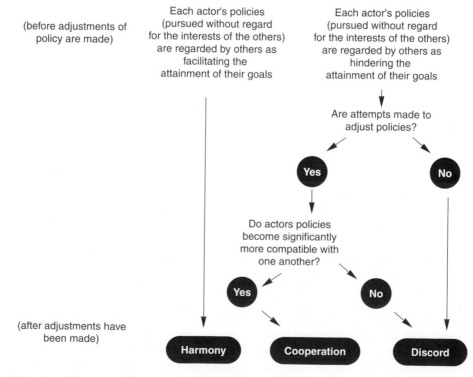

FIGURE 1 *Harmony, Cooperation and Discord*

defending the Navigation Acts, Smith declared: "As defence is of much more importance than opulence, the act of navigation is, perhaps, the wisest of all the commercial regulations of England" (1776/1976, p. 487). Waltz summarizes the point by saying that "in anarchy there is no automatic harmony" (1959, p. 182).

Yet this insight tells us nothing definitive about the prospects for cooperation. For this we need to ask a further question about situations in which harmony does not exist. Are attempts made by actors (governmental or nongovernmental) to adjust their policies to each others' objectives? If no such attempts are made, the result is discord: a situation in which governments regard each others' policies as hindering the attainment of their goals, and hold each other responsible for these constraints.

Discord often leads to efforts to induce others to change their policies; when these attempts meet resistance, policy conflict results. Insofar as these attempts at policy adjustment succeed in making policies more compatible, however, cooperation ensues. The policy coordination that leads to cooperation need not involve bargaining or negotiation at all. What Lindblom calls "adaptive" as opposed to "manipulative" adjustment can take place: one country may shift its policy in the direction of another's preferences without regard for the effect of its action on the other state, defer to the other country, or partially shift its policy in order to avoid adverse consequences for its partner. Or nonbargained manipulation—such as one actor confronting another with a *fait accompli*—may occur (Lindblom, 1965, pp. 33–34 and ch. 4). Frequently, of course, negotiation and bargaining indeed take place, often accompanied by other actions that are designed to induce others to adjust their policies to one's own. Each government pursues what it perceives as its self-interest, but looks for bargains that can benefit all parties to the deal, though not necessarily equally.

Harmony and cooperation are not usually distinguished from one another so clearly. Yet, in the study of world politics, they should be. Harmony is apolitical. No communication is necessary, and no influence need be exercised. Cooperation, by contrast, is highly political: somehow, patterns of behavior must be altered. This change may be accomplished through negative as well as positive inducements. Indeed, studies of international crises, as well as game-theoretic experiments and simulations, have shown that under a variety of conditions strategies that involve threats and punishments as well as promises and rewards are more effective in attaining cooperative outcomes than those that rely entirely on persuasion and the force of good example (Axelrod, 1981, 1984; Lebow, 1981; Snyder and Diesing, 1977).

Cooperation therefore does not imply an absence of conflict. On the contrary, it is typically mixed with conflict and reflects partially successful efforts to overcome conflict, real or potential. Cooperation takes place only in situations in which actors perceive that their policies are actually or potentially in conflict, not where there is harmony. Cooperation should not be viewed as the absence of conflict, but rather as a reaction to conflict or potential conflict. Without the specter of conflict, there is no need to cooperate.

The example of trade relations among friendly countries in a liberal international political economy may help to illustrate this crucial point. A naive observer, trained only to appreciate the overall welfare benefits of trade, might assume that trade relations would be harmonious: consumers in importing countries benefit from cheap foreign goods and increased competition, and producers can increasingly take advantage of the division of labor as their export markets expand. But harmony does not normally ensue. Discord on trade issues may prevail because governments do not even seek to reduce the adverse consequences of their own policies for others, but rather strive in certain respects to increase the severity of those effects. Mercantilist governments have sought in the twentieth century as well as the seventeenth to manipulate foreign trade, in conjunction with warfare, to damage each other economically and to gain productive resources themselves (Wilson, 1957; Hirschman, 1945/1980). Governments may desire "positional goods," such as high status (Hirsch, 1976), and may therefore resist even mutually beneficial cooperation if it helps others more than themselves. Yet even when neither power nor positional motivations are present, and when all participants would benefit in the aggregate from liberal trade, discord tends to predominate over harmony as the initial result of independent governmental action.

This occurs even under otherwise benign conditions because some groups or industries are forced to incur adjustment costs as changes in comparative advantage take place. Governments often respond to the ensuing demands for protection by attempting, more or less effectively, to cushion the burdens of adjustment for groups and industries that are politically influential at home. Yet unilateral measures to this effect almost always impose adjustment costs abroad, and discord continually threatens. Governments enter into international negoti-

ations in order to reduce the conflict that would otherwise result. Even substantial potential common benefits do not create harmony when state power can be exercised on behalf of certain interests and against others. In world politics, harmony tends to vanish: attainment of the gains from pursuing complementary policies depends on cooperation.

Observers of world politics who take power and conflict seriously should be attracted to this way of defining cooperation, since my definition does not relegate cooperation to the mythological world of relations among equals in power. Hegemonic cooperation is not a contradiction in terms. Defining cooperation in contrast to harmony should, I hope, lead readers with a Realist orientation to take cooperation in world politics seriously rather than to dismiss it out of hand. To Marxists who also believe in hegemonic power theories, however, even this definition of cooperation may not seem to make it relevant to the contemporary world political economy. From this perspective, mutual policy adjustments cannot possibly resolve the contradictions besetting the system because they are attributable to capitalism rather than to problems of coordination among egoistic actors lacking common government. Attempts to resolve these contradictions through international cooperation will merely transfer issues to a deeper and even more intractable level. Thus it is not surprising that Marxian analyses of the international political economy have, with few exceptions, avoided sustained examinations of the conditions under which cooperation among major capitalist countries can take place. Marxists see it as more important to expose relationships of exploitation and conflict between major capitalist powers on the one hand and the masses of people in the periphery of world capitalism on the other. And, from a Leninist standpoint, to examine the conditions for international cooperation without first analyzing the contradictions of capitalism, and recognizing the irreconcilability of conflicts among capitalist countries, is a bourgeois error.

This is less an argument than a statement of faith. Since sustained international coordination of macroeconomic policies has never been tried, the statement that it would merely worsen the contradictions facing the system is speculative. In view of the lack of evidence for it, such a claim could even be considered rash. Indeed, one of the most perceptive Marxian writers of recent years, Stephen Hymer (1972), recognized explicitly that capitalists face problems of collective action and argued that they were seeking, with at least temporary prospects of success, to overcome them. As he recognized, any success in internationalizing capital could pose grave threats to socialist aspirations and, at the very least, would shift contradictions to new points of tension. Thus even were we to agree that the fundamental issue is posed by the contradictions of capitalism rather than the tensions inherent in a state system, it would be worthwhile to study the conditions under which cooperation is likely to occur.

INTERNATIONAL REGIMES AND COOPERATION

One way to study cooperation and discord would be to focus on particular actions as the units of analysis. This would require the systematic compilation of a data set composed of acts that could be regarded as comparable and coded according to the degree of cooperation that they reflect. Such a strategy has some attractive features. The problem with it, however, is that instances of cooperation and discord could all too easily be isolated from the context of beliefs and behavior within which they are embedded. This [writer] does not view cooperation atomistically as a set of discrete, isolated acts, but rather seeks to understand patterns of cooperation in the world political economy. Accordingly, we need to examine actors' expectations about future patterns of interaction, their assumptions about the proper nature of economic arrangements, and the kinds of political activities they regard as legitimate. That is, we need to analyze cooperation within the context of international institutions, broadly defined . . . in terms of practices and expectations. Each act of cooperation or discord affects the beliefs, rules, and practices that form the context for future actions. Each act must therefore be interpreted as embedded within a chain of such acts and their successive cognitive and institutional residues.

This argument parallels Clifford Geertz's discussion of how anthropologists should use the concept of culture to interpret the societies they investigate. Geertz sees culture as the "webs of significance" that people have created for themselves. On their surface, they are enigmatical; the observer has to interpret them so that they make sense. Culture, for Geertz, "is a context, something within which [social events] can be intelligibly described" (1973, p. 14). It makes little sense to describe naturalistically what goes on at a Balinese cock-fight unless one understands the meaning of the event for Balinese culture. There is not a world culture in the fullest sense, but even in world politics, human beings spin webs of significance. They develop implicit standards for behavior, some of which emphasize the principle of sovereignty and legitimize the pursuit of self-interest, while others rely on quite different principles. Any act of cooperation or apparent cooperation needs to be interpreted within the context of related actions, and of prevailing expectations and shared beliefs, before its meaning can be properly understood. Fragments of political behavior become comprehensible when viewed as part of a larger mosaic.

The concept of international regime not only enables us to describe patterns of cooperation; it also helps to account for both cooperation and discord. Although regimes themselves depend on conditions that are conducive to interstate agreements, they may also facilitate further efforts to coordinate policies. . . . To understand international cooperation, it is necessary to comprehend how institutions and rules not only reflect, but also affect, the facts of world politics.

Defining and Identifying Regimes

When John Ruggie introduced the concept of international regimes into the international politics literature in 1975, he defined a regime as "a set of mutual expectations, rules and regulations, plans, organizational energies and financial commitments, which have been accepted by a group of states" (p. 570). More recently, a collective definition, worked out at a conference on the subject, defined international regimes as "sets of implicit or explicit principles, norms, rules and decision-making procedures around which actors' expectations converge in a given area of international relations. Principles are beliefs of fact, causation, and rectitude. Norms are standards of behavior defined in terms of

rights and obligations. Rules are specific prescriptions or proscriptions for action. Decision-making procedures are prevailing practices for making and implementing collective choice" (Krasner, 1983, p. 2).

This definition provides a useful starting-point for analysis, since it begins with the general conception of regimes as social institutions and explicates it further. The concept of norms, however, is ambiguous. It is important that we understand norms in this definition simply as standards of behavior defined in terms of rights and obligations. Another usage would distinguish norms from rules and principles by stipulating that participants in a social system regard norms, but not rules and principles, as morally binding regardless of considerations of narrowly defined self-interest. But to include norms, thus defined, in a definition of necessary regime characteristics would be to make the conception of regimes based strictly on self-interest a contradiction in terms. Since this [writer] regards regimes as largely based on self-interest, I will maintain a definition of norms simply as standards of behavior, whether adopted on grounds of self-interest or otherwise. Only [later] will the possibility again be taken seriously that some regimes may contain norms and principles justified on the basis of values extending beyond self-interest, and regarded as obligatory on moral grounds by governments.

The principles of regimes define, in general, the purposes that their members are expected to pursue. For instance, the principles of the postwar trade and monetary regimes have emphasized the value of open, nondiscriminatory patterns of international economic transactions; the fundamental principle of the nonproliferation regime is that the spread of nuclear weapons is dangerous. Norms contain somewhat clearer injunctions to members about legitimate and illegitimate behavior, still defining responsibilities and obligations in relatively general terms. For instance, the norms of the General Agreement on Tariffs and Trade (GATT) do not require that members resort to free trade immediately, but incorporate injunctions to members to practice nondiscrimination and reciprocity and to move toward increased liberalization. Fundamental to the nonproliferation regime is the norm that members of the regime should not act in ways that facilitate nuclear proliferation.

The rules of a regime are difficult to distinguish from its norms; at the margin, they merge into one another. Rules are, however, more specific: they indicate in more detail the specific rights and obligations of members. Rules can be altered more easily than principles or norms, since there may be more than one set of rules that can attain a given set of purposes. Finally, at the same level of specificity as rules, but referring to procedures rather than substances, the decisionmaking procedures of regimes provide ways of implementing their principles and altering their rules.

An example from the field of international monetary relations may be helpful. The most important principle of the international balance-of-payments regime since the end of World War II has been that of liberalization of trade and payments. A key norm of the regime has been the injunction to states not to manipulate their exchange rates unilaterally for national advantage. Between 1958 and 1971 this norm was realized through pegged exchange rates and procedures for consultation in the event of change, supplemented with a variety of devices

to help governments avoid exchange-rate changes through a combination of borrowing and internal adjustment. After 1973 governments have subscribed to the same norm, although it has been implemented more informally and probably less effectively under a system of floating exchange rates. Ruggie (1983b) has argued that the abstract principle of liberalization, subject to constraints imposed by the acceptance of the welfare state, has been maintained throughout the postwar period: "embedded liberalism" continues, reflecting a fundamental element of continuity in the international balance-of-payments regime. The norm of nonmanipulation has also been maintained, even though the specific rules of the 1958-71 system having to do with adjustment have been swept away.

The concept of international regime is complex because it is defined in terms of four distinct components: principles, norms, rules, and decisionmaking procedures. It is tempting to select one of these levels of specificity—particularly, principles and norms or rules and procedures—as *the* defining characteristic of regimes (Krasner, 1983; Ruggie, 1983b). Such an approach, however, creates a false dichotomy between principles on the one hand and rules and procedures on the other. As we have noted, at the margin norms and rules cannot be sharply distinguished from each other. It is difficult if not impossible to tell the difference between an "implicit rule" of broad significance and a well-understood, relatively specific operating principle. Both rules and principles may affect expectations and even values. In a strong international regime, the linkages between principles and rules are likely to be tight. Indeed, it is precisely the linkages among principles, norms, and rules that give regimes their legitimacy. Since rules, norms, and principles are so closely intertwined, judgments about whether changes in rules constitute changes *of* regime or merely changes *within* regimes necessarily contain arbitrary elements.

Principles, norms, rules, and procedures all contain injunctions about behavior: they prescribe certain actions and proscribe others. They imply obligations, even though these obligations are not enforceable through a hierarchical legal system. It clarifies the definition of regime, therefore, to think of it in terms of injunctions of greater or lesser specificity. Some are far-reaching and extremely important. They may change only rarely. At the other extreme, injunctions may be merely technical, matters of convenience that can be altered without great political or economic impact. In-between are injunctions that are both specific enough that violations of them are in principle identifiable and that changes in them can be observed, and sufficiently significant that changes in them make a difference for the behav-ior of actors and the nature of the international political economy. It is these intermediate injunctions—politically consequential but specific enough that violations and changes can be identified—that I take as the essence of international regimes.[2]

A brief examination of international oil regimes, and their injunctions, may help us clarify this point. The pre-1939 international oil regime was dominated by a small number of international firms and contained explicit injunctions about where and under what conditions companies could produce oil, and where and how they should market it. The rules of the Red Line and Achnacarry or "As-Is" agreements of 1928 reflected an "anti-competitive ethos": that is, the basic principle that competition was destructive to the system and the norm that firms should not engage in it (Turner, 1978, p. 30). This principle and this norm both persisted after World War II, although an intergovernmental regime with explicit rules was not established, owing to the failure of the Anglo-American Petroleum Agreement. . . . Injunctions against price-cutting were reflected more in the practices of companies than in formal rules. Yet expectations and practices of major actors were strongly affected by these injunctions, and in this sense the criteria for a regime—albeit a weak one—were met. As governments of producing countries became more assertive, however, and as formerly domestic independent companies entered international markets, these arrangements collapsed; after the mid-to-late 1960s, there was no regime for the issue-area as a whole, since no injunctions could be said to be accepted as obligatory by all influential actors. Rather, there was a "tug of war" (Hirschman, 1981) in which all sides resorted to self-help. The Organization of Petroleum Exporting Countries (OPEC) sought to create a producers' regime based on rules for prorationing oil production, and consumers established an emergency oil-sharing system in the new International Energy Agency to counteract the threat of selective embargoes.

If we were to have paid attention only to the principle of avoiding competition, we would have seen continuity: whatever the dominant actors, they have always sought to cartelize the industry one way or another. But to do so would be to miss the main point, which is that momentous changes have occurred. At the other extreme, we could have fixed our attention on very specific particular arrangements, such as the various joint ventures of the 1950s and 1960s or the specific provisions for controlling output tried by OPEC after 1973, in which case we would have observed a pattern of continual flux. The significance of the most important events—the demise of old cartel arrangements, the undermining of the international majors' positions in the 1960s, and the rise of producing governments to a position of influence in the 1970s—could have been missed. Only by focusing on the intermediate level of relatively specific but politically consequential injunctions, whether we call them rules, norms, or principles, does the concept of regime help us identify major changes that require explanation.

As our examples of money and oil suggest, we regard the scope of international regimes as corresponding, in general, to the boundaries of issue-areas, since governments establish regimes to deal with problems that they regard as so closely linked that they should be dealt with together. Issue-areas are best defined as sets of issues that are in fact dealt with in common negotiations and by the same, or closely coordinated, bureaucracies, as opposed to issues that are dealt with separately and in uncoordinated fashion. Since issue-areas depend on actors' perceptions and behavior rather than on inherent qualities of the subject-matters, their boundaries change gradually over time. Fifty years ago, for instance, there was no oceans issue-area, since particular questions now grouped under that heading were dealt with separately; but there was an international monetary issue-area even then (Keohane and Nye, 1977, ch. 4). Twenty years ago trade in cotton textiles had an international regime of its own—the Long-Term Agreement on Cotton Textiles—and was treated separately from trade in synthetic fibers (Aggarwal, 1981). Issue-areas are defined and redefined by changing patterns of human intervention; so are international regimes.

Self-Help and International Regimes

The injunctions of international regimes rarely affect economic transactions directly: state institutions, rather than international organizations, impose tariffs and quotas, intervene in foreign exchange markets, and manipulate oil prices through taxes and subsidies. If we think about the impact of the principles, norms, rules, and decision-making procedures of regimes, it becomes clear that insofar as they have any effect at all, it must be exerted on national controls, and especially on the specific interstate agreements that affect the exercise of national controls (Aggarwal, 1981). International regimes must be distinguished from these specific agreements; . . . a major function of regimes is to facilitate the making of specific cooperative agreements among governments.

Superficially, it could seem that since international regimes affect national controls, the regimes are of superior importance—just as federal laws in the United States frequently override state and local legislation. Yet this would be a fundamentally misleading conclusion. In a well-ordered society, the units of action—individuals in classic liberal thought—live together within a framework of constitutional principles that define property rights, establish who may control the state, and specify the conditions under which subjects must obey governmental regulations. In the United States, these principles establish the supremacy of the federal government in a number of policy areas, though not in all. But world politics is decentralized rather than hierarchic: the prevailing principle of sovereignty means that states are subject to no superior government (Ruggie, 1983a). The resulting system is sometimes referred to as one of "self-help" (Waltz, 1979).

Sovereignty and self-help mean that the principles and rules of international regimes will necessarily be weaker than in domestic society. In a civil society, these rules "specify terms of exchange" within the framework of constitutional principles (North, 1981, p. 203). In world politics, the principles, norms, and rules of regimes are necessarily fragile because they risk coming into conflict with the principle of sovereignty and the associated norm of self-help. They may promote cooperation, but the fundamental basis of order on which they would rest in a well-ordered society does not exist. They drift around without being tied to the solid anchor of the state.

Yet even if the principles of sovereignty and self-help limit the degree of confidence to be placed in international agreements, they do not render cooperation impossible. Orthodox theory itself relies on mutual interests to explain forms of cooperation that are used by states as instruments of competition. According to balance-of-power theory, cooperative endeavors such as political-military alliances necessarily form in self-help systems (Waltz, 1979). Acts of cooperation are accounted for on the grounds that mutual interests are sufficient to enable states to overcome their suspicions of one another. But since even orthodox theory relies on mutual interests, its advocates are on weak ground in objecting to interpretations of system-

wide cooperation along these lines. There is no logical or empirical reason why mutual interests in world politics should be limited to interests in combining forces against adversaries. As economists emphasize, there can also be mutual interests in securing efficiency gains from voluntary exchange or oligopolistic rewards from the creation and division of rents resulting from the control and manipulation of markets.

International regimes should not be interpreted as elements of a new international order "beyond the nation-state." They should be comprehended chiefly as arrangements motivated by self-interest: as components of systems in which sovereignty remains a constitutive principle. This means that, as Realists emphasize, they will be shaped largely by their most powerful members, pursuing their own interests. But regimes can also affect state interests, for the notion of self-interest is itself elastic and largely subjective. Perceptions of self-interest depend both on actors' expectations of the likely consequences that will follow from particular actions and on their fundamental values. Regimes can certainly affect expectations and may affect values as well. Far from being contradicted by the view that international behavior is shaped largely by power and interests, the concept of international regime is consistent both with the importance of differential power and with a sophisticated view of self-interest. Theories of regimes can incorporate Realist insights about the role of power and interest, while also indicating the inadequacy of theories that define interests so narrowly that they fail to take the role of institutions into account.

Regimes not only are consistent with self-interest but may under some conditions even be necessary to its effective pursuit. They facilitate the smooth operation of decentralized international political systems and therefore perform an important function for states. In a world political economy characterized by growing interdependence, they may become increasingly useful for governments that wish to solve common problems and pursue complementary purposes without subordinating themselves to hierarchical systems of control.

CONCLUSIONS

In this chapter international cooperation has been defined as a process through which policies actually followed by governments come to be regarded by their partners as facilitating realization of their own objectives, as the result of policy coordination. Cooperation involves mutual adjustment and can only arise from conflict or potential conflict. It must therefore be distinguished from harmony. Discord, which is the opposite of harmony, stimulates demands for policy adjustments, which can either lead to cooperation or to continued, perhaps intensified, discord.

Since international regimes reflect patterns of cooperation and discord over time, focusing on them leads us to examine long-term patterns of behavior, rather than treating acts of cooperation as isolated events. Regimes consist of injunctions at various levels of generality, ranging from principles to norms to highly specific rules and decisionmaking procedures. By investigating the evolution of the norms and rules of a regime over time, we can use the concept of international regime both to explore continuity and to investigate change in the world political economy.

From a theoretical standpoint, regimes can be viewed as intermediate factors, or "intervening variables," between fundamental characteristics of world politics such as the international distribution of power on the one hand and the behavior of states and nonstate actors such as multinational corporations on the other. The concept of international regime helps us account for cooperation and discord. To understand the impact of regimes, it is not necessary to posit idealism on the part of actors in world politics. On the contrary, the norms and rules of regimes can exert an effect on behavior even if they do not embody common ideals but are used by self-interested states and corporations engaging in a process of mutual adjustment.

NOTES

1. Historically hegemonies have usually arisen only after major wars. The two principal modern powers that could be considered hegemonic leaders—Britain after 1815 and the United States after 1945—both emerged victorious from world conflicts. I am assuming, in regarding hegemony as unlikely in the foreseeable future, that any world war would have such disastrous consequences that no country would emerge as hegemonic over a world economy resembling that of the present. For a discussion of the cycle of hegemony, see Gilpin (1981) and Modelski (1978 and 1982).
2. Some authors have defined "regime" as equivalent to the conventional concept of international system. For instance, Puchala and Hopkins (1983) claim that "a regime exists in every substantive issue-area in international relations where there is discernibly patterned behavior" (p. 63). To adopt this definition would be to make either "system" or "regime" a redundant term. At the opposite extreme, the concept of regime could be limited to situations with

genuine normative content, in which governments followed regime rules *instead of* pursuing their own self-interests when the two conflicted. If this course were chosen, the concept of regime would be just another way of expressing ancient "idealist" sentiments in international relations. The category of regime would become virtually empty. This dichotomy poses a false choice between using "regime" as a new label for old patterns and defining regimes as utopias. Either strategy would make the term irrelevant.

QUESTIONS

1. Provide a detailed explanation of the effects of harmony, cooperation, and discord on the international system.

2. How does Keohane's view of interdependence differ from that of Robert Gilpin's view in "War and Change in World Politics" (page 88)?

LIBERAL PERSPECTIVE OF SEPTEMBER 11

15.   The Globalization of Informal Violence, Theories of World Politics, and "the Liberalism of Fear"

Robert O. Keohane

Robert O. Keohane discusses how the events of September 11, 2001, have altered our assumptions about the nature of national security. Keohane applies his theories of interdependence and power to place recent events in a larger theoretical context. He also offers a new neutral phrase, "informal violence," to replace the term *terrorism* because the latter term is burdened with such negative connotations.

Robert Keohane is a professor of political science at Duke University. He is the author of many books, among which is *Power and Interdependence: World Politics in Transition.*

The attacks on the United States on September 11, 2001, have incalculable consequences for domestic politics and world affairs. Reliable predictions about these consequences are impossible. However, it may be worthwhile, even at this early point, to reflect on what these acts of violence reveal about the adequacy of our theories of world politics. In what respects have our assumptions and our

Reprinted by permission of the author.

analytical models helped us to understand these events, and responses to them? And in what ways have we been misled by our theories?

In this short article, I will not attempt to be comprehensive. Instead, I will focus instead on specific issues on which my commentary may be of some value, without presuming that these are the most important issues to address. For instance, the attacks of September 11 reveal that all mainstream theories of world politics are relentlessly secular with respect to motivation. They ignore the impact of religion, despite the fact that world-shaking political movements have so often been fueled by religious fervor. None of them takes very seriously the human desire to dominate or to hate—both so strong in history and in classical realist thought. Most of them tend to assume that the world is run by those whom Joseph Schumpeter (1950 [1942]: 137) called "rational and unheroic" members of the bourgeoisie. After September 11 we need also to keep in mind another motivation: the belief, as expressed by Osama bin Laden, that terrorism against "infidels" will assure one "a supreme place in heaven."[1] However, since I have few insights into religious motivations in world politics, I will leave this subject to those who are more qualified to address it.

In the next section of this article I define the phrase, "the globalization of informal violence." In referring to a general category of action, I substitute this phrase for "terrorism," since the latter concept has such negative connotations that it is very difficult to define in an analytically neutral and consistent way that commands general acceptance.[2] Even as the United Nations Security Council has passed resolutions against terrorism, it has been unable to define the term. Since everyone is against terrorism, the debate shifts to its definition, as each party seeks to define its enemy's acts, but not its own, as terrorist. Nevertheless, deliberately targeted surprise attacks on arbitrarily chosen civilians, designed to frighten other people, are clearly acts of terror. The attacks on the World Trade Center of September 11, 2001, were therefore terrorist acts and I refer to them as such.

This paper has three themes. First, the events of September 11 illustrate starkly how our assumptions about security are conceived in terms of increasingly obsolescent views of geographical space. Secondly, the globalization of informal violence can be analyzed by exploring patterns of asymmetrical interdependence and their implications for power. Thirdly, United States responses to the attacks tell us quite a bit about the role of multilateral institutions in contemporary world politics.

My argument is that our theories provide important components of an adequate post-September 11 conceptualization of world politics, but that we need to alter some of our assumptions in order to rearrange these components into a viable theoretical framework. Effective wielding of large-scale violence by non-state actors reflects new patterns of asymmetrical interdependence, and calls into question some of our assumptions about geographical space as a barrier. Responses to these actions reveal the significance of international institutions as well as the continuing central role of states. In thinking about these issues, students of world politics can be usefully reminded of Judith N. Shklar's concept of the "liberalism of fear," and her argument that the most basic function of a liberal state is to protect its citizens from the fear of cruelty.

1. THE GLOBALIZATION OF INFORMAL VIOLENCE AND THE RECONCEPTUALIZATION OF SPACE

The various definitions of globalization in social science all converge on the notion that human activities across regions and continents are being increasingly linked together, as a result both of technological and social change (Held et al.: 15). Globalism as a state of affairs has been defined as "a state of the world involving networks of interdependence at multicontinental distances, linked through flows of capital and goods, information and ideas, people and force, as well as environmentally and biologically relevant substances" (Keohane and Nye 2001: 229).

When globalism is characterized as multidimensional, as in these definitions, the expansion of terrorism's global reach is an instance of globalization (Held et al. 1999: 80; Keohane and Nye 2001: 237). Often, globalism and globalization have been defined narrowly as economic integration on a global scale; but whatever appeal such a definition may have had, it has surely disappeared after September 11. To adopt it would be to imply that globalized informal violence, which takes advantage of modern technologies of communication, transportation, explosives, and potentially biology, somehow threatens to *hinder* or *reduce* the *level* of globalism. But like military technology between 1914 and 1945, globalized informal violence strengthens one dimension of globalism—the networks through which means of violence flow—while potentially weakening globalism along other dimensions, such as economic and social exchange. As in the past, not all aspects of globalization go together.

I define informal violence as violence by non-state actors, capitalizing on secrecy and surprise to inflict great harm with small material capabilities. Such violence is "informal" because it is not wielded by formal state institutions and it is typically not announced in advance, as in a declaration of war. Such violence becomes globalized when the networks of non-state actors operate on an intercontinental basis, so that acts of force in one society can be initiated and controlled from very distant points of the globe.

The implications of the globalization of *formal* violence were profound for traditional conceptions of foreign policy in an earlier generation, particularly in the United States, which had so long been insulated by distance from invasion and major direct attack. The great expositors of classical realist theories of foreign policy in the United States, such as Walter Lippmann, began with the premise that defense of the "continental homeland" is "a universally recognized vital interest." Before World War II, threats to the homeland could only stem from other states that secured territory contiguous to that of the United States or that controlled ocean approaches to it. Hence the Monroe Doctrine of 1823 was the cornerstone of American national security policy. As Lippmann recognized in 1943, changes in the technologies of formal violence meant that security policy needed to be more ambitious: the United States would have to maintain coalitions with other great powers that would "form a combination of indisputably preponderant power" (Lippmann 1943: 88, 101). Nevertheless, Lippmann was able to retain a key traditional concept: that of a geographically defined defensive perimeter, which can be thought of as a set of concentric circles. If the United States were to control not only its own area but the circle surrounding that area, comprising littoral regions of Europe and Asia, its homeland would be secure.

The American strategists of the 1950s —led by Bernard Brodie, Thomas Schelling, and Albert Wohlstetter—had to rethink the concept of a defensive perimeter, as intercontinental ballistic missiles reduced the significance of distance: that is, as formal violence became globalized. John Herz (1959: 107–108) argued that nuclear weapons forced students of international politics to rethink sovereignty, territoriality, and the protective function of the state:

> "With the advent of the atomic weapon, whatever remained of the impermeability of states seems to have gone for good. . . Mencius, in ancient China, when asked for guidance in matters of defense and foreign policy by the ruler of a small state, is said to have counseled: 'dig deeper your moats; build higher your walls; guard them along with your people.' This remained the classical posture up to our age, when a Western sage, Bertrand Russell, could still, even in the interwar period, define power as a force radiating from one center and diminishing with the distance from that center until it finds an equilibrium with that of similar geographically anchored units. Now that power can destroy power from center to center everything is different."

September 11 signifies that informal violence has become globalized, just as formal, state-controlled violence became globalized, for the superpowers, during the 1950s. The globalization of informal violence was not *created* by September 11. Indeed, earlier examples, extending back to piracy in the 17th century, can be easily found. But the significance of globalization—of violence as well as economically and socially—is not its absolute newness but its increasing magnitude as a result of sharp declines in the costs of global communications and transportation (Keohane and Nye 2001: 243–45).

Contemporary theorists of world politics face a challenge similar to that of this earlier generation: to understand the nature of world politics, and its connections to domestic politics, when what Herz called the "hard shell" of the state (Herz 1959: 22) has been shattered. Geographical space, which has been seen as a natural *barrier* and a locus for human barriers, now must be seen as a *carrier* as well.

The corollary to the barrier conception of geographical space was scorn for the geopolitical significance of weak countries, without nuclear weapons, far from the defensive perimeter, consigned to "the obscurity that they justly deserve." One of the finest hours of American realism was its opposition to the war in Vietnam on just these grounds. Walter Lippmann and Hans J. Morgenthau opposed the war not for moralistic reasons, but because of Vietnam's unimportance to the national interests of the United States. For Lippmann, the key to a successful foreign policy is achieving a "balance, with a comfortable surplus of power in reserve, [between] the nation's commitment and the nation's power" (Lippmann 1943: 9). Going abroad in search of monsters to destroy upset that balance.

The globalization of informal violence, carried out by networks of non-state actors, defined by commitments rather than by territory, has profoundly changed these fundamental foreign policy assumptions.[3] On traditional grounds of national interest, Afghanistan should be one of the least important places in the world for American foreign policy—and until the Soviet invasion of 1979, and again after the collapse of the Soviet Union in 1991 until September 11, the United States all but ignored it. Yet in October 2001 it became the theatre of war. Globalization means, among other things, that threats of violence to our homeland can occur from anywhere. The barrier conception of geographical space, already anachronistic with respect to thermonuclear war and called into question by earlier acts of globalized informal violence, was finally shown to be thoroughly obsolete on September 11.[4]

2. INTERDEPENDENCE AND POWER

Another way to express the argument made above is that networks of interdependence, involving transmission of informal violence, have now taken a genuinely global form. Using this language helps us to see the relevance for the globalization of informal violence of the literature on interdependence and power, which was originally developed to understand international political economy. In that literature, interdependence is conceptualized as mutual dependence, and power is conceptualized in terms of *asymmetrical, interdependence.*[5] This literature has also long been clear that "military power dominates economic power in the sense that economic means alone are likely to be ineffective against the serious use of military force" (Keohane and Nye 2001: 14).

September 11 revealed how much the United States could be hurt by informal violence, to an extent that had been anticipated by some government reports but that had not been incorporated into the plans of the government.[6] The long-term vulnerability of the United States is not entirely clear, but the availability of

means of mass destruction, the extent of hatred for the United States, and the ease of entering the United States from almost anywhere in the world, all suggest that vulnerability may be quite high.

If the United States were facing a territorial state with conventional objectives, this vulnerability might not be a source of worry. After all, the United States has long been much more vulnerable, in technological terms, to a nuclear attack from Russia. But the United States was not *asymmetrically vulnerable.* On the contrary, the United States either had superior nuclear capability or "mutual assured destruction" (MAD) kept vulnerability more or less symmetrical. Russia has controlled great *force,* but has not acquired power over the United States from its arsenal.

With respect to terrorism, however, two asymmetries, which do not normally characterize relationships between states, favored wielders of informal violence in September 2001 First there was an *asymmetry of information.* It seems paradoxical that an "information society" such as that of the contemporary United States would be at an informational disadvantage with respect to networks of individuals whose communications seem to occur largely through hand-written messages and face-to-face contacts. But an information society is also an open society. Potential terrorists had good information about their targets, while before September 11 the United States had poor information about the identity and location of terrorist networks within the United States and other western societies. Perhaps equally important, the United States was unable coherently to process the information that its various agencies had gathered. Secondly, there is an *asymmetry in beliefs.* Some of Osama bin Laden's followers apparently believed that they would be rewarded in the afterlife for committing suicidal attacks on civilians. Others were duped into participating in the attacks without being told of their suicidal purpose. Clearly, the suicidal nature of the attacks made them more difficult to prevent and magnified their potential destructive power. Neither volunteering for suicide missions nor deliberately targeting civilians is consistent with secular beliefs widely shared in the societies attacked by al-Qaeda.

The United States and its allies have enormous advantages in resources, including military power, economic resources, political influence, and technological capabilities. Furthermore, communications media, largely based in the West, give greater weight to the voices of people in the wealthy democracies than to those of the dispossessed in developing countries. Hence the asymmetries in information and beliefs that I have mentioned are, in a sense, exceptional. They do not confer a permanent advantage on the wielders of informal violence. Yet they were sufficient to give the terrorists at least a short-term advantage, and they make terrorism a long-term threat.

Our failure to anticipate the impact of terrorist attacks does not derive from a fundamental conceptual failure in thinking about power. On the contrary, the power of terrorists, like that of states, derives from asymmetrical patterns of interdependence. Our fault has rather been our failure to understand that the most powerful state ever to exist on this planet could be vulnerable to small bands of terrorists due to patterns of asymmetrical interdependence. *We have over-emphasized states and we have over-aggregated power.*

Power comes not simply out of the barrel of a gun, but from asymmetries in vulnerability interdependence—some of which, it turns out, favor certain non-state actors more than most observers anticipated. The networks of interdependence along which power can travel are multiple, and they do not cancel one another out. Even a state that is overwhelmingly powerful on many dimensions can be highly vulnerable on others. We learned this lesson in the 1970s with respect to oil power; we are re-learning it now with respect to terrorism.

3. INSTITUTIONS AND LEGITIMACY

Institutionalist theory implies that multilateral institutions should play significant roles wherever interstate cooperation is extensive in world politics Yet a reader of the American press immediately after the September 11, 2001, attack on the World Trade Center and the Pentagon, might well have thought this claim weirdly divorced from reality. Immediate reactions centered on domestic security, military responses, and the creation of a broad international coalition against terrorism. Although the United Nations Security Council did act on September 12, passing resolution 1368, its response attracted relatively little attention. Indeed, President Bush's speech to Congress of September 20 did not mention the United Nations, although the President did praise NATO and made a generic reference to international organizations. And coverage of the United Nations was virtually nonexistent in the *New York Times.*

But theory is not tested by the immediate reactions of policymakers, much less by those of the press. Social science theory purports to elucidate underlying structures of social reality, which generate incentives for action. Kenneth Waltz rightly looks for confirmation of his theory of the balance of power "through observation of difficult cases." The theory is confirmed, he claims, where states ally with each other, "in accordance with the expectations the theory gives rise to, even though they have strong reasons not to cooperate with one another" (Waltz 1979: 125). Realists rightly argue that if leaders seem to be compelled toward actions that theory suggests—as, for instance, Winston Churchill was when Britain allied with the Soviet Union in 1941 and American leaders when they built NATO after World War II—this counts for their theory. Indeed, the most demanding test of theory comes when policymakers are initially unreceptive to the arguments on which the theory is based. If they nevertheless turn to the policy measures that the theory anticipates, it gains support.

The terrorist attacks of September 11 therefore pose a fruitful test for institutionalist theory. Before September 11, the Bush Administration had been pursuing a notably unilateralist policy with respect to several issues, including global warming, trade in small arms, money laundering, and tax evasion. Its leading policymakers all had realist proclivities: they emphasized the decisive use of force and had not been public supporters of international institutions. Their initial inclinations, if their public statements and those of the President are any guide, did not lead them to emphasize the role of the United Nations.

Nevertheless, the United States returned to the Security Council. On September 28, 2001, the Security Council unanimously adopted Resolution 1373, on the motion of the United States. This resolution used the mandatory provisions of Chapter VII of the United Nations Charter to require all states to "deny safe haven" both to terrorists and to those who

"provide safe haven" to terrorists. Resolution 1373 also demanded that states prevent potential terrorists from using their territories, and "prevent and suppress the financing of terrorist acts." It did not, as noted above, define terrorism. Furthermore, the United States continued to engage the United Nations, indeed delegating to it the task of bringing Afghan factions together in Germany in a meeting that culminated in an agreement in December 2001.

Why should the United States have relied so extensively on the United Nations? The UN, in Stalin's famous phrase, has no divisions. The United States, not the UN, carried out the significant military actions. Transnational banks, central banks, and states in their capacities as bank regulators, froze funds allegedly belonging to terrorists. Even before the September 28 Security Council resolution, allies of the United States had already invoked Article 5 of NATO's Charter.

Inis L. Claude proposed one answer almost 35 years ago (Claude 1967). States seek "collective legitimation" for their policies in the United Nations. Only the UN can provide the breadth of support for an action that can elevate it from the policy of one country or a limited set of countries, to a policy endorsed on a global basis. In contemporary jargon, the "transaction costs" of seeking support from over 150 countries around the world are higher than those of going to the Security Council, ready to meet at a moment's notice. But more important than these costs is the fact that the institution of the United Nations can confer a certain degree of legitimacy on a policy favored by the United States.

What does legitimacy mean in this context? Legally, decisions of the United Nations Security Council on issues of involving the use of violence are legitimate since members of the United Nations, through the Charter, have authorized such decisions. In a broader popular and normative sense, decisions are legitimate for a given public insofar as members of that public believe that they should be obeyed. As Weber pointed out, the sources of such legitimacy may include tradition, charisma or rational-legal authority (Weber 1978: 954); they may also include appeal to widely accepted norms. People in various parts of the world may believe that their governments should obey decisions of the Security Council because they were made through a process that is normatively as well as legally acceptable. Or they may regard its decisions as legitimate insofar as they are justified on the basis of principles—such as collective opposition to aggression— that they regard as valid.

Why is legitimacy important? In part, because people will voluntarily support a legitimacy policy, without requiring material inducements.[7] But it would be naive to believe that leaders of most countries will be persuaded, by Security Council action, of the wisdom or righteousness of the policy and will therefore support it for normative reasons. To explain the impact of Security Council resolutions, we need also to look for self-interested benefits for leaders.

Even if the leaders are entirely cynical, the adoption of a legitimate UN resolution will change their calculations. If they lead democratic societies in which publics accept the legitimacy of UN action, they will benefit more politically from supporting policies endorsed by the United Nations, than from supporting policies not so endorsed. If they exercise rule over people who are unsympathetic to the policies and who do not accept them merely due to UN endorsement, the legal status of Security Council resolutions may change their calculations. Chapter VII decisions are mandatory, which means that states defying the Security Council run the risk of facing sanctions themselves, as in the Gulf War. Leaders of countries with unsympathetic populations can point out that, however distasteful it may be to take action against Osama bin Laden and his network, it could be more costly to be cut off from essential supplies and markets, to suffer disruption of transportation and banking services, or even to become a target of military action.

The general point is one that has often been made by institutional theory: international institutions work largely by altering the costs of state strategies. Of course, there is no guarantee that institutions will be sufficiently important to ensure that strategies change: they are only one element in a mixture of calculations. Yet as the use of the United Nations by the United States indicates, they are an element that should not be overlooked.

The general issue of whether the United States should secure multilateral endorsement of its policies takes us back to issues of interdependence and power. The focused terrorist attacks on the United States have made the United States more dependent on other states for assistance in its struggle. Reciprocity requires that in return for such assistance, the United States provide benefits to its partners. Some of these benefits are bilateral, but others are more efficiently provided through multilateral institutions. Using these institutions, the United States can send stronger signals and make more credible commitments. Hence terrorism directed against the United States is likely to make the United States more responsive to its partners—both partners in crucial regions, such as Pakistan, and the most important entities on a global basis, such as China, Russia and the European Union. Terrorism may also make the United States more receptive to the use of multilateral institutions even when they limit American freedom of action.

In the short run, multilateralism may be a beneficiary of the globalization of informal violence. A major reason for a government to commit itself to a multilateral policy is that it can thereby induce other governments to make valuable reciprocal commitments. The United States has greater need for commitments from other states now than it had before September 11, and is therefore more inclined to make reciprocal commitments of its own. Greater multilateralism with respect to security issues is the direct result. Indirectly, due to issue-linkage, more American concessions on other issues can also be expected. These concessions will surely entail, as an indirect result, more multilateralism on these issues, as a way of improving relations with states whose help the United States needs to fight terrorism, and the support of whose people the United States seeks.

Yet at this point a note of caution is necessary. The United States has been notably reluctant to permit the United Nations, or its own allies, to restrict its military freedom of action in Afghanistan. In fact, requests by Great Britain to send in troops to protect relief operations were rebuffed by the United States on the advice of its military commanders. Another interpretation of the delegation of inter-factional negotiations to the United Nations is that the United States seeks to be able to leave Afghanistan promptly after the defeat of the Tal-iban and the capture or killing of Bin Laden and al-Qaeda fighters. Even more cynically, it can be feared that American policymakers wish to be able to lay the blame for inevitable political difficulties as the door of the UN.

One can easily imagine a more pessimistic scenario for the next few years. The United States government could decide that its security required radical measures that would not be supported even by many of its NATO allies, such as an attack on Iraq without strong evidence of Iraqi complicity in prior attacks on the United States. In such an eventuality, American actions would not be legitimated either by the United Nations or by NATO. Having acted unilaterally, the United States would not be moved to rely more heavily on international institutions, and multilateralism could suffer a serious blow.

Even if the multilateral path is chosen, it is hardly likely to be sufficient. It is unlikely that multilateral organizations will be the key *operating agencies* in dealing with the globalization of informal violence: they are too cumbersome for that. The state, with its capacity for decisive, forceful action and the loyalty it commands from citizens, will remain a necessary part of the solution to threats of informal violence. *Jejeune* declarations of the "death of the state" are surely among the casualties of the terrorist offensive But multilateral organizations will be an essential part of the process of legitimizing action by states.

It should be evident that these arguments about multilateral institutions and networks are not "anti-realist." On the contrary, they rest on an appreciation of the role of power, and of state action, in world politics; on an understanding that new threats create new alliances; and on a belief that structures matter. Analysts who are sensitive to the role of multilateral institutions need not regard them as operating independently from states, nor should they see such institutions as a panacea for our new ills. But sensitivity to the role of multilateral institutions helps us see how these institutions can play a role: not only by reducing transaction costs but also by generating opportunities for signaling commitments and providing collective legitimacy for effective action.

4. THE "LIBERALISM OF FEAR"

Judith N. Shklar's "liberalism of fear" envisages liberal democracy as "more a recipe for survival than a project for the perfectibility of mankind." It seeks to avoid the worst outcomes, and therefore declares that "the first right is to be protected against the fear of cruelty" (Shklar 1984: 4; 237). The liberalism of fear certainly speaks to our condition today, as it did to that of victims of the Nazis such as Judith Shklar. It raises both an analytical and a normative issue. Analytically, it leads us to ask about the protective role of the state, facing the globalization of informal violence. Normatively, it should make us think about our own role as students of world politics.

The erosion of the concept of a protected homeland within a defensive perimeter, discussed above, makes the "liberalism of fear" more relevant to Americans than it has been in almost two centuries. Suddenly, the task of protecting citizens from the fear of cruelty has become a demanding project for the state, not one that a superpower can take for granted.

Judith Shklar looked to the state as the chief threat. "No liberal," she declared, "ever forgets that governments are coercive" (Shklar 1984: 244). In this respect, the "liberalism of fear" shares a blind spot with the most popular theories of world politics, including realism, institutionalism and some forms of constructivism. All of these views share a common fault: they do not sufficiently take account of how globalization facilitates the agency of non-state entities and networks. After September 11 no liberal should be able to forget that non-state actors, operating within the borders of liberal states, can be as coercive and fear-inducing as states.

Recognition of the dangers of informal violence may lead the United States toward a broader vision of its global interests. As we have seen, classical realist thinking drew a bright line between geographical areas important to the national interest and those parts of the world that were insignificant from the standpoint of interests. Now that attacks against the United States can be planned and fostered within countries formerly viewed as insignificant, this bright line has been blurred.

One of the implications of this blurring of lines is that the distinction between self-defense and humanitarian intervention may become less clear. Future military actions in failed states, or attempts to bolster states that are in danger of failing, may be more likely to be described *both* as self-defense and as humanitarian or public-spirited. When the only arguments for such policies were essentially altruistic ones, they commanded little support, so the human and material price that American leaders were willing to pay to attain them was low. Now, however, such policies can be framed in terms of American self-interest, properly understood. Sound arguments from self interest are more persuasive than arguments from responsibility or altruism.

More generally, recognition of the dangers of informal violence will force a redefinition of American national interests, which could take different forms. Such a redefinition could lead Americans to support measures to reduce poverty, inequality and injustice in poor countries. The Marshall Plan is a useful if imperfect analogy. In 1947 the United States redefined its self-interest, taking responsibility for helping to build a democratic and capitalist Europe, open to other capitalist democracies. The United States invested very large resources in this project, with great success. The task now in the less developed countries is much more daunting, both in sheer magnitude and since the political systems of most of these countries are weaker than those of European countries in 1947.[8] But the resources available to the United States and other democratic countries are also much greater than they were in 1947.

Any widely appealing vision of American interests will need to be based on core values that can be generalized. Individual freedom, economic opportunity, and representative democracy constitute such values. The ability to drive gas-guzzling sports utility vehicles (SUVs) does not. In the end, "soft power" (Nye 1990) depends not merely on the desire of people in one country to imitate the institutions and practices prevailing in another, but also their ability to do so. Exhibiting a glamorous lifestyle that others have no possibility of attaining is more likely to generate hostility and a feeling of "sour grapes" than support. To relate successfully to people in poor countries during the 21st century, Americans will have to distinguish between their values and their privileges.

The attachment of Americans to a privileged lifestyle raises the prospect of a defensive and reactionary broadening of American national interests. Recall that a virtue of classical realism was to link commitments to a relatively limited set of interests, defined partly by geography. Ideology and a self-serving attempt to preserve privileges could define a different set of interests. Opponents—not merely those who have attacked the United States—would be demonized. Deals would continue to be cut with corrupt and repressive regimes to keep cheap oil flowing to the United States. The United States would rely exclusively on military power and bilateral deals rather than also on economic assistance, trade benefits, and efforts at cultural understanding. The costs would include estrangement from our democratic allies and hatred of the United States in much of the world. Ultimately, such a vision of national interest is a recipe for isolation and continual conflict—an environment in which liberal democracy could be threatened by the emergence of a garrison state at home.

Normatively, thinking about the "liberalism of fear" reminds our generation that in a globalized world, we cannot take liberal societies for granted. People such as Judith Shklar, who experienced Nazism, understood the fear of cruelty in their bones. Those of us who grew up in the United States during the Cold War experienced such fear only in our imaginations, although nuclear threats and wars such as those in Korea and Vietnam gave our imaginations plenty to work with. The generations that have come of age in the United States since the mid-to-late 1980s—essentially, those people under 35—have been able to take the basics of liberalism for granted, as if the United States were insulated from the despair of much of the world's population. The globalization of informal violence means that we are not so insulated. We are linked with hateful killers by real physical connections, not merely those of cyberspace. Neither isolationism nor unilateralism is a viable option.

Hence, the liberalism of fear means that we who study international interdependence and multilateral institutions will need to redouble our efforts. We should pay less attention to differentiating our views from those of other schools of international relations; more to both synthesis and disaggregation. We need to synthesize insights from classical realism, institutionalism, and constructivism, but we also need to take alternative worldviews—including religious world views—more seriously. We need to examine how purposes are shaped by ideas and how calculations of power interact with institutions, to produce outcomes in world politics. We need, at the same time, to disaggregate strands of asymmetrical interdependence, with their different implications for power; and to differentiate international institutions and networks from one another, in their effects and their potential for good or ill.

CONCLUSION

The terrorist attacks on New York and Washington force us to rethink our theories of world politics. Globalism should not be equated with economic integration. The agents of globalization are not simply the high-tech creators of the internet, or multinational corporations, but also small bands of fanatics, travelling on jet aircraft and inspired by fundamentalist religion. The globaliza-

tion of informal violence has rendered problematic our conventional assumptions about security threats. It should also lead us to question the classical realist distinction between important parts of the world, in which great powers have interests, and insignificant places, which were thought to present no security threats although they may raise moral dilemmas. Indeed, we need to reconceptualize the significance for homeland security of geographical space, which can be as much a carrier of malign informal violence as a barrier to it.

Most problematic are the assumptions in international relations theory about the roles played by states. There has been too much "international relations," and too little "world politics," not only in work on security but also in much work on international institutions. States no longer have a monopoly on the means of mass destruction: more people died in the attacks on the World Trade Center and the Pentagon than in the Japanese attack on Pearl Harbor in 1941. Indeed, it would be salutary for us to change the name of our field, from "international relations" to "world politics."[9] The language of "international" relations enables us to slip back into state-centric assumptions too easily. Asymmetrical interdependence is not merely an interstate phenomenon.

Yet as the state loses its monopoly on means of mass destruction, the response to terrorism is strengthening the powers of states, and the reliance of people on government. Even as states acquire more authority, they are likely to cooperate more extensively with each other on security issues, using international institutions to do so. Ironically, as states acquire more authority, they will be forced to learn better how to relate to networks—both hostile networks and networks that they may use instrumentally—and to rely more heavily on multilateral institutions. These institutions, in turn, will have to define their tasks in ways that emphasize their advantages—in conferring collective legitimacy on actions—while minimizing the impact of their liabilities, as cumbersome organizations without unity of command.

One result of these apparently paradoxical changes is closer linkages between traditional security issues and other issues. The artificial but convenient separation of the field into security and political economy may be one of the casualties of the struggle against terrorism. Areas formerly seen as "nonsecurity areas," such as air transport, transnational finance, and migration, have become more important to security, and more tightly subject therefore to state regulation.

Finally, the globalization of informal violence indicates how parochial have been some of the disputes among various schools of international relations theory. Analysis of the ramifications of the attacks on the United States must come to grips not only with structures of power, but also with changing subjective ideas and their impact on strategies. It must be concerned with international institutions, and with non-state actors and networks—elements of world politics emphasized by different schools of thought. And it must probe the connections between domestic politics and world politics. We do not face a *choice* between these perspectives, but rather the task of *synthesizing* them into a comprehensive, yet coherent, view.

Our understanding of world politics has often advanced under the pressure of events, such as those of World War II,

the Nuclear Revolution, and the growth of economic interdependence over the last fifty years. Perhaps the globalization of informal violence will refocus our attention for a new period of intellectual creativity, as sober thinking about global governance and classic political realism converge on problems identified so well by the "liberalism of fear."

NOTES

1. Statement by Osama bin Laden, *New York Times,* October 8, 2001, p. B7.
2. The best definitional discussion of terrorism that I know of is by Alex Schmid, who defines it as "an anxiety-inspiring method of repeated violent action, employed by (semi)clandestine individual, group or state actors, for idiosyncratic, criminal or political reasons, whereby—in contrast to assassination—the direct targets of violence are not the main targets" (Schmid 1993:8,12).
3. A few pessimistic and prescient observers understood that terrorism could pose a threat to the United States homeland despite our dominance in military power. See Carter and Perry 1999, and the Hart-Rudman Report, Phase I, September 15, 1999, Conclusion 1.
4. Another implication of this change is that the bright line between humanitarian intervention—to save *others* from human rights abuses—and self-defense—to protect *ourselves*—has become blurred.
5. In 1977 Keohane and Nye distinguished between two types of dependence, which they labelled (following the contemporary literature on economic interdependence) sensitivity and vulnerability dependence. Sensitivity dependence refers to "liability to costly effects imposed from outside before policies are altered to try to change the situation." Vulnerability dependence, in contrast, refers to "an actor's liability to suffer costs imposed by external events even after policies have been altered. This language seems inappropriate

in the contemporary situation, since in ordinary language, the attacks on an unprepared United States on September 11 demonstrated how vulnerable the country was. But the distinction between levels of dependence before and after policy change remains important. See Keohane and Nye 2001: 11; the text is unchanged from the 1st edition, 1977.

6. My colleague Ole Holsti has pointed out to me that in surveys conducted by the Chicago Council on Foreign Relations in 1994 and 1998, the public more often regarded international terrorism as a "critical" foreign policy issue than did leaders. Indeed, 69% and 84%, respectively, of the public regarded terrorism as a critical issue in those years, compared to 33% and 61 % of the elites. See Holsti 2000: 21.

7. Douglas North links legitimacy to the costs of enforcing rules. "The costs of mainte-nance of an existing order are inversely related to the perceived legitimacy of the existing system. To the extent that the participants believe the system fair, the costs of enforcing the rules and property rights are enormously reduced" (North 1981: 53).

8. It is tempting in hindsight to forget that the political systems of European countries were not terribly strong in 1947. Germany was still under occupation, Italy had recently been Fascist, and France and Italy had very large, pro-Soviet communist parties. Nevertheless, these countries had relatively highly educated populations, they had some history of democratic or at least liberal politics, and their administrative bureaucracies were quite effective.

9. This is a point that the late Susan Strange repeatedly emphasized.

BIBLIOGRAPHY

Carter, Ashton B. and William Perry. 1999. *Preventive Defense: A New Security Strategy for America.* Washington, D.C.: Brookings.

Claude, Inis L. 1967. *The Changing United Nations.* New York: Random House.

Hart, Gary, Warren Rudman, et al., 1999. *Phase I Report on the Emerging Global Security Environment for the First Quarter of the 21st Century,* United States Commission on National Security/21st Century (Washington, D.C.: September 15). "Hart-Rudman Report."

Held, David and Anthony McGrew, David Goldblatt, and Jonathan Perraton. 1999. *Global Transformations.* Stanford: Stanford University Press.

Holsti, Ole. 2000. "Public Opinion and Foreign Policy." In Robert Lieber, ed., *Eagle Rules?* (New York: Longman): 16–46.

Keohane, Robert O. and Joseph S. Nye. 2001. *Power and Interdependence.* 3rd edition. New York: Addison Wesley Longman.

Lippmann, Walter. 1943. *U.S. Foreign Policy: Shield of the Republic.* Boston: Little, Brown.

North, Douglas C. 1981. *Structure and Change in Economic History.* New York: W.W. Norton.

Nye, Joseph S. 1990. *Bound to Lead: The Changing Nature of American Power.* New York: Basic Books.

Schmid, Alex P. 1993. "The Response Problem as a Definition Problem," in Schmid and Crelinsten, 1993: 7–13.

Schmid, Alex P. and Ronald D. Crelinsten. 1993. *Western Responses to Terrorism.* London: Frank Cass.

Schumpeter, Joseph. 1950 [1942]. *Capitalism, Socialism and Democracy.* New York: Harper and Row.

Shklar, Judith N. *Ordinary Vices.* 1984. Cambridge: the Belknap Press of Harvard University Press.

Waltz, Kenneth N. 1979. *Theory of International Politics.* Reading, MA: Addison-Wesley.
Weber, Max. 1978. *Economy and Society,* edited by Guenther Roth and Claus Wittich. Berkeley: University of California Press.

QUESTIONS

1. Do you believe that Robert Keohane's use of the phrase "informal violence" is a useful alternative to the term *terrorism*? Has the term *terrorism* become too politicized to be useful as an analytical term? If so, why?

2. Why is terrorism an example of asymmetric power?

Chapter 4

CLASS SYSTEM THEORY

COMPONENTS OF CLASS SYSTEM THEORY

Focus of Analysis ········▶	• Capitalist world system
Major Actors ········▶	• States • Transnational class coalitions • Multinational corporations • International organizations
Behavior of States ········▶	• Class struggle • Accumulation of wealth for capitalist class
Goal of States ········▶	• Enhance wealth of capitalist class
View of Human Nature ········▶	• Selfish and dominating but reformable
Condition of International System ········▶	• Domination of capitalist world system • Cycle of exploitation/dependency
Key Concepts ········▶	• Capitalist world system; Class struggle; Dependency theory; Dialectical materialism; Imperialism; Neo-imperialism; North–South conflict; Proletariat; Transnational class coalitions; Uneven development

INTRODUCTION

The next system-level theory is what we have termed *class system theory*. This paradigm is also known as the radical, globalist, or neo-marxist theory. "Class system" seems a particularly good title, since advocates of this theory contend that it is classes, and the divisions between them, that define and determine the course of international politics.

Class system theory is based on four important concepts. First, proponents contend, economic factors are the driving force of international politics. Political and military power are the direct result of the underlying economic strength of the dominant class. Second, class system theory focuses on the development of the capitalist world economy and how it both creates and perpetuates uneven development between advanced capitalist states and poor, less developed states. Third, theorists point to an international class structure in which the advanced industrialized states in the center of the world capitalist system dominate and exploit poorer states, occupying the periphery of this system. Finally, transnational class coalitions represent the primary actors in international politics. States are important, but only as agents of the dominant class. Nonstate actors, most notably multinational corporations, allow capitalist elites to maintain the exploitative economic links that bind core countries with those on the periphery.

Economic forces, then, are a key part of the framework of class system theory. Unlike economic liberals, however, class system theorists emphasize the exploitative nature of international economic ties between states. They believe there is a systemwide hierarchy of classes and states that is rooted in the unequal distribution of wealth. According to class system theory, the structure and process of international relations is largely the result of the struggle between rich and poor countries over the control and distribution of economic resources. The tension between rich and poor countries is often referred to as the **North–South conflict.** The North represents the wealthy industrialized states that lie primarily in the northern hemisphere, while the South depicts the less developed countries, generally located in the southern hemisphere.

When conflict arises among states, it is caused, according to class system theory, by the clash of opposing economic interests—namely, the clash between capitalist and noncapitalist states. War is the result of capitalist states attempting to increase their wealth and power through imperialist foreign policies—policies in which strong capitalist states seek to exploit weaker noncapitalist states. Presumably, these conflicts will continue until the international status quo is radically altered, socialism replaces capitalism as the dominant socioeconomic system, and a more equitable distribution of wealth among nations is attained. However, beneficiaries of the "capitalist world system," the dominant capitalist class, certainly have a stake in preventing such radical change and preserving the current arrangement: keeping the rich wealthy, while the poor remain poor.

Class system theorists acknowledge that states are important actors, but they also emphasize that the dominant class exerts significant influence and often controls government policymakers. Unlike realism, which holds that states pursue national security interests, class system theory argues that states act in accordance with the wishes of the dominant economic class within the state. If the dominant class is capitalist, a state's foreign policy will be oriented to enhance the wealth and influence of the capitalist class.

With the diminished position of individual states, or groups of states, and emphasis on class conflict, class system theory also attributes a greater role to nonstate actors, such as multinational corporations and international institutions. These nonstate actors are important because they foster transnational class coalitions. The idea of **transnational class coalitions** suggests that economic classes form close ties across national boundaries. It is important not to confuse the notion of transnational class coalitions with the liberal theory presented in the previous chapter. Unlike liberals, who focus on the positive aspects of increasing international economic linkages, class system theorists emphasize the exploitative nature of the global economic system and the role that transnational actors, such as multinational corporations, play in this exploitation.

Multinational corporations (MNCs) are companies that have production facilities or branches in several countries. With headquarters in the advanced states, MNCs are the mechanism by which the capitalist class penetrates the poor countries. Rather than assisting in the development of these poor countries, multinational corporations exploit lesser developed countries as a source of cheap labor and inexpensive natural resources. MNCs then transfer profits from the lesser developed states to the base of operations in advanced capitalist states. These profits enable the capitalist class to increase global influence and sustain a dominant position in the world.

At this point, we might ask why the dominant class of a capitalist society doesn't exhibit a more selfless, "share the wealth" attitude. More broadly, why are some countries rich ("core" states) and some poor (periphery or semi-periphery states)? Here, we see some similarity to realism in that class system theory also suggests that human nature tends toward self-interest and the need to dominate others. However, unlike the realists, most class system theorists believe that if society were based more on an equal distribution of wealth, the aggressive and negative aspects of human nature might be reformed and perfected.

MARXISM

Most class system theorists rely on the fundamental assumptions of marxism, and on its critique of capitalism, as the intellectual basis for their theories about international relations. Karl Marx was not an international relations scholar but a German social and economic theorist. Together with his lifelong collaborator Friedrich Engels, Marx wrote *Manifesto of the Communist Party* (1848) and *Das Kapital* (*The Capital*, 1867), providing a social and economic doctrine that served as a basis for many theories of international relations. Marx and Engels created a body of political, social, and economic prescriptions that formed the ideological foundation of modern communist parties and strongly influenced many twentieth-century socialists and class system theorists.

According to Marx, the driving force of history is the struggle between economic classes. He termed this condition **dialectical materialism.** The dialectic, as it is called, suggests that history moves through stages—from feudalism to capitalism to socialism and, finally, to communism. The transition from one stage to the next is often prompted by the struggle between economic classes, as we have pointed out, as well as by the development and spread of technology. Politics, then, both domestic and international, would be best understood in terms of the structure and interaction of economic classes.

In the capitalist phase of Marx's dialectic, human interaction is characterized by the strong exploiting the weak, the struggle between the oppressed and the oppressors. He contends that capitalist society is divided into three basic classes. The dominant class, made up of wealthy capitalists, owns and controls the means of production, that is, factories and land. Although the capitalist class represents the smallest percentage of society, it is this ownership of both the factories and the land that enables it to control and exploit the other classes and amass even greater wealth and power.

The second class consists largely of workers living in the cities and working in these capitalist-owned factories. Marx wrote that the workers, or **proletariat,** are nothing more than "wage slaves," paid subsistence wages and exploited by capitalist factory owners whose sole motivation is greed. In a similar plight, the third class is made up of peasants who work the land. Capitalist land owners exploit peasant farm labor in return for allowing the peasantry to live on their land.

The division of society into these three classes represents the core of marxist theory, emphasizing the history of society as the history of **class struggle,** in which the oppressed worker and peasant classes attempt to free themselves from the domination of the wealthy capitalist class. As competition for wealth increases among the capitalists, this clash, leading from capitalism to socialism, is, according to Marx, inevitable. A redistribution of wealth within society would take place under the leadership of the proletariat.

IMPERIALISM

John A. Hobson, a British economist and journalist, wrote *Imperialism: A Study* in 1902, focusing on the imperialist policies of the European colonial empires. Classical **imperialism** is the policy of expanding a state's power and authority by conquering and controlling territories called colonies. Hobson stripped away any notion of imperialism as *noblesse oblige,* that is, a wealthy nation's duty or noble obligation to "assist" poorer, less developed nations. According to Hobson, imperialism is an extension of the capitalist search and competition for cheap labor and raw materials, and occurs when wealthy states exert political and economic control and influence over weaker nations or territories. Such a pattern is often sanctioned, even facilitated, by the powerful state's government and foreign policy. Hobson argued that imperialism was designed to increase the wealth and power of strong states at the *expense* of weaker states.

Hobson said that far from any selfless desire to promote growth in these under-developed areas, capitalists invest abroad because of the potential for higher profits. Reinvestment at home would not yield the same benefits as exploitation of raw materials and cheap labor in these colonies. The foreign and domestic policies of a state are often guided by the ruling class—the wealthy capitalists—and, therefore, facilitate this system of imperialism.

V. I. Lenin, founder of the Communist Party of the Soviet Union, used Hobson's writings as the basis for his notion that imperialism is, in fact, "the highest stage of capitalism." He contended that international politics was simply the "international-ization of the class system." Lenin asserted that in order to survive, capitalism needed to expand constantly. Having exploited the workers in their own states, European capitalists sought new markets, cheap raw materials, and greater profits. The acqui-sition of colonies fulfilled these requirements.

The problem with this "scramble for colonies" was that, by the late nineteenth century, most areas in the world were already colonized. Once this occurred, the ex-pansion of one imperialist power could come only at the expense of other imperi-alist powers. This process, according to Lenin, led to world war between the great European imperialist states. World War I, he reasoned, was simply the final stage of capitalist imperialism.

This link, between imperialism and the inevitability of war due to imperialism, is one of Lenin's fundamental contributions to international relations theory. We now see that, although their explanations are quite different, both class system the-orists and neo-realists view the causes of war as coming from the nature of and conditions in the international system itself. For neo-realists, the problem is anarchy; for class system theorists, it is imperialism and economic dependence.

DEPENDENCY THEORY

Dependency theory, as part of the class system paradigm, is discussed in the article by Immanuel Wallerstein. He developed dependency theory to explain the uneven development in wealth between poor and rich countries. **Uneven development** is defined as the propensity of capitalism to create and perpetuate an unequal dis-persal of global wealth and prosperity. **Dependency theory** asserts that trade, foreign investment, and even foreign aid between advanced, industrialized coun-tries and poor, less developed states is inherently exploitative, works to the disad-vantage of the poor nations, and perpetuates the dependency of these less devel-oped countries.

With respect to dependency theory, Wallerstein suggests that relations between states in the international system can be classified as part of a system of depen-dency and exploitation. The term **neo-imperialism** is used to describe the less overt control now exercised by the North over exports and raw materials in developing nations. Though distinct from the imperialist practices of the European colonial em-pires, the economic and political influence exercised by advanced capitalist powers over less developed countries is simply a new, more subtle form of imperialism.

In conjunction with dependency theory, Wallerstein also developed the notion of a **capitalist world system,** dividing states into three categories: core (wealthy), periphery (poor), and semi-periphery (less developed). In many ways, the relationship between these three categories of countries parallels that between different classes within capitalist society. Dominant core nations are wealthy, with economies geared more toward technologically or economically advanced businesses—from high technology manufacturing to banking and global finance. These countries control the global means of production. Machinery for manufacturing, tools for agricultural production, and world monetary systems are in the hands of these core nations.

To support their dominant position, core nations depend on the raw materials and cheap labor of periphery, or poor, states. Like the underclass or the proletariat in a capitalist society, periphery states depend on the orders and work provided by core countries for their survival. Indeed, core countries exploit the cheap labor and raw materials to maintain a high profit margin and to sustain their own dominant position in the international system. Semi-periphery states, or less developed countries, are important when the cost of labor in core countries becomes too high, and they also serve as markets for excess production and investment capital.

Using Wallerstein's outline of the capitalist world system, let us look at the positions of core, periphery, and semi-periphery countries with respect to one another; this should help to explain why and how such a system is maintained. This theory not only describes the hierarchical international system in which the rich states continue to dominate poor, less developed states but also provides an explanation for the uneven rates of development between the North and the South.

Dominant core countries have a stake in preserving this cycle of dependency and exploitation that exists with periphery and semi-periphery states and pursue foreign and domestic policies to further that goal. Poor and less developed countries are virtually locked into a position of dependency. As we discussed earlier with regard to transnational class coalitions, class system theorists suggest that strong capitalist nations have allies in these poor nations. Small groups of capitalist elites in the peripheral states act as liaisons to and partners with leaders, policymakers, and business executives in the core countries. These elites have more in common with the capitalists of foreign nations than with the underclass of their own state. They too, then, have a stake in preserving the status quo—the dependency and exploitation—of their own country.

CONTEMPORARY CLASS SYSTEM THEORY

The selection by Fred Halliday provides us with an example of how the major assumptions of class system theory can be used to develop an innovative and provocative explanation for the collapse of the Soviet Union and the end of the Cold War. His analysis emphasizes the vitality of Western capitalism and the inability of the Soviet Union to compete effectively.

Realist theoreticians treated the Cold War as a continuation of traditional power politics, but Halliday focuses on the ideological and socioeconomic aspects of superpower conflict. He argues that the structure of the international system is actually the result of specific historical conditions. The conditions that prevailed in the Cold War environment depended on the dominance of two contending political, economic, and ideological systems locked in a struggle for ascendancy.

Though Halliday's analysis of the Cold War acknowledges that the United States and the Soviet Union were engaged in a broad bipolar conflict, that conflict was actually motivated and propelled by competition on three distinct levels. Two of these, socioeconomic and ideological, were at least as important as, if not ultimately more important than, the third, traditional military competition. Despite his mistrust and criticism of capitalism, Halliday, unlike many class system theorists, at least acknowledges the vitality of capitalism as a dynamic economic and social system.

The last article is written by Noam Chomsky, one of the most prominent political dissidents and leftist theorists of the last several decades. Chomsky presents a class system analysis of the U.S. war against terrorism. The author contends that American armed intervention in Afghanistan and previous U.S. military actions could equally be classified as terrorist acts. Chomsky urges Americans to reassess the long-term implications of America's military attacks abroad and change U.S. policy accordingly.

A CRITIQUE OF CLASS SYSTEM THEORY

Like the proponents of all our system-level theories, class system theorists tend to emphasize the unique contributions of their own paradigm as a model to assess and interpret international relations. This theory does, indeed, have certain strengths. While both realism and liberalism tend to focus primarily on the interaction of wealthy, powerful states, only class system theory examines the so-called pattern of dependence that distinguishes the relationship between rich and poor countries.

Perhaps, for this reason, class system theory, though out of favor in Western circles, remains popular and widely accepted by scholars in less developed nations. Today, many prominent class system theorists are, in fact, from Latin America. This theory, with its emphasis on the North–South conflict and problems of development, poverty, and other social-welfare issues, is one of the few paradigms that tries to provide an explanation for the disparities in wealth and development worldwide.

Class system theory must be credited with at least some success in providing an explanation for these and other problems facing less developed states. Certainly, poor countries are more vulnerable to shifts in the international marketplace, relying on exports of primary products—raw materials and natural resources—to sustain themselves economically. Moreover, class system theory contains a valuable critique of the excesses of capitalism and its impact on less developed countries. It is difficult to deny that some vestiges of imperialism are still in place today. Many people living in less developed parts of the world resent not only the economic but

---

KEY CONCEPTS

Capitalist world system   is a concept of class system theory that focuses on the exploitative nature of the global spread of capitalism. This system divides states into three categories: core (wealthy), periphery (poor), and semi-periphery (less developed). Core nations are wealthy, advanced powers that control the global means of production and use their wealth and power to exploit and dominate those states residing in the semi-periphery and periphery of the global economic system.

Class struggle   is the marxist theory that history is a story of struggle between economic classes in which the oppressed worker and peasant classes attempt to free themselves from the domination of the wealthy capitalist class.

Dependency theory   is a concept associated with class system theorists that asserts that trade, foreign investment, and even foreign aid between advanced industrialized countries and poor, lesser developed states is inherently exploitative and works to the disadvantage of the poor nations.

Dialectical materialism   is a theory developed by Karl Marx positing that history moves through stages—from feudalism to capitalism to socialism and, finally, to communism. The transition from one stage to the next is often prompted by the struggle between economic classes as well as by the development and spread of technology.

Imperialism   is the policy of expanding a state's power and authority by conquering and controlling territories, called colonies.

(continued)

---

also the cultural penetration of their countries. Capitalism, from their vantage point, is closely linked to Western—particularly American—culture and viewed as a threat to indigenous cultural traditions and ways of life.

Though there is merit to the arguments in favor of class system theory, critics are not without ammunition. Many critics argue that class system theory exaggerates the role of the world capitalist system in limiting development and ignores the impact that policies adopted in the less developed states have on their own economic development.

Specifically, class system theory fails to address the impact that different development strategies have had on various countries facing similar problems with economic development. Dependency theory can account only for those countries that have failed to develop. How could, for example, Immanuel Wallerstein explain the remarkable economic growth of many countries occupying what he describes as the semi-periphery? Rapid and successful industrial development in Taiwan, Singapore, Hong Kong, South Korea, and Brazil is difficult for class system theorists to

(continued from previous page)

Neo-imperialism is the process of the international system in which the advanced industrial states' control of exports and raw materials in developing nations is simply a more subtle form of domination than the previous imperalist practices of the European colonial empires. The economic and political influence exercised by the advanced capitalist powers over less developed countries is simply a new, more insidious form of imperialism.

North–South conflict is a phrase used to characterize the tension between rich and poor countries. *North* represents the wealthy industrialized states that lie primarily in the northern hemisphere, while *South* is the term used for the less developed countries mainly located in the southern hemisphere.

Proletariat is a marxist term for industrial workers living in urban areas and working in capitalist-owned factories. Marx wrote that the workers are nothing more than "wage slaves," paid subsistence wages and exploited by capitalist factory owners whose sole motivation is greed.

Transnational class coalitions is a concept of class system theory contending that economic classes form close ties across national boundaries. Unlike liberals who focus on the positive aspects of increasing international economic linkages, class system theorists emphasize the exploitative nature of the global economic system and the role that transnational actors, like multinational corporations, play in this exploitation.

Uneven development is the propensity of capitalism to create and perpetuate an unequal dispersal of global wealth and prosperity.

explain or dismiss. These newly industrialized countries (NICs) are the rising economic powers of the late twentieth century and already compete successfully with major capitalist powers in the North. Clearly, these countries illustrate that, contrary to the suppositions of class system theory, capitalism can be beneficial and bring prosperity to developing countries.

In addition to ignoring the progress of these economically vibrant nations, some class system theorists have been criticized for being ahistorical—a potential trap for any theorist of international relations. Critics point out that class system theorists rely on case studies that conform to and confirm their particular paradigm while ignoring states that fall outside these parameters.

This theoretical blind eye is especially true with respect to weaknesses of communist nations. While focusing on North–South relations, class system theorists fail to account for a significant percentage of the globe. The former Soviet Union and Eastern European states, even China, present some difficulties for the class system paradigm. Certainly, during the Cold War era, the Soviet Union maintained policies of imperialism in the subjugation and exploitation of Eastern Europe. Imperialist domination of other states is, evidently, not limited solely to capitalist powers.

Class system theory also falls short in explaining the failure of marxist principles and communist doctrine in the former USSR and Eastern Bloc nations, as well as the capitalist reforms now under way in these countries. Though advocates might suggest that true marxist doctrine was never fully implemented in the region, surely this cannot be considered true of communist China. Even in this most ideologically committed nation, the Chinese government has turned to free enterprise and open markets to stimulate its formerly stagnant socialized economy.

Despite these flaws, class system theory still provides important insights into the economic development process and remains a highly popular explanation of global politics, particularly among scholars in less developed countries. Like any theory, it is important for students to decide for themselves which explanation, if any, provides the most accurate description of international relations.

16.   Manifesto of the Communist Party

Karl Marx and Friedrich Engels

In this excerpt, Karl Marx and Friedrich Engels generate the framework for what we call class system theory. Marx and Engels argue that history is based largely on class struggle, that the capitalist economic system created a world situation in which wealth and the control of wealth is in the hands of a few, and that growing tension among the classes during various stages of development will finally be resolved by a transformation to political and economic socialism. This selection is from *Manifesto of the Communist Party* (1848).

Karl Marx (1818–1883) and Friedrich Engels (1820–1895) were two of the founders of the Communist movement in Europe during the nineteenth century. Their other works include *Das Kapital (The Capital), The German Ideology*, and *The Poverty of Philosophy*.

A spectre is haunting Europe—the spectre of Communism. All the Powers of old Europe have entered into a holy alliance to exorcise this spectre: Pope and Czar, Metternich and Guizot, French Radicals and German police-spies.

Where is the party in opposition that has not been decried as Communistic by its opponents in power? Where the Opposition that has not hurled back the branding reproach of Communism, against the more advanced opposition parties, as well as against its reactionary adversaries?

Two things result from this fact.

I. Communism is already acknowledged by all European Powers to be itself a Power.

II. It is high time that Communists should openly, in the face of the whole world, publish their views, their aims, their tendencies, and meet this nursery tale of the Spectre of Communism with a Manifesto of the party itself.

To this end, Communists of various nationalities have assembled in London, and sketched the following Manifesto, to be published in the English, French, German, Italian, Flemish and Danish languages.

I. Bourgeois and Proletarians[1]

The history of all hitherto existing society[2] is the history of class struggles.

Freeman and slave, patrician and plebeian, lord and serf, guild-master[3] and journeyman, in a word, oppressor and oppressed, stood in constant opposition to one another, carried on an uninterrupted, now hidden, now open fight, a fight that each time ended, either in a revolutionary re-constitution of society at large, or in the common ruin of the contending classes.

In the earlier epochs of history, we find almost everywhere a complicated arrangement of society into various orders, a manifold gradation of social rank. In ancient Rome we have patricians, knights, plebeians, slaves; in the Middle Ages, feudal lords, vassals, guild-masters, journeymen, apprentices, serfs; in almost all of these classes, again, subordinate gradations.

The modern bourgeois society that has sprouted from the ruins of feudal society has not done away with clash antagonisms. It has but established new classes, new conditions of oppression, new forms of struggle in place of the old ones.

Our epoch, the epoch of the bourgeoisie, possesses, however, this distinctive feature: it has simplified the class antagonisms: Society as a whole is more and more splitting up into two great hostile camps, into two great classes directly facing each other: Bourgeoisie and Proletariat.

From the serfs of the Middle Ages sprang the chartered burghers of the earliest towns. From these burgesses the first elements of the bourgeoisie were developed.

The discovery of America, the rounding of the Cape, opened up fresh ground for the rising bourgeoisie. The East-Indian and Chinese markets, the colonisation of America, trade with the colonies, the increase in the means of exchange and in commodities generally, gave to commerce, to navigation, to industry, an impulse never before known, and thereby, to the revolutionary element in the tottering feudal society, a rapid development.

The feudal system of industry, under which industrial production was monopolised by closed guilds, now no longer sufficed for the growing wants of the new markets. The manufacturing system took its place. The guild-masters were pushed on one side by the manufacturing middle class; division of labour between the different corporate guilds vanished in the face of division of labour in each single workshop.

Meantime the markets kept ever growing, the demand ever rising. Even manufacture no longer sufficed. Thereupon, steam and machinery revolutionised industrial production. The place of manufacture was taken by the giant, Modern Industry, the place of the industrial middle class, by industrial millionaires, the leaders of whole industrial armies, the modern bourgeois.

Modern industry has established the world-market, for which the discovery of America paved the way. This market has given an immense development to commerce, to navigation, to communication by land. This development has, in its turn, reacted on the extension of industry; and in proportion as industry, commerce, navigation, railways extended, in the same proportion the bourgeoisie developed, increased its capital, and pushed into the background every class handed down from the Middle Ages.

We see, therefore, how the modern bourgeoisie is itself the product of a long course of development, of a series of revolutions in the modes of production and of exchange.

Each step in the development of the bourgeoisie was accompanied by a corresponding political advance of that class. An oppressed class under the sway of the feudal nobility, an armed and self-governing association in the mediaeval commune,[4] here independent urban republic (as in Italy and Germany), there taxable "third estate" of the monarchy (as in France), afterwards, in the period of manufacture proper, serving either the semi-feudal or the absolute monarchy as a counterpoise against the nobility, and, in fact, corner-stone of the great monarchies in general, the bourgeoisie has at last, since the establishment of Modern Industry and of the world-market, conquered for itself, in the modern representative State, exclusive political sway. The executive of the modern State is but a committee for managing the common affairs of the whole bourgeoisie.

The bourgeoisie, historically, has played a most revolutionary part.

The bourgeoisie, wherever it has got the upper hand, has put an end to all feudal, patriarchal, idyllic relations. It has pitilessly torn asunder the motley feudal ties that bound man to his "natural superiors," and has left remaining no other nexus between man and man than naked self-interest, than callous "cash payment." It has drowned the most heavenly ecstasies of religious fervour, of chivalrous enthusiasm, of philistine sentimentalism, in the icy water of egotistical calculation. It has resolved personal worth into exchange value, and in place of the numberless indefeasible chartered freedoms, has set up that single, unconscionable freedom— Free Trade. In one word, for exploitation, veiled by religious and political illusions, it has substituted naked, shameless, direct, brutal exploitation.

The bourgeoisie has stripped of its halo every occupation hitherto honoured and looked up to with reverent awe. It has converted the physician, the lawyer, the priest, the poet, the man of science, into its paid wage-labourers.

The bourgeoisie has torn away from the family its sentimental veil, and has reduced the family relation to a mere money relation.

The bourgeoisie has disclosed how it came to pass that the brutal display of vigour in the Middle Ages, which Reactionists so much admire, found its fitting complement in the most slothful indolence. It has been the first to show what man's activity can bring about. It has accomplished wonders far surpassing Egyptian pyramids, Roman aqueducts, and Gothic cathedrals; it has conducted expeditions that put in the shade all former Exoduses of nations and crusades.

The bourgeoisie cannot exist without constantly revolutionising the instruments of production, and thereby the relations of production, and with them the whole relations of society. Conservation of the old modes of production in unaltered form, was, on the contrary, the first condition of existence for all earlier industrial classes. Constant revolutionising of production, uninterrupted disturbance of all social conditions, everlasting uncertainty and agitation distinguish the bourgeois epoch from all earlier ones. All fixed, fast-frozen relations, with their train of ancient and venerable prejudices and opinions, are swept away, all new-formed ones become antiquated before they can ossify. All that is solid melts into air, all that is holy is profaned, and man is at last compelled to face with sober senses, his real conditions of life, and his relations with his kind.

The need of a constantly expanding market for its products chases the bourgeoisie over the whole surface of the globe. It must nestle everywhere, settle everywhere, establish connexions everywhere.

The bourgeoisie has through its exploitation of the world-market given a cosmopolitan character to production and consumption in every country. To the great chagrin of Reactionists, it has drawn from under the feet of industry the national ground on which it stood. All old-established national industries have been destroyed or are daily being destroyed. They are dislodged by new industries, whose introduction becomes a life and death question for all civilised nations, by industries that no longer work up indigenous raw material, but raw material drawn from the remotest zones; industries whose products are consumed, not only at home, but in every quarter of the globe. In place of the old wants, satisfied by the productions of the country, we find new wants, requiring for their satisfaction the products of distant lands and climes. In place of the old local and national seclusion and self-sufficiency, we have intercourse in every direction, universal interdependence of nations. And as in material, so also in intellectual production. The intellectual creations of individual nations become common property. National one-sidedness and narrow-mindedness become more and more impossible, and from the numerous national and local literatures, there arises a world literature.

The bourgeoisie, by the rapid improvement of all instruments of production, by the immensely facilitated means of communication, draws all, even the most barbarian, nations into civilisation. The cheap prices of its commodities are the heavy artillery with which it batters down all Chinese walls, with which it forces the barbarians' intensely obstinate hatred of foreigners to capitulate. It compels all nations, on pain of extinction, to adopt the bourgeois mode of production; it compels them to introduce what it calls civilisation into their midst, i.e., to become bourgeois themselves. In one word, it creates a world after its own image.

The bourgeoisie has subjected the country to the rule of the towns. It has created enormous cities, has greatly increased the urban population as compared with the rural, and has thus rescued a considerable part of the population from the idiocy of rural life. Just as it has made the country dependent on the towns, so it has made barbarian and semi-barbarian countries dependent on the civilised ones, nations of peasants on nations of bourgeois, the East on the West.

The bourgeoisie keeps more and more doing away with the scattered state of the population, of the means of production, and of property. It has agglomerated population, centralised means of production, and has concentrated property in a few hands. The necessary consequence of this was political centralisation. Independent, or but loosely connected provinces, with separate interests, laws, governments and systems of taxation, became lumped together into one nation, with one government, one code of laws, one national class-interest, one frontier and one customs-tariff.

The bourgeoisie, during its rule of scarce one hundred years, has created more massive and more colossal productive forces than have all preceding generations together. Subjection of Nature's forces to man, machinery, application of chemistry to industry and agriculture, steam-navigation, railways, electric telegraphs, clearing of whole continents for cultivation, canalisation of rivers, whole populations conjured out of the ground—what earlier century had even a presentiment that such productive forces slumbered in the lap of social labour?

We see then: the means of production and of exchange, on whose foundation the bourgeoisie built itself up, were generated in feudal society. At a certain stage in the development of these means of production and of exchange, the conditions under which feudal society produced and exchanged, the feudal organisation of agriculture and manufacturing industry, in one word, the feudal relations of property became no longer compatible with the already developed productive forces; they became so many fetters. They had to be burst asunder; they were burst asunder.

Into their place stepped free competition, accompanied by a social and political constitution adapted to it, and by the economical and political sway of the bourgeois class.

A similar movement is going on before our own eyes. Modern bourgeois society with its relations of production, of exchange and of property, a society that has conjured up such gigantic means of production and of exchange, is like the sorcerer, who is no longer able to control the powers of the nether world whom he has called up by his spells. For many a decade past the history of industry and commerce is but the history of the revolt of modern productive forces against modern conditions of production, against the property relations that are the conditions for the existence of the bourgeoisie and of its rule. It is enough to mention the commercial crises that by their periodical return put on its trial, each time more threateningly, the existence of the entire bourgeois society. In these crises a great part not only of the existing products, but also of the previously created productive forces, are periodically destroyed. In these crises there breaks out an epidemic that, in all earlier epochs, would have seemed an absurdity—the epidemic of over-production. Society suddenly finds itself put back into a state of momentary barbarism; it appears as if a famine, a universal war of devastation had cut off the supply of every means of subsistence; industry and commerce seem to be destroyed; and why? Because there is too much civilisation, too much means of subsistence, too much industry, too much commerce. The productive forces at the disposal of society no longer tend to further the development of the conditions of bourgeois property; on the contrary, they have become too powerful for these conditions, by which they are fettered, and so soon as they overcome these fetters, they bring disorder into the whole of bourgeois society, endanger the existence of bourgeois property. The conditions of bourgeois society are too narrow to comprise the wealth created by them. And how does the bourgeoisie get over these crises? On the one hand by enforced destruction of a mass of productive forces; on the other, by the conquest of new markets, and by the more thorough exploitation of the old ones. That is to say, by paving the way for more extensive and more destructive crises, and by diminishing the means whereby crises are prevented.

The weapons with which the bourgeoisie felled feudalism to the ground are now turned against the bourgeoisie itself.

But not only has the bourgeoisie forged the weapons that bring death to itself; it has also called into existence the men who are to wield those weapons—the modern working class—the proletarians.

In proportion as the bourgeoisie, i.e., capital, is developed, in the same proportion is the proletariat, the modern working class, developed—a class of labourers, who live only so long as they find work, and who find work only so long as their labour increases capital. These labourers, who must sell themselves piece-meal, are a commodity, like every other article of commerce, and are consequently exposed to all the vicissitudes of competition, to all the fluctuations of the market.

Owing to the extensive use of machinery and to division of labour, the work of the proletarians has lost all individual character, and consequently, all charm for the workman. He becomes an appendage of the machine, and it is only the most simple, most monotonous, and most easily acquired knack, that is required of him. Hence, the cost of production of a workman is restricted, almost entirely, to the means of subsistence that he requires for his maintenance, and for the propagation of his race. But the price of a commodity, and therefore also of labour,[5] is equal to its cost of production. In proportion, therefore, as the repulsiveness of the work increases, the wage decreases. Nay more, in proportion as the use of machinery and division of labour increases, in the same proportion the burden of toil also increases, whether by prolongation of the working hours, by increase of the work exacted in a given time or by increased speed of the machinery, etc.

Modern industry has converted the little workshop of the patriarchal master into the great factory of the industrial capitalist. Masses of labourers, crowded into the factory, are organised like soldiers. As privates of the industrial army they are placed under the command of a perfect hierarchy of officers and sergeants. Not only are they slaves of the bourgeois class, and of the bourgeois State; they are daily and hourly enslaved by the machine, by the over-looker, and, above all, by the individual bourgeois manufacturer himself. The more openly this despotism proclaims gain to be its end and aim, the more petty, the more hateful and the more embittering it is.

The less the skill and exertion of strength implied in manual labour, in other words, the more modern industry becomes developed, the more is the labour of men superseded by that of women. Differences of age and sex have no longer any distinctive social validity for the working class. All are instruments of labour, more or less expensive to use, according to their age and sex.

No sooner is the exploitation of the labourer by the manufacturer, so far, at an end, that he receives his wages in cash, than he is set upon by the other portions of the bourgeoisie, the landlord, the shopkeeper, the pawnbroker, etc.

The lower strata of the middle class—the small tradespeople, shopkeepers, and retired tradesmen generally, the handicraftsmen and peasants—all these sink gradually into the proletariat, partly because their diminutive capital does not suffice for the scale on which Modern Industry is carried on, and is swamped in the competition with the large capitalists, partly because their specialised skill is rendered worthless by new methods of production. Thus the proletariat is recruited from all classes of the population.

The proletariat goes through various stages of development. With its birth begins its struggle with the bourgeoisie. At first the contest is carried on by individual labourers, then by the workpeople of a factory, then by the operatives of one trade, in one locality, against the individual bourgeois who directly exploits them. They direct their attacks not against the bourgeois conditions of production, but against the instruments of production themselves; they destroy imported wares that compete with their labour, they smash to pieces machinery, they set factories ablaze, they seek to restore by force the vanished status of the workman of the Middle Ages.

At this stage the labourers still form an incoherent mass scattered over the whole country, and broken up by their mutual competition. If anywhere they unite to form more compact bodies, this is not yet the consequence of their own active union, but of the union of the bourgeoisie, which class, in order to attain its own political ends, is compelled to set the whole proletariat in motion, and is moreover yet, for a time, able to do so. At this stage, therefore, the proletarians do not fight their enemies, but the enemies of their enemies, the remnants of absolute monarchy, the landowners, the non-industrial bourgeois, the petty bourgeoisie. Thus the whole historical movement is concentrated in the hands of the bourgeoisie; every victory so obtained is a victory for the bourgeoisie.

But with the development of industry the proletariat not only increases in number; it becomes concentrated in greater masses, its strength grows, and it feels that strength more. The various interests and conditions of life within the ranks of the proletariat are more and more equalised, in proportion as machinery obliterates all distinctions of labour, and nearly everywhere reduces wages to the same low level. The growing competition among the bourgeois, and the resulting commercial crises, make the wages of the workers ever more fluctuating. The unceasing improvement of machinery, ever more rapidly developing, makes their livelihood more and more precarious; the collisions between individual workmen and individual bourgeois take more and more the character of collisions between two classes. Thereupon the workers begin to form combinations (Trades Unions) against the bourgeois; they club together in order to keep up the rate of wages; they found permanent associations in order to make provision beforehand for these occasional revolts. Here and there the contest breaks out into riots.

Now and then the workers are victorious, but only for a time. The real fruit of their battles lies, not in the immediate result, but in the ever-expanding union of the workers. This union is helped on by the improved means of communication that are created by modern industry and that place the workers of different localities in contact with one another. It was just this contact that was needed to centralise the numerous local struggles, all of the same character, into one national struggle between classes. But every class struggle is a political struggle. And that union, to attain which the burghers of the Middle Ages, with their miserable highways, required centuries, the modern proletarians, thanks to railways, achieve in a few years.

This organisation of the proletarians into a class, and consequently into a political party, is continually being upset again by the competition between the workers themselves. But it ever rises up again, stronger, firmer, mightier. It compels legislative recognition of particular interests of the workers, by taking advantage of the divisions among the bourgeoisie itself. Thus the ten-hours' bill in England was carried.

Although collisions between the classes of the old society further, in many ways, the course of development of the proletariat. The bourgeoisie finds itself involved in a constant battle. At first with the aristocracy; later on, with those portions of the bourgeoisie itself, whose interests have become antagonistic to the progress of industry; at all times, with the bourgeoisie of foreign countries. In all these battles it sees itself compelled to appeal to the proletariat, to ask for its help, and thus, to drag it into the political arena. The bourgeoisie itself, therefore, supplies the proletariat with its own elements of political and general education, in other words, it furnishes the proletariat with weapons for fighting the bourgeoisie.

Further, as we have already seen, entire sections of the ruling classes are, by the advance of industry, precipitated into the proletariat, or are at least threatened in their conditions of existence. These also supply the proletariat with fresh elements of enlightenment and progress.

Finally, in times when the class struggle nears the decisive hour, the process of dissolution going on within the ruling class, in fact within the whole range of society, assumes such a violent, glaring character, that a small section of the ruling class cuts itself adrift, and joins the revolutionary class, the class that holds the future in its hands. Just as, therefore, at an earlier period, a section of the nobility went over to the bourgeoisie, so now a portion of the bourgeoisie goes over to the proletariat, and in particular, a portion of the bourgeois ideologists, who have raised themselves to the level of comprehending theoretically the historical movement as a whole.

Of all the classes that stand face to face with the bourgeoisie today, the proletariat alone is a really revolutionary class. The other classes decay and finally disappear in the face of Modern Industry; the proletariat is its special and essential product.

The lower middle class, the small manufacturer, the shopkeeper, the artisan, the peasant, all these fight against the bourgeoisie, to save from extinction their existence as fractions of the middle class. They are therefore not revolutionary, but conservative. Nay more, they are reactionary, for they try to roll back the wheel of history. If by chance they are revolutionary, they are so only in view of their impending transfer into the proletariat, they thus defend not their present, but their future interests, they desert their own standpoint to place themselves at that of the proletariat.

The "dangerous class," the social scum, that passively rotting mass thrown off by the lowest layers of old society, may, here and there, be swept into the movement by a proletarian revolution; its conditions of life, however, prepare it far more for the part of a bribed tool of reactionary intrigue.

In the conditions of the proletariat, those of old society at large are already virtually swamped. The proletarian is without property; his relation to his wife and children has no longer anything in common with the bourgeois family-relations; modern industrial labour, modern subjection to capital, the same in England as in France, in America as in Germany, has stripped him of every trace of national character. Law, morality, religion, are to him so many bourgeois prejudices, behind which lurk in ambush just as many bourgeois interests.

All the preceding classes that got the upper hand, sought to fortify their already acquired status by subjecting society at large to their conditions of appropriation. The proletarians cannot become masters of the productive forces of society, except by abolishing their own previous mode of appropriation, and thereby also every other previous mode of appropriation. They have nothing of their own to secure and to fortify; their mission is to destroy all previous securities for, and insurances of, individual property.

All previous historical movements were movements of minorities, or in the interests of minorities. The proletarian movement is the self-conscious, independent movement of the immense majority, in the interests of the immense majority. The proletariat, the lowest stratum of our present society, cannot stir, cannot raise itself up, without the whole superincumbent strata of official society being sprung into the air.

Though not in substance, yet in form, the struggle of the proletariat with the bourgeoisie is at first a national struggle. The proletariat of each country must, of course, first of all settle matters with its own bourgeoisie.

In depicting the most general phases of the development of the proletariat, we traced the more or less veiled civil war, raging within existing society, up to the point where that war breaks out into open revolution, and where the violent overthrow of the bourgeoisie lays the foundation for the sway of the proletariat.

Hitherto, every form of society has been based, as we have already seen, on the antagonism of oppressing and oppressed classes. But in order to oppress a class, certain conditions must be assured to it under which it can, at least, continue its slavish existence. The serf, in the period of serfdom, raised himself to membership in the commune, just as the petty bourgeois, under the yoke of feudal absolutism, managed to develop into a bourgeois. The modern labourer, on the contrary, instead of rising with the progress of industry, sinks deeper and deeper below the conditions of existence of his own class. He becomes a pauper, and pauperism develops more rapidly than population and wealth. And here it becomes evident, that the bourgeoisie is unfit any longer to be the ruling class in society, and to impose its conditions of existence upon society as an over-riding law. It is unfit to rule because it is incompetent to assure an existence to its slave within his slavery, because it cannot help letting him sink into such a state, that it has to feed him, instead of being fed by him. Society can

no longer live under this bourgeoisie, in other words, its existence is no longer compatible with society.

The essential condition for the existence, and for the sway of the bourgeois class, is the formation and augmentation of capital; the condition for capital is wage-labour. Wage-labour rests exclusively on competition between the labourers. The advance of industry, whose involuntary promoter is the bourgeoisie, replaces the isolation of the labourers, due to competition, by their revolutionary combination, due to association. The development of Modern Industry, therefore, cuts from under its feet the very foundation on which the bourgeoisie produces and appropriates products. What the bourgeoisie, therefore, produces, above all, is its own grave-diggers. Its fall and the victory of the proletariat are equally inevitable.

NOTES

1. By *bourgeoisie* is meant the class of modern Capitalists, owners of the means of social production and employers of wage-labour. By *proletariat*, the class of modern wage-labourers who, having no means of production of their own, are reduced to selling their labour-power in order to live. [*Engels, English edition of 1888*]

2. That is, all *written* history. In 1847, the pre-history of society, the social organisation existing previous to recorded history, was all but unknown. Since then, Haxthausen discovered common ownership of land in Russia, Maurer proved it to be the social foundation from which all Teutonic races started in history, and by and by village communities were found to be, or to have been the primitive form of society everywhere from India to Ireland. The inner organisation of this primitive Communistic society was laid bare, in its typical form, by Morgan's crowning

discovery of the true nature of the *gens* and its relation to the *tribe*. With the dissolution of these primaeval communities society begins to be differentiated into separate and finally antagonistic classes. I have attempted to retrace this process of dissolution in: "Der Ursprung der Familie, des Privateigenthums und des Staats" [*The Origin of the Family, Private Property and the State*], 2nd edition, Stuttgart 1886. [*Engels, English edition of 1888*]

3. Guild-master, that is, a full member of a guild, a master within, not a head of a guild. [*Engels, English edition of 1888*]

4. "Commune" was the name taken, in France, by the nascent towns even before they had conquered from their feudal lords

and masters local self-government and political rights as the "Third Estate." Generally speaking, for the economical development of the bourgeoisie, England is here taken as the typical country; for its political development, France. [*Engels, English edition of 1888*]

This was the name given their urban communities by the townsmen of Italy and France, after they had purchased or wrested their initial rights of self-government from their feudal lords. [*Engels, German edition of 1890*]

5. Subsequently Marx pointed out that the worker sells not his labour but his labour power.

QUESTIONS

1. Describe in detail the various stages of development in Marx and Engels' discussion of class struggle.

2. Can a link be made on the basis of security between class struggle and the anarchic nature of the international system described by Hans Morgenthau in "Politics among Nations" (page 63)? Explain.

17.   Imperialism: The Highest Stage of Capitalism

Vladimir I. Lenin

In this excerpt, Lenin explains how imperialism is the inevitable by-product of capitalism. According to Lenin, the colonial empires of Western capitalist nations can be maintained only by the extension of boundaries and exploitation of outlying territories. Since the number of new territories was limited, the struggle to attain more colonies ultimately caused capitalist states to war with one another. This selection is from *Imperialism, The Highest Stage of Capitalism* (1952).

Reprinted by permission of Foreign Languages Press.

Vladimir Ilyich Lenin (1870–1924) was leader of the Bolshevik Revolution that brought an end to czarist Russia in 1917. He subsequently ruled the Soviet Union until his death.

IMPERIALISM, AS A SPECIAL STAGE OF CAPITALISM

Imperialism emerged as the development and direct continuation of the fundamental characteristics of capitalism in general. But capitalism only became capitalist imperialism at a definite and very high stage of its development, when certain of its fundamental characteristics began to change into their opposites, when the features of the epoch of transition from capitalism to a higher social and economic system had taken shape and revealed themselves all along the line. Economically, the main thing in this process is the displacement of capitalist free competition by capitalist monopoly. Free competition is the fundamental characteristic of capitalism, and of commodity production generally; monopoly is the exact opposite of free competition, but we have seen the latter being transformed into monopoly before our eyes, creating large-scale industry and forcing out small industry, replacing large-scale by still larger-scale industry, and carrying concentration of production and capital to the point where out of it has grown and is growing monopoly: cartels, syndicates and trusts, and merging with them, the capital of a dozen or so banks, which manipulate thousands of millions. At the same time the monopolies, which have grown out of free competition, do not eliminate the latter, but exist over it and alongside of it, and thereby give rise to a number of very acute, intense antagonisms, frictions and conflicts. Monopoly is the transition from capitalism to a higher system.

If it were necessary to give the briefest possible definition of imperialism we should have to say that imperialism is the monopoly stage of capitalism. Such a definition would include what is most important, for, on the one hand, finance capital is the bank capital of a few very big monopolist banks, merged with the capital of the monopolist combines of industrialists; and, on the other hand, the division of the world is the transition from a colonial policy which has extended without hindrance to territories unseized by any capitalist power, to a colonial policy of monopolistic possession of the territory of the world which has been completely divided up.

But very brief definitions, although convenient, for they sum up the main points, are nevertheless inadequate, since very important features of the phenomenon that has to be defined have to be especially deduced. And so, without forgetting the conditional and relative value of all definitions in general, which can never embrace all the concatenations of a phenomenon in its complete development, we must give a definition of imperialism that will include the following five of its basic features: 1) the concentration of production and capital has developed to such a high stage that it has created monopolies which play a decisive role in economic life; 2) the merging of bank capital with industrial capital, and the creation, on the basis of this "finance capital," of a financial oligarchy; 3) the export of capital as distinguished from the export of commodities acquires exceptional importance; 4) the formation of international monopolist capitalist combines which share the world among themselves, and 5) the territorial division of the whole world among the biggest capitalist powers is completed. Imperialism is capitalism in that stage of development in which the dominance of monopolies and finance capital has established itself; in which the export of capital has acquired pronounced importance; in which the division of the world among the international trusts has begun; in which the division of all territories of the globe among the biggest capitalist powers has been completed. . . .

THE PLACE OF IMPERIALISM IN HISTORY

We have seen that in its economic essence imperialism is monopoly capitalism. This in itself determines its place in history, for monopoly that grows out of the soil of free competition, and precisely out of free competition, is the transition from the capitalist system to a higher social-economic order. We must take special note of the four principal types of monopoly, or principal manifestations of monopoly capitalism, which are characteristic of the epoch we are examining.

Firstly, monopoly arose out of a very high stage of development of the concentration of production. This refers to the monopolist capitalist combines, cartels, syndicates and trusts. We have seen the important part these play in present-day economic life. At the beginning of the twentieth century, monopolies had acquired complete supremacy in the advanced countries, and although the first steps towards the formation of the cartels were first taken by countries enjoying the protection of high tariffs (Germany, America), Great Britain, with

her system of free trade, revealed the same basic phenomenon, only a little later, namely, the birth of monopoly out of the concentration of production.

Secondly, monopolies have stimulated the seizure of the most important sources of raw materials, especially for the basic and most highly cartelized industries in capitalist society: the coal and iron industries. The monopoly of the most important sources of raw materials has enormously increased the power of big capital, and has sharpened the antagonism between cartelized and non-cartelized industry.

Thirdly, monopoly has sprung from the banks. The banks have developed from humble middlemen enterprises into the monopolists of finance capital. Some three to five of the biggest banks in each of the foremost capitalist countries have achieved the "personal union" of industrial and bank capital, and have concentrated in their hands the control of thousands upon thousands of millions which form the greater part of the capital and income of entire countries. A financial oligarchy, which throws a close network of dependence relationships over all the economic and political institutions of present-day bourgeois society without exception—such is the most striking manifestation of this monopoly.

Fourthly, monopoly has grown out of colonial policy. To the numerous "old" motives of colonial policy, finance capital has added the struggle for the sources of raw materials, for the export of capital, for "spheres of influence," i.e., for spheres for profitable deals, concessions, monopolist profits and so on, and finally, for economic territory in general. When the colonies of the European powers in Africa, for instance, comprised only one-tenth of that territory (as was the case in 1876), colonial policy was able to develop by methods other than those of monopoly—by the "free grabbing" of territories, so to speak. But when nine-tenths of Africa had been seized (by 1900), when the whole world had been divided up, there was inevitably ushered in the era of monopoly ownership of colonies and, consequently, of particularly intense struggle for the division and the redivision of the world.

The extent to which monopolist capital has intensified all the contradictions of capitalism is generally known. It is sufficient to mention the high cost of living and the tyranny of the cartels. This intensification of contradictions constitutes the most powerful driving force of the transitional period of history, which began from the time of the final victory of world finance capital.

Monopolies, oligarchy, the striving for domination instead of striving for liberty, the exploitation of an increasing number of small or weak nations by a handful of the richest or most powerful nations—all these have given birth to those distinctive characteristics of imperialism which compel us to define it as parasitic or decaying capitalism. More and more prominently there emerges, as one of the tendencies of imperialism, the creation of the "rentier state," the usurer state, in which the bourgeoisie to an ever increasing degree lives on the proceeds of capital exports and by "clipping coupons." It would be a mistake to believe that this tendency to decay precludes the rapid growth of capitalism. It does not. In the epoch of imperialism, certain branches of industry, certain strata of the bourgeoisie and certain countries betray, to a greater or lesser degree, now one and now another of these tendencies. On the whole, capitalism is growing far more rapidly than before; but this growth is not only becoming more and more uneven in general, its unevenness also manifests itself, in particular, in the decay of the countries which are richest in capital (England).

QUESTIONS

1. How does Lenin explain the evolution of imperialism from capitalism?

2. According to Lenin, there are four principle manifestations of monopoly capitalism. Explain them.

---

18.   The Capitalist World Economy

Immanuel Wallerstein

In this article, Immanuel Wallerstein presents the key elements of the capitalist world economy. Concepts such as the core and periphery zones of goods and services and the socialization of the productive process are also discussed. This selection is from the journal *Contemporary Marxism* (1984).

Immanuel Wallerstein is director of the Fernand Braudel Center at the State University of New York, Binghamton, and a senior research scholar at Yale University. His works include *World Inequality* (1975) and *Historic Capitalism* (1983), as well as contributions to various professional journals.

1. THE NATURE OF THE WORLD-ECONOMY

1.1. The concept world-economy (*économie-monde* in French) should be distinguished from that of world economy (*économie mondiale*) or international economy. The latter concept presumes there are a series of separate "economies" which are "national" in scope, and that under certain circumstances these "national economies" trade with each other, the sum of these (limited) contacts being called the international economy. Those who use this latter concept argue that the limited contacts have been expanding in the 20th century. It is thus asserted that the world has become "one world" in a sense it wasn't prior to the 20th century.

By contrast, the concept "world-economy" assumes that there exists an "economy" wherever (and if but only if) there is an ongoing extensive and relatively complete social division of labor with an integrated set of production processes which relate to each other through a "market" which has been "instituted" or "created" in some complex way. Using such a concept, the world-economy is not new in the 20th century, nor is it a coming together of "national economies," none of the latter constituting complete divisions of labor. Rather, a world-economy, capitalist in form, has been in existence in at least part of the globe since the 16th century. Today, the entire globe is operating within the framework of this singular social division of labor we are calling the capitalist world-economy.

1.2. The capitalist world-economy has, and has had since its coming into existence, boundaries far larger than that of any political unit. Indeed, it seems to be one of the basic defining features of a capitalist world-economy that there exists no political entity with ultimate authority in all its zones.

Rather, the political superstructure of the capitalist world-economy is an interstate system within which and through which political structures called "sovereign states" are legitimized and constrained. Far from meaning the total autonomy of decision-making, the term "sovereignty" in reality implies a formal autonomy combined with real limitations on this autonomy, which are implemented both via the explicit and implicit rules of the interstate system and via the power of other states in the interstate system. No state in the interstate system, even the single most powerful one at any given time, is totally autonomous—but obviously some enjoy far greater autonomy than others.

1.3. The world-economy is a complex of cultures—in the sense of languages, religions, ideologies—but this complex is not haphazard. There exists a *Weltanschauung* of imperium, albeit one with several variants, and there exist cultures of resistance to this imperium.

1.4. The major social institutions of the capitalist world-economy—the states, the classes, the "peoples," and the households—are all shaped (even created) by the ongoing workings of the world-economy. None of them are primordial, in the sense of permanent, pre-existing, relatively fixed structures to which the workings of the capitalist world-economy are exogenous.

1.5. The capitalist world-economy is a *historical* social system. It came into existence, and its genesis must be explained. Its existence is defined by certain patterns—both cyclical rhythms and secular trends—which must be explicated. It is highly probable that it will one day go out of existence (become transformed into another type of historical social system), and we can therefore assess the historical alternatives that are before us.

2. THE PATTERNS OF THE WORLD-ECONOMY

All historical structures constantly evolve. However, the use of any concept is a capturing in fixed form of some continuing pattern. We could not discern the world, interpret it, or consciously change it unless we used concepts, with all the limitations that any reification, however slight, implies.

2.1. The world-economy has a capitalist mode of production. This is an empirical statement. Although there have been other world-economies (as defined above) known in history, the modern one of which we are speaking is the only one which has survived over a long period of time without either disintegrating or being transformed into a world-empire (with a singular political structure). This modern one has had a capitalist mode of production—that is, its economy has been dominated by those who operate on the primacy of endless accumulation, such entrepreneurs (or controllers of production units) driving

from the arena those who seek to operate on other premises. Since only one world-economy has survived over a long period of time, and since this one has been capitalist in form, we may suspect that the two phenomena are theoretically linked: that a world-economy to survive must have a capitalist mode of production, and inversely that capitalism cannot be the mode of production except in a system that has the form of a world-economy (a division of labor more extensive than any one political entity).

2.2. The capitalist world-economy has operated via a social relationship called capital/labor, in which the surplus created by direct producers has been appropriated by others either at the point of production or at the most immediate market place, in either case by virtue of the fact that the appropriators control the "capital" and that their "rights" to the surplus are legally guaranteed. The extractors of surplus-value may in many cases be individuals, but they have tended increasingly to be collective entities (private or state corporations).

2.3. Once surplus-value has been extracted, it has yet to be "distributed" among a network of beneficiaries. The exchange processes of the "market" are one mode through which this redistribution occurs. In particular, the structure of the world-economy permits an unequal exchange of goods and services (primarily trans-state), such that much of the surplus-value extracted in the peripheral zones of the world-economy is transferred to the core zones.

2.4. The exchange of products containing unequal amounts of social labor we may call the core/periphery relationship. This is pervasive, continuing, and constant. There tend to be geographical localizations of productive activities such that core-like production activities and periphery-like production activities tend each to be spatially grouped together. We can thus, for shorthand purposes, refer to some states as core states and others as peripheral states.

2.5. Insofar as some states function as loci of mixed kinds of production activities (some core-like, some periphery-like), we can speak of such states as semi-peripheral. There always exist semi-peripheral zones.

2.6. While the pattern of a spatial hierarchy of production processes within the capitalist world-economy is a constant, the position of any given state is not, since there have been regular partial relocations of core-like and periphery-like economic activities.

2.7. Since what makes a production process core-like or periphery-like is the degree to which it incorporates labor-value, is mechanized, and is highly profitable, and all these characteristics shift over time for any given product because of "product cycles," it follows that no product is inherently core-like or periphery-like, but has that characteristic for a given time. Nonetheless, there are always some products which are core-like and others which are periphery-like at any given time.

2.8. Because the imperatives of accumulation operate via the individual decisions of entrepreneurs, each seeking to maximize his profit—the so-called anarchy of production—there is an inherent tendency to the expansion of absolute volume of production in the world-economy. Profit can, however, only be realized if there is effective demand for the global product. World effective demand, however, is a function of the sum of political arrangements in the various states (the result of prior class struggles), which determine the real distribution of the global surplus. These arrangements are stable for intermediate periods of time. Consequently, world supply expands at a steady rate while world demand remains relatively fixed for intermediate periods. Such a system must result, and historically has resulted, in recurring bottlenecks of accumulation, which are translated into periods of economic stagnation. The A-phases of expansion and the B-phases of stagnation seem to have occurred historically in cycles of 40–55 years (sometimes called "Kondratieff cycles").

2.9. Each period of stagnation has created pressures to restructure the network of production processes and the social relations that underlie them in ways that would overcome the bottlenecks to accumulation. Among the mechanisms that have operated to renew expansion are:

a. reduction of production costs of former core-like products by further mechanization and/or relocation of these activities in lower-wage zones;

b. creation of new core-like activities ("innovation"), which promise high initial rates of profit, thus encouraging new loci of investment;

c. an intensified class struggle both within the core states and between groups located in different states such that there may occur at the end of the process some political redistribution of world surplus to workers in core zones (often by means of fully proletarianizing hitherto semi-proletarian households) and to bourgeois in semi-peripheral and peripheral zones, thereby augmenting world effective demand;

d. expansion of the outer boundaries of the world-economy, thereby creating new pools of direct producers who can be involved in world production as semi-proletarianized workers receiving wages below the cost of reproduction.

2.10. States in which core-like activities occur develop relatively strong state apparatuses which can advance the interests of their bourgeoisies, less by protection (a mechanism of the medium-strong seeking to be stronger) than by preventing other states from erecting political barriers to the profitability of these activities. In general, states seek to shape the world market in ways that will advance the interests of some entrepreneurs against that of others.

2.11. There seem to be cycles as well, within the interstate system. On three separate occasions, one state has been able to achieve what may be called a hegemonic position in the world-economy: the United Provinces, 1620–1650; the United Kingdom, 1815–1873; the United States, 1945–1967. When producers located within a given state can undersell producers located in other core states in the latter's "home market," they can over time transform this production advantage into one in the commercial arena and then into one in the financial arena. The combined advantages may be said to constitute hegemony and are reflected as well in a political-military advantage in the interstate system. Such hegemonies are relatively short-lived, since the production advantages cannot be sustained indefinitely and mechanisms of the balance of power intrude to reduce the political advantage of the single most powerful state.

2.12. The core states in general, and the hegemonic state when one exists in particular, seek to reinforce the advantages of their producers and to legitimize their role in the interstate system by imposing their cultural dominance on the world. To some extent, this occurs in the easily visible form of language, religion, and mores, but more importantly this occurs in the form of seeking to impose modes of thought and analysis, including in particular the paradigms that inform philosophy and the sciences/social sciences.

3. THE SECULAR TRENDS OF THE WORLD-ECONOMY

The patterns of the world-economy may be at first glance cyclical in form, but they are not perfectly cyclical. The world-economy has a historical development which is structural and can be analyzed in terms of its secular trends.

3.1. The drive to accumulate leads to the constant deepening of the capitalist development. The search to reduce long-term costs of production leads to a steady increase in the degree to which production is mechanized. The search for the least expensive source of factors of production (including as an expense delays in time in acquiring access) leads to a steady increase in the degree to which these factors (land, labor, and goods) are commodified. The desire to reduce barriers to the process of accumulation leads to a steady increase in the degree to which economic transactions are contractualized. It is important to recognize two things about these processes of mechanization, commodification, and contractualization.

3.1.1. While there are regular increases in the world-economy taken as a whole of the degree of mechanization, commodification, and contractualization, the pattern is not linear but stepwise, each significant advance leading to overall expansion, and each overall stagnation leading to a restructuring of the world-economy such that there is further advance.

3.1.2. The capitalist development of the world-economy at the world level is far from complete in the 20th century. These processes are still in full operation.

3.2. The recurring stagnations of the world-economy, which have led to the regular restructuring of this world-economy, have involved as part of restructuring the expansion of the "outer" boundaries of the world-economy, a process which, however, has been nearly completed as of now. This expansion, which was central to world history of the past several hundred years, gradually eliminated from the globe other kinds of historical social systems, creating the historically unique situation of there being, for all effects and purposes, a single social division of labor on the earth.

3.3. The steady but still incomplete commodification of labor, side by side with the now largely completed expansion of the outer boundaries of the world-economy, accounts for the shape of two of the major institutional structures of the capitalist world-economy: the classes and the households.

3.3.1. The commodification of labor ultimately means a structure in which direct producers have no access to the means of production except by selling their labor-power on a market; that is, they become proletarians. Although the percentage of direct producers who are full-lifetime proletarians has been growing worldwide over time, nonetheless, even today such proletarians are still probably no more than half of the world's work force.

3.3.2. The commodification of land and capital ultimately means a structure in which controllers of land or capital (including "human capital") have no access to the maintenance and reproduction of land and capital except by pursuing an active policy of maximizing the accumulation of capital; that is, they become bourgeois. In the 20th century, there are very few who control land or capital—directly (individually) or indirectly (collectively)—who are not bourgeois, that is, persons whose economic raison d'être is the accumulation of capital.

3.3.3. Hence, we have a situation in which *a part but not all* of the direct producers are (full-lifetime) proletarians (the other part we may designate as "semi-proletarians"), but *most* of the controllers of land and capital are bourgeois.

3.3.4. The creation of two large worldwide classes has led to the molding of appropriate household structures as the member-units of these classes. We mean by household the unit which, over a longish (30–50 year) period, pools the income of all its members, from whatever source and in whatever form is this income.

3.3.5. The "semi-proletarian" household, so extensive in peripheral zones of the world-economy, permits the wage-employment of some of its members for parts of their lives at wages below the proportionate cost of reproduction by pooling this wage-income with that received from subsistence, petty commodity, rental, and transfer income. This is what is meant by "super-exploitation" (since in this case the employer of the wage-laborer is receiving not merely the surplus-value created by the wage-laborer, but that which other members of the household are creating).

3.3.6. The proletarian household, tending to receive wage-income approximating the real costs of reproduction (no less but also not much more) tends to move in the direction of more "nucleated" households, sloughing off *affines* and others not defined as pulling their full weight.

3.3.7. The bourgeois household, seeking to maximize the use of capital, the direct control of which tends to increase by age, and utilizing the family structure as the primary mechanism of avoiding social redistribution, tends to take the form of extended, multilocal households.

3.4. The steady (now largely completed) expansion of the outer boundaries of the world-economy, combined with the continuing competition among bourgeois for advantage in the capitalist world-economy, accounts for the shape of the other two major institutional structures of the capitalist world-economy: the states and the peoples.

3.4.1. The drive of bourgeois for competitive advantage has led to increasing definition ("power") of the states as political structures and increasing emphasis on their constraint by the interstate system. This push for a "strong" state (strong vis-à-vis both other internal loci of power and vis-à-vis other states and external nonstate forces) has been greatest and therefore most efficacious in those states with core-like production activities. The strong state has been the principal mechanism by which the bourgeois controlling these core-like production activities have been able (a) to limit and moderate the economic demands of their national work forces, (b) to shape the world market so as to compete effectively with bourgeoisies located in other states, and (c) to incorporate new zones into the world-economy, thus constantly re-creating new centers of peripheral production activities.

3.4.2. The increasing definition of state structures has led to the shaping, reshaping, creation, destruction, revival of "people." To the extent that these "peoples" are defined by themselves (and by others) as controlling or having the "moral" right to control state structures, these "peoples" become "nations." To the extent that they are not defined as having the right to control a state structure, these people become "minorities" or "ethnic groups." Defining given states as nation-states is an aid in strengthening the state. Such a definition requires emphasizing one "people" and deemphasizing, even destroying (conceptually or literally), others. This is particularly important for semi-peripheral states seeking to transform their structural role in the world-economy. Various groups have interests supporting and opposing any particular nation-state definition. "Nationalism" is a mechanism both of imperium/integration and of resistance/liberation. The people are not haphazardly defined but neither are they simple and unfixed derivations from a historical past. They are solidarity groupings whose boundaries are a matter of constant social transmittal/redefinition.

3.5. As the classes come to be defined vis-à-vis the developing division of labor in the world-economy and the peoples come to be defined vis-à-vis the increasing rationalized interstate system, the locational concentration of various oppressed groups gives rise over time to anti-systemic movements. These movements have organized in two main forms around two main themes: the social movement around "class" and the national movement around "nation" or people.

3.5.1. The seriously anti-systemic (or revolutionary) forms of such movements first emerged in *organized* form in the

19th century. Their general objective, human equality, was by definition incompatible with the functioning of the capitalist world-economy, a hierarchical system based on uneven development, unequal exchange, and the appropriation of surplus-value. However, the political structure of the capitalist world-economy—the fact that it was not a single unit but a series of sovereign states—pressed the movements to seek the transformation of the world-system via the achievement of political power within separate states. The organization of these anti-systemic movements at the state level had contradictory effects.

3.5.2. Organization at the state level for the social movement was ideologically confusing from the beginning, as it counterposed the logical and ideological necessity of worldwide struggle (proletarian internationalism) against the immediate political need of achieving power within one state. Either the social movement resisted "nationalism" and was rendered inefficacious or it utilized nationalism and then faced ambiguously the so-called "national question"—that is, the "nationalisms" of the "minorities" within the boundaries of the state. Whatever the tactic of a given social movement, the achievement of partial or total state power involved power in a structure constrained by the interstate system, hence unable by itself to transform the system entirely (that is, to withdraw totally from the capitalist world-economy).

3.5.3. Organization at the state level created dilemmas for the national movements as well. The smaller the zone within which the national movement defined itself, the easier the access to state power but the less consequential. Hence, all national movements have oscillated in terms of the unit of definition, and the various "pan-" movements have had limited success. But defeats of "pan-" movements have tended to dilute the anti-systemic thrust of particular national movements.

3.5.4. In general, both social and national movements have had a difficult time reconciling long-run anti-systemic objectives and short-run "developmentalist" or "catching-up" objectives, which tend to reinforce rather than undermine the world-system. Nonetheless, the collective momentum of the social and national movements over time has been anti-systemic in effect, despite the "reformism" or "revisionism" of the various movements taken separately. Furthermore, the collective momentum of these movements has been such as to confound increasingly the social and national movements, which has in fact been a source of additional strength.

3.6. The unfolding of the institutional structures of the world-system—the classes, the states, the peoples, the households—has been reflected in the cultural mosaic of the world-system, whose pattern has been increasingly that of the tension between imperium and resistance.

3.6.1. As the axial division of labor became more pronounced and more unequal, the need to facilitate its operation through the allocation of work forces and the justification of inequality led to an ideology of racism that became the central organizing cultural theme of the world bourgeoisie. The existence of superior groups (whether in particular instances these groups were defined as Caucasians or Anglosaxons or other variants on this theme) became a method of simple *triage* in job and income allocation.

3.6.2. Whereas racism has served as a mechanism of worldwide control of direct producers, the bourgeoisie of strong core states (and particularly of the hegemonic power) sought also to direct the activities of the bourgeois of other states and various middle strata worldwide into channels that would maximize the close integration of production processes and the smooth operation of the interstate system such that the accumulation of capital was facilitated. This required the creation of a world bourgeois cultural framework that could be grafted onto "national" variations. This was particularly important in terms of science and technology, but quite important too in the realm of political ideas and of the social sciences.

3.6.3. The concept of a neutral "universal" culture to which the cadres of the world division of labor would be "assimilated" (the passive tense being important here) hence came to serve as one of the pillars of the world-system as it historically evolved. The exaltation of progress, and later of "modernization," summarized this set of ideas, which served less as true norms of social action than as status-symbols of obeisance and of participation in the world's upper strata.

3.6.4. Resistance to this cultural assimilationism was to be found among competitive bourgeois in semi-peripheral and nonhegemonic core states and took the form of asserting the autonomy of "national" traditions and/or antipathy to structural generalizations in the domain of ideas. It also took the form of reinforcing alternative world linguistic groupings to the hegemonic one (in practice, of English).

3.6.5. More fundamental cultural resistance on the part of anti-systemic movements has come slowly to take the form of positing civilizational alternatives to dominant cultural forms. In particular, it has counterdistinguished civilizations (plural) to civilization (singular and imperial).

4. THE SYSTEM IN CRISIS

4.1. A system that has cyclical patterns has recurring downturns, whatever we wish to call them. We have argued the regularity of world economic stagnations as one of the patterns of the capitalist world-economy. But insofar as there are also mechanisms that regularly bring these stagnations to an end and relaunch world economic expansion, we cannot count these cyclical downturns as crises, however much they are perceived as such by the individuals living through them.

4.2. Rather, a "crisis" is a situation in which the restitutive mechanisms of the system are no longer functioning well, and therefore the system will either be transformed fundamentally or disintegrate. It is in this sense that we could talk for example of the "crisis of feudalism" in Europe in the period 1300–1450, a crisis whose resolution was the historic emergence of a capitalist world-economy located in that particular geographic arena. We may say that this capitalist world-economy in turn entered into a long "crisis" of a comparable nature in the 20th century, a crisis in the midst of which we are living.

4.3. The causes of the crisis are internal to the system, the result of the contradictions built into the processes.

4.3.1. One of the mechanisms whereby the world-economy has overcome its downturn phases has been the expansion of the outer boundaries of the world-economy, but this is a process which has inbuilt limits which are nearly reached.

4.3.2. Another of the mechanisms whereby the world-economy has overcome its downturn phases has been the expansion of world effective demand, in part through proletarianization of the direct producers, in part by redistribution of the surplus among the world bourgeoisie.

4.3.2.1. Proletarianization is also a process that has inbuilt limits. While they have hardly yet been reached, the process has been speeding up, and one can foresee it reaching its asymptote within the coming century.

4.3.2.2. Redistribution of the surplus among the bourgeoisie is itself the result of bourgeoisification, which has entailed an increase of the total percentage of the world population who are bourgeois. If one distinguishes between the small group of bourgeois who control most of the fixed capital and the much larger group of bourgeois who control principally human capital, the growth and social concentration of the latter group have resulted in their acquisition of considerable political power in core states. They have been able, as the price of their political support for the world-system as a system, to ensure that an increasing proportion of the appropriated surplus will be redistributed to them, reducing over the long run the rate of profit to the holders of fixed capital.

4.4. Increasing proletarianization and the increasing constraint on individual mobility because of the degree to which definitions of peoples have been linked to position in the world-economy have led to the rise of the anti-systemic movements. These movements have a cumulative effect which may be said to draw a logarithmic curve. We have entered into the phase of acute escalation.

4.5. The fact that we are in a systemic crisis and have been in one at least since the Russian Revolution—which was its symbolic detonator and has always been seen as such—does not mean that the capitalist development of the world-economy has come to an end. Quite the contrary. It is as vigorous as ever, perhaps more so. This is indeed the prime cause of the crisis. The very vigor of capitalist development has been and will continue to be the main factor that exacerbates the contradictions of the system.

4.6. It is therefore not the case that the crisis will be imminently resolved. A crisis of a system is a long, slow, difficult process, and for it to play itself out over a 150-year period is scarcely surprising. We have little perspective on it as we are amidst it, and we therefore tend to exaggerate each minor fork in the road. There is some constructive value in being overly optimistic in a short run, but the negative side of such exaggeration is the disillusionments it breeds. A crisis is best navigated by a cool, long-run strategy. It cannot however be totally planned, as the crisis itself gives rise to new possibilities of human action.

5. PROSPECTIVES

There are three different logics which are playing themselves out in the present world crisis. The outcome will be the result of their interaction.

5.1. There is the logic of socialism.

5.1.1. The capitalist development of the world-economy itself moves toward the socialization of the productive process. There is an *organizational* (as opposed to a political) imperative in which the full achievement of capitalist relations of production—through its emphasis on the increase of relative surplus-value and the maximum efficiency (free flow) of the factors of production—pushes toward a fully planned single productive organizational network in the world-economy.

5.1.2. Furthermore, the political logic of the appropriation of surplus by the few leads to the growth of the anti-systemic movements and therefore toward the spread of socialist values among the world's direct producers.

5.1.3. Finally, the structure of the world-economy (multiple states within the division of labor) has created the possibility of socialist political movements coming to power in individual states, seeking to "construct socialism." Despite the fact that their continued location in the capitalist world-economy and the interstate system seriously constrains the kinds of transformations they can effectuate within boundaries of a given state, their attempts to approximate in various ways a socialist order create additional institutional pressures on the world-system to move in the direction of socialism.

5.2. There is also the logic of domination.

5.2.1. Insofar as the powerful have, by definition, more power than the mass of the world population, and insofar as the process of transformation is slow and contradictory, it creates much opportunity for the ruling strata (the world bourgeoisie) to invent modes of continuity of power and privilege. The adoption of new social roles and new ideological clothing may be a route for existing dominant strata to perpetuate themselves in a new system. It is certainly the logic of domination that dominant groups seek to survive even a "crisis." As the landowning hero of di Lampedusa's *Il Gattopardo* says: "We must

change everything in order that everything remain the same."

5.2.2. In the process of the world bourgeoisie seeking to retain their power, they may engage in policies which lead to a nuclear world war. This could bring about a demise of the present system in a manner that would destroy much of the forces of production and thereby make a socialist world order far less structurally feasible.

5.3. There is a logic of the civilizational project.

5.3.1. While the capitalist world-economy has been the first and only social system that has managed to eliminate from the earth all contemporaneous social systems, this has been historically true only for a very recent period of time. We could regard it as simply the conquest by Western Europeans of the globe. In this case, in the long run of history, the political and technological supremacy of the West constitutes a short interval and, from the perspective of alternative "civilizational" centers, might be thought of as a transitory and aberrant interlude. There is thus a drive for a restituted civilizational balance, which the very process of capitalist development of the world-economy makes more urgent and more realizable.

5.3.2. How a restituted civilizational balance fits in, however, with world socialism on the one hand and the drive of world ruling strata to survive on the other is not at all clear.

5.4. We live facing real historical alternatives. It is clear that the capitalist world-economy cannot survive, and that as a historical social system it is in the process of being superseded. The forces at play are also clear, as are the secular trends. We can struggle for our preferences. We can analyze probabilities. But we cannot foretell, because we cannot yet know for certain how the conjuncture of forces at play will constrain the directions of change and even less can we know what new possibilities of human liberation they will afford. The only thing of which we may be certain is that our present activity will be a major factor in the outcome of the crisis.

QUESTIONS

1. Explain how Wallerstein defines the development of the core and periphery zone in the capitalist world economy.

2. Discuss how Hans Morgenthau ("Politics among Nations," page 63) and Kenneth Waltz ("Man, the State, and War," page 12) might respond to Wallerstein's thesis.

19.   A Singular Collapse:
The Soviet Union, Market Pressure,
and Inter-State Competition

Fred Halliday

In this article, Fred Halliday examines "how far and in what ways" the ideological and economic competition between the United States and the Soviet Union contributed to the final collapse of the communist system. Halliday concludes that the Soviet Union collapsed because it was ultimately unable to compete with the consumerism and capitalist policies of the West. This selection is from the journal *Contention* (1991).

Fred Halliday is a professor of international relations at the London School of Economics. His books include *The World at 2000: Perils and Promises* (2000) and *Islam and the Myth of Confrontation* (1996).

INTRODUCTION: NEW LIGHT ON OLD QUESTIONS

The collapse of the Soviet system within the U.S.S.R. and internationally in the late 1980s, in addition to its manifold implications for global politics and policy, has raised a range of important and unresolved issues, analytically and within social and international theory. The first question is that of explanation, of providing why a political and socio-economic system that was broadly equal to its rival in military terms should have collapsed rapidly and unequivocally, and in the

Reprinted by permission of the publisher from *Contention*, Vol. I, No. 2, pp. 121–139, Fall 1991.

absence of significant international military conflict.[1] No explanation in terms of a single factor is possible, and there is much that will only become clearer with the passage of time. What is being attempted here is a provisional analysis of the causes of the collapse of the communist system, focusing on the international dimensions of this process. The internal weaknesses of the system played a major role in its demise, not least the paralysis at both economic and political levels that characterized it,[2] but an analysis of the international factors is of relevance for several reasons—first, because so much has been said and written about how international competition did contribute to the failure of communism and it is worth now assessing these claims; second, because, despite talk of its "failure," this system did not fall because of internal pressures alone; third, because a discussion of the historical question, why communism collapsed, may cast light on underlying theoretical issues pertaining to interstate and intersystemic competition.

The communist leaderships were engaged in a project that was both national and international: it was international as a result of systemic pressure from other states, but it was also ideologically international, an attempt to constitute a model society on an international scale, and to promote similar movements in other countries. Yet if the overall failure of communism includes its failure to spread worldwide, a better starting point to analyze why the regimes collapsed is the record of internal, top-down transformation which the regimes promoted. The elites in the central committees and politbureaus of the ruling parties sought to transform the societies in accordance with a theoretical blueprint of where socialist society should be going. This project was a failure, not only in reaching its goal, but also because much of what had apparently been achieved was impermanent and superficial. The claims that "developed socialism" or some sort of more perfect society had been reached were false, and so too were the apparently less apologetic claims that these societies were in some implicitly teleological sense "in transition" to a new socio-economic model and represented a permanent advance beyond what capitalism could provide.

This failure is as true for attempts to create a viable and self-sustaining planned economy as it is for those to forge politically viable one-party systems, and for attempts to reform attitudes regarding major areas of ideological importance, notably work, gender, religion, and ethnicity. The simplest explanation of the collapse is to say that such a project was, in an absolute sense, a "failure": this is the conclusion that many in the communist countries now draw, as those who deny the efficacy of "social engineering" have always done. There are, however, reasons to resist this conclusion. In terms of the capacities of states to transform society from above, the record is not so absolute.

First, it is far too early to say how much of the legacy of communist rule will endure and whether some of it may not in fact survive. Second, it is wrong to take as evidence of the failure of communism the emergence of forces that appear to mark a return to pre-communist forms of behavior, since many of these have a character that has been shaped by the very impact of communist transformation—ethnic conflict being an obvious case. Similarly, as many who have analyzed the emergence of Gorbachev have shown, the change in Soviet society is in some respects a product of the achievements of communism—expansion in education and urbanization being obvious contributory factors.[3] Third, even if much or all of what is associated with communist rule does disappear, say in a decade or two, the historical fact of the communist achievement over some decades will remain: this was evident in socioeconomic transformation, the raising of living standards and the implementation of a widespread social welfare system, the sustenance and reproduction of a political system and, not least, a considerable success in the most testing area of all, inter-state competition. It may be that the success of the latter—Soviet victory in World War II, plus four decades of rivalry with the West thereafter—provided part of the illusion of communism's overall efficacy, at home and abroad. However, the record of interstate competition alone would suggest that the characterization of the communist record as a "failure" is simplistic. Such a verdict would have come as rather a surprise to, for example, the 250,000 Germans captured at Stalingrad as it would have to military planners in the Pentagon during the 1970s and early 1980s. The achievement was substantial, even if temporary.

THE NATURE OF COLD WAR

If the events of 1989 signal the end of the Cold War, they make it more possible to address the question of what the Cold War was, and how as one specific instance it pertains to broader conceptions of interstate competition. Despite its apparent distinctiveness, the Cold War has been treated by most writers as merely another chapter in a longer history of international competition. The term "cold war" tended to be used in two ways: one to denote particular periods of intense East-West rivalry, 1947–53, the classic original "Cold War" and, though this is more disputed, the period 1979–84, the "Second Cold War." The other usage denotes not specific periods but the more protracted rivalry of the two systems, capitalist and communist, as it developed after 1945 and originated in 1917.[4]

The academic literature has tended to focus on historical questions pertaining to the first, narrower sense of cold war, of who originated the intensified conflict in 1947 or 1979 and why, and this is the basis of the debate between orthodox, revisionist and post-revisionist historians on the origins of the cold war. Less articulated has been the theoretical debate, on what kind of conflict this cold war in the broader sense was, and what its implications are for international and other social theory. In one view, there was no problem: the Cold War was a strategic rivalry between great powers like any other and susceptible to conventional "realist" analysis. This explanation had several things to recommend it: it had considerable explanatory power; it drew attention to what were undoubtedly points of comparison between historic great power conflicts and the Soviet-American one, most obviously competition for spheres of influence and military power; it provided a way of creating academic distance from the rival ideological claims of both sides to be representing one or other set of universal values; it distinguished itself from the orthodox Marxist view that in some way the Cold War represented an internationalized political conflict, class struggle on a world scale.

Yet it can be questioned how far this conventional description of the Cold War did accord with reality and, not least, how far it can be seen to provide a basis for understanding communism's collapse. One initial novelty about East-West rivalry in the postwar epoch was the role of nuclear weapons, the limits these placed upon direct territorial competition between the core blocs and the peculiarly intense but controlled competition of the arms race. While the two blocs were involved in wars in the Third World to challenge hegemony or take territory in core states of the other bloc, it was not possible. More important, if often overstated by the two competitors themselves, was the fact that the Cold War involved not just relative degrees of power and strategic advantage, but also competition about the way in which society and political systems were to be organized. It involved a drive by both sides to produce a homogeneous world, not just in the conventional International Relations sense of states that performed in roughly similar ways on the international stage, but in terms of internal political and socioeconomic organization. It was heterogeneity in this latter domain that lay at the core of the Cold War and which, for all its strategic and other similarities with great power conflicts of the past, made it distinctive.

What was involved in the Cold War was the confrontation of two societies, including but not solely involving, the United States. Both U.S.-led capitalism and Soviet-led communism sought nothing less than to create worlds in their own image: although, for four decades both were checked by the military and political strength of the other, the endurance of this universalizing drive was evident. Soviet communism gave up its global political aspirations at some point after the mid-1970s—with the collapse of Eurocommunism and the paralysis of Third World socialist and socialist-oriented regimes. Western capitalism did not give up and, with greater resources and determination, sustained its pressure, and in the end prevailed. Nothing bore this underlying nature of the conflict out more clearly than the manner in which it ended. Had the Cold War been a traditional great power conflict alone it could have ended with a truce, negotiated distribution of power and military strength. This was what had existed in Europe after 1945 and what was attempted, without success, in the Third World. Ultimately, the denouement came in the apparently paralyzed, "balanced" core, namely Europe, and as a result of a change of policy at the core. It came because one system was no longer able to sustain itself in the face of the other, and it was as a result of this, of one side in effect collapsing, that the Cold War could be said to have ended.

THE ROLE OF EXTERNAL COMPETITION

It is now possible to address the main question of this analysis, one of both historical and theoretical importance, namely how far and in what ways external competition contributed to the evolution and final collapse of the communist system.[5] As already noted, that system was not destroyed by war, nor was its collapse solely exogenous. Internal factors, most importantly the paralysis of the economies and political systems, played a major part. But external forces, including economic ones, did contribute to the final collapse of 1989. Two kinds of factors conventionally evolved in analysis of interstate competition—"traditional" and contemporary—can be examined: the conclusion will be that, above all, it was neither of these but competition in the fields of perceived economic and ideological performance that determined the outcome.

The cold war was not the first case of international competition between heterogeneous states. The fate of the Ottoman and Chinese empires in the latter half of the nineteenth centuries up to their final disappearances during World War I are two classic earlier instances of this. Here too military competition, administrative reform as a response to interstate competition, and rising dissension within all contributed to the collapse of the weaker system. As in the cold war, the erosion was gradual, not cataclysmic, and involved military, economic and diplomatic dimensions. Yet for all the similarities, the differences between these earlier cases of intersystemic competition and the later cold war are rather greater. At the military level, the Soviet system was far more an equal of its rival than were the Ottoman and Qing (Manchu) empires, and there was no equivalent of the incursions and annexations that preceded the collapse of the latter. Indeed, in the postwar period the Soviet system survived the military challenges at the margin—Korea, Vietnam, even Afghanistan—comparatively well. Economically, the contest was even more different: whereas the Ottoman and Qing (Manchu) empires had been eroded by foreign trade, capitulations, debt and so forth, the Soviet system used interaction with the western economies as a means of retaining power. Loans to, trade with, and investment in these countries did not weaken, but rather strengthened, the power of the communist states. It was not the "market," in any direct sense of intervention within these societies and economies, that contributed to their ultimate demise.[6]

INTERNATIONAL FACTORS IN COLD WAR

The other set of international factors often cited are more recent and more singular, those which are commonly held to be responsible for the collapse of the communist regimes, and in particular for the crisis of the U.S.S.R., in the late 1980s. These revolve around the argument that in one way or another the pressure that the West placed upon the communist system for the mid-1970s onwards, embodied in the policies of the Second Cold War, was such that the Soviet system could not endure. Breaking this general argument down, three specific factors are often cited: the burden of the arms race, the economic and CoCom technological embargoes, and the anticommunist guerrilla movements in the Third World Soviet allies. On their own, or in some kind of combination, these were, it is frequently argued, the forms of international competition and pressure that brought the U.S.S.R. to its knees.

(I) The Arms Race

Enough is now known for us to be able to outline the history and significance of the East-West arms race. In summary form, its record was as follows: (A) from the late 1940s onwards, the U.S.S.R. and the U.S.A. were engaged in an arms race, conventional and nuclear, involving growing expenditures, and a technological race, in which, for all major dimensions except space in the late 1950s, the U.S.A. was in the lead in the technological field, and remained, in most dimensions, in the lead in the quantitative domain;[7] (B) despite this U.S. lead, the relative burden on the U.S.A. was significantly less, representing between 5% and 10% of GNP, whereas for the U.S.S.R.

arms expenditure represented between 10% and 20% throughout this period—some Soviet officials now say it was as high as 25%; (C) despite the lack of a direct U.S.-Soviet military confrontation, conventional or nuclear, this arms race represented, in a Clausewitzian sense, a continuation of politics by other means: it reflected a search for an elusive but strategically meaningful measure of "superiority" over the other, it embodied a pursuit by both sides of prestige and status in the international arena, and it constituted a means of pressure on the budget and hence on the state-society relationship within the other bloc.[8]

Given the burden on the U.S.S.R. and its evident inability to compete with the U.S.A., it is frequently argued that it was this which forced the U.S.S.R. into strategic retreat in the mid-1980s. At least three variants of this argument can be noted: an economic one, that the level of expenditure on arms and the diversion of resources to the military sector were such that the U.S.S.R. could not continue to compete, and needed a drastic reduction in military expenditure in order to divert resources for domestic economic reorganization; a technological argument, that it was the continued U.S. lead, acutely represented in the early 1980s by two developments, the strategic defense initiative ("Star Wars") and cruise missiles, which forced the Soviet leadership to realize that it could not continue to compete; and a political argument, that the dangers of nuclear war and the costs involved forced the Soviets to abandon the idea of the world as one divided between two camps, locked in social conflict, in favor of a stress on the common interests of human kind. All three are, in varying degrees, found in the writings of Soviet and Western writers and each must have

played a role. Gorbachev himself has consistently evoked the third, political argument. The power of nuclear weapons and the accident of Chernobyl in 1986 certainly served to reinforce this awareness of the dangers of nuclear energy and, by extension, nuclear weapons.

Important as it is, there are reasons to qualify the import of the arms race explanation as the major factor behind the Soviet collapse. Certainly, the economic argument must have considerable force: indeed, the very quantitative figure of 10% or 20% of Soviet GNP being spent on defense understates the qualitative and distorting impact, with the allocation of the best administrative and scientific personnel and of key material resources to this sector. On the other hand, military expenditure at 10% or more of GNP is far from being an adequate explanation for the failings of the Soviet economy. The very high rate of military expenditure as a percentage of GNP is but another way of saying that GNP itself was rather low—the figures for overall expenditure as between the U.S. and the U.S.S.R. show that in absolute terms the U.S.A. was outspending the U.S.S.R.[9] The focus must, therefore, be as much on the efficiency and allocative mechanisms of the civilian sector as on the claim of the military on GNP: had the Soviet GNP been rather higher and the remaining 80% of the Soviet economy been more efficiently organized, the "burden" of military expenditure would have been less and would, given reasonable efficiency and growth rates, have represented a lower percentage of GNP anyway.

Similar problems arise with the technological argument: the assumption of much analysis of the arms race and of the conventional Soviet approach prior to this was that, more or less, the U.S.S.R.

was compelled by the necessities of inter-state competition to match the U.S.A. in qualitative and quantitative terms. Previously, the U.S.S.R. had imitated U.S. advances—as in the MIRVing of missiles after 1972 and the development of a submarine-launched intercontinental capacity. By the late 1970s this was no longer possible: the challenges of SDI and of cruise missiles were that the U.S.S.R. had no comparable riposte antidote. In particular, it could not compete in the technology of the third industrial revolution. Yet the U.S.S.R. could have produced some countermeasures to these U.S. challenges—a few low flying missiles plus decoys would have done much to invalidate SDI. A policy of what is termed "minimum deterrence" could have made a substantial difference and enabled the U.S.S.R. to escape from its self-defeating pursuit of "rough parity." It was perhaps not so much at the military level as such, but what the new technologies symbolized about the overall retardation of the system, that forced the Soviet leaders into retreat. The third argument relevant to the arms race, the political argument about the threat to humanity of nuclear weapons, has much validity and it is to the credit of Gorbachev that he articulated it more clearly than anyone else: but it does not entail the overall process of political and social change within the U.S.S.R. that has accompanied the adoption of these universal values associated with "new thinking." It is conceivable that the U.S.S.R. would have opted out of the nuclear arms race as previously pursued but insisted on preserving its distinctive political and socio-economic system. To explain the latter involves looking beyond the realm of the arms race and its economic, technical, and political costs.

(II) Economic Pressures

The second set of factors commonly adduced to explain the Soviet retreat is the economic, and in particular the impact on the U.S.S.R. of Western embargoes and restrictions in the field of high technology. Most postwar discussion of the relationship between trade and security in the East-West context has operated with the assumption that increased commercial interaction between the two blocs would contribute to the stability of the Soviet bloc: the argument, as it developed in the 1970s, was between those who believed that greater trade, by making the Soviet Union more secure, would reduce areas of conflict between it and the West, and those who thought it would encourage combative behavior. If the former view, drawing on theories of "interdependence," was dominant in the early 1970s, it was the latter view that prevailed in the period of the Second Cold War.

On the basis of the partial evidence available, it would appear that economic interaction and pressure of various kinds were a factor in the collapse of the communist system, but that the most important factor was the inability of the centrally planned regimes to make use of the advantages that trade with the capitalist world brought. In the case of certain Eastern European countries— Poland is the most striking example— the opening up to the West in the early 1970s had short-term gains, in terms of availability of consumer goods and investment, but led to a longer-run crisis, with foreign debt and increased pressure on domestic earnings once debt repayment became necessary. The centrally planned economic system could not make use of such external support adequately to develop its own economy, and ended up being trapped by its international commitments. In the case of the U.S.S.R., all the evidence suggests that straightforward commercial interaction with the capitalist world had the effect of strengthening the existing system in the short run: most obviously, wheat imports provided a means of offsetting failures in agriculture. The rise in the price of oil in the 1970s gave the U.S.S.R. a windfall profit for much of the decade: however, as Soviet writers have recently pointed out, the longer-run consequences of these profits were inhibiting, since they enabled the central planners and managers to postpone changes that might otherwise have had to be introduced more rapidly.

The same applied in the field of technology: the record of technological innovation in the U.S.S.R. is by no means as bleak as is often suggested, but there is no doubt that most of the major technological innovations of recent decades originated in the West. Here the U.S.S.R. was at a disadvantage in two respects. It did not make any major innovations itself and was therefore compelled, in the civilian and military spheres, to copy or simply steal new technologies from the capitalist world. The degree of Soviet insulation from the international market was never as great as conventional images suggest: the industrialization of the 1930s relied heavily on capital goods imports from Britain and Germany; the history of Soviet aerospace is one of reproduction of Western planes and technologies. Yet in this pursuit of technological development, the U.S.S.R. was always behind. Even more important, however, it was unable to make proper use of the technologies it did have: there was little interaction between the military and civilian sectors; the system of central planning contained built-in disincentives for innovation and encouraged the use of inefficient and traditional methods of production; political and ideological constraints inhibited the use of information technology throughout the system. The pattern of "conservative modernization" identified as endemic to the centrally planned economies operated in this regard.[10] Hence the third industrial revolution, which began in the early 1970s, outstripped it more than ever.

The factor of economic pressure and its political impact is important even when it comes to the embargoes. Here it has been argued that Soviet behavior in the international arena was affected by Western restrictions, both those of a strictly national security kind, through CoCom, and broader political embargoes announced in the wake of Afghanistan. The former, it was said, would make it more difficult for the U.S.S.R. to compete in the arms race, the latter would act as disincentives for unwelcome Soviet foreign policy actions. Given the degree to which the U.S.S.R. protested about these restrictions, it would seem that their impact was considerable.[11] Yet these pressures in themselves can hardly explain the change in Soviet orientation from the mid-1980s onwards: the U.S.S.R., faced with a dire technological lag in the military sphere, could have made substantial concessions without placing their overall strategy in question; in the short run at least, they did not respond to Western political sanctions by making major foreign policy concessions and were indeed more intransigent up to 1985 than had hitherto been the case. The very same factors that diminished the import of Western commercial and technological impact served to lessen the impact of their withdrawal: the centralized political and economic system could absorb the denial, just as it could inhibit the diffusion, of the new technologies.

(III) Erosion of the Bloc

A third major factor adduced to explain the retreat of Soviet power is the cost of supporting its Third World allies, at both the economic and military levels. Soviet writers themselves now complain openly about the costs, economic and diplomatic, of backing Third World allies and have reversed the earlier Khrushchevite view that national liberation and Third World revolutionary movements made a positive contribution to the power of the U.S.S.R.;[12] the concept of "imperial overstretch" would seem to apply here and provide a comparative perspective on the Soviet retreat. The character of Soviet relations with Third World allies, resting on substantial economic subsidies in return for political and strategic rewards, made this set of relationships especially burdensome. For U.S. strategic planners in the early 1980s the weakest link of the Soviet system lay in the Third World, which is why there evolved the doctrine of support for anti-communist guerrilla movements.

On closer examination, however, the pressure of Third World commitments seems different and in some ways smaller than at first sight appeared. The greatest cost to the U.S.S.R. of its Third World commitments was in the diplomatic field, e.g., Soviet support for revolutionary allies and movements worsened U.S.-Soviet relations, and the invasion of Afghanistan provided a means by which the West could for the first time weaken the U.S.S.R.'s relationship with the Third World as a whole. The other factors nor-mally adduced, economic and military, may have been less significant. First, the figures for Soviet "aid" to the Third World comprise a variety of forms of support, including, in the case of the largest commitment, Cuba, major long-term trading agreements: though these gave Cuba far better terms of trade than it could have gotten on the world market (high prices for sugar, low for oil), they were not net transfers in the ordinary sense. There were benefits to the U.S.S.R.—getting sugar and nickel that were paid for in rubles, rather than having to pay in hard currency. In other cases, the Third World ally was able to provide the U.S.S.R. with valuable imports—Afghan gas being one example. Second, despite Soviet over-stated claims, the amount of aid was in comparative terms very low— 0.25% of GNP, roughly equivalent to the U.S. record.[13] Politically convenient as it may now be within the U.S.S.R. to blame Third World allies, who certainly were also mismanaging their economies, for the economic woes of the U.S.S.R., this was not a major factor in the economic crisis of the Soviet system.

As with military expenditure within the U.S.S.R. itself, the focus of criticism must go back to the overall system of planning and production and the inefficiencies it contained, which were, incidentally, reproduced by Soviet aid programs within Third World states themselves. The strategic cost of sustaining Third World allies in the 1980s was certainly rising, but if the purpose of U.S. support to Third World anti-communist movements was to weaken the U.S.S.R. at its weakest point this did not happen. One of the major reasons for Soviet and Western involvement in Afghanistan was the demonstration effect of a ruling communist party being overthrown: the impact on Eastern Europe of Kabul's falling was, both sides believed, potentially enormous. Yet in the end it was not in Nicaragua or Afghanistan that Soviet allies were first overthrown, but in Eastern Europe. It was what happened in Warsaw, Berlin, and Prague that affected developments in Managua, Aden, and Kabul and not the other way around.

COMPETITION: THE EXTERNAL IN PERSPECTIVE

The argument so far has identified two categories of external factors, the traditional-imperial ones and the East-West Cold War ones, which can be considered to have played a role in eroding and undermining Soviet power. While both categories have some explanatory power, we have argued that they alone are inadequate. If this is true, it encourages a reexamination of the reasons for the collapse of Soviet power, at both the historical and the theoretical levels: i.e., a reexamination both of what actually happened, and of how our conception of interstate competition may need modifying in the light of the Soviet case.

What needs explanation is that an international system of states collapsed in the absence of the most evident forms of threat: it was not defeated in war; it did not face overwhelming political challenges from below (Poland being the only, partial, exception); it was not, despite its manifold economic and social problems, unable to meet the basic economic demands of its citizenry. It did not, therefore, "collapse," "fail," "break down" in any absolute sense. What occurred, rather, was that the leadership of the most powerful state in the system decided to introduce a radically new set of policies, within the U.S.S.R. and within the system as a whole: it was not that

the ruled could not go on being ruled in the old way so much as that the rulers could not go on ruling in the old way. The question is what it was that led these rulers, who cannot be accused of lacking a desire to retain power or of being covert supporters of the West, to introduce the changes they did.

Two kinds of reason, one endogenous and the other exogenous, seem to have been responsible. They can be termed, in summary form, socioeconomic paralysis and lack of international competitiveness. The internal paralysis was evident in a wide range of spheres: falling growth rates, rising social problems, growing corruption and disillusionment, ecological crises. Not only could the system not go on reproducing the rates of growth and improvement in welfare provision characteristic of earlier phases—the 1930s, the 1950s—but it seemed to have run out of steam in a comprehensive manner. This was increasingly clear not just to the leadership but to the growing body of educated people produced by the system. These phenomena are often referred to in the Soviet literature as "stagnation," yet in many ways this is a simplistic term:[14] it understates the degree to which there was continued progress in some spheres, not least the lessening of political repression; it still contains within it the teleological assumption that the system could, under other circumstances, have continued to grow and develop.

Most important, however, "stagnation" leaves out what was also a major factor in forcing the Soviet leadership, faced with this trend, to introduce change, namely the awareness of the system's *comparative* failure vis-à-vis the West. It is here, in the perceived inability of the Soviet system to catch up, let alone overtake, the West that a central aspect of the Soviet collapse must be seen. It was a failure to compete internationally that, on top of the internal crisis, led to the post-1985 changes in the U.S.S.R.: once begun, an attempt to reform the system the better to survive and compete quickly capsized into an attempt to save the state as such.

The awareness of the system's inability to compete in the 1980s was the final in several stages of such loss of hope. The first, historical, disappointment was that immediately after 1917 when the Bolsheviks realized that their revolution would not be reproduced in Germany. This realization led to a double redefinition of strategy—temporary abandonment of the idea of world revolution, proclamation of the idea that a socialist regime *could* be built in the U.S.S.R. With the victories in World War II and the increase in the number of Third World pro-Soviet allies, it appeared for the 1950s and 1960s as if the initial encirclement of the U.S.S.R. could be overcome concomitant with the development of socialism within the U.S.S.R. itself. The successes of post-war reconstruction and space technology in the 1950s seemed to confirm this: hence the new, secularly optimistic, program of Khrushchev which combined continued rivalry with the West in the Third World with a policy of socio-economic development designed to "catch up with and overtake" the West in two decades. It would seem, difficult as it is to believe now, that this perspective, modified by Brezhnev, dominated Soviet thinking until the early 1980s: there were continued advances in the Third World, the U.S.S.R. attained "rough parity" with the U.S.A. in the arms race, and at home it was official policy to state that the U.S.S.R. was now at a new stage, one of "developed socialism."

The reality was, however, rather different, as each of the major areas of interstate and interbloc competition showed. In the most public and privileged area of competition, the military, the U.S.S.R. was always inferior in numbers and quality, except for its conventional strength in Eastern Europe. If this was the area where the Soviet Union was to compete the most, it was evidently not doing anything like well enough.

The international system created by the U.S.S.R. was also markedly weaker quantitatively and qualitatively than that created by the West. Not only was the international capitalist market far stronger in terms of economic output, technological change, and number of countries included within it, but its degree of integration was greater: despite all the talk of a new socialist "system," one of the paradoxes of planning within the U.S.S.R. and the Soviet international system more generally was its inability to integrate sectors beyond giving them separate, if supposedly coordinated, production targets. In many respects, not least innovation and pricing, it remained dependent on the capitalist system, and ineffectually imitative of it. In the military sphere a similar disparity and qualitative inferiority prevailed in the comparison between NATO and the Warsaw Pact. For all the talk of constituting an alternative world order, the Soviet one was less integrated and much weaker overall.[15]

This failure to compete in international terms would, in itself, have been a major problem, given the fact that underlying East-West rivalry and Cold War was an attempt by both sides to provide a basis for a new international "order," to demonstrate the superiority of the one over the other. But this external blockage, one going right back to 1917 and only obscured by subsequent international triumphs, was compounded by the internal limits of the system in many spheres: the failure to match levels of output in the West, the growing gap in living standards between developed socialist and developed capitalist states and, obscured by rhetoric about "socialist" democracy, the contrast between a substantial degree of democratic success in the West and continuing if less brutal centralized political control in the East. Had the U.S.S.R. been able to rival the West successfully in other spheres, these internal deficiencies, those denoted by "stagnation," might have been concealed the longer: but it was the failure at the international level combined with that at home that forced the leadership to face up to them.

Here we come to a central feature of the collapse: almost impossible to believe as it may now be, it would seem that up to the early 1980s this contrast in internal achievement was hidden from, or at least not recognized by, most Soviet observers, in the leadership or elsewhere. The underlying self-confidence of the Soviet system, a product of the revolution's historic claims and of victory in World War II, seemed to have lasted up to that time; but at some point in the early 1980s it began to erode, first amongst the leadership and then within the population as a whole. The awareness of how people lived in the West and of the enormous gap in living standards produced a situation in which the self-confidence that had lasted from 1917 evaporated in the space of a few short years. The lack of political freedom played its part through Helsinki and Western pressure: but the evidence suggests that it was the economic which played the major role in getting this

process going. Once the living standards gap became evident then the residual legitimacy of the communist political system was swept away and that of the alternative system, the Western variant of pluralism, was enhanced.

Here it is worth looking at the mechanism by which this change of attitude occurred. The insulation of Soviet society was both physical—lack of communication, radio jamming, absence of travel, punishment of those who sought contact with the outside world—and psychological—a belief that whatever went wrong, "*u nas lushche*"—"things are better with us."[16] Those who traveled abroad or had access to comparative data were condemned to silence, even when they realized the truth. Here the change of heart of the leadership, one encouraged by broader awareness in the society, was of pivotal importance and opened the floodgates to popular discontent: the breaking of the secular self-confidence of the top leadership must certainly have been encouraged by the failures of international competition in the military and economic spheres, but it would appear that the very perception of the contrast in living standards, highlighting the reality of internal paralysis in the late 1970s, and the growing military gap associated with the third industrial revolution, played the crucial part. In Gorbachev's case, for example, it would seem that his visits to Canada provided such an occasion: it would only take five minutes in an average Canadian supermarket for the point to become clear, and for the specific experience of shortages and administrative problems he experienced in running the Stavropol region to be set in its decisive, internationalized, context.

Once this change had occurred, then the process of broader awareness followed inexorably. The liberalization of the political system within the U.S.S.R. allowed of greater information about the capitalist world, almost all of it favorable when not uncritical, and for a more negative assessment of the record of the U.S.S.R. It is noticeable too how, in speeches made after 1985, Gorbachev himself would make telling comparisons with the capitalist world, in the field of social indicators—infant mortality, hospital conditions, alcoholism, availability of basic foods—as well as in broader macroeconomic and political terms.[17] His own process of self-education seems to have followed such a path: already dissatisfied with socialist performance, he came into office in 1985 apparently believing that the socialist system could reform itself by applying technology in a more intense way, the better to "accelerate" production; but by 1989 he had moved much further on both the economic and political fronts, in the face of the evident inability of the system to reform itself within orthodox socialist political and economic parameters. In other words, the international comparison that had brought him to the point of initiating major reform in 1985 pushed him after 1985 to envisage a much more radical reform of the system. The fact that, through forcing the comparison onto the Soviet public, he had unleashed widespread additional dissatisfaction, only served to confirm this trend.

THREE LEVELS OF INTERNATIONAL COMPETITION

This analysis of East-West competition up to the late 1980s has a number of implications for theories of interstate and intersociety competition in particular. No one analyzing East-West conflict can deny the relevance within it of conventional, interstate, forms of competition—at the military, economic, and political levels. The rivalry of the Soviet and U.S. systems in the postwar period involved a comprehensive competition in which the innovation was not the role of states but rather the way in which this interstate competition developed into new domains—the arms race, on the one hand, the comprehensive mobilization of ideological resources on the other. Given its strong position in the economic field, it was natural that the West should seek to use its economic strength to place pressure on the U.S.S.R. for security reasons: the international political economy of East-West relations was, in essence, one of the uses of economic instruments by the stronger bloc, that of Western states, for political and military ends.

This interstate competition, comprehensive as it was, is not sufficient to explain how, why, and when the communist system collapsed, how the West succeeded in prevailing over the East. We have seen how earlier cases of intersystemic conflict—the Ottoman and Manchu cases—provide at best partial points of comparison: despite some similarities, theirs was fundamentally a very different story. The specifically Cold War instruments of interstate competition—arms race, embargoes, Third World harassment—do not, in themselves, explain why the Soviet leadership took the decisions it did after 1985. To analyze this rivalry it is necessary to take a broader look at East-West conflict as a whole, one that encompasses the competition of systems, i.e. capitalism and "communism," within which state competition plays an important, but not exclusive, role.

In this perspective, it becomes possible to distinguish three dimensions of competition which are interrelated but analytically distinct: the level of activities of states; that of social and economic entities, most notably businesses; and what can, in the broadest sense, be termed the "ideological," the perception of and belief about the political, economic levels and culture of another society. In addressing the question of "how" the West put pressure on the East this tripartite distinction may be helpful. Operating on the first level, Western state action had effects, but it was not the only story. Paradoxically, the ability of Western states directly to put such pressure is now greater than ever before as the linking of economic assistance to socioeconomic change within the U.S.S.R. and Eastern Europe show: *perestroika* has created the conditions for such a socioeconomic intervention by the Group of 7, not resulted from it. In the case of Eastern Europe, Western firms—industrial enterprises, banks—also played a role, especially in dealings with Poland in the early 1970s and in the handling of the Soviet oil output. In the opening up that took place from late 1989 onwards, West German business enterprises have taken a lead, somewhat coordinated with but separate from, that of the Bonn government itself. It would be analytically misleading either to reduce state policy in East-West relations to the wishes of multinational corporations, or to see the latter as acting simply within parameters laid down by or at the behest of Western states. Their actions are parallel and usually—though not always—convergent: the generally negative response of sectors of the business community to political embargoes was evidence enough of divergence in this regard.

The ideological dimension is, perhaps, of even greater importance: its role in the collapse of communism and in the East-West rivalry that preceded it was in some ways decisive. Here capitalism operated not just through states or firms, but through the society as a whole. What above all forced the leadership of the CPSU to change course, and what destroyed the support or acquiescence of the peoples of Eastern Europe and the U.S.S.R. to communism, was, on top of the difference in political achievement, the perceived contrast in political and economic standards and in living conditions between East and West. This ideological dimension is certainly something that states help to promote and regulate, and which their information and propaganda organs disseminate; it is something that rests upon political record and on economic performance, on the output and sales policies of business corporations. But it is something distinct, encompassing as it does the perception of political system, popular culture, the media, fashion, and, in broad terms the image of what constitutes a good life, in the eyes of the leadership and population of the rival system. Moreover, the dissemination of images pertaining to this is not simply the result of state or business enterprise decisions: it takes place in an uncoordinated but pervasive way, through television and film, through popular music, through impressions gained from travel and personal encounter. It is informal and diffuse, but constitutes the most potent interface between two societies. The abandonment by the majority of the inhabitants of East Germany of any belief in a separate socialist way or entity was above all a product of this encounter: years of exposure to West German images on television, followed by the direct encounter itself, the *Reiseshock*.

Insofar as this distinction is valid, and the importance of ideological and perceptual factors in international relations is accepted, then it suggests another interpretation of the Cold War and its end, and of international relations more generally. Relations between states retain their importance, and the particular mechanisms of conflict and resource mobilization at any one time are open to analysis on a contingent basis. The denial of state efficacy and the premature reduction of its role are as misleading as the insistence that all international relations can be seen, or deemed, to be ones between states. At the same time, international competition involves two other major dimensions: the unofficial and the ideological. The latter has always operated—it would be impossible to follow the history of Christianity, its diffusion and division, without it. But the ideological has a special salience in a world where material well-being, fashion and consumerism together with political freedoms occupy a special role in the constitution of specific societies, and in an international situation characterized by immediate transmission of sound and images. There is clearly a relationship between power in one domain and power in the ideological domain—through control of images and their means of diffusion. Never was Gramsci's conception of hegemony, in the sense of ideological and cultural factors as instruments of domination, so relevant as in analyzing the international system today. If communism surrendered without firing a shot, it was because the instrument of international competition in the late twentieth century was as much the T-shirt as the gunboat.

POSTSCRIPT: THE END OF THE SOVIET UNION

The denouncement of the August crisis in the U.S.S.R. has unexpectedly accelerated the process analysed here. A last-ditch attempt to save the old regime only brought forward the collapse of the traditional centers of power, and of the Soviet Union itself: it showed how discredited, and divided, the old centers were and, through their implication in the coup attempt, confirmed that discrediting. Leaders and led no longer believed in the system. The goal of those brought to office by the coup is both to complete the abandonment of the U.S.S.R.'s pre-existing international role and to integrate the remnants, as far as possible, into the political and economic structures of the capitalist West. The victory of the West, promoted at all three levels analyzed above, has now been reinforced.

NOTES

1. See my "The Ends of Cold War," *New Left Review*, 180(March–April 1990): 5–23; George Schopflin, "Why Communism Collapsed," *International Affairs*, 66, 1(1990): 3–16.
2. For the argument as to why, on economic grounds, the state socialist model could not work, despite initial successes and a margin for reform, see Wlodzimierz Brus and Kazimierz Laski, *From Marx to Market* (Oxford: The Clarendon Press, 1989).
3. Moshe Lewin, *The Gorbachev Phenomenon* (Berkeley: University of California Press, 1988), is a lucid overview of the social and economic preconditions for the breakdown of the Brezhnevite order in the 1980s.
4. Fred Halliday, *The Making of the Second Cold War* (London: Verso, 1983), chapter 1, on the different meanings of "cold war."
5. Theda Skoepol, *States and Social Revolutions* (Princeton: Princeton University Press, 1979), remains a classic discussion of this question.

6. On the Ottoman background see Roger Owen, *The Middle East in the World Economy, 1800–1914* (Oxford: Oxford University Press, 1981): Caglar Keyder, *State and Class in Turkey, A Study in Capitalist Development* (London: Verso, 1987).

7. On the arms race see my *The Making of the Second Cold War*, chapter 3.

8. This was conventionally known as the "arms race theory of arms control."

9. U.S. expenditure in 1971 was $120 billions, as against Soviet $94 billions, in 1980 $111 billions as against $107. Total Soviet plus allies expenditure was only half that of its opponents, NATO plus Far Eastern allies (China, Japan) expenditure: in 1980 $120 billions for the WTO as against $243 billions. All data from *SIPRI Yearbook* (Stockholm: SIPRI, 1981), figures in constant 1978 prices. U.S. expenditure was conventionally understated by a number of accounting devices: one calculation was that the 1980 figure of $127 billions should be adjusted upwards to $223 billions, i.e., from 5.2% to 9.5% of GNP: James Cypher, "Rearing America," *Monthly Review*, 33, 6 (November 1981): 11–27.

10. See Brus-Laski.

11. For a Soviet view of the Western embargo see Igor Artemiev, "International Economic Security," in Igor Artemiev and Fred Halliday, *International Economic Security: Soviet and British Approaches* (London: Chatham House Discussion Paper, no. 7, 1988).

12. Fred Halliday, *From Kabul to Managua* (New York: Pantheon, 1989). (UK title *Cold War, Third World*. London: Hutchinson/Radius, 1989), chapter 4, for the rethinking of Soviet policy towards the Third World.

13. According to OECD DAC figures.

14. On "stagnation" see Mikhail Gorbachev, *Perestroika: New Thinking for Our Country and the World* (London: Collins, 1987), chapter 1.

15. On the NATO-WTO comparison see note 14 above. The degree of economic integration between the Eastern European Comecon members was far less than that within the EEC: most trade was on a bilateral, Soviet-East European, basis.

16. Hedrick Smith, *The Russians* (London: Sphere, 1976), gives a powerful evocation of this attitude in the period prior to the collapse of Soviet confidence.

17. Gorbachev's *Perestroika* is replete with calls for the Soviet economy to rise to "world standards," i.e., those of the West.

QUESTIONS

1. What are the three levels of international competition identified by Halliday?

2. Does Halliday's conclusion about the collapse of the Soviet Union prove or disprove George Kennan's policy on containment ("The Sources of Soviet Conduct," page 76)? Explain.

CLASS SYSTEM PERSPECTIVE OF SEPTEMBER 11

20.   The New War Against Terror

Noam Chomsky

In this speech, delivered to the Technology & Culture Forum at the Massachusetts Institute of Technology on October 18, 2001, Noam Chomsky offers a critical evaluation of the United States' war on terrorism. Chomsky asserts that U.S. actions in Afghanistan and previous U.S. military interventions could also be classified as terrorist acts. He urges Americans to reassess the long-term implications of America's military attacks abroad and change U.S. policy accordingly.

Noam Chomsky is the Ferrari P. Ward Chair of Modern Language and Linguistics at the Massachusetts Institute of Technology. He is the author of many books and articles. Among his recent work is *9-11*, which contains an analysis of the U.S. war on terrorism.

Everyone knows it's the TV people who run the world [crowd laughter]. I just got orders that I'm supposed to be here, not there. Well the last talk I gave at this forum was on a light pleasant topic. It was about how humans are an endangered species and given the nature of their institutions they are likely to destroy themselves in a fairly short time. So this time there is a little relief and we have a pleasant topic instead, the new war on terror. Unfortunately, the world keeps coming up with things that make it more and more horrible as we proceed.

I'm going to assume 2 conditions for this talk.

• The first one is just what I assume to be recognition of fact. That is that the events of September 11 were a horrendous atrocity probably the most devastating instant human toll of any crime in history, outside of war.

• The second assumption has to do with the goals. I'm assuming that our goal is that we are interested in reducing the likelihood of such crimes whether they are against us or against someone else.

If you don't accept those two assumptions, then what I say will not be addressed to you. If we do accept them, then a number of questions arise, closely related ones, which merit a good deal of thought.

THE 5 QUESTIONS

One question, and by far the most important one is what is happening right now? Implicit in that is what can we do about it? The 2nd has to do with the very common assumption that what happened on September 11 is a historic event, one which will change history. I tend to agree with that. I think it's true. It was a historic event and the question we should be asking is exactly why? The 3rd question has to do with the title, The War Against Terrorism. Exactly what is it? And there is a related question, namely what is terrorism? The 4th question which is narrower but important has to do with the origins of the crimes of September 11th. And the 5th question that I want to talk a little about is what policy options there are in fighting this war against terrorism and dealing with the situations that led to it.

I'll say a few things about each. Glad to go beyond in discussion and don't hesitate to bring up other questions. These are ones that come to my mind as prominent but you may easily and plausibly have other choices.

1. WHAT'S HAPPENING RIGHT NOW?

Starvation of 3 to 4 Million People

Well let's start with right now. I'll talk about the situation in Afghanistan. I'll just keep to uncontroversial sources like the New York Times [crowd laughter]. According to the New York Times there are 7 to 8 million people in Afghanistan on the verge of starvation. That was true actually before September 11th. They were surviving on international aid. On September 16th, the Times reported, I'm quoting it, that the United States demanded from Pakistan the elimination of truck convoys that provide much of the food and other supplies to Afghanistan's civilian population. As far as I could determine there was no reaction in the United States or for that matter in Europe. I was on national radio all over Europe the next day. There was no reaction in the United States or in Europe to my knowledge to the demand to impose massive starvation on millions of people. The threat of military strikes right after September . . . around that time forced the removal of international aid workers that crippled the assistance programs. Actually, I am quoting again from the New York Times. Refugees reaching

Pakistan after arduous journeys from AF are describing scenes of desperation and fear at home as the threat of American led military attacks turns their long running misery into a potential catastrophe. The country was on a lifeline and we just cut the line. Quoting an evacuated aid worker, in the New York Times Magazine.

The World Food Program, the UN program, which is the main one by far, were able to resume after 3 weeks in early October, they began to resume at a lower level, resume food shipments. They don't have international aid workers within, so the distribution system is hampered. That was suspended as soon as the bombing began. They then resumed but at a lower pace while aid agencies leveled scathing condemnations of US airdrops, condemning them as propaganda tools which are probably doing more harm than good. That happens to be quoting the London Financial Times but it is easy to continue. After the first week of bombing, the New York Times reported on a back page inside a column on something else, that by the arithmetic of the United Nations there will soon be 7.5 million Afghans in acute need of even a loaf of bread and there are only a few weeks left before the harsh winter will make deliveries to many areas totally impossible, continuing to quote, but with bombs falling the delivery rate is down to 1/2 of what is needed. Casual comment. Which tells us that Western civilization is anticipating the slaughter of, well do the arithmetic, 3–4 million people or something like that. On the same day, the leader of Western civilization dismissed with contempt, once again, offers of negotiation for delivery of the alleged target, Osama bin Laden, and a request for some evidence to substantiate the demand for total capitulation. It was dismissed. On the same day the Special Rapporteur of the UN in charge of food pleaded with the United States to stop the bombing to try to save millions of victims. As far as I'm aware that was unreported. That was Monday. Yesterday the major aid agencies OXFAM and Christian Aid and others joined in that plea. You can't find a report in the New York Times. There was a line in the Boston Globe, hidden in a story about another topic, Kashmir.

Silent Genocide

Well we could easily go on . . . but all of that . . . first of all indicates to us what's happening. Looks like what's happening is some sort of silent genocide. It also gives a good deal of insight into the elite culture, the culture that we are part of. It indicates that whatever, what will happen we don't know, but plans are being made and programs implemented on the assumption that they may lead to the death of several million people in the next few months. . . .

2. WHY WAS IT A HISTORIC EVENT?

National Territory Attacked

Alright let's turn to the slightly more abstract question, forgetting for the moment that we are in the midst of apparently trying to murder 3 or 4 million people, not Taliban of course, their victims. Let's go back . . . turn to the question of the historic event that took place on September 11th. As I said, I think that's correct. It was a historic event. Not unfortunately because of its scale, unpleasant to think about, but in terms of the scale it's not that unusual. I did say it's the worst . . . probably the worst instant human toll of any crime. And that may be true. But there are ter-

rorist crimes with effects a bit more drawn out that are more extreme, unfortunately. Nevertheless, it's a historic event because there was a change. The change was the direction in which the guns were pointed. That's new. Radically new. So, take US history.

The last time that the national territory of the United States was under attack, or for that matter, even threatened was when the British burned down Washington in 1814. There have been many . . . it was common to bring up Pearl Harbor but that's not a good analogy. The Japanese, what ever you think about it, the Japanese bombed military bases in 2 US colonies not the national territory; colonies which had been taken from their inhabitants in not a very pretty way. This is the national territory that's been attacked on a large scale, you can find a few fringe examples but this is unique.

During these close to 200 years, we, the United States expelled or mostly exterminated the indigenous population, that's many millions of people, conquered half of Mexico, carried out depredations all over the region, Caribbean and Central America, sometimes beyond, conquered Hawaii and the Philippines, killing several 100,000 Filipinos in the process. Since the Second World War, it has extended its reach around the world in ways I don't have to describe. But it was always killing someone else, the fighting was somewhere else, it was others who were getting slaughtered. Not here. Not the national territory.

3. WHAT IS THE WAR AGAINST TERRORISM?

Well, let's go to the third question, 'What is the war against terrorism?' and a side question, 'What's terrorism?'. The war against terrorism has been described in high places as a struggle against a plague, a cancer which is spread by barbarians, by "depraved opponents of civilization itself." That's a feeling that I share. The words I'm quoting, however, happen to be from 20 years ago. Those are . . . that's President Reagan and his Secretary of State. The Reagan administration came into office 20 years ago declaring that the war against international terrorism would be the core of our foreign policy . . . describing it in terms of the kind I just mentioned and others. And it was the core of our foreign policy. The Reagan administration responded to this plague spread by depraved opponents of civilization itself by creating an extraordinary international terrorist network, totally unprecedented in scale, which carried out massive atrocities all over the world, primarily . . . well, partly nearby, but not only there. I won't run through the record, you're all educated people, so I'm sure you learned about it in High School. [crowd laughter]

Reagan-US War Against Nicaragua

But I'll just mention one case which is totally uncontroversial, so we might as well not argue about it, by no means the most extreme but uncontroversial. It's uncontroversial because of the judgments of the highest international authorities the International Court of Justice, the World Court, and the UN Security Council. So this one is uncontroversial, at least among people who have some minimal concern for international law, human rights, justice and other things like that. And now I'll leave you an exercise. You can estimate the size of that category by simply asking how often this uncontroversial case has been mentioned in the commentary of the last month. And it's a

particularly relevant one, not only because it is uncontroversial, but because it does offer a precedent as to how a law abiding state would respond to . . . did respond in fact to international terrorism, which is uncontroversial. And was even more extreme than the events of September 11th. I'm talking about the Reagan-US war against Nicaragua which left tens of thousands of people dead, the country ruined, perhaps beyond recovery.

Nicaragua's Response

Nicaragua did respond. They didn't respond by setting off bombs in Washington. They responded by taking it to the World Court, presenting a case, they had no problem putting together evidence. The World Court accepted their case, ruled in their favor, ordered the . . . condemned what they called the "unlawful use of force," which is another word for international terrorism, by the United States, ordered the United States to terminate the crime and to pay massive reparations. The United States, of course, dismissed the court judgment with total contempt and announced that it would not accept the jurisdiction of the court henceforth. Then Nicaragua then went to the UN Security Council which considered a resolution calling on all states to observe international law. No one was mentioned but everyone understood. The United States vetoed the resolution. It now stands as the only state on record which has both been condemned by the World Court for international terrorism and has vetoed a Security Council resolution calling on states to observe international law. Nicaragua then went to the General Assembly where there is technically no veto but a negative US vote amounts to a veto. It passed a similar resolution with only the

United States, Israel, and El Salvador opposed. The following year again, this time the United States could only rally Israel to the cause, so 2 votes opposed to observing international law. At that point, Nicaragua couldn't do anything lawful. It tried all the measures. They don't work in a world that is ruled by force.

This case is uncontroversial but it's by no means the most extreme. We gain a lot of insight into our own culture and society and what's happening now by asking 'how much we know about all this? How much we talk about it? How much you learn about it in school? How much it's all over the front pages?' And this is only the beginning. The United States responded to the World Court and the Security Council by immediately escalating the war very quickly, that was a bipartisan decision incidentally. The terms of the war were also changed. For the first time there were official orders given . . . official orders to the terrorist army to attack what are called "soft targets," meaning undefended civilian targets, and to keep away from the Nicaraguan army. They were able to do that because the United States had total control of the air over Nicaragua and the mercenary army was supplied with advanced communication equipment, it wasn't a guerilla army in the normal sense and could get instructions about the disposition of the Nicaraguan army forces so they could attack agricultural collectives, health clinics, and so on . . . soft targets with impunity. Those were the official orders.

What was the Reaction Here?

What was the reaction? It was known. There was a reaction to it. The policy was regarded as sensible by left liberal opinion. So Michael Kinsley who represents the left in mainstream discussion, wrote an article in which he said that we shouldn't be too quick to criticize this policy as Human Rights Watch had just done. He said a "sensible policy" must "meet the test of cost benefit analysis"—that is, I'm quoting now, that is the analysis of "the amount of blood and misery that will be poured in, and the likelihood that democracy will emerge at the other end." Democracy as the US understands the term, which is graphically illustrated in the surrounding countries. Notice that it is axiomatic that the United States, US elites, have the right to conduct the analysis and to pursue the project if it passes their tests. And it did pass their tests. It worked. When Nicaragua finally succumbed to superpower assault, commentators openly and cheerfully lauded the success of the methods that were adopted and described them accurately. So I'll quote *Time* Magazine just to pick one. They lauded the success of the methods adopted: "to wreck the economy and prosecute a long and deadly proxy war until the exhausted natives overthrow the unwanted government themselves," with a cost to us that is "minimal," and leaving the victims "with wrecked bridges, sabotaged power stations, and ruined farms," and thus providing the U.S. candidate with a "winning issue": "ending the impoverishment of the people of Nicaragua." The New York Times had a headline saying "Americans United in Joy" at this outcome.

Terrorism Works—Terrorism is not the Weapon of the Weak

That is the culture in which we live and it reveals several facts. One is the fact that terrorism works. It doesn't fail. It works. Violence usually works. That's world history. Secondly, it's a very serious analytic error to say, as is commonly done, that terrorism is the weapon of the weak. Like other means of violence, it's primarily a weapon of the strong, overwhelmingly, in fact. It is held to be a weapon of the weak because the strong also control the doctrinal systems and their terror doesn't count as terror. Now that's close to universal. I can't think of a historical exception, even the worst mass murderers view the world that way. So pick the Nazis. They weren't carrying out terror in occupied Europe. They were protecting the local population from the terrorisms of the partisans. And like other resistance movements, there was terrorism. The Nazis were carrying out counter terror. Furthermore, the United States essentially agreed with that. After the war, the US army did extensive studies of Nazi counter terror operations in Europe. First I should say that the US picked them up and began carrying them out itself, often against the same targets, the former resistance. But the military also studied the Nazi methods published interesting studies, sometimes critical of them because they were inefficiently carried out, so a critical analysis, you didn't do this right, you did that right, but those methods with the advice of Wermacht officers who were brought over here became the manuals of counter insurgency, of counter terror, of low intensity conflict, as it is called, and are the manuals, and are the procedures that are being used. So it's not just that the Nazis did it. It's that it was regarded as the right thing to do by the leaders of western civilization, that is us, who then proceeded to do it themselves. Terrorism is not the weapon of the weak. It is the weapon of those who are against 'us' whoever 'us' happens to be. And if you can find a historical exception to that, I'd be interested in seeing it.

Nature of our Culture—How We Regard Terrorism

Well, an interesting indication of the nature of our culture, our high culture, is the way in which all of this is regarded. One way it's regarded is just suppressing it. So almost nobody has ever heard of it. And the power of American propaganda and doctrine is so strong that even among the victims it's barely known. I mean, when you talk about this to people in Argentina, you have to remind them. Oh, yeh, that happened, we forgot about it. It's deeply suppressed. The sheer consequences of the monopoly of violence can be very powerful in ideological and other terms.

The Idea that Nicaragua Might Have The Right To Defend Itself

Well, one illuminating aspect of our own attitude toward terrorism is the reaction to the idea that Nicaragua might have the right to defend itself. Actually I went through this in some detail with database searches and that sort of thing. The idea that Nicaragua might have the right to defend itself was considered outrageous. There is virtually nothing in mainstream commentary indicating that Nicaragua might have that right. And that fact was exploited by the Reagan administration and its propaganda in an interesting way. Those of you who were around in that time will remember that they periodically floated rumors that the Nicaraguans were getting MIG jets, jets from Russia. At that point the hawks and the doves split. The hawks said, 'ok, let's bomb 'em.' The doves said, 'wait a minute, let's see if the rumors are true. And if the rumors are true, then let's bomb them. Because they are a threat to the United States.' Why, incidentally were they getting MIGs. Well they tried to get jet planes from European countries but the United States put pressure on its allies so that it wouldn't send them means of defense because they wanted them to turn to the Russians. That's good for propaganda purposes. Then they become a threat to us. Remember, they were just 2 days march from Harlingen, Texas. We actually declared a national emergency in 1985 to protect the country from the threat of Nicaragua. And it stayed in force. So it was much better for them to get arms from the Russians. Why would they want jet planes? Well, for the reasons I already mentioned. The United States had total control over their airspace, was over flying it and using that to provide instructions to the terrorist army to enable them to attack soft targets without running into the army that might defend them. Everyone knew that that was the reason. They are not going to use their jet planes for anything else. But the idea that Nicaragua should be permitted to defend its airspace against a superpower attack that is directing terrorist forces to attack undefended civilian targets, that was considered in the United States as outrageous and uniformly so. Exceptions are so slight, you know I can practically list them. I don't suggest that you take my word for this. Have a look. That includes our own senators, incidentally.

The Coalition—Including Algeria, Russia, China, Indonesia

Now that's pretty impressive and that has to do with the coalition that is now being organized to fight the war against terror. And it's very interesting to see how that coalition is being described. So have a look at this morning's Christian Science Monitor. That's a good newspaper. One of the best international newspapers, with real coverage of the world. The lead story, the front-page story, is about how the United States, you know people used to dislike the United States but now they are beginning to respect it, and they are very happy about the way that the US is leading the war against terror. And the prime example, well in fact the only serious example, the others are a joke, is Algeria. Turns out that Algeria is very enthusiastic about the US war against terror. The person who wrote the article is an expert on Africa. He must know that Algeria is one of the most vicious terrorist states in the world and has been carrying out horrendous terror against its own population in the past couple of years, in fact. For a while, this was under wraps. But it was finally exposed in France by defectors from the Algerian army. It's all over the place there and in England and so on. But here, we're very proud because one of the worst terrorist states in the world is now enthusiastically welcoming the US war on terror and in fact is cheering on the United States to lead the war. That shows how popular we are getting.

And if you look at the coalition that is being formed against terror it tells you a lot more. A leading member of the coalition is Russia which is delighted to have the United States support its murderous terrorist war in Chechnya instead of occasionally criticizing it in the background. China is joining enthusiastically. It's delighted to have support for the atrocities it's carrying out in western China against, what it called, Muslim secessionists. Turkey, as I mentioned, is very happy with the war against terror. They are experts. Algeria, Indonesia delighted to have even more US support for atrocities it is carrying out in Ache and elsewhere. Now we can run through the list, the list of the states that have joined the coalition against terror is quite impressive. They have a characteristic in common. They are certainly among the leading terrorist states in the world. And they happen to be led by the world champion.

What is Terrorism?

Well that brings us back to the question, what is terrorism? I have been assuming we understand it. Well, what is it? Well, there happen to be some easy answers to this. There is an official definition. You can find it in the US code or in US army manuals. A brief statement of it taken from a US army manual, is fair enough, is that terror is the calculated use of violence or the threat of violence to attain political or religious ideological goals through intimidation, coercion, or instilling fear. That's terrorism. That's a fair enough definition. I think it is reasonable to accept that. The problem is that it can't be accepted because if you accept that, all the wrong consequences follow. For example, all the consequences I have just been reviewing. Now there is a major effort right now at the UN to try to develop a comprehensive treaty on terrorism. When Kofi Annan got the Nobel prize the other day, you will notice he was reported as saying that we should stop wasting time on this and really get down to it.

But there's a problem. If you use the official definition of terrorism in the comprehensive treaty you are going to get completely the wrong results. So that can't be done. In fact, it is even worse than that. If you take a look at the definition of Low Intensity Warfare which is official US policy you find that it is a very close paraphrase of what I just read. In fact, Low Intensity Conflict is just another name for terrorism. That's why all countries, as far as I know, call whatever horrendous acts they are carrying out, counter terrorism. We happen to call it Counter Insurgency or Low Intensity Conflict. So that's a serious problem. You can't use the actual definitions. You've got to carefully find a definition that doesn't have all the wrong consequences.

Why did the United States and Israel Vote Against a Major Resolution Condemning Terrorism?

There are some other problems. Some of them came up in December 1987, at the peak of the first war on terrorism, that's when the furor over the plague was peaking. The United Nations General Assembly passed a very strong resolution against terrorism, condemning the plague in the strongest terms, calling on every state to fight against it in every possible way. It passed unanimously. One country, Honduras abstained. Two votes against; the usual two, United States and Israel. Why should the United States and Israel vote against a major resolution condemning terrorism in the strongest terms, in fact pretty much the terms that the Reagan administration was using? Well, there is a reason. There is one paragraph in that long resolution which says that nothing in this resolution infringes on the rights of people struggling against racist and colonialist regimes or foreign military occupation to continue with their resistance with the assistance of others, other states, states outside in their just cause. Well, the United States and Israel can't accept that. The main reason that they couldn't at the time was because of South Africa. South Africa was an ally, officially called an ally. There was a terrorist force in South Africa. It was called the African National Congress. They were a terrorist force officially. South Africa in contrast was an ally and we certainly couldn't support actions by a terrorist group struggling against a racist regime. That would be impossible.

And of course there is another one. Namely the Israeli occupied territories, now going into its 35th year. Supported primarily by the United States in blocking a diplomatic settlement for 30 years now, still is. And you can't have that. There is another one at the time. Israel was occupying Southern Lebanon and was being combated by what the U.S. calls a terrorist force, Hizbullah, which in fact succeeded in driving Israel out of Lebanon. And we can't allow anyone to struggle against a military occupation when it is one that we support so therefore the U.S. and Israel had to vote against the major UN resolution on terrorism. And I mentioned before that a U.S. vote against . . . is essentially a veto. Which is only half the story. It also vetoes it from history. So none of this was every reported and none of it appeared in the annals of terrorism. If you look at the scholarly work on terrorism and so on, nothing that I just mentioned appears. The reason is that it has got the wrong people holding the guns. You have to carefully hone the definitions and the scholarship and so on so that you come out with the right conclusions; otherwise it is not respectable scholarship and honorable journalism. Well, these are some of problems that are hampering the effort to develop a comprehensive treaty against terrorism. Maybe we should have an academic conference or something to try to see if we can figure out a way of defining terrorism so that it comes out with just the

right answers, not the wrong answers. That won't be easy.

4. WHAT ARE THE ORIGINS OF THE SEPTEMBER 11 CRIME?

Well, let's drop that and turn to the 4th question, What are the origins of the September 11 crimes? Here we have to make a distinction between 2 categories which shouldn't be run together. One is the actual agents of the crime, the other is kind of a reservoir of at least sympathy, sometimes support that they appeal to even among people who very much oppose the criminals and the actions. And those are 2 different things.

Category 1: The Likely Perpetrators

Well, with regard to the perpetrators, in a certain sense we are not really clear. The United States either is unable or unwilling to provide any evidence, any meaningful evidence. There was a sort of a play a week or two ago when Tony Blair was set up to try to present it. I don't exactly know what the purpose of this was. Maybe so that the US could look as though it's holding back on some secret evidence that it can't reveal or that Tony Blair could strike proper Churchillian poses or something or other. Whatever the PR [public relations] reasons were, he gave a presentation which was in serious circles considered so absurd that it was barely even mentioned. So the Wall Street Journal, for example, one of the more serious papers had a small story on page 12, I think, in which they pointed out that there was not much evidence and then they quoted some high US official as saying that it didn't matter whether there was any evidence because they were going to do it anyway. So why bother with the evidence? The more ideological press, like the New York Times and others, they had big front-page headlines. But the Wall Street Journal reaction was reasonable and if you look at the so-called evidence you can see why. But let's assume that it's true. It is astonishing to me how weak the evidence was. I sort of thought you could do better than that without any intelligence service [audience laughter]. In fact, remember this was after weeks of the most intensive investigation in history of all the intelligence services of the western world working overtime trying to put something together. And it was a prima facie, it was a very strong case even before you had anything. And it ended up about where it started, with a prima facie case. So let's assume that it is true. So let's assume that, the actual perpetrators come from the radical Islamic, here called, fundamentalist networks of which the bin Laden network is undoubtedly a significant part. Whether they were involved or not nobody knows. It doesn't really matter much.

Where did they come from?

That's the background, those networks. Well, where do they come from? We know all about that. Nobody knows about that better than the CIA because it helped organize them and it nurtured them for a long time. They were brought together in the 1980's actually by the CIA and its associates elsewhere: Pakistan, Britain, France, Saudi Arabia, Egypt, China was involved, they may have been involved a little bit earlier, maybe by 1978. The idea was to try to harass the Russians, the common enemy. According to President Carter's National Security Advisor, Zbigniew Brzezinski, the US got involved in mid 1979. Do you remember, just to put the dates right, that Russia invaded Afghanistan in December 1979. Ok. According to Brzezinski, the US support for the mojahedin fighting against the government began 6 months earlier. He is very proud of that. He says we drew the Russians into, in his words, an Afghan trap, by supporting the mojahedin, getting them to invade, getting them into the trap. Now then we could develop this terrific mercenary army. Not a small one, maybe 100,000 men or so bringing together the best killers they could find, who were radical Islamist fanatics from around North Africa, Saudi Arabia . . . anywhere they could find them. They were often called the Afghanis but many of them, like bin Laden, were not Afghans. They were brought by the CIA and its friends from elsewhere. Whether Brzezinski is telling the truth or not, I don't know. He may have been bragging, he is apparently very proud of it, knowing the consequences incidentally. But maybe it's true. We'll know someday if the documents are ever released. Anyway, that's his perception. By January 1980 it is not even in doubt that the US was organizing the Afghanis and this massive military force to try to cause the Russians maximal trouble. It was a legitimate thing for the Afghans to fight the Russian invasion. But the US intervention was not helping the Afghans. In fact, it helped destroy the country and much more. The Afghanis, so called, had their own . . . it did force the Russians to withdrew, finally. Although many analysts believe that it probably delayed their withdrawal because they were trying to get out of it. Anyway, whatever, they did withdraw.

Meanwhile, the terrorist forces that the CIA was organizing, arming, and training were pursuing their own agenda, right away. It was no secret. One of the first acts was in 1981 when they assassinated the President of Egypt, who was one of the most enthusiastic of their creators. In 1983, one suicide bomber, who may or may not have been connected, it's pretty shadowy, nobody knows. But one suicide bomber drove the US army-military out of Lebanon. And it continued. They have their own agenda. The US was happy to mobilize them to fight its cause but meanwhile they are doing their own thing. They were clear very about it. After 1989, when the Russians had withdrawn, they simply turned elsewhere. Since then they have been fighting in Chechnya, Western China, Bosnia, Kashmir, South East Asia, North Africa, all over the place.

They Are Telling Us What They Think

They are telling us just what they think. The United States wants to silence the one free television channel in the Arab world because it's broadcasting a whole range of things from Powell over to Osama bin Laden. So the US is now joining the repressive regimes of the Arab world that try to shut it up. But if you listen to it, if you listen to what bin Laden says, it's worth it. There is plenty of interviews. And there are plenty of interviews by leading Western reporters, if you don't want to listen to his own voice, Robert Fisk and others. And what he has been saying is pretty consistent for a long time. He's not the only one but maybe he is the most eloquent. It's not only consistent over a long time, it is consistent with their actions. So there is every reason to take it seriously. Their prime enemy is what they call the corrupt and oppressive authoritarian brutal regimes of the Arab world and when

the say that they get quite a resonance in the region. They also want to defend and they want to replace them by properly Islamist governments. That's where they lose the people of the region. But up till then, they are with them. From their point of view, even Saudi Arabia, the most extreme fundamentalist state in the world, I suppose, short of the Taliban, which is an offshoot, even that's not Islamist enough for them. Ok, at that point, they get very little support, but up until that point they get plenty of support. Also they want to defend Muslims elsewhere. They hate the Russians like poison, but as soon as the Russians pulled out of Afghanistan, they stopped carrying out terrorist acts in Russia as they had been doing with CIA backing before that within Russia, not just in Afghanistan. They did move over to Chechnya. But there they are defending Muslims against a Russian invasion. Same with all the other places I mentioned. From their point of view, they are defending the Muslims against the infidels. And they are very clear about it and that is what they have been doing.

Why did they turn against the United States?

Now why did they turn against the United States? Well that had to do with what they call the US invasion of Saudi Arabia. In 1990, the US established permanent military bases in Saudi Arabia which from their point of view is comparable to a Russian invasion of Afghanistan except that Saudi Arabia is way more important. That's the home of the holiest sites of Islam. And that is when their activities turned against the Unites States. If you recall, in 1993 they tried to blow up the World Trade Center. Got part of the way, but not the whole way and that was only part of it. The plans were to blow up the UN building, the Holland and Lincoln tunnels, the FBI building. I think there were others on the list. Well, they sort of got part way, but not all the way. One person who is jailed for that, finally, among the people who were jailed, was a Egyptian cleric who had been brought into the United States over the objections of the Immigration Service, thanks to the intervention of the CIA which wanted to help out their friend. A couple years later he was blowing up the World Trade Center. And this has been going on all over. I'm not going to run through the list but it's, if you want to understand it, it's consistent. It's a consistent picture. It's described in words. It's revealed in practice for 20 years. There is no reason not to take it seriously. That's the first category, the likely perpetrators.

Category 2: What about the reservoir of support?

What about the reservoir of support? Well, it's not hard to find out what that is. One of the good things that has happened since September 11 is that some of the press and some of the discussion has begun to open up to some of these things. The best one to my knowledge is the Wall Street Journal which right away began to run, within a couple of days, serious reports, searching serious reports, on the reasons why the people of the region, even though they hate bin Laden and despise everything he is doing, nevertheless support him in many ways and even regard him as the conscience of Islam, as one said. Now the Wall Street Journal and others, they are not surveying public opinion. They are surveying the opinion of their friends: bankers, professionals, international law-

yers, businessmen tied to the United States, people who they interview in Mac-Donalds restaurant, which is an elegant restaurant there, wearing fancy American clothes. That's the people they are interviewing because they want to find out what their attitudes are. And their attitudes are very explicit and very clear and in many ways consonant with the message of bin Laden and others. They are very angry at the United States because of its support of authoritarian and brutal regimes; its intervention to block any move towards democracy; its intervention to stop economic development; its policies of devastating the civilian societies of Iraq while strengthening Saddam Hussein; and they remember, even if we prefer not to, that the United States and Britain supported Saddam Hussein right through his worst atrocities, including the gassing of the Kurds, bin Laden brings that up constantly, and they know it even if we don't want to. And of course their support for the Israeli military occupation which is harsh and brutal. It is now in its 35th year. The US has been providing the overwhelming economic, military, and diplomatic support for it, and still does. And they know that and they don't like it. Especially when that is paired with US policy towards Iraq, towards the Iraqi civilian society which is getting destroyed. Ok, those are the reasons roughly. And when bin Laden gives those reasons, people recognize it and support it.

Now that's not the way people here like to think about it, at least educated liberal opinion. They like the following line which has been all over the press, mostly from left liberals, incidentally. I have not done a real study but I think right wing opinion has generally been more honest. But if you look at say at the New York Times at the first op-ed they ran by Ronald Steel, serious left liberal intellectual. He asks Why do they hate us? This is the same day, I think, that the Wall Street Journal was running the survey on why they hate us. So he says "They hate us because we champion a new world order of capitalism, individualism, secularism, and democracy that should be the norm everywhere." That's why they hate us. The same day the Wall Street Journal is surveying the opinions of bankers, professionals, international lawyers and saying 'look, we hate you because you are blocking democracy, you are preventing economic development, you are supporting brutal regimes, terrorist regimes and you are doing these horrible things in the region.' A couple days later, Anthony Lewis, way out on the left, explained that the terrorist seek only "apocalyptic nihilism," nothing more and nothing we do matters. The only consequence of our actions, he says, that could be harmful is that it makes it harder for Arabs to join in the coalition's anti-terrorism effort. But beyond that, everything we do is irrelevant.

Well, you know, that's got the advantage of being sort of comforting. It makes you feel good about yourself, and how wonderful you are. It enables us to evade the consequences of our actions. It has a couple of defects. One is it is at total variance with everything we know. And another defect is that it is a perfect way to ensure that you escalate the cycle of violence. If you want to live with your head buried in the sand and pretend they hate us because they're opposed to globalization, that's why they killed Sadat 20 years ago, and fought the Russians, tried to blow up the World Trade Center in 1993. And these are all people who are in the midst of . . . corporate globalization

but if you want to believe that, yeh . . . comforting. And it is a great way to make sure that violence escalates. That's tribal violence. You did something to me, I'll do something worse to you. I don't care what the reasons are. We just keep going that way. And that's a way to do it. Pretty much straight, left-liberal opinion.

5. What are the Policy Options?

What are the policy options? Well, there are a number. A narrow policy option from the beginning was to follow the advice of really far out radicals like the Pope [audience laughter]. The Vatican immediately said look it's a horrible terrorist crime. In the case of crime, you try to find the perpetrators, you bring them to justice, you try them. You don't kill innocent civilians. Like if somebody robs my house and I think the guy who did it is probably in the neighborhood across the street, I don't go out with an assault rifle and kill everyone in that neighborhood. That's not the way you deal with crime, whether it's a small crime like this one or really massive one like the US terrorist war against Nicaragua, even worse ones and others in between. And there are plenty of precedents for that. In fact, I mentioned a precedent, Nicaragua, a lawful, a law abiding state, that's why presumably we had to destroy it, . . . which followed the right principles. Now of course, it didn't get anywhere because it was running up against a power that wouldn't allow lawful procedures to be followed. But if the United States tried to pursue them, nobody would stop them. In fact, everyone would applaud. And there are plenty of other precedents.

Leaderless Resistance

You know, it could be that the people who did it, killed themselves. Nobody knows this better than the CIA. These are decentralized, nonhierarchic networks. They follow a principle that is called Leaderless Resistance. That's the principle that has been developed by the Christian Right terrorists in the United States. It's called Leaderless Resistance. You have small groups that do things. They don't talk to anybody else. There is a kind of general background of assumptions and then you do it. Actually people in the anti war movement are very familiar with it. We used to call it affinity groups. If you assume correctly that whatever group you are in is being penetrated by the FBI, when something serious is happening, you don't do it in a meeting. You do it with some people you know and trust, an affinity group and then it doesn't get penetrated. That's one of the reasons why the FBI has never been able to figure out what's going on in any of the popular movements. And other intelligence agencies are the same. They can't. That's leaderless resistance or affinity groups, and decentralized networks are extremely hard to penetrate. And it's quite possible that they just don't know. When Osama bin Laden claims he wasn't involved, that's entirely possible. In fact, it's pretty hard to imagine how a guy in a cave in Afghanistan, who doesn't even have a radio or a telephone could have planned a highly sophisticated operation like that. Chances are it's part of the background. You know, like other leaderless resistance terrorist groups. Which means it's going to be extremely difficult to find evidence.

Establishing Credibility

And the US doesn't want to present evidence because it wants to be able to do it, to act without evidence. That's a crucial part of the reaction. You will notice that the US did not ask for Security Council authorization which they probably could have gotten this time, not for pretty reasons, but because the other permanent members of the Security Council are also terrorist states. They are happy to join a coalition against what they call terror, namely in support of their own terror. Like Russia wasn't going to veto, they love it. So the US probably could have gotten Security Council authorization but it didn't want it. And it didn't want it because it follows a long-standing principle which is not George Bush, it was explicit in the Clinton administration, articulated and goes back much further and that is that we have the right to act unilaterally. We don't want international authorization because we act unilaterally and therefore we don't want it. We don't care about evidence. We don't care about negotiation. We don't care about treaties. We are the strongest guy around; the toughest thug on the block. We do what we want. Authorization is a bad thing and therefore must be avoided. There is even a name for it in the technical literature. It's called establishing credibility. You have to establish credibility. That's an important factor in many policies. It was the official reason given for the war in the Balkans and the most plausible reason.

You want to know what credibility means, ask your favorite Mafia Don. He'll explain to you what credibility means. And it's the same in international affairs, except it's talked about in universities using big words, and that sort of thing.

But it's basically the same principle. And it makes sense. And it usually works. The main historian who has written about this in the last couple years is Charles Tilly with a book called Coercion, Capital, and European States. He points out that violence has been the leading principle of Europe for hundreds of years and the reason is because it works. You know, it's very reasonable. It almost always works. When you have an overwhelming predominance of violence and a culture of violence behind it. So therefore it makes sense to follow it. Well, those are all problems in pursuing lawful paths. And if you did try to follow them you'd really open some very dangerous doors. Like the US is demanding that the Taliban hand over Osama bin Laden. And they are responding in a way which is regarded as totally absurd and outlandish in the west, namely they are saying, Ok, but first give us some evidence. In the west, that is considered ludicrous. It's a sign of their criminality. How can they ask for evidence? I mean if somebody asked us to hand someone over, we'd do it tomorrow. We wouldn't ask for any evidence. [crowd laughter].

Haiti

In fact it is easy to prove that. We don't have to make up cases. So for example, for the last several years, Haiti has been requesting the United States to extradite Emmanuel Constant. He is a major killer. He is one of the leading figures in the slaughter of maybe 4000 or 5000 people in the years in the mid 1990's, under the military junta, which incidentally was being, not so tacitly, supported by the Bush and the Clinton administrations contrary to illusions. Anyway he is a leading killer. They have plenty of

evidence. No problem about evidence. He has already been brought to trial and sentenced in Haiti and they are asking the United States to turn him over. Well, I mean do your own research. See how much discussion there has been of that. Actually Haiti renewed the request a couple of weeks ago. It wasn't even mentioned. Why should we turn over a convicted killer who was largely responsible for killing 4000 or 5000 people a couple of years ago. In fact, if we do turn him over, who knows what he would say. Maybe he'll say that he was being funded and helped by the CIA, which is probably true. We don't want to open that door. And he is not he only one.

Reactions in Afghanistan

Well, what about the reactions in Afghanistan. The initial proposal, the initial rhetoric was for a massive assault which would kill many people visibly and also an attack on other countries in the region. Well the Bush administration wisely backed off from that. They were being told by every foreign leader, NATO, everyone else, every specialist, I suppose, their own intelligence agencies that that would be the stupidest thing they could possibly do. It would simply be like opening recruiting offices for bin Laden all over the region. That's exactly what he wants. And it would be extremely harmful to their own interests. So they backed off that one. And they are turning to what I described earlier which is a kind of silent genocide. It's a . . . well, I already said what I think about it. I don't think anything more has to be said. You can figure it out if you do the arithmetic.

A sensible proposal which is kind of on the verge of being considered, but it has been sensible all along, and it is being raised, called for by expatriate Afghans and allegedly tribal leaders internally, is for a UN initiative, which would keep the Russians and Americans out of it, totally. These are the 2 countries that have practically wiped the country out in the last 20 years. They should be out of it. They should provide massive reparations. But that's their only role. A UN initiative to bring together elements within Afghanistan that would try to construct something from the wreckage. It's conceivable that that could work, with plenty of support and no interference. If the US insists on running it, we might as well quit. We have a historical record on that one.

You will notice that the name of this operation . . . remember that at first it was going to be a Crusade but they backed off that because PR (public relations) agents told them that that wouldn't work [audience laughter]. And then it was going to be Infinite Justice, but the PR agents said, wait a minute, you are sounding like you are divinity. So that wouldn't work. And then it was changed to enduring freedom. We know what that means. But nobody has yet pointed out, fortunately, that there is an ambiguity there. To endure means to suffer. [audience laughter]. And a there are plenty of people around the world who have endured what we call freedom. Again, fortunately we have a very well-behaved educated class so nobody has yet pointed out this ambiguity. But if its done there will be another problem to deal with. But if we can back off enough so that some more or less independent agency, maybe the UN, maybe credible NGO's (non governmental organizations) can take the lead in trying to reconstruct something from the wreckage, with plenty of assistance

and we owe it to them. Them maybe something would come out. Beyond that, there are other problems.

An Easy Way To Reduce The Level Of Terror

We certainly want to reduce the level of terror, certainly not escalate it. There is one easy way to do that and therefore it is never discussed. Namely stop participating in it. That would automatically reduce the level of terror enormously. But that you can't discuss. Well we ought to make it possible to discuss it. So that's one easy way to reduce the level of terror.

Beyond that, we should rethink the kinds of policies, and Afghanistan is not the only one, in which we organize and train terrorist armies. That has effects. We're seeing some of these effects now. September 11th is one. Rethink it.

Rethink the policies that are creating a reservoir of support. Exactly what the bankers, lawyers and so on are saying in places like Saudi Arabia. On the streets it's much more bitter, as you can imagine. That's possible. You know, those policies aren't graven in stone.

And further more there are opportunities. It's hard to find many rays of light in the last couple of weeks but one of them is that there is an increased openness. Lots of issues are open for discussion, even in elite circles, certainly among the general public, that were not a couple of weeks ago. That's dramatically the case. I mean, if a newspaper like USA Today can run a very good article, a serious article, on life in the Gaza Strip . . . there has been a change. The things I mentioned in the Wall Street Journal . . . that's change. And among the general public, I think there is much more openness and willingness to think about things that were under the rug and so on. These are opportunities and they should be used, at least by people who accept the goal of trying to reduce the level of violence and terror, including potential threats that are extremely severe and could make even September 11th pale into insignificance. Thanks.

QUESTIONS

1. What key assumptions of class system theory can you identify in this excerpt by Noam Chomsky?

2. How does Chomsky's evaluation of U.S. foreign policy complement or differ from Lenin's critique of imperialism ("Imperalism: The Highest Stage of Capitalism," page 210)?

Chapter 5

POSTMODERNISM

COMPONENTS OF POSTMODERNISM

Focus of Analysis ········▶	• Social construction and impact of ideas, discourse, group identities, and gender on international relations
View of Human Nature ········▶	• A product of cultural and social circumstances • Constantly changing and evolving
Behavior of States ········▶	• Driven by beliefs, norms, and social identities
Goals of Postmodernism ········▶	• Broaden the agenda of international relations theory • Expose the power relationships of contemporary discourse in global politics
Key Concepts ········▶	• Androcentric; Constructivism; Deconstruction; Epistemology; Gender; Gender roles; Hermeneutics; Positivism; Postmodernism; Post modern feminist; Social constructivism; Subtext

INTRODUCTION

The fourth and newest system-level theory of international relations is known as **postmodernism**. This paradigm incorporates a rather diverse array of theories developed over the last twenty-five years, including constructivism, feminism, critical theory, and poststructuralism. Although these theories offer distinct views of international relations, they are united by their rejection of empirically based positivist traditions that are the cornerstone of the first three theories of international relations presented in this text.

Unlike realism, liberalism, and class system theory, postmodernism focuses primarily on the importance of ideas and culture in shaping our understanding of international politics. Postmodernists argue that traditional theories of international relations are inherently subjective and merely reflect the biases and motivations of the people who created the theories in the first place. Many postmodernists argue that it is impossible to construct an objective or unbiased theory of international relations and therefore focus on how our understanding of international relations is shaped by our beliefs and social identities.

At the root of the argument between postmodernism and mainstream IR theory is a difference over epistemology. **Epistemology** is the study of the origin, nature, and limits of human knowledge. Put another way, epistemology focuses on how we know or attain knowledge. Traditional theorists of international relations (realists, liberals, and class system theorists) believe that it is possible to acquire objective knowledge of the world. These mainstream approaches rest upon the assumption that it is possible to develop rational and testable theories to explain international relations. This can be accomplished by relying on the methodologies developed by the natural sciences and adopting them to explain social phenomena such as domestic and international politics. This school of thought is called positivism.

Positivism is a philosophical movement characterized by an emphasis upon science and scientific method as the only dependable sources of knowledge. Positivists believe that reliable knowledge can be acquired only through experimental investigation and empirical observation. So traditional IR theory is based on the belief that it is possible to identify objective facts and use them as a basis for developing testable hypotheses upon which we can form theories of international relations.

Postmodernists, on the other hand, question the validity of positivist epistemology. The postmodernist critique of conventional IR theory can be divided into three basic parts. The first part involves hermeneutics and its effect on theory development. **Hermeneutics** is the study of how we interpret, explain, and draw meaning from language. Postmodernists differ with traditional theorists over the value of language as a tool for understanding the world in which we live. The positivist views the world and reality as constructed through the orderly system of language, while postmodernists distrust the reliance on language as the path to knowledge.

Second, many postmodernists argue that there is no such thing as objective, value-free theory. Theory is merely the product of our perception of reality. In fact, postmodernists contend that theory simply reflects the values of the individuals who construct the theories. Therefore, they are skeptical about whether the methodology of the natural sciences can be applied to the social sciences. Postmodernists emphasize the difference between theories in the natural science such as chemistry and biology as opposed to social science theories such as political science. In chemistry, elements have distinct properties and react in particular ways that can be replicated in laboratory settings. These chemical reactions occur regardless of what we believe or want to happen. Social scientists, on the other hand, study human interactions that cannot be isolated in controlled laboratory conditions. Thus, the study of human beings is far more complex and subject to influences outside of the control of the social scientists. So when social science scholars study IR theory, there is an unavoidable relationship between theory and practice, between what political leaders think about how the world works and how they behave in the world.

Third, postmodernists' uncertainty about the objectivity of language and the ability of theorists to produce value-neutral theory caused them to search for alternative ways to interpret IR theory. This skepticism regarding the ability of language to represent an objective view of reality led them to the literary and philosophical theory of deconstruction. **Deconstruction** is a theory about language and literature that postmodernists adapted to analyze theories of international relations. Deconstruction is an analytical method that seeks to take apart, or "de-construct," verbal and written language in search of the hidden meanings implanted inside. Deconstruction offers social and political context to our understanding of language. It is a view of language as it exists not only in books but in speech, in history, and in culture. For the deconstructionist, language creates human reality. Language provides the broader cultural background that gives meaning to social conventions and concepts. In short, deconstruction is used by postmodernists to demonstrate that language and therefore knowledge is a human construct that is subjective.

In the chapter's first reading, Yosef Lapid introduces the basic underpinnings of postmodernism. Lapid presents both the promises and potential problems associated with postmodernism. The author begins by asserting that the postmodernist paradigm represents a serious challenge to our understanding of social science and consequently our study of international relations theory. Lapid reminds us that we need to be aware of the potential weaknesses of mainstream analytical methodology used in traditional theories of international relations. The author concludes with a warning that uncritical acceptance of postmodernism can lead to theoretical relativism, in which all theories are considered equal regardless of their intellectual merit.

As noted earlier, the postmodernist paradigm represents a diverse and wide number of images in international relations. In order not to overwhelm students by presenting examples of all the key theories within postmodernism, we limited our attention to the two most influential and widely known branches of postmodernism. Therefore, we will focus on constructivist and feminist theories of postmodernism.

CONSTRUCTIVISM

The first branch of postmodernism is called constructivism. **Constructivism** is based on the claim that our understanding of reality is socially "constructed." By this we mean that constructivists place great attention on the role of ideas and beliefs in shaping our understanding of the world. They emphasize the identities and interests of individuals and states and the ways in which those preferences are a product of society. Constructivists examine the processes by which leaders, groups, and states alter their preferences, shape their identities, and learn new behavior.

Constructivists share the postmodernist position that knowledge is not just about what we observe but also about the meaning given to those observations. This view rests on the principle of social constructivism. **Social constructivism** is the study of how people's identities, values, and ideas are defined by their group affiliations. Social constructivism examines how ideas and identities are created, how they change, and how they shape the manner in which states act on the international stage. The constructivist approach to international relations centers on states as social actors whose actions adhere to international and domestic rules. Put simply, constructivists assert that the behavior of states is driven by rules, norms, institutions, and identities. Like other postmodernists, constructivists place great emphasis on the malleability of world politics and how social norms shape and change the nature of international relations. For example, conventional IR theory concepts such as power, anarchy, and state sovereignty are not objective (empirical) phenomena but are actually ideas given meaning by us. The constructivist approach is to study how these ideas and values came into being and how they affect the way states act.

The constructivist view of international relations is based on five basic assumptions. First, constructivists contend that ideas, beliefs, and identities of individuals and groups are key to understanding the nature and course of international relations.

Second, constructivists believe that people's identities, ideas, and values are created or "constructed" in large part by their group affiliations. In other words, who you are and what you believe is in large measure the result of where you live and to what groups you belong. A young Afghan's view of the world will be dramatically different from that of a young American's. The values, ideas, and goals of each are, in part, the product of their distinct cultures, group affiliations, and social upbringing.

Third, constructivism places greater emphasis on social factors than on material factors such as military and economic power. Constructivists assert that people create social reality. This means that social factors such as ideas, values, and identities are most important in understanding international politics.

Fourth, constructivists contend that conflict or cooperation between states is largely the result of their values, views and ideas about each other and their place in the international system. For example, one of the architects of constructivism, Alexander Wendt, has argued that the realist principle of anarchy does not offer a satisfactory explanation of why conflict occurs between states. Realists argue that anarchy is an objective reality, whereas Wendt believes anarchy is subjective. Therefore, according to Wendt, anarchy exists only when people believe it exists. Most importantly, constructivists examine how anarchy is understood by states and how this understanding has shaped and continues to shape their actions.

Fifth, constructivists place great emphasis on explaining change in international relations. Change is a focal point for constructivists because their theory of the social construction of ideas holds that the way people and groups view the world can change dramatically over time. Overall, constructivists believe that concepts such as nation and sovereignty, democracy and terrorism are all socially constructed ideas with socially constructed definitions, and are not permanent, objective truths that are impervious to changing interpretations.

The last assumption may demonstrate why constructivism has drawn more serious scholarly attention since the end of the Cold War. Stephen Walt, a noted scholar of international relations theory (see his article in Chapter 1, "International Relations: One World, Many Theories," page 29), pointed out that constructivism is the only theory that offered a plausible explanation for the end of the Cold War between the United States and the Soviet Union. Constructivists argued that the end of the Cold War was a direct result of former Soviet President Mikhail Gorbachev's embracing of new ideas and the gradual decline of the acceptance of communist ideology by elites within the Soviet Union.

In his selection, Alexander Wendt critiques realism and offers constructivism as an alternative theory of international relations. Wendt offers a brief overview of the major assumptions of the constructivist approach and contends that postmodernists are united by their focus on how world politics is socially constructed. Wendt stresses the ultimate subjectivity of interests and their links to changing identities. Finally, he emphasizes the importance of ideas and culture in shaping the behavior of states.

FEMINIST THEORY

Before we begin our discussion of the feminist branch of postmodernism it must be noted that not all feminist IR theorists fit into the postmodernist paradigm. In fact, many feminist IR theorists remain positivists and reject the fundamental principles of the theoretical approach of postmodernism. The point here is to emphasize the diversity within the feminist approach to international relations theory and that this chapter spotlights a major but not exclusive view of feminist writings on IR theory.

The analysis and articles presented here examine international relations and established theories of international relations from a feminist viewpoint. That is, they introduce the element of gender into our understanding of foreign policy and the behavior of states. Gender, with respect to political science, does not narrowly adhere to the traditional biological delineation between men and women. Rather, the term **gender** encompasses the social and cultural distinctions as well as the differences in conventional roles between the two sexes, not simply clinical or biological classifications. Further, when we associate a particular role with an individual or group, we generally mean the function or behavior patterns normally connected with a particular position. Hence, **gender roles** are the jobs, tasks, and activities that are traditionally associated with either men or women as a group.

A key component of feminist theory is its questioning of the validity of the distribution of power, a key component in the behavior of and relations between states as the system currently stands. Feminist theorists do not believe that the accumulation of power, balance-of-power politics, and domination implicit in such an arrangement represent reasonable standards for the conduct of international affairs. Feminist theory also argues that the current system fails to promote the interests and roles of women in the world community. Traditional theorists' ignoring of women's contributions and issues renders the entire history and present system of, as well as the approach to, international politics one-sided, masculinist, and not fully representative.

Feminist theory may be viewed as a multifaceted effort to change the course and conduct of international relations in a way that incorporates the unique character and contributions of women. One aspect of feminist theory is its emphasis on the unique perspective and contributions that women bring to human relations and its analysis of these relations. This approach highlights the distinctions between men and women in terms of role, interests, capabilities, and so forth, arguing that women do not need to compete with or surpass men on every issue. Emphasis is placed on positive differences rather than negative competition. Feminist theorists argue that differences in women's expertise and perspective on various issues bring vitality, expand possibilities, and offer a new breadth of understanding to accepted norms and established theories of international affairs. For example, women's traditional skills and experience as primary caregiver and nurturer in the family setting and in society would presumably give them a greater range of abilities in the public spheres of conflict resolution, negotiation, and diplomacy. Overall, women's greater capacity to bond, form lasting relationships, and empathsize with others provides them with a natural advantage over men in these situations—a point never considered in traditional international relations theories.

Postmodern Feminist IR Theory

As in constructivism, social identity is a primary principle for **postmodern feminist** theory. Feminist postmodernists emphasize the social construction of gender roles and their impact on the structure of society and international relations. Postmodern feminists remind us that gender-based concepts and attitudes are social constructs that are created and rooted in interconnected systems of male dominated power. Consequently, feminists focus on the gender-related—often oppressive—themes and subtexts that litter a field dominated by men since its inception and still dominated by men today. A **subtext** is a hidden, underlying meaning or interpretation that can presumably be discerned by close examination of the words and phrases chosen by the author. Thus, both overtly and unconsciously, the analysis, worldview, and terminology widely used and accepted in the study and practice of international affairs is dominated by a male perspective.

Feminist theorists often use the term **androcentric** (male-centered) to describe the idea that mainstream theories of international relations (particularly realism) ignore alternative viewpoints and, instead, rely on essentially masculine interpretations of world affairs. The male approach—filled with images of power, strength, domination, and war—is quite distinct from the female approach—characterized by images of peace, equity, social justice, and environmental balance. By recognizing these inherent and pervasive inequalities and exposing the hidden masculinist agenda in the world political system, these feminist theorists hope to create a broader overall setting for enlightened discourse. And, since women have historically been outsiders in this global power game, this new approach would likely benefit peripheral nations (Third World, less-industrialized societies) that have also commonly found themselves on the fringes of political influence.

Obviously, feminist theory encompasses several viewpoints in a progressive dialogue on international relations theory. There is, however, agreement within the ranks of the debate on some key issues. To begin, the frameworks for both the practice of and theorizing about international affairs have been constructed to fit male conceptions of the world, life, and human interaction. In addition to setting up these frameworks, men have played and continue to play the primary role within them. Feminist theorists generally agree that the inclusion of women, in any of the forms mentioned above, would have a significant, positive impact on the policy-making process and the policies themselves. Such changes would stem from the perspective and experience of women in society and would benefit the world community by promoting greater equality throughout the system, as well as policies emphasizing nonviolent solutions and alternatives.

Writings in Feminist Theory

The articles selected for this chapter represent a sampling of the work being done on feminist theories of international relations. J. Ann Tickner's piece offers a frank discussion about the tensions between feminists and traditional IR theorists. The author examines the theoretical and methodological differences between feminist scholars and others. Tickner contends that feminists do not fit into the conventional state-centric and structural approaches and that this is one of the primary reasons why feminist IR theory is so misunderstood by conventional scholars in the field. Finally, Tickner explains how feminist perspectives of the conventional concept of security can contribute to our understanding of contemporary international politics.

In the next reading, Robert Keohane responds to J. Ann Tickner's article by providing an explanation of why feminist theory lacks widespread acceptance by mainstream IR theorists. In fact, Keohane asserts that much of the fault lies with feminists themselves. He decries the excessive politicization of the debate between feminists and traditional theorists and argues that this problem prevents serious discussion on feminist IR scholarship. Keohane concludes that feminist IR theorists must do more than offer critiques of mainstream IR theory. Instead, feminists need to develop systematic, testable, and falsifiable hypotheses because this will facilitate a more constructive scholarly dialogue between feminists and traditional IR theorists.

The selection by Birgit Locher and Elisabeth Prügl offers some unique insights into the similarities and differences between constructivist and feminist approaches to IR theory. The authors acknowledge that both theories share a fundamental agreement on the importance of the role of social construction of ideas and identities in understanding international politics. Many feminists agree that gender is a social construct, and this position forms the cornerstone of commonality between constructivist and feminist approaches to IR theory. But the authors contend that constructivism ignores key feminist epistemological insights and that there are profound differences between feminists and constructivists.

The final reading, by Saba Gul Khattak, is an interesting example of a policy-relevant feminist analysis of the utility and impact of the use of force. The author uses the U.S. bombing of Afghanistan in the aftermath of the events of September 11, 2001, to demonstrate the importance of understanding the problem from the perspective of Afghans in general and gender in particular.

KEY CONCEPTS

Androcentric   (male-centered) describes the idea that traditional theories of international relations (particularly realism) ignore alternative viewpoints and, instead, rely on essentially masculine interpretations of world affairs.

Constructivism   is a postmodernist theory of international relations that is based on the claim that our understanding of reality is socially constructed. Constructivists place great attention on the role of ideas and beliefs in shaping our understanding of the world. They emphasize the identities and interests of individuals and states and the ways in which those preferences are socially constructed.

Deconstruction   is a theory about language and literature developed in the 1970s that postmodernists have adapted to analyze theories of international relations. Deconstruction is an analytical method that seeks to take apart or "de-construct" verbal and written language in search of the hidden meanings embedded inside.

Epistemology   is the study of the origin, nature, and limits of human knowledge.

Gender   encompasses the social and cultural distinctions, as well as the differences in traditional roles, between the two sexes, not simply clinical or biological classifications.

(continued)

A Critique of Feminist Theory

One of the greatest strengths and contributions of postmodern feminist theory is that it examines the construction and role of gender that mainstream international relations theory ignores. It stands to reason that if men have dominated the course and conduct of international relations, and men have designed theories on this subject, that overall perceptions have been gender influenced. Just as two people witnessing the same event might describe it differently because of their unique backgrounds and preconceptions, it is likely that the predominance of men in international affairs has had an effect on the foreign policy behavior of states and theories about world politics.

Feminist theory has also made important headway both in uncovering the masculinist approach to international relations theory and in promoting the interests, goals, and equality of women in the field. Essentially, feminist theorists have moved beyond isolating the gender inequities in our traditional ways of looking at things and have also established various methods for redressing these inequities. These

(continued from previous page)

Gender roles   are the jobs, tasks, and activities that are traditionally associated to either men or women as a group.

Hermeneutics   is the study of how we interpret, explain, and draw meaning from language.

Positivism   is a philosophical movement characterized by an emphasis upon science and scientific method as the only dependable sources of knowledge. Positivists believe that reliable knowledge can only be acquired through experimental investigation and empirical observation. Traditional IR theory is based on the positivist epistemology.

Postmodernism   is the name of the paradigm that incorporates the following theories: constructivism, feminism, critical theory, and poststructuralism. Postmodernism asserts that it is impossible to construct an objective or unbiased theory of international relations and instead spotlights how our understanding of international relations is shaped by our beliefs and social identities. Postmodernists believe that reality is shaped by perceptions and that knowledge is highly subjective.

Social constructivism   is the study of how people's identities, values, and ideas are developed by their group affiliations.

Subtext   is a hidden, underlying meaning or interpretation that can presumably be discerned by close examination of the words and phrases chosen by the author.

methods seek to incorporate a greater number of issues important and relevant to women's lives or to expand the percentage of women in the foreign policy establishment. As the disparities in power and influence between men and women equalize, the nature and conduct of international politics may very well change.

A major criticism of the feminist paradigm, however, is its failure to provide a comprehensive theoretical construct for analyzing international relations. Conventional theorists might suggest it is not sufficiently rigorous, lacking an organized, cohesive framework. As a prescriptive theory, feminism falls into the trap of focusing too much of its efforts on how the situation in world politics, and the study of world politics, might be changed. What feminist theory does *not* supply are the explanatory and theoretical tools to conduct a thorough analysis.

We might also question some of the standards that are established in the context of feminist theory. Are feminists guilty of relying on their own stereotypes of gender characteristics? By using selective characterizations—women are more cooperative and peaceful, while men are more violent and aggressive—feminist theorists risk reinforcing the same gender stereotyping they are trying to overcome.

Despite our initial point, crediting feminist theory with uncovering gender bias in a male dominated field, there are skeptics who question the utility of this view. Critics contend that international relations theory should explain and predict behavior based on how the world actually operates. Since men hold the vast majority of leadership positions, scholars must study their behavior. Critics also point out that gender may not provide a sufficient explanation for past and contemporary international politics. Larger forces (human nature, disparities in wealth and power, anarchic world system, to name just a few) shape the behavior of various actors on the world stage, irrespective of gender. As evidence, critics point to the fact that when women have assumed leadership positions and confronted the same global problems that men have confronted, their actions have been similar to men's.

Feminist theorists respond to these arguments in a number of ways. First, feminists contend that illustrating that women and men behave differently is not engaging in stereotypes. It simply challenges scholars to appreciate the extent to which traditional theories of international relations rely solely on male conceptions of reality and ignore the perspectives and concerns of women. Second, they argue that feminist theories of international relations should not be judged by conventional, male-dominated rules of objectivity and analysis. Feminism is an innovative approach that seeks to inject a "feminine" perspective into the study of international relations. With this new perspective come new ways of analyzing global politics that cannot, and should not, be judged merely on how well the theories hold up to conventional social science methodologies and practices.

Whether we agree or disagree with these critics, feminist theory is now an important perspective in the field of international relations. In our study of how individuals behave in a global setting, differences between the sexes cannot be ignored. As men and women address gender issues in practice within society at large, it must certainly be time to address them in theory.

CRITIQUE OF POSTMODERNISM

Even a cursory reading of this chapter makes it clear to the reader that postmodernism is a complex, diverse, and intellectually challenging view of international relations theory. Broadly speaking, postmodernism provides an engaging critique of the social sciences more generally and to IR theory specifically. The postmodernist evaluation of positivism reminds us of the limits of IR theory and offers a useful lesson that IR theory is not an exact discipline that contains immutable truths that can be relied upon with certainty. Its emphasis on the subjectivity of ideas, theories, and even methodology is an important counterweight to mainstream conceptions of IR theory. Moreover, both the constructivist and feminist branches of postmodernism point out that language, group identities, and gender roles are socially constructed concepts that have a profound impact on the conduct of our lives.

In general, postmodernists concentrate on important questions that the other paradigms sometimes ignore. Specifically, constructivists focus on why and how change occurs in international politics. Feminists ask whether gender roles affect our view of global politics and whether our understanding of international relations has been narrowed by male-dominated cultures. What this demonstrates is that theories are important not just for the answers they supply but for the questions they ask. The postmodernists have broadened the agenda of IR theory by posing some very valuable questions that the other paradigms had customarily de-emphasized or disregarded. Criticism of postmodernist theory centers on three major problems. First, postmodernism rejects the positivist underpinnings of mainstream IR theory but it doesn't present any clear alternative with which to replace it. Second, postmodernism is merely a critique of traditional IR theory and nothing more. For that reason, critics contend that postmodernism is more accurately viewed as a radical approach to the study of theory in general than it is a cogent theory of international relations. Third, many mainstream IR theorists question the intellectual rigor of postmodernists who shun mainstream social science methodology and rely solely on non-falsifiable assertions regarding the nature and course of international relations. Finally, the postmodernist emphasis on the social construction of reality and the lack of objective truths leads many to wonder whether postmodernism is simply an anti-intellectual exercise that leads us nowhere.

Postmodernists respond by saying that traditional approaches to IR theory are too constraining and that the value of postmodernism cannot be judged by the conventional methods employed by mainstream IR theorists. Instead, postmodernism represents an attempt to broaden the horizon of international relations theory and employ new viewpoints and methods for understanding the changing nature of international relations. This debate is sure to continue for many years, but one thing remains certain: The postmodernist image of global politics has assumed its position as one of the major systemic theories of international relations.

21.   The Third Debate: On the Prospects of International Theory in a Post-Positivist Era

Yosef Lapid

In this article, Yoseph Lapid contends that IR theory has gone through three successive debates: the idealist vs. realist, the history vs. science and the current 'third debate' between positivist and post-positivists. The author then examines the strengths and weaknesses of the post-positivist (postmodernist) perspective.

Yosef Lapid is a professor of government at New Mexico State University. He is co-editor of *Identities, Borders, Orders: Rethinking International Relations Theory* (2001).

> "The search for a better theory forms the third debate . . . [It] is potentially the richest, most promising and exciting that we have ever had in international relations."
>
> —MICHAEL BANKS (1986:17)

Excursions into metatheory are notoriously controversial in the social sciences. One finds, on the one hand, the conviction that such concerns "are too important to be taken for granted and too much a part of our ongoing research enterprises to be left to philosophers to think about." Furthermore, "Those who try to ignore philosophy only succeed in reinventing it." One finds, on the other hand, a prescription for a rigorous philosophy-avoidance strategy for the practicing social scientist. Especially in the early stages of theorizing, so this argument goes, misplaced pursuits of epistemology and philosophy of science are bound to be inconclusive and are likely to come at the expense of actual research.

Be that as it may, it is hardly disputable that the demise of the empiricist-positivist promise for a cumulative behavioral science recently has forced scholars from nearly all the social disciplines to reexamine the ontological, epistemological, and axiological foundations of their scientific endeavors. As a result, the human sciences are currently undergoing an acute bout of self-doubt and heightened metatheoretical ferment. Indeed, some of the most highly prized premises of Western academic discourse concerning the nature of our social knowledge, its acquisition, and its utility—including shibboleths such as "truth," "rationality," "objectivity," "reality," and "consensus"—have come under renewed critical reflection. . . .

As we shall see shortly, this far-reaching and still evolving intellectual transition in the philosophical and social disciplines has left its mark on international relations scholarship. Following the "idealism versus realism" schism of the 1920s and 1930s, and transcending the more recent "history versus science"

From *International Studies Quarterly* (1989), 33, 235–251.

exchange of the 1950s and 1960s, in the late 1980s the discipline stands in the midst of a third discipline-defining debate. It is noteworthy that in terms of methodological and theoretical innovations the field of international relations was and still is "an absorber and importer, not a producer in its own right." Hence, *prima facie,* there are reasons to suspect that just as the "second debate"—the "history versus science" controversy—was wedded to the ascendance of positivism in Western social science, so is the "third debate" linked, historically and intellectually, to the confluence of diverse anti-positivistic philosophical and sociological trends.

Submitting that the third debate in international relations theory parallels the intellectual ferment that other social sciences are presently undergoing and that this debate constitutes a diffuse and still maturing disciplinary effort to reassess theoretical options in a "post-positivist" era, this essay explores the debate's etiology and assesses its implications for current and future prospects for theoretical growth. . . .

THE THIRD DEBATE: DISARRAY OR THEORETICAL RESTRUCTURING?

Few observers would seriously contest the suggestion that the field of international studies has experienced in recent years sustained theoretical effervescence. But beyond a vague uneasiness over the fact that no reduction seems to be obtaining in the diversity of conceptualizations and higher-order theories, one looks in vain for a more specific consensus on the current state and future direction of the discipline. . . . We find at the pessimistic end of the spectrum scholars who are either reluctant or unable to detect a coherent pattern in the rampant theoretical speculation. Such observers deplore the dazing pace with which new ideas are superficially introduced into international relations theory, only to be discarded subsequently with inexplicable urgency. They seem thoroughly confused by the "amount of debris on the battlefield of international relations theory" and feel understandably frustrated at facing this vast intellectual disarray "with few guides on making choices." Hence, they conclude that "in both theory and practice international politics can bring on despair. This is an occupational hazard in the field for which there is no remedy."

Others, to be sure, would strongly disagree with such a gloomy reading. They would counter that the lively chorus of contending theoretical voices in the field of international relations constitutes a "dialogue" or a "debate" with the power to transform the international relations discipline. Yet even among this group there is conspicuously little agreement about who is debating whom, along what lines of contention, and with what prospects of success. . . . But . . . it is imperative to highlight some notable commonalities among those who do acknowledge a coherent and consequential pattern in the current intellectual cacophony in the international relations field. For at a minimum one finds, for example, a shared recognition that the third debate marks a clear end to the positivist epistemological consensus that was hardly shaken in the course of the "history versus science" controversy. Whereas the second debate was preoccupied with quarrels over the methodology narrowly defined, the third debate is typically expected to facilitate trailblazing ideas about the nature and progression of knowledge in the international relations field. One also finds a shared appreciation that theory in this field is "in the process of being restructured," a restructuring which is recognized more-over as being "linked directly to a similar set of debates occurring in contemporary social and political theory."

THE THIRD DEBATE:
A POST-POSITIVIST PROFILE

Especially when compared with the simplistic coherence of the positivist philosophical movement, post-positivism is not a unitary philosophical platform. It presents itself as a rather loosely patched-up umbrella for a confusing array of only remotely related philosophical articulations. Hence, if one wishes to refer meaningfully to post-positivism as an alternative in philosophical position—perhaps ushering in a new era in international relations theory—one first must identify some areas of convergence in the general ideas presented by this "new philosophy of science."

A detailed analysis of such convergent post-positivist views is, however, well beyond the scope of this paper. I will deliberately restrict my attention to three themes which seem to have been particularly influential in determining the tone, agenda, and mood of the current debate in international relaposttions theory. These themes—the preoccupation with meta-scientific units (paradigmatism), the concern with underlying premises and assumptions (perspectivism), and the drift towards methodological pluralism (relativism)—are, of course, interrelated. They will, however, be treated separately here to elucidate more clearly their distinct impact on the current theoretical debate.

The Concern with Meta-Scientific Units (Paradigmatism)

Post-positivism has wrought a notable change in the understanding and choice of proper units of analysis in the study of scientific development. In sharp contrast to the positivist choice of the empirically corroborated law or generalization as the fundamental unit of scientific achievement, the new philosophy of science insists that only relatively long-lived, large-scale, and multi-tiered constructs—such as "paradigms," "research-programmes," "research traditions," "super-theories," "global theories," and "weltanschauungen"—should qualify as basic knowledge-producing, knowledge-accumulating, and knowledge-conserving units. For theories do not come to us separately; hence they should not be handled as self-contained entities.

Above all, the new philosophical posture portrays scientific knowledge as a triadic complex consisting of 1) a "phenomenic" axis covering the empirical content of scientific theories; 2) an "analytic" axis covering hypotheses, explanations, and theoretical models; and 3) a "thematic" axis covering reality-defining assumptions, epistemological premises, and other types of distinctly "ideological" or "metaphysical" ingredients. The novelty of this underlying post-positivist project—postulating an irreducibly three-dimensional space for scientific knowledge—is the explicit negation of the cardinal positivist premise which affirms the "eliminability of the human" and places (or replaces) the scientist "at the center of the social-intellectual-ethical complex known as science."

Paradigmatism thus asserts that meta-scientific constructs come and go in complete packages. It follows that only broader conjunctures of interrelated theories, including their unstated premises and underlying assumptions, can qualify as proper units of development and appraisal in science. It follows, furthermore, that empirical evidence in the usual sense of registering "objectively" what one sees is of only limited utility in scientific evaluative appraisal. For in sharp contrast with the phenomenic axis, the thematic axis—although challengeable perhaps in some other way—is not refutable by direct empirical observation. This partially explains why science is not "one great totalitarian engine taking everyone relentlessly to the same inevitable goal." At the same time it also raises the challenge of formulating alternative, "rational" criteria of evaluative appraisal which acknowledge and confront rather than deny or ignore the non-empirical nature of at least one integral component of all scientific knowledge.

Returning to our principal concern with international relations theory, I submit that "paradigmatism"—in the specific sense of an enhanced post-positivist concern with meta-scientific constructs which incorporate integral thematic components as a precondition of scientific intelligibility—presents itself as one of the most notable characteristics of the third debate. For even a cursory glance at the literature reveals that studies involving bivariate and multivariate relations, which flourished throughout the 1960s and early 1970s, now are held in general disrepute. The intellectual exchange is no longer between individual scholars or isolated theories, but between "models," "paradigms," "research programs," and "research traditions," or "discourses." The chosen unit differs in accordance with respective preferences for Kuhnian (1962), Lakatosian (1970), Laudanian (1984), or other more fashionally "post-modernist"

constructs. But we find in each case a remarkable concurrence with the underlying tenet which postulates that significant theoretical modifications and choices must always take into account the supportive meta-scientific domains in which they are holistically embedded.

It is in this general context, I suggest, that one can best understand the marked popularity of countless efforts to recast the fragmented theoretical turnout of the international relations field in terms of contending meta-theoretical constructs. There is also the related propensity to go beyond simple shopping lists of would-be paradigms or perspectives by launching more ambitious projects of paradigm demolition, paradigm synthesis or paradigm proliferation. And, arguably, such is the logic that also informs, for instance, Kratochwil and Ruggie's (1986) choice of the historically evolving "research program" (international organization) over the isolated theory (regimes) as their prime unit of evaluative appraisal.

The common denominator of these endeavors is the implicit belief that the substitution of new meta-theoretical constructs for more traditional units of scientific appraisal is somehow essential to locating and stimulating genuine theoretical growth. Fortunately—as indicated by the tendency to up-grade theoretical revisions to would-be "paradigm clashes" or putative "progressive" or "degenerative problem-shifts"—the impact of paradigmatism on current theoretical preoccupations in the international relations field has started penetrating well beyond a technical recasting of its fragmented theoretical corpus into revamped and more fashionably holistic blueprints. New questions are being raised about the dynamics of emergence, persistence, and the decline of meta-theoretical constructs in the field. The extent to which contending paradigms are truly "incommensurable"—incompatible and even incommunicable with one another—is more seriously examined. And the potential for fruitful dialogue between or syntheses of contending paradigmatic approaches is more systematically explored.

Most important, in this process of expanding paradigmatism the third debate has progressively taken the format of "a discourse about the choice of analytic frameworks." In this more sophisticated sense paradigmatism focuses on the difficult task of formulating and applying valid—as opposed to invalid—evaluative procedures at the paradigmatic level. Needless to say, for the time being these promising developments have expressed themselves mainly in a far greater sensitivity to, rather than the actual resolution of, new and hereto ignored sets of metatheoretical problems. But given this, it is still possible to summarize by reiterating the remarkable role played by the postpositivist reformulation of the unit of scientific appraisal in determining the specifically "inter-paradigmatic" profile of the current debate in international relations theory. This I submit differentiates in a fundamental rather than a faddish way the current controversy from its two predecessors in the field.

THE FOCUS ON PREMISES AND ASSUMPTIONS: PERSPECTIVISM

In addition to the reformulation of the unit of scientific achievement, post-positivism also invokes a deliberate shift to the thematic level of underlying ontological, epistemological, and axiological premises and assumptions. Such a refocusing is considered necessary in view of the remarkable willingness of both natural and social scientists to disregard empirical data that appear to contradict theories that (for them) have reached thematic status. Sometimes, therefore, impasses in the growth of knowledge may be created and reproduced less by observational mistakes (in the phenomenic axis) or by narrowly defined theoretical flaws (in the analytic axis) than by generalized crises of basic presuppositions (the thematic axis).

Once a set of guiding assumptions is elevated to thematic status, the perspectivist argument suggests, it becomes highly resistant to both evidence and logical criticism. And occasionally, under the fiat of premises that endure in the face of all negative tests, the entire process of theorizing may be forced to proceed along unacceptably restrictive or misleading lines. . . .

Highlighting assumptions as an important source of our scientific ignorance is different, however, from submitting that they always serve to distort theoretical inquiry. To the contrary, *similar* sets of assumptions invariably serve as enabling sources of valid scientific knowledge. Perspectivism submits, in short, that we are encapsulated in sets of presuppositions which may hinder *or* facilitate theoretical growth. And if guiding assumptions are the source of both our ignorance and our knowledge, it follows that "the focal point of challenge in science should become our weltanschauungen".

It should not be difficult to establish that the current debate in international relations theory also is characterized by a shift of attention toward the domain of thematic premises and assumptions. This refocusing expresses itself in a manifest eagerness of international relations scholars, from even radically opposed theoretical camps, to leave the phenomenic and analytic planes in order to devote more energetic attention to the "hidden" domain of key underlying assumptions. Perspectivism is implicit, for instance, in insights concerning the "inescapability of theory" and in ensuing concerns with becoming "the prisoner of unstated assumptions." It is manifest also in a more explicit sensitivity to the need "to become clearly aware of the perspective which gives rise to theorizing."

To be sure, the perspectivist accent is most audible among a small but vocal group of "post-positivist," "post-structuralist," and "post-modernist" critics of mainstream international relations theory. As indicated by Richard Ashley's recent work, these "rebels" utilize "deconstructive" and "genealogical" tools deliberately designed to automatically "target" assumptive theoretical headquarters. These intellectual technologies postulate that meaning and understanding are not intrinsic to the world but, on the contrary, are continuously constructed, defended, and challenged. Their main purpose is to "problemize" answers, make "strange" what has become familiar, and reverse the process of construction in order to reveal how problematic are the taken-for-granted structures ("anarchy" for instance) of our social and political world.

The growing fascination with the thematic component of our current knowledge of world politics is by no means restricted to an elite vanguard of post-modernist rebels. Robert Jervis (1988) has recently demonstrated that modernists can be quite effective—and, of course, far more accessible than their post-modernist colleagues—in exposing major assumptive traps in current theory. . . .

Although it is possible to argue that the preoccupation with underlying assumptions is anything but new to international relations theory, my point is that this preoccupation has acquired new significance in the context of the third debate. Perspectivism, as defined in this study, denotes something more fundamental than a ritualistic insistence that "we must examine our assumptions about the behavior of the actors in international arenas more carefully." It refers to more than "a rejection of empiricism in favor of a theoretical approach that accepts the place of data in a subordinate position." On the basis of these brief illustrations, it seems reasonable to conclude that perspectivism in the sense of a strong post-positivist focus on thematic premises and assumptions has been internalized as a foremost characteristic of the third debate in international relations theory.

The Drift Toward Methodological Pluralism: Relativism

"The current fierce attack on science, objectivity, truth, and even rationality and logic," says J.O. Wisdom, "may well be the fiercest ever mounted in history (1987: 159;). The new epistemology associated with Fleck, Polanyi, Kuhn, Feyerabend and others is, indeed, often attacked as having extremely relativistic implications. This new relativism is far more radical than previous versions because it is "second order," that is, "it questions not individual assertions for their lack of evidence but the implied and embedded standards, criteria, norms and principles that *make judgments possible and give them privileged status*" (D'Amico, 1986: 139; my emphasis). By undermining objectivity and truth, this relativization of philosophical thinking has greatly complicated the task of providing effective legitimation of knowledge and has rendered problematic the demarcation of science from non-science.

The massive move towards relativism has had at least three noteworthy ramifications. First, all versions of *methodological monism* seeking to institutionalize standardized, explicit, and unchanging criteria for regulating scientific domains—including the positivist conception of the scientific method—have been rendered suspect by this new intellectual climate. Far from consenting that epistemic criteria are destined to remain essentially unchanged over time and place, the new epistemology unapologetically suggests that it is itself socially mutable and historically contingent. And, following methodologically from such epistemological relativism, "a vigorous pluralism is called for. When it comes to the theoretical ideas 'let the hundred flowers bloom.' "

Second, the growing recognition of a multitude of potentially fruitful research strategies also has facilitated a better understanding of science as a polymorphic as opposed to monolithic entity. As the end product of scientific activity, social knowledge is now more typically seen as a complex of equally privileged but only loosely integratable forms. . . .

Finally, the post-positivist endorsement of epistemological and methodological diversity has undermined the classic fascination with scientific consensus, resulting in "a new-wave preoccupation with scientific dissensus." This intriguing eclipse of consensus as a prime desideratum in social science is of primary importance, for its signals a collapse of the highly influential Kuhnian equation of an inability to achieve paradigmatic consensus with an inability to achieve the significant theoretical growth.

Returning to our main focus of interest, we note that the post-positivist bent toward relativism and its ensuing methodological ramifications have clearly influenced the tone and substance of the third debate in international relations theory. It is hardly accidental, for instance, that despite high emotional and intellectual stakes, the current controversy has not been characterized by the focused intransigence that marked the two previous debates. In tune with the post-positivist "plea for tolerance in matters theoretical," scholars have resisted the temptation to seize upon the current intellectual transition as an opportunity to impose a new set of exclusive epistemological principles and prescriptions.

Reflecting a deepening suspicion of methodological monism, even scholars who are otherwise sympathetic to positivist orthodoxy now feel obliged to concede the dangers of "monolithic dogmatism." The discipline as a whole now seems favorably disposed to consider alternative epistemologies "rather than replacement of one kind of science by another." . . .

Finally, it was perhaps inevitable that the expanding acceptance of a polymorphic image of science and the growing popularity of methodological pluralism also would lead to a reexamination of scientific dissensus and its relationship to scientific progress. As a result, the search for "un-Kuhnian" versions of progress is already well underway in international relations theory. Irrespective of other disagreements concerning the theoretical prospects of the field, one now finds considerable consensus that "the way forward for [international relations theory] that finds itself in difficulties is not to pursue 'normalcy' of the Kuhnian kind but to work towards a diversity of strong paradigms."

THE GROUNDS FOR POST-POSITIVIST OPTIMISM

Granted that some post-positivist messages have been trickling down from the new philosophy of science, why should these tenets translate into greater optimism about the prospects of international relations theory? On what basis and in what sense can one posit that the third debate "provides stimulus, hope, and even excitement in the demanding business of analyzing international relations"? (Banks, 1985:20). What are the new promises of international relations theory from a post-positivist standpoint, and what is the post-positivist substitute for the embattled and rapidly fading El Dorado of positivist science?

In seeking an answer to this question it will be useful to take a second look at the three post-positivist themes that surfaced in our previous discussion. Closer scrutiny suggests that, under certain conditions, each of them can provide fertile ground for rejuvenated theoretical optimism. To begin, the preoccupation with meta-scientific constructs provides an attractive substitute for the positivist choice of the empirically corroborated law or generalization as the fundamental unit of scientific achievement. For despite many valiant efforts, scholars were ultimately forced to concede the manifest absence of cumulative progress defined in the rigorous terms of the empiricist-positivist scientific blueprint.

Provided that one is willing to live with charitable definitions of "paradigms" or "research programs," it is possible to document a rather impressive record of actual and forthcoming theoretical growth in international relations theory. . . . And if the popularity of Lakatos's methodology continues to rise

among theorists, one may safely anticipate that we will soon have as many, if not more, correspondingly reconstructed "research programs." . . .

The belief that social scientists are invariably better equipped to cut through assumptive as opposed to empirical impasses is perhaps overly optimistic. By pointing, nonetheless, to the nonempirical sphere of thematic premises and pre-suppositions, perspectivism has facilitated a relative "liberation of theory from observation." And this liberation was destined to be interpreted by at least some scholars as a good reason for renewed hopefulness. "Having passed through a phase in which facts have dominated theory," one of them notes approvingly, "the logic of our scholarship is carrying us into a phase in which theory dominates facts" (Banks, 1986:9).

This takes us directly to perhaps the richest mine of optimism embedded in the post-positivist credos of the third debate. Like other social scientists, international relations theorists can derive renewed confidence in their scientific credentials from the post-positivist move toward relativism and methodological pluralism. For the positivist scientific promise was arrogant and brutal in its simplicity: "This is the model of a scientific enterprise, take it or leave it."

For too long the tragedy of international relations scholars was, of course, that they proved incapable of either fruitfully adopting or decisively rejecting the grail of positivist science. Via positivism the discipline became locked in a sterile and frustrating worshipful relationship to the natural sciences. Presently emerging from this self-imposed positivist trap, many scholars are favorably impressed by the new latitude of maneuver offered by a multitude of post-positivist idioms of enquiry. And although notably lacking the exclusive luster of the positivist "mantle of science," the post-positivist counterpart—or counterparts—are far more accommodating in their acknowledged posture of tolerance and humility.

The endorsement of methodological pluralism, the emergence of a polymorphic image of science, and the reassuring notion that in the social sciences even permanent dissensus is not a scientific disaster have neutralized the once intimidating bite of the positivist "anti-scientific" label. Small wonder that currently issued verdicts of condemnation to "a life of intellectual pluralism" no longer carry their traditional message of scientific despair. Following a necessary period of digestion of post-positivist ideas, it is now more fashionable to posit that "much of the strength of the discipline comes from the plurality of its theoretical orientations."

Arguably it is this feeling of an exceptional "opening up" of international theory which above all sustains the hope that, by presenting unprecedented theoretical potentialities, the impact of the third debate may exceed by far the significance of the two previous ones. For some the main opportunity is to overcome U.S.-inspired nationalistic parochialism and create a "genuinely international theory applicable to all." Others seem more concerned with related problems of paradigmatic sectarianism, identifying opportunities for new and more energetic syntheses of realism and Liberalism or realism and Marxism.

Still others have identified opportunities for revamping the empiricist-positivist orthodoxy with "holistic" or "interpretive" correctives; grounding political realism and international theory in the supposedly superior principles of a "realist philosophy of science"; endorsing the epistemological foundations of critical theory as "the next stage in the development of International Relations theory"; and adopting a "post-structuralist discourse" which, we are told, "expands the agenda of social theory, posing questions that other discourses must *refuse* to ask."

Other interpretations of the precise nature of the post-positivist promise are readily available. What seems common to many of these theoretical projects is their striking ambition. In their combined effect the themes of paradigmatism, perspectivism, and relativism—in conjunction with the post-positivist plea for tolerance in matters theoretical—apparently have generated a reservoir of energy which seems to be best released by theorizing on a grandiose scale. Indeed, as Rosenau remarks, "this is not a time for nit-picking, for finding fault with rogue definitions, imprecise formulations and skewed data" (1986:850).

THE LIMITS OF POST-POSITIVIST OPTIMISM

How durable and consequential will the current season of hope be in the international relations discipline? Are we truly on the verge of a new era in international theory or is it more likely that the adrenaline rush of the third debate, like others, will have only negligible long-term implications? A definitive answer to this question would be risky and premature at this point, for we must keep in mind that the current surge of optimism is admittedly heuristic. It is, in other words, an enthusiasm of newly initiated departures rather than a sober celebration of safe arrivals. Hence prudence and fairness and the post-positivist spirit of tolerance itself demand a patient awaiting of further, more substantive, research findings.

Having acknowledged this it is nonetheless appropriate to add some observations on the hazards of excessive post-positivist optimism. In referring to possible problems and difficulties, my purpose is not to deprecate the revitalizing theoretical energy released by the third debate. It is rather to further delimit its scope in the spirit of constructive criticism. For clarity and consistency we will return, for the last time, to the three post-positivist trademarks of the third debate. Starting with "paradigmatism," one should notice in particular the danger of misappropriating this valuable post-positivist corrective for propaganda and polemical uses. Philosophers of science have long suspected, in fact, that one major reason social scientists turn to philosophy is to fabricate a more "respectable" anchor for the claim of being a "progressive science." There are reasons to suspect that such a line of reasoning may stand behind some current attempts to reconstruct the corpus of international theory in terms of "paradigms," "research programs," and other meta-scientific units of analysis.

Consider the fact that, as typically applied to the international relations field, Lakatos's methodology of scientific appraisal has consistently resulted in rather optimistic readings of both its past theoretical growth and its future prospects. . . .

But the problem goes far beyond cavalier invocations of would-be philosophical authorities. With the consolidation of international relations as a "dividing discipline," contending sets of criteria for judging scientific acceptability proliferate. Ironically, this opens up tempting opportunities for instant scientific redemption of vast bodies of theoretical literature by simple shifts of epistemic standards of appraisal. Would-be scientific contributions such as Allison's "models" of foreign policy decision-making, which might be considered unacceptable if judged by strict positivist criteria, may appear more promising if "interpretive" or "hermeneutical" standards are invoked. Without questioning the considerable merits of multiple criteria for evaluating claims, scholars in the field should beware lest they come to resemble the proverbial archer who shoots his arrow and then draws a bull's eye around it. . . . Especially if seen as a miracle drug, enthusiastic paradigmatism which makes light of the critical distinction between promising and misleading lines of inquiry at the meta-scientific level might lead us straight into new but equally damaging traps at the paradigmatic level.

A more sober look at the true merits of post-positivist perspectivism reveals at least three noteworthy risks. First, the preprogramming capacity of assumptive frameworks is often vastly exaggerated or reified. Perspectivism can play a constructive role only in so far as it acknowledges the historic and dynamic character of cognitive schemes and assumptive frameworks. Otherwise, "we lock the subject into himself unable ever to see more than he knows." This reminder seems particularly pertinent in view of the still popular rehearsals of rigid matrixes of underlying assumptions which mechanistically incapacitate realist thinking about contemporary world affairs. Seen in this simplistic manner—but *not* otherwise—perspectivism as revealed in the debate over realism may justifiably be dismissed as a source of confusion."

This takes us to a second set of hazards, namely that of embedding the fixation on guiding assumptions in a superficial understanding of the ramifications of what has been popularized by Kuhn and by Feyerabend as the "incommensurability" thesis. This in turn can result in equally damaging denials *or* exaggerations of the problem of comparison and communication between sets of thematic assumptions. Rather than defining the problem away by assuming automatic commensuration (portraying "models" as merely different "facets" of the same complex "reality"), and instead of building up the problem to "suicidal" proportions (by insisting that "genuine" paradigms "are defined by their fundamental incommensurabilities with other interpretations"), scholars interested in understanding the implications of postpositivist perspectivism for international theory must pay considerably more attention to philosophical efforts to devise new roads to commensurability.

A third danger which merits brief mention in this context lurks in the often-voiced concern that the shift of focus toward the lofty domain of guiding assumptions will come at the expense of empirical or lower level theoretical studies. Should it drift into such parasitic directions, the post-positivist "liberation of theory from data" could indeed lead us "into the dead end of metatheory" (Skocpol, 1987:12).

Finally, we will briefly examine the notorious pitfalls of post-positivist relativism. To be sure, methodological pluralism richly benefits from all the virtues of relativism. Unfortunately, it also suffers from some of its worse vices. If adopted uncritically or taken to its logical conclusion, methodological pluralism may deteriorate into a condition of epistemological anarchy under which almost any position can legitimately claim equal hearing. And to the extent that such an equality between different types of knowledge prevails, mere theoretical proliferation becomes practically indistinguishable from genuine theoretical growth.

It is hardly a secret, of course, that the international relations field is already seriously afflicted by some of the hazards of unreflective methodological pluralism. . . . The "Newton syndrome" and the seemingly universal desire to engage in grandiose theorizing have already resulted in an excessive fragmentation of the field. To borrow an apt metaphor, the field of international relations indeed "resembles nothing as much as the Learnean Hydra; each time one conceptual head is lopped off, another two appear in its place." If the relativistic excesses of methodological pluralism and fickle allegiances lead to hopeless theoretical incoherence, the optimistic message of post-positivist pluralism ironically may result in a backlash of some new dogmatic version of methodological monism.

IN LIEU OF CONCLUSION: A "PIANISSIMO" BRAVO?

Much more could be said on the promises and hazards of post-positivism in international relations theory. It is certainly useful to note that the third debate offers as many dead ends as it opens promising paths for future research. But acknowledging such hazards is not to deny that theoretical creativity may be greater today than at any time since the emergence of international relations as a distinct discipline. For we must keep in mind Isaiah Berlin's brilliant insight concerning the propensity of all great liberating ideas to turn into "suffocating straitjackets." When all angles are carefully considered, the hazards are not sufficient to seriously challenge the conclusion that the third debate has indeed generated some unparalleled theoretical potentialities. . . .

Whether these theoretical potentialities will bear fruit in the foreseeable future remains to be seen, but one thing seems reasonably clear. For many years the international relations discipline has had the dubious honor of being among the least self-reflexive of the Western social science. . . . The third debate is the beginning of a slow but progressive loss of patience with this posture of intellectual hibernation. The debate has stimulated theoretical and epistemological ferment in international relations theory, forging links with other disciplines undergoing a similar process. It has called attention to new notions of scientific objectivity, forcing a reconsideration of the role of the international relations theorist in the scientific process. It has called into question received criteria for evaluating theoretical constructs (such as empirical validity, prediction, and explanation), allowing theories to be reexamined in terms of their historical context, their ideological underpinnings, the forms of society which they foster or sustain, and the metaphors and literacy tropes that inform their construction.

Although the controversy fueled by post-positivist ideas in some ways has aggravated the dangers of epistemological anarchism, it also has alerted scholars to the problem of understanding "the notion of criticism where known methods of refutation are inapplicable." Although we may be unable to disprove a "themata" or a "weltanschauung" with traditional empirical or logical methods, we may find them to be overly restrictive or impossible to work with, as shown by Jervis's (1988) critique of the "anarchy/

game theory" framework or by Kratochwill and Ruggie's rebuff of positivism in the context of regime analysis (1986: 766).* . . .

In the space cleared by the weakening of deeply rooted urges for firm foundations, invariant truths, and unities of knowledge, an optimistic hope is now being planted—as hinted by the demand to make room for new "problematiques" and "to open up the field to critical approaches which have hitherto been marginalised, neglected, or dismissed by the discipline"—that, as in other social disciplines, knowledge in the field of international relations may be cumulative "not in possessing ever-more-refined answers about fixed questions but in possessing an ever-rich repertoire of questions." In this process, the discipline's level of reflexivity and its means for sustaining critical and self-conscious direction have been vitally enriched. . . .

"The task," as highlighted by the third debate, is neither the discovery of some ahistorical and universal scientific method nor the attainment of some objectively validated truth about world politics. It is rather a matter of promoting a more reflexive intellectual environment in which debate, criticism, and novelty can freely circulate. The international relations scholarly community—like all communities of inquiry—is communicatively constituted, and its success is partially conditioned by its ability to sustain and enhance the quality of argument in the context of deeply entrenched paradigmatic diversity. . . . we can agree, I hope, that the "exclusive and chloroforming world of the 1950s . . . is one to which few friends of International Relations or social science more generally would want to return" (Halliday, 1987:216). And on this minimal basis I for one am prepared to add a pianissimo "bravo" to the cheers of those already celebrating the would-be splendors of post-positivism in international relations theory.

NOTE

* Wisdom calls this "the enabling criterion." It asks whether a weltanschauung "can do its job or gets in the way of its own goal" (Wisdom, 1987:161).

REFERENCES

Banks, M. (1985) Where We Are Now. *Review of International Studies* 11:215–33.

Banks, M. (1986) The International Relations Discipline: Asset or Liability for Conflict Resolution. In *International Conflict Resolution*, edited by E. E. Azar and J. M. Burton, pp. 5–27. Boulder: Lynne Rienner Publishers.

D'Amico, R.(1986) Going Relativist. *Telos* 67:135–45.

Halliday, F. (1987) State and Society in International Relations: A Second Agenda. *Millennium* 16(2):216–29.

Jervis, R. (1988) Realism, Game Theory, and Cooperation. *World Politics* XL(3):317–49.

Kratochwil, F. and J. G. Ruggie. (1986) International Organization: A State of the Art on the Art of the State. *International Organization* 40(4):753–75.

Kuhn, T. S. (1962) *The Structure of Scientific Revolution.* Chicago: University of Chicago Press.

Lakatos, I. (1970) Falsification and the Methodology of Scientific Research Programmes. In *Criticism and the Growth of Knowledge,* edited by I. Lakatos and A. Musgrave. Cambridge: Cambridge University Press.

Laudan, L. (1984) *Science and Values.* Berkeley: University of California Press.

Rosenau, J. N. (1986) Before Cooperation: Hegemons, Regimes, and Habit-Driven Actors in World Politics. *International Organization* 40(4):849–94.

Skocpol, T. (1987) The Dead End of Metatheory. *Contemporary Sociology* 16(1):10–12.

Wisdom, J. O. (1987) *Challengeability in Modern Science.* Dorset: Blackmore Press.

QUESTIONS

1. How does Lapid define the third debate and does this categorization make sense from a theoretical standpoint?

2. What is the difference between positivism and post-positivism?

22. Anarchy Is What States Make of It: The Social Construction of Power Politics

Alexander Wendt

In this excerpt, Alexander Wendt introduces the constructivist view that world politics is socially constructed. The author contends that the constructivist approach is based on two assumptions: first, that the fundamental structures of international politics are social; second, that these structure shape the identities and interests of states.

Alexander Wendt received his Ph.D. in 1989 from the Univ. of Minnesota. He has taught at Yale University and Dartmouth College and is currently a member of the political science department at the University of Chicago. He is also the author of *Social Theory of International Politics* (1999).

The debate between realists and liberals has reemerged as an axis of contention in international relations theory.[1] Revolving in the past around competing theories of human nature, the debate is more concerned today with the extent to which state action is influenced by "structure" (anarchy and the distribution of power) versus "process" (interaction and learning) and institutions. Does the absence of centralized political authority force states to play competitive power politics? Can international regimes overcome this logic, and under what conditions? What in anarchy is given and immutable, and what is amenable to change?

The debate between "neorealists" and "neoliberals" has been based on a shared commitment to "rationalism."[2] Like all social theories, rational choice directs us to ask some questions and not others, treating the identities and interests of agents as exogenously given and focusing on how the behavior of agents generates outcomes. As such, rationalism offers a fundamentally behavioral conception of both process and institutions: they change behavior but not identities and interests.[3] In addition to this way of framing research problems, neorealists and neoliberals share generally similar assumptions about agents: states are the dominant actors in the system, and they define security in "self-interested" terms. Neorealists and neoliberals may disagree about the extent to which states are motivated by relative versus absolute gains, but both groups take the self-interested state as the starting point for theory.

This starting point makes substantive sense for neorealists, since they believe anarchies are necessarily "self-help" systems, systems in which both central authority and collective security are absent. The self-help corollary to anarchy does enormous work in neorealism, generating the inherently competitive dynamics of the security dilemma and collective action problem. Self-help is not seen as an "institution" and as such occupies a privileged explanatory role vis-à-vis process, setting the terms for, and unaffected by, interaction. Since states failing to conform to the logic of self-help will be driven from the system, only simple learning or behavioral adaptation is possible; the complex learning

Reprinted by permission of MIT Press Journals from *International Organizations* 46:2 (Spring 1992), pp. 391–425. © 1992 by the World Peace Foundation and the Massachusetts Institute of Technology.

involved in redefinitions of identify and interest is not.[4] Questions about identify- and interest-formation are therefore not important to students of international relations. A rationalist problématique, which reduce process to dynamics of behavioral interaction among exogenously constituted actors, defines the scope of systemic theory.

By adopting such reasoning, liberals concede to neorealists the causal powers of anarchic structure, but they gain the rhetorically powerful argument that process can generate cooperative behavior, even in an exogenously given, self-help system. Some liberals may believe that anarchy does, in fact, constitute states with self-interested identities exogenous to practice. Such "weak" liberals concede the causal powers of anarchy both rhetorically and substantively and accept rationalism's limited, behavioral conception of the causal powers of institutions. They are realists before liberals (we might call them "weak realists"), since only if international institutions can change powers and interests do they go beyond the "limits" of realism.[5]

Yet some liberals want more. When Joseph Nye speaks of "complex learning," or Robert Jervis of "changing conceptions of self and interest," or Robert Keohane of "sociological" conceptions of interest, each is asserting an important role for transformations of identity and interest in the liberal research program and, by extension, a potentially much stronger conception of process and institutions in world politics.[6] "Strong" liberals should be troubled by the dichotomous privileging of structure over process, since transformations of identity and interest through process are transformations of structure. Rationalism has little to offer such an argument, which is in part why, in an important article, Fried-

rich Kratochwil and John Ruggie argued that its individualist ontology contradicted the intersubjectivist epistemology necessary for regime theory to realize its full promise.[7] Regimes cannot change identities and interests if the latter are taken as given. Because of this rationalist legacy, despite increasingly numerous and rich studies of complex learning in foreign policy, neoliberals lack a systematic theory of how such changes occur and thus must privilege realist insights about structure while advancing their own insights about process.

The irony is that social theories which seek to explain identities and interests do exist. Keohane has called them "reflectivist";[8] because I want to emphasize their focus on the social construction of subjectivity and minimize their image problem, following Nicholas Onuf I will call them "constructivist."[9] Despite important differences, cognitivists, poststructuralists, standpoint and postmodern feminists, rule theorists, and structurationists share a concern with the basic "sociological" issue bracketed by rationalists—namely, the issue of identity- and interest-formation. Constructivism's potential contribution to a strong liberalism has been obscured, however, by recent epistemological debates between modernists and postmodernists. . . .[10] Real issues animate this debate, which also divides constructivists. With respect to the substance of international relations, however, both modern and postmodern constructivists are interested in how knowledgeable practices constitute subjects, which is not far from the strong liberal interest in how institutions transform interests. They share a cognitive, intersubjective conception of process in which identities and interests are endogenous to interaction, rather than a rationalist-behavioral one in which they are exogenous.

My objective in this article is to build a bridge between these two traditions (and, by extension, between the realist-liberal and rationalist-reflectivist debates) by developing a constructivist argument, drawn from structurationist and symbolic interactionist sociology, on behalf of the liberal claim that international institutions can transform state identities and interests.[11] In contrast to the "economic" theorizing that dominates mainstream systemic international relations scholarship, this involves a "sociological social psychological" form of systemic theory in which identities and interests are the dependent variable.[12] Whether a "communitarian liberalism" is still liberalism does not interest me here. What does is that constructivism might contribute significantly to the strong liberal interest in identity- and interest-formation and thereby perhaps itself be enriched with liberal insights about learning and cognition which it has neglected.

My strategy for building this bridge will be to argue against the neorealist claim that self-help is given by anarchic structure exogenously to process. Constructivists have not done a good job of taking the causal powers of anarchy seriously. This is unfortunate, since in the realist view anarchy justifies disinterest in the institutional transformation of identities and interests and thus building systemic theories in exclusively rationalist terms; its putative causal powers must be challenged if process and institutions are not to be subordinated to structure. I argue that self-help and power politics do not follow either logically or causally from anarchy and that if today we find ourselves in a self-help world, this is due to process, not structure. There is no "logic" of anarchy apart from the practices that create and instantiate one structure of identities and interests rather than another; structure has no existence or causal powers apart from process. Self-help and power politics are institutions, not essential features of anarchy. *Anarchy is what states make of it*.

In the subsequent sections of this article, I critically examine the claims and assumptions of neorealism, develop a positive argument about how self-help and power politics are socially constructed under anarchy, and then explore three ways in which identities and interests are transformed under anarchy: by the institution of sovereignty, by an evolution of cooperation, and by intentional efforts to transform egoistic identities into collective identities.

ANARCHY AND POWER POLITICS

Classical realists such as Thomas Hobbes, Reinhold Niebuhr, and Hans Morgenthau attributed egoism and power politics primarily to human nature, whereas structural realists or neorealists emphasize anarchy. The difference stems in part from different interpretations of anarchy's causal powers. Kenneth Waltz's work is important for both. In *Man, the State, and War,* he defines anarchy as a condition of possibility for or "permissive" cause of war, arguing that "wars occur because there is nothing to prevent them."[13] It is the human nature or domestic politics of predator states, however, that provide the initial impetus or "efficient" cause of conflict which forces other states to respond in kind.[14] Waltz is not entirely consistent about this, since he slips without justification from the permissive causal claim that in anarchy war is always possible to the active causal claim that "war may at any moment occur."[15] But despite Waltz's concluding call for third-image theory, the efficient causes that initialize anarchic systems are from the first and second images. This is reversed in Waltz's *Theory of International Politics,* in which first- and second-image theories are spurned as "reductionist," and the logic of anarchy seems by itself to constitute self-help and power politics as necessary features of world politics.[16]

This is unfortunate, since whatever one may think of first- and second-image theories, they have the virtue of implying that practices determine the character of anarchy. In the permissive view, only if human or domestic factors cause A to attack B will B have to defend itself. Anarchies may contain dynamics that lead to competitive power politics, but they also may not, and we can argue about when particular structures of identity and interest will emerge. In neorealism, however, the role of practice in shaping the character of anarchy is substantially reduced, and so there is less about which to argue: self-help and competitive power politics are simply given exogenously by the structure of the state system.

I will not here contest the neorealist description of the contemporary state system as a competitive, self-help world;[17] I will only dispute its explanation. I develop my argument in three stages. First, I disentangle the concepts of self-help and anarchy by showing that self-interested conceptions of security are not a constitutive property of anarchy. Second, I show how self-help and competitive power politics may be produced causally by processes of interaction between states in which anarchy plays only a permissive role. In both of these stages of my argument, I self-consciously bracket the first- and second-image determinants of state identity, not because they are unimportant (they are indeed important), but because like Walz's objective, mine is to clarify the "logic" of anarchy. Third, I reintroduce first- and second-image determinants to assess their effects on identity-formation in different kinds of anarchies.

Anarchy, Self-Help, and Intersubjective Knowledge

Waltz defines political structure on three dimensions: ordering principles (in this case, anarchy), principles of differentiation (which here drop out), and the distribution of capabilities.[18] By itself, this definition predicts little about state behavior. It does not predict whether two states will be friends or foes, will recognize each other's sovereignty, will have dynastic ties, will be revisionist or status quo powers, and so on. These factors, which are fundamentally intersubjective, affect states' security interests and thus the character of their interaction under anarchy. In an important revision of Waltz's theory, Stephen Walt implies as much when he argues that the "balance of threats," rather than the balance of power, determines state action, threats being socially constructed.[19] Put more generally, without assumptions about the structure of identities and interests in the system, Waltz's definition of structure cannot predict the content or dynamics of anarchy. Self-help is one such intersubjective structure and, as such, does the decisive explanatory work in the theory. The question is whether self-help is a logical or contingent feature of anarchy. In this section, I develop the concept of a "structure of identity and interest" and show that no particular one follows logically from anarchy.

A fundamental principle of constructivist social theory is that people act toward objects, including other actors, on the basis of the meanings that the objects have for them.[20] States act differently toward enemies than they do toward friends because enemies are threatening and friends are not. Anarchy and the distribution of power are insufficient to tell us which is which. U.S. military power has a different significance for Canada than for Cuba, despite their similar "structural" positions, just as British missiles have a different significance for the United States than [did] Soviet missiles. The distribution of power may always affect states' calculations, but how it does so depends on the intersubjective understandings and expectations, on the "distribution of knowledge," that constitute their conceptions of self and other.[21] If society "forgets" what a university is, the powers and practices of professor and student cease to exist; if the United States and Soviet Union decide that they are no longer enemies, "the cold war is over." It is collective meanings that constitute the structures which organize our actions.

Actors acquire identities—relatively stable, role-specific understandings and expectations about self—by participating in such collective meanings.[22] Identities are inherently relational: "Identity, with its appropriate attachments of psychological reality, is always identity within a specific, socially constructed world," Peter Berger argues.[23] Each person has many identities linked to institutional roles, such as brother, son, teacher, and citizen. Similarly, a state may have multiple identities as "sovereign," "leader of the free world," "imperial power," and so on.[24] The commitment to and the salience of particular identities vary, but each identity is an inherently social definition of the actor grounded in the theories which actors collectively hold about themselves and one another and which constitute the structure of the social world.

Identities are the basis of interest. Actors do not have a "portfolio" of interests that they carry around independent of social context; instead, they define their interests in the process of defining situations.[25] As Nelson Foote puts it: "Motivation . . . refer[s] to the degree to which a human being, as a participant in the ongoing social process in which he necessarily finds himself, defines a problematic situation as calling for the performance of a particular act, with more or less anticipated consummations and consequences, and thereby his organism releases the energy appropriate to performing it."[26] Sometimes situations are unprecedented in our experience, and in these cases we have to construct their meaning, and thus our interests, by analogy or invent them de novo. More often they have routine qualities in which we assign meanings on the basis of institutionally defined roles. When we say that professors have an "interest" in teaching, research, or going on leave, we are saying that to function in the role identity of "professor," they have to define certain situations as calling for certain actions. This does not mean that they will necessarily do so (expectations and competence do not equal performance), but if they do not, they will not get tenure. The absence or failure of roles makes defining situations and interests more difficult, and identity confusion may result. This seems to be happening today in the United States and the former Soviet Union: without the cold war's mutual attributions of threat and hostility to define their identities, these states seem unsure of what their "interests" should be.

An institution is a relatively stable set or "structure" of identities and interests.

Such structures are often codified in formal rules and norms, but these have motivational force only in virtue of actors' socialization to and participation in collective knowledge. Institutions are fundamentally cognitive entities that do not exist apart from actors' ideas about how the world works.[27] This does not mean that institutions are not real or objective, that they are "nothing but" beliefs. As collective knowledge, they are experienced as having an existence "over and above the individuals who happen to embody them at the moment."[28] In this way, institutions come to confront individuals as more or less coercive social facts, but they are still a function of what actors collectively "know." Identities and such collective cognitions do not exist apart from each other; they are "mutually constitutive."[29] On this view, institutionalization is a process of internalizing new identities and interests, not something occurring outside them and affecting only behavior; socialization is a cognitive process, not just a behavioral one. Conceived in this way, institutions may be cooperative or conflictual, a point sometimes lost in scholarship on international regimes, which tends to equate institutions with cooperation. There are important differences between conflictual and cooperative institutions to be sure, but all relatively stable self-other relations—even those of "enemies"—are defined intersubjectively.

Self-help is an institution, one of various structures of identity and interest that may exist under anarchy. Processes of identity-formation under anarchy are concerned first and foremost with preservation or "security" of the self. Concepts of security therefore differ in the extent to which and the manner in which the self is identified cognitively with the other, and, I want to suggest, it is upon this cognitive variation that the meaning of anarchy and the distribution of power depends. Let me illustrate with a standard continuum of security systems.[30]

At one end is the "competitive" security system, in which states identify negatively with each other's security so that ego's gain is seen as alter's loss. Negative identification under anarchy constitutes systems of "realist" power politics: risk-averse actors that infer intentions from capabilities and worry about relative gains and losses. At the limit—in the Hobbesian war of all against all—collective action is nearly impossible in such a system because each actor must constantly fear being stabbed in the back.

In the middle is the "individualistic" security system, in which states are indifferent to the relationship between their own and others' security. This constitutes "neoliberal" systems: states are still self-regarding about their security but are concerned primarily with absolute gains rather than relative gains. One's position in the distribution of power is less important, and collective action is more possible (though still subject to free riding because states continue to be "egoists").

Competitive and individualistic systems are both "self-help" forms of anarchy in the sense that states do not positively identify the security of self with that of others but instead treat security as the individual responsibility of each. Given the lack of a positive cognitive identification on the basis of which to build security regimes, power politics within such systems will necessarily consist of efforts to manipulate others to satisfy self-regarding interests.

This contrasts with the "cooperative" security system, in which states identify positively with one another so that the security of each is perceived as the responsibility of all. This is not self-help in any interesting sense, since the "self" in terms of which interests are defined is the community; national interests are international interests.[31] In practice, of course, the extent to which states' identification with the community varies, from the limited form found in "concerts" to the full-blown form seen in "collective security" arrangements.[32] Depending on how well developed the collective self is, it will produce security practices that are in varying degrees altruistic or prosocial. This makes collective action less dependent on the presence of active threats and less prone to free riding. Moreover, it restructures efforts to advance one's objectives, or "power politics," in terms of shared norms rather than relative power.

On this view, the tendency in international relations scholarship to view power and institutions as two opposing explanations of foreign policy is therefore misleading, since anarchy and the distribution of power only have meaning for state action in virtue of the understandings and expectations that constitute institutional identities and interests. Self-help is one such institution, constituting one kind of anarchy but not the only kind. Waltz's three-part definition of structure therefore seems underspecified. In order to go from structure to action, we need to add a fourth: the intersubjectively constituted structure of identities and interests in the system.

This has an important implication for the way in which we conceive of states in the state of nature before their first encounter with each other. Because states do not have conceptions of self and other, and thus security interests, apart from or prior to interaction, we assume too much about the state of nature if we concur with Waltz that, in virtue of anarchy, "international political systems, like economic markets, are formed by the coaction of self-regarding units."[33] We also assume too much if we argue that, in virtue of anarchy, states in the state of nature necessarily face a "stag hunt" or "security dilemma."[34] These claims presuppose a history of interaction in which actors have acquired "selfish" identities and interests; before interaction (and still in abstraction from first- and second-image factors) they would have no experience upon which to base such definitions of self and other. To assume otherwise is to attribute to states in the state of nature qualities that they can only possess in society.[35] Self-help is an institution, not a constitutive feature of anarchy.

What, then, *is* a constitutive feature of the state of nature before interaction? Two things are left if we strip away those properties of the self which presuppose interaction with others. The first is the material substrate of agency, including its intrinsic capabilities. For human beings, this is the body; for states, it is an organizational apparatus of governance. In effect, I am suggesting for rhetorical purposes that the raw material out of which members of the state system are constituted is created by domestic society before states enter the constitutive process of international society, although this process implies neither stable territoriality nor sovereignty, which are internationally negotiated terms of individuality (as discussed further below). The second is a desire to preserve this material substrate, to survive. This does not entail "self-regardingness," however, since actors do not have a self prior to interaction with an other; how they view the meaning and requirements of this survival therefore depends on the processes by which conceptions of self evolve.

This may all seem very arcane, but there is an important issue at stake: are the foreign policy identities and interests of states exogenous or endogenous to the state system? The former is the answer of an individualistic or undersocialized systemic theory for which rationalism is appropriate; the latter is the answer of a fully socialized systemic theory. Waltz seems to offer the latter and proposes two mechanisms, competition and socialization, by which structure conditions state action.[36] The content of his argument about this conditioning, however, presupposes a self-help system that is not itself a constitutive feature of anarchy. As James Morrow points out, Waltz's two mechanisms condition behavior, not identity and interest.[37] This explains how Waltz can be accused of both "individualism" and "structuralism."[38] He is the former with respect to systemic constitutions of identity and interest, the latter with respect to systemic determinations of behavior.

Anarchy and the Social Construction of Power Politics

If self-help is not a constitutive feature of anarchy, it must emerge causally from processes in which anarchy plays only a permissive role.[39] This reflects a second principle of constructivism: that the meanings in terms of which action is organized arise out of interaction.[40] This being said, however, the situation facing states as they encounter one another for

the first time may be such that only self-regarding conceptions of identity can survive; if so, even if these conceptions are socially constructed, neorealists may be right in holding identities and interests constant and thus in privileging one particular meaning of anarchic structure over process. In this case, rationalists would be right to argue for a weak, behavioral conception of the difference that institutions make, and realists would be right to argue that any international institutions which are created will be inherently unstable, since without the power to transform identities and interests they will be "continuing objects of choice" by exogenously constituted actors constrained only by the transaction costs of behavioral change.[41] Even in a permissive causal role, in other words, anarchy may decisively restrict interaction and therefore restrict viable forms of systemic theory. I address these causal issues first by showing how self-regarding ideas about security might develop and then by examining the conditions under which a key efficient cause—predation—may dispose states in this direction rather than others.

Conceptions of self and interest tend to "mirror" the practices of significant others over time. This principle of identity-formation is captured by the symbolic interactionist notion of the "looking-glass self," which asserts that the self is a reflection of an actor's socialization.

Consider two actors—ego and alter—encountering each other for the first time. Each wants to survive and has certain material capabilities, but neither actor has biological or domestic imperatives for power, glory, or conquest (still bracketed), and there is no history of security or insecurity between the two. What should they do? Realists would probably argue that each should act on the basis of worst-case assumptions about the other's intentions, justifying such an attitude as prudent in view of the possibility of death from making a mistake. Such a possibility always exists, even in civil society; however, society would be impossible if people made decisions purely on the basis of worst-case possibilities. Instead, most decisions are and should be made on the basis of probabilities, and these are produced by interaction, by what actors *do*.

In the beginning is ego's gesture, which may consist, for example, of an advance, a retreat, a brandishing of arms, a laying down of arms, or an attack.[42] For ego, this gesture represents the basis on which it is prepared to respond to alter. This basis is unknown to alter, however, and so it must make an inference or "attribution" about ego's intentions and, in particular, given that this is anarchy, about whether ego is a threat.[43] The content of this inference will largely depend on two considerations. The first is the gesture's and ego's physical qualities, which are in part contrived by ego and which include the direction of movement, noise, numbers, and immediate consequences of the gesture. The second consideration concerns what alter would intend by such qualities were it to make such a gesture itself. Alter may make an attributional "error" in its inference about ego's intent, but there is also no reason for it to assume a priori—before the gesture—that ego is threatening, since it is only through a process of signaling and interpreting that the costs and probabilities of being wrong can be determined.[44] Social threats are constructed, not natural.

Consider an example. Would we assume, a priori, that we were about to be attacked if we are ever contacted by members of an alien civilization? I think not. We would be highly alert, of course, but whether we placed our military forces on alert or launched an attack would depend on how we interpreted the import of their first gesture for our security—if only to avoid making an immediate enemy out of what may be a dangerous adversary. The possibility of error, in other words, does not force us to act on the assumption that the aliens are threatening: action depends on the probabilities we assign, and these are in key part a function of what the aliens do; prior to their gesture, we have no systemic basis for assigning probabilities. If their first gesture is to appear with a thousand spaceships and destroy New York, we will define the situation as threatening and respond accordingly. But if they appear with one spaceship, saying what seems to be "we come in peace," we will feel "reassured" and will probably respond with a gesture intended to reassure them, even if this gesture is not necessarily interpreted by them as such.[45]

This process of signaling, interpreting, and responding completes a "social act" and begins the process of creating intersubjective meanings. It advances the same way. The first social act creates expectations on both sides about each other's future behavior: potentially mistaken and certainly tentative, but expectations nonetheless. Based on this tentative knowledge, ego makes a new gesture, again signifying the basis on which it will respond to alter, and again alter responds, adding to the pool of knowledge each has about the other, and so on over time. The mechanism here is reinforcement; interaction rewards actors for holding certain ideas about each other and discourages them from holding others. If repeated long enough, these "reciprocal typifications" will create relatively stable concepts of self and other regarding the issue at stake in the interaction.[46]

It is through reciprocal interaction, in other words, that we create and instantiate the relatively enduring social structures in terms of which we define our identities and interests. Jeff Coulter sums up the ontological dependence of structure on process this way: "The parameters of social organization themselves are reproduced only in and through the orientations and practices of members engaged in social interactions over time. . . . Social configurations are not 'objective' like mountains or forests, but neither are they 'subjective' like dreams or flights of speculative fancy. They are, as most social scientists concede at the theoretical level, intersubjective constructions."[47]

The simple overall model of identity- and interest-formation proposed in Figure 1 applies to competitive institutions no less than to cooperative ones. Self-help security systems evolve from cycles of interaction in which each party acts in ways that the other feels are threatening to the self, creating expectations that the other is not to be trusted. Competitive or egoistic identities are caused by such insecurity; if the other is threatening, the self is forced to "mirror" such behavior in its conception of the self's relationship to that other. Being treated as an object for the gratification of others precludes the positive identification with others necessary for collective security; conversely, being treated by others in ways that are empathic with respect to the security of the self permits such identification.

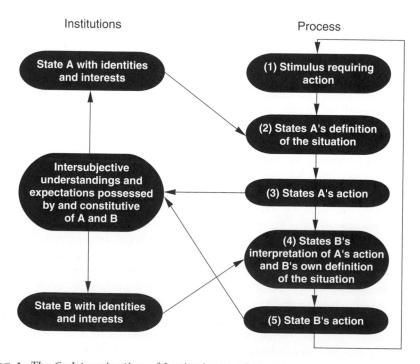

FIGURE 1 *The Codetermination of Institutions and Process*

Competitive systems of interaction are prone to security "dilemmas," in which the efforts of actors to enhance their security unilaterally threatens the security of the others, perpetuating distrust and alienation. The forms of identity and interest that constitute such dilemmas, however, are themselves ongoing effects of, not exogenous to, the interaction; identities are produced in and through "situated activity."[48] We do not *begin* our relationship with the aliens in a security dilemma; security dilemmas are not given by anarchy or nature. Of course, once institutionalized such a dilemma may be hard to change (I return to this below), but the point remains: identities and interests are constituted by collective meanings that are always in process. As Sheldon Stryker emphasizes, "The social process is one of constructing and reconstructing self and social relationships."[49] If states find themselves in a self-help system, this is because their practices made it that way. Changing the practices will change the intersubjective knowledge that constitutes the system.

Predator States and Anarchy as Permissive Cause

The mirror theory of identity-formation is a crude account of how the process of creating identities and interests might work, but it does not tell us why a system of states—such as, arguably, our own—would have ended up with self-regarding and not collective identities. In this section, I examine an efficient cause, predation, which, in conjunction with anarchy as a permissive cause, may generate a self-help system. In so doing, however, I show the key role that the structure of identities and interests plays in mediating anarchy's explanatory role.

The predator argument is straightforward and compelling. For whatever reasons—biology, domestic politics, or systemic victimization—some states may become predisposed toward aggression. The aggressive behavior of these predators or "bad apples" forces other states to engage in competitive power politics, to meet fire with fire, since failure to do so may degrade or destroy them. One predator will best a hundred pacifists because anarchy provides no guarantees. This argument is powerful in part because it is so weak: rather than making the strong assumption that all states are inherently power-seeking (a purely reductionist theory of power politics), it assumes that just one is power-seeking and that the others have to follow suit because anarchy permits the one to exploit them.

In making this argument, it is important to reiterate that the possibility of predation does not in itself force states to anticipate it a priori with competitive power politics of their own. The possibility of predation does not mean that "war may at any moment occur"; it may in fact be extremely unlikely. Once a predator emerges, however, it may condition identity- and interest-formation in the following manner.

In an anarchy of two, if ego is predatory, alter must either define its security in self-help terms or pay the price. This follows directly from the above argument, in which conceptions of self mirror treatment by the other. In an anarchy of many, however, the effect of predation also depends on the level of collective identity already attained in the system. If predation occurs right after the first encounter in the state of nature, it will force others with whom it comes in contact to defend themselves, first individually and then collectively *if* they come to perceive a common threat. The emergence of such a defensive alliance will be seriously inhibited if the structure of identities and interests has already evolved into a Hobbesian world of maximum insecurity, since potential allies will strongly distrust each other and face intense collective action problems; such insecure allies are also more likely to fall out amongst themselves once the predator is removed. If collective security identity is high, however, the emergence of a predator may do much less damage. If the predator attacks any member of the collective, the latter will come to the victim's defense on the principle of "all for one, one for all," even if the predator is not presently a threat to other members of the collective. If the predator is not strong enough to withstand the collective, it will be defeated and collective security will obtain. But if it is strong enough, the logic of the two-actor case (now predator and collective) will activate, and balance-of-power politics will reestablish itself.

The timing of the emergence of predation relative to the history of identity-formation in the community is therefore crucial to anarchy's explanatory role as a permissive cause. Predation will always lead victims to defend themselves, but whether defense will be collective or not depends on the history of interaction within the potential collective as much as on the ambitions of the predator. Will the disappearance of the Soviet threat renew old insecurities among the members of the North Atlantic Treaty Organization? Perhaps, but not if they have reasons independent of that threat for identifying their security with one another. Identities and interests are relationship-specific, not intrinsic attributes of a "portfolio"; states may be competitive in some relationships and solidary in oth-

ers. "Mature" anarchies are less likely than "immature" ones to be reduced by predation to a Hobbesian condition, and maturity, which is a proxy for structures of identity and interest, is a function of process.[50]

The source of predation also matters. If it stems from unit-level causes that are immune to systemic impacts (causes such as human nature or domestic politics taken in isolation), then it functions in a manner analogous to a "genetic trait" in the constructed world of the state system. Even if successful, this trait does not select for other predators in an evolutionary sense so much as it teaches other states to respond in kind, but since traits cannot be unlearned, the other states will continue competitive behavior until the predator is either destroyed or transformed from within. However, in the more likely event that predation stems at least in part from prior systemic interaction—perhaps as a result of being victimized in the past (one thinks here of Nazi Germany or the Soviet Union)—then it is more a response to a learned identity and, as such, might be transformed by future social interaction in the form of appeasement, reassurances that security needs will be met, systemic effects on domestic politics, and so on. In this case, in other words, there is more hope that process can transform a bad apple into a good one.

The role of predation in generating a self-help system, then, is consistent with a systematic focus on process. Even if the source of predation is entirely exogenous to the system, it is what states *do* that determines the quality of their interactions under anarchy. In this respect, it is not surprising that it is classical realists rather than structural realists who emphasize this sort of argument. The former's emphasis on unit-level causes of power politics leads more easily to a permissive view of anarchy's explanatory role (and therefore to a processual view of international relations) than does the latter's emphasis on anarchy as a "structural cause";[51] neorealists do not need predation because the system is given as self-help.

This raises anew the question of exactly how much and what kind of role human nature and domestic politics play in world politics. The greater and more destructive this role, the more significant predation will be, and the less amenable anarchy will be to formation of collective identities. Classical realists, of course, assumed that human nature was possessed by an inherent lust for power or glory. My argument suggests that assumptions such as this were made for a reason: an unchanging Hobbesian man provides the powerful efficient cause necessary for a relentless pessimism about world politics that anarchic structure alone, or even structure plus intermittent predation, cannot supply. One can be skeptical of such an essentialist assumption, as I am, but it does produce determinate results at the expense of systemic theory. A concern with systemic process over structure suggests that perhaps it is time to revisit the debate over the relative importance of first-, second-, and third-image theories of state identity-formation.[52]

Assuming for now that systemic theories of identity-formation in world politics are worth pursuing, let me conclude by suggesting that the realist-rationalist alliance "reifies" self-help in the sense of treating it as something separate from the practices by which it is produced and sustained. Peter Berger and Thomas Luckmann define reification as follows: "[It] is the apprehension of the products of human activity *as if* they were something else than human products—such as facts of nature, results of cosmic laws, or manifestations of divine will. Reification implies that man is capable of forgetting his own authorship of the human world, and further, that the dialectic between man, the producer, and his products is lost to consciousness. The reified world is . . . experienced by man as a strange facticity, an *opus alienum* over which he has no control rather than as the *opus proprium* of his own productive activity."[53] By denying or bracketing states' collective authorship of their identities and interests, in other words, the realist-rationalist alliance denies or brackets the fact that competitive power politics help create the very "problem of order" they are supposed to solve—that realism is a self-fulfilling prophecy. Far from being exogenously given, the intersubjective knowledge that constitutes competitive identities and interests is constructed every day by processes of "social will formation."[54] It is what states have made of themselves.

INSTITUTIONAL TRANSFORMATIONS OF POWER POLITICS

Let us assume that processes of identity- and interest-formation have created a world in which states do not recognize rights to territory or existence—a war of all against all. In this world, anarchy has a "realist" meaning for state action: be insecure and concerned with relative power. Anarchy has this meaning only in virtue of collective, insecurity-producing practices, but if those practices are relatively stable, they do constitute a system that may resist change. The fact that worlds of power politics are socially constructed, in other words, does not guarantee they are malleable, for at least two reasons.

The first reason is that once constituted, any social system confronts each of its members as an objective social fact that reinforces certain behaviors and discourages others. Self-help systems, for example, tend to reward competition and punish altruism. The possibility of change depends on whether the exigencies of such competition leave room for actions that deviate from the prescribed script. If they do not, the system will be reproduced and deviant actors will not.

The second reason is that systemic change may also be inhibited by actors' interests in maintaining relatively stable role identities. Such interest are rooted not only in the desire to minimize uncertainty and anxiety, manifested in efforts to confirm existing beliefs about the social world, but also in the desire to avoid the expected costs of breaking commitments made to others—notably domestic constituencies and foreign allies in the case of states—as part of past practices. The level of resistance that these commitments induce will depend on the "salience" of particular role identities to the actor.[55] The United States, for example, is more likely to resist threats to its identity as "leader of anti-communist crusades" than to its identity as "promoter of human rights." But for almost any role identity, practices and information that challenge it are likely to create cognitive dissonance and even perceptions of threat, and these may cause resistance to transformations of the self and the thus to social change.

For both systemic and "psychological" reasons, then, intersubjective understandings and expectations may have a self-perpetuating quality, constituting path-dependencies that new ideas about self and other must transcend. This does not change the fact that through practice agents are continuously producing and reproducing identities and interest, continuously "choosing now the preferences [they] will have later."[56] But it does mean that choices may not be experienced with meaningful degrees of freedom. This could be a constructivist justification for the realist position that only simple learning is possible in self-help systems. The realist might concede that such systems are socially constructed and still argue that after the corresponding identities and interests have become institutionalized, they are almost impossible to transform.

In the remainder of this article, I examine three institutional transformations of identity and security interest through which states might escape a Hobbesian world of their own making. In so doing, I seek to clarify what it means to say that "institutions transform identities and interest," emphasizing that the key to such transformations is relatively stable practice.

Sovereignty, Recognition, and Security

In a Hobbesian state of nature, states are individuated by the domestic processes that constitute them as states and by their material capacity to deter threats from other states. In this world, even if free momentarily from the predations of others, state security does not have any basis in social recognition—in intersubjective understandings or norms that a state has a right to its existence, territory, and subjects. Security is a matter of national power, nothing more.

The principle of sovereignty transforms this situation by providing a social basis for the individuality and security of states. Sovereignty is an institution, and so it exists only in virtue of certain intersubjective understandings and expectations; there is no sovereignty without an other. These understandings and expectations not only constitute a particular kind of state—the "sovereign" state—but also constitute a particular form of community, since identities are relational. The essence of this community is a mutual recognition of one another's right to exercise exclusive political authority within territorial limits. These reciprocal "permissions"[57] constitute a spatially rather than functionally differentiated world—a world in which fields of practice constitute and are organized around "domestic" and "international" spaces rather than around the performance of particular activities.[58] The location of the boundaries between these spaces is of course sometimes contested, war being one practice through which states negotiate the terms of their individuality. But this does not change the fact that it is only in virtue of mutual recognition that states have "territorial property rights."[59] This recognition functions as a form of "social closure" that disempowers nonstate actor and empowers and helps stabilize interaction among states.[60]

Sovereignty norms are now so taken for granted, so natural, that it is easy to overlook the extent to which they are both presupposed by an ongoing artifact of practice. When states tax "their" "citizens" and not others, when they "protect" their markets against foreign "imports," when they kill thousands of Iraqis in one kind of war and then refuse to "intervene" to kill even one person in another kind, a "civil" war, and

when they fight a global war against a regime that sought to destroy the institution of sovereignty and then give Germany back to the Germans, they are acting against the background of, and thereby reproduced, shared norms about what it means to be a sovereign state.

If states stopped acting on those norms, their identity as "sovereigns" (if not necessarily as "states") would disappear. The sovereign state is an ongoing accomplishment of practice, not a once-and-for-all creation of norms that somehow exist apart from practice.[61] Thus, saying that "the institution of sovereignty transforms identities" is shorthand for saying that "regular practices produce mutually constituting sovereign identities (agents) and their associated institutional norms (structures)." Practice is the core of constructivist resolutions of the agent-structure problem. This ongoing process may not be politically problematic in particular historical contexts and, indeed, once a community of mutual recognition is constituted, its members—even the disadvantaged ones—may have a vested interest in reproducing it. In fact, this is part of what having an identity means. But this identity and institution remain dependent on what actors do: removing those practices will remove their intersubjective conditions of existence.

This may tell us something about how institutions of sovereign states are reproduced through social interaction, but it does not tell us why such a structure of identity and interest would arise in the first place. Two conditions would seem necessary for this to happen: (1) the density and regularity of interactions must be sufficiently high and (2) actors must be dissatisfied with preexisting forms of identity and interaction. Given these conditions, a norm of mutual recognition is relatively undemanding in terms of social trust, having the form of an assurance game in which a player will acknowledge the sovereignty of the others as long as they will in turn acknowledge that player's own sovereignty. Articulating international legal principles such as those embodied in the Peace of Augsburg (1555) and the Peace of Westphalia (1648) may also help by establishing explicit criteria for determining violations of the nascent social consensus.[62] But whether such a consensus holds depends on what states do. If they treat each other as if they were sovereign, then over time they will institutionalize that mode of subjectivity; if they do not, then that mode will not become the norm.

Practices of sovereignty will transform understandings of security and power politics in at least three ways. First, states will come to define their (and our) security in terms of preserving their "property rights" over particular territories. We now see this as natural, but the preservation of territorial frontiers is not, in fact, equivalent to the survival of the state or its people. Indeed, some states would probably be more secure if they would relinquish certain territories—the "Soviet Union" of some minority republics, "Yugoslavia" of Croatia and Slovenia, Israel of the West Bank, and so on. The fact that sovereignty practices have historically been oriented toward producing distinct territorial spaces, in other words, affects states' conceptualization of what they must "secure" to function in that identity, a process that may help account for the "hardening" of territorial boundaries over the centuries.[63]

Second, to the extent that states successfully internalize sovereignty norms, they will be more respectful toward the territorial rights of others. This restraint is *not* primarily because of the costs of violating sovereignty norms, although when violators do get punished (as in the Gulf War) it reminds everyone of what these costs can be, but because part of what it means to be a "sovereign" state is that one does not violate the territorial rights of others without "just cause." A clear example of such an institutional effect, convincingly argued by David Strang, is the markedly different treatment that weak states receive within and outside communities of mutual recognition.[64] What keeps the United States from conquering the Bahamas, or Nigeria from seizing Togo, or Australia from occupying Vanuatu? Clearly, power is not the issue, and in these cases even the cost of sanctions would probably be negligible. One might argue that great powers simply have no "interest" in these conquests, and this might be so, but this lack of interest can only be understood in terms of their recognition of weak states' sovereignty. I have no interest in exploiting my friends, not because of the relative costs and benefits of such action but because they are my friends. The absence of recognition, in turn, helps explain the Western states' practices of territorial conquest, enslavement, and genocide against Native American and African peoples. It is in *that* world that only power matters, not the world of today.

Finally, to the extent that their ongoing socialization teaches states that their sovereignty depends on recognition by other states, they can afford to rely more on the institutional fabric of international society and less on individual national means—especially military power—to protect their security. The intersubjective understandings embodied in the institution of sovereignty, in other words, may redefine the meaning of others' power for the security of the self. In policy terms, this means that states can be less worried about short-term survival and relative power and can thus shift their resources accordingly. Ironically, it is the great powers, the states with the greatest national means, that may have the hardest time learning this lesson; small powers do not have the luxury of relying on national means and may therefore learn faster that collective recognition is a cornerstone of security.

None of this is to say that power becomes irrelevant in a community of sovereign states. Sometimes states *are* threatened by others that do not recognize their existence or particular territorial claims, that resent the externalities from their economic policies, and so on. But most of the time, these threats are played out within the terms of the sovereignty game. The fates of Napoleon and Hitler show what happens when they are not.

Cooperation among Egoists and Transformations of Identity

We began this section with a Hobbesian state of nature. Cooperation for joint gain is extremely difficult in this context, since trust is lacking, time horizons are short, and relative power concerns are high. Life is "nasty, brutish, and short." Sovereignty transforms this system into a Lockean world of (mostly) mutually recognized property rights and (mostly) egoistic rather than competitive conceptions of security, reducing the fear that what states already have will be seized at any moment by potential collaborators, thereby enabling them to contemplate more direct forms of

cooperation. A necessary condition for such cooperation is that outcomes be positively interdependent in the sense that potential gains exist which cannot be realized by unilateral action. States such as Brazil and Botswana may recognize each other's sovereignty, but they need further incentives to engage in joint action. One important source of incentives is the growing "dynamic density" of interaction among states in a world with new communications technology, nuclear weapons, externalities from industrial development, and so on.[65] Unfortunately, growing dynamic density does not ensure that states will in fact realize joint gains; interdependence also entails vulnerability and the risk of being "the sucker," which if exploited will become a source of conflict rather than cooperation.

This is the rationale for the familiar assumption that egoistic states will often find themselves facing prisoners' dilemma, a game in which the dominant strategy, if played only once, is to defect. As Michael Taylor and Robert Axelrod have shown, however, given iteration and a sufficient shadow of the future, egoists using a tit-for-tat strategy can escape this result and build cooperative institutions.[66] The story they tell about this process on the surface seems quite similar to George Herbert Mead's constructivist analysis of interaction, part of which is also told in terms of "games."[67] Cooperation is a gesture indicating ego's willingness to cooperate; if alter defects, ego does likewise, signaling its unwillingness to be exploited; over time and through reciprocal play, each learns to form relatively stable expectations about the other's behavior, and through these, habits of cooperation (or defection) form. Despite similar concerns with communication, learning, and habit-formation, however, there is an important difference between the game-theoretic and constructivist analysis of interaction that bears on how we conceptualize the causal powers of institutions.

In the traditional game-theoretic analysis of cooperation, even an iterated one, the structure of the game—of identities of interests—is exogenous to interaction and, as such, does not change.[68] A "black box" is put around identity- and interest-formation, and analysis focuses instead on the relationship between expectations and behavior. The norms that evolve from interaction are treated as rules and behavioral regularities which are external to the actors and which resist change because of the transaction costs of creating new ones. The game-theoretic analysis of cooperation among egoists is at base behavioral.

A constructivist analysis of cooperation, in contrast, would concentrate on how the expectations produced by behavior affect identifies and interests. The process of creating institutions is one of internalizing new understandings of self and other, of acquiring new role identities, not just of creating external constraints on the behavior of exogenously constituted actors.[69] Even if not intended as such, in other words, the process by which egoists learn to cooperate is at the same time a process of reconstructing their interests in terms of shared commitments to social norms. Over time, this will tend to transform a positive interdependence of *outcomes* into a positive interdependence of *utilities* or collective interest organized around the norms in question. These norms will resist change because they are tied to actors' commitments to their identities and interests, not merely because of transaction costs. A constructivist analysis of "the cooperation problem," in other

words, is at base cognitive rather than behavioral, since it treats the intersubjective knowledge that defines the structure of identities and interests, of the "game," as endogenous to and instantiated by interaction itself.

The debate over the future of collective security in Western Europe may illustrate the significance of this difference. A weak liberal or rationalist analysis would assume that the European states' "portfolio" of interests has not fundamentally changed and that the emergence of new factors, such as the collapse of the Soviet threat and the rise of Germany, would alter their cost-benefit ratios for pursuing current arrangements, thereby causing existing institutions to break down. The European states formed collaborative institutions for good, exogenously constituted egoistic reasons, and the same reasons may lead them to reject those institutions; the game of European power politics has not changed. A strong liberal or constructivist analysis of this problem would suggest that four decades of cooperation may have transformed a positive interdependence of outcomes into a collective "European identity" in terms of which states increasingly define their "self"-interests.[70] Even if egoistic reasons were its starting point, the process of cooperating tends to redefine those reasons by reconstituting identities and interests in terms of new intersubjective understandings and commitments. Changes in the distribution of power during the late twentieth century are undoubtedly a challenge to these new understandings, but it is not as if West European states have some inherent, exogenously given interest in abandoning collective security if the price is right. Their identities and security interests are continuously in process, and if collective identities become "embedded," they will be as resistant to change as egoistic ones.[71] Through participation in new forms of social knowledge, in other words, the European states of 1990 might no longer be the states of 1950.

Critical Strategic Theory and Collective Security

The transformation of identity and interest through and "evolution of cooperation" faces two important constraints. The first is that the process is incremental and slow. Actors' objectives in such a process are typically to realize joint gains within what they take to be a relatively stable context, and they are therefore unlikely to engage in substantial reflection about how to change the parameters of that context (including the structure of identities and interests) and unlikely to pursue policies specifically designed to bring about such changes. Learning to cooperate may change those parameters, but this occurs as an unintended consequence of policies pursued for other reasons rather than as a result of intentional efforts to transcend existing institutions.

A second, more fundamental, constraint is that the evolution of cooperation story presupposes that actors do not identify negatively with one another. Actors must be concerned primarily with absolute gains; to the extent that antipathy and distrust lead them to define their security in relativistic terms, it will be hard to accept the vulnerabilities that attend cooperation.[72] This is important because it is precisely the "central balance" in the state system that seems to be so often afflicted with such competitive thinking, and realists can therefore argue that the possibility of cooperation within one "pole" (for example, the West) is parasitic on the dominance of competition between poles (the East–West conflict). Relations between the poles may be amenable to some positive reciprocity in areas such as arms control, but the atmosphere of distrust leaves little room for such cooperation and its transformative consequences.[73] The conditions of negative identification that make an "evolution of cooperation" most needed work precisely against such a logic.

This seemingly intractable situation may nevertheless be amenable to quite a different logic of transformation, one driven more by self-conscious efforts to change structures of identity and interest than by unintended consequences. Such voluntarism may seem to contradict the spirit of constructivism, since would-be revolutionaries are presumably themselves effects of socialization to structures of identity and interest. How can they think about changing that to which they owe their identity? The possibility lies in the distinction between the social determination of the self and the personal determination of choice, between what Mead called the "me" and the "I."[74] The "me" is that part of subjectivity which is defined in terms of others; the character and behavioral expectations of a person's role identity as "professor," or of the United States as "leader of the alliance," for example, are socially constituted. Roles are not played in mechanical fashion according to precise scripts, however, but are "taken" and adapted in idiosyncratic ways by each actor.[75] Even in the most constrained situations, role performance involves a choice by the actor. The "I" is the part of subjectivity in which this appropriation and reaction to roles and its corresponding existential freedom lie.

The fact that roles are "taken" means that, in principle, actors always have a capacity for "character planning"—for engaging in critical self-reflection and choices designed to bring about changes in their lives.[76] But when or under what conditions can this creative capacity be exercised? Clearly, much of the time it cannot: if actors were constantly reinventing their identities, social order would be impossible, and the relative stability of identities and interests in the real world is indicative of our propensity for habitual rather than creative action. The exceptional, conscious choosing to transform or transcend roles has at least two preconditions. First, there must be a reason to think of oneself in novel terms. This would most likely stem from the presence of new social situations that cannot be managed in terms of preexisting self-conceptions. Second, the expected costs of intentional role change—the sanctions imposed by others with whom one interacted in previous roles—cannot be greater than its rewards.

When these conditions are present, actors can engage in self-reflection and practice specifically designed to transform their identities and interests and thus to "change the games" in which they are embedded. Such "critical" strategic theory and practice has not received the attention it merits from students of world politics (another legacy of exogenously given interests perhaps), particularly given that one of the most important phenomena in [recent] world politics, Mikhail Gorbachev's policy of "New Thinking," [was] arguably precisely that.[77] Let me therefore use this policy as an example of how states might transform a competitive security system into a cooperative one, dividing the transformative process into four stages.

The first stage in intentional transformation is the breakdown of consensus about identity commitments. In the So-viet case, identity commitments centered on the Leninist theory of imperialism, with its belief that relations between capitalist and socialist states are inherently conflictual, and on the alliance patterns that this belief engendered. In the 1980s, the consensus within the Soviet Union over the Leninist theory broke down for a variety of reasons, principal among which seem to have been the state's inability to meet the economic-technological-military challenge from the West, the government's decline of political legitimacy at home, and the reassurance from the West that it did not intend to invade the Soviet Union, a reassurance that reduced the external costs of role change.[78] These factors paved the way for a radical leadership transition and for a subsequent "unfreezing of conflict schemas" concerning relations with the West.[79]

The breakdown of consensus makes possible a second stage of critical examination of old ideas about self and other and, by extension, of the structures of interaction by which the ideas have been sustained. In periods of relatively stable role identities, ideas and structures may become reified and thus treated as things that exist independently of social action. If so, the second stage is one of denaturalization, of identifying the practices that reproduce seemingly inevitable ideas about self and other; to that extent, it is a form of "critical" rather than "problem-solving" theory.[80] The result of such a critique should be an identification of new "possible selves" and aspirations.[81] New Thinking [embodies] such critical theorizing. Gorbachev [wanted] to free the Soviet Union from the coercive social logic of the cold war and engage the West in far-reaching cooperation. Toward this end, he ... rejected the Leninist belief in the inherent conflict of interest between socialist and capitalist states and, perhaps more important, . . . recognized the crucial role that Soviet aggressive practices played in sustaining that conflict.

Such rethinking paves the way for a third stage of new practice. In most cases, it is not enough to rethink one's own ideas about self and other, since old identities have been sustained by systems of interaction with *other* actors, the practices of which remain a social fact for the transformative agent. In order to change the self, then, it is often necessary to change the identities and interests of the others that help sustain those systems of interaction. The vehicle for inducing such change is one's own practice and, in particular, the practice of "altercasting"—a technique of interactor control in which ego uses tactics of self-presentation and stage management in an attempt to frame alter's definitions of social situations in ways that create the role which ego desires alter to play.[82] In effect, in altercasting ego tries to induce alter to take on a new identity (and thereby enlist alter in ego's effort to change itself) by treating alter *as if* it already had that identity. The logic of this follows directly from the mirror theory of identity-formation, in which alter's identity is a reflection of ego's practices; change those practices and ego begins to change alter's conception of itself.

What these practices should consist of depends on the logic by which the preexisting identities were sustained. Competitive security systems are sustained by practices that create insecurity and distrust. In this case, transformative practices should attempt to teach other states that one's own state can be trusted and should not be viewed as a threat to their security. The fastest way to do this is to make unilateral initiatives

and self-binding commitments of sufficient significance that another state is faced with "an offer it cannot refuse."[83] Gorbachev . . . tried to do this by withdrawing from Afghanistan and Eastern Europe, implementing asymmetric cuts in nuclear and conventional forces, calling for "defensive defense," and so on. In addition, he . . . skillfully cast the West in the role of being morally required to give aid and comfort to the Soviet Union, . . . emphasized the bonds of common fate between the Soviet Union and the West, and . . . indicated that further progress in East–West relations is contingent upon the West assuming the identity being projected onto it These actions are all dimensions of altercasting, the intention of which is to take away the Western "excuse" for distrusting the Soviet Union, which, in Gorbachev's view, . . . helped sustain competitive identities in the past.

Yet by themselves such practices cannot transform a competitive security system, since if they are not reciprocated by alter, they will expose ego to a "sucker" payoff and quickly wither on the vine. In order for critical strategic practice to transform competitive identities, it must be "rewarded" by alter, which will encourage more such practice by ego, and so on.[84] Over time, this will institutionalize a positive rather than a negative identification between the security of self and other and will thereby provide a firm intersubjective basis for what were initially tentative commitments to new identities and interests.

Notwithstanding . . . rhetoric about the end of the cold war, skeptics may still doubt whether Gorbachev (or some future leader) will succeed in building an intersubjective basis for a new Soviet (or Russian) role identity. There are important domestic, bureaucratic, and cognitive-ideological sources of resistance in both East and West to such a change, not the least of which is the shakiness of the democratic forces' domestic position. But if my argument about the role of intersubjective knowledge in creating competitive structures of identity and interest is right, then at least New Thinking shows a greater appreciation—conscious or not—for the deep structure of power politics than we are accustomed to in international relations practice.

CONCLUSION

All theories of international relations are based on social theories of the relationship between *agency, process,* and *social structure.* Social theories do not determine the content of our international theorizing, but they do structure the questions we ask about world politics and our approaches to answering those questions. The substantive issue at stake in debates about social theory is what kind of foundation offers the most fruitful set of questions and research strategies for explaining the revolutionary changes that seem to be occurring in the late twentieth century international system. Put simply, what should systemic theories of international relations look like? How should they conceptualize the relationship between structure and process? Should they be based exclusively on "microeconomic" analogies in which identities and interests are exogenously given by structure and process is reduced to interactions within those parameters? Or should they also be based on "sociological" and "social psychological" analogies in which identities and interests and therefore the meaning of structure are endogenous to pro-

cess? Should a behavioral-individualism or a cognitive-constructivism be the basis for systemic theories of world politics?

This article notwithstanding, this question is ultimately an empirical one in two respects. First, its answer depends in part on how important interaction among states is for the constitution of their identities and interests. On the one hand, it may be that domestic or genetic factors, which I have systematically bracketed, are in fact much more important determinants of states' identities and interests than are systemic factors. To the extent that this is true, the individualism of a rationalist approach and the inherent privileging of structure over process in this approach become more substantively appropriate for systemic theory (if not for first- and second-image theory), since identities and interests are *in fact* largely exogenous to interaction among states. On the other hand, if the bracketed factors are relatively unimportant or if the importance of the international system varies historically (perhaps with the level of dynamic density and interdependence in the system), then such a framework would not be appropriate as an exclusive foundation for general systemic theory.

Second, the answer to the question about what systemic theories should look like also depends on how easily state identities and interests can change as a result of systemic interaction. Even if interaction is initially important in constructing identities and interests, once institutionalized its logic may make transformation extremely difficult. If the meaning of structure for state action changes so slowly that it becomes a defacto parameter within which process takes place, then it may again be substantively appropriate to adopt the rationalist assumption that identities and interests are given (although again, this may vary historically).

We cannot address these empirical issues, however, unless we have a framework for doing systemic research that makes state identity and interest an issue for both theoretical and empirical inquiry. Let me emphasize that this is *not* to say we should never treat identities and interests as given. The framing of problems and research strategies should be question-driven rather than method-driven, and if we are not interested in identity- and interest-formation, we may find the assumptions of a rationalist discourse perfectly reasonable. Nothing in this article, in other words, should be taken as an attack on rationalism per se. By the same token, however, we should not let this legitimate analytical stance become a de facto ontological stance with respect to the content of third-image theory, at least not until after we have determined that systemic interaction does not play an important role in processes of state identity- and interest-formation. We should not choose our philosophical anthropologies and social theories prematurely. By arguing that we cannot derive a self-help structure of identity and interest from the principle of anarchy alone—by arguing that anarchy is what states make of it—this article has challenged one important justification for ignoring processes of identity- and interest-formation in world politics. As such, it helps set the stage for inquiry into the empirical issues raised above and thus for a debate about whether communitarian or individualist assumptions are a better foundation for systemic theory.

I have tried to indicate by crude example what such a research agenda might look like. Its objective should be to assess the causal relationship between practice and interaction (as independent variable) and the cognitive structures at the level of individual states and of systems of states which constitute identities and interests (as dependent variable)—that is, the relationship between what actors *do* and what they *are*. We may have some a priori notion that state actors and systemic structures are "mutually constitutive," but this tells us little in the absence of an understanding of how the mechanics of dyadic, triadic, and *n*-actor interaction shape and are in turn shaped by "stocks of knowledge" that collectively constitute identities and interests and, more broadly, constitute the structures of international life. Particularly important in this respect is the role of practice in shaping attitudes toward the "giveness" of these structures. How and why do actors reify social structures, and under what conditions do they denaturalize such reifications?

The state-centrism of this agenda may strike some, particularly postmodernists, as "depressingly familiar."[85] The significance of states relative to multinational corporations, new social movements, transnationals, and intergovernmental organizations is clearly declining, and "postmodern" forms of world politics merit more research attention than they have received. But I also believe, with realists, that in the medium run sovereign states will remain the dominant political actors in the international system. Any transition to new structures of global political authority and identity—to "postinternational" politics—will be mediated by and path-dependent on the particular institutional resolution of the tension between unity and diversity, or particularism and universality, that is the sovereign state.[86] In such a world there should continue to be a place for theories of anarchic interstate politics, alongside other forms of international theory; to that extent, I am a statist and a realist. I have argued in this article, however, that statism need not be bound by realist ideas about what "state" must mean. State identities and interests can be collectively transformed within an anarchic context by many factors—individual, domestic, systemic, or transnational—and as such are an important dependent variable. Such a reconstruction of state-centric international theory is necessary if we are to theorize adequately about the emerging forms of transnational political identity that sovereign states will help bring into being. To that extent, I hope that statism, like the state, can be historically progressive.

I have argued that the proponents of strong liberalism and the constructivists can and should join forces in contributing to a process-oriented international theory. Each group has characteristic weaknesses that are complemented by the other's strengths. In part because of the decision to adopt a choice-theoretic approach to theory construction, neoliberals have been unable to translate their work on institution-building and complex learning into a systemic theory that escapes the explanatory priority of realism's concern with structure. Their weakness, in other words, is a lingering unwillingness to transcend, at the level of systemic theory, the individualist assumption that identities and interests are exogenously given. Constructivists bring to this lack of resolution a systematic communitarian ontology in which intersubjective knowledge constitutes identities and interests. For their part, however, constructivists have often devoted too much effort to questions of ontology and con-

stitution and not enough effort to the causal and empirical questions of how identities and interests are produced by practice in anarchic conditions. As a result, they have not taken on board neoliberal insights into learning and social cognition.

An attempt to use a structurationist–symbolic interactionist discourse to bridge the two research traditions, neither of which subscribes to such a discourse, will probably please no one. But in part this is because the two "sides" have become hung up on differences over the epistemological status of social science. The state of the social sciences and, in particular, of international relations, is such that epistemological prescriptions and conclusions are at best premature. Different questions involve different standards of inference; to reject certain questions because their answers cannot conform to the standards of classical physics is to fall into the trap of method-driven rather than question-driven social science. By the same token, however, giving up the artificial restrictions of logical positivist conceptions of inquiry does not force us to give up on "Science." Beyond this, there is little reason to attach so much importance to epistemology. Neither positivism, nor scientific realism, nor poststructuralism tells us about the structure and dynamics of international life. Philosophies of science are not theories of international relations. The good news is that strong liberals and modern and postmodern constructivists are asking broadly similar questions about the substance of international relations that differentiate both groups from the neorealist-rationalist alliance. Strong liberals and constructivists have much to learn from each other if they can come to see this through the smoke and heat of epistemology.

NOTES

1. See, for example, Joseph Grieco, "Anarchy and the Limits of Cooperation: A Realist Critique of the Newest Liberal Institutionalism," *International Organization* 42 (Summer 1988), pp. 485-507; Joseph Nye, "Neorealism and Neoliberalism," *World Politics* 40 (January 1988), pp. 235-51; Robert Keohane, "Neoliberal Institutionalism: A Perspective on World Politics," in his collection of essays entitled *International Institutions and State Power* (Boulder, Colo.: Westview Press, 1989), pp. 1-20; John Mearsheimer, "Back to the Future: Instability in Europe After the Cold War," *International Security* 13 (Summer 1990), pp. 5-56, along with subsequent published correspondence regarding Mearsheimer's article; and Emerson Niou and Peter Ordeshook, "Realism Versus Neoliberalism: A Formulation," *American Journal of Political Science* 35 (May 1991), pp. 481-511.

2. See Robert Keohane, "International Institutions: Two Approaches," *International Studies Quarterly* 32 (December 1988), pp. 379-96.

3. Behavioral and rationalist models of man and institutions share a common intellectual heritage in the materialist individualism of Hobbes, Locke, and Bentham. On the relationship between the two models, see Jonathan Turner, *A Theory of Social Interaction* (Stanford, Calif.: Stanford University Press, 1988), pp. 24-31; and George Homans, "Rational Choice Theory and Behavioral Psychology," in Craig Calhoun et al., eds., *Structures of Power and Constraint* (Cambridge: Cambridge University Press, 1991), pp. 77-89.

4. On neorealist conceptions of learning, see Philip Tetlock, "Learning in U.S. and Soviet Foreign Policy," in George Breslauer and Philip Tetlock, eds., *Learning in U.S. and Soviet Foreign Policy* (Boulder, Colo.: Westview Press, 1991), pp. 24-27. On the difference between behavioral and cognitive learning, see ibid., pp. 20-61; Joseph Nye, "Nuclear Learning and U.S.-Soviet Security Regimes," *International Organization* 41 (Summer 1987), pp. 371-402; and Ernst Haas, *When Knowledge Is Power* (Berkeley: University of California Press, 1990), pp. 17-49.

5. See Stephen Krasner, "Regimes and the Limits of Realism: Regimes as Autonomous Variables," in Stephen Krasner, ed., *International Regimes* (Ithaca, N.Y.: Cornell University Press, 1983), pp. 355-68.

6. See Nye, "Nuclear Learning and U.S.-Soviet Security Regimes"; Robert Jervis, "Realism, Game Theory, and Cooperation," *World Politics* 40 (April 1988), pp. 340-44; and Robert Keohane, "International Liberalism Reconsidered," in John Dunn, ed., *The Economic Limits to Modern Politics* (Cambridge: Cambridge University Press, 1990), p. 183.

7. Friedrich Kratochwil and John Ruggie, "International Organization: A State of the Art on an Art of the State," *International Organization* 40 (Autumn 1986), pp. 753-75.

8. Keohane, "International Institutions."

9. See Nicholas Onuf, *World of Our Making* (Columbia: University of South Carolina Press, 1989).

10. On Science, see Keohane, "International Institutions"; and Robert Keohane, "International Relations Theory: Contributions of a Feminist Standpoint," *Millennium* 18 (Summer 1989), pp. 245-53. On Dissent, see R. B. J. Walker, "History and Structure in the Theory of International Relations," *Millennium* 18 (Summer 1989), pp. 163-83; and Richard Ashley and R. B. J. Walker, "Reading Dissidence/Writing the Discipline: Crisis and the Question of Sovereignty in International Studies," *International Studies Quarterly* 34 (September 1990), pp. 367-416. For an excellent critical assessment of these debates, see Yosef Lapid, "The Third Debate: On the Prospects of International Theory in a Post-Positivist Era," *International Studies Quarterly* 33 (September 1989), pp. 235-54.

11. The fact that I draw on these approaches aligns me with modernist constructivists,

even though I also draw freely on the substantive work of postmodernists, especially Richard Ashley and Rob Walker. For a defense of this practice and a discussion of its epistemological basis, see my earlier article, "The Agent-Structure Problem in International Relations Theory," *International Organization* 41 (Summer 1987), pp. 335–70; and Ian Shapiro and Alexander Wendt, "The Difference That Realism Makes: Social Science and the Politics of Consent," . . . in *Politics and Society*. Among modernist constructivists, my argument is particularly indebted to the published work of Emanuel Adler, Friedrich Kratochwil, and John Ruggie, as well as to an unpublished paper by Naeem Inayatullah and David Levine entitled "Politics and Economics in Contemporary International Relations Theory," Syracuse University, Syracuse, N.Y., 1990.

12. See Viktor Gecas, "Rekindling the Sociological Imagination in Social Psychology," *Journal for the Theory of Social Behavior* 19 (March 1989), pp. 97–115.

13. Kenneth Waltz, *Man, the State, and War* (New York: Columbia University Press, 1959), p. 232.

14. Ibid., pp. 169–70.

15. Ibid., p. 232. This point is made by Hidemi Suganami in "Bringing Order to the Causes of War Debates," *Millennium* 19 (Spring 1990), p. 34, fn. 11.

16. Kenneth Waltz, *Theory of International Politics* (Boston: Addison-Wesley, 1979).

17. The neorealist description is not unproblematic. For a powerful critique, see David Lumsdaine, *Ideals and Interests: The Foreign Aid Regime, 1949–1989* (Princeton, N.J.: Princeton University Press).

18. Waltz, *Theory of International Politics,* pp. 79–101.

19. Stephen Walt, *The Origins of Alliances* (Ithaca, N.Y.: Cornell University Press, 1987).

20. See, for example, Herbert Blumer, "The Methodological Position of Symbolic Interactionism," in his *Symbolic Interactionism: Perspective and Method* (Englewood Cliffs, N.J.: Prentice-Hall, 1969), p. 2. Throughout this article, I assume that a theoretically productive analogy can be made between individuals and states. . . .

21. The phrase "distribution of knowledge" is Barry Barnes's, as discussed in his work *The Nature of Power* (Cambridge: Polity Press, 1988); see also Peter Berger and Thomas Luckmann, *The Social Construction of Reality* (New York: Anchor Books, 1966). The concern of recent international relations scholarship on "epistemic communities" with the cause-and-effect understandings of the world held by scientists, experts, and policymakers is an important aspect of the role of knowledge in world politics; see Peter Haas, "Do Regimes Matter? Epistemic Communities and Mediterranean Pollution Control," *International Organization* 43 (Summer 1989), pp. 377–404; and Ernst Haas, *When Knowledge Is Power.* My constructivist approach would merely add to this an equal emphasis on how such knowledge also *constitutes* the structures and subjects of social life.

22. For an excellent short statement of how collective meanings constitute identities, see Peter Berger, "Identity as a Problem in the Sociology of Knowledge," *European Journal of Sociology,* vol. 7, no. 1, 1966, pp. 32–40. . . .

23. Berger, "Identity as a Problem in the Sociology of Knowledge," p. 111.

24. While not normally cast in such terms, foreign policy scholarship on national role conceptions could be adapted to such identity language. See Kal Holsti, "National Role Conceptions in the Study of Foreign Policy," *International Studies Quarterly* 14 (September 1970), pp. 233–309; and Stephen Walker, ed., *Role Theory and Foreign Policy Analysis* (Durham, N.C.: Duke University Press, 1987) . . . .

25. On the "portfolio" conception of interests, see Barry Hindess, *Political Choice and Social Structure* (Aldershot, U.K.:

Edward Elgar, 1989), pp. 2–3. The "definition of the situation" is a central concept in interactionist theory.

26. Nelson Foote, "Identification as the Basis for a Theory of Motivation," *American Sociological Review* 16 (February 1951), p. 15.

27. In neo-Durkheimian parlance, institutions are "social representations." See Serge Moscovici, "The Phenomenon of Social Representations," in Rob Farr and Serge Moscovici, eds., *Social Representations* (Cambridge: Cambridge University Press, 1984), pp. 3–69. See also Barnes, *The Nature of Power. . . .*

28. Berger and Luckmann, *The Social Construction of Reality*, p. 58.

29. See Giddens, *Central Problems in Social Theory*; and Alexander Wendt and Raymond Duvall, "Institutions and International Order," in Ernst-Otto Czempiel and James Rosenau, eds., *Global Changes and Theoretical Challenges* (Lexington, Mass.: Lexington Books, 1989), pp. 51–74.

30. Security systems might also vary in the extent to which there is a functional differentiation or a hierarchical relationship between patron and client, with the patron playing a hegemonic role within its sphere of influence in defining the security interests of its clients. I do not examine this dimension here; for preliminary discussion, see Alexander Wendt, "The States System and Global Militarization," Ph.D. diss., University of Minnesota, Minneapolis, 1989; and Alexander Wendt and Michael Barnett, "The International System and Third World Militarization," unpublished manuscript, 1991.

31. This amounts to an "internationalization of the state." For a discussion of this subject, see Raymond Duvall and Alexander Wendt, "The International Capital Regime and the Internationalization of the State," unpublished manuscript, 1987. See also R. B. J. Walker, "Sovereignty, Identity, Community: Reflections on the Horizons of Contemporary Political Practice," in R. B. J. Walker and Saul Mendlovitz, eds., *Contending Sovereignties* (Boulder, Colo.: Lynne Rienner, 1990), pp. 159–85.

32. On the spectrum of cooperative security arrangements, see Charles Kupchan and Clifford Kupchan, "Concerts, Collective Security, and the Future of Europe," *International Security* 16 (Summer 1991), pp. 114–61; and Richard Smoke, "A Theory of Mutual Security," in Richard Smoke and Andrei Kortunov, eds., *Mutual Security* (New York: St. Martin's Press, 1991), pp. 59–111. These may be usefully set alongside Christopher Jencks' "Varieties of Altruism," in Jane Mansbridge, ed., *Beyond Self-Interest* (Chicago: University of Chicago Press, 1990), pp. 53–67.

33. Waltz, *Theory of International Politics,* p. 91.

34. See Waltz, *Man, the State, and War;* and Robert Jervis, "Cooperation Under the Security Dilemma," *World Politics* 30 (January 1978), pp. 167–214.

35. My argument here parallels Rousseau's critique of Hobbes. For an excellent critique of realist appropriations of Rousseau, see Michael Williams, "Rousseau, Realism, and Realpolitik," *Millennium* 18 (Summer 1989), pp. 188–204. Williams argues that far from being a fundamental starting point in the state of nature, for Rousseau the stag hunt represented a stage in man's fall. On p. 190, Williams cites Rousseau's description of man prior to leaving the state of nature: "Man only knows himself; he does not see his own well-being to be identified with or contrary to that of anyone else; he neither hates anything nor loves anything; but limited to no more than physical instinct, he is no one, he is an animal." For another critique of Hobbes on the state of nature that parallels my constructivist reading of anarchy, see Charles Landesman, "Reflections on Hobbes: Anarchy and Human Nature," in Peter Caws, ed., *The Causes of Quarrel* (Boston: Beacon, 1989), pp. 139–48.

36. Waltz, *Theory of International Politics*, pp. 74–77.

37. See James Morrow, "Social Choice and System Structure in World Politics," *World Politics* 41 (October 1988), p. 89. Waltz's behavioral treatment of socialization may be usefully contrasted with the more cognitive approach taken by Ikenberry and the Kupchans in the following articles: G. John Ikenberry and Charles Kupchan, "Socialization and Hegemonic Power," *International Organization* 44 (Summer 1989), pp. 283–316; and Kupchan and Kupchan, "Concerts, Collective Security, and the Future of Europe." Their approach is close to my own, but they define socialization as an elite strategy to induce value change in others, rather than as a ubiquitous feature of interaction in terms of which all identities and interests get produced and reproduced.

38. Regarding individualism, see Richard Ashley, "The Poverty of Neorealism," *International Organization* 38 (Spring 1984), pp. 225–86; Wendt, "The Agent-Structure Problem in International Relations Theory"; and David Dessler, "What's at Stake in the Agent-Structure Debate?" *International Organization* 43 (Summer 1989), pp. 441–74. Regarding structuralism, see R. B. J. Walker, "Realism, Change, and International Political Theory," *International Studies Quarterly* 31 (March 1987), pp. 65–86; and Martin Hollis and Steven Smith, *Explaining and Understanding International Relations* (Oxford: Clarendon Press, 1989). The behavioralism evident in neorealist theory also explains how neorealists can reconcile their structuralism with the individualism of rational choice theory. On the behavioral-structural character of the latter, see Spiro Latsis, "Situational Determinism in Economics," *British Journal for the Philosophy of Science* 23 (August 1972), pp. 207–45.

39. The importance of the distinction between constitutive and causal explanations is not sufficiently appreciated in constructivist discourse. See Wendt, "The Agent-Structure Problem in International Relations Theory," pp. 362–65; Wendt,

"The States System and Global Militarization," pp. 110–13; and Wendt, "Bridging the Theory/Meta-Theory Gap in International Relations," *Review of International Studies* 17 (October 1991), p. 390.

40. See Blumer, "The Methodological Position of Symbolic Interactionism," pp. 2–4.

41. See Robert Grafstein, "Rational Choice: Theory and Institutions," in Kristen Monroe, ed., *The Economic Approach to Politics* (New York: Harper Collins, 1991), pp. 263–64. A good example of the promise and limits of transaction cost approaches to institutional analysis is offered by Robert Keohane in his *After Hegemony* (Princeton, N.J.: Princeton University Press, 1984).

42. Mead's analysis of gestures remains definitive. See Mead's *Mind, Self, and Society*. See also the discussion of the role of signaling in the "mechanics of interaction" in Turner's *A Theory of Social Interaction,* pp. 74–79 and 92–115.

43. On the role of attribution processes in the interactionist account of identity-formation, see Sheldon Stryker and Avid Gottlieb, "Attribution Theory and Symbolic Interactionism," in John Harvey et al., eds., *New Directions in Attribution Research,* vol. 3 (Hillsdale, N.J.: Lawrence Erlbaum, 1981), pp. 425–58; and Kathleen Crittenden, "Sociological Aspects of Attribution," *Annual Review of Sociology,* vol. 9, 1983, pp. 425–46. On attributional processes in international relations, see Shawn Rosenberg and Gary Wolfsfeld, "International Conflict and the Problem of Attribution," *Journal of Conflict Resolution* 21 (March 1977), pp. 75–103.

44. This discussion of the role of possibilities and probabilities in threat perception owes much to Stewart Johnson's comments on an earlier draft of my article.

45. On the role of "reassurance" in threat situations, see Richard Ned Lebow and Janice Gross Stein, "Beyond Deterrence,"

Journal of Social Issues, vol. 43, no. 4, 1987, pp. 5–72.

46. On "reciprocal typifications," see Berger and Luckmann, *The Social Construction of Reality,* pp. 54–58.

47. Jeff Coulter, "Remarks on the Conceptualization of Social Structure," *Philosophy of the Social Sciences* 12 (March 1982), pp. 42–43.

48. See C. Norman Alexander and Mary Glenn Wiley, "Situated Activity and Identity Formation," in Morris Rosenberg and Ralph Turner, eds., *Social Psychology: Sociological Perspectives* (New York: Basic Books, 1981), pp. 269–89.

49. Sheldon Stryker, "The Vitalization of Symbolic Interactionism," *Social Psychology Quarterly* 50 (March 1987), p. 93.

50. On the "maturity" of anarchies, see Barry Buzan, *People, States, and Fear* (Chapel Hill: University of North Carolina Press, 1983).

51. A similar intuition may lie behind Ashley's effort to reappropriate classical realist discourse for critical international relations theory. See Richard Ashley, "Political Realism and Human Interests," *International Studies Quarterly* 38 (June 1981), pp. 204–36.

52. Waltz has himself helped open up such a debate with his recognition that systemic factors condition but do not determine state actions. See Kenneth Waltz, "Reflections on *Theory of International Politics:* A Response to My Critics," in Robert Keohane, ed., *Neorealism and Its Critics* (New York: Columbia University Press, 1986), pp. 322–45. The growing literature on the observation that "democracies do not fight each other" is relevant to this question, as are two other studies that break important ground toward a "reductionist" theory of state identity: William Bloom's *Personal Identity, National Identity and International Relations* (Cambridge: Cambridge University Press, 1990) and Lumsdaine's *Ideals and Interests.*

53. See Berger and Luckmann, *The Social Construction of Reality,* p. 89. See also Douglas Maynard and Thomas Wilson, "On the Reification of Social Structure," in Scott McNall and Gary Howe, eds., *Current Perspectives in Social Theory,* vol. 1 (Greenwich, Conn.: JAI Press, 1980), pp. 287–322.

54. See Richard Ashley, "Social Will and International Anarchy," in Hayward Alker and Richard Ashley, eds., *After Realism,* work in progress, Massachusetts Institute of Technology, Cambridge, and Arizona State University, Tempe, 1992.

55. On the relationship between commitment and identity, see Foote, "Identification as the Basis for a Theory of Motivation"; Howard Becker, "Notes on the Concept of Commitment," *American Journal of Sociology* 66 (July 1960), pp. 32–40; and Stryker, *Symbolic Interactionism.* On role salience, see Stryker, ibid.

56. James March, "Bounded Rationality, Ambiguity, and the Engineering of Choice," *Bell Journal of Economics* 9 (Autumn 1978), p. 600.

57. Haskel Fain, *Normative Politics and the Community of Nations* (Philadelphia: Temple University Press, 1987).

58. This is the intersubjective basis for the principle of functional nondifferentiation among states, which "drops out" of Waltz's definition of structure because the latter has no explicit intersubjective basis. In international relations scholarship, the social production of territorial space has been emphasized primarily by post-structuralists. See, for example, Richard Ashley, "The Geopolitics of Geopolitical Space: Toward a Critical Social Theory of International Politics," *Alternatives* 12 (October 1987), pp. 403–34; and Simon Dalby, *Creating the Second Cold War* (London: Pinter, 1990). But the idea of space as both product and constituent of practice is also prominent in structurationist discourse. See Giddens, *Central Problems in Social Theory;* and Derek Gregory and John Urry, eds., *Social Relations and Spatial Structures* (London: Macmillan, 1985).

59. See John Ruggie, "Continuity and Transformation in the World Polity: Toward a Neorealist Synthesis," *World Politics* 35 (January 1983), pp. 261–85.

60. For a definition and discussion of "social closure," see Raymond Murphy, *Social Closure* (Oxford: Clarendon Press, 1988).

61. See Richard Ashley, "Untying the Sovereign State: A Double Reading of the Anarchy Problematique," *Millennium* 17 (Summer 1988), pp. 227–62.

62. See William Coplin, "International Law and Assumptions About the State System," *World Politics* 17 (July 1965), pp. 615–34.

63. See Anthony Smith, "States and Homelands: The Social and Geopolitical Implications of National Territory," *Millennium* 10 (Autumn 1981), pp. 187–202.

64. David Strang, "Anomaly and Commonplace in European Expansion: Realist and Institutional Accounts," *International Organization* 45 (Spring 1991), pp. 143–62.

65. On "dynamic density," see Ruggie, "Continuity and Transformation in the World Polity"; and Waltz, "Reflections on *Theory of International Politics.*" The role of interdependence in conditioning the speed and depth of social learning is much greater than the attention to which I have paid it. On the consequences of interdependence under anarchy, see Helen Milner, "The Assumption of Anarchy in International Relations Theory: A Critique," *Review of International Studies* 17 (January 1991), pp. 67–85.

66. See Michael Taylor, *Anarchy and Cooperation* (New York: Wiley, 1976); and Robert Axelrod, *The Evolution of Cooperation* (New York: Basic Books, 1984).

67. Mead, *Mind, Self, and Society.*

68. Strictly speaking, this is not true, since in iterated games the addition of future benefits to current ones changes the payoff structure of the game at T1, in this case from prisoners' dilemma to an assurance game. This transformation of interest takes place entirely within the actor, however, and as such is not a function of interaction with the other.

69. In fairness to Axelrod, he does point out that internationalization of norms is a real possibility that may increase the resilience of institutions. My point is that this important idea cannot be derived from an approach to theory that takes identities and interests as exogenously given.

70. On "European identity," see Barry Buzan et al., eds., *The European Security Order Recast* (London: Pinter, 1990), pp. 45–63.

71. On "embeddedness," see John Ruggie, "International Regimes, Transactions, and Change: Embedded Liberalism in a Postwar Economic Order," in Krasner, *International Regimes,* pp. 195–232.

72. See Grieco, "Anarchy and the Limits of Cooperation."

73. On the difficulties of creating cooperative security regimes given competitive interests, see Robert Jervis, "Security Regimes," in Krasner, *International Regimes,* pp. 173–94; and Charles Lipson, "International Cooperation in Economic and Security Affairs," *World Politics* 37 (October 1984), pp. 1–23.

74. See Mead, *Mind, Self, and Society.* . . .

75. Turner, "Role-Taking."

76. On "character planning," see Jon Elster, *Sour Grapes: Studies in the Subversion of Rationality* (Cambridge: Cambridge University Press, 1983), p. 117. . . .

77. For useful overviews of New Thinking, see Mikhail Gorbachev, *Perestroika: New Thinking for Our Country and the World* (New York: Harper & Row, 1987); Vendulka Kubalkova and Albert Cruickshank, *Thinking New About Soviet "New Thinking"* (Berkeley: Institute of International Studies, 1989); and Allen Lynch, *Gorbachev's International Outlook: Intellectual Origins and Political Consequences* (New York: Institute for East–West Security Studies, 1989). . . .

78. For useful overviews of these factors, see Jack Snyder, "The Gorbachev Revolution: A Waning of Soviet Expansionism?" *World Politics* 12 (Winter 1987–88), pp. 93–

121; and Stephen Meyer, "The Sources and Prospects of Gorbachev's New Political Thinking on Security," *International Security* 13 (Fall 1988), pp. 124-63.

79. See Daniel Bar-Tal et al., "Conflict Termination: An Epistemological Analysis of International Cases," *Political Psychology* 10 (June 1989), pp. 233-55. . . .

80. See Robert Cox, "Social Forces, States and World Orders: Beyond International Relations Theory," In Keohane, *Neorealism and Its Critics,* pp. 204-55. See also Brian Fay, *Critical Social Science* (Ithaca, N.Y.: Cornell University Press, 1987).

81. Hazel Markus and Paula Nurius, "Possible Selves," *American Psychologist* 41 (September 1986), pp. 954-69.

82. See Goffman, *The Presentation of Self in Everyday Life;* Eugene Weinstein and Paul Deutschberger, "Some Dimensions of Altercasting," *Sociometry* 26 (December 1963), pp. 454-66; and Walter Earle, "International Relations and the Psychology of Control: Alternative Control Strategies and Their Consequences," *Political Psychology* 7 (June 1986), pp. 369-75.

83. See Volker Boge and Peter Wilke, "Peace Movements and Unilateral Disarmament: Old Concepts in a New Light," *Arms Control* 7 (September 1986), pp. 156-70; Zeev Maoz and Daniel Feisenthal, "Self-Binding Commitments, the Inducement of Trust, Social Choice, and the Theory of International Cooperation," *International Studies Quarterly* 31 (June 1987), pp. 177-200; and V. Sakamoto, "Unilateral Initiative as an Alternative Strategy," *World Futures,* vol. 24, nos. 1-4, 1987, pp. 107-34.

84. On rewards, see Thomas Milburn and Daniel Christie, "Rewarding in International Politics," *Political Psychology* 10 (December 1989), pp. 625-45.

85. Yale Ferguson and Richard Mansbach, "Between Celebration and Despair: Constructive Suggestions for Future International Theory," *International Studies Quarterly* 35 (December 1991), 375.

86. For excellent discussions of this tension, see Walker, "Sovereignty, Identity, Community"; and R. B. J. Walker, "Security, Sovereignty, and the Challenge of World Politics," *Alternatives* 15 (Winter 1990), pp. 3-27. On institutional path dependencies, see Stephen Krasner, "Sovereignty: An Institutional Perspective," *Comparative Political Studies* 21 (April 1988), pp. 66-94.

QUESTIONS

1. What does Wendt mean by the phrase "social structures"? Why is it central to understanding his theory?

2. How does Wendt explain the social construction of the Cold War?

23.   You Just Don't Understand: Troubled Engagements Between Feminists and IR Theorists

J. Ann Tickner

In this reading, J. Ann Tickner explains why the feminist perspective on international relations continues to remain outside the mainstream of traditional approaches to IR theory. The author argues that one of the primary problems is that feminist perspectives do not accept the conventional state-centric approaches or methodologies typically used by IR theorists. Tickner illustrates these differences by contrasting the feminist approach to security issues with that of conventional IR theory. The author concludes with suggestions for how this discussion between Feminist and conventional IR theorists might be pursued in a more constructive fashion.

Dr. J. Ann Tickner is Professor of International Relations at the University of Southern California and Director of the Center for International Relations and Social Science. Her major publications include *Gendering World Politics: Issues and Approaches in the Post–Cold War Era* (2001) and *Gender in International Relations: Feminist Perspectives on Achieving Global Security* (1992).

Since feminist approaches to international relations first made their appearance in the late 1980s, courses on women and world politics and publications in this area have proliferated rapidly, as have panels at professional meetings.[1] Yet, the effect on the mainstream discipline, particularly in the United States, continues to be marginal, and the lack of attention paid to feminist perspectives by other critical approaches has also been disappointing (Sylvester, 1994b:ch. 4). While feminist scholars, as well as a few IR theorists, have called for conversations and dialogue across paradigms (Keohane, 1989; Peterson, 1992b:184), few public conversations or debates have occurred.[2] These continuing silences have led one scholar working in this area to conclude that most women are homeless as far as the canons of IR knowledge are concerned (Sylvester, 1994a:316).

Linguist Deborah Tannen, from whose widely read book the title of this article is taken, asserts that everyday conversations between women and men are cross-cultural and fraught with all the misunderstandings and talking at cross-purposes that cross-cultural communications frequently incur (Tannen, 1990).[3] The lack of sustained dialogue or substantively focused debates between feminists and scholars of international relations is troubling. Could this reluctance to engage in similarly difficult cross-cultural conversations be due to the very different realities and epistemologies with which feminists and international relations scholars are working?

Although critical engagement is rare, evidence of awkward silences and miscommunications can be found in the oral questions and comments IR-trained feminists frequently encounter when presenting their work to IR audiences. Having

From *International Studies Quarterly* (1997), Vol. 41, pp. 611–632. Reprinted by permission of Blackwell Publishing.

articulated what seems to her (or him)[4] to be a reasoned feminist critique of international relations, or some suggestions as to the potential benefits of looking at IR through "gender-sensitive" lenses, a feminist scholar is often surprised to find that her audience does not engage with what, to her at least, are the main claims of her presentation. Questioners may assert that her presentation has little to do with the discipline of international relations or the practice of international politics.[5] Prefaced by affirmations that the material presented is genuinely interesting and important, questions such as the following are frequently asked: What does this talk have to do with solving "real-world" problems such as Bosnia, Northern Ireland or nuclear proliferation?[6] Why does gender have anything to do with explaining the behavior of states in the international system? Isn't IR a gender-neutral discipline? More unsettling are comments suggesting that the presentation is personally insulting to the audience, or that the material is more suitable for bedside reading than for serious scholarly discussion.

Furthermore, to scholars trained in conventional scientific methodologies, feminist approaches appear to be atheoretical—merely criticism, devoid of potential for fruitful empirical research. Therefore, they ask: Where is your research program? or: Why can't women just as well be subsumed under established theoretical approaches? Assuming the idealist notion that women are more peaceful than men lurks somewhere behind the presenter's remarks, a questioner may challenge this unasserted claim by referring to Margaret Thatcher or Golda Meier. Believing these questions to be indications of an audience unfamiliar with, or even threatened by, feminist subject matter, a frustrated presenter may well wish to declare: You just don't understand.

These often unsatisfactory oral engagements illustrate a gendered estrangement that inhibits more sustained conversations, both oral and written, between feminists and other international relations scholars. I am not saying that this is an estrangement that pits men against women. A majority of IR women scholars do not work with feminist approaches, and some men do use gender as a category of analysis. Nevertheless, I do believe, and will argue below, that these theoretical divides evidence socially constructed gender differences. Understanding them as such may be a useful entry point for overcoming silences and miscommunications, thus beginning more constructive dialogues.

In this article I explore the implications and apparent presuppositions of some of these frequently asked questions. I will demonstrate that feminists and IR scholars are drawing on very different realities and using different epistemologies when they engage in theorizing about international relations. It is my belief that these differences themselves are gendered, with all the difficulties of cross-cultural communication that this implies.

While misunderstandings occur in both directions, I will focus on feminist responses to questions and comments from conventional IR scholars because these are less familiar to IR audiences. Because I believe it is where the greatest misunderstandings occur, I have chosen to engage with methodologically conventional IR scholars—whom I define as realists, neorealists, neoliberals, peace researchers, behavioralists, and empiricists committed to data-based methods of testing, rather than with recent critical approaches, associated with post-positivist methodologies as defined in the third debate (Lapid, 1989).[7] I realize there are significant differences between these conventional approaches. However, none of them has used gender as a category of analysis; it is in this sense, as well as in their shared commitment to a scientific methodology, that I have grouped them together.

There are three types of misunderstandings embedded in the questions outlined above; first, misunderstandings about the meaning of gender as manifested in the more personal reactions; second, the different realities or ontologies that feminists and nonfeminists see when they write about international politics, evident in comments that feminist scholars are not engaging the subject matter of IR; third, the epistemological divides that underlie questions as to whether feminists are doing theory at all.

Summarizing some work from a variety of feminist approaches, I will discuss each of these issues in the first part of this article. The second part offers some feminist perspectives on security and suggests how these perspectives might contribute to new ways of understanding contemporary security problems. This is not intended as an extensive feminist analysis of security but, rather, as a more concrete illustration of some of the issues raised in part one—that is, how misunderstandings can occur when feminists analyze IR issues. In conclusion, I will offer some thoughts on how these troubling feminist/nonfeminist IR engagements might be pursued more constructively.

SOURCES OF MISUNDERSTANDING

Gender: Is the Personal International?

Responding to a call to change the name of the International Brotherhood of Teamsters to include a recognition of its 30 percent female membership, James Hoffa asserted that the name should remain because "the definition of brotherhood is that it's neutral" (*New York Times*, 1996). While scholars of international relations, aware of the need to pay attention to gender-sensitive language, would probably want to claim some distance from this statement, it does indicate how, all too often, claims of gender neutrality mask deeply embedded masculinist assumptions which can naturalize or hide gender differences and gender inequalities. As documented above, even amongst the most sophisticated audiences, feminist challenges to these assumptions can often appear threatening, even when "male-bashing" is not intended.[8] Deborah Tannen has suggested that the reason gender differences are more troubling than other cross-cultural differences is that they occur where the home and hearth are: "[W]e enact and create our gender, and our inequality, with every move that we make" (Tannen, 1990: 283). Feminist scholars claim that gender differences permeate all facets of public and private life, a socially constructed divide which they take to be problematic in itself; IR scholars, however, may believe that gender is about interpersonal relations between women and men, but not about international politics.

Given that most contemporary feminist scholarship takes gender—which embodies relationships of power inequality—as its central category of analysis, the fact that the meaning of gender is so often misunderstood is, I believe, central to problems of misunderstanding and miscommunication. Almost all feminists who write about international relations use gender in a social constructivist sense, a move that many see not only as necessary for overcoming gender discrimination, but also as a way of opening avenues for communication by avoiding some of the threatened responses illustrated above.

As Sandra Harding (1986:17–8) has suggested, gendered social life is produced through three distinct processes: assigning dualistic gender metaphors to various perceived dichotomies, appealing to these gender dualisms to organize social activity, and dividing necessary social activities between different groups of humans. She refers to these three aspects of gender as gender symbolism, gender structure, and individual gender.

Feminists define gender, in the symbolic sense, as a set of variable but socially and culturally constructed characteristics—such as power, autonomy, rationality, and public—that are stereotypically associated with masculinity. Their opposites—weakness, dependence, emotion, and private—are associated with femininity. There is evidence to suggest that both women and men assign a more positive value to masculine characteristics. Importantly, definitions of masculinity and femininity are relational and depend on each other for their meaning; in other words, what it means to be a "real man" is not to display "womanly" weaknesses. Since these characteristics are social constructions, it is entirely possible for Margaret Thatcher to act like an iron lady or a "real man"; in fact, many feminists would argue that such behavior is necessary for both women and men to succeed in the tough world of international politics. As Tannen (1990:43) claims, girls and boys grow up in different worlds of words, but gender goes beyond language: it is a symbolic system that shapes many aspects of our culture. As Carol Cohn (1993:229) has suggested, even if real men and women do not fit these gender "ideals,"

the existence of this system of meaning affects us all—both our interpretations of the world and the way the world understands us.

As Joan Scott (1986:1069) claims, while the forms gender relations take across different cultures may vary, they are almost always unequal; therefore, gender, in the structural sense, is a primary way of signifying relationships of power. Although gender is frequently seen as belonging in the household and, therefore, antithetical to the "real" business of politics, a reason why it is often seen as irrelevant to IR, Scott argues that it is constructed in the economy and the polity through various institutional structures that have the effect of "naturalizing," and even legalizing, women's inferior status. Recent feminist writings that deal with issues of race and class problematize these power relationships still further.[9]

Individual gender relations enter into and are constituent elements in every aspect of human experience (Flax, 1987: 624). Jane Flax reminds us that, while feminism is about recovering women's activities, it must also be aware of how these activities are constituted through the social relations in which they are situated. Therefore, gender is not just about women; it is also about men and masculinity, a point that needs to be emphasized if scholars of international relations are to better understand why feminists claim that it is relevant to their discipline and why they believe that a gendered analysis of its basic assumptions and concepts can yield fruitful results.

Theorizing the International: Are Feminists Really "Doing" IR?

Deborah Tannen (1990:97) claims that women are more comfortable than men with an ethnographic style of individually oriented story-telling typical of anthropology, a difference that fits IR scholarship as well. International relations, particularly after the move toward science in the post–World War II period in the United States, has generally shied away from level-one analysis, preferring a more systemic or state-oriented focus. Coming out of literatures that are centrally concerned with individuals and social relations, and that are more explicitly normative, feminist perspectives, on the other hand, demonstrate a preference for more humanistically oriented methodologies. Although their focus is different, their discomfort with structural IR is similar to that captured in Martin Wight's famous title, "Why Is There No International Theory?"

In "Why Is There No International Theory?" Martin Wight (1995) remarked on the absence of an international theoretical tradition comparable to the very rich historical tradition of Western political philosophy.[10] According to Wight, the reason for this absence can be found in the character of the international system. Theorizing the international would mean speculating about a society or community of states. Since he saw the international system as evidencing the absence of society, a "realm of necessity" characterized by "recurrence and repetition," Wight (1995:32) claimed that there could be no "progressive" international theory, only a "theory of survival" marked by "an intellectual and moral poverty."[11] Wight is, of course, using theory in an explicitly normative sense, not fashionable amongst contemporary, more scientific theoretical approaches. He is postulating a "theory of the good life" (Wight, 1995:32), a progressive theory of social relations that calls for societal improvements, improvements, Wight claims, that can take place only within a political space such as the state.

While many contemporary feminist theorists would take issue with Wight's views on equating progressive theory with a tradition of Western political thought that has generally either excluded women altogether or treated them as less than fully human (Okin, 1980),[12] his reasons for claiming the poverty of international theory have relevance for problems feminists encounter when theorizing the international. With an ontology based on unitary states operating in an asocial, anarchical international environment, there is little in realist theory that provides an entry point for feminist theories, grounded as they are in an epistemology that takes social relations as its central category of analysis.[13]

As demonstrated above, much of contemporary feminism is also committed to progressive or emancipatory goals, particularly the goal of achieving equality for women through the elimination of unequal gender relations. Drawing on earlier literatures, such as those on women in the military and women and development, feminist writings on international relations have focused on individuals in their social, political, and economic settings, rather than on decontextualized unitary states and anarchical international structures. They investigate how military conflict and the behavior of states in the international system are constructed through, or embedded in, unequal gendered structural relations and how these affect the life chances of individuals, particularly women. These very different foci evoke the kind of questions introduced above about what is the legitimate subject matter of the discipline.

Returning to Martin Wight's discomfort with the realist tradition, with which feminists might find some common ground, could we find an entry point for feminist theorizing about the international system in approaches that start with different assumptions? Given a high level of economic interdependence, the growth of transnational nonstate actors, and the proliferation of international institutions, many IR scholars, particularly liberals with progressivist views of the international arena, prefer to work in the Grotian or Kantian traditions which postulate not an anarchy, but an international society of states within which a discussion of social relations becomes possible. Writing in the Kantian tradition, Andrew Linklater (1982) offers a critique of Wight. While acknowledging the tension between man as a universal category and citizens bound by loyalties to their states, Linklater postulates a Kantian resolution: "[B]ecause modern citizens are more than mere members of their communities, since they are responsive to universalistic moral claims, it is within their power to transform international relations in a direction which realises their capacity to lead free lives" (Linklater, 1982:18). "Kant held that all men were bound together by the necessary obligation to so arrange their social and political lives that they could gradually realise a condition of universal justice and perpetual peace. ... [These] were essential or categorical ends which men were under an unconditional obligation to promote by virtue of their rational nature" (Linklater, 1982:97).

The Kantian ethic, a progressive interpretation of international relations, is one of the important foundations of the so-called idealist tradition, a tradition to which feminist writings in international relations are often mistakenly assigned by international relations scholars.[14] In spite of its commitment to emancipatory goals of justice and peace which, in theory at least, could include the elimination of unjust social relations, this tradition is also problematic for feminists (Sylvester, 1994b:94). Western theories of universal justice, built on a rather abstract concept of rationality, have generally been constructed out of a definition of human nature that excludes or diminishes women. Feminists assert that the universalism they defend is defined by identifying the experience of a special group, (elite men), as paradigmatic of human beings as a whole (Benhabib, 1987: 81). Most Western political theorists were quite explicit in their claims that women either were not capable of, or should not be encouraged in, the attainment of enlightenment, autonomy, and rationality. For example, while Kant viewed the development of rationality as necessary for the formation of a moral character, he denied that women were capable of such achievements; he also recommended against the education of women because it would inhibit man's development (Tuana, 1992:52–3).[15]

While IR scholars might argue that Kant's views on women were a time-bound premise which can safely be discarded in today's more gender-sensitive climate, feminists believe that the Western philosophical tradition is too deeply implicated in masculinist assumptions to serve as a foundation for constructing a gender-sensitive IR. Therefore, the gender biases of this tradition, which are fundamental to its normative orientation, must be exposed and challenged. For this reason, feminists claim that works that have served as foundational texts for international relations must be reexamined for evidence of gender biases which call into question the gender neutrality frequently claimed in response to feminist critiques. In the words of one feminist theorist, "all forms of feminist theorizing are normative in the sense that they help us to question certain meanings and interpretations in IR theory" (Sylvester, 1994a:318). However, challenging the core assumptions, concepts, and ontological presuppositions of the field with claims of gender bias are bound to result in miscommunications and to make conversations with international theorists difficult.

Epistemological Divides: Where Is Your Research Program?

International Theory

In his commentary on Wight's piece, discussed earlier, Hans Morgenthau (1995) asserted that international theory could be progressive but in a rather different sense: "[T]he ideal toward which these theories try to progress is ultimately international peace and order to be achieved through scientific precision and predictability in understanding and manipulating international affairs" (Morgenthau, 1995:40). For Morgenthau, the purpose of theory was "to bring order and meaning into a mass of unconnected material and to increase knowledge through the logical development of certain propositions empirically established" (Morgenthau, 1995:46). Unlike Wight, Morgenthau, motivated by countering German fascism of the 1930s, was making the case for a scientific international theory, a type of theory that has strongly influenced mainstream international relations, at least in the United States.[16]

As I shall discuss below, this view of the purposes of theory is one that feminists have found problematic. However, feminists often misunderstand or ignore the rationale for the search for more scientific theories offered by early realists such as Morgenthau. Most of the founding fathers of American realism in the post–World War II period were European intellectuals fleeing from Nazi persecution. Flagrant violations of international law and abuses of human rights in the name of German nationalism motivated Morgenthau, and other early realists, to dissociate the realm of morality and values from the realpolitik of international politics. Painting a gloomy picture of "political man," and the dangers of an anarchic international system, Morgenthau claimed that war was always a possibility. However, he believed that the search for deeper explanations of the laws that govern human action could contribute to lessening the chances that such disasters would recur in the future.[17] Defending science against ideologically charged claims, which he associated with European fascism of the 1930s, Morgenthau believed that only by a more "scientific" understanding of its causes could the likelihood of war be diminished.

According to Stanley Hoffmann (1977), Morgenthau shaped these truths as a guide to those in power; thus, the growth of the discipline cannot be separated from the growing American role in world affairs in the post–World War II era. Speaking to and moving among foreign policy elites, this "American discipline" was, and is, aimed at an audience very different from feminist international relations. This difference—to which I return below—also causes misunderstandings.

The scientific turn in postwar realism was also adopted by behavioralists, neorealists, liberal institutionalists, and some peace researchers, all of whom drew on models from the natural sciences and from economics to build their theories. Seeking scientific respectability, international theorists turned to the natural sciences for their methodologies; many of them were also defending the autonomy of rational inquiry against totalitarian ideologies, this time of postwar Communism. Theories were defined as sets of logically related, ideally casual propositions, to be empirically tested or falsified in the Popperian sense. Scientific research programs were developed from realist assumptions about the international system serving as the "hard core" (Lakatos and Musgrave, 1970). While international theorists never sought the precision of Newton's grand schemes of deterministic laws and inescapable forces, they did claim that the international system is more than the constant and regular behavior of its parts (Hollis and Smith, 1990:50). Popular in the discipline, structural theories account for behavior by searching for causes. These theorists believe that events are governed by the laws of nature; in other words, behavior is generated by structures external to the actors themselves (Hollis and Smith, 1990:3).[18] In all these endeavors, theorists have generally assumed the possibility as well as the desirability of conducting systematic and cumulative scientific research.

Borrowing from economics, game theory and rational choice theory became popular for explaining the choices and optimizing behavior of self-interested states in an anarchical international system as well as a means for interpreting the actions of their foreign policy decision makers. Given the dangers and unpredictability of such a system, theory building was motivated by the desire to control and predict (Waltz, 1979:6)[19] The search for systematic inquiry could, hopefully, contribute to the effort of diminishing the likelihood of future conflict. Broadly defined as positivist, this turn to science represents a view of the creation of knowledge based on four assumptions: first, a belief in the unity of science—that is, the same methodologies can apply in the natural and social worlds; second, that there is a distinction between facts and values, with facts being neutral between theories; third, that the social world has regularities like the natural world; and fourth, that the way to determine the truth of statements is by appeal to neutral facts or an empiricist epistemology (Smith, 1997:168).[20]

Feminist Theory

Since it entered the field of international relations in the late 1980s, feminist theory has often, but not exclusively, been located within the critical voices of the "third debate," a term articulated by Yosef Lapid (1989). Although they are not all postmodern, or even post-Enlightenment, in their normative orientation at least, an assumption sometimes implied by conventional scholars, many contemporary feminist international relations scholars would identify themselves as post-positivists in terms of Lapid's articulation of the term and in terms of the definition of positivism outlined above. While there is no necessary connection between feminist approaches and post-positivism, there is a strong resonance for a variety of reasons including a commitment to epistemological pluralism as well as to certain ontological sensitivities. With a preference for hermeneutic, historically based, humanistic and philosophical traditions of knowledge cumulation, rather than those based on the natural sciences, feminist theorists are often skeptical of empiricist methodologies that claim neutrality of facts. While many feminists do see structural regularities, such as gender and patriarchy, they define them as socially constructed and variable across time, place, and cultures, rather than as universal and natural.

Agreeing with Robert Cox's assertion that theory is always for someone and for some purpose, the goal of feminist approaches is similar to that of critical theory as defined by Cox. While not all historians would accept this link, Cox asserts that critical theory "stands apart from the prevailing order of the world and asks how that order came about": it can, therefore, be a guide to strategic action for bringing about an alternative order (Cox, 1981:129–30).

Cox contrasts critical theory with conventional theory which he labels "problem-solving"—a type of conversation that Tannen associates with men (1990:ch.2). Problem-solving takes the world as it finds it and implicitly accepts the prevailing order as its framework (Cox, 1981:130). Since feminist theorists believe that the world is characterized by gender hierarchies that are detrimental to women, they would be unlikely to take such an epistemological stance. In the words of one feminist scholar who defines herself as a post-positivist, "postpositivism compels our attention to context and historical process, to contingency and uncertainty, to how we construct, rather than dis-cover, our world(s)" (Peterson, 1992a:57).

In constructing their approaches to international theory, feminists draw on a variety of philosophical traditions and literatures outside international relations and political science within which most IR scholars are trained. While IR feminists are seeking genuine knowledge that can help them to better understand the issues with which they are concerned, the IR training they receive rarely includes such knowledge. Hence, they, like scholars in other critical approaches, have gone outside the discipline to seek what they believe are more appropriate method-

ologies for understanding the social construction and maintenance of gender hierarchies. This deepens the level of misunderstanding and miscommunication and, unfortunately, often leads to negative stereotyping on all sides of these epistemological divides.

Feminist theories, variously identified as Marxist, radical, psychoanalytic, socialist, standpoint, existentialist, and postmodern, describe the causes and consequences of women's oppression and prescribe strategies for removing it;[21] thus, many of them are progressive in the sense in which Martin Wight was using the term. While psychoanalytic traditions look for causes of women's inequality in socialization practices of early childhood, radicals, Marxists, and socialists look for explanations in structures of patriarchy which "naturalize" women's oppression, or in the labor market with its gender discriminations and divisions between public (paid) and private (unpaid/domestic) work. As Carole Pateman (1994:21) has emphasized, feminism is more than a derivation from other bodies of political and social theory because it is centered on an investigation of the forms of power that men exercise over women.

All these feminist theoretical approaches, upon which IR feminists have drawn, are grounded in social and political theory and sociological traditions many of which lie outside the discipline of international relations. Therefore, while international theorists are often justifiably frustrated when feminists cannot provide a brief overview of feminist theory, feminists find communication on this issue with scholars trained in social scientific methodologies equally difficult because of the lack of agreement as to what counts as legitimate scientific inquiry. Since all these feminist approaches question the claim that women can simply be added to existing theoretical frameworks, it is predictable that misunderstandings will compound when those working within the scientific tradition suggest that feminist approaches can be incorporated into conventional IR methodologies. Indeed, feminists have a legitimate fear of cooptation; so often women's knowledge has been forgotten or subsumed under more dominant discourses.[22]

Incorporation can also be a source of misunderstanding when international theorists, responding to challenges of gender blindness, have attempted to make women more visible in their texts. For, as Emily Rosenberg (1990) tells us, efforts to integrate women into existing theories and consider them equally with men can only lead to a theoretical cul-de-sac which further reinforces gender hierarchies. For example, in international relations, when we add exceptional women—the famous few such as Margaret Thatcher or Golda Meier who succeed in the tough world of international politics by acting like men—to existing frameworks, it tends to imply, without the claim being made overtly, that the problem of their absence lies with women themselves. Conversely, if we go looking for women working in "women's spheres," such as peace groups, it only reinforces the socially constructed boundaries between activities differentially deemed appropriate for women and for men; moreover, it contributes to the false claim that women are more peaceful than men, a claim that disempowers both women and peace. Although feminists are frequently told that they are implying that women are more peaceful than men, many are actually quite suspicious of this association of women with peace. Besides being derivative of an essentialized position about women's "nature," to which most contemporary feminists do not subscribe, this association tends to brand women as naive and unrealistic, thereby further delegitimizing their voices in the world of foreign policy making (Sylvester, 1987; Elshtain, 1990).

Feminists are arguing for moving beyond knowledge frameworks that construct international theory without attention to gender and for searching deeper to find ways in which gender hierarchies serve to reinforce socially constructed institutions and practices that perpetuate different and unequal role expectations, expectations that have contributed to fundamental inequalities between women and men in the world of international politics. Therefore, including gender as a central category of analysis transforms knowledge in ways that go beyond adding women; importantly, but frequently misunderstood, this means that women cannot be studied in isolation from men.

While most feminists are committed to the emancipatory goal of achieving a more just society, which, for them, includes ending the oppression of women, the Kantian project of achieving this goal through Enlightenment knowledge is problematic because of feminist claims that this type of knowledge is gendered. Feminists assert that dichotomies, such as rational/irrational, fact/value, universal/particular, and public/private, upon which Western Enlightenment knowledge has been built and which they see as gendered, separate the mind (rationality) from the body (nature) and, therefore, diminish the legitimacy of women as "knowers." Susan Heckman has claimed that, "since the Enlightenment, knowledge has been defined in terms of 'man,' the subject, and espouses an epistemology that is radically homocentric." Since Enlightenment epistemology places women in an inferior position, outside the realm of rationality, challenging the priority of "man" in the modern episteme must be fundamental to any feminist program (Heckman, 1990:2). Similarly, Patricia Hill Collins (1989) claims that Black women would be unlikely to subscribe to an epistemology that has, for the most part, excluded Blacks and other minorities. Black women, she claims, prefer, and consider more legitimate, knowledge construction based on concrete experience of everyday lives, stories, and dialogues. These subjective epistemological positions are unsettling for scholars trained in scientific methodologies based on more abstract knowledge claims.

In her critique of the natural sciences, Evelyn Fox Keller (1985:89) asserts that modern Enlightenment science has incorporated a belief system that equates objectivity with masculinity and a set of cultural values that simultaneously elevates what is defined as scientific and what is defined as masculine. Throughout most of the history of the modern West, men have been seen as the knowers; what has counted as legitimate knowledge, in both the natural and social sciences, has generally been knowledge based on the lives of men in the public sphere. The separation of the public and private spheres, reinforced by the scientific revolution of the seventeenth century, has resulted in the legitimation of what are perceived as the "rational" activities (such as politics, economics, and justice) in the former while devaluing the "natural" activities (such as household management, child-rearing,

and care-giving) of the latter (Peterson, 1992b:202).

As Carole Pateman (1988:90) argues, in the seventeenth century women began to be deprived of the economic basis for independence by the separation of the workplace from the household and the consolidation of the patriarchal structures of capitalism. The separation of public and private spheres has also engendered a division between reason and feeling as the household, the "natural" site of women's existence, became associated with moral sentiments as opposed to self-interest, more characteristic of the public world (Tronto, 1993:52–6), a split that has been particularly evident in rationalist theories of international relations. Feminists believe that the legitimation of particular types of knowledge, intensified by this public/private divide, shapes and restricts the kinds of questions that get asked and how they get answered.[23]

Stephen Toulmin (1990) analyzes the coincidence of the birth of the modern scientific method and the birth of the modern nation-state. He contrasts the scientific method with a "pre-modern" or "early modern" humanistic tradition, incorporating writers such as Erasmus and Montaigne, whose skeptical tolerance for ambiguity and diversity in knowledge accumulation seems more compatible with feminist thinking than with the rationalist universalism of the scientific revolution. Most feminists claim that knowledge is socially constructed, contingent, and shaped by context, culture, and history. According to Sandra Harding (1991:59), the subject of knowledge is never simply an individual capable of transcending historical location: in other words, there is no impartial, value-neutral Archimedean perspective. Feminist analysis insists that the inquirer be placed in the same critical plane as the subject matter (Harding, 1987:9). Even the best forms of knowledge cannot be divorced from their political consequences, a claim that can only appear unsettling to proponents of scientific methodologies who frequently label such knowledge claims as relativist and lacking in objectivity.

Feminists argue, however, that broadening the base from which knowledge is constructed, that is, including the experiences of women, can actually enhance objectivity.[24] Arguing from a modified standpoint position,[25] Sandra Harding explores the question as to whether objectivity and socially situated knowledge is an impossible combination. She concludes that adopting a feminist standpoint actually strengthens standards of objectivity. While it requires acknowledging that all human beliefs are socially situated, it also requires critical evaluation to determine which social situations tend to generate the most objective knowledge claims. Harding argues for what she calls "strong objectivity" which extends the task of scientific research to include a systematic examination of powerful background beliefs and making strange what has hitherto appeared as familiar (Harding, 1991:142, 149).

Likewise, Donna Haraway argues for what she calls "embodied objectivity" or "situated knowledge." For Haraway, situated knowledge does not mean relativism but shared conversations leading to "better accounts of the world" (Haraway, 1988:580).[26] Indeed, feminists frequently use the metaphor of conversation both as a preferred methodology and in their calls for engagement with IR scholars. Since conversational or dialogic methodologies come out of a her-

meneutic tradition, conversation is not a metaphor social scientists are likely to employ; indeed, it is one that would appear quite strange as a basis for theory construction.[27]

This brief overview of a variety of feminist epistemologies suggests that they are quite different from those prevailing in conventional international relations. Since all feminist approaches are concerned with social relations, particularly the investigation of the causes and consequences of unequal relationships between women and men, the questions they ask about international relations are likely to be quite different from those of international theorists primarily concerned with the interaction of states in the international system. While feminist theories might fit more comfortably into what Hollis and Smith (1990) term the "inside," or hermeneutical approach, feminists construct their knowledge about international relations not so much from the perspectives of "insiders" but from voices of the disempowered and marginalized not previously heard.[28] The sounds of these unfamiliar voices and the issues they raise sometimes cause conventional scholars to question whether feminists even belong within the same discipline.

As Sandra Harding (1991:123) tells us, an important task of feminist theory is to make strange what has previously appeared familiar, or to challenge us to question what has hitherto appeared as "natural." In international relations, this has involved an examination of the basic assumptions and concepts of the field, taken as unproblematic—and gender-neutral—by conventional international theorists. While critical approaches more generally have often been accused of indulging in criticism rather than producing new research programs (Walt,

1991: 223), feminists would argue that a critical examination is necessary because feminist research agendas cannot be built without first exposing and questioning the gender biases of the field. As an example of one such conceptual reexamination and its implications for different kinds of investigations and understandings, I shall now outline some feminist perspectives on security. Rather than attempt to offer a comprehensive analysis of the subject, I use these observations to illustrate more concretely some of the sources of misunderstanding discussed above; this section is also intended to suggest potential feminist research agendas.[29]

FEMINIST PERSPECTIVES ON SECURITY

I have chosen to focus on security because it has been central to the discipline of international relations since its inception in the early twentieth century. It is also an important issue for feminists who write about international relations. However, as I have indicated, since feminist perspectives are constructed out of very different ontologies and epistemologies, their definition of security, explanations of insecurity, and prescriptions for security enhancement are areas where divergence from conventional international theory is significant. Thus, they offer a good illustration of some of the misunderstandings outlined above. I shall begin by defining what certain feminist scholars mean by security and insecurity; I shall outline some of the kinds of empirical evidence feminists use when analyzing security. Then, drawing on some of the feminist approaches discussed earlier, I will illustrate some of the types of explanations feminist theories

offer for some contemporary insecurities, thereby demonstrating potential avenues for further research. While these research agendas may be different from conventional analyses of security, they too claim to seek greater understanding of "real-world" security issues.

What Is Security?

Scholars in the realist paradigm, within which much of the analysis of security has taken place, define security in political/military terms, as the protection of the boundaries and integrity of the state and its values against the dangers of a hostile international environment, Martin Wight's "realm of necessity" (Wolfers, 1962). In their search for more parsimonious explanations, neorealists emphasize the anarchical structure of the system rather than domestic factors as being the primary determinant of states' insecurities. States are postulated as unitary actors whose internal characteristics, beyond an assessment of their relative capabilities, are not seen as necessary for understanding their vulnerabilities or security-enhancing behavior (Waltz, 1979). States' efforts to increase their power or engage in balance-of-power activities are explained as attempts to improve their security. In the United States, security studies, defined largely in terms of the bipolar nuclear confrontation between the United States and the former Soviet Union, became an important subfield within the discipline. For security specialists, this definition of security remains in place in the post–Cold War era. Security specialists believe that military power remains a central element of international politics and that the traditional agenda of security studies is, therefore, expanding rather than shrinking (Walt, 1991:222).

In the 1980s, a trend toward broadening the definition of security emerged as peace researchers, those concerned with poverty in the South, environmentalists, and certain European policy makers began to define security in economic and environmental as well as political/military terms (Independent Commission, 1982; Ullman, 1983; Mathews, 1989; Buzan, 1991). While this trend continues to gain strength after the end of the Cold War, the issue remains controversial.[30] It is, however, a definition more compatible with most contemporary feminist scholarship that also finds traditional definitions of security too narrow for what they consider to be the security issues of the post–Cold War world. There are, however, important differences between the new security literature and feminist perspectives since very little of the new security literature has paid attention to women or gender.

Many IR feminists define security broadly in multidimensional and multilevel terms—as the diminution of all forms of violence, including physical, structural, and ecological (Tickner, 1992; Peterson and Runyan, 1993). Since women are marginal to the power structures of most states, and since feminist perspectives on security take women's security as their central concern, most of these definitions start with the individual or community rather than the state or the international system. According to Christine Sylvester (1994b), security is elusive and partial and involves struggle and contention; it is a process rather than an ideal in which women must act as agents in the provision of their own security. Speaking from the margins, feminists are sensitive to the various ways in which social hierarchies manifest themselves across societies and history. Striving for security involves exposing these different social hierarchies, understanding how they construct and are constructed by the international order, and working to denaturalize and dismantle them.

These feminist definitions of security grow out of the centrality of social relations, particularly gender relations, for feminist theorizing. Coming out of different literatures and working with definitions based on different ontologies as well as different normative goals, feminist writings on security open themselves up to criticism that their work does not fall within the subject matter of international relations. Feminists would respond by asserting that structural inequalities, which are central contributors to the insecurity of individuals, are built into the historical legacy of the modern state and the international system of which it is a part. Calling into question realist boundaries between anarchy and danger on the outside and order and security on the inside, feminists believe that state-centric or structural analyses miss the interrelation of insecurity across levels of analysis. Since "women's space" inside households has also been beyond the reach of law in most states, feminists are often quite suspicious of boundaries that mark states as security providers. They would argue that Martin Wight's political space, within which theorizing the good life is possible, requires radical restructuring before it can be regarded as offering a safe space for women.[31] I shall now outline some of the evidence feminists draw on when defining the kinds of personal and structural insecurities they believe must be overcome in order to create a more secure world.

Questioning the role of states as adequate security providers leads feminists to analyze power and military capabilities differently from conventional international relations scholars. Rather than seeing military capability as an assurance against outside threats to the state, militaries frequently are seen as antithetical to individuals', particularly women's, security—as winners in the competition for resources for social safety nets on which women depend disproportionately to men, as definers of an ideal type of militarized citizenship, usually denied to women (Tobias, 1990), or as legitimators of a kind of social order that can sometimes even valorize state violence.

Consequently, when analyzing political/military dimensions of security, feminists tend to focus on the consequences of what happens during wars rather than on their causes (Pettman, 1996:87–106). They draw on evidence to emphasize the negative impact of contemporary military conflicts on civilian populations. According to the United Nations' *Human Development Report,* there has been a sharp increase in the proportion of civilian casualties of war—from about 10 percent at the beginning of the century to 90 percent today. While the *Report* does not break down these casualties by sex, it claims that this makes women among the worst sufferers even though they constitute only 2 percent of the world's regular army personnel (United Nations, 1995:45). As mothers, family providers, and care-givers, women are particularly penalized by economic sanctions associated with military conflict, such as the UN boycott put in place against Iraq after the Gulf War. Women and children (about 18 million at the end of 1993) constitute about 80 percent of the total refugee population, a population whose numbers increased from 3 million to 27 million between 1970 and 1994, mainly due to military

conflict (United Nations, 1995:14).[32] Feminists also draw attention to issues of rape in war; as illustrated by the Bosnian case, rape is not just an accident of war but is, or can be, a systematic military strategy. Cynthia Enloe (1993:119) has described social structures in place around most army bases where women are often kidnapped and sold into prostitution.

For feminists writing about security, economic dimensions and issues of structural violence have been as important as issues of military conflict.[33] According to the *Human Development Report*, in no country are women doing as well as men. While figures vary from state to state, on an average, women earn three quarters of men's earnings. Of the 1.3 billion people estimated to be in poverty today, 70 percent are women: the number of rural women living in absolute poverty rose by nearly 50 percent over the past two decades (United Nations, 1995:36). Women receive a disproportionately small share of credit from formal banking institutions. For example, in Latin America, women constitute only 7–11 percent of the beneficiaries of credit programs; while women in Africa contribute up to 80 percent of total food production, they receive less than 10 percent of the credit to small farmers and 1 percent of total credit to agriculture (United Nations, 1995:4, 39). While women actually work more hours than men in almost all societies, their work is under-remunerated and undervalued because much of it takes place outside the market economy, in households or subsistence sectors. Whether women are gatherers of fuel and firewood or mothers of sick children, their lives are severely impacted by resource shortages and environmental pollution.

These are some of the issues with which feminists writing about security, defined in both political/military and economic terms, are concerned. They are not, however, issues considered relevant to conventional state-centric security concerns. Challenging both the traditional notion of the state as the framework within which security should be defined and analyzed, and the conventional boundaries between security inside and anarchy outside the state, feminists embed their analyses in a system of relations that cross these boundaries. Challenging the notion of discrete levels of analysis, they argue that inequalities between women and men, inequalities that contribute to all forms of insecurity, can only be understood and explained within the framework of a system shaped by patriarchal structures that extend from the household to the global economy. I shall now elaborate on some of the ways feminists explain these persistent inequalities.

Explaining Insecurity

Feminists claim that inequalities, which decrease individuals', particularly women's, security, cannot be understood using conventional tools of analysis. Theories that construct structural explanations that aspire to universality typically fail to recognize how unequal social structures impact in different ways on the security of different groups. Feminists believe that only by introducing gender as a category of analysis can the differential impact of the state system and the global economy on the lives of women and men be analyzed and understood. Feminists also caution that searching for universal laws may miss the ways in which gender hierarchies manifest themselves in a variety of ways across time and culture; therefore, theories must be sensitive to history, context, and contingency.

Questioning the neutrality of facts and concepts, feminists have challenged international theory's claim that the state can be taken as given in its theoretical investigations. Feminists assert that only by analyzing the evolution of the modern state system and its changing political, economic, and social structures can we begin to understand its limitations as a security provider. The particular insecurities of women cannot be understood without reference to historical divisions between public and private spheres. As Spike Peterson and other feminists have pointed out, at the time of the foundation of the modern Western state, and coincidentally with the beginnings of capitalism, women were not included as citizens but consigned to the private space of the household; thus, they were removed both from the public sphere of politics and the economic sphere of production (Peterson, 1992a: 40–4). As a result, women lost much of their existing autonomy and agency, becoming more dependent on men for their economic security.

Consequently, the term *citizen* has also been problematic for women. As Carole Pateman (1988) has pointed out, women were not included in the original social contract by most contract theorists in the Western tradition; rather, they were generally subsumed under male heads of households with no legal rights of their own. In most parts of the world women are still struggling for full equality. Gaining the right to vote much later than men in most societies,[34] women continue to be under-represented in positions of political and economic power and are usually excluded from military combat even in societies committed to formal equality. Therefore, terms such as *citizen, head of household,* and *breadwinner* are not neutral but are associated with men. In spite of the fact that many women do work outside the household, the association of women with housewife, care-giver, and mother has become naturalized, thereby decreasing women's economic security and autonomy. While these issues may appear irrelevant to the conduct of international politics, feminists claim that these gender-differentiated roles actually support and legitimate the international security-seeking behavior of the state.

For example, feminists have argued that unequal gender relations are important for sustaining the military activities of the state. Thus, what goes on in wars is not irrelevant to their causes and outcomes. The notion that (young) males fight wars to protect vulnerable groups such as women and children who cannot be expected to protect themselves has been an important motivator for the recruitment of military forces and support for wars. Feminists have challenged this protector/protected relationship with evidence of the high increase in civilian casualties documented above.[35] As feminists have pointed out, if women are thought to be in need of protection, it is often their protectors who provide the greatest threat. Judith Stiehm (1982) claims that this dependent, asymmetric relationship leads to feelings of low self-esteem and little sense of responsibility on the part of women. For men, the presence of able-bodied, competent adults who are seen as dependent and incapable can contribute to misogyny. Anne Orford (1996) tells us that accounts of sexual assault by peacekeepers have emerged in many UN peacekeeping operations. However, such violence against

women is usually dismissed as a "natural" outcome of the right of young soldiers to enjoy themselves. This type of behavior may also be aggravated by the misogynist training of soldiers who are taught to fight and kill through appeals to their masculinity; such behavior further erodes the notion of protection.

Whereas feminist analysis of military security has focused on the gendered structures of state institutions, issues of economic security and insecurity have emphasized the interrelationship between activities in markets and households. Feminists claim that women's particular economic insecurities can only be understood in the context of patriarchal structures, mediated through race, class, and ethnicity, which have the effect of consigning women to households or low-paying jobs. Public/private boundaries have the effect of naturalizing women's unremunerated work in the home to the detriment of women's autonomy and economic security. Women's disproportionate numbers at the bottom of the socioeconomic scale cannot be explained by market conditions alone; they also require an understanding that certain types of work such as teaching, nursing, and other forms of care-giving are often considered "natural" for women to perform (Peterson and Runyan, 1993:37; Pettman, 1996: 165–8). Moreover, the clustering of women in low-paying or non-waged work in subsistence or households cannot be understood by using rational choice models, because women may have internalized the ideas behind traditional systems of discrimination, and thus may themselves view their roles as natural (Nussbaum and Glover, 1995:91). In other words, social expectations having to do with gender roles can reinforce economic inequalities between women and men and exacerbate women's insecurities. Such issues can only be explained by using gender as a category of analysis; since they take them as given, rational actor models miss the extent to which opportunities and choices are constrained by the social relations in which they are embedded.

Many of these issues seem far removed from the concerns of international relations. But, employing bottom-up rather than top-down explanations, feminists claim that the operation of the global economy and states' attempts to secure benefits from it are built on these unequal social relations between women and men which work to the detriment of women's (and certain men's) security. For example, states that successfully compete in attracting multinational corporations often do so by promising them a pool of docile cheap labor consisting of young unmarried women who are not seen as "breadwinners" and who are unlikely to organize to protest working conditions and low wages (Enloe, 1990:151–76). When states are forced to cut back on government spending in order to comply with structural adjustment programs, it is often the expectation that women, by virtue of their traditional role as care-givers, will perform the welfare tasks previously assumed by the state without remuneration. According to Caroline Moser (1991: 105), structural adjustment programs dedicated to economic "efficiency" are built on the assumption of the elasticity of women's unpaid labor.

In presenting some feminist perspectives on security and some explanations for insecurity, I have demonstrated how feminists are challenging levels of analysis and boundaries between inside and outside which they see, not as discrete constructs delineating boundaries

between anarchy and order, but as contested and mutually constitutive of one another. Through a reexamination of the state, feminists demonstrate how the unequal social relations on which most states are founded both influence their external security-seeking behavior and are influenced by it. Investigating states as gendered constructs is not irrelevant to understanding their security-seeking behaviors as well as whose interests are most served by these behaviors. Bringing to light social structures that support war and "naturalize" the gender inequalities manifested in markets and households is not irrelevant for understanding their causes. Feminists claim that the gendered foundations of states and markets must be exposed and challenged before adequate understandings of, and prescriptions for, women's (and certain men's) security broadly defined can be formulated.

CONCLUSIONS

Feminist theorists have rarely achieved the serious engagement with other IR scholars for which they have frequently called. When they have occurred, conversations have often led to misunderstandings and other kinds of miscommunication, such as awkward silences and feminist resistances to suggestions for incorporation into more mainstream approaches. In this article I have tried to reconstruct some typical conversational encounters and to offer some hypotheses as to why estrangement seems so often to be the result. Although I realize that these encounters demonstrate misunderstandings on both sides, I have emphasized some feminist perspectives because they are less likely to be familiar to IR scholars. While it is all too easy to account for these troubled engagements between IR scholars and feminists solely in terms of differences in ontologies and epistemologies, it must be acknowledged that power differences play an important role also. Inequalities in power between mainstream and feminist IR allow for greater ignorance of feminist approaches on the part of the mainstream than is possible for feminists with respect to conventional IR, if they are to be accorded any legitimacy within the profession. Because of this power differential, feminists are suspicious of cooptation or attempts to label certain of their approaches as more compatible than others.

Understanding that all these problems are inherent in calling for one more effort at renewed conversation, I have tried to suggest and analyze reasons for the frequent failures or avoidance of such efforts, comparing these failures to problems of cross-cultural communications. Lack of understanding and judgments of irrelevance are two major causes of the silence with which feminist approaches have generally been received by the discipline of international relations. Contemporary feminist perspectives on international relations are based on ontologies and epistemologies that are quite different from those that inform the conventional discipline. Since they grow out of ontologies that take individuals or groups embedded in and changed by social relations, such relationally defined feminist approaches do not fit comfortably within conventional levels of analysis theorizing or the state-centric and structural approaches which grow out of such theorizing. They are also informed by different normative concerns. Moreover, feminists claim that normative international theories, such as the Grotian and Kantian traditions, are

based on literatures that have often diminished or excluded women.

Feminist epistemologies that inform these new ways of understanding international relations are also quite different from those of conventional international theory. But, as I have argued, feminists cannot be anything but skeptical of universal truth claims and explanations associated with a body of knowledge from which women have frequently been excluded as knowers and subjects. However, this does not mean that feminists are abandoning theory or the search for better knowledge. Although they draw on epistemologies quite different from conventional international relations, they also are seeking better understanding of the processes that inform international political, economic, and social relations. Building knowledge that does not start from the position of the detached universal subject involves being sensitive to difference while striving to be as objective as possible. By starting thought from women's lives, feminists claim they are actually broadening the base from which knowledge is constructed. While feminist perspectives do not claim to tell us everything we need to know about the behavior of states or the workings of the global economy, they are telling us things that too often remained invisible.

Feminists often draw on the notion of conversation when pursuing their goal of shareable understandings of the world. Skeptical of the possibility of arriving at one universal truth, they advocate seeking understanding through dialogues across boundaries and cultures in which the voices of others, particularly those on the margins, must be seen as equally valid as one's own.[36] This method of truth-seeking, motivated by the attempt to separate valid knowledge from what feminists see as power-induced distortions, is far removed from more scientific methodologies and from a discipline whose original goal was to better understand the behavior of states in order to offer advice to their policy makers. Therefore, feminists must understand that their preferred methodologies and the issues they raise are alien to the traditional discipline; and IR scholars must realize that speaking from the perspective of the disempowered appears increasingly urgent in a world where the marginalized are the most likely victims of war and the negative effects of economic globalization.

Seeking greater understanding across theoretical divides, and the scientific and political cultures that sustain them, might be the best model if feminist international theory is to have a future within the discipline. Feminist theorists may claim that conventional IR has little to offer as to how to make cross-paradigm communications more effective and mutually successful. But feminists must understand that methodologies relevant to the investigations of their preferred issues are not normally part of a graduate curriculum in IR in the United States; therefore, they appear strange, unfamiliar, and often irrelevant to those so trained. However, feminists, along with other critical scholars, are pioneering the effort to look beyond conventional training and investigate the relevance of other disciplines and literatures for these methodologies. Conversations will not be successful until the legitimacy of these endeavors is more widely recognized and acknowledged as part of the discipline of international relations.

Asking the question as to how we open lines of communication, Deborah Tannen (1990:120–1) suggests that men and women must try to take each other on their own terms rather than apply the standards of one group to the behavior of the other. Additionally, she claims that this is not an easy task because all of us tend to look for a single "right" way of doing things. Could this be a model for beginning more productive conversations between feminists and IR theorists?

NOTES

1. In defining this literature as new, I am referring to recent work that is critiquing international relations theory from a variety of feminist perspectives and reconstructing international relations through gender-sensitive lenses. For some examples see Enloe, 1990, Grant and Newland, 1991, Peterson, 1992a, Tickner, 1992, Sylvester, 1994b, and Pettman, 1996. Of course, I am aware of the impossibility of trying to represent a very rich and diverse literature adequately in one paper.

2. One recent article that does engage in a critique of some feminist literature is Jones (1996). Certain introductory IR texts have begun to incorporate feminist approaches. See for examples Rourke (1993) and Goldstein (1994). As yet, feminist articles in mainstream U.S./IR journals have been rare. There has been some recognition of critical approaches other than feminism by the mainstream; however, they have often been dismissed or assessed quite negatively, particularly postmodernism. For a more constructive engagement see Keohane (1988) and the response by Walker (1989).

3. While *You Just Don't Understand* is a popular, somewhat stereotypical book, it is, I believe, a useful entry point for offering insights into the problems of gendered cross-cultural communications. It comes out of a rich tradition of gender-sensitive discourse analysis many of whose classics are cited in Tannen's bibliography.

4. I am not saying that men cannot engage in feminist or gender analysis; indeed, gender is not just about women. However, it is usually women and feminists who write about gender issues. The main reason for this is that what it means to be human has generally been equated with (often Western elite) men. As feminists point out, women have often been rendered less than fully human, or even invisible, by this move. Revelations of the gender biases of medical research are an important illustration of this.

5. I am drawing on fairly widely shared experiences that I and other feminist scholars have had when speaking to IR audiences. I cannot analyze these engagements more systematically since these types of comments rarely appear in print.

6. That this happens frequently is supported by the title of an article by Marysia Zalewski (1995), "Well, What Is the Feminist Perspective on Bosnia?" Zalewski suggests that the reason for the frequency of such questions is that feminist theory has only recently infiltrated the discipline. I believe that their frequency is the result of a much deeper level of misunderstanding.

7. For examples of where I have engaged more systematically with some of these approaches I have defined as conventional see Tickner, 1988, 1992, 1994.

8. Conversely, dangers lurk in the uncritical switch to gender-neutral language when it is used even when the speaker is clearly not speaking for or about women. See Okin, 1989:10–3, for elaboration of this point.

9. For example, as Bell Hooks (1984) claims, nonwhite women would not subscribe to the feminist goal of making women equal to men who are themselves victims of racist oppression. I am aware of the importance of including class and race differences when defining and analyzing gender and women's oppression. However, I do not believe this should prevent us from making testable, generalizeable claims about the gendering of the disci-pline of international relations. For a useful discussion of this issue more generally see Martin, 1994.

10. It is interesting to note that certain IR feminists have expressed some affinity with classical realism and/or more sociological approaches associated with the English School. Whitworth (1989:268) claims that the classical realism of Morgenthau acknowledges that meaning is contingent and socially constructed, thus creating a space, in theory if not in practice, for the analysis of gender. The authors chosen by James Der Derian for his edited volume *International Theory* (1995), which includes Wight's piece, illustrate the link between the English School and some other contemporary critical perspectives. It also includes American scholars of the scientific tradition. I have chosen to cite from this volume, rather than going back to the original sources, for this reason.

11. Here Wight is presenting a realist world-view. However, it is difficult to place Wight exclusively within any one of the three theoretical traditions that he himself outlined. For further elaboration of this point see Yost, 1994.

12. Feminist perspectives on international relations have focused on the explicitly gendered writings of political philosophers, such as Hobbes and Machiavelli, whose works have served as foundational texts for the discipline. See, for example, Grant, 1991, and Sylvester, 1994a.

13. For further elaboration on these ontological distinctions, as well as on the problems of articulating a world politics beyond the state, see Walker, 1992.

14. Feminists believe that labeling their work as idealism is often a mistake. They claim they are describing a reality rarely acknowledged in the discipline. I use the term *so-called* when referring to idealism because the label was invented by realists and it is one that has contributed to the delegitimation of the idealist tradition. It is interesting to note that the language of the realist/idealist debate

has gendered connotations. Communitarian, liberal, or cosmopolitan might serve as better definitions of this rich tradition. However, women's voices and gender analysis have been absent also from international law from which the cosmopolitan and communitarian traditions have drawn inspiration (see Charlesworth, Chinkin, and Wright, 1991).

15. I am aware that the exclusion of women from traditions of universalist ethics and justice is quite a different issue from postulating a universalist ethic that could include women. Indeed, this is an important and contentious issue in feminist theories of justice. For positions on both sides of this debate see various chapters in Nussbaum and Glover, 1995.

16. Just as he was not considered scientific enough by many subsequent international theorists, Morgenthau was himself ambivalent about the turn to science in American international theory. For evidence of this ambivalence see Morgenthau, 1946. For an analysis of the reasons for the preference for scientific methodologies in the U.S. see Hoffmann, 1977.

17. For a feminist critique of Morgenthau's six principles of political realism see Tickner, 1988.

18. Hollis and Smith (1990) identify two traditions in international theory, "inside" and "outside." Since "inside" theories are interpretive or hermeneutical, feminist theories would probably fit more comfortably into this tradition, although it too presents problems for feminists. A tradition constructed out of the beliefs and intentions of human actors has rarely included women as actors.

19. What level of prediction is desirable or possible is a matter of some contention amongst international theorists. Claims that international theorists failed to predict the end of the Cold War has added fuel to this debate (see Gaddis, 1992–93).

20. Not all IR theorists, who associate themselves with the scientific tradition, would agree with all parts of this definition. Few social scientists believe that their work is value-free or that universally valid generalizations are possible; nevertheless, they would probably agree that these are useful standards to which to aspire. Most would believe, however, that systematic social scientific research is possible and desirable and that methodologies borrowed from the natural sciences can be useful, although some have recognized the problems of applying natural science methods to the social sciences. I am indebted to an anonymous reviewer and to Harvey Starr for these observations.

21. One must be wary of putting feminist perspectives into boxes, however. There is considerable overlap amongst approaches, and many theorists draw on a variety of intellectual traditions. The interdisciplinarity of feminism compounds the difficulties and limitations of categorizations. I am also aware that, as with my definition of conventional theory, I am conflating divergent bodies of scholarship. The unifying theme upon which I draw is that most feminist approaches take gender as a central category of analysis and seek to understand the sources of women's oppression and how to end it. For a useful introductory overview of feminist theories see Tong, 1989.

22. This issue of cooptation is evidenced in Weber's (1994) critique of Keohane (1989) which called for an alliance between neoliberal institutionalism and standpoint feminism.

23. Carol Cohn (1987) makes this point with respect to issues of nuclear strategy. She claims that the rationalist, depersonalized, and technocratic language of defense intellectuals has limited the kind of questions that can be asked and has restricted the kinds of policy options that are seen as legitimate.

24. As Sandra Harding (1991:123) emphasizes, women's experiences alone are not a reliable guide for deciding which knowledge claims are preferable because women

tend to speak in socially acceptable ways. Nevertheless, Harding believes that women's lives are the place from which feminist research should begin.

25. I use the term *modified* to indicate that Harding takes into consideration postmodern critiques of an essentialized standpoint which, they say, speaks from the position of privileged Western women. Standpoint feminism comes out of Hegel's notion of the master/slave relationship and out of Marxist theory more generally. Hegel and Marxists claim that the slave (or the proletariat) have, by necessity, a more comprehensive understanding of the position of both the master (or the capitalist) and the slave.

26. Christine Sylvester's method of empathetic cooperation draws on this idea of shared conversations (see Sylvester, 1994a, 1994b).

27. Tannen's (1990:ch.3) distinction between "report-talk" and "rapport talk" may be relevant to this discussion of the gendering of scientific methods. According to Tannen, for most men, talk is a means of preserving independence, whereas, for most women, it is a way of establishing connections.

28. It is important to stress that feminists recognize the multiplicity of women's voices mediated by class, race, and cultural positions. Debate on the problems of essentialism is one of the most vital in feminist theory today. For an elaboration of the issues at stake see Martin, 1994.

29. I have offered a more systematic analysis of security from a feminist perspective in *Gender in International Relations* (Tickner, 1992; see also Peterson, 1992a, and Peterson and Runyan, 1993).

30. Walt (1991) makes a case for continuing to define security narrowly. For a critique of Walt's position see Kolodziej, 1992.

31. I am aware that women's relations to the state vary across race, class, and culture. I am also aware that the state may not be a safe space for men in racially or ethnically divided societies. Mona Harrington (1992) has offered an interesting challenge to feminists' often negative views of the state. Harrington argues for a reformulated "feminist" state which could provide the necessary protection against global capitalism and international institutions which, she argues, increasingly, have no democratic accountability. This challenge seems to have saliency in an era of "globalization" and its negative effects on marginalized populations documented by the *Human Development Report* (United Nations, 1995). I cite the 1995 edition because it focused specifically on women and gender issues. The UN's recent disaggregation of data by sex has significantly advanced the potential for research on women worldwide.

32. Although the majority of refugees in camps are women left alone to care for children and, therefore, acting as heads of households, they usually do not have refugee status in their own right but only as wives within families (Moser, 1991: 96).

33. The term *structural violence* was first introduced by Johan Galtung in the 1970s to explain decreased life expectancy of individuals due to structures that cause economic deprivation (see Galtung, 1971).

34. The suffrage has still not been extended to women in all societies. Kuwait and Saudi Arabia are states where women are still denied the vote, an issue that did not receive much attention when the rationale of fighting for democracy was used to justify the Gulf War to the American public.

35. For an extensive analysis of women's relationship to war throughout history see Elshtain, 1987.

36. Jef Huysmans (1995:486) suggests that this dialogic approach, typical of latemodern or postmodern approaches to IR, is inspired by the liberal idea of pluralism and a democratic ethos.

REFERENCES

Benhabib, S. (1987) "The Generalized and the Concrete Other." In *Feminism as Critique: Essays on the Politics of Gender in Late-Capitalist Societies*, edited by S. Benhabib and D. Cornell, pp. 77–95. Cambridge: Polity Press.

Buzan, B. (1991) *People, States and Fear,* 2nd ed., Boulder, CO: Lynne Rienner.

Charlesworth, H., C. Chinkin, and S. Wright (1991) Feminist Approaches to International Law. *American Journal of International Law* 85:613–645.

Cohn, C. (1987) Sex and Death in the Relational World of Defense Intellectuals. *Signs: Journal of Women in Culture and Society* 12(4):687–718.

Cohn, C. (1993) "Wars, Wimps, and Women: Talking Gender and Thinking War." In *Gendering War Talk,* edited by M. Cooke and A. Wollacott, pp. 227–246. Princeton, NJ: Princeton University Press.

Collins, P. H. (1989) The Social Construction of Black Feminist Thought. *Signs: Journal of Women in Culture and Society* 14(4):745–773.

Cox, R. (1981) Social Forces, States and World Orders: Beyond International Theory. *Millennium* 10(2):126–155.

Der Derian, J. (1995) *International Theory: Critical Investigations.* New York: New York University Press.

Elshtain, J. B. (1987) *Women and War.* New York: Basic Books.

Elshtain, J. B. (1990) "The Problem with Peace." In *Women, Militarism and War*, edited by J. B. Elshtain and S. Tobias, pp. 255–266. Savage, MD: Rowman and Littlefield.

Enloe, C. (1990) *Bananas, Beaches and Bases: Making Feminist Sense of International Politics.* Berkeley: University of California Press.

Enloe, C. (1993) *The Morning After: Sexual Politics at the End of the Cold War.* Berkeley: University of California Press.

Flax, J. (1987) Postmodernism and Gender Relations in Feminist Theory. *Signs: Journal of Women in Culture and Society* 12(4):621–643.

Gaddis, J. (1992–93) International Relations Theory and the End of the Cold War. *International Security* 17(3):5–58.

Galtung, J. (1971) A Structural Theory of Imperialism. *Journal of Peace Research* 8:81–117.

Goldstein, J. (1994) *International Relations.* New York: Harper Collins.

Grant, R. (1991) "The Sources of Gender Bias in International Relations Theory." In *Gender and International Relations*, edited by R. Grant and K. Newland, pp. 8–26. Indianapolis: Indiana University Press.

Grant, R., and K. Newland, eds. (1991) *Gender and International Relations.* Indianapolis: Indiana University Press.

Haraway, D. (1988) Situated Knowledges: The Science Question in Feminism and the Privilege of Partial Perspective. *Feminist Studies* 14:575–599.

Harding, S. (1986) *The Science Question in Feminism.* Ithaca, NY: Cornell University Press.

Harding S. (1987) "Introduction: Is There a Feminist Method?" In *Feminism and Methodology*, edited by S. Harding, pp. 1–14. Bloomington: Indiana University Press.

Harding, S. (1991) *Whose Science? Whose knowledge? Thinking from Women's Lives.* Ithaca, NY: Cornell University Press.

Harrington, M. (1992) "What Exactly Is Wrong with the Liberal State as an Agent of Change?" In *Gendered States*, edited by V. S. Peterson. Boulder, CO: Lynne Rienner.

Heckman, S. (1990) *Gender and Knowledge: Elements of a Postmodern Feminism.* Boston: Northeastern University Press.

Hoffmann, S. (1977) An American Social Science: International Relations. *Daedalus* 106(3): 41–60.

Hollis, M., and S. Smith (1990) *Explaining and Understanding International Relations.* Oxford: Oxford University Press.

Hooks, B. (1984) *Feminist Theory: From Margin to Center.* Boston: South End Press.

Huysmans, J. (1995) Post-Cold War Implosion and Globalisation: Liberalism Running Past Itself? *Millennium* 24(3):471–487.

Independent Commission on Disarmament and Security Issues (1982) *Common Security: A Blueprint for Survival.* New York: Simon and Schuster.

Jones, A. (1996) Does "Gender" Make the World Go Round? Feminist Critiques of International Relations. *Review of International Studies* 22:405–429.

Keller, E. F. (1985) *Reflections on Gender and Science.* New Haven, CT: Yale University Press.

Keohane, R. (1988) International Institutions: Two Approaches. *International Studies Quarterly* 36:379–396.

Keohane, R. (1989) International Relations Theory: Contributions of a Feminist Standpoint. *Millennium* 18:245–253.

Kolodziej, E. (1992) Renaissance in Security Studies? Caveat Lector! *International Studies Quarterly* 36:421–438.

Lakatos, I., and A. Musgrave (1970) *Criticism and the Growth of Knowledge.* Cambridge: Cambridge University Press.

Lapid, Y. (1989) The Third Debate: On the Prospects of International Theory in a Post-Positivist Era. *International Studies Quarterly* 33:235–254.

Linklater, A. (1982) *Men and Citizens in the Theory of International Relations.* London: Macmillan.

Martin, J. R. (1994) Methodological Essentialism, False Difference, and Other Dangerous Traps. *Signs: Journal of Women in Culture and Society* 19(3):630–657.

Mathews, J. (1989) Redefining Security. *Foreign Affairs* 68(2):162–177.

Morgenthau, H. (1946) *Scientific Man Vs Power Politics.* Chicago: University of Chicago Press.

Morgenthau, H. (1995) "The Intellectual and Political Functions of Theory." In *International Theory: Critical Investigations,* edited by J. Der Derian, pp. 36–52. New York: New York University Press.

Moser, C. (1991) "Gender Planning in the Third World: Meeting Practical and Strategic Needs." In *Gender and International Relations,* edited by R. Grant and K. Newland, pp. 83–121. Indianapolis: Indiana University Press.

New York Times (1996) "Cause for Sibling Rivalry at Teamsters," by Peter Kilborn, July 17, p. A16.

Nussbaum, M., and J. Glover, eds. (1995) *Women, Culture and Development: A Study of Human Capabilities.* Oxford: Oxford University Press.

Okin, S. M. (1980) *Women in Western Political Thought.* Princeton, NJ: Princeton University Press.

Okin, S. M. (1989) *Justice, Gender and the Family.* New York: Basic Books.

Orford, A. (1996) The Politics of Collective Security. *Michigan Journal of International Law* 17(2):373–409.

Pateman, C. (1988) *The Sexual Contract.* Stanford, CA: Stanford University Press.

Pateman, C. (1994) The Rights of Man and Early Feminism. *Schweizerisches Jahrbuch für Politische Wissenschaft* 34:19–31.

Peterson, V. S. (1992a) *Gendered States: Feminist (Re)Visions of International Relations Theory.* Boulder, CO: Lynne Rienner.

Peterson, V. S. (1992b) Transgressing Boundaries: Theories of Knowledge, Gender and International Relations. *Millennium* 21(2): 183–206.

Peterson, V. S., and A. S. Runyan (1993) *Global Gender Issues.* Boulder, CO: Westview Press.

Pettman, J. (1996) *Worlding Women: A Feminist International Politics*. New York: Routledge.

Rosenberg, E. (1990) Gender. *Journal of American History* 77(1):116–124.

Rourke, J. (1993) *International Politics on the World Stage*, 4th ed. Guilford, CT: Dushkin Publishing Group.

Scott, J. (1986) Gender: A Useful Category of Historical Analysis. *American Historical Review* 91: 1053–1075.

Smith, S. (1997) "New Approaches to International Theory." In *The Globalization of World Politics*, edited by J. Baylis and S. Smith, pp. 165–190. Oxford: Oxford University Press.

Stiehm, J. (1982) The Protected, the Protector, the Defender. *Women's Studies International Forum* 5(3/4):367–376.

Sylvester, C. (1987) Some Dangers in Merging Feminist and Peace Projects. *Alternatives* 12(4):493–509.

Sylvester, C. (1994a) Empathetic Cooperation: A Feminist Method for IR. *Millennium* 23(2): 315–334.

Sylvester, C. (1994b) *Feminist Theory and International Relations in a Postmodern Era*. Cambridge: Cambridge University Press.

Tannen, D. (1990) *You Just Don't Understand: Women and Men in Conversation*. New York: William Morrow.

Tickner, J. A. (1988) Hans Morgenthau's Principles of Political Realism: A Feminist Reformulation. *Millennium* 17(3):429–440.

Tickner, J. A. (1992) *Gender in International Relations: Feminist Perspectives on Achieving Global Security*. New York: Columbia University Press.

Tickner, J. A. (1994) "Feminist Perspectives on Peace and World Security in the Post–Cold War Era." In *Peace and World Security Studies: A Curriculum Guide*, 6th ed., edited by M. Klare, pp. 43–54. Boulder, CO: Lynne Rienner.

Tobias, S. (1990) "Shifting Heroisms: The Uses of Military Service in Politics." In *Women, Militarism and War*, edited by J.B. Elshtain and S.Tobias, pp.163–185. Savage, MD: Rowman and Littlefield.

Tong, R. (1989) *Feminist Thought: A Comprehensive Introduction*. Boulder, CO: Westview Press.

Toulmin, S. (1990) *Cosmopolis: The Hidden Agenda of Modernity*. Chicago: University of Chicago Press.

Tronto, J. (1993) *Moral Boundaries: A Political Argument for an Ethic of Care*. New York: Routledge.

Tuana, N. (1992) "Reading Philosophy as a Woman." In *Against Patriarchal Thinking*, edited by M. Pellikaan-Engel, pp. 47–54. Amsterdam: VU University Press.

Ullman, R. (1983) Redefining Security. *International Security* 8(1):129–153.

United Nations (1995) *Human Development Report*. Oxford: Oxford University Press.

Walker, R. B. J. (1989) History and Structure in the Theory of International Relations. *Millennium* 18(2):163–183.

Walker, R. B. J. (1992) "Gender and Critique in the Theory of International Relations." In *Gendered States*, edited by V. S. Peterson, pp.179–202. Boulder, CO: Lynne Rienner.

Walt, S. (1991) The Renaissances of Security Studies. *International Studies Quarterly* 35:211–239.

Waltz, K. (1979) *Theory of International Politics*. Reading, MA: Addison-Wesley.

Weber, C. (1994) Good Girls, Little Girls and Bad Girls. *Millennium* 23(2):337–348.

Whitworth, S. (1989) Gender in the Inter-Paradigm Debate. *Millennium* 18(2):265–272.

Wight, M. (1995) "Why Is There No International Theory?" In *International Theory: Critical Investigations*, edited by J. Der Derian, pp.15–35. New York: New York University Press.

Wolfers, A. (1962) *Discord and Colloboration: Essays on International Politics*. Baltimore, MD: Johns Hopkins University Press.

Yost, D. (1994) Political Philosophy and the Theory of International Relations. *International Affairs* 70(2):263-290.

Zalewski, M. (1995) "Well, What is the Feminist Perspective on Bosnia?" *International Affairs* 71(2):339-356.

QUESTIONS

1. According to Tickner, why does the feminist perspective on international relations continue to remain outside the mainstream of traditional approaches to IR theory?

2. How would a feminist analysis of global terrorism differ from that of a realist?

24.   Beyond Dichotomy: Conversations Between International Relations and Feminist Theory

Robert O. Keohane

The following reading presents Robert Keohane's response to J. Ann Tickner's (reading 23) contention that feminist perspectives on international relations are misunderstood by conventional IR theorists. Keohane asserts that much of the fault lies with feminists themselves. He decries the excessive politicization of the debate between feminists and traditional theorists and asserts that this problem prevents serious discussion on feminist IR scholarship. Keohane concludes that feminist IR theorists must do more than offer critiques of mainstream IR theory.

Robert Keohane is James B. Duke Professor of political science at Harvard University. He is the author of numerous books and articles.

Ann Tickner's article in this journal, "You Just Don't Understand: Troubled Engagements Between Feminists and IR Theorists," seeks to generate a missing debate: between feminist students of international relations and what she denotes (1997:613) as "methodologically conventional IR scholars," who seek knowledge through scientific, or positivist, methodologies. Professor Tickner points out that the states at the heart of international relations theory are deeply gendered hierarchies, and that such hierarchies also structure transnational relations. Conventional definitions of "security" miss the real personal insecurity suffered by peo-

From *International Studies Quarterly* (1998), Vol. 42 (1), pp. 194-199. Reprinted by permission of Blackwell Publishing.

ple, especially women, who are excluded from power, autonomy, and even from respect, as a result of gendered patterns of social relations. Tickner suggests a research agenda for understanding the connections that she asserts between these unequal social relations, on the one hand, and distributional outcomes and external security-seeking behavior, on the other. These are important contributions, and I hope that Tickner's thoughtful argument will provoke deep reflection and wide discussion.

The absence of sustained responses by established IR theorists frustrates Professor Tickner, for good reason. She suggests that one of the reasons for IR theorists' silence is ignorance of the contributions that feminist thinking has made. Another reason, however, may be that the politicization of debate on issues related to feminist scholarship has meant that IR scholars fear that if they engage seriously in this debate, they will not provoke a serious discussion but will instead become targets for ad hominem attacks on their motives. My own experience unfortunately provides some support for such fears. On the whole, feminist scholars met my own 1989 efforts to point up connections between institutionalist theory and feminist analysis with silence; the most prominent discussion (to my knowledge) accused me of attempts at manipulation and cooptation, but failed to deal with the substantive issues that I had raised (Weber, 1994). Weber's rhetoric about "good girls and bad girls" was amusing, but it did not constitute a serious attempt to discuss real issues.

Since the issues are important ones, and Tickner's article is a major statement, I have accepted the editor's invitation to engage once again in this conversation. My first response is to welcome work that has introduced concepts of gender into international relations. Clearly, gender permeates social life, and is likely therefore to have profound, and largely unnoticed, effects on the actions of states and on transnational relations. Tickner's book, *Gender in International Relations* (1992), is probably the most important work about gender and international relations to date, and certainly the pioneering feminist statement on the issue. Ann Tickner is a bridge-builder between scholars with broadly common purposes but very different preoccupations. Her work helps in an insightful way to cross barriers to synergistic syntheses of orientations in the study of world politics. At what is called, ironically in light of feminist theory, the "domestic" level, societies construct gendered roles, whose impact on international and transnational behavior is virtually unknown to us, because we haven't studied it. Tickner is right to tell us that we need to do so. At the end of this essay, I will return to the research program that Tickner suggests and outline some possible directions that I think scholarly work, informed both by IR theory and by feminism, could take.

THREE MISLEADING DICHOTOMIES

Taking scholarly work seriously, however, involves not only trying to read it sympathetically, but also offering criticism of arguments that do not seem convincing. My starting point is to accept an insight of much feminist writing: conceptual *dichotomies* create misleading stereotypes. Professor Tickner mentions four: rational/irrational, fact/value, universal/particular, and public/private. As feminists point out, gender—the social construction of sexual differences—operates largely through the use of such stereotypes.

What I will argue here is that Professor Tickner herself relies too much on three key *dichotomies*, which seem to me to have misleading implications, and to hinder constructive debate. The first of these *dichotomies* contrasts "critical theory" with "problem-solving" theory. "Problem-solving [theory] takes the world as it finds it and implicitly accepts the prevailing order as its framework" (1997:619). The second *dichotomy* pits "hermeneutic, historically-based, humanistic and philosophical traditions" against positivist epistemologies modeled on the natural sciences. Finally, Tickner contrasts a view that emphasizes the social construction of reality with an atomistic, asocial conception of behavior governed by the laws of nature (1997:616, 618–9). International relations theory is portrayed as problem-solving, positivist, and asocial; feminist theory as critical, post-positivist, and sociological.

These *dichotomies* have some rhetorical force; arguably, recent international relations theory has been insufficiently critical, too committed to covering law epistemology, and too mechanistic and asocial, in its reliance on states as actors and on economic logic to analyze their behavior. But few major IR theorists fit the stereotype of being at the problem-solving, positivist, and asocial ends of all three *dichotomies*. As Tickner herself points out, Hans J. Morgenthau had a deeply normative purpose: to prevent the recurrence of war generated by ideologies such as fascism and communism. Since Morgenthau was a refugee from Nazism, he hardly accepted the prevailing world order of the late 1930s and early 1940s as the framework for his analysis! Kenneth N. Waltz, the leader in neorealist theory, has famously relied on "socializa-

tion" as a major (although insufficiently specified) process in world politics, which makes him a poor candidate for a proponent of "asocial" theories. And Stephen Walt—one of Tickner's targets—has been highly critical of game-theoretic methodology.

The problem with Tickner's *dichotomies* however, goes much deeper. The *dichotomies* should be replaced by continua, with the dichotomous characterizations at the poles. Each analyst of world politics has to locate herself or himself somewhere along the dimensions between critical and problem-solving theory, nomothetic and narrative epistemology, and a social or structural conception of international relations. In my view, none of the ends of these continua are the optimal places to rest one's perspective.

Criticism of the world, by itself, becomes a jeremiad, often resting implicitly on a utopian view of human potential. Without analysis, furthermore, it constitutes merely the opinion of one or a number of people. On the other hand, implicit or complacent acceptance of the world as it is would rob the study of international relations of much of its meaning. How could one identify "problems" without criticism at some level? The issue is not problem-solving vs. critical theory—a convenient device for discarding work that one does not wish to accept—but how deeply the criticism should go. For example, most students of war study it because they hope to expose its evils or to control it in some way: few do so to glorify war as such. But the depth of the critique varies. Does the author reject certain acts of warfare, all warfare, all coercion, or the system of states itself? The deeper the criticism, the more wide-ranging the questions. Narrowly problem-solving work, as in much policy analysis, often ignores the most important causal factors in a situation because they are not manipulable in the short run. However, the more critical and wide-ranging an author's perspective, the more difficult it is to do comparative empirical analysis. An opponent of some types of war can compare the causes of different wars, as a way to help to eliminate those that are regarded as pernicious; but the opponent of the system of states has to imagine the counterfactual situation of a system without states.

The second *dichotomy*—positivist vs. post-positivist—is also misleading. There is a wide range of adherence, in international relations, to more or less nomothetic theoretical claims, and to aspirations of greater or less adherence to canons associated with natural science. Scientific success is not the attainment of objective truth, but the attainment of wider agreement on descriptive facts and causal relationships, based on transparent and replicable methods. Even those who seek scientific generalization recognize the importance of descriptive work, and of investigating issues that are not amenable to statistical analysis, due to their complexity, contingency, and lack of homogeneity between the units to be compared (King, Keohane, and Verba, 1994). No serious students of international relations expect to discover meaningful universal laws that operate deterministically, since they recognize that no generalization is meaningful without specification of its scope conditions.

The point is that a sophisticated view of science overcomes the objectivist-subjectivist *dichotomy*, and forces the investigator to make interrelated choices about purposes, subject matter, and methods. One can recognize that knowledge is socially constructed without giving up on efforts to widen intersubjective agreement about important issues, and to specify more fully the conditions under which some important outcomes are more or less likely to occur. For instance, our current knowledge of the conditions under which various strategies in international crises lead to war or settlement (Gelpi, 1997; Huth, 1996) is surely an advance over aphorisms such as "to achieve peace, prepare for war," or "deterrence does (or does not) work." But it would be foolish to believe that one could understand the Cuban Missile Crisis simply on the basis of generalizations, however valid, about crisis management. Narratives, and an understanding of personal psychology, play an essential role in understanding unique events. Finally, the social-asocial *dichotomy* is misleading because social behavior consists of individual choices constrained by social, economic, and political structures, and by institutions. Choices are made on the basis of normative, descriptive, and causal beliefs, all of which are deeply socially constructed. It is a platitude that our beliefs are culturally conditioned and transmitted. Hence all human action is in a profound sense social. Yet as Marx said, people make their own history, but not "as they please." Choices are made within structures of demography, material scarcity, and power—and within institutions that affect the incentives and opportunities available to actors, as well as constraining them.

It seems ill-advised to locate oneself on the extreme end of any of these three continua: it is not sensible to choose between critical and problem-solving theory; commitment to nomothetic, objective science and attention to particularity; emphasis on social construction of reality and on constraints—material, political, and institutional. Aspects of all of these loci of attention can enrich the study of international relations. On each continuum, trade-offs exist: movements along the continuum achieve gains on one dimension, but incur losses on another. Where to locate oneself depends, among other things, on the condition of world politics at the moment, the state of our knowledge of the issues, and the nature of the problem to be investigated.

RESEARCH DIRECTIONS

Recent constructivist work in international relations (Finnemore, 1996; Katzenstein, 1996) has demonstrated how theoretical imagination and empirical exploration can be enhanced, and made more persuasive to the community of international relations scholars, by a commitment to a relatively conventional epistemology. As Katzenstein, Jepperson, and Wendt suggest, "[T]he literature is prone to conflate substantive and theoretical differences with methodological ones, as if a theoretical departure necessarily depends on some methodological uniqueness. It need not" (Katzenstein, Jepperson, and Wendt, 1996:68). Constructivist work in international relations has articulated new concepts, identified puzzles unexplained by previous theory, and begun to articulate interesting hypotheses about behavior. Since this work is exploratory, the concepts are not always clearly specified and the evidence is often fragmentary rather than comprehensive; but the procedures begin followed are consistent with a broad conception of the scientific method. Other scholars, not previously committed to these views, are paying more attention to work of scholars such as Finnemore and Katzenstein than to arguments that conflate similar theoretical innovations with dismissal of the desirability of systematic, disciplined efforts to evaluate propositions with evidence.

Careful scientific work does not have to aggregate homogeneous units, much less use quantitative data. When events are unique—whether the subject is dinosaur extinction, a murder, or a particular path-dependent sequence of political actions—the investigator may have to act more like a detective than like a statistician. Both the basic method of social science remains the same: make a conjecture about causality; formulate that conjecture as an hypothesis, consistent with established theory (and perhaps deduced from it, at least in part); specify the observable implications of the hypothesis; test for whether those implications obtain in the real world; and overall, ensure that one's procedures are publicly known and replicable. Relevant evidence has to be brought to bear on hypotheses generated by theory for the theory to be meaningful.

Feminists give us wise advice to dispense with sexist *dichotomies*. I think that conversations among students of international relations—nonfeminist, feminist, neofeminist, quasi-feminist, and postfeminist—will be advanced if we extend this advice to common but misleading *dichotomies* about theory and method in our own discipline. We need more cogent contingent generalizations above international relations—scientific because based on publicly known methods and checked by a community of scholars, working both critically and cooperatively. These generalizations will not stand forever—no science does—but if successful they could command wider intersubjective agreement, forming the basis for more discriminating and subtle analysis. The questions asked, and the methods, will reflect our preoccupations and critical dissatisfactions as members of particular societies at a particular time: hence the findings will indeed be socially constructed. Furthermore, insofar as these generalizations are worthwhile, they will not claim excessive comprehensiveness: events that follow pathways created by individual actions are unlikely to be meaningfully explained by covering laws. Most of all, we should all be sufficiently humble to recognize that the points on which we have chosen to place our emphasis—the trade-offs we accept—are not privileged.

Ann Tickner refers to criticisms of feminist thinkers by international relations scholars for allegedly not having a research program, and suggests a response: a research program that links gendered hierarchies—domestically and transnationally—with classic external behavior, such as actions affecting war and peace. It seems to me that such a research program could be enormously fruitful. We now have much reason to believe that democracies behave differently, in international relations, than autocracies. Do countries with highly inegalitarian gendered hierarchies behave differently from those with less inequality at home? Like democracies, are they less inclined to fight each other? Feminists can be interpreted, in neopositivist terms, as proposing a new explanatory variable for the study of international relations: the degree to which socially constructed gendered hierarchies are important. Analysis of the effects of gendered hierarchies could proceed by issue area, by historical time period, by country, or through a combination of the three.

Since we know that intentionality and consequences are not tightly linked in international relations, we should not assume that the consequences in international relations of more egalitarian practices within some societies will necessarily be benign. Supposing that increased gender equality leads to less aggression, we might well expect that countries with relatively less hierarchical internal structures would not fight each other. But their relationships with states with more inegalitarian gender relationships would need to be investigated. Perhaps states with less gender hierarchy could resolve conflict more easily; but it is also possible that they would be more easily bullied, or would become more moralistic, leading eventually to more serious crises and perhaps warfare. To continue with the democracy analogy, democracies are quite warlike toward nondemocracies, although they are disinclined to fight other democracies. It would be worthwhile to explore such questions, with an open mind about what the answers will be.

Comparable questions could be posed about transnational relations. To what extent do gendered inequalities within societies extend to transnational relations—as, for instance, in tolerating or even encouraging the operation of brothels near military bases, or in the hiring practices of Japanese-based multinational enterprises operating in the United States? Once again, however, questions will not be enough: feminist IR scholars will need to supply answers that will convince others—including those not ideologically predisposed to being convinced. Specifying their propositions, and providing systematically gathered evidence to test these propositions, will be essential: scientific method, in the broadest sense, is the best path to-ward convincing current nonbelievers of the validity of the message that fem-inists are seeking to deliver. We will only "understand" each other if IR scholars are open to the important questions that feminist theories raise, and if feminists are willingto formulate their hypotheses in ways that are testableand falsifiable—with evidence.

REFERENCES

Finnemore, M. (1996) *National Interests in International Society*. Ithaca, NY: Cornell Uni-versity Press.

Gelpi, C. (1997) "Crime and Punishment: The Role of Norms in Crisis Bargaining." *American Political Science Review* 91:339–360.

Huth, P. (1996) *Standing Your Ground: Territorial Disputes and International Conflict*. Ann Arbor: University of Michigan Press.

Jepperson, R. L., P. J. Katzenstein, and A. Wendt (1996) "Norms, Identity and Culture in Na-tional Security." In Katzenstein, 1996:33-75.

Katzenstein, P. J., Ed. (1996) *The Culture of National Security: Norms and Identity in World Politics*. New York: Columbia University Press.

King, G., R. O. Keohane, and S. Verba (1994) *Designing Social Inquiry: Scientific Inference in Qualitative Research*. Princeton, NJ: Princeton University Press.

Tickner, J. A. (1992) *Gender in International Relations: Feminist Perspectives on Achieving Global Security*. New York: Columbia University Press.

Tickner, J. A. (1997) "You Just Don't Understand: Troubled Engagements Between Feminists and IR Theorists." *International Studies Quarterly* 41:611–632.

Weber, C. (1994) "Good Girls, Little Girls and Bad Girls." *Millennium* 23:337-348.

QUESTIONS

1. According to Keohane, what are the primary weaknesses of feminist ap-proaches to IR theory?

2. How might a proponent of feminist IR theory respond to Keohane's critique?

---

25. Feminism and Constructivism: Worlds Apart or Sharing the Middle Ground

Birgit Locher and Elisabeth Prügl

The selection by Birgit Locher and Elisabeth Prügl offers some unique insights into the similarities and differences between constructivist and feminist approaches to IR theory. The authors acknowledge that both theories share a fundamental agree-ment on the importance of the role of social construction of ideas and identities in

From *International Studies Quarterly* (2001), Vol. 45, pp. 111-129. Reprinted by permission of Black-well Publishing.

understanding international politics. However, the authors also contend that constructivism ignores key feminist epistemological insights and that there are profound differences between feminists and constructivists.

Elisabeth M. Prügl is Graduate Director in the Department of International Relations and Associate Professor of International Relations at Florida International University.

Birgit Locher is a lecturer at Bremes University.

Seeking greater understanding across theoretical divides, and the scientific and political cultures that sustain them, might be the best model if feminist international theory is to have a future within the discipline.

—J. A. Tickner (1997:630)

We will only "understand" each other if IR scholars are open to the important questions that feminist theories raise, and if feminists are willing to formulate their hypotheses in ways that are testable—and falsifiable—with evidence.

—R. O. Keohane (1998:197)

The imagery of increasingly better understanding based on clearer and more open communication and rational tactics misses a crucial issue. This is that what structures these debates "remains unspeakable [and unhearable] within the very terms in which the [debates] proceed." I use Judith Butler's point here to argue that it seems incongruous to expect a fruitful outcome (for feminists) from a debate between feminists and mainstream International Relations theorists if the debate is structured around representations of woman as

derivative, marginal and intellectually suspect.

—M. Zalewski (1998:864)

"You just don't understand"—this is how Ann Tickner (1997) entitled her description of the "troubled engagements between feminists and IR theorists," which, she argues, have been characterized by misunderstanding and a disregard for feminist interventions. Tickner locates the reasons for the trouble in differing ontologies and epistemologies. Robert Keohane's response to Tickner seems to confirm her argument: "IR scholars" will understand only if feminists renounce "ideology" and commit themselves to "the basic method of social science" narrowly conceived as hypothesis testing (Keohane, 1998:196). In light of this position, Marysia Zalewski's conclusion is compelling: feminists and mainstream international relations (IR) scholars will never understand each other as long as the quest for understanding is based on "the politics, epistemologies and ontologies of the other," on a logic that maintains woman in "repression, censorship and nonrecognition" (Zalewski, 1998:864, quoting Irigaray). Indeed, many feminists have found it possible to go on with their empirical research only after shaking off the strictures of the discipline (e.g. Enloe, 1989, 1993; Moon, 1997). Others continue the work of deconstructing the discipline and the practices it gives rise to (e.g. Weber, 1999). Apparently, they eschew the very goal of shared epistemologies and ontologies: "We will never convert someone who is not already converted. We will never touch the heart that lives on another planet" (Zalewski, 1998:864, quoting Hélène Cixous).

In this article we seek to move forward a debate that seems to have reached a dead end. Taking up again Tickner's quest to find a terrain of understanding between feminists and IR theorists, we suggest that the third (or fourth, see Wæver, 1996) debate of the late 1990s has provided a new basis for an engagement between feminists and the mainstream. Specifically, we argue that constructivism shares ontological grounds with feminism and thus provides a unique window of opportunity for understanding.

With ideas and concepts borrowed from sociology, constructivism made a prominent appearance in IR in the late 1980s. Since then, the U.S. mainstream has appointed it the grand alternative to rationalist approaches, whereas in Europe it is more frequently seen as occupying the middle ground between rational-choice approaches and postmodernism (Adler, 1997; Katzenstein, Keohane, and Krasner, 1998; Checkel, 1998; Price and Reus-Smit, 1998). In positioning constructivism as a new middle, Europeans avoid the silencing of postmodern approaches typical in the United States. But describing constructivism as a third force occupying a consensual middle ground is perilous for other reasons. Advocates of such a positioning skirt basic questions of epistemology, ontology, and axiology while morphing fundamental incompatibilities into questions of ranking and ordering variables and of more rigorous and more parsimonious explanations of reality. In effect, they fail to take seriously the postpositivist critique.

In using the language of a middle ground we are thus entering treacherous territory and some words of caution are in order. We do not advocate a theory merger following the path of "shotgun wedding, unhappy marriage, no-fault divorce" that Shelton and Aggar (1993) identified in the troubled relationship of feminism and Marxism. This would risk papering over considerable diversity among feminists and constructivists as well as making light of profound differences between the two. Furthermore, it would risk styling feminism as supplementary to constructivism, thus reproducing its marginality by framing it as derivative. As Ann Tickner reminds us (1997:620), feminism is a rich body of theory that offers much more than adding the particularity of women and gender to a general picture. Or, in Cynthia Weber's words (1994:337), feminism does not need a father theory; it is neither a "good girl" nor a "little" or a "bad girl." Thus, although our primary goal is to seek points of dialogue, as Tickner suggests in the epigraph, we also want to reveal points of friction that emerge from the othering of women that Zalewski finds characteristic.

We base our dialogue on the idea that feminism and constructivism share an ontology and develop the notion of a "feminist constructivism" that defines our own standpoint. Many feminists in IR agree that gender, one of their most important analytical categories,[1] is a social construct. Indeed, feminists in IR were talking about social construction long before the notion captured a broad audience. We argue in this article that constructivist ontology forms a "planet" on which both feminists and (at least some) IR theorists could live and talk.

However, many feminists are profoundly uncomfortable with the styling of constructivism as the grand alternative or new middle ground, and most self-identified constructivists have followed the example of most of their rationalist colleagues in ignoring feminist literature and gender analysis. Our challenge is therefore to stake out a middle ground that does not obliterate feminism and to search for a terrain that enables engagement on equal terms.

We believe that a dialogue between feminism and constructivism is important because the two approaches add to each other and in combination can yield better theoretical and empirical understandings of the world. Elsewhere (Locher and Prügl, 2001) we argue that constructivism contributes to feminism a theory of agency. Here we reverse the emphasis, showing that feminism contributes to constructivism an understanding of power as an integral element of processes of construction. Because they leave the social construction of power undertheorized, constructivists lack the tools to explain how gender and power reproduce, how and why certain constructs emerge as more influential than others. They miss an important part of the empirical reality of international politics. Furthermore, constructivists not sensitive to power as a social and gendered construct risk epistemological inconsistencies. If constructivism wants to be more than liberalism in a new cloth, if it wants to retain its critical potential, it needs to take seriously the epistemological critiques of feminists and postmodernists.[2]

We proceed in two stages. First, we explore the intersections of feminist and constructivist thought in the area of ontology, highlighting compatibilities and problems. Second, we explore feminist and constructivist epistemologies by problematizing the position of the knowing subject. We conclude by probing the empirical relevance of our theoretical arguments. We locate ourselves on the borderlines between feminism and constructivism, attempting an engagement based on empathetic cooperation, a feminist method Christine Sylvester has proposed for IR. This approach entails "a process of positional slippage that occurs when one listens seriously to the concerns, fears, and agendas of those one is unaccustomed to heeding when building social theory, taking on board rather than dismissing, finding in the concerns of others borderlands of one's own concerns and fears" (Sylvester, 1994:317). In adopting such shifting positions we negotiate our own ambiguous standpoints not only between constructivism and feminism but also between the U.S. and the German academic worlds that we have experienced and that separate us now.

AN ONTOLOGY OF BECOMING

The new enthusiasm in the United States about constructivism as the alternative to rational choice and as a middle ground between utilitarian approaches and postmodernism in the European debate imposes an unwarranted homogeneity on constructivist scholarship. In practice, self-identified constructivists subscribe to a diverse set of sometimes incompatible propositions. Contention exists around core assumptions and philosophical foundations. Some subsume constructivism under writings probing ideational causation (e.g., Yee, 1996), some take norms and social context as its crucial explanatory variables (e.g., Finnemore, 1996; Katzenstein, 1996;

Risse-Kappen, 1996), some consider institutionalization and intersubjectivity its key concerns (Ruggie, 1998a, 1998b), whereas others find its central preoccupation to be language (Onuf, 1989; Fierke, 1997). Some constructivists draw their insights from philosophical realism, some from the sociological classics (Durkheim and Weber, often via Anthony Giddens), some from Wittgenstein and speech act theory, some from the writings of French poststructuralists.[3]

But what diverse constructivisms do have in common is an ontology: a way to depict the world. Constructivists describe the world not as one that is, but as one that is in the process of becoming; they replace a "positional" with a "transformational ontology" (Dessler, 1989:444; Ruggie, 1998a:863; Kubálková, Onuf, and Kowert, 1998; see also Wendt, 1987:355). Taking their clues from sociology, constructivists argue that international life is social: international relations are constructed when people talk, follow rules and norms, are guided by world views or institutions, perform rituals, and engage in various social practices. The constructivist focus of inquiry therefore is social phenomena, such as norms, rules, institutions, language, or productions. These phenomena mediate agency (ontologically privileged in behavioralist and rational choice approaches) and structure (ontologically privileged in structural realism and world systems theory). Rather than subscribing to the incompatibility of explanations from different levels of analysis, constructivists argue that agency and structure are co-constituted.[4] Structures reproduce through the practices of knowledgeable agents while at the same time enabling these practices.[5] Depending on their orientation, constructivists variously take norms, rules, institutions,

or language as the media of this reproduction. These social forms are intimately implicated in world politics not only because of their regulative, but also because of their constitutive, effects: they guide conduct while at the same time creating objects and agents.

An ontology of becoming allows constructivists to account for aspects of world politics that neorealism and neoliberalism obscure. First, constructivists have put in the center of attention the constitution of international agents. No longer are sovereign states and other international agents considered as given and preexisting entities, but national interests, state identities, social movments, and transnational networks appear in need of explanation (e.g., Wendt, 1994; Risse-Kappen, 1995a; Finnemore, 1996; Kowert, 1998; Neumann, 1999). Second, because they focus on the construction of interests and identities, constructivists can explain shifts in strategies. For example, war making and negotiations are not instrumental tools toward an end but constitute the enactment of diverse games and rules on which reasoning actors draw (Fierke, 1996; Duffy, Frederking, and Tucker, 1998). Third, in combining agency and structure, constructivists have been able to develop rich understandings of social change. This has made the approach attractive to those who seek to explain the transition from the medieval to the Westphalian system, the end of the Cold War, or the transformation of world politics through the strengthening of "global civil society" (Koslovski and Kratochwil, 1994; Klotz and Lynch, 1996; Ruggie, 1998a).[6]

Like constructivism, feminism is diverse in range and orientation, and not all feminists employ a constructivist ontology. Yet, among Western feminists the contention that gender, and indeed woman, is a social construct has been influential. Liberal ideas of women's equality, socialist ideas of a sexual division of labor, the Freudian suggestion that identities are produced, and functionalist ideas on sex roles all had come together by the middle of the twentieth century to thoroughly undermine any suggestion that gender was a biological or natural given (Connell, 1987). Writers in the second wave of the feminist movement in Europe and North America linked these insights to an analysis of women's subordination, suggesting that gender not only was a social construct, but also created women's oppression. Simone de Beauvoir's *The Second Sex*, published in France in 1949 and in the United States in 1952, was a landmark documenting this relationship, drawing on structuralist thinking. Increasingly, and in parallel to movement slogans that suggested "the personal is political" and "the political is personal," feminist writings explored gender messages in areas beyond households and personal identities: in myths, ideologies, and patriarchal institutions, such as the family, the state, and the division of labor (e.g., Barrett, 1988). Working in different research traditions, feminists approached these themes in very different ways.

When we juxtapose feminism and constructivism in the following, we primarily refer to the writings of feminists that are self-identified scholars of international relations, many affiliated with European and North American associations of international relations or political science, teaching in various (mostly U.S., Canadian, British, and Australian) universities. They constitute a community of scholars who read and refer to each other's work. A set of programmatic writings (including Enloe, 1989; Tickner, 1992; Peterson, 1992a; Sylvester, 1994; Whitworth, 1994) helped create this network of scholars about a decade ago and still provide an important point of reference. Yet, while feminist IR scholars share a (sometimes vague) commitment to the field of international relations, most are committed to the notion of social construction, albeit on the basis of diverse theoretical and empirical orientations (compare Steans, 1998).

Starting from critical theory, social construction appears as an interaction of the Coxian triad of material conditions, institutions, and ideas in the works of Sandra Whitworth (1994) and Deborah Stienstra (1994). In this perspective, social construction designates an opposition to the material world and is characterized by malleability and context dependency. V. Spike Peterson combines the structuralist notion of a fundamental dichotomy between genders with an understanding that people are socialized into their genders while social expectations and ideologies reproduce notions of masculinity and femininity. She refers to gender as a "systematic social construction that dichotomizes identities, behaviors, and expectations as masculine and feminine." It is, according to her, not "simply a trait of individuals but an institutionalized feature of social life" (1992b:194; see also Peterson and Runyan, 1993:5–7). Tickner (1992:6), following Connell (1987), introduces the notion of "hegemonic masculinity," a cluster of character traits including toughness, courage, power, independence, and physical strength that define a cultural ideal. Sustained through its opposition to devalued masculinities and femininities, hegemonic masculinity perpetuates masculinized power structures, including those that frame international relations as a practice and a field. The notion of hegemonic masculinity has lent itself to studying identities in international affairs by employing an understanding of social construction as discursive. Charlotte Hooper (1998, 2000), for example, analyzes discursive practices of world politics and discourses of globalization as sites of social construction. Similarly, Christine Sylvester (1994, 1998) draws on discourse theories to develop an understanding of social construction that privileges "temporary homesteads" over stable identities. For her, "socially constructed" means "that men and women are the stories that have been told about 'men' and 'women' and the constraints and opportunities that have hereby arisen as we take to our proper places" (Sylvester, 1994:4). Cynthia Enloe (1989, 1993) perhaps most explicitly combines the modern and postmodern tendencies revealed in these approaches. She claims that relationships between governments depend on the construction and reconstruction of gender and that such relations produce certain notions of femininity and masculinity. Gender in her work emerges as constitutive of international relations and vice versa, global politics create gender.

We would do force to these writings if we were to subsume them under the label "feminist constructivist." But we do borrow from them eclectically to develop our own feminist constructivist position. This position insists that agents make world politics but also understands masculinities and femininities as an effect of such politics. It furthermore suggests that the focus on identity does not exhaust feminist constructivist approaches to IR. Such approaches can subsume as well studies of socialization, institutions, norms, and other social phenomena currently underrepresented in the study of gender in IR.

Feminist constructivists share with other constructivists in IR an ontology of becoming. This, however, does not preclude differences. First, IR feminists insist that gender is pervasive in an international world that is socially constructed: "the personal is international" and "the international is personal" (Enloe, 1989:196). Thus, gender inheres in all international politics. It has shaped and enabled processes of state formation, war and peace, and revolutions (Peterson, 1992a; Tétreault, 1994; Pettman, 1996). It has informed international political economics (Marchand and Parpart, 1995; Han and Ling, 1998; Chin, 1998; Adler, 1999), is pervasive in international organizations and the practices of global governance (Whitworth, 1994; Stienstra, 1994; Meyer and Prügl, 1999; Prügl, 1999), and has shaped foreign policies (Moon, 1997). For IR feminists it is impossible to talk about any of these processes without talking about gender. In contrast, constructivists tend to consider gender subtexts in IR as marginal to explanations of most phenomena that interest them and gender politics outside the realm of power politics.

At the core of this divergence are different conceptions of power. Unlike most constructivists, IR feminists consider power a social construct and gender a code for power. Many have adopted (explicitly Tickner, 1992:7, 1997:615; Grant and Newland, 1991) Joan Scott's definition of gender as consisting of two elements: social construction and power. According to Scott, "gender is a constitutive element of social relationships based on perceived differences between the sexes, and gender is a primary way of signifying relationships of power" (1986:1067). The first part asserts a reality of social construction: gender creates social forms based on a binary construction of masculinity and femininity. The second part infuses power into social construction: messages of gender always also express messages of super- and subordination. Few constructivists in IR have similarly theorized power as a social construct, often treating it either as a material quantity or as located in the institutions of the state.

Among feminists in IR, two approaches to power stand out. The first conceives of gender constructions as part of a larger system of subordination, typically capitalism or, less commonly, patriarchy, or some intersection of the two. It is tied to the Gramscian tradition as elaborated by Robert Cox and often employed by those feminists whose empirical work focuses on the global political economy. Here gender constructions emerge as an ideology, revealed in beliefs, ideas, and institutions that stabilize the system. Power is located in such ideologies and in this way is external to identities. Indeed, writings in this tradition are rarely concerned with identity formation as an exclusionary process but instead treat gender as a social status that intersects with other statuses (e.g., class, ethnicity) to realize various contextually specific forms of super- and subordination. According to authors taking this approach, states, firms, and international organizations play a crucial role in the construction of gender. They create and diffuse a hegemonic ideology that facilitates certain forms of capitalism, and gender constructs are part of this ideology (e.g., Whitworth, 1994; Stienstra, 1994; Chin, 1998; various chapters in Kofman and Youngs, 1996).

A second group of IR feminists does not describe power as ideology but sees it located in the formation of identities. These writers argue that the subordination of women is enmeshed in modernist discourses that understand the self as the source of agency and create this self in opposition to an "other" that provides a reference point of what the self is not. Coded in terms of race, ethnicity, gender, and other status markers, the self emerges through a denigration of this "other." Gender is a particularly powerful code because it is co-constituted with sex, its presumably "natural" correlate. Binary metaphysics, language, and symbolic order structurally connect gender and sex, merging biology and culture and creating an all-embracing and apparently natural gendered reality. As a code for power, gender and sex thus contribute to anchoring modern identities. Gender constructions are not ideologies that impose themselves from the outside but a foundational aspect of the modern subject, a necessary ingredient in the formation of identities. Drawing on the understanding of gender dichotomies as an underlying element of subject formation, IR feminists have argued that such dichotomies map onto the pervasive oppositions that organize modern science, politics, and international relations: subject/object, fact/value, public/private, protector/protected (Tickner, 1992:6–8; Peterson, 1992b:202). They have explored in particular the way in which gendered others and naturalized identities have enabled particular security practices, finding a connection between the construction of hegemonics masculinities and the legitimization of wars (see various chapters in Zalewski and Parpart, 1998; Elshtain, 1987; Cohn, 1987; Tickner, 1992:ch. 2; Weber, 1998).

Constructivists have dealt with power in various ways, but only a few have taken the analysis of power as far as feminists have (compare also Doty, 1997).

First are those who have not put power in the center of their analysis but have implied two conventional understandings: domestically, power means legitimate authority; internationally, power is a material resource. In both cases, power is treated as a quantity that actors (states, militaries, interest groups) have and that they use differently depending on political cultures or identities (e.g., various articles in Katzenstein, 1996; also Wendt, 1994). Understanding power as a quantity would take feminists no further than to say that women don't have it. It tells little about how power is constructed and reproduced. A second way in which constructivists have talked about power is by suggesting that institutions both create the world and delimit possibilities (e.g., Wendt and Duvall, 1989). The suggestion that institutions delimit the world is familiar to critical feminist theorists; the idea that power both enables and constrains is a central element of feminist writings concerned with identities. A third constructivist understanding of power pushes the issue further and reformulates, in constructivist language, the insight of feminist critical theorists: all rules and institutions always entail rule, that is, they systematically distribute privilege to create patterns of subordination (Onuf, 1989:75). In this understanding institutions exercise power in providing guides to practice, but these guides are always tainted, promoting formations of rule such as hierarchy, hegemony, or heteronomy (Onuf, 1989). Such a conceptualization of power lends itself to showing systematic forces of subordination aligned along the axes of gender, race, and other statuses. It enables an investigation both of gendered power in institutions and of the way in which agents participate in reproducing or challenging it.

In sum then, although feminists and constructivists in IR tend to share an ontology of becoming, different groups of constructivists differ in the status they accord power in the process of becoming. Because feminists consider power as always present in social construction and because they understand gender as a code for power, they treat gender as a core variable in analyzing international relations. Some constructivist accounts resonate with such feminist understandings, but those that take power as a quantity rather than a process fall short. Whereas for many IR scholars constructivism thus mainly offers a departure from the fixed and stable entities of utilitarian approaches, for IR feminists social construction entails a new understanding of "power politics." This difference has epistemological implications. Because the premise of socially constructed genders sheds light on the political purposes enmeshed in science projects, IR feminists, unlike many other constructivists, have retained an interest in epistemology. They have used an ontology of becoming as a springboard toward refiguring knowledge creation and toward the realization of feminist values within the field of international relations.

EPISTEMOLOGICAL CONSIDERATIONS: WHO KNOWS?

Neo-Kantian philosophers have sought to locate grounds of knowledge in the human mind. Underlying their epistemologies is a model of consciousness whose reference point is historical individuality conceived as a trait of human nature. Interpretations of the world are possible because of the presumed unity of the human condition (Delanty, 1997:46–47).

Although social scientists have disputed each other intensely on methodological grounds, writers in the orthodox positivist and in most variations of the hermeneutic traditions have shared these epistemological assumptions. Since they locate grounds of knowledge in the mind, their claims over scientific legitimacy often remain at the level of abstract logic, disembodied from the knower and the social and historical context in which he/she is embedded. Such epistemologies are problematized in both constructivist and feminist accounts.

In the middle of the twentieth century there was a profound shift in the epistemological premises that formed the base for the Western philosophical tradition. The "linguistic turn," associated with Wittgenstein's *Philosophical Investigations* (1953/1958), launched a powerful and widely echoed critique not only of the subject-object split but also of the dominant correspondence theory of truth and language. Breaking away from the common understanding that linguistic statements of the world can be assessed against reality to see if they correspond, Wittgenstein proposed instead that language itself constitutes the world (Fierke and Jørgensen, 2001:4–5). Reality appears as a linguistic construction that is created through and not outside language. Despite differences, many contemporary philosophers share the constructivist premises of the later Wittgenstein's philosophy of language. They include, for example, J. L. Austin, John Searle, Anthony Giddens, Hans-Georg Gadamer, Jürgen Habermas, Richard Rorty, Peter Winch, and Francois Lyotard as key figures whose ideas have profoundly influenced constructivist thinking (Fierke and Jørgensen, 2001:5).

Since Wittgenstein, philosophers and theorists of various kinds have contributed to the relocation of grounds of knowledge from the (individual and atomistic) mind and the realm of abstract logic to the larger social context. Claims to know, so goes the postpositivist argument, involve a relation to a socially constituted normative order. Based on this argument, critical theorists have contested the idea of an ethically neutral and value-free science and have attempted a reconceptualization of the normative foundations of science. Habermas (1979, 1984, 1987, 1988) argued that knowledge is constructed through interactions of subjects who negotiate in communicative exchanges common definitions of the world. Interpretations of reality come about through a communicative affirmation or challenge of validity claims. Knowledge is always produced in specific social and historical contexts, reflecting the interests and culture of the groups in question. What counts as knowledge can be assessed against standards of rationality but is ultimately tied to a particular social and historical location.

Similarly, Rorty (1979) has pleaded for an end to epistemology, considering it a figment of the modern separation of mind and body that has created humans as a "glassy essence" occupied with mirroring a material truth "out there." He suggests that philosophy should be "edifying," its purpose not to found truth claims but to keep the conversation going. Adopting a pragmatist orientation (but not Habermas' "universal pragmatics"), Rorty considers "truth" as "no more and no less than the best idea we currently have about how to explain what is going on" (1979:385). There is no Archimedean point from which to judge such truth. The focus of "epistemology" thus shifts from assessing the relation between human beings and their objects of inquiry to the relation between alternative standards of justification and to the historical changes of such standards (1979:389–390).

Although the linguistic turn has thus had profound implications in philosophical debates about epistemology, there is today little agreement (and indeed little discussion) about epistemology among constructivists in IR (Klotz and Lynch, 1998; Ruggie, 1998a: 880–882). Whereas Kratochwil and Ruggie (1986) insisted that an intersubjective ontology contradicts a positivist epistemology, many others consider constructivism part of the "normal science" camp, depending on "no special methodology or epistemology" (Jepperson, Wendt, and Katzenstein, 1996:65; see also Hopf 1998:182). Dessler's (1989) and Wendt's (1987, 1999) efforts to ground constructivism in scientific realism serve the purpose of legitimizing a positivist research program that stands in profound tension the ontological premises of constructivism. On the other hand, some constructivists have developed Kantian (Onuf, 1989:38–40) and pragmatist epistemologies (Adler, 1997: 326) that are committed to the idea of social science (as a methodology), yet recognize that all insights are socially embedded and therefore temporary. They acknowledge that an ontology of becoming does not except scientists. Scientific investigation, like any other social practice, constructs a world; scientists thus are caught in the "double hermeneutic" of construction. Ironically, this acknowledgement does not lead to a broad discussion of epistemology. Rather, once constructivists have acknowledged the social embeddedness of science, epistemology fades into the background. Questions of what constitutes knowledge, how knowledge claims can be jus-

tified, and what purpose knowledge creation serves have largely dropped out of constructivist debates.

Different takes on epistemology also depict tendencies in the geographically and intellectually differentiated IR debates in the United States and Europe. The U.S. debate deals to a certain extent with "science questions" because it has defined constructivism in opposition to rationalism, which in the U.S. context is largely associated with positivist epistemologies. In contrast, the European (and especially the German) IR community tends to view constructivism as epistemologically compatible with utilitarian approaches: they are both part of a general postpositivist enterprise. This in turn has led to the apparent consensus that epistemological questions need no further investigation and that the real challenge for constructivists consists of empirical studies through which theoretical claims and hypotheses can be tested against each other (Risse-Kappen, 1995b:182; see also Zangl and Zürn, 1996:358–362). The omission of epistemological issues in the German IR discussion is actually presented as one of its strengths and advantages over the U.S. debate (Risse-Kappen, 1995b; for a critique see Jaeger, 1996, and Zehfuß, 1998).

The difference between the U.S. and German IR debates concerning epistemological issues has to be seen in the light of the rather distinct intellectual histories of the social sciences in these countries. With Max Weber's writings (1951) or, at the latest, since the famous "Positivismusstreit" of the Frankfurt School in the 1960s, orthodox positivist positions lost their dominance in the German social sciences, whereas such thinking remained much more influential in the United States until lately. Whereas the main epistemological division in the United States appears between positivism and postpositivism, many scholars in the German debate would locate it between the broad fields of postpositivism on the one hand and postmodernism on the other. The two debates are obviously informed by different understandings of the term "postpositivism": in the United States it indicates a radical shift away from claims to objective, value-free, universal knowledge that, among others, are considered inherent in rationalist approaches. In Germany, postpositivism is understood as a much broader category that, as Risse-Kappen (1995b) argues, offers space for the *homo economicus* as well as the *homo sociologicus*. Here a postpositivist approach is seen to encompass "normal science" standards but leaves out postmodernism and its various theoretical variations. Since postmodern thinking is rather marginal within the German IR community (but see, for example, Albert, 1994, 1999; Diez, 1996), a divide along those lines does not provoke epistemological battles.[7]

Whereas epistemology is thus a secondary matter for most IR constructivists, it continues to be a central topic in feminist debates. Supposedly epistemological orientations that separate empiricist, standpoint, and postmodern feminists have been broadly popularized in IR (Sylvester, 1992, 1994). The labels are somewhat unfortunate, since they conflate methodology, epistemology, and ontology. Arguably feminist empiricists favor certain methods, postmodern feminists subscribe to a particular (constructivist) ontology, and only standpoint feminists have put forward a specific epistemology. Thus, it is not surprising (or contradictory) that many feminists have combined postmodern and standpoint orientations (including Sylvester, 1992; Harding, 1986;

Haraway, 1988), that there are few instances of "pure" feminist empiricism, and that feminist philosophers of science have argued for a feminist empiricism based on "naturalized" epistemologies that "ground" knowledge in epistemic communities and demand that standards of scientific critique be subject to public scrutiny (Nelson, 1993; Longino, 1993).

In political science, one of the most influential feminist epistemological formulations has centered on the notion of a "feminist standpoint," a concept profoundly indebted to critical theory. When Nancy Hartsock introduced the term in 1983, she argued that material circumstances set limits to what can be known, that the perspective of the ruling group is "partial and perverse" but structures the material relations in which all are forced to participate. Consequently, oppressed groups must struggle for their own vision to expose existing relations as inhumane. Along the same lines, Sandra Harding called for a "critical evaluation to determine which social situations tend to generate the most objective knowledge claims" (1991:142). She argued that "women's experiences, informed by feminist theory, provide a potential grounding for more complete and less distorted knowledge claims than do men's" (1987:184f). In this way the feminist standpoint provided a vehicle for women's liberation.

The notion of a feminist standpoint has received considerable scrutiny for its ontological premises. Many denounced the essentialist assumption of a common biology, the same psychosocial situation, or a shared experience of motherhood and domestic work that seemed to underlie its diverse theorizations. Hartsock has denied the charge of essentialism pointing to her Marxist epistemology, which views knowledge as historically specific and accomplished through practice. But she also (1998:239) has acknowledged that her original conceptualization did not allow theoretical space for differences arising from race or sexual orientation and has argued the need for pluralizing the notion of a standpoint. This was not a minor concession. In abandoning a unitary feminist standpoint, feminists have lost a grounding of knowledge in the privileged position of the subordinate that provided Hartsock a measure for truth. If there is no unitary feminist standpoint but many standpoints of groups involved in different relationships of power, whose truth claims should be considered the right ones?

In order to counteract the relativism this step seemed to imply, some feminists have sought to develop a new understanding of objectivity. Harding (1991) introduced the notion of "strong objectivity," demanding that knowledge claims be evaluated in relation to the social situation that generated them. Haraway was thinking along similar lines when she suggested that "feminist objectivity means quite simply situated knowledges" (1988:581). Like Harding, she suggested that knowledge claims emerged from particular social situations and needed to be judged against such situations. Haraway elaborates that the purpose of doing science is not only searching for truth, but providing new visions, alternative accounts that make a difference in the world. The value of knowledge is thus measured against the futures it can produce. In this understanding knowledge creation retains common scholarly practices such as comparison, critique, and defense, but the standards are changed. Truth is not simply a matter of correspondence but emerges (however provisionally) from arguments and discursive exchanges

that are critically aware of location, not simply of the array of oppressions subsumed under labels such as race, sex, and class, but more importantly of "the sense of being *for* some worlds and not others" (Haraway, 1997:37).

In aligning themselves with a pragmatist philosophy of science, some constructivists in IR share with feminists a "conception of truth as situated, perspectival, and discursive" (Hekman, 1997: 356). In the words of Price and Reus-Smit (1998:272), constructivists make "small-t" truth claims that are empirically and logically plausible yet always also contingent and partial. Or in Adler's formulation, interpretation is "an intrinsic part of a scientific enterprise" (1997: 328). But although these constructivists follow feminists in "grounding" knowledge in social contexts, they do not take Haraway's additional step of critically reflecting on the location from which their knowledge issues, of thinking through the political and ethical implications of their knowledge claims. By failing to problematize the partiality of their claims, they avoid responsibility for their political effects.

But once it is acknowledged that claims to know create not only a social but also a political reality, at least two additional issues arise for a constructivist epistemology. First is the necessity to be aware of the larger sociopolitical context in which knowledge is created and of the way in which such knowledge relates to the perpetuation of specific constellations of super- and subordination. Critical theorists have extensively discussed this issue, putting in the center of epistemological questioning not truth but interests. Epistemology then turns from probing philosophical justifications of truth claims as they relate to an objective reality to probing political justifications of knowledge claims as they relate to a constructed reality. The epistemological issue for social scientists is not only the search for better correspondences but also the political questioning of "*Cui bono?*"—the specification of the political purposes that their knowledge serves. Few constructivists have been willing to "pollute" their science with an explication of political agendas, retaining the fiction that the knowledge they produce reflects an objective reality and not a provisional and partial set of propositions emerging from a particular sociopolitical context.

The second issue for feminists centers around the question "Who knows?" For Adler the relevant standards from which to judge truth are those developed by a "community of scientists" who engage in "choice, deliberation, judgement and interpretation" (Adler 1997:328–329). Thus the epistemic privilege of science is preserved. This allows constructivists to put aside epistemological considerations and continue in their construction of knowledge by whatever methods the scientific community finds acceptable in the particular historical context. However, if truth claims are dependent on the consensus of a "community of scientists," as Adler, Ruggie, Risse and other constructivists claim, then the question how these communities are constituted is important. Feminists have pointed out that these communities are rather exclusive, not only in the sense of excluding people who lack power, but even more so in excluding the standpoints of those less privileged, the ways of knowing that make sense from their perspective. If the purpose of science is not only searching for truth but also providing visions of a better world, then subjugated knowledges constitute an important source of understanding

and a creative resource to envision what could be.

In problematizing the position of the knower, feminist writings have extensively worked through the epistemological implications of an ontology of becoming. Feminist epistemology points away from the solitary human mind toward socially constituted and politically legitimized groups of knowers. It problematizes the privileged access to knowledge accorded a scientific community that employs agreed-upon methodologies (whether logically positivist or interpretive). It gives legitimacy to many communities of knowers committed to a diverse range of standards of justification and creating a scientific debate that consists of a variety of open, transitory, limited, and partial knowledge claims. From our feminist constructivist perspective, it is the discursive encounter of such knowledge claims, issuing from people's diverse locations, that can produce emancipatory knowledge. Thus, feminist epistemology needs to "start from women's lives" (Harding, 1991:150), giving purpose to the search for truth and to world-changing practices.

In taking seriously questions regarding the grounds of knowledge within an ontology of becoming, constructivists (like feminists) thus find themselves not only on the terrain of epistemology but also on the terrain of ethics and politics. The problem of justification shifts from abstractly evaluating truth claims to assessing in context their political and ethical implications. As Hartsock (1997: 373) argues, "the criteria for privileging some knowledges over others are ethical and political rather than purely 'epistemological.'" Or, in Haraway's (1997:36) echo of Marx, the point of science is "to make a difference in the world, to cast our lot for some ways of life and not others." What these ways of life should be cannot be known with certainty in advance; they are themselves a product of ongoing critical construction that should benefit from a science committed to social critique.

CONCLUSION

In probing the overlapping terrains of constructivism and feminism in IR we have found grounds for understanding in an ontology of becoming. Shared ontological commitments lead constructivists and feminists to a shared research focus centering on concepts such as norms, rules, identities, and institutions. Yet, despite these common ontological starting points, feminists and constructivists have pursued quite different research paths. Feminist research differs in particular from the type of constructivist research that has excised the focus on power. One could argue that this constitutes a diversity to be celebrated. Feminist interventions would then just add one point of view to a pluralism of constructivisms. Contrary to this perspective we have argued that some constructivist approaches encounter logical problems precisely because their epistemology does not follow through on the premises of their social ontology. Furthermore, their failure to conceptualize power as social and pervasive leads them to miss an important part of the reality of power politics. In lieu of a conclusion we would like to probe the empirical relevance of our theoretical arguments. If constructivists incorporated feminist insights, how would their research change? What do feminists do in their empirical research that constructivists are missing? We see at least two major areas of empirical research

where feminist constructivists have made unique contributions.

To begin with, whereas power has virtually dropped out of most constructivist accounts, feminist constructivists empirically investigate power in the process of construction. The significance of this type of inquiry becomes evident in a comparison of research on state identities. Constructivists have focused on the importance of understanding state identities in order to explain national interests and state practices (e.g., Wendt, 1999; Jepperson et al., 1996). Indeed, national interest, emerging from state identity, replaces the classical realist variable, power (simply understood in terms of material resources), as the key explanatory variable in these constructivists' accounts of state action. Yet, their treatments of identity rarely explain why states adopt one identity over another or how identity construction proceeds. As Kowert and Legro observe in their critical reprise to the Katzenstein volume on norms and identity in world politics, "about the *process* of identity construction, the authors have relatively little to say" (1996:469). Feminists and other constructivists, especially those who heed poststructuralist insights on the nexus of power and knowledge and those who are aware of the Onufian linking of rules and rule (e.g., Weldes, 1996; Laffey and Weldes, 1997; Alexander, 2000), find an answer to this question in a social understanding of power.

Feminists specifically probe the way in which gender, race, class, and other status distinctions serve as codes of super- and subordination that powerfully suggest preferred forms of identification. For example, feminist analyses of diverse nationalisms show that gender constructs, such as the framing of the nation as a female body raped by a colonial power, or the eroticizing of the nation as a loved woman's body, have enabled specific political projects, such as national liberation or national defense, associating transgressions of state boundaries with sexual danger (Pettman, 1996:49; Yuval-Davis and Anthias, 1989). Focusing on identity construction of developmental states, Christine Chin (1998) has interpreted practices surrounding foreign domestic labor in Malaysia as defining a middle-class identity that constitutes the Malaysian state as modern, and Leslie Ann Jeffrey (2000) has interpreted the punitive Thai prostitution policy as enabling an image of the Thai state as modern and efficient. Both emphasize that this identity is made possible through the subjection of particular female subjects. In the area of security policy, Steve Niva has explained the U.S. approach to the Gulf War as an exercise to restore American manhood after the trauma of Vietnam (Niva, 1998). In all these analyses, identity is not simply an explanatory variable but a complex outcome of discursive strategies that encode power by evoking privileged understandings of masculinity at the expense of femininity.

There is more at stake here than the privileging of one identity over others. The emphasis in this feminist work is less on identity as an explanatory variable than on the process of identification, on the way in which identity formation evokes gendered power, on the way in which gender is structurally pervasive in all practices and discourses. Thus, what is at stake is not a moral claim to "be nicer to women" but an ontological and epistemological claim about what power is about and how power works.[8] By ignoring gender,

constructivists miss a key element of this picture.

A second and related area where feminist constructivist approaches have contributed to empirical work in international relations concerns the epistemological privileging of certain communities as the prototypical participants in and knowers of world politics. Breaking away from (neo-)realist state-centrism, constructivists have focused extensively on nonstate actors. For example, some have researched local, national, and transnational nongovernmental organizations (NGOs) fighting for human rights (chapters in Risse, Ropp, and Sikkink, 1999), for peace (Risse-Kappen, 1994; Evangelista, 1998), or against apartheid (Klotz, 1995). Others have investigated the role of social movements in political transformation processes (Chilton, 1995) and discussed the influence of activists organized in transnational advocacy networks in areas such as violence against women and nature protection (chapters in Keck and Sikkink, 1998). This broadening of perspective toward including diverse sets of actors has stimulated novel and creative empirical research and helped to provide a more complex but also more comprehensive account of international politics.

Despite these advances, constructivists severely limit themselves because of their positivist inclinations and because they ignore feminist epistemological insights. In most cases, constructivists approach NGOs, movements, and advocacy networks as "objects" of inquiry and describe the knowledge and world views of these objects. The primary purpose for including them often is to probe whether their existence "makes a difference," that is, whether their activities can explain certain policy outcomes. In taking this approach constructivists refuse to attribute to NGOs, movements, and advocacy networks a status as creators of knowledge equal to that of scholars; that is, they refuse to endow them with a true "subject" quality. This not only reinforces the dominant top-down bias in IR scholarship and serves to maintain epistemological privilege but also prevents scholars from seriously engaging with the knowledge proposed by such nonstate actors. What does this knowledge reveal when juxtaposed with hegemonic conceptions? What kinds of exclusions, injustices, inequalities, and shortages of care in the existing world does this knowledge uncover? What kind of a future does this knowledge promise? What new kinds of exclusions and inequalities are embedded in this knowledge?

These are precisely the questions that are at the center of feminist constructivist inquiry. Feminists have validated diverse and unusual bodies of knowledge about political and international life—not only those of NGOs, but also those of Philippinas working as nannies and domestic servants abroad, of sex workers servicing foreign soldiers in Korea and tourists in Thailand, of home-based workers forming international alliances to gain recognition as employees, of participants in the Greenham Commons peace camp in England or in foreign-funded women's cooperatives in Zimbabwe (Enloe, 1989; Pettman, 1996; Chin, 1998; Moon, 1997; Prügl, 1999; Sylvester, 1992, 1999). These stories reveal the ugly underbelly of a globalizing economy, the insecurities created by U.S. security policies, the exclusionary biases in international labor codes, and the dependencies emerging from development policies. They reveal that gender is present in all aspects of international affairs, that it is a structural feature of international life. In feminist research, these stories gain a status perhaps more valid than the stories of those who occupy power positions in the making or the study of international politics. By moving beyond the "high politics" of the official knowledge constructors of IR, feminist writings of this kind broaden the ontological terrain of disciplinary international relations, subverting its exclusionary boundaries and revealing hidden aspects of international politics that many constructivists fail to recognize. In giving a voice to those considered marginal in international politics feminist writings validate their knowledge and position it to disrupt hegemonic accounts. But more than that, the interpretations of those on the margins serve to frame feminist projects, juxtaposing what is with what ought to be, rarely yielding prescriptions for a better future, but providing a powerful point of departure for a better understanding of the world.

NOTES

1. Others are "women" and "sex," in addition to "race," "class," "ethnicity," and other markers of difference

2. In this paper we skirt the question of how feminism relates to postmodernism. Clearly many feminist insights into power are indebted to poststructuralist theorizing, and there are feminists in IR who more faithfully adhere to poststructuralist principles than we do in the paper. Although we are aware that the emphasis on "texts," in particular in the work of Derrida, is difficult to reconcile with the constructivist focus on "agency," we believe that a constructivist reformulation of poststructuralist insights on power need not diminish their force.

3. For a categorization of constructivists (including some feminists) according to

philosophical bases, see Ruggie, 1998a (880–882). Price and Reus-Smit distinguish "modernists" and "postmodernists" (1998: 267ff). Ruggie does not identify Wittgenstein as providing philosophical roots separate from the sociological classics and thereby papers over substantial differences. For a forceful argument in favor of a Wittgensteinian constructivism, see Fierke, 1996, 1997 (45); also Onuf, 1989.

4. For a summary of the protracted agent-structure debate, see Gould, 1998.

5. The writings of Anthony Giddens have provided inspiration for many constructivists in IR on this issue. See Giddens, 1984. Giddens is discussed in Onuf, 1989 (36) and Wendt, 1987 (356).

6. Note that this ability to explain change is lost in approaches that take norms or culture as explanatory variables (Kowert and Legro, 1996). This lies at the basis of Finnemore and Sikkink's puzzling statement that "like other theoretical frameworks in international relations (IR), much of the macrotheoretical equipment of constructivism is better at explaining stability than change" (1998:888).

7. An exception was the debate between Thomas Diez and Tanja A. Börzel on the meaning of postmodern approaches for studying European integration in the *Zeitschrift für Internationale Beziehungen* (Diez, 1996; Börzel, 1997).

8. We are grateful to an anonymous reviewer for clarifying this point and for suggesting this formulation.

REFERENCES

Adler, E. (1997) Seizing the Middle Ground: Constructivism in World Politics. *European Journal of International Relations* 3:319–363.

Adler, L. (1999) Discourses of Flexibility and the Rise of the "Temp" Industry, or How I Met the "Kelly Girl" Commuting between Public and Private. *International Feminist Journal of Politics* 1:210–236.

Albert, M. (1994) "Postmoderne" und Theorie der internationalen Beziehungen ["Postmodernity" and Theory of International Relations]. *Zeitschrift für Internationale Beziehungen* 1:45–63.

Albert, M. (1999) Territorium und Identität: Kollektive Identitäten und moderner Nationalstaat [Territory and Identity: Collective Identities and the Modern Nation-State]. *Österreichische Zeitschrift für Politikwissenschaft* 3.255–268.

Alexandar, K. H. (2000) "Constructivist International Relations Theory: Reflections, Critical Evaluation, and Suggestions for Future Research." Paper presented at the annual meeting of the International Studies Association, Los Angeles, March 14–18.

Barrett, M. (1988) *Women's Oppression Today: The Marxist/Feminist Encounter.* London: Verso.

Börzel, T. A (1997) Zur (Ir-)Relevanz der "Postmoderne" für die Integrationsforschung: Eine Replik auf Thomas Diez' Beitrag "Postmoderne und europäische Integration" [On the (Ir-)Relevance of "Postmodernity" for Integration Research: A Response to Thomas Diez' "Postmodernity and European Integration"]. *Zeitschrift für Internationale Beziehungen* 4:125–137.

Checkel, J. T. (1998) The Constructivist Turn in International Relations Theory. *World Politics* 50:324–348.

Chilton, P. (1995) "Mechanisms of Change: Social Movements, Transnational Coalitions, and the Transformation Processes in Eastern Europe." In *Bringing Transnational Relations Back In*, edited by T. Risse-Kappen, pp. 189–226. Cambridge: Cambridge University Press.

Chin, C. B. N. (1998) *In Service and Servitude: Foreign Female Domestic Workers and the Malaysian "Modernity" Project.* New York: Columbia University Press.

Cohn, C. (1987) Sex and Death in the Rational World of Defense Intellectuals. *Signs: Journal of Women in Culture and Society* 12:687-718.

Connell, R. W. (1987) *Gender and Power: Society, the Person and Sexual Politics.* Stanford: Stanford University Press.

de Beauvoir, S. [1952] (1989) *The Second Sex.* New York: Vintage Books.

Delanty, G. (1997) *Social Science: Beyond Constructivism and Realism.* Buckingham, U.K.: Open University Press.

Dessler, D. (1989) What's at Stake in the Agent-Structure Debate? *International Organization* 43:441-473.

Diez, T. (1996) Postmoderne und europäische Integration. Die Dominanz des Staatsmodells, die Verantwortung gegenüber dem Anderen und die Konstruktion eines alternativen Horizonts [Postmodernity and European Integration: The Dominance of the State Model, the Responsibility towards the Other, and the Construction of an Alternative Horizon]. *Zeitschrift für Internationale Beziehungen* 3:255-281.

Doty, R. L. (1997) Aporia: A Critical Exploration of the Agent-Structure Problematique in International Relations Theory. *European Journal of International Relations* 3:365-392.

Duffy, G., B. K. Frederking, and S. A. Tucker (1998) Language Games: Dialogical Analysis of the INF Negotiations. *International Studies Quarterly* 42:271-294.

Elshtain, J. B. (1987) *Women and War.* New York: Basic Books.

Enloe, C. (1989) *Bananas, Beaches and Bases: Making Feminist Sense of International Politics.* Berkeley and Los Angeles: University of California Press.

Enloe, C. (1993) *The Morning After: Sexual Politics at the End of the Cold War.* Berkeley and Los Angeles: University of California Press.

Evangelista, M. (1998) *Taming the Bear: Transnational Relations and the Demise of the Soviet Threat.* Ithaca: Cornell Univeristy Press.

Fierke, K. M. (1996) Multiple Identities, Interfacing Games: The Social Construction of Western Action in Bosnia. *European Journal of International Relations* 2:467-497.

Fierke, K. M. (1997) "At the Boundary: Language, Rules and Social Construction." In *The Aarhus-Norsminde Papers: Constructivism, International Relations and European Studies*, edited by K. E. Jørgensen, pp. 43-51. Aarhus, Denmark: Aarhus University, Department of Political Science.

Fierke, K. M., and K. E. Jørgensen (2001) "Introduction." In *Constructing International Relations: Towards a New Generation*, edited by K. Fierke and K. E. Jørgensen, pp.3-9. Armonk, NY: M. E. Sharpe.

Finnemore, M. (1996) *National Interests in International Society.* Ithaca: Cornell University Press.

Finnemore, M., and K. Sikkink (1998) International Norm Dynamics and Political Change. *International Organization* 52:887-917.

Giddens, A. (1984) *The Constitution of Society: Outline of a Theory of Structuration.* Berkeley and Los Angeles: University of California Press.

Gould, H. D. (1998) "What *Is* at Stake in the Agent-Structure Debate?" In *International Relations in a Constructed World*, edited by V. Kubálková, N. G. Onuf, and P. Kowert, pp. 79-98. Armonk, NY: M. E. Sharpe.

Grant, R., and K. Newland, Eds. (1991) *Gender and International Relations.* Bloomington: Indiana University Press.

Habermas, J. (1979) *Communication and the Evolution of Society.* London: Heinemann.

Habermas, J. (1984) *The Theory of Communicative Action*, vol. 1: *Reason and the Rationalization of Society.* London: Heinemann.

Habermas, J. (1987) *The Theory of Communicative Action*, vol. 2: *Lifeworld and System: A Critique of Functionalist Reason.* Cambridge, U.K.: Polity Press.

Habermas, J. (1988) *On the Logic of the Social Sciences.* Cambridge, U.K.: Polity Press.

Han, J. and L. H. M. Ling (1998) Authoritarianism in the Hypermasculinized State: Hybridity, Patriarchy, and Capitalism in Korea. *International Studies Quarterly* 42:53-78.

Haraway, D. (1988) Situated Knowledges: The Science Question in Feminism and the Privilege of Partial Perspective. *Feminist Studies* 14:575-599.

Haraway, D. (1997) *Modest_Witness@Second_Millenium.FemaleMan_Meets_OncoMouse: Feminism and Technoscience.* New York: Routledge.

Harding, S. (1986) *The Science Question in Feminism.* Ithaca: Cornell University Press.

Harding, S., ed. (1987) *Feminism and Methodology.* Bloomington: Indiana University Press.

Harding, S. (1991) *Whose Science? Whose Knowledge? Thinking from Women's Lives.* Ithaca: Cornell University Press.

Hartsock, N. C. M. (1983) *Money, Sex, and Power: Toward a Feminist Historical Materialism.* New York and London: Longman.

Hartsock, N. C. M. (1997) Comment on Hekman's "Truth and Method: Feminist Standpoint Theory Revisited": Truth or Justice? *Signs: Journal of Women in Culture and Society* 22:367-373.

Hartsock, N. C. M. (1998) *The Feminist Standpoint Revisited and Other Essays.* Boulder, CO: Westview.

Hekman, S. (1997) Truth and Method: Feminist Standpoint Theory Revisited. *Signs: Journal of Women in Culture and Society* 22:341-365.

Hooper, C. (1998) "Masculinist Practices and Gender Politics: The Operation of Multiple Masculinities in International Relations." In *The "Man" Question in International Relations*, edited by M. Zalewski and J. Parpart, pp. 28-53. Boulder, CO: Westview Press.

Hooper, C. (2000) "Masculinities in Transition: The Case of Globalization." In *Gender and Global Restructuring: Sightings, Sites and Resistances*, edited by M. Marchand and A. S. Runyan, pp. 59-73. London: Routledge.

Hopf, T. (1998) The Promise of Constructivism in International Relation Theory. *International Security* 23:171-200.

Jaeger, H. M. (1996) Konstruktionsfehler des Konstruktivismus in den Internationalen Beziehungen [Construction Mistakes of Constructivism in International Relations]. *Zeitschrift für Internationale Beziehungen* 3:313-340.

Jeffrey, L. A. (2000) "The Middle Class and the Material Girls: Thai National Identity in a Globalized Era." Paper presented at the annual meeting of the International Studies Association, Los Angeles, March 14-18.

Jepperson, R. L., A. Wendt, and P. J. Katzenstein (1996) "Norms, Identity and Culture in National Security." In *The Culture of National Security: Norms and Identity in World Politics*, edited by P. J. Katzenstein, pp. 33-75. New York: Columbia University Press.

Katzenstein, P. J., ed. (1996) *The Culture of National Security: Norms and Identity in World Politics.* New York: Columbia University Press.

Katzenstein, P J., R. O. Keohane, and S. D. Krasner (1998) "International Organization" and the Study of World Politics. *International Organization* 52:645-685.

Keck, M. E., and K. Sikkink (1998) *Activists beyond Borders: Advocacy Networks in International Politics.* Ithaca: Cornell University Press.

Keohane, R. O. (1998) Beyond Dichotomy: Conversations between International Relations and Feminist Theory. *International Studies Quarterly* 42:193-198.

Klotz, A. (1995) *Norms in International Relations: The Struggle against Apartheid.* Ithaca: Cornell University Press.

Klotz, A., and C. Lynch (1996) "Constructivism: Past Agendas and Future Directions." Paper presented at the annual meeting of the American Political Science Association, San Francisco.

Klotz, A., and C. Lynch (1998) "Conflicted Constructivism? Positivist Leanings vs. Interpretivist Meanings." Paper presented at the annual meeting of the International Studies Association, Minneapolis, March 17-21.

Kofman, E., and G. Youngs, eds. (1996) *Globalization, Theory and Practice.* London and New York: Wellington House.

Koslovski, R., and F. Kratochwil (1994) Understanding Change in International Politics: The Soviet Empire's Demise and the International System. *International Organization* 48: 215-247.

Kowert, P. (1998) "Agent versus Structure in the Construction of National Identify." *In International Relations in a Constructed World*, edited by V. Kubálková, N. G. Onuf, and P. Kowert, pp. 101-122. Armonk NY: M. E. Sharpe.

Kowert, P., and J. Legro (1996) "Norms, Identity, and Their Limits: A Theoretical Reprise." In *The Culture of National Security: Norms and Identity in World Politics*, edited by P. J. Katzenstein, pp. 451-497. New York: Columbia University Press.

Kratochwil, F., and J. G. Ruggie (1986) International Organization: A State of the Art on an Art of the State. *International Organization* 40: 753-775.

Kubálková, V., N. G. Onuf, and P. Kowert (1998) "Constructing Constructivism." In *International Relations in a Constructed World*, edited by V. Kubálková, N. G. Onuf, and P. Kowert, pp. 3-21 Armonk, NY: M. E. Sharpe.

Laffey, M., and J. Weldes (1997) Beyond Belief: Ideas and Symbolic Technologies in the Study of International Relations. *European Journal of International Relations* 3:193-237.

Locher, B., and E. Prügl (2001) "Feminism: Constructivism's Other Pedigree." In *Constructing International Relations: Toward a New Generation*, edited by K. M. Fierke and K. E. Jørgensen, pp. 71-85. Armonk, NY: M. E. Sharpe.

Longino, H. (1993) "Subjects, Power and Knowledge: Description and Prescription in Feminist Philosophies of Science." In *Feminist Epistemologies*, edited by L. Alcoff and E. Potter, pp. 101-120. New York: Routledge.

Marchand, M., and J. L. Parpart (1995) *Feminism/Postmodernism/Development.* London: Routledge.

Meyer, M. K., and E. Prügl, eds. (1999) *Gender Politics in Global Governance.* Lanham, MD: Rowman and Littlefield.

Moon, K. H. S. (1997) *Sex among Allies: Military Prostitution in U.S.-Korea Relations.* New York: Columbia University Press.

Nelson, L. H. (1993) "Epistemological Communities." In *Feminist Epistemologies*, edited by L. Alcoff and E. Potter, pp. 121-159. New York: Routledge.

Neumann, I. B. (1999) *Uses of the Other: "The East" in European Identity Formation.* Minneapolis: University of Minnesota Press.

Niva, S. (1998) "Tough and Tender: New World Order Masculinity and the Gulf War." In *The "Man" Question in International Relations*, edited by M. Zalewski and J. Parpart, pp. 109-128. Boulder, CO: Westview.

Onuf, N. G. (1989) *World of Our Making: Rules and Rule in Social Theory and International Relations.* Columbia: University of South Carolina Press.

Peterson, V. S., ed. (1992a) *Gendered States: Feminist (Re)Visions of International Relations Theory.* Boulder, CO: Lynne Rienner.

Peterson, V. S., (1992b) Transgressing Boundaries: Theories of Knowledge, Gender and International Relations. *Millennium: Journal of International Studies* 21:183-206.

Peterson, V. S., and A. S. Runyan (1993) *Global Gender Issues.* Boulder, CO: Westview Press.

Pettman, J. J. (1996) *Worlding Women: A Feminist International Politics.* London: Routledge.

Price, R., and C. Reus-Smit (1998) Dangerous Liaisons? Critical International Theory and Constructivism. *European Journal of International Relations* 4:259-294.

Prügl, E. (1999) *The Global Construction of Gender: Home-Based Work in the Political Economy of the 20th Century.* New York: Columbia University Press.

Risse, T., S. C. Ropp, and K. Sikkink, eds. (1999) *The Power of Human Rights: International Norms and Domestic Change,* Cambridge: Cambridge University Press.

Risse-Kappen, T. (1994) Ideas Do Not Float Freely: Transnational Coalitions, Domestic Structures, and the End of the Cold War. *International Organization* 48:185-214.

Risse-Kappen, T. (1995a) *Cooperation among Democracies: The European Influence on U.S. Foreign Policy.* Princeton: Princeton University Press.

Risse-Kappen, T. (1995b) Reden ist nicht billig. Zur Debatte um Kommunikation und Rationalität [Talk Is Not Cheap: A Contribution to the Debate on Communication and Rationality]. *Zeitschrift für Internationale Beziehungen* 2:171-184.

Risse-Kappen, T. (1996) "Collective Identity in a Democratic Community: The Case of NATO." In *The Culture of National Security: Norms and Identity in World Politics,* edited by P. J. Katzenstein, pp. 357-399. New York: Columbia University Press.

Rorty, R. (1979) *Philosophy and the Mirror of Nature.* Princeton: Princeton University Press.

Ruggie, J. G. (1998a) What Makes the World Hang Together? Neo-Utilitarianism and the Social Constructivist Challenge. *International Organization* 52:855-885.

Ruggie, J. G. (1998b) *Constructing the World Polity: Essays on International Institutionalization.* New York: Routledge.

Scott, J. W. (1986) Gender: A Useful Category of Historical Analysis. *American Historical Review* 91:1053-1075.

Shelton, B. A., and B. Aggar (1993) "Shotgun Wedding, Unhappy Marriage, No-Fault-Divorce? Rethinking the Feminism-Marxism Relationship." In *Theory on Gender/Feminism on Theory,* edited by P. England, pp. 25-41. New York: Aldine de Gruyter.

Steans, J. (1998) *Gender and International Relations: An Introduction.* New Brunswick: Rutgers University Press.

Stienstra, D. (1994) *Women's Movements and International Organizations.* New York: St. Martin's Press.

Sylvester, C. (1992) "The Emperors' Theories and Transformations: Looking at the Field through Feminist Lenses." In *Transformations in the Global Political Economy,* edited by D. C. Pirages and C. Sylvester, pp. 230-253. London: Macmillan.

Sylvester, C. (1994) *Feminist Theory and International Relations in a Postmodern Era.* Cambridge: Cambridge University Press.

Sylvester, C. (1998) "'Masculinity,' 'Feminity,' and 'International Relations': Or Who Goes to the 'Moon' with Bonaparte and the Adder?" In *The 'Man' Question in International Relations,* edited by J. Parpart and M. Zalewski, pp. 185-198. Boulder, CO: Westview.

Sylvester, C. (1999) "Progress" in Zimbabwe. *International Feminist Journal of Politics* 1: 89-118.

Tétreault, M. A. (1994) "Women and Revolution in Vietnam." In *Women and Revolution in Africa, Asia, and the New World,* edited by M. A. Tétreault, pp. 111-136. Columbia: University of South Carolina Press.

Tickner, J. A. (1992) *Gender in International Relations: Feminist Perspectives on Acheiving Global Security.* New York: Columbia University Press.

Tickner, J. A. (1997) You Just Don't Understand: Troubled Engagements between Feminists and IR Theorists, *International Studies Quarterly* 41:611-632.

Wæver, O. (1996) "The Rise and Fall of the Inter-paradigm Debate." In *International Theory: Positivism and Beyond,* edited by S. Smith, K. Booth and M. Zalewski, pp.149-185. Cambridge: Cambridge University Press.

Weber, C. (1994) Good Girls, Little Girls and Bad Girls: Male Paranoia in Robert Keohane's Critique of Feminist International Relations. *Millennium: Journal of International Studies* 23:337–349.

Weber, C. (1998) Performative States. *Millennium: Journal of International Studies* 27:77–95.

Weber, C. (1999) *Faking It: U.S. Hegemony in a "Post-Phallic" Era.* Minneapolis: University of Minnesota Press.

Weber, M.(1951) *Gesammelte Aufsätze zur Wissenchaftslehre* [Collected Essays on the Methodology of the Social Sciences], 2nd ed. Tübingen, Germany: Mohr.

Weldes, J. (1996) Constructing National Interests. *European Journal of International Relations* 2:275–318.

Wendt, A. (1987) The Agent-Structure Problem in International Relations Theory. *International Organization* 41:335–370.

Wendt, A. (1994) Collective Identity Formation and the International State. *American Political Science Review* 88:384–396.

Wendt, A. (1999) *Social Theory of International Politics.* Cambridge: Cambridge University Press.

Wendt, A., and R. Duvall (1989) "Institutions and International Order." In *Global Changes and Theoretical Challenges: Approaches to the World Politics for the 1990s*, edited by E. Czempiel and J. N. Rosenau, pp 51–73. Lexington, MA: Lexington Books.

Whitworth, S. (1994) *Feminism and International Relations: Towards a Political Economy of Gender in Interstate and Non-governmental Institutions.* London: Macmillan.

Wittgenstein, L. [1953] (1958) *Philosophical Investigations*, trans. G. E. M. Anscombe. Oxford: Blackwell Publishers.

Yee, A. S. (1996) The Effects of Ideas on Policies. *International Organization* 50:69–108.

Yuval-Davis, N. and F. Anthias, eds. (1989) *Women-Nation-State.* London: Macmillan.

Zalewski, M. (1998) Where Is Woman in International Relations? "To Return as a Woman and Be Heard." *Millenium: Journal of International Studies.* 27: 847–867.

Zalewski, M., and J. Parpart, eds. (1998) *The "Man" Question in International Relations.* Boulder, CO: Westview Press.

Zangl, B., and M. Zürn (1996) Argumentatives Handeln bei internationalen Verhandlungen: Moderate Anmerkungen zur post-realistischen Debatte [Argumentative Acion in International Negotiations: Moderate Remarks on the Post-realist Debate]. *Zeitschrift für Internationale Beziehungen* 3:341–366.

Zehfuss, M. (1998) Sprachlosigkeit schränkt ein: Zur Bedeutung von Sprache in konstruktivistischen Theorien [Speechlessness Limits: The Significance of Speech in Constructivist Theories]. *Zeitschrift für Internationale Beziehungen* 5:109–137.

QUESTIONS

1. What are the fundamental assumptions shared by both constructivists and feminists?

2. What are the key epistemological insights of feminism that the author claims are ignored by constructivists?

POSTMODERNIST PERSPECTIVE OF SEPTEMBER 11

26. The U.S. Bombing of Afghanistan: A Women-Centered Perspective

Saba Gul Khattak

This excerpt by Saba Gul Khattak is a fine example of a policy-relevant feminist analysis of the utility and impact of the use of force. The author uses the U.S. bombing of Afghanistan in the aftermath of the events of September 11, 2001, to demonstrate the importance of understanding the problem from the perspective of both Afghans in general and gender in particular.

Saba Gul Khattak is a Deputy Director and Research Fellow for the Sustainable Development Policy Institute in Pakistan.

How do we analyze the US bombing of Afghanistan? Is this bombing a ceremonial reaffirmation of power? Is it about avenging the 11th September hijackings, the subsequent destruction and damage of the WTC and the Pentagon respectively and the death of thousands of innocent people? Is it about the display and exhibition of US armaments for international buyers? Is about ensuring oil supply lines and warm water ports a la Carter Doctrine? Is it primarily about ridding the world of terrorism and terrorists? Is it about restoring peace and eventually democracy in Afghanistan? Is it about, in addition to all this, liberating Afghan women from the oppression of the Taliban (though not the patriarchal culture that kept them back whether in Afghanistan or in refugee camps in Pakistan)? Is it about the American resolve not to live in fear? Or, it is about Osama Bin Laden?

Why are answers to this issue important? Why must we establish the primacy of one answer and through that hierarchy talk about US goals and priorities? This is probably because we feel an urgent need to make sense of international politics. But to make sense of the recent and continuing madness, we cannot restrict ourselves to mainstream explanations, whether they spring from liberal, progressive or left oriented perspectives.

In the present context, to attempt to understand the American bombing of Afghanistan, we need to look at the issue from the Afghan perspective, and within that perspective, through the lens of gender. This short piece is based upon qualitative interviews with Afghan women refugees who have experienced not only the American bombing and violence of the Northern Alliance but also other types of violence prior to the October 7th bombing. In that context, for the Afghans the bombing and its motivation are not connected with the shock that the US and some others around the world have experienced. For the Afghans, the bombing represents yet another wave of violence in a 21-year history of relentless conflict. It has, once again, driven them out of their homes and their country, making them insecure refugees

From the Social Science Research Council, New York, NY.

or IDPs (internally displaced persons) because no country will allow them in.

According to Trinh T. Minh-ha (1994: 12), the story of refugees "exposes power politics in its most primitive form . . . the ruthlessness of major powers, the brutality of nation states, the avarice and prejudice of people." The story of Afghan refugees contains tales of terror unleashed by major powers, neighboring states as well as their own people. Therefore, at one level it does not matter whether the bombs are manufactured in the USA or the former USSR. What matters to the people is what the bombs do to them when they are dropped. As one Afghan woman in Pakistan, a recent refugee from the bombing, explained, "Jung sho-Kabul taa raalo" (fighting erupted and it reached Kabul) or as another woman put it in an understated way, "the circumstances became unbearable," meaning the bombing was horrendous. For the women then, what mattered was that they had to flee their homes in order to be secure. This was the case much more for women than men who have some sensitivity to whose bombs are raining, although many have learnt to distance themselves from the warring factions. For many of the poor displaced women and their children, the removal of the Taliban and killing and looting carried out by the Northern Alliance is not tantamount to liberation, nor does the promise of democracy hold meaning. What they underscore is their need for peace (qaraar - araami). For example, one respondent, when asked if her son will wage/continue the jihad (holy war), promptly emphasized that he will only work to establish peace. This is a contrast to the mother of twenty years ago who was willing to sacrifice her son's life for the war.

For many of the poor Afghan women, the first and foremost concern (as for everyone else) is security for themselves and their family. Side by side with this is their need for a home and longing for the lost home, both in the context of geographical as well as symbolic space. This need usually goes unrecognized as the home is not accorded any importance in the context of international politics despite being integral to state formation and its continuation. It is the nation-state that constitutes the basic unit of analysis, entirely ignoring the fact that the edifice of social life in a state is built upon the construct of the home.

One associates wars with battlefields and with men, whether they ride horses, tanks, jeeps or helicopters and planes. Wars are associated with wide-open spaces, public spaces. This makes it appropriate to target and bomb countries and makes it possible to talk in terms of "targeted bombing," "carpet bombing" and "collateral damage." Homes are associated with women and with the family hence they belong to the private sphere and are generally considered outside the purview of war. However, homes are targeted in times of war and conflict. This is because the destruction of home and villages is debilitating and used as an instrument of war to spread fear and intimidation. The tendency of marauding armies in the past to murder, loot and burn that which they could not carry with them resulted in the destruction of entire villages and communities. While this has been widely documented, and has been currently experienced by Afghans at the hands of foreigners as well as their own people, very few people have looked at the issues that emerge out of these acts of violence.

The destruction of home and community has implications that go beyond the physical being of these places. These range from ideas of self, of identity, creativity, interpersonal relations and one's world-view. Some of these issues have been addressed and analyzed by anthropologists in the context of recent conflicts. However, these accounts are generally restricted to documenting and observing changes in human relations in the context of individual violence such as murder, rape and ritualistic violence. One seldom comes across accounts that make the connection between the violence of war and conflict in conjunction with the dislocation of people from their homes.

The leaving of home is not only about acquiring security, it is also symbolic of leaving behind a sense of identity, a culture, a personal and collective history. Indeed, the word home has several connotations for women, hence, its leaving, its destruction and its making are important. Home is the source of primary identity for women not only because both are associated predominantly with the private sphere but also because home is the locus of self, culture and belonging. This is true for men as well as women; however, due to the historical role that women play in the making of home, they identify much more with it.

Women's understanding and representations of home involve multiple themes that relate to both physical as well as imagined and intangible aspects. Aside from being a reflection of self, social and economic status, home represents the space where women can be happy and secure, where they can be creative and where they enjoy familial support. At the same time, due to the extreme degree of violence and destruction that has been perpetrated due to the war, home and country are no longer the symbols of protection and security. Both mirror the peril they contain for the very people they need to shelter and protect. This peril has been experienced several times, leading to double and triple trauma as the Afghan refugees keep fleeing back from their country and their homes in the face of constant bombings and fighting. This process has also rendered some women completely homeless so that they are unable to conceptualize the presence of a place that may be called home. As one Afghan woman refugee said, "we have no home anywhere. We left everything behind … and it (home) has been blown to smithereens." Her husband and she are presently renting a small room in a 4-room mud house (shared with three other families) in a squatter settlement from which she does not leave due to having no prior experience of going out, but where she is acutely uncomfortable because men of the other families come and go as and when they like, leaving no privacy or space for purdah ["modest seclusion"—ED.]. This is certainly not the home in which she can be "at home."

The themes that emerge from the interviews are about the destruction resulting from war, deaths due to rockets and bombs and the yearning to go back to the place that was home and that lies destroyed. Many talk about the pain of returning under successive governments only to find out that the same destruction and senseless war continued and they were as insecure as they had been previously. There is thus a sense of betrayal that is not alleviated by the sense of alienation in Pakistan. Their house is not "home"—it is a place, a mud house, a rented house, a camp or a tent. It is not home. There are constant thoughts of returning home and this prevents them from coming to terms with the present. Their refusal to accept their move as final (something their hosts also do not want them to do) makes them feel that the present is "temporary" even though it has affected their lives very deeply and permanently.

We also conclude that displacement, whether within one's country or outside of it, has implications not only about physical security but also anxieties about non-material aspects that form the basis of our identities, of who we are. These issues involve shifting identities, ruptures in their meanings and our perceptions of ourselves and others' perceptions of us. These identities also have to do with being men and women. For many women, memory is an important coping mechanism. Memory serves to preserve their class and social identities but also their national identities and association with their country as something beautiful. However, simultaneously the memory of violence prevents them from narrativizing their individual experience into collective history or collective consciousness.

I do not wish to end on a note of pessimism. As a social scientist, I would like to see new spaces being created by Afghan refugee women in the midst of the tremendous violence they face. I am confident that these spaces and a new

politics will eventually emerge; however, for the time being, we need to recognize that having undergone multiple traumas at multiple levels, they require respite and a breathing space—a space and time for personal and collective healing to take place and for creativity to be able to take off. They need to be able to narrativize their collective experience and make sense of their loss and sorrow by giving it meaning. At present they need time-out. For us to expect towering narratives of courage, indigenous exotic wisdom and survival is to begin to impose a new colonizing idea and discourse upon them.

While we try to make sense of international politics as it plays itself out in the life or lives of countries and their people, Afghan women try to make sense of the loss of relatives and home inflicted upon them by yet another unknown enemy-an enemy without form. As they make a safe passage into a hostile country or end up in a camp on the borders of their own country that is being bombed day in and out, their primary concern is with their own security and with trying to recreate the lost home and recover the sense of security that comes with the sense of being at home.

QUESTIONS

1. How does a "women-centered perspective" on the U.S. military intervention in Afghanistan differ from that of a male-centered perspective? Is this distinction useful in formulating IR theory?

2. Describe the elements of the feminist perspective on international relations. How do they differ from the traditionalist view?

State-Level International Relations Theories

In Part I, we discussed system-level theories of international relations, focusing on the nature of the global system and how it shapes the behavior of states within it. Now, we turn our attention to the theories that fall under Waltz's second level of analysis—the state level. State-level theories, as noted in Chapter 1, concentrate on the individual attributes of states rather than the overall system in which they operate. The primary concern here is with the domestic, political, and cultural characteristics of a state. The key assumption is that the internal character and institutions of a state have a direct bearing on its foreign policy.

There are two primary state-level theories presented in this book; each focuses on the role of the state and its impact on international relations: political culture theory and decision-making process theory. In the first chapter, we examine the tenets of political culture theory, as well as its strengths and weaknesses. Some political culture theorists argue that the type of government a state has is a broad determining factor in its behavior and foreign policy. On a basic level, these theorists suggest that, generally, democracies tend to be inherently peaceful, while authoritarian regimes are likely to pursue more aggressive policies.

A second group of political culture theorists acknowledges that these differences between regimes can be important, but believes that it is the cultural and civilizing aspects of a society that shape and guide foreign policy. For these theorists, the traditions, customs, values, and beliefs that characterize a particular group of people also have an influence on the political behavior of that group or its governing body.

The theory presented in the following chapter, decision-making process theory, emphasizes the importance of how decisions are made and the impact of the bureaucracy itself on the government's decision-making process. The implication is that the structure of the government—with its various departments and competing interests—can have substantial sway over not just the policy-making process but the policies themselves.

In the next two chapters, we take a closer look at one of the primary actors on the world stage—the state. From this level of analysis, we examine how states and governments can influence the course of events in international relations. Types of political systems, bureaucratic structure, and unique characteristics of different cultures and civilizations are just some of the important features we will discuss as part of the state level of analysis.

Chapter 6

POLITICAL CULTURE THEORY

COMPONENTS OF POLITICAL CULTURE THEORY

Focus of Analysis ········▶	• Domestic political and cultural characteristics of states or civilizations
Major Influences ········▶	• Type of government or civilization
Behavior of States ········▶	• (Regimists) Behavior based on type of government • (Civilizationists) Competitive, based on cultural values
Basis of a State's ········▶ **Foreign Policy**	• Assumes that a state's foreign policy reflects the dominant values, attitudes, and beliefs of society/civilizations
Key Concepts ········▶	• Authoritarian regimes; Civilization; Civilizationist perspective; Cultural fault line; Culture; Elitism; End of history; Foreign policy; Government; Liberal democracies; Pluralism; Political culture; Regimist perspective; Sovereignty; State

INTRODUCTION

Before we begin our discussion of political culture theory, it might be helpful to answer a few fundamental questions about states and how they operate, as well as to define some commonly used terms. Though it may seem fairly basic, let us first ask, What is a state, and how does a state differ from a government?

We can all list the names of any number of states throughout the world—France, Singapore, the United States, Kenya, and so forth. All are very different, yet all are considered states. A **state** or country (these terms are synonymous) is a political, legal, and territorial entity. A state consists of an internationally recognized territory, a permanent population, and a government that has control over the people within its acknowledged boundaries. In theory, states are sovereign. That is, the government is the supreme authority within the state and does not answer to any outside power. This **sovereignty** is recognized by international law and by other states through diplomatic relations, and often by membership in the United Nations. Though this definition may sound complex, if we refer back to our examples, we see they all fit this description. Each state has specific borders recognized by other states in the international community, and also has specific and unique political, economic, and military structures and goals.

On a broad level, the interaction of states is guided by each state's government. **Government** is a public institution that has the authority to create, implement, and enforce rules, laws, and decisions within a state's territorial borders. These rules, laws, and decisions maintain order within society as well as project and protect the state's interests abroad. The number of branches within any particular system of government can vary but commonly consists of at least a leadership branch, a bureaucratic or administrative branch, and a judicial branch.

Governments present themselves and their interests to the international community using foreign policy. **Foreign policy** consists of the decisions and strategies used by governments to guide their interaction with other states in the international system. Typically, foreign policy promotes the political, economic, and military interests of the state. The way foreign policy is made depends, in large part, on the type of government that exists in any given country.

Returning to our discussion of political culture theory, this paradigm actually contains two distinct aspects. First, we will look at the **regimist perspective,** which emphasizes the nature of a state's government—democratic or authoritarian—as a vital factor in its foreign policy and behavior within the global system. Second, the **civilizationist perspective** of political culture theory acknowledges some points made by proponents of the regime category, but stresses the importance of culture and civilization in determining a state's behavior in the international system and the future of world politics.

Before we begin our discussion of either the regimists or civilizationists, as we will call them, it might be helpful to take a look at several fundamental terms. First, **culture** refers to a particular social group's commonly shared behavior patterns, including language, traditions, values, customs, institutions, and beliefs. **Political culture** points specifically to the dominant values, attitudes, and beliefs that affect the politics and behavior of individual governments. This set of common attitudes and values about politics is fostered by the collective history of the political system and becomes embedded in the national character. It is important to remember that political culture reflects the *dominant* values and beliefs of a society, which are not necessarily representative of the beliefs of all people within that society.

Political culture can be shaped by a wide array of factors—ideological, religious, social, and economic—that may influence a country's behavior. Political culture often varies dramatically from state to state, with each reflecting its own unique approach to politics and the role of government. The political culture of the United States, for example, reflects a common belief in democracy, individual rights, capitalism, and the separation of church and state, among many other things. On the other hand, the political culture of North Korea emphasizes order, obedience, deference to authority, and the sacrifice of individual rights in favor of the community as a whole.

Political culture theorists—both regimists and civilizationists—argue that a state's political culture has a substantial influence over its foreign policy. The political culture establishes broad guidelines within which leaders make foreign policy, and creates an attitudinal environment in which every political system operates. While not normally responsible for specific policies, political culture broadly affects the range of policy options available to individual leaders.

THE REGIMISTS

Political culture theorists who emphasize the importance of regimes argue that it is the inherent differences between various types of government that can, indeed, influence state behavior on the world stage and, consequently, international politics. Unlike system-level theorists—who point to the characteristics of the system as a whole as the central force in international politics—political culture theorists suggest that the domestic characteristics of state governments are key determinants of world politics.

Let's look at the two primary types of governments and how their differences affect both their respective foreign policies and foreign policy-making processes. **Liberal democracies** (or "open" societies), in which the citizenry has a voice in government through duly elected representatives from two or more political parties, generally take a more pluralistic approach to foreign policy-making. **Pluralism** describes a political system in which decisions and policies are formulated on the basis of many different viewpoints or interests. Not just political parties, but other special interest groups (business, labor, or environmental groups, or even certain factions within the bureaucracy) can make their opinions known by contacting leaders directly or through more indirect means (media campaigns, etc.). Though the ultimate decisions on these matters do rest with a fairly small leadership circle, the people can, and often do, influence the course and content of the policy-making process.

Conversely, in **authoritarian regimes** (or "closed" societies), decisions and policies are made by an individual or small group of leaders. The people in these states generally have no meaningful impact on the political agenda or foreign policy of the country. Under this system of decision making, sometimes called **elitism,** the policies that control the actions of the state and those who live within it are created and directed by a small ruling elite. This group formulates both the domestic and foreign policy agendas. The decisions are not completely without parameters—leaders in closed societies do face political limitations, economic or military power obstacles, bureaucratic inertia or public and/or private resistance, etc.—but these are minor when compared with the variety of interests represented in a liberal democracy.

The selection taken from Bruce Russett's book *Controlling the Sword* makes the case for proponents of the regime aspect of political culture theory, emphasizing the differences between these two types of governments. Liberal democracies, Russett suggests, are less "warlike" than authoritarian or totalitarian regimes. He looks not only at empirical evidence about whether democracies go to war less often, but also at domestic factors that might make democratic states more or less reticent to engage in conflict.

Studies and empirical research into what types of nations (democratic or authoritarian) go to war and how often they go to war have shown that democracies are just as likely to engage in conflict as any other type of regime. The important difference to note here, however, is that liberal democracies rarely, if ever, make war with one another. They actually tend to bond together, forming protective, generally defensive, political-military alliances. According to Russett, the specific structure, nature, and characteristics common to democratic governments all contribute to promote a more peaceful, less aggressive foreign policy.[1]

Political culture regimists point to a number of other broader political and social ideals associated with liberal democracies that contribute to a less warlike foreign policy. Respect for human rights and the rule of law (international law, in this case), as well as the tradition of resolution through negotiation, tend to promote both peace and greater stability.

In the next selection, Francis Fukuyama agrees with the points made by Russett about the impact of a state's regime on the course of its foreign policy and behavior in the world community. Fukuyama contends that ideological competition has been the driving force of conflict between the major powers in the twentieth century. These wars have been fought largely to secure a dominant position for what one might call the great "isms" of the day. Clashes occurred between western political and economic liberalism and its two ideological antagonists, fascism and communism. Fascism was defeated and discredited at the end of World War II with the victory over Nazi Germany by the allied powers and, forty-five years later, communism was dealt a severe blow with the collapse of the Soviet empire.

The success of western liberalism over its two ideological opponents led Fukuyama to take the regimist position on political culture theory a step further, concluding that "what we may be witnessing is not just the end of the Cold War, or the passing of a particular period in postwar history, but the **end of history** as such: that is, the end point of mankind's ideological evolution and the universalization of western liberal democracy as the final form of human government."[2] Western liberal democracy has triumphed over its ideological rivals, and—since history is marked by the clash of ideas—history, according to Fukuyama, has come to an end.

---

[1] Many institutional transnationlists introduced in our analysis of system-level theories, such as, Immanuel Kant and Woodrow Wilson, have been strong advocates of the positive contribution made to the stability of the international system by liberal democratic regimes. Kant, in his work *Perpetual Peace*, published in 1795, argued that the accountability of democratic leaders to the people for their decisions makes them more cautions about taking steps that could lead to armed conflict. Understandably, the people tend to be equally cautious in supporting a bellicose foreign policy, since they would be called upon to do any fighting should the need arise.

[2] Francis Fukuyama, "The End of History?" *The National Interest*, Number 16/Summer 1989, p. 4.

While this victory is "incomplete" and many nations, particularly in the third world, have not yet or not fully adopted western economic and political liberalism, Fukuyama believes the course of history will inevitably lead to the expansion and broad acceptance of these ideals. Prior to this point, the world can be divided into two major categories based on levels of liberal democratic development. Relations among liberal democratic countries in the "post-historical" stage are characterized by cooperation and stability. The non-democratic nations, classified as "still in history," continue to struggle with ethnic and nationalist conflicts. International conflict, Fukuyama argues, will revolve around these states, while relations among post-historical states—largely in the West—will be limited primarily to peaceful economic and technological competition.

Fukuyama's thesis about the triumph of liberal democracy and what this means for the future of international relations has been hotly debated. Critics disagree with Fukuyama on a number of issues. They argue that the end of the Cold War does not necessarily represent the end of political rivalries among states—either post-historical or still in history. Indeed, as we will discuss in more detail later, Samuel P. Huntington believes that the post–Cold War period may well lead to greater instability and conflict in world politics.

THE CIVILIZATIONISTS

The second perspective on political culture theory focuses on Samuel Huntington's examination of the impact of broad cultural factors on the behavior of individual states, or even groups of states that share a common culture. Samuel Huntington stresses the importance of culture in international relations. Huntington outlined this new theory of international politics for the post-Cold War world in his 1993 *Foreign Affairs* article "The Clash of Civilizations?" Unlike proponents of the regimist position, who are concerned primarily with the differences between democratic and authoritarian governments, Huntington focuses on the broader cultural attributes that both unite and divide people, states, and the world.

His view of civilization is a key component of this thesis. Huntington defines **civilization** as the "highest cultural grouping of people and the broadest level of cultural identity people have, short of that which distinguishes them from other species." Civilization, then, is composed of those elements that bind people together, such as common language, religion, customs, institutions, and identification with a particular culture. According to these criteria, states can be grouped together into eight major civilizations: Western, Confucian, Japanese, Islamic, Hindu, Slavic-Orthodox, Latin American, and African.

Now, let us see how Huntington applies the concept of civilization to his political culture theory of international relations. To begin, Huntington agrees with two points regarding the end of the Cold War in Fukuyama's article "The End of History?" First, Huntington accepts that the end of the Cold War was a turning point in global politics, setting the stage for new theories to explain recent developments in international relations. Second, he agrees, too, that this event also signaled the diminished relevance of ideology as a source of conflict between western countries. But, as we noted in the preceding section, Huntington draws the line well before Fukuyama, stating that conflicts themselves have not ended and that we are by no means at an end of history.

"The Clash of Civilizations?" lays out a theoretical framework suggesting that cultural differences have supplanted ideological differences as the most important source of conflict among peoples and states. Conflicts, Huntington contends, are most likely to develop between groups that are part of different civilizations. Likewise, cooperation occurs more frequently within civilizations rather than between them.

This argument centers on the idea that cultural differences between the eight civilizations—Western, Confucian, Japanese, Islamic, Hindu, Slavic-Orthodox, Latin American, and African—are more serious and could even be more dangerous than the traditional ideological and economic clashes characterizing past wars. Huntington asserts that advances in global communication and increasing economic and social interaction between people in different regions of the world have enhanced the awareness and importance of "civilization." In addition, modernization has eroded the relevance of local and national cultural identifications while magnifying the significance of this broader grouping.

As we noted, Huntington believes increasing "civilization consciousness" implies that cooperation will occur with greatest frequency among states within a particular civilization. Conflict is more likely to occur between groups in different civilizations. This is because cultural issues like religion and social traditions are more fundamental and less easily resolved through compromise and negotiation. Conflict will likewise most often occur along cultural fault lines. A **cultural fault line** is found where different civilizations share a common border; this includes both borders between different states as well as the more tenuous ones found within states. According to Huntington, cultural fault lines now represent the most probable new "flash points for crisis and bloodshed."[3]

To support his theory, Huntington points to several contemporary ethnic and religious conflicts in the world. Among those flash points are the current warfare in the former Yugoslavia, where Western and Islamic civilizations meet within a confined geographic area. Christian and Muslim factions now battle for control over territory they once shared peacefully under a communist regime that suppressed these ethnic tensions. Also, the continued unrest between Israel and its Arab neighbors attests to not only the vehemence with which civilizations can clash but also the prolonged nature of these feuds. One other example might be found in India and Pakistan; both countries have been plagued by violence between Hindu and Muslim peoples within each state's own borders.

Clearly, there is no shortage of examples worldwide where one might find Huntington's clash of civilizations. But what do these clashes mean for the West and for western civilization? Taking a fairly dim view of the future, Huntington fears that conflict on a global scale—what he refers to as the "West versus the Rest"—is a possibility. Western political, economic, and cultural dominance is increasingly challenged by Confucian and Islamic states. These particular civilizations are increasingly more willing and able to assert their own economic, political, and military power against western-oriented institutions and ideals. Huntington believes that the West will have

---

[3] Samuel Huntington, "The Clash of Civilizations?" *Foreign Affairs*, Summer 1993, p. 29.

to learn to "accommodate" these rising nonwestern civilizations and "coexist" with countries "whose values and interests differ significantly from those of the West."[4]

The "Clash of Civilizations" thesis has been subjected to a remarkable amount of criticism from a variety of sources. Here, we offer an article by Stephen Walt that forcefully critiques Huntington's civilizationist theory. Walt questions the emphasis on civilizations as a source of either unity among or division between peoples. He contests Huntington's notion that civilizations are cohesive groupings, united in purpose. Huntington, according to Walt, glosses over significant economic, social, and political cleavages that exist within all of what Huntington has called civilizations. Similarly, Walt says, Huntington ignores examples of cooperation between states representing different civilizations.

But we might ask why Walt sees cooperation between civilizations where Huntington sees conflict. In a fashion reminiscent of realism, Walt argues that even in the post–Cold War environment, states remain the primary actors on the international political stage. The individual geopolitical and economic self-interests of the state supersede any fidelity toward a particular civilization. In addition, Walt suggests that economic and technological modernization and secularism actually enhance rather than prohibit cooperation between states.

In the end, Walt's argument echoes the realist view that international politics will continue to be dominated by states vying for geopolitical and economic position. Though we see many cases of this competition along the fault lines of Huntington's civilizations, contemporary history has also shown that when circumstances warrant cooperation between states and peoples, the differences of civilizations can be set aside in the interests of *realpolitic.*

The final two selections in this chapter offer examples of how political culture theory can be applied to recent events. In the short piece by Francis Fukuyama entitled "The west has won," the author defends his "end of history" thesis by noting that terrorism perpetrated by radical Islam is merely a backlash against modernity and does not represent a viable alternative to liberal democratic values. The final article by Benjamin Barber is a civilizationist critique of the utility of realism in the post–September 11 era. Barber argues that nonstate actors are motivated by dramatically different interests than states are. Therefore, traditional realist assumptions cannot be relied upon as useful guidelines for understanding the current global war on terrorism. Instead, Barber contends, we must focus on the social, political, cultural and economic conditions under which terrorism thrives.

A Critique of Political Culture Theory

Certainly, the article by Stephen Walt provides a thorough critique of the "civilizationist" perspective of political culture theory offered by Samuel Huntington. It might be useful, however, to review here the major points both for and against what we call the regimist viewpoint of political culture theory.

---

[4] Huntington, p. 49.

KEY CONCEPTS

Authoritarian regimes   are societies in which dominant political authority and power resides in an individual or small group of leaders who are not responsible to the people under their control.

Civilization   is composed of those elements that bind people together such as common language, religion, customs, institutions, and identification with a particular culture. Samuel P. Huntington defines civilization as the "highest cultural grouping of people and the broadest level of cultural identity people have short of that which distinguishes them from other species."

Civilizationist perspective,   as used in this book, is one of two major divisions of political culture theory and is based on the theory set forth by Samuel P. Huntington in his article, "The Clash of Civilizations?" The civilizationist perspective stresses that the "principal conflicts of global politics will occur between nations and groups of different civilizations."

Cultural fault line   is found where different civilizations share a common border; this includes both borders between different states as well as the more tenuous ones found within states. This term was coined by Samuel P. Huntington.

Culture   refers to commonly shared behavior patterns, including language, traditions, values, customs, institutions, and religious beliefs of a particular social group.

Elitism   exists where a small group of people control, rule, or dominate the actions of a state. This group formulates both the domestic and foreign policy agendas.

End of history   is a phrase used by Francis Fukuyama to describe the triumph of western economic and political liberalism over its ideological alternatives, such as fascism and Marxism-Leninism, and the coming universalization of western liberal democracy.

(continued)

There is little doubt that the type of government and the larger cultural attributes of a country have an impact on the course of international politics. As Bruce Russett and Francis Fukuyama indicated, considerable evidence shows that democracies do behave differently from authoritarian regimes. The virtual absence of war between democratic regimes speaks volumes about the cooperative nature of these governments. Critics have argued, though, that peace among democracies may be the result of particular geopolitical factors rather than the influence of shared common values. Regimists do, however, provide substantial evidence—both quantitative and qualitative—that democracies more commonly resort to negotiation than do authoritarian regimes as a means of conflict resolution.

(continued from previous page)

Foreign policy   is the strategy used by a government to make decisions and guide its interaction with other states in the international system. Typically, foreign policy promotes the political, economic, and military interests of the state.

Government   is a public institution that has the authority to create, implement, and enforce rules, laws, and decisions within a state's territorial borders. These rules, laws, and decisions maintain order within society, as well as project and protect the state's interests abroad.

Liberal democracies   are states in which the citizenry has a voice in government through duly elected representatives from two or more political parties.

Pluralism   is a political system in which decisions and policies are formulated on the basis of many different viewpoints or interests.

Political culture   refers to the dominant values, attitudes, and beliefs that affect the politics and behavior of individual governments.

Regimist perspective,   as used in this text, is one of two major divisions of political culture theory. Regimists argue that democracies and authoritarian regimes behave differently in foreign affairs. Their analysis focuses on regime type as a vital factor in determining a state's foreign policy and behavior within the global system.

Sovereignty   exists when the domestic government is the supreme authority within the state and does not answer to any outside power. This sovereignty is recognized by international law and by other states through diplomatic relations and often by membership in the United Nations.

State   is a political, legal, and territorial entity. A state consists of an internationally recognized territory, a permanent population, and a government that has control over the people within its acknowledged boundaries.

The civilizationist perspective of political culture theory outlined in Samuel P. Huntington's "The Clash of Civilizations?" is perhaps the most innovative and ambitious attempt to codify international relations theory in the post–Cold War era. His idea that conflict between civilizations will supplant ideological conflict as the dominant force in international politics offers a unique look into the domestic-level explanations of what drives the actions of states and groups of states.

The question remains, however, whether civilization consciousness is truly a uniting or dividing force among states. Are cultural, religious, and ethnic factors vitally important sources of states' actions? Can the principles of liberal democracy bring states and peoples together? Or could the actions of states be shaped more by systemic factors, compelling all governments—irrespective of regime or civilization—to act in similar manners? Or might it be some combination?

27.   Controlling the Sword

Bruce Russett

In this excerpt, Bruce Russett discusses the reasons why democracies are not likely to go to war with each other. He lays out the causes, limitations, and implications of a democratic world system. Russett also criticizes the realist view that states are motivated primarily by a quest for power. This selection is from *Controlling the Sword: The Democratic Governance of National Security* (1990).

Bruce Russett is a professor of international relations and world politics at Yale University. He has authored many books on international relations, including *Power and Community in World Politics* (1974), *Interest and Ideology* (1975), *Prisoners of Insecurity* (1983), *Grasping the Democratic Peace: Principles for a Post–Cold War World* (1993), and *World Politics: The Menu for Choice* (2003).

Two apparent facts about contemporary international patterns of war and peace stare us in the face. The first is that some states expect, prepare for, and fight wars against other states. The second is that some states do *not* expect, prepare for, or fight wars *at least against each other.* The first is obvious to everyone. The second is widely ignored, yet it is now true on a historically unprecedented scale, encompassing wide areas of the earth. In a real if still partial sense, peace is already among us. We need only recognize it, and try to learn from it.

An understanding of why some states do not engage in hostility may lead us to an attainable basis for an alternative system of security, one that does not depend on acceptance of a world state to enforce peace or on a particular configuration of strategy and weaponry to provide a peace of sorts through some form of stable deterrence. . . .

PEACE AMONG DEMOCRACIES

I refer to the peace among the industrialized and democratically governed states, primarily in the northern hemisphere. These states—members of the Organization for Economic Cooperation and Development (OECD: Western Europe, North America, Japan, Australia, and New Zealand), plus a few scattered less-industrialized democratic states—constitute a vast zone of peace, with more than three quarters of a billion people. Not only has there been no war among them for 45 years (see table on page 383), there has been little expectation of or preparation for war among them either. By war I mean large-scale organized international violence with, by a conventional social science definition, at least 1,000 battle deaths. In fact, even much smaller-scale violence between these countries has been virtually absent. The nearest exception is Greece and Turkey, with their brief and limited violent clashes over Cyprus; they are, however, among the poorest countries of this group, and only sporadically democratic.

In the years before 1945 many of these states fought often and bitterly—but always when at least one of the

Harvard University Press, United Kingdom.

Distribution of International Wars, 1945–1989.

| | FOUGHT IN | | |
FOUGHT BY	OECD COUNTRIES	COMMUNIST COUNTRIES	LDCS
OECD countries	0	1	7
Communist countries	0	3	3
LDCs (less developed countries)	0	1	19

Source: Small and Singer, 1982, updated to 1989. Includes all interstate and colonial wars (not civil wars) with more than 1000 battle deaths.

states in any warring pair was ruled by an authoritarian or totalitarian regime. Despite that past, war among them is now virtually unthinkable. What had been seemingly the most permanent enmities—for instance, between France and Germany—have for the past two or three decades appeared well buried. Individual citizens may not love each other across national boundaries, but neither do they expect the other's state to attack, or wish to mount an attack on it. Expectations of peace are thus equally important; these peoples make few preparations for violence between them; peace for them means more than just the prevention of war through threat and deterrence. This condition has been characterized as a "security community," or as "stable peace" (Deutsch et al., 1957; Boulding, 1979). In duration and expectation it differs from the simple absence of war that may prevail between some other states, including nondemocratic ones in the third world. By the standards of world history this is an extraordinary achievement.

It is not easy to explain just why this peace has occurred. Partly it is due to the network of *international law and institutions* deliberately put into place in order to make a repetition of the previous world wars both unthinkable and impossible. But that network is strongest in Western Europe, often excluding the countries in North America and the Far East; even in the strongest instance the institutions typically lack full powers to police and coerce would-be breakers of the peace; and, as we shall see below, even powerful institutions cannot guarantee peace if the underlying preconditions of peace are lacking.

In part it is due to favorable *economic conditions* associated with advanced capitalism. Fairly steady economic growth, a high absolute level of prosperity, relative equality of incomes within and across the industrial states, and a dense network of trade and investment across national borders all make the resort to violence dubious on cost-benefit grounds; a potential aggressor who already is wealthy risks much from the large-scale destructiveness of modern war, for only moderate gain (Mueller, 1989). But the condition of peace among these rich states has not been endangered by such periods of postwar recession and stagnation as have occurred, and in other parts of the world, especially Latin America, there are democratic states that are not wealthy but are still at peace with one another.

Partly, too, peace is the result of a perceived *"external" threat* faced by the industrialized democracies; they maintain peace among themselves in order not to invite intervention by the communist powers. Where peace among them is threatened, it may be enforced by the dominant "hegemonic" power of the United States (Weede, 1984). But the external threat also has waxed and waned without affecting the peace among these states; indeed, their peace became even more stable during the very time, over the past two decades, when the cold war abated and Europeans, especially, ceased to have much fear of Soviet attack. All these explanations, therefore, are at best only partial ones, and we are driven back to observing that the period of peace among the highly industrialized states essentially coincides with the period when they all have been under democratic rule.[1]

Conceptually and empirically the competing explanations overlap somewhat and reinforce one another, especially for the post–World War II era. International law has served to legitimate widely many of the domestic legal principles of human rights associated with liberal democracy; all advanced capitalist industrial states have been, since World War II, democratic (though not all democratic states are economically advanced); most of them have also been part of the American "hegemonic" alliance system (which has also included nondemocratic and economically less-developed countries). While this overlap prevents a definitive test, all the alternative hypotheses find their predictions falsified by at least one warring pair: the British-Argentine war in 1982, between two capitalist (Argentina only moderately advanced) states allied with the United States. World Wars I and II of course included many industrial capitalist countries as warring pairs. Analysts as different as Joseph Schumpeter and Karl Kautsky predicted peace among advanced capitalist states; Lenin did not. Nor is it simply part of a general statement that politically or culturally similar

countries do not fight one another (Russett, 1968, ch. 12; Wilkinson, 1980, ch. 9). An empirical correlation between cultural similarity and relative absence of war exists, but it is a weak one. There are several examples of wars or threats of war within Eastern Europe and Latin America in recent decades; by contrast, a reduction in regional enmities is associated with parallel democratization (for example, Argentina and Brazil). . . .

By a democratic state I mean one with the conditions of public contestation and participation, essentially as identified by Robert Dahl (1971), with a voting franchise for a substantial fraction of male citizens (in the nineteenth and early twentieth centuries; wider thereafter), contested elections, and an executive either popularly elected or responsible to an elected legislature. While scholars who have found this pattern differ slightly in their definitions, agreement on the condition of virtual absence of war among democracies ("liberal," "libertarian," or "polyarchic" states) is now overwhelming (Wallensteen, 1973; Small and Singer, 1976; Rummel, 1983, 1985; Chan, 1984; Weede, 1984; Doyle, 1986; Maoz and Abdolali, 1989). This simple fact cries out for explanation: What is there about democratic governments that so inhibits their people from fighting one another?

In exploring that question we should be clear about what is not implied. The condition of peace *between* democratic states does not mean that democratic states are ipso facto peaceful with *all* countries. . . .

INTERNAL PEACE AND INTERNATIONAL PEACE

There are powerful norms against the use of lethal force both within democratic states and between them. Within them is of course the basic norm of liberal democratic theory—that disputes can be resolved without force through democratic political processes which in some balance are to ensure both majority rule and minority rights. A norm of equality operates both as voting equality and certain egalitarian rights to human dignity. Democratic government rests on the consent of the governed, but justice demands that consent not be abused. Resort to organized lethal violence, or the threat of it, is considered illegitimate, and unnecessary to secure one's "legitimate" rights. Dissent within broad limits by a loyal opposition is expected and even needed for enlightened policy-making, and the opposition's basic loyalty to the system is to be assumed in the absence of evidence to the contrary.

All participants in the political process are expected to share these norms. In practice the norms do sometimes break down, but the normative restraints on violent behavior—by state and citizens—are fully as important as the state's monopoly on the legitimate use of force in keeping incidents of the organized use of force rare. Democracy is a set of institutions and norms for peaceful resolution of conflict. The norms are probably more important than any particular institutional characteristic (two-party/multiparty, republican/parliamentary) or formal constitutional provision. Institutions may precede the development of norms. If they do, the basis for restraint is likely to be less secure.

Democracy did not suddenly emerge full-blown in the West, nor by any linear progression. Only over time did it come to mean the extension of a universal voting franchise, formal protection for the rights of ethnic, racial, and religious minorities, and the rights of groups to organize for economic and social action.

The rights to organize came to imply the right to carry on conflict—but non-violently, as by strikes, under the principle that each side in the conflict had to recognize the right of the other to struggle, so long as that struggle was constrained by law, mutual self-interest, and mutual respect. The implicit or explicit contract in the extension of such rights was that the beneficiaries of those rights would in turn extend them to their adversaries.

To observe this is not to accept democratic theory uncritically, or to deny that it is part of a belief structure that, in Gramsci's view of cultural hegemony, may serve to legitimate dominant-class interests and provide subordinate classes with a spurious sense of their own political efficacy.[2] As such, it may exaggerate belief in the "reasonableness" of both the demands of one's own state in international politics and those of other democratic states. But it is precisely beliefs and perceptions that are primarily at issue here; insofar as the other state's demands are considered ipso facto reasonable according to a view of one's own system that extends to theirs, popular sentiment for war or resistance to compromise is undermined.

Politics within a democracy is seen as a largely nonzero-sum enterprise: by cooperating, all can gain something even if all do not gain equally, and the winners today are restrained from crushing the losers; indeed, the winners may, with shifting coalitions, wish tomorrow to ally with today's losers. If the conflicts degenerate to physical violence, either by those in control of the state or by insurgents, all can lose. In international politics—the anarchy of a self-help system with no superordinate governing authority—these norms are not the same. "Realists" remind us of the powerful norms of legitimate self-defense and the acceptability of military deterrence, norms much more extensive internationally than within democratic states. Politics between nations takes on a more zero-sum hue. True, we know we all can lose in nuclear war or in a collapse of international commerce, but we worry much more about comparative gains and losses. The essence of "realist" politics is that even when two states both become more wealthy, if one gains much more wealth than the other it also gains more power, more potential to coerce the other; thus the one which is lagging economically only in relative terms may be an absolute loser in the power contest.

The principles of anarchy and self-help in a zero-sum world are seen most acutely in "structural realist" theories of international relations. Specifically, a bipolar system of two great states or alliances, each much more powerful than any others in the international system, is seen as inherently antagonistic. The nature of the great powers' internal systems of government is irrelevant; whatever they may work out with or impose on some of their smaller allies, their overall behavior with other great powers is basically determined by the structure of the international system and their position in that structure. Athens and Sparta, or the United States and the Soviet Union, are doomed to compete and to resist any substantial accretion to the other's power. To fail to compete is to risk the death of sovereignty, or death itself. Through prudence and self-interest they may avoid a full-scale war that might destroy or cripple both of them (the metaphor of two scorpions in a bottle), but the threat of war is never absent, and can never be absent. "Peace," such as it is, can come only from deterrence, eternal vigilance, and probably vi-

olent competition between their "proxies" elsewhere in the world. By this structural realist understanding, the kind of stable peace that exists between the democratic countries can never exist on a global scale (Waltz, 1979).

Efforts to establish norms against the use of lethal violence internationally have been effective only to a limited degree. The Kellogg-Briand Pact of 1928 to outlaw war was a failure from the outset, as have been efforts to outlaw "aggressive" war. Despite its expression of norms and some procedures for the pacific settlement of disputes, the United Nations Charter fully acknowledges "the inherent right of individual or collective self-defense if an armed attack occurs" (Article 51). It could hardly do otherwise in the absence of superordinate authority. The norm of national self-defense—including collective self-defense on behalf of allies, and defense of broadly conceived "vital" interests even when national survival is not at stake—remains fully legitimate to all but tiny pacifist minorities. While there is some cross-cultural variation in the readiness of different peoples to use lethal force in different modes of self-defense, these differences are not strongly linked to form of government. Citizens of small democracies who perceive themselves as beleaguered (such as Israel), or citizens of large powerful democracies with imperial histories or a sense of global responsibilities for the welfare of others (such as Britain or the United States) are apt to interpret national or collective interest quite broadly. Especially across international cultural barriers, perversions of the "right" of self-defense come easily.

Yet democratic peoples exercise that right within a sense that somehow they and other peoples *ought* to be able to satisfy common interests and work out compromise solutions to their problems, without recourse to violence or threat of it. After all, that is the norm for behavior to which they aspire within democratic systems. Since other people living in democratic states are presumed to share those norms of live and let live, they can be presumed to moderate their behavior in international affairs as well. That is, they can be respected as self-governing peoples, and expected to offer the same respect to other democratic countries in turn. The habits and predispositions they show in their behavior in internal politics can be presumed to apply when they deal with like-minded outsiders. If one claims the principle of self-determination for oneself, normatively one must accord it to others perceived as self-governing. Norms do matter. Within a transnational democratic culture, as within a democratic nation, others are seen as possessing rights and exercising those rights in a spirit of enlightened self-interest. Acknowledgment of those rights both prevents us from wishing to dominate them and allows us to mitigate our fears that they will try to dominate us.

Realism has no explanation for the fact that certain kinds of states—namely, democratic ones—do not fight or prepare to fight one another. One must look instead to the liberal idealist vision of Immanuel Kant's *Perpetual Peace,* embodied also in Woodrow Wilson's vision of a peaceful world of democratic states. This same vision inspired American determination to root out fascism and establish the basis for democratic governments in West Germany and Japan after World War II (and partly also explains and was used to justify interventions in Vietnam, Grenada, Nicaragua, and so on).

Democratic states, with their wide variety of active interest groups in shifting coalitions, also present the opportunity for the formation of transnational coalitions in alliance with groups in other democracies. This may seem a form of "meddling"; it also provides another channel for resolution of international conflict. International anarchy is not supplanted by institutions of common government, but conflicts of interest within the anarchy can be moderated fairly peacefully on the principle of self-determination within an international society.

How much importance should we attribute to perceptions among the public in general, and how much to those of the elites including, in particular, the leaders of the state? Decisions for war, and indeed most major decisions in national security matters, are taken by the leaders and debated largely among the elites. They have some ability to mold mass opinion. Nevertheless, the elites in a democracy know that the expenditure of blood and treasure in any extended or costly international conflict will not be popular, and can be sustained only with the support of the general public. Whereas there may be leads and lags either way, . . . long-term serious differences between public opinion and official foreign policy are rare. Hence the elites will be somewhat constrained by popular views of the reasonableness of engaging in violent conflict with a particular foreign country. . . .

RELATIONS WITH NONDEMOCRATIC STATES

When we look within the construct of democratic ideology, it is apparent that the restraints on behavior that operate between separately governed democratic peoples do not apply to their relations with nondemocratic states. If other self-governing (democratic) peoples can be presumed to be worthy of being treated in a spirit of compromise and as in turn acting in that spirit, the same presumption does not apply to authoritarian states. According to democratic norms, authoritarian states do not rest on the proper consent of the governed, and thus they cannot properly represent the will of their peoples—if they did, they would not need to rule through undemocratic, authoritarian institutions. Rulers who control their own people by such means, who do not behave in a just way that respects their own people's right to self-determination, cannot be expected to behave better toward peoples outside their states. "Because non-liberal governments are in a state of aggression with their own people, their foreign relations become for liberal governments deeply suspect. In short, fellow liberals benefit from a presumption of amity; nonliberals suffer from a presumption of enmity" (Doyle, 1986, p. 1161). Authoritarian governments are expected to aggress against others if given the power and the opportunity. By this reasoning, democracies must be eternally vigilant against them, and may even sometimes feel the need to engage in preemptive or preventive (defensively motivated) war against them.

Whereas wars against other democratic states are neither expected nor considered legitimate, wars against authoritarian states may often be expected and "legitimated" by the principles outlined above. Thus an international system composed of both democratic and authoritarian states will include both zones of peace (actual and expected, among the democracies) and zones of war or at best deterrence between democratic states and authoritarian ones and, of course, between authoritarian states. Two states may avoid war even if one of them is not a democracy, but chiefly because of the power of one or both states to deter the other from the use of lethal force: the one-sided deterrence of dominance, or mutual deterrence between those more or less equally powerful. If the democratic state is strong, its "forbearance" may permit war to be avoided.

Of course, democracies have not fought wars only out of motivations of self-defense, however broadly one may define self-defense to include "extended deterrence" for the defense of allies and other interests or to include anticipation of others' aggression. Many of them have also fought imperialist wars to acquire or hold colonies (like the French in Vietnam) or, since World War II, to retain control of states formally independent but within their spheres of influence (like the Americans in Vietnam). In these cases they have fought against people who on one ground or another could be identified as not self-governing.[3] . . .

HUMAN RIGHTS AND INFORMATION

Whatever the faults of Western liberal (bourgeois) democracy, a world of spreading democratic ideology and practice offers some significant possibilities also for spreading peace. Those possibilities can be enhanced by attention to implementing a broad definition of human rights and institutionalizing a freer flow of information.[4] Human rights and information are elements both of greater global democratization and of direct and indirect contributions to international peace. In a world of imperfect democratization, such elements can help reduce those imperfections, and can compensate for some of them in the avoidance of war.

1. Recent American governments have tended, in different ways, to emphasize a commitment to human rights. In the Carter administration this began with an emphasis on political rights and civil liberties throughout the world; American standards were applied both to communist countries and to Third World states. Those governments found wanting did not appreciate the criticism. American attention to human rights in the Soviet Union reflected and perhaps hastened the decline of détente; despite some successes in the Third World, American pressures often angered allies thought to be strategically important, and the pressures were lessened. During the early years of the Reagan administration, official policy on human rights seemed to be turned most critically toward the Soviet Union and its allies, with abuses by American allies typically overlooked, tolerated, or even abetted. American allies were said to be merely authoritarian states, not totalitarian ones. The frequent ineffectiveness or hypocrisy of American policy on human rights has given the whole concept a bad name to some otherwise sympathetic and liberal-minded people. But the forces strengthening human rights can at least be assisted by low-key persuasion and good example.

Efforts to promote human rights internationally have not been uniformly ineffective or hypocritical. Third world states sometimes do relax the worst of their oppression in response to external pressures, whether those pressures come from governments, international organizations, or private transnational organizations like Amnesty International and Americas Watch. External pressures can contribute to the legitimacy of internal opposition. Some of the rhetoric and liberalizing action of Gorbachev owes a great debt to the power and attractiveness of Western concepts of human rights. Western efforts to reiterate those concepts and their implications—for Eastern Europe as well as for the Soviet Union itself—can hardly be abandoned. An image of the Soviet government as willing to grant a fairly high degree of autonomy to its own citizens but not to its neighbors would hardly fit the image of a state with the "liberal," "live-and-let-live" policy essential to the basis of international peace being discussed in these pages.

Yet political concessions in the form of domestic human rights policies cannot be *demanded* of another great power. The principle of noninterference in the internal governance of other states (in international law, statist and positivist norms), dating from the end of the Thirty Years War, does help to defuse one major source of interstate conflict and cannot lightly be cast aside. Hectoring or badgering the leaders of another great power is likely to poison political relations and exacerbate other conflicts; linkage of human rights concessions to important arms control measures is likely to hobble efforts to reduce real dangers of inadvertent escalation of conflict. The failure to reach human rights goals should not become a reason to forgo arms control agreements or, worse, used as an excuse to prevent arms control agreements.

International discussions on human rights are properly a dialogue, wherein the normatively persuasive elements are not solely those of Western advocates. A broad conception of human rights most certainly requires great emphasis on the kind of political rights stressed in American statements. Movement toward a more democratic world requires continued repetition of that message. It also requires a recognition of the legitimacy of some of the rights stressed by others: economic rights, to employment, housing, and some basic standard of material life (Beitz, 1979; Kim, 1984) Justice demands political liberty, and it also demands a decent level of economic well-being. Political and social peace within democratic countries has been bought in part by this recognition; severe dismantlement of the welfare state would inflame class and ethnic conflict, and most elected political leaders know it. Internationally, recognition of the multi-faceted nature of human rights is essential if the dialogue is to be one of mutual comprehension and persuasion. This is a way in which political rights, economic rights, and international peace are bound inextricably together.

Increasing worldwide adherence to democratic political norms and practices cannot alone bear all the weight of sustaining peace. Greater prosperity and economic justice, especially in the Third World, must also bear a major part. This conviction has often been expressed (for example, Brandt, 1980; Shue, 1980); cynics often dismiss it. But it is unlikely to be merely a coincidence that, as noted earlier, the industrial democracies are rich as well as democratic. The distribution of material rewards within them, while hardly ideal, is nevertheless far more egalitarian than that within many Third World countries, or between First and Third World peoples. That relatively just distribution does affect the cost-benefit analysis of those who would drastically alter it by violence; both rich and poor know they could lose badly. Some such calculation, including but not limited to the normative demands of justice, must apply to cement peace between nations. The broader human rights

dialogue, incorporating political, cultural, and economic rights, constitutes a key element of global democratization where the domestic institutions of democracy are imperfect.

2. Another aspect of a stable international peace—reinforcing but not fully contained in concepts of political democracy and human rights—concerns practices and institutions for international communication and cooperation. This has several elements.

One is *economic:* a freer flow of goods and services between communist and capitalist countries, especially including the Soviet Union. Henry Kissinger's détente policy envisaged such a network of interdependence, giving the Soviet Union a greater material stake in peaceful relations with the capitalist world, and increased Soviet interest in Western products and markets makes the vision all the more plausible. The vision is consistent with traditional liberal prescriptions for trade and international cooperation (Rosecrance, 1986). While it is not a sufficient condition for peace, and possibly not even a necessary one, it certainly can make an important contribution.

Economic exchange is also a medium and an occasion for the exchange of *information*. Facilitation of a freer flow of information is a second major element. Without a free flow of information outward there can be no confidence in the outside world that democratic practices are really being followed within a country, and sharp restrictions on the flow of information into one's own country are incompatible with the full democratic competition of ideas inside it. Cultural exchanges and free travel across state boundaries can help ease misunderstandings of the other's reasoning, goals, and intent. Across the spectrum from academic game theory to concrete social experience, we know that the prospects for cooperation are much enhanced if the relevant actors can communicate their preferences and actions clearly. This too is not a sufficient condition, and it is easy to trivialize or ridicule the idea by imagining that communication alone can solve international problems. But without the dependable exchange of information, meaningful cooperation is virtually impossible in a world of complex problems and complex national governing systems.[5]

It is in this sense that *institutions*— especially what Keohane (1984) calls "information rich" institutions—are valuable as a means to discover and help achieve shared and complementary interests. Global organizations such as UN agencies are important purveyors of relevant information. Regional organizations, especially among culturally similar countries, may be much less important as instruments of coercion or enforcement than as a means of spotlighting major human rights violations and upholding the moral force of higher norms. The European Commission on Human Rights and the European Court of Human Rights have done this effectively, the Inter-American Commission on Human Rights and the Inter-American Court of Human Rights to a lesser degree (Weston et al., 1987). Transnational and populist legal norms serve to counter statist ones, and principles of democratic rights become incorporated, often through treaties, into international law and thereby into other states' domestic law (see MacDougal et al., 1980; Falk, 1981; Boyle, 1985).

The element of information exchange relates directly to progress on *security* issues. Arms control and disarmament agreements require confidence that compliance with the agreements can be verified. Arrangements for ensuring verification must be established on a long-term, reliable basis. Without verification the agreements are continually hostage both to real fears that the agreements are being violated and to pernicious charges by those who are opposed to the agreements whether or not they are being violated. An authoritarian government can more easily, if it wishes, pursue long-term strategies of aggressive expansion than can a pluralistic democracy with many power centers and voices. "Democratic governments can also have their military buildups, of course, but cannot mask them because a public atmosphere of fear or hostility will have to be created to justify the sacrifices; they can threaten other countries, but only after their action has been justified in the open." (Luttwak, 1987, p. 235). Liberalization of the Soviet Union allows its external partners and adversaries to feel less apprehensive, and to feel more confident that they will have early warning of any newly aggressive policy.

A dense, informal network of information exchange which extends across a wide range of issues and is beyond the control of any government will help, as will some formal institutions for information-sharing. Just as substantial freedom of information is essential to democratic processes within a country, it is essential to peaceful collaboration between autonomous, self-determining peoples organized as nation-states.

Certain specific kinds of multilateral institutions can be important in controlling crises. One possibility is to create crisis management centers, of the kind already established by the United States and the Soviet Union but extended to include other nuclear powers whose actions might cascade a crisis. Another is to strengthen the information and communications base—now sadly inadequate—of the United Nations, and especially of the Secretary General, so that in some future event like the Cuban missile crisis he could act as an informed and timely mediator. Yet another possibility is to have observation satellites operated by third parties (other countries, or international organizations) to monitor military activities and arms control compliance by a variety of electronic means (Boudreau, 1984; Florini, 1988). As long as nuclear weapons exist, even in a world of substantial political liberalization, reliable means of information exchange will be essential. . . .

THE COMING TEST?

Realist theories about the inherently antagonistic structure of international relations have never been tested in a world where all the major states were governed more or less democratically. Thus we never have had a proper test of some realist propositions against liberal idealist ones.[6] Perhaps we are about to see one. Even if liberal idealist theories are correct, it is not clear whether some threshold of democratic norms and practices must be crossed to achieve peace, or whether (Rummel, 1983, 1985) it is merely a matter of greater *degree* of democratization bringing a greater *likelihood* of peace between states. . . .

NOTES

1. These attempted explanations are considered at greater length in Russett and Starr, 1989, ch. 14. For the European states, Duroselle, 1988, credits democracy and also the demise of colonialism and therefore the end of colonial rivalries. Small and Singer, 1976, p. 67, noted that in their data—ending in 1965—relatively few democracies were contiguous and therefore had much opportunity to fight. Many more contiguous democracies have emerged since then—but no wars.

2. If one or both governments is not broadly representative despite the cultural belief that it is, the possibility of irreconcilable conflicts of interest between them is increased.

3. There also have been cases of covert intervention (rather than overt attack) against some radical but elected Third World governments (Guatemala, Chile) justified by a cold war ideology and public belief that the government in question was allying itself with the major nondemocratic adversary.

4. Any discussion of human rights, as of democracy, is inevitably colored by one's historical context, including mine as a privileged member of society in a powerful capitalist country, governed by democratic procedures as understood in the Western liberal tradition. My perspective on these matters is nevertheless one of the moderate historicism: that whereas all are in some sense conventions, they can be substantially grounded across ages and cultures. See Bernstein, 1983, and Haskell, 1987.

5. A balanced assessment of functionalist benefits in the range of Soviet-American exchanges is Jangotch, 1985. In a very different context, see Russett, 1963. Specifically on the conflict-reducing effects of East-West trade, see Gasiorowski and Polachek, 1982.

6. Neither realist nor liberal idealist theories are fully adequate, but the dominance of realist thinking in contemporary academic as well as government circles has tended to diminish attention to realism's analytical and empirical weaknesses. See Nye, 1988; Vasquez, 1988. Note that the theoretical perspective of this chapter attends neither to the international-system level of analysis nor to the individual nation-state, but rather to the nature of *relations* between two states. For the distinction, see Russett and Starr, 1989, ch. 1. The whole analysis of this book, that domestic politics importantly influence foreign policy, is outside the mainstream of realist thinking.

QUESTIONS

1. Are democracies more or less prone to war than other systems of government?

2. How might realists respond to this essay?

28. The End of History?

Francis Fukuyama

In this article, Francis Fukuyama presents his view on the "end of history," in which ideological conflict is no longer the driving force behind relations among major powers. He suggests that the two ideologies that most challenged liberalism—fascism and Marxist-Leninist doctrine—are no longer a threat. Written in 1989, Fukuyama's article notes broad-based democratic capitalist reform programs in both the Soviet Union and China, though both nations maintained the ideological trappings of communism. Fukuyama also discusses the role of nationalism and religious fundamentalism in this global ideological shift. This selection is from the journal *The National Interest* (1989).

Francis Fukuyama is a former deputy director of the United States Department of State policy planning staff. He is the Bernard L. Schwartz Professor of International Political Economy at Johns Hopkins University. He is the author of several articles and books including his most recent publication, *Our Posthuman Future: Consequences of the Biotechnology Revolution* (2002).

In watching the flow of events over the past decade or so, it is hard to avoid the feeling that something very fundamental has happened in world history. The past year has seen a flood of articles commemorating the end of the Cold War, and the fact that "peace" seems to be breaking out in many regions of the world. Most of these analyses lack any larger conceptual framework for distinguishing between what is essential and what is contingent or accidental in world history, and are predictably superficial. If Mr. Gorbachev were ousted from the Kremlin or a new Ayatollah proclaimed the millennium from a desolate Middle Eastern capital, these same commentators would scramble to announce the rebirth of a new era of conflict.

And yet, all of these people sense dimly that there is some larger process at work, a process that gives coherence and order to the daily headlines. The twentieth century saw the developed world descend into a paroxysm of ideological violence, as liberalism contended first with the remnants of absolutism,

Reprinted by permission of the publisher.

then bolshevism and fascism, and finally an updated Marxism that threatened to lead to the ultimate apocalypse of nuclear war. But the century that began full of self-confidence in the ultimate triumph of Western liberal democracy seems at its close to be returning full circle to where it started: not to an "end of ideology" or a convergence between capitalism and socialism, as earlier predicted, but to an unabashed victory of economic and political liberalism.

The triumph of the West, of the Western *idea,* is evident first of all in the total exhaustion of viable systematic alternatives to Western liberalism. In the past decade, there have been unmistakable changes in the intellectual climate of the world's two largest communist countries, and the beginnings of significant reform movements in both. But this phenomenon extends beyond high politics and it can be seen also in the ineluctable spread of consumerist Western culture in such diverse contexts as the peasants' markets and color television sets now omnipresent throughout China, the cooperative restaurants and clothing stores opened in the past year in Moscow, the Beethoven piped into Japanese department stores, and the rock music enjoyed alike in Prague, Rangoon, and Tehran.

What we may be witnessing is not just the end of the Cold War, or the passing of a particular period of postwar history, but the end of history as such: that is, the end point of mankind's ideological evolution and the universalization of Western liberal democracy as the final form of human government. This is not to say that there will no longer be events to fill the pages of *Foreign Affairs*'s yearly summaries of international relations, for the victory of liberalism has occurred primarily in the realm of

ideas or consciousness and is as yet incomplete in the real or material world. But there are powerful reasons for believing that it is the ideal that will govern the material world *in the long run.* To understand how this is so, we must first consider some theoretical issues concerning the nature of historical change.

I

The notion of the end of history is not an original one. Its best known propagator was Karl Marx, who believed that the direction of historical development was a purposeful one determined by the interplay of material forces, and would come to an end only with the achievement of a communist utopia that would finally resolve all prior contradictions. But the concept of history as a dialectical process with a beginning, a middle, and an end was borrowed by Marx from his great German predecessor, Georg Wilhelm Friedrich Hegel.

For better or worse, much of Hegel's historicism has become part of our contemporary intellectual baggage. The notion that mankind has progressed through a series of primitive stages of consciousness on his path to the present, and that these stages corresponded to concrete forms of social organization, such as tribal, slave-owing, theocratic, and finally democratic-egalitarian societies, has become inseparable from the modern understanding of man. Hegel was the first philosopher to speak the language of modern social science, insofar as man for him was the product of his concrete historical and social environment and not, as earlier natural right theorists would have it, a collection of more or less fixed "natural" attributes. The mastery and transformation of man's natural environment through the application of science and technology was originally not a Marxist concept, but a Hegelian one. Unlike later historicists whose historical relativism degenerated into relativism *tout court,* however, Hegel believed that history culminated in an absolute moment—a moment in which a final, rational form of society and state became victorious.

It is Hegel's misfortune to be known now primarily as Marx's precursor, and it is our misfortune that few of us are familiar with Hegel's work from direct study, but only as it has been filtered through the distorting lens of Marxism. In France, however, there has been an effort to save Hegel from his Marxist interpreters and to resurrect him as the philosopher who most correctly speaks to our time. Among those modern French interpreters of Hegel, the greatest was certainly Alexandre Kojève, a brilliant Russian emigre who taught a highly influential series of seminars in Paris in the 1930s at the *Ecole Practique des Hautes Etudes.*[1] While largely unknown in the United States, Kojève had a major impact on the intellectual life of the continent. Among his students ranged such future luminaries as Jean-Paul Sartre on the Left and Raymond Aron on the Right; postwar existentialism borrowed many of its basic categories from Hegel via Kojève.

Kojève sought to resurrect the Hegel of the *Phenomenology of Mind,* the Hegel who proclaimed history to be at an end in 1806. For as early as this Hegel saw in Napoleon's defeat of the Prussian monarchy at the Battle of Jena the victory of the ideals of the French Revolution, and the imminent universalization of the state incorporating the principles of liberty and equality. Kojève, far from rejecting Hegel in light of the turbulent events of the next century and a half, insisted that the latter had been essentially correct.[2] The Battle of Jena marked the end of history because it was at that point that the *vanguard* of humanity (a term quite familiar to Marxists) actualized the principles of the French Revolution. While there was considerable work to be done after 1806—abolishing slavery and the slave trade, extending the franchise to workers, women, blacks, and other racial minorities, etc.—the basic *principles* of the liberal democratic state could not be improved upon. The two world wars in this century and their attendant revolutions and upheavals simply had the effect of extending those principles spatially, such that the various provinces of human civilization were brought up to the level of its most advanced outposts, and of forcing those societies in Europe and North America at the vanguard of civilization to implement their liberalism more fully.

The state that emerges at the end of history is liberal insofar as it recognizes and protects through a system of law man's universal right to freedom, and democratic insofar as it exists only with the consent of the governed. For Kojève, this so-called "universal homogenous state" found real-life embodiment in the countries of postwar Western Europe—precisely those flabby, prosperous, self-satisfied, inward-looking, weak-willed states whose grandest project was nothing more heroic than the creation of the Common Market.[3] But this was only to be expected. For human history and the conflict that characterized it was based on the existence of "contradictions": primitive man's quest for mutual recognition, the dialectic of the master and slave, the transformation and mastery of nature, the struggle for the universal recognition of rights, and the dichotomy between proletarian and capitalist. But in the universal homogenous state, all prior contradictions are resolved and all human needs are satisfied. There is no struggle or conflict over "large" issues, and consequently no need for generals or statesmen; what remains is primarily economic activity. And indeed, Kojève's life was consistent with his teaching. Believing that there was no more work for philosophers as well, since Hegel (correctly understood) had already achieved absolute knowledge, Kojève left teaching after the war and spent the remainder of his life working as a bureaucrat in the European Economic Community, until his death in 1968.

To his contemporaries at mid-century, Kojève's proclamation of the end of history must have seemed like the typical eccentric solipsism of a French intellectual, coming as it did on the heels of World War II and at the very height of the Cold War. To comprehend how Kojève could have been so audacious as to assert that history has ended, we must first of all understand the meaning of Hegelian idealism.

II

For Hegel, the contradictions that drive history exist first of all in the realm of human consciousness, i.e. on the level of ideas[4]—not the trivial election year proposals of American politicians, but ideas in the sense of large unifying world views that might best be understood under the rubric of ideology. Ideology in this sense is not restricted to the secular and explicit political doctrines we usually associate with the term, but can include religion, culture, and the complex of moral values underlying any society as well.

Hegel's view of the relationship between the ideal and the real or material worlds was an extremely complicated one, beginning with the fact that for him the distinction between the two was only apparent.[5] He did not believe that the real world conformed or could be made to conform to ideological preconceptions of philosophy professors in any simple-minded way, or that the "material" world could not impinge on the ideal. Indeed, Hegel the professor was temporarily thrown out of work as a result of a very material event, the Battle of Jena. But while Hegel's writing and thinking could be stopped by a bullet from the material world, the hand on the trigger of the gun was motivated in turn by the ideas of liberty and equality that had driven the French Revolution.

For Hegel, all human behavior in the material world, and hence all human history, is rooted in a prior state of consciousness—an idea similar to the one expressed by John Maynard Keynes when he said that the views of men of affairs were usually derived from defunct economists and academic scribblers of earlier generations. This consciousness may not be explicit and self-aware, as are modern political doctrines, but may rather take the form of religion or simple cultural or moral habits. And yet this realm of consciousness *in the long run* necessarily becomes manifest in the material world, indeed creates the material world in its own image. Consciousness is cause and not effect, and can develop autonomously from the material world; hence the real subtext underlying the apparent jumble of current events is the history of ideology.

Hegel's idealism has fared poorly at the hands of later thinkers. Marx reversed the priority of the real and the ideal completely, relegating the entire realm of consciousness—religion, art, culture, philosophy itself—to a "superstructure" that was determined entirely by the prevailing material mode of production. Yet another unfortunate legacy of Marxism is our tendency to retreat into materialist or utilitarian explanations of political or historical phenomena, and our disinclination to believe in the autonomous power of ideas. A recent example of this is Paul Kennedy's hugely successful *The Rise and Fall of the Great Powers,* which ascribes the decline of great powers to simple economic overextension. Obviously, this is true on some level: an empire whose economy is barely above the level of subsistence cannot bankrupt its treasury indefinitely. But whether a highly productive modern industrial society chooses to spend 3 or 7 percent of its GNP on defense rather than consumption is entirely a matter of that society's political priorities, which are in turn determined in the realm of consciousness.

The materialist bias of modern thought is characteristic not only of people on the Left who may be sympathetic to Marxism, but of many passionate anti-Marxists as well. Indeed, there is on the Right what one might label the *Wall Street Journal* school of deterministic materialism that discounts the importance of ideology and culture and sees man as essentially a rational, profit-maximizing individual. It is precisely this kind of individual and his pursuit of material incentives that is posited as the basis for economic life as such in economic textbooks.[6] One small example will illustrate the problematic character of such materialist views.

Max Weber begins his famous book, *The Protestant Ethic and the Spirit of Capitalism,* by noting the different economic performance of Protestant and Catholic communities throughout Europe and America, summed up in the proverb that Protestants eat well while Catholics sleep well. Weber notes that according to any economic theory that posited man as a rational profit-maximizer, raising the piece-work rate should increase labor productivity. But in fact, in many traditional peasant communities, raising the piece-work rate actually had the opposite effect of *lowering* labor productivity: at the higher rate, a peasant accustomed to earning two and one-half marks per day found he could earn the same amount by working less, and did so because he valued leisure more than income. The choices of leisure over income, or of the militaristic life of the Spartan hoplite over the wealth of the Athenian trader, or even the ascetic life of the early capitalist entrepreneur over that of a traditional leisured aristocrat, cannot possibly be explained by the impersonal working of material forces, but come preeminently out of the sphere of consciousness—what we have labeled here broadly as ideology. And indeed, a central theme of Weber's work was to prove that contrary to Marx, the material mode of production, far from being the "base," was itself a "superstructure" with roots in religion and culture, and that to understand the emergence of modern capitalism and the profit motive one had to study their antecedents in the realm of the spirit.

As we look around the contemporary world, the poverty of materialist theories of economic development is all too apparent. The *Wall Street Journal* school of deterministic materialism habitually points to the stunning economic success of Asia in the past few decades as evidence of the viability of free market economics, with the implication that all societies would see similar development were they simply to allow their populations to pursue their material self-interest freely. Surely free markets and stable political systems are a necessary precondition to capitalist economic growth. But just as surely the cultural heritage of those Far Eastern societies, the ethic of work and saving and family, a religious heritage that does not, like Islam, place restrictions on certain forms of economic behavior, and other deeply ingrained moral qualities, are equally important in explaining their economic performance.[7] And yet the intellectual weight of materialism is such that not a single respectable contemporary theory of economic development addresses consciousness and culture seriously as the matrix within which economic behavior is formed.

Failure to understand that the roots of economic behavior lie in the realm of consciousness and culture leads to the common mistake of attributing material causes to phenomena that are essentially ideal in nature. For example, it is commonplace in the West to interpret the reform movements first in China and most recently in the Soviet Union as the victory of the material over the ideal—that is, a recognition that ideological incentives could not replace material ones in stimulating a highly productive modern economy, and that if one wanted to prosper one had to appeal to baser forms of self-interest. But the deep defects of socialist economies were evident thirty or forty years ago to anyone who chose to look. Why was it that these countries moved away from central planning only in the 1980s? The answer must be found in the consciousness of the elites and leaders ruling them, who decided to opt for the "Protestant" life of wealth and risk over the "Catholic" path of poverty

and security.[8] That change was in no way made inevitable by the material conditions in which either country found itself on the eve of the reform, but instead came about as the result of the victory of one idea over another.[9]

For Kojève, as for all good Hegelians, understanding the underlying processes of history requires understanding developments in the realm of consciousness or ideas, since consciousness will ultimately remake the material world in its own image. To say that history ended in 1806 meant that mankind's ideological evolution ended in the ideals of the French or American Revolutions: while particular regimes in the real world might not implement these ideals fully, their theoretical truth is absolute and could not be improved upon. Hence it did not matter to Kojève that the consciousness of the postwar generation of Europeans had not been universalized throughout the world; if ideological development had in fact ended, the homogenous state would eventually become victorious throughout the material world.

I have neither the space nor, frankly, the ability to defend in depth Hegel's radical idealist perspective. The issue is not whether Hegel's system was right, but whether his perspective might uncover the problematic nature of many materialist explanations we often take for granted. This is not to deny the role of material factors as such. To a literal-minded idealist, human society can be built around any arbitrary set of principles regardless of their relationship to the material world. And in fact men have proven themselves able to endure the most extreme material hardships in the name of ideas that exist in the realm of the spirit alone, be it the divinity of cows or the nature of the Holy Trinity.[10]

But while man's very perception of the material world is shaped by his historical consciousness of it, the material world can clearly affect in return the viability of a particular state of consciousness. In particular, the spectacular abundance of advanced liberal economies and the infinitely diverse consumer culture made possible by them seem to both foster and preserve liberalism in the political sphere. I want to avoid the materialist determinism that says that liberal economics inevitably produces liberal politics, because I believe that both economics and politics presuppose an autonomous prior state of consciousness that makes them possible. But that state of consciousness that permits the growth of liberalism seems to stabilize in the way one would expect at the end of history if it is underwritten by the abundance of a modern free market economy. We might summarize the content of the universal homogenous state as liberal democracy in the political sphere combined with easy access to VCRs and stereos in the economic.

III

Have we in fact reached the end of history? Are there, in other words, any fundamental "contradictions" in human life that cannot be resolved in the context of modern liberalism, that would be resolvable by an alternative political-economic structure? If we accept the idealist premises laid out above, we must seek an answer to this question in the realm of ideology and consciousness. Our task is not to answer exhaustively the challenges to liberalism promoted by every crackpot messiah around the world, but only those that are embodied in important social or political forces and movements, and which are therefore part of world history. For our purposes, it matters very little what strange thoughts occur to people in Albania or Burkina Faso, for we are interested in what one could in some sense call the common ideological heritage of mankind.

In the past century, there have been two major challenges to liberalism, those of fascism and of communism. The former[11] saw the political weakness, materialism, anomie, and lack of community of the West as fundamental contradictions in liberal societies that could only be resolved by a strong state that forged a new "people" on the basis of national exclusiveness. Fascism was destroyed as a living ideology by World War II. This was a defeat, of course, on a very material level, but it amounted to a defeat of the idea as well. What destroyed fascism as an idea was not universal moral revulsion against it, since plenty of people were willing to endorse the idea as long as it seemed the wave of the future, but its lack of success. After the war, it seemed to most people that German fascism as well as its other European and Asian variants were bound to self-destruct. There was no material reason why new fascist movements could not have sprung up again after the war in other locales, but for the fact that expansionist ultranationalism, with its promise of unending conflict leading to disastrous military defeat, had completely lost its appeal. The ruins of the Reich chancellory as well as the atomic bombs dropped on Hiroshima and Nagasaki killed this ideology on the level of consciousness as well as materially, and all of the proto-fascist movements spawned by the German and Japanese examples like the Peronist movement in Argentina or Subhas Chandra Bose's Indian National Army withered after the war.

The ideological challenge mounted by the other great alternative to liberalism, communism, was far more serious. Marx, speaking Hegel's language, asserted that liberal society contained a fundamental contradiction that could not be resolved within its context, that between capital and labor, and this contradiction has constituted the chief accusation against liberalism ever since. But surely, the class issue has actually been successfully resolved in the West. As Kojève (among others) noted, the egalitarianism of modern America represents the essential achievement of the classless society envisioned by Marx. This is not to say that there are not rich people and poor people in the United States, or that the gap between them has not grown in recent years. But the root causes of economic inequality do not have to do with the underlying legal and social structure of our society, which remains fundamentally egalitarian and moderately redistributionist, so much as with the cultural and social characteristics of the groups that make it up, which are in turn the historical legacy of premodern conditions. Thus black poverty in the United States is not the inherent product of liberalism, but is rather the "legacy of slavery and racism" which persisted long after the formal abolition of slavery.

As a result of the receding of the class issue, the appeal of communism in the developed Western world, it is safe to say, is lower today than any time since the end of the First World War. This can be measured in any number of ways: in the declining membership and electoral pull of the major European communist parties, and their overtly revisionist programs; in the corresponding electoral success of conservative parties from Britain and Germany to the United States and Japan, which are unabashedly pro-market and anti-statist; and in an intellectual climate whose most "advanced" members no longer believe that bourgeois society is something that ultimately needs to be overcome. This is not to say that the opinions of progressive intellectuals in Western countries are not deeply pathological in any number of ways. But those who believe that the future must inevitably be socialist tend to be very old, or very marginal to the real political discourse of their societies.

One may argue that the socialist alternative was never terribly plausible for the North Atlantic world, and was sustained for the last several decades primarily by its success outside of this region. But it is precisely in the non-European world that one is most struck by the occurrence of major ideological transformations. Surely the most remarkable changes have occurred in Asia. Due to the strength and adaptability of the indigenous cultures there, Asia became a battleground for a variety of imported Western ideologies early in this century. Liberalism in Asia was a very weak reed in the period after World War I; it is easy today to forget how gloomy Asia's political future looked as recently as ten or fifteen years ago. It is easy to forget as well how momentous the outcome of Asian ideological struggles seemed for world political development as a whole.

The first Asian alternative to liberalism to be decisively defeated was the fascist one represented by Imperial Japan. Japanese fascism (like its German version) was defeated by the force of American arms in the Pacific war, and liberal democracy was imposed on Japan by a victorious United States. Western capitalism and political liberalism when transplanted to Japan were adapted and transformed by the Japanese in such a way as to be scarcely recognizable.[12] Many Americans are now aware that Japanese industrial organization is very different from that prevailing in the United States or Europe, and it is questionable what relationship the factional maneuvering that takes place with the governing Liberal Democratic Party bears to democracy. Nonetheless, the very fact that the essential elements of economic and political liberalism have been so successfully grafted onto uniquely Japanese traditions and institutions guarantees their survival in the long run. More important is the contribution that Japan has made in turn to world history by following in the footsteps of the United States to create a truly universal consumer culture that has become both a symbol and an underpinning of the universal homogeneous state. V. S. Naipaul travelling in Khomeini's Iran shortly after the revolution noted the omnipresent signs advertising the products of Sony, Hitachi, and JVC, whose appeal remained virtually irresistible and gave the lie to the regime's pretensions of restoring a state based on the rule of the *Shariah*. Desire for access to the consumer culture, created in large measure by Japan, has played a crucial role in fostering the spread of economic liberalism throughout Asia, and hence in promoting political liberalism as well.

The economic success of the other newly industrializing countries (NICs) in Asia following on the example of Japan is by now a familiar story. What is important from a Hegelian standpoint is that political liberalism has been following economic liberalism, more slowly than many had hoped but with seeming inevitability. Here again we see the victory of the idea of the universal homogenous state. South Korea had developed into a modern, urbanized society with an increasingly large and well-educated middle class that could not possibly be isolated from the larger democratic trends around them. Under these circumstances it seemed intolerable to a large part of this population that it should be ruled by an anachronistic military regime while Japan, only a decade or so ahead in economic terms, had parliamentary institutions for over forty years. Even the former socialist regime in Burma, which for so many decades existed in dismal isolation from the larger trends dominating Asia, was buffeted in the past year by pressures to liberalize both its economy and political system. It is said that unhappiness with strongman Ne Win began when a senior Burmese officer went to Singapore for medical treatment and broke down crying when he saw how far socialist Burma had been left behind by its ASEAN neighbors.

But the power of the liberal idea would seem much less impressive if it had not infected the largest and oldest culture in Asia, China. The simple existence of communist China created an alternative pole of ideological attraction, and as such constituted a threat to liberalism. But the past fifteen years have seen an almost total discrediting of Marxism-Leninism as an economic system. Beginning with the famous third plenum of the Tenth Central Committee in 1978, the Chinese Communist party set about decollectivizing agriculture for the 800 million Chinese who still lived in the countryside. The role of the state in agriculture was reduced to that of a tax collector, while production of consumer goods was sharply increased in order to give peasants a taste of the universal homogeneous state and thereby an incentive to work. The reform doubled Chinese grain output in only five years, and in the process created for Deng Xiaoping a solid political base from which he was able to extend the reform to other parts of the economy. Economic statistics do not begin to describe the dynamism, initiative, and openness evident in China since the reform began.

China could not now be described in any way as a liberal democracy. At present, no more than 20 percent of its economy has been marketized, and most importantly it continues to be ruled by a self-appointed Communist party which has given no hint of wanting to devolve power. Deng has made none of Gorbachev's promises regarding democratization of the political system and there is no Chinese equivalent of *glasnost*. The Chinese leadership has in fact been much more circumspect in criticizing Mao and Maoism than Gorbachev with respect to Brezhnev and Stalin, and the regime continues to pay lip service to Marxism-Leninism as its ideological underpinning. But anyone familiar with the outlook and behavior of the new technocratic elite now governing China knows that Marxism and ideological principle have become virtually irrelevant as guides to policy, and that bourgeois consumerism has a real meaning in that country for the first time since the revolution. The various slowdowns in the pace of reform, the campaigns against "spiritual pollution" and crackdowns on political dissent are more properly seen as tactical adjustments made in the process of managing what is an extraordinarily difficult political transition. By ducking the question of political reform while putting the economy on a new footing, Deng has managed to avoid the breakdown of authority that has accompanied Gorbachev's *perestroika*. Yet the pull of the liberal idea continues to be very strong as economic power devolves and the economy becomes more open to the outside world. There are

currently over 20,000 Chinese students studying in the U.S. and other Western countries, almost all of them the children of the Chinese elite. It is hard to believe that when they return home to run the country they will be content for China to be the only country in Asia unaffected by the larger democratizing trend. The student demonstrations in Beijing that broke out first in December 1986 and recurred recently on the occasion of Hu Yao-bang's death were only the beginning of what will inevitably be mounting pressure for change in the political system as well.

What is important about China from the standpoint of world history is not the present state of the reform or even its future prospects. The central issue is the fact that the People's Republic of China can no longer act as a beacon for illiberal forces around the world, whether they be guerrillas in some Asian jungle or middle class students in Paris. Maoism, rather than being the pattern for Asia's future, became an anachronism, and it was the mainland Chinese who in fact were decisively influenced by the prosperity and dynamism of their overseas co-ethnics—the ironic ultimate victory of Taiwan.

Important as these changes in China have been, however, it is developments in the Soviet Union—the original "homeland of the world proletariat"—that have put the final nail in the coffin of the Marxist-Leninist alternative to liberal democracy. It should be clear that in terms of formal institutions, not much has changed in the four years since Gorbachev has come to power: free markets and the cooperative movement represent only a small part of the Soviet economy, which remains centrally planned; the political system is still dominated by the Communist party, which has only begun to democratize internally and to share power with other groups; the regime continues to assert that it is seeking only to modernize socialism and that its ideological basis remains Marxism-Leninism; and, finally, Gorbachev faces a potentially powerful conservative opposition that could undo many of the changes that have taken place to date. Moreover, it is hard to be too sanguine about the chances for success of Gorbachev's proposed reforms, either in the sphere of economics or politics. But my purpose here is not to analyze events in the short-term, or to make predictions for policy purposes, but to look at underlying trends in the sphere of ideology and consciousness. And in that respect, it is clear that an astounding transformation has occurred.

Emigres from the Soviet Union have been reporting for at least the last generation now that virtually nobody in that country truly believed in Marxism-Leninism any longer, and that this was nowhere more true than in the Soviet elite, which continued to mouth Marxist slogans out of sheer cynicism. The corruption and decadence of the late Brezhnev-era Soviet state seemed to matter little, however, for as long as the state itself refused to throw into question any of the fundamental principles underlying Soviet society, the system was capable of functioning adequately out of sheer inertia and could even muster some dynamism in the realm of foreign and defense policy. Marxism-Leninism was like a magical incantation which, however absurd and devoid of meaning, was the only common basis on which the elite could agree to rule Soviet society.

What has happened in the four years since Gorbachev's coming to power is a revolutionary assault on the most funda-

mental institutions and principles of Stalinism, and their replacement by other principles which do not amount to liberalism *per se* but whose only connecting thread is liberalism. This is most evident in the economic sphere, where the reform economists around Gorbachev have become steadily more radical in their support for free markets, to the point where some like Nikolai Shmelev do not mind being compared in public to Milton Friedman. There is a virtual consensus among the currently dominant school of Soviet economists now that central planning and the command system of allocation are the root cause of economic inefficiency, and that if the Soviet system is ever to heal itself, it must permit free and decentralized decision-making with respect to investment, labor, and prices. After a couple of initial years of ideological confusion, these principles have finally been incorporated into policy with the promulgation of new laws on enterprise autonomy, cooperatives, and finally in 1988 on lease arrangements and family farming. There are, of course, a number of fatal flaws in the current implementation of the reform, most notably the absence of a thoroughgoing price reform. But the problem is no longer a *conceptual* one: Gorbachev and his lieutenants seem to understand the economic logic of marketization well enough, but like the leaders of a Third World country facing the IMF, are afraid of the social consequences of ending consumer subsidies and other forms of dependence on the state sector.

In the political sphere, the proposed changes to the Soviet constitution, legal system, and party rules amount to much less than the establishment of a liberal state. Gorbachev has spoken of democratization primarily in the sphere of internal party affairs, and has shown little intention of ending the Communist party's monopoly of power; indeed, the political reform seeks to legitimize and therefore strengthen the CPSU's rule.[13] Nonetheless, the general principles underlying many of the reforms—that the "people" should be truly responsible for their own affairs, that higher political bodies should be answerable to lower ones, and not vice versa, that the rule of law should prevail over arbitrary police actions, with separation of powers and an independent judiciary, that there should be legal protection for property rights, the need for open discussion of public issues and the right of public dissent, the empowering of the Soviets as a forum in which the whole Soviet people can participate, and of a political culture that is more tolerant and pluralistic—come from a source fundamentally alien to the USSR's Marxist-Leninist tradition, even if they are incompletely articulated and poorly implemented in practice.

Gorbachev's repeated assertions that he is doing no more than trying to restore the original meaning of Leninism are themselves a kind of Orwellian doublespeak. Gorbachev and his allies have consistently maintained that intraparty democracy was somehow the essence of Leninism, and that the various liberal practices of open debate, secret ballot elections, and rule of law were all part of the Leninist heritage, corrupted only later by Stalin. While almost anyone would look good compared to Stalin, drawing so sharp a line between Lenin and his successor is questionable. The essence of Lenin's democratic centralism was centralism, not democracy; that is, the absolutely rigid, monolithic, and disciplined dictatorship of a hierarchically organized vanguard Communist party, speaking in the name of the *demos*. All of Lenin's vicious polemics against Karl Kautsky, Rosa Luxemburg, and various other Menshevik and Social Democratic rivals, not to mention his contempt for "bourgeois legality" and freedoms, centered around his profound conviction that a revolution could not be successfully made by a democratically run organization.

Gorbachev's claim that he is seeking to return to the true Lenin is perfectly easy to understand: having fostered a thorough denunciation of Stalinism and Brezhnevism as the root of the USSR's present predicament, he needs some point in Soviet history on which to anchor the legitimacy of the CPSU's continued rule. But Gorbachev's tactical requirements should not blind us to the fact that the democratizing and decentralizing principles which he has enunciated in both the economic and political spheres are highly subversive of some of the most fundamental precepts of both Marxism and Leninism. Indeed, if the bulk of the present economic reform proposals were put into effect, it is hard to know how the Soviet economy would be more socialist than those of other Western countries with large public sectors.

The Soviet Union could in no way be described as a liberal or democratic country now, nor do I think that it is terribly likely that *perestroika* will succeed such that the label will be thinkable any time in the near future. But at the end of history it is not necessary that all societies become successful liberal societies, merely that they end their ideological pretensions of representing different and higher forms of human society. And in this respect I believe that something very important has happened in the

Soviet Union in the past few years: the criticisms of the Soviet system sanctioned by Gorbachev have been so thorough and devastating that there is very little chance of going back to either Stalinism or Brezhnevism in any simple way. Gorbachev has finally permitted people to say what they had privately understood for many years, namely, that the magical incantations of Marxism-Leninism were nonsense, that Soviet socialism was not superior to the West in any respect but was in fact a monumental failure. The conservative opposition in the USSR, consisting both of simple workers afraid of unemployment and inflation and of party officials fearful of losing their jobs and privileges, is outspoken and may be strong enough to force Gorbachev's ouster in the next few years. But what both groups desire is tradition, order, and authority; they manifest no deep commitment to Marxism-Leninism, except insofar as they have invested much of their own lives in it.[14] For authority to be restored in the Soviet Union after Gorbachev's demolition work, it must be on the basis of some new and vigorous ideology which has not yet appeared on the horizon.

If we admit for the moment that the fascist and communist challenges to liberalism are dead, are there any other ideological competitors left? Or put another way, are there contradictions in liberal society beyond that of class that are not resolvable? Two possibilities suggest themselves, those of religion and nationalism.

The rise of religious fundamentalism in recent years within the Christian, Jewish, and Muslim traditions has been widely noted. One is inclined to say that the revival of religion in some way attests to a broad unhappiness with the impersonality and spiritual vacuity of liberal consumerist societies. Yet while the emptiness at the core of liberalism is most certainly a defect in the ideology—indeed, a flaw that one does not need the perspective of religion to recognize[15]—it is not at all clear that it is remediable through politics. Modern liberalism itself was historically a consequence of the weakness of religiously-based societies which, failing to agree on the nature of the good life, could not provide even the minimal preconditions of peace and stability. In the contemporary world only Islam has offered a theocratic state as a political alternative to both liberalism and communism. But the doctrine has little appeal for non-Muslims, and it is hard to believe that the movement will take on any universal significance. Other less organized religious impulses have been successfully satisfied within the sphere of personal life that is permitted in liberal societies.

The other major "contradiction" potentially unresolvable by liberalism is the one posed by nationalism and other forms of racial and ethnic consciousness. It is certainly true that a very large degree of conflict since the Battle of Jena has had its roots in nationalism. Two cataclysmic world wars in this century have been spawned by the nationalism of the developed world in various guises, and if those passions have been muted to a certain extent in postwar Europe, they are still extremely powerful in the Third World. Nationalism has been a threat to liberalism historically in Germany, and continues to be one in isolated parts of "post-historical" Europe like Northern Ireland.

But it is not clear that nationalism represents an irreconcilable contradiction in the heart of liberalism. In the first place, nationalism is not one single phenomenon but several, ranging from mild cultural nostalgia to the highly organized and elaborately articulated doctrine of National Socialism. Only systematic nationalisms of the latter sort can qualify as a formal ideology on the level of liberalism or communism. The vast majority of the world's nationalist movements do not have a political program beyond the negative desire of independence *from* some other group or people, and do not offer anything like a comprehensive agenda for socio-economic organization. As such, they are compatible with doctrines and ideologies that do offer such agendas. While they may constitute a source of conflict for liberal societies, this conflict does not arise from liberalism itself so much as from the fact that the liberalism in question is incomplete. Certainly a great deal of the world's ethnic and nationalist tension can be explained in terms of peoples who are forced to live in unrepresentative political systems that they have not chosen.

While it is impossible to rule out the sudden appearance of new ideologies or previously unrecognized contradictions in liberal societies, then, the present world seems to confirm that the fundamental principles of socio-political organization have not advanced terribly far since 1806. Many of the wars and revolutions fought since that time have been undertaken in the name of ideologies which claimed to be more advanced than liberalism, but whose pretensions were ultimately unmasked by history. In the meantime, they have helped to spread the universal homogenous state to the point where it could have a significant effect on the overall character of international relations.

IV

What are the implications of the end of history for international relations? Clearly, the vast bulk of the Third World remains very much mired in history, and will be a terrain of conflict for many years to come. But let us focus for the time being on the larger and more developed states of the world who after all account for the greater part of world politics. Russia and China are not likely to join the developed nations of the West as liberal societies any time in the foreseeable future, but suppose for a moment that Marxism-Leninism ceases to be a factor driving the foreign policies of these states—a prospect which, if not yet here, the last few years have made a real possibility. How will the overall characteristics of a de-ideologized world differ from those of the one with which we are familiar at such a hypothetical juncture?

The most common answer is—not very much. For there is a very widespread belief among many observers of international relations that underneath the skin of ideology is a hard core of great power national interest that guarantees a fairly high level of competition and conflict between nations. Indeed, according to one academically popular school of international relations theory, conflict inheres in the international system as such, and to understand the prospects for conflict one must look at the shape of the system—for example, whether it is bipolar or multipolar—rather than at the specific character of the nations and regimes that constitute it. This school in effect applies a Hobbesian view of politics to international relations, and assumes that aggression and insecurity are universal characteristics of human societies rather than the product of specific historical circumstances.

Believers in this line of thought take the relations that existed between the participants in the classical nineteenth century European balance of power as a model for what a de-ideologized contemporary world would look like. Charles Krauthammer, for example, recently explained that if as a result of Gorbachev's reforms the USSR is shorn of Marxist-Leninist ideology, its behavior will revert to that of nineteenth century imperial Russia.[16] While he finds this more reassuring than the threat posed by a communist Russia, he implies that there will still be a substantial degree of competition and conflict in the international system, just as there was say between Russia and Britain or Wilhelmine Germany in the last century. This is, of course, a convenient point of view for people who want to admit that something major is changing in the Soviet Union, but do not want to accept responsibility for recommending the radical policy redirection implicit in such a view. But is it true?

In fact, the notion that ideology is a superstructure imposed on a substratum of permanent great power interest is a highly questionable proposition. For the way in which any state defines its national interest is not universal but rests on some kind of prior ideological basis, just as we saw that economic behavior is determined by a prior state of consciousness. In this century, states have adopted highly articulated doctrines with explicit foreign policy agendas legitimizing expansionism, like Marxism-Leninism or National Socialism.

The expansionist and competitive behavior of nineteenth-century European states rested on no less ideal a basis; it just so happened that the ideology driving it was less explicit than the doctrines of the twentieth century. For one thing, most "liberal" European societies were illiberal insofar as they believed in the legitimacy of imperialism, that is, the right of one nation to rule over other nations without regard for the wishes of the ruled. The justifications for imperialism varied from nation to nation, from a crude belief in the legitimacy of force, particularly when applied to non-Europeans, to the White Man's Burden and Europe's Christianizing mission, to the desire to give people of color access to the culture of Rabelais and Molière. But whatever the particular ideological basis, every "developed" country believed in the acceptability of higher civilizations ruling lower ones—including, incidentally, the United States with regard to the Philippines. This led to a drive for pure territorial aggrandizement in the latter half of the century and played no small role in causing the Great War.

The radical and deformed outgrowth of nineteenth-century imperialism was German fascism, an ideology which justified Germany's right not only to rule over non-European peoples, but over *all* non-German ones. But in retrospect it seems that Hitler represented a diseased bypath in the general course of European development, and since his fiery defeat, the legitimacy of any kind of territorial aggrandizement has been thoroughly discredited.[17] Since the Second World War, European nationalism has been defanged and shorn of any real relevance to foreign policy, with the consequence that the nineteenth-century model of great power behavior has become a serious anachronism. The most extreme form of nationalism that any Western European state has mustered since 1945 has been Gaullism, whose self-assertion has been confined largely to the realm of nuisance politics and culture. International life for the part of the world that has reached the end of history is far more preoccupied with economics than with politics or strategy.

The developed states of the West do maintain defense establishments and in the post-war period have competed vigorously for influence to meet a worldwide communist threat. This behavior has been driven, however, by an external threat from states that possess overtly expansionist ideologies, and would not exist in their absence. To take the "neo-realist" theory seriously, one would have to believe that "natural" competitive behavior would reassert itself among the OECD states were Russia and China to disappear from the face of the earth. That is, West Germany and France would arm themselves against each other as they did in the 1930s, Australia and New Zealand would send military advisers to block each others' advances in Africa, and the U.S.-Canadian border would become fortified. Such a prospect is, of course, ludicrous: minus Marxist-Leninist ideology, we are far more likely to see the "Common Marketization" of world politics than the disintegration of the EEC into nineteenth-century competitiveness. Indeed, as our experience in dealing with Europe on matters such as terrorism or Libya prove, they are much further gone than we down the road that denies the legitimacy of the use of force in international politics, even in self-defense.

The automatic assumption that Russia shorn of its expansionist communist ideology should pick up where the czars left off just prior to the Bolshevik Revolution is therefore a curious one. It assumes that the evolution of human consciousness has stood still in the meantime, and that the Soviets, while picking up currently fashionable ideas in the realm of economics, will return to foreign policy views a century out of date in the rest of Europe. This is certainly not what happened to China after it began its reform process. Chinese competitiveness and expansionism on the world scene have virtually disappeared: Beijing no longer sponsors Maoist insurgencies or tries to cultivate influence in distant African countries as it did in the 1960s. This is not to say that there are not troublesome aspects to contemporary Chinese foreign policy, such as the reckless sale of ballistic missile technology in the Middle East; and the PRC continues to manifest traditional great power behavior in its sponsorship of the Khmer Rouge against Vietnam. But the former is explained by commercial motives and the latter is a vestige of earlier ideologically-based rivalries. The new China far more resembles Gaullist France than pre–World War I Germany.

The real question for the future, however, is the degree to which Soviet elites have assimilated the consciousness of the universal homogenous state that is post-Hitler Europe. From their writings and from my own personal contacts with them, there is no question in my mind that the liberal Soviet intelligentsia rallying around Gorbachev has arrived at the end-of-history view in a remarkably short time, due in no small measure to the contacts they have had since the Brezhnev era with the larger European civilization around them. "New political thinking," the general rubric for their views, describes a world dominated by economic concerns, in which there are no ideological grounds for major conflict between nations, and in which, consequently, the use of military force becomes less legitimate. As Foreign Minister Shevardnadze put it in mid-1988:

> The struggle between two opposing systems is no longer a determining tendency of the present-day era. At the modern stage, the ability to build up material wealth at an accelerated rate on the basis of front-ranking science and high-level techniques and technology, and to distribute it fairly, and through joint efforts to restore and protect the resources necessary for mankind's survival acquires decisive importance.[18]

The post-historical consciousness represented by "new thinking" is only one possible future for the Soviet Union, however. There has always been a very strong current of great Russian chauvinism in the Soviet Union, which has found freer expression since the advent of *glasnost*. It may be possible to return to traditional Marxism-Leninism for a while as a simple rallying point for those who want to restore the authority that Gorbachev has dissipated. But as in Poland, Marxism-Leninism is dead as a mobilizing ideology: under its banner people cannot be made to work harder, and its adherents have lost confidence in themselves. Unlike the propagators of traditional Marxism-Leninism, however, ultra-nationalists in the USSR believe in their Slavophile cause passionately, and one gets the sense that the fascist alternative is not one that has played itself out entirely there.

The Soviet Union, then, is at a fork in the road: it can start down the path that was staked out by Western Europe forty-five years ago, a path that most of Asia has followed, or it can realize its own uniqueness and remain stuck in history. The choice it makes will be highly important for us, given the Soviet Union's size and military strength, for that power will continue to preoccupy us and slow our realization that we have already emerged on the other side of history.

V

The passing of Marxism-Leninism first from China and then from the Soviet Union will mean its death as a living ideology of world historical significance. For while there may be some isolated true believers left in places like Managua, Pyongyang, or Cambridge, Massachusetts, the fact that there is not a single large state in which it is a going concern undermines completely its pretensions to being in the vanguard of human history. And the death of this ideology means the growing "Common Marketization" of international relations, and the diminution of the likelihood of large-scale conflict between states.

This does not by any means imply the end of international conflict *per se*. For the world at that point would be divided between a part that was historical and a part that was post-historical. Conflict between states still in history, and between those states and those at the end of history, would still be possible. There would still be a high and perhaps rising level of ethnic and nationalist violence, since those are impulses incompletely played out, even in parts of the post-historical world. Palestinians and Kurds, Sikhs and Tamils, Irish Catholics and Walloons, Armenians and Azeris, will continue to have their unresolved grievances. This implies that terrorism and wars of national liberation will continue to be an important item on the international agenda. But large-scale conflict must involve large states still caught in the grip of history, and they are what appear to be passing from the scene.

The end of history will be a very sad time. The struggle for recognition, the willingness to risk one's life for a purely abstract goal, the worldwide ideological struggle that called forth daring, courage, imagination, and idealism, will be replaced by economic calculation, the endless solving of technical problems, environmental concerns, and the satisfaction of sophisticated consumer demands. In the post-historical period there will be neither art nor philosophy, just the perpetual caretaking of the museum of human history. I can feel in myself, and see in others around me, a powerful nostalgia for the time when history existed. Such nostalgia, in fact, will continue to fuel competition and conflict even in the post-historical world for some time to come. Even though I recognize its inevitability, I have the most ambivalent feelings for the civilization that has been created in Europe since 1945, with its north Atlantic and Asian offshoots. Perhaps this very prospect of centuries of boredom at the end of history will serve to get history started once again.

Notes

1. Kojève's best-known work is his *Introduction à la lecture de Hegel* (Paris: Editions Gallimard, 1947), which is a transcript of the *Ecole Practique* lectures from the 1930s. This book is available in English entitled *Introduction to the Reading of Hegel* arranged by Raymond Queneau, edited by Allan Bloom, and translated by James Nichols (New York: Basic Books, 1969).

2. In this respect Kojève stands in sharp contrast to contemporary German interpreters of Hegel like Herbert Marcuse who, being more sympathetic to Marx, regarded Hegel ultimately as an historically bound and incomplete philosopher.

3. Kojève alternatively identified the end of history with the postwar "American way of life," toward which he thought the Soviet Union was moving as well.

4. This notion was expressed in the famous aphorism from the preface to the *Philosophy of History* to the effect that "everything that is rational is real, and everything that is real is rational."

5. Indeed, for Hegel the very dichotomy between the ideal and material worlds was itself only an apparent one that was ultimately overcome by the self-conscious subject; in his system, the material world is itself only an aspect of mind.

6. In fact, modern economists, recognizing that man does not always behave as a *profit* maximizer, posit a "utility" function, utility being either income or some other good that can be maximized: leisure, sexual satisfaction, or the pleasure of philosophizing. That profit must be replaced with a value like utility indicates the cogency of the idealist perspective.

7. One need look no further than the recent performance of Vietnamese immigrants in the U.S. school system when compared to their black or Hispanic classmates to realize that culture and consciousness are absolutely crucial to explain not only economic behavior but virtually every other important aspect of life as well.

8. I understand that a full explanation of the origins of the reform movements in China and Russia is a good deal more complicated than this simple formula would suggest. The Soviet reform, for example, was motivated in good measure by Moscow's sense of *insecurity* in the technological-military realm. Nonetheless, neither country on the eve of its reforms was in such a state of *material* crisis that one could have predicted the surprising reform paths ultimately taken.

9. It is still not clear whether the Soviet peoples are as "Protestant" as Gorbachev and will follow him down that path.

10. The internal politics of the Byzantine Empire at the time of Justinian revolved

around a conflict between the so-called monophysites and monothelites, who believed that the unity of the Holy Trinity was alternatively one of nature or of will. This conflict corresponded to some extent to one between proponents of different racing teams in the Hippodrome in Byzantium and led to a not insignificant level of political violence. Modern historians would tend to seek the roots of such conflicts in antagonisms between social classes or some other modern economic category, being unwilling to believe that men would kill each other over the nature of the Trinity.

11. I am not using the term "fascism" here in its most precise sense, fully aware of the frequent misuse of this term to denounce anyone to the right of the user. "Fascism" here denotes any organized ultra-nationalist movement with universalistic pretensions—not universalistic with regard to its nationalism, of course, since the latter is exclusive by definition, but with regard to the movement's belief in its right to rule other people. Hence Imperial Japan would qualify as fascist while former strongman Stoessner's Paraguay or Pinochet's Chile would not. Obviously fascist ideologies cannot be universalistic in the sense of Marxism or liberalism, but the structure of the doctrine can be transferred from country to country.

12. I use the example of Japan with some caution, since Kojève late in his life came to conclude that Japan, with its culture based on purely formal arts, proved that the universal homogeneous state was not victorious and that history had perhaps not ended. See the long note at the end of the second edition of *Introduction à la Lecture de Hegel, 462–3.*

13. This is not true in Poland and Hungary, however, whose Communist parties have taken moves toward true power-sharing and pluralism.

14. This is particularly true of the leading Soviet conservative, former Second Secretary Yegor Ligachev, who has publicly recognized many of the deep defects of the Brezhnev period.

15. I am thinking particularly of Rousseau and the Western philosophical tradition that flows from him that was highly critical of Lockean or Hobbesian liberalism, though one could criticize liberalism from the standpoint of classical political philosophy as well.

16. See his article, "Beyond the Cold War," *New Republic*, December 19, 1988.

17. It took European colonial powers like France several years after the war to admit the illegitimacy of their empires, but decolonialization was an inevitable consequence of the Allied victory which had been based on the promise of a restoration of democratic freedoms.

18. *Vestnik Ministerstva Inostrannikh Del SSSR* no. 15 (August 1988), 27–46. "New thinking" does of course serve a propagandistic purpose in persuading Western audiences of Soviet good intentions. But the fact that it is good propaganda does not mean that its formulators do not take many of its ideas seriously.

QUESTIONS

1. According to Fukuyama, what are the major factors promoting the end of history?

2. Compare and contrast this article with Fred Halliday's "A Singular Collapse," page 224. Specifically, do Fukuyama and Halliday agree on the role and importance of ideology in international politics?

29.   The Clash of Civilizations?

Samuel P. Huntington

In this article, Samuel P. Huntington argues that world politics is entering a new phase in which the great divisions among humankind and the dominating source of international conflict will be cultural. Civilizations—the highest cultural groupings of people—are differentiated from one another by religion, history, language, and tradition. These divisions are deep and increasing in importance. From Yugoslavia to the Middle East to Central Asia, the fault lines of civilizations are the battle lines of the future. In this emerging era of cultural conflict, the United States must forge alliances with similar cultures to spread its values wherever possible. In the final analysis, all civilizations will have to learn to tolerate each other. This selection is from the journal *Foreign Affairs* (1993).

Samuel P. Huntington is Eaton Professor of the Science of Government and director of the John M. Olin Institute for Strategic Studies at Harvard University. He has written many books, including *The Soldier and the State* (1975), *Political Order in Changing Societies* (1968), *The Third Wave: Democratization in the Late Twentieth Century* (1991), and has contributed to numerous political science and international studies journals.

THE NEXT PATTERN OF CONFLICT

World politics is entering a new phase, and intellectuals have not hesitated to proliferate visions of what it will be— the end of history, the return of traditional rivalries between nation states, and the decline of the nation state from the conflicting pulls of tribalism and globalism, among others. Each of these visions catches aspects of the emerging reality. Yet they all miss a crucial, indeed a central, aspect of what global politics is likely to be in the coming years.

It is my hypothesis that the fundamental source of conflict in this new world will not be primarily ideological or primarily economic. The great divisions among humankind and the dominating source of conflict will be cultural. Nation states will remain the most powerful actors in world affairs, but the principal conflicts of global politics will occur between nations and groups of different civilizations. The clash of civilizations will dominate global politics. The fault lines between civilizations will be the battle lines of the future.

Conflict between civilizations will be the latest phase in the evolution of conflict in the modern world. For a century and a half after the emergence of the modern international system with the Peace of Westphalia, the conflicts of the Western world were largely among princes—emperors, absolute monarchs and constitutional monarchs attempting to expand their bureaucracies, their armies, their mercantilist economic strength and, most important, the territory they ruled. In the process they created nation states, and beginning with the French Revolution the principal lines of conflict were between nations rather than princes. In 1793, as R. R. Palmer put it, "The wars of kings were over; the wars of peoples had begun." This nineteenth-century pattern lasted until the end of World War I. Then, as a result of the Russian Revolution and the reaction against it, the conflict of nations yielded to the conflict of ideologies, first among communism, fascism-Nazism and liberal democracy, and then between communism and liberal democracy. During the Cold War, this latter conflict became embodied in the struggle between the two superpowers, neither of which was a nation state in the classical European sense and each of which defined its identity in terms of its ideology.

These conflicts between princes, nation states and ideologies were primarily conflicts within Western civilization, "Western civil wars," as William Lind has labeled them. This was as true of the Cold War as it was of the world wars and the earlier wars of the seventeenth, eighteenth and nineteenth centuries. With the end of the Cold War, international politics moves out of its Western phase, and its centerpiece becomes the interaction between the West and non-Western civilizations and among non-Western civilizations. In the politics of civilizations, the peoples and governments of non-Western civilizations no longer remain the objects of history as targets of Western colonialism but join the West as movers and shapers of history.

THE NATURE OF CIVILIZATIONS

During the Cold War the world was divided into the First, Second and Third Worlds. Those divisions are no longer relevant. It is far more meaningful now to group countries not in terms of their political or economic systems or in terms of their level of economic development but rather in terms of their culture and civilization.

What do we mean when we talk of a civilization? A civilization is a cultural entity. Villages, regions, ethnic groups, nationalities, religious groups, all have distinct cultures at different levels of cultural heterogeneity. The culture of a village in southern Italy may be different from that of a village in northern Italy, but both will share in a common Italian culture that distinguishes them from German villages. European communities, in turn, will share cultural features that distinguish them from Arab or Chinese communities. Arabs, Chinese and Westerners, however, are not part of any broader cultural entity. They constitute civilizations. A civilization is thus the highest cultural grouping of people and the broadest level of cultural identity people have short of that which distinguishes humans from other species. It is defined both by common objective elements, such as language, history, religion, customs, institutions, and by the subjective self-identification of people. People have levels of identity: a resident of Rome may define himself with varying degrees of intensity as a Roman, an Italian, a Catholic, a Christian, a European, a Westerner. The civilization to which he belongs is the broadest level of identification with which he intensely identifies. People can and do redefine their identities and, as a result, the composition and boundaries of civilizations change.

Civilizations may involve a large number of people, as with China ("a civilization pretending to be a state," as Lucian Pye put it), or a very small number of people, such as the Anglophone Caribbean. A civilization may include several nation states, as is the case with Western, Latin American and Arab civilizations, or only one, as is the case with Japanese civilization. Civilizations obviously blend and overlap, and may include subcivilizations. Western civilization has two major variants, European and North American, and Islam has its Arab, Turkic and Malay subdivisions. Civilizations are nonetheless meaningful entities, and while the lines between them are seldom sharp, they are real. Civilizations are dynamic; they rise and fall; they divide and merge. And, as any student of history knows, civilizations disappear and are buried in the sands of time.

Westerners tend to think of nation states as the principal actors in global affairs. They have been that, however, for only a few centuries. The broader reaches of human history have been the history of civilizations. In *A Study of History,* Arnold Toynbee identified 21 major civilizations; only six of them exist in the contemporary world.

WHY CIVILIZATIONS WILL CLASH

Civilization identity will be increasingly important in the future, and the world will be shaped in large measure by the interactions among seven or eight major civilizations. These include Western, Confucian, Japanese, Islamic, Hindu, Slavic-Orthodox, Latin American and possibly African civilization. The most important conflicts of the future will occur along the cultural fault lines separating these civilizations from one another.

Why will this be the case?

First, differences among civilizations are not only real; they are basic. Civilizations are differentiated from each other by history, language, culture, tradition and, most important, religion. The people of different civilizations have different views on the relations between God and man, the individual and the group, the citizen and the state, parents and children, husband and wife, as well as differing views of the relative importance of rights and responsibilities, liberty and authority, equality and hierarchy. These differences are the product of centuries. They will not soon disappear. They are far more fundamental than differences among political ideologies and political regimes. Differences do not necessarily mean conflict, and conflict does not necessarily mean violence. Over the centuries, however, differences among civilizations have generated the most prolonged and the most violent conflicts.

Second, the world is becoming a smaller place. The interactions between peoples of different civilizations are increasing; these increasing interactions intensify civilization consciousness and awareness of differences between civilizations and commonalities within civilizations. North African immigration to France generates hostility among Frenchmen and at the same time increased receptivity to immigration by "good" European Catholic Poles. Americans react far more negatively to Japanese investment than to larger investments from Canada and European countries. Similarly, as Donald Horowitz has pointed out, "An Ibo may be . . . an Owerri Ibo or an Onitsha Ibo in what was the Eastern region of Nigeria. In Lagos, he is simply an Ibo. In London, he is a Nigerian. In New York, he is an African." The interactions among peoples of different civilizations enhance the civilization-consciousness of people that, in turn, invigorates differences and animosities stretching or thought to stretch back deep into history.

Third, the processes of economic modernization and social change throughout the world are separating people from longstanding local identities. They also weaken the nation state as a source of identity. In much of the world religion has moved in to fill this gap, often in the form of movements that are labeled "fundamentalist." Such movements are found in Western Christianity, Judaism, Buddhism and Hinduism, as well as in Islam. In most countries and most religions the people active in fundamentalist movements are young, college-educated, middle-class technicians, professionals and business persons. The "unsecularization of the world," George Weigel has remarked, "is one of the dominant social facts of life in the late twentieth century." The revival of religion, "la revanche de Dieu," as Gilles Kepel labeled it, provides a basis for identity and commitment that transcends national boundaries and unites civilizations.

Fourth, the growth of civilization-consciousness is enhanced by the dual role of the West. On the one hand, the West is at a peak of power. At the same time, however, and perhaps as a result, a return to the roots phenomenon is occurring among non-Western civilizations. Increasingly one hears references to trends toward a turning inward and "Asianization" in Japan, the end of the Nehru legacy and the "Hinduization" of India, the failure of Western ideas of socialism and nationalism and hence "re-Islamization" of the Middle East, and now a debate over Westernization versus Russianization in Boris Yeltsin's country. A West at the peak of its power confronts non-Wests that increasingly have the desire, the will and the resources to shape the world in non-Western ways.

In the past, the elites of non-Western societies were usually the people who were most involved with the West, had been educated at Oxford, the Sorbonne or Sandhurst, and had absorbed Western attitudes and values. At the same time, the populace in non-Western countries often remained deeply imbued with the indigenous culture. Now, however, these relationships are being reversed. A de-Westernization and indigenization of elites is occurring in many non-Western countries at the same time that Western, usually American, cultures, styles and habits become more popular among the mass of the people.

Fifth, cultural characteristics and differences are less mutable and hence less easily compromised and resolved than political and economic ones. In the former Soviet Union, communists can become democrats, the rich can become poor and the poor rich, but Russians cannot become Estonians and Azeris cannot become Armenians. In class and ideological conflicts, the key question was "Which side are you on?" and people could and did choose sides and change sides. In conflicts between civilizations, the question is "What are you?" That is a given that cannot be changed. And as we know, from Bosnia to the Caucasus to the Sudan, the wrong answer to that question can mean a bullet in the head. Even more than ethnicity, religion discriminates sharply and exclusively among people. A person can be half-French and half-Arab and simultaneously even a citizen of two countries. It is more difficult to be half-Catholic and half-Muslim.

Finally, economic regionalism is increasing. The proportions of total trade that were intraregional rose between 1980 and 1989 from 51 percent to 59 percent in Europe, 33 percent to 37 percent in East Asia, and 32 percent to 36 percent in North America. The importance of regional economic blocs is likely to continue to increase in the future. On the one hand, successful economic regionalism will reinforce civilization-consciousness. On the other hand, economic regionalism may succeed only when it is rooted in a common civilization. The European Community rests on the shared foundation of European culture and Western Christianity. The success of the North American Free Trade Area depends on the convergence now underway of Mexican, Canadian and American cultures. Japan, in contrast, faces difficulties in creating a comparable economic entity in East Asia because Japan is a society and civilization unique to itself. However strong the trade and investment links Japan may develop with other East Asian countries, its cultural differences with those countries inhibit and perhaps preclude its promoting regional economic integration like that in Europe and North America.

Common culture, in contrast, is clearly facilitating the rapid expansion of the economic relations between the People's Republic of China and Hong Kong, Taiwan, Singapore and the overseas Chinese communities in other Asian countries. With the Cold War over, cultural commonalities increasingly overcome ideological differences, and mainland China and Taiwan move closer together. If cultural commonality is a prerequisite for economic integration, the principal East Asian economic bloc of the future is likely to be centered on China. This bloc is, in fact, already coming into existence. As Murray Weidenbaum has observed,

> Despite the current Japanese dominance of the region, the Chinese-based economy of Asia is rapidly emerging as a new epicenter for industry, commerce and finance. This strategic area contains substantial amounts of technology and manufacturing capability (Taiwan), outstanding entrepreneurial, marketing and services acumen (Hong Kong), a fine communications network (Singapore), a tremendous pool of financial capital (all three), and very large endowments of land, resources and labor (mainland China). . . . From Guangzhou to Singapore, from Kuala Lumpur to Manila, this influential network—often based on extensions of the traditional clans—has been described as the backbone of the East Asian economy.[1]

Culture and religion also form the basis of the Economic Cooperation Organization, which brings together ten non-Arab Muslim countries: Iran, Pakistan, Turkey, Azerbaijan, Kazakhstan, Kyrgyzstan, Turkmenistan, Tadjikistan, Uzbekistan and Afghanistan. One impetus to the revival and expansion of this organization, founded originally in the 1960s by Turkey, Pakistan and Iran, is the realization by the leaders of several of these countries that they had no chance of admission to the European Community. Similarly, Caricom, the Central American Common Market and Mercosur rest on common cultural foundations. Efforts to build a broader Caribbean-Central American economic entity bridging the Anglo-Latin divide, however, have to date failed.

As people define their identity in ethnic and religious terms, they are likely to see an "us" versus "them" relation existing between themselves and people of different ethnicity or religion. The end of ideologically defined states in Eastern Europe and the former Soviet Union permits traditional ethnic identities and animosities to come to the fore. Differences in culture and religion create differences over policy issues, ranging from human rights to immigration to trade and commerce to the environment. Geographical propinquity give rise to conflicting territorial claims from Bosnia to Mindanao. Most important, the efforts of the West to promote its values of democracy and liberalism as universal values, to maintain its military predominance and to advance its economic interests engender countering responses from other civilizations. Decreasingly able to mobilize support and form coalitions on the basis of ideology, governments and groups will increasingly attempt to mobilize support by appealing to common religion and civilization identity.

The clash of civilizations thus occurs at two levels. At the micro-level, adjacent groups along the fault lines between civilizations struggle, often violently, over the control of territory and each other. At the macro-level, states from different civilizations compete for relative military and economic power, struggle over the control of international institutions and third parties, and competitively promote their particular political and religious values. . . .

CIVILIZATION RALLYING: THE KIN-COUNTRY SYNDROME

Groups or states belonging to one civilization that become involved in war with people from a different civilization naturally try to rally support from other members of their own civilization. As the post–Cold War world evolves, civilization commonality, what H. D. S. Greenway has termed the "kin-country" syndrome, is replacing political ideology and traditional balance of power considerations as the principal basis for cooperation and coalitions. It can be seen gradually emerging in the post–Cold War conflicts in the Persian Gulf, the Caucasus and

Bosnia. None of these was a full-scale war between civilizations, but each involved some elements of civilizational rallying, which seemed to become more important as the conflict continued and which may provide a foretaste of the future.

. . . In the Gulf War one Arab state invaded another and then fought a coalition of Arab, Western and other states: While only a few Muslim governments overtly supported Saddam Hussein, many Arab elites privately cheered him on, and he was highly popular among large sections of the Arab publics. Islamic fundamentalist movements universally supported Iraq rather than the Western-backed governments of Kuwait and Saudi Arabia. Forswearing Arab nationalism, Saddam Hussein explicitly invoked an Islamic appeal. He and his supporters attempted to define the war as a war between civilizations. "It is not the world against Iraq," as Safar Al-Hawali, dean of Islamic Studies at the Umm Al-Qura University in Mecca, put it in a widely circulated tape. "It is the West against Islam." Ignoring the rivalry between Iran and Iraq, the chief Iranian religious leader, Ayatollah Ali Khamenei, called for a holy war against the West: "The struggle against American aggression, greed, plans and policies will be counted as a jihad, and anybody who is killed on that path is a martyr." "This is a war," King Hussein of Jordan argued, "against all Arabs and all Muslims and not against Iraq alone."

The rallying of substantial sections of Arab elites and publics behind Saddam Hussein caused those Arab governments in the anti-Iraq coalition to moderate their activities and temper their public statements. Arab governments opposed or distanced themselves from subsequent Western efforts to apply pressure on Iraq, including enforcement of a no-fly zone in the summer of 1992 and the bombing of Iraq in January 1993. The Western-Soviet-Turkish-Arab only anti-Iraq coalition of 1990 had by 1993 become a coalition of almost only the West and Kuwait against Iraq.

Muslims contrasted Western actions against Iraq with the West's failure to protect Bosnians against Serbs and to impose sanctions on Israel for violating U.N. resolutions. The West, they alleged, was using a double standard. A world of clashing civilizations, however, is inevitably a world of double standards: people apply one standard to their kin-countries and a different standard to others. . . .

Civilization rallying to date has been limited, but it has been growing, and it clearly has the potential to spread much further. As the conflict . . . in the Persian Gulf . . . continued, the positions of nations and the cleavages between them increasingly were along civilizational lines. Populist politicians, religious leaders and the media have found it a potent means of arousing mass support and of pressuring hesitant governments. In the coming years, the local conflicts most likely to escalate into major wars will be those, as in Bosnia and the Caucasus, along the fault lines between civilizations. The next world war, if there is one, will be a war between civilizations.

THE WEST VERSUS THE REST

The West is now at an extraordinary peak of power in relation to other civilizations. Its superpower opponent has disappeared from the map. Military conflict among Western states is unthinkable, and Western military power is unrivaled. Apart from Japan, the West faces no eco-nomic challenge. It dominates international political and security institutions and with Japan international economic institutions. Global political and security issues are effectively settled by a directorate of the United States, Britain and France, world economic issues by a directorate of the United States, Germany and Japan, all of which maintain extraordinarily close relations with each other to the exclusion of lesser and largely non-Western countries. Decisions made at the U.N. Security Council or in the International Monetary Fund that reflect the interests of the West are presented to the world as reflecting the desires of the world community. The very phrase "the world community" has become the euphemistic collective noun (replacing "the Free World") to give global legitimacy to actions reflecting the interests of the United States and other Western powers.[2] Through the IMF and other international economic institutions, the West promotes its economic interests and imposes on other nations the economic policies it thinks appropriate. In any poll of non-Western peoples, the IMF undoubtedly would win the support of finance ministers and a few others, but get an overwhelmingly unfavorable rating from just about everyone else, who would agree with Georgy Arbatov's characterization of IMF officials as "neo-Bolsheviks who love expropriating other people's money, imposing undemocratic and alien rules of economic and political conduct and stifling economic freedom."

Western domination of the U.N. Security Council and its decisions, tempered only by occasional abstention by China, produced U.N. legitimation of the West's use of force to drive Iraq out of Kuwait and its elimination of Iraq's sophisticated weapons and capacity to produce such weapons. It also produced the quite unprecedented action by the United States, Britain and France in getting the Security Council to demand that Libya hand over the Pan Am 103 bombing suspects and then to impose sanctions when Libya refused. After defeating the largest Arab army, the West did not hesitate to throw its weight around in the Arab world. The West in effect is using international institutions, military power and economic resources to run the world in ways that will maintain Western predominance, protect Western interests and promote Western political and economic values.

That at least is the way in which non-Westerners see the new world, and there is a significant element of truth in their view. Differences in power and struggles for military, economic and institutional power are thus one source of conflict between the West and other civilizations. Differences in culture, that is basic values and beliefs, are a second source of conflict. V. S. Naipaul has argued that Western civilization is the "universal civilization" that "fits all men." At a superficial level much of Western culture has indeed permeated the rest of the world. At a more basic level, however, Western concepts differ fundamentally from those prevalent in other civilizations. Western ideas of individualism, liberalism, constitutionalism, human rights, equality, liberty, the rule of law, democracy, free markets, the separation of church and state, often have little resonance in Islamic, Confucian, Japanese, Hindu, Buddhist or Orthodox cultures. Western efforts to propagate such ideas produce instead a reaction against "human rights imperialism" and a reaffirmation of indigenous values, as can be seen in the support for religious fundamentalism by the younger generation in non-Western cultures. The very notion that there could be a "universal civilization" is a Western idea, directly at odds with the particularism of most Asian societies and their emphasis on what distinguishes one people from another. Indeed, the author of a review of 100 comparative studies of values in different societies concluded that "the values that are most important in the West are least important worldwide."[3] In the political realm, of course, these differences are most manifest in the efforts of the United States and other Western powers to induce other peoples to adopt Western ideas concerning democracy and human rights. Modern democratic government originated in the West. When it has developed in non-Western societies it has usually been the product of Western colonialism or imposition.

The central axis of world politics in the future is likely to be, in Kishore Mahbubani's phrase, the conflict between "the West and the Rest" and the responses of non-Western civilizations to Western power and values.[4] Those responses generally take one or a combination of three forms. At one extreme, non-Western states can, like Burma and North Korea, attempt to pursue a course of isolation, to insulate their societies from penetration or "corruption" by the West, and, in effect, to opt out of participation in the Western-dominated global community. The costs of this course, however, are high, and few states have pursued it exclusively. A second alternative, the equivalent of "band-wagoning" in international relations theory, is to attempt to join the West and accept its values and institutions. The third alternative is to attempt to "balance" the West by developing economic and military power and cooperating with other non-Western societies against the West, while preserving indigenous values and institutions; in short, to modernize but not to Westernize.

THE TORN COUNTRIES

In the future, as people differentiate themselves by civilization, countries with large numbers of peoples of different civilizations, such as the Soviet Union and Yugoslavia, are candidates for dismemberment. Some other countries have a fair degree of cultural homogeneity but are divided over whether their society belongs to one civilization or another. These are torn countries. Their leaders typically wish to pursue a bandwagoning strategy and to make their countries members of the West, but the history, culture and traditions of their countries are non-Western. The most obvious and prototypical torn country is Turkey. The late twentieth-century leaders of Turkey have followed in the Attatürk tradition and defined Turkey as a modern, secular, Western nation state. They allied Turkey with the West in NATO and in the Gulf War; they applied for membership in the European Community. At the same time, however, elements in Turkish society have supported an Islamic revival and have argued that Turkey is basically a Middle Eastern Muslim society. In addition, while the elite of Turkey has defined Turkey as a Western society, the elite of the West refuses to accept Turkey as such. Turkey will not become a member of the European Community, and the real reason, as President Özal said, "is that we are Muslim and they are Christian and they don't say that." Having rejected Mecca, and then being rejected by Brussels, where does Turkey look? Tashkent may be the answer. The end of the Soviet Union gives Turkey the opportunity to become the leader of a revived Turkic civilization involving seven countries from the borders of Greece to those of China. Encouraged by the West, Turkey is making strenuous efforts to carve out this new identity for itself. . . .

To redefine its civilization identity, a torn country must meet three requirements. First, its political and economic elite has to be generally supportive of and enthusiastic about this move. Second, its public has to be willing to acquiesce in the redefinition. Third, the dominant groups in the recipient civilization have to be willing to embrace the convert. . . .

THE CONFUCIAN-ISLAMIC CONNECTION

The obstacles to non-Western countries joining the West vary considerably. They are least for Latin American and East European countries. They are greater for the Orthodox countries of the former Soviet Union. They are still greater for Muslim, Confucian, Hindu and Buddhist societies. Japan has established a unique position for itself as an associate member of the West: it is in the West in some respects but clearly not of the West in important dimensions. Those countries that for reason of culture and power do not wish to, or cannot, join the West compete with the West by developing their own economic, military and political power. They do this by promoting their internal development and by cooperating with other non-Western countries. The most prominent form of this cooperation is the Confucian-Islamic connection that has emerged to challenge Western interests, values and power.

Almost without exception, Western countries are reducing their military power; under Yeltsin's leadership so also is Russia. China, North Korea and several Middle Eastern states, however, are significantly expanding their military capabilities. They are doing this by the import of arms from Western and non-Western sources and by the development of indigenous arms industries. One result is the emergence of what Charles Krauthammer has called "Weapon States," and the Weapon States are not Western states. Another result is the redefinition of arms control, which is a Western concept and a Western goal. During the Cold War the primary purpose of arms control was to establish a stable military balance between the United States and its allies and the Soviet Union and its allies. In the post–Cold War world the primary objective of arms control is to prevent the development by non-Western societies of military capabilities that could threaten Western interests. The West attempts to do this through international agreements, economic pressure and controls on the transfer of arms and weapons technologies.

The conflict between the West and the Confucian-Islamic states focuses largely, although not exclusively, on nuclear, chemical and biological weapons, ballistic missiles and other sophisticated means for delivering them, and the guidance, intelligence and other electronic capabilities for achieving that goal. The West promotes nonproliferation as a universal norm and nonproliferation treaties and inspections as means of realizing that norm. It also threatens a variety of sanctions against those who promote the spread of sophisticated weapons and proposes some benefits for those who do not. The attention of the West fo-

cuses, naturally, on nations that are actually or potentially hostile to the West.

The non-Western nations, on the other hand, assert their right to acquire and to deploy whatever weapons they think necessary for their security. They also have absorbed, to the full, the truth of the response of the Indian defense minister when asked what lesson he learned from the Gulf War: "Don't fight the United States unless you have nuclear weapons." Nuclear weapons, chemical weapons and missiles are viewed, probably erroneously, as the potential equalizer of superior Western conventional power. China, of course, already has nuclear weapons; Pakistan and India have the capability to deploy them. North Korea, Iran, Iraq, Libya and Algeria appear to be attempting to acquire them. A top Iranian official has declared that all Muslim states should acquire nuclear weapons, and in 1988 the president of Iran reportedly issued a directive calling for development of "offensive and defensive chemical, biological and radiological weapons." . . .

A Confucian-Islamic military connection has thus come into being, designed to promote acquisition by its members of the weapons and weapons technologies needed to counter the military power of the West. It may or may not last. At present, however, it is, as Dave McCurdy has said, "a renegades' mutual support pact, run by the proliferators and their backers." A new form of arms competition is thus occurring between Islamic-Confucian states and the West. In an old-fashioned arms race, each side developed its own arms to balance or to achieve superiority against the other side. In this new form of arms competition, one side is developing its arms and the other side is attempting not to balance but to limit and prevent that arms build-up while at the same time reducing its own military capabilities.

IMPLICATIONS FOR THE WEST

This article does not argue that civilization identities will replace all other identities, that nation states will disappear, that each civilization will become a single coherent political entity, that groups within a civilization will not conflict with and even fight each other. This paper does set forth the hypotheses that differences between civilizations are real and important; civilization-consciousness is increasing; conflict between civilizations will supplant ideological and other forms of conflict as the dominant global form of conflict; international relations, historically a game played out within Western civilization, will increasingly be de-Westernized and become a game in which non-Western civilizations are actors and not simply objects; successful political, security and economic international institutions are more likely to develop within civilizations than across civilizations; conflicts between groups in different civilizations will be more frequent, more sustained and more violent than conflicts between groups in the same civilization; violent conflicts between groups in different civilizations are the most likely and most dangerous source of escalation that could lead to global wars; the paramount axis of world politics will be the relations between "the West and the Rest"; the elites in some torn non-Western countries will try to make their countries part of the West, but in most cases face major obstacles to accomplishing this; a central focus of conflict for the immediate future will be between the West and several Islamic-Confucian states.

This is not to advocate the desirability of conflicts between civilizations. It is to set forth descriptive hypotheses as to what the future may be like. If these are plausible hypotheses, however, it is necessary to consider their implications for Western policy. These implications should be divided between short-term advantage and long-term accommodation. In the short term it is clearly in the interest of the West to promote greater cooperation and unity within its own civilization, particularly between its European and North American components; to incorporate into the West societies in Eastern Europe and Latin America whose cultures are close to those of the West; to promote and maintain cooperative relations with Russia and Japan; to prevent escalation of local inter-civilization conflicts into major inter-civilization wars; to limit the expansion of the military strength of Confucian and Islamic states; to moderate the reduction of Western military capabilities and maintain military superiority in East and Southwest Asia; to exploit differences and conflicts among Confucian and Islamic states; to support in other civilizations groups sympathetic to Western values and interests; to strengthen international institutions that reflect and legitimate Western interests and values and to promote the involvement of non-Western states in those institutions.

In the longer term other measures would be called for. Western civilization is both Western and modern. Non-Western civilizations have attempted to become modern without becoming Western. To date only Japan has fully succeeded in this quest. Non-Western civilizations will continue to attempt to acquire the wealth, technology, skills, machines and weapons that are part of being modern. They will also attempt to reconcile this modernity with their traditional culture and values. Their economic and military strength relative to the West will increase. Hence the West will increasingly have to accommodate these non-Western modern civilizations whose power approaches that of the West but whose values and interests differ significantly from those of the West. This will require the West to maintain the economic and military power necessary to protect its interests in relation to these civilizations. It will also, however, require the West to develop a more profound understanding of the basic religious and philosophical assumptions underlying other civilizations and the ways in which people in those civilizations see their interests. It will require an effort to identify elements of commonality between Western and other civilizations. For the relevant future, there will be no universal civilization, but instead a world of different civilizations, each of which will have to learn to coexist with the others.

NOTES

1. Murray Weidenbaum, *Greater China: The Next Economic Superpower?*, St. Louis: Washington University Center for the Study of American Business, Contemporary Issues, Series 57, February 1993, pp. 2–3.
2. Almost invariably Western leaders claim they are acting on behalf of "the world community." One minor lapse occurred during the run-up to the Gulf War. In an interview on *Good Morning America*, Dec. 21, 1990, British Prime Minister John Major referred to the actions "the West" was taking against Saddam Hussein. He quickly corrected himself and subsequently referred to "the world community." He was, however, right when he erred.
3. Harry C. Triandis, *The New York Times*, Dec. 25, 1990, p. 41, and "Cross-Cultural Studies of Individualism and Collectivism," Nebraska Symposium on Motivation, vol. 37, 1989, pp. 41–133.
4. Kishore Mahbubani, "The West and the Rest," *The National Interest*, Summer 1992, pp. 3–13.

QUESTIONS

1. What are Huntington's primary criticisms of Fukuyama's essay "The End of History?"

2. In your opinion, does Huntington underestimate the importance of nationalism in international relations?

30. Building up New Bogeymen

Stephen M. Walt

Stephen M. Walt reviews Samuel Huntington's Clash of Civilizations thesis and offers a constructive critique of his cultural clash theory. Among Walt's criticisms is the notion that Huntington's thesis does not stand up to close scrutiny. Huntington

From *Foreign Policy* (Spring 1997), Issue 106, pp. 176–190.

does not explain why loyalties suddenly shift from the level of nation-states to that of "civilizations," and he does not explain why this alleged shift will lead to greater intercivilizational conflict.

Stephen M. Walt is Academic Dean and Robert and Rince Belfer Professor of International Affairs of the John F. Kennedy School of Government at Harvard University. His recent publications include: "Beyond bin Ladin: Reshaping U.S. Foreign Policy." *International Security*, Winter 2001-02; and "The Enduring Relevance of the Realist Tradition," in *Political Science: State of the Discipline* (W.W. Norton, 2002).

Samuel Huntington's *The Clash of Civilizations and the Remaking of World Order* is an ambitious attempt to formulate a conceptual framework that can help citizens and policymakers to make sense of the post–Cold War world. Instead of focusing on power and ideology—as we did during the Cold War—Huntington's paradigm emphasizes cultural competition.

Huntington's central thesis is straightforward. "In the post–Cold War world," he writes, "the most important distinctions among peoples are not ideological, political, or economic. They are cultural." Identities and loyalties are shifting from the state to the broader cultural entity of "civilization," and this shift is creating a radically different world order. "For the first time in history," he maintains, "global politics has become multipolar and multicivilizational." As a result, conflicts between civilizations will be more frequent than conflicts within them, and "the most pervasive, important, and dangerous conflicts will . . . [be] between peoples belonging to different cultural entities."

There are at least three reasons why The Clash of Civilizations is likely to enjoy a longer shelf life than some other efforts to formulate a post–Cold War paradigm. First, Huntington presents his argument with great skill and with a keen eye for the apt anecdote. Huntington has always been an adroit conceptualizer, and his knack for subsuming diverse phenomena into simple and memorable frameworks is evident through- out the book. He is also a master of the scholarly sound bite, as in his observation that "in Islam, God is Caesar; in China and Japan, Caesar is God; in Orthodoxy, God is Caesar's junior partner." These stylistic felicities make the book a lively read and greatly enhance the seductiveness of its argument.

Second, cultural explanations are very much in vogue these days, whether the subject is foreign policy, educational performance, gender roles, or family values. Huntington's arguments are thus in step with current intellectual fashions, even if many intellectuals will probably recoil from some of his conclusions.

Third, Huntington's arguments possess a powerful prima facie plausibility. We all know that cultural differences can foster misunderstanding and suspicion, and even a superficial reading of history reveals that groups from different cultural backgrounds have fought on countless occasions. A brief read of any newspaper seems to offer further support for a cultural perspective: "Western" Croats, Muslims, and "Orthodox" Serbs are at odds in Bosnia; Muslims and Hindus are quarreling over Kashmir; "Orthodox" Russians and Armenians have been fighting Muslim Chechens and Azerbaijanis;

and trouble may now be brewing between China and its various non-Sinic neighbors. At first glance, therefore, recent events seem to be remarkably in sync with Huntington's assertions.

Yet despite these strengths, the book's central thesis does not stand up to close scrutiny. Huntington does not explain why loyalties are suddenly shifting from the level of nation-states to that of "civilizations," and he does not explain why this alleged shift will lead to greater intercivilizational conflict. Moreover, some of his central claims are contradicted by both historical and contemporary evidence. Finally, Huntington's focus on the broad concept of civilization has led him to overlook or obscure the far more potent role of nationalism. As a result, The Clash of Civilizations is an unreliable guide to the emerging world order and a potentially dangerous blueprint for policy.

A Blueprint for Policy?

Huntington begins by defining a civilization as the "highest cultural grouping of people and the broadest level of cultural identity . . . defined by . . . language, history, religion, customs, institutions, and by the subjective selfidentification of people." Drawing upon the work of historians such as William McNeill, Fernand Braudel, Carroll Quigley, and Oswald Spengler, Huntington identifies six contemporary civilizations (Hindu, Islamic, Japanese, Orthodox, Sinic, and Western) and two possible candidates (African and Latin American). Five of these eight civilizations have a dominant core state (India, Japan, Russia, China, and the United States), but the African, Islamic, and Latin American civilizations do not.

According to Huntington, the future world order will be shaped by several powerful trends. First, the era of Western dominance is coming to an end, and several non-Western states are emerging as great powers in their own right. Second, these new great powers increasingly reject Western values in favor of their own cultural norms, and the continuing decline in the West's material superiority will erode its cultural appeal even more. Thus, Huntington rejects the belief that modernization is leading to cultural convergence between the West and "the rest." Third, as different civilizations become more tightly connected by markets and media and as universalist ideologies like Marxism-Leninism or liberalism cease to command belief, the broad cultural values embodied in each civilization will become more important as sources of personal and political identity. Taken together, these trends herald the emergence of a new multipolar world in which each of the great powers is the core state of a different civilization. For Huntington, the end of the Cold War is the critical historical divide between the old world of national rivalries and the new world of clashing civilizations.

What will world politics look like in this multipolar, multicivilizational world? Huntington recognizes that states remain the key actors in world politics, but he believes that they increasingly define their interests in civilizational terms. As a result, "they cooperate with and ally themselves with states with similar or common culture and are more often in conflict with countries of different culture." Or, as he says elsewhere, "alignments defined by ideology and superpower relations are giving way to alignments defined by culture and civilization." It follows that conflicts will occur either in "cleft countries" defined as states where large segments of the population belong to different civilizations, like Ukraine—or in the "fault-line wars" that occur along the boundaries between two or more civilizations. The latter conflicts are likely to be especially complex, as local antagonists try to rally support from their cultural brethren and especially from the core state (if there is one). The chief danger is the possibility that one or more of these "fault-line wars" will escalate into a great-power conflict that transcends civilizational boundaries.

For the West, two dangers are especially salient. The first is Islam, where a demographic explosion, a cultural resurgence, and the absence of a strong core state combine to create a high propensity for conflict. Huntington recognizes that Islam is deeply divided and relatively weak (its share of world economic product is less than one fourth that of the West), but these facts do not afford him much comfort. Indeed, he sees Islam and the West as very nearly at war already, observing that "dedicated Islamic militants exploit the open societies of the West and plant car bombs at selected targets. Western military professionals exploit the open skies of Islam and drop smart bombs on selected targets." He believes that the challenge from Islam is inherently cultural and likely to be prolonged.

The second challenge arises from Asia, and especially from China. If the Islamic threat is partly a reflection of the unruly energies of millions of mobilized young Muslims, the Asian threat derives from the order and discipline that has fueled Asia's economic ascendance. Asian societies are rejecting the individualistic culture of the West, their economic success has reinforced their self-confidence and desire for greater global influence, and Huntington sees a clash of interests—and thus, a clash of civilizations—as virtually inevitable.

Huntington's prescriptions follow directly from his basic framework. In a world characterized by civilizational divisions, he favors greater political, economic, and military integration among the member states of the West; advocates expanding NATO to include other Western states (such as the Czech Republic, Hungary, and Poland); and wants to bring Latin America into the Western fold while preventing Japan from moving toward China. Because the Sinic and Islamic civilizations pose the greatest threats, the West should also accept Russian hegemony among the Orthodox countries and strive to limit the growth of Sinic and Islamic power. On the home front, the United States must prevent advocates of "multiculturalism" from undermining the West's cultural traditions and encourage immigrants to embrace Western values. Huntington also warns that Western intervention in the affairs of other civilizations will be "the single most dangerous source of instability," but he does not suggest that we abstain from such activities entirely.

This summary does not do full justice to Huntington's often insightful analysis. He neatly debunks claims of cultural convergence and bolsters his own arguments with numerous examples of cross-cultural conflict. His analysis of the dynamics of "fault-line" conflicts is especially intriguing, as is his discussion of the conflictive character of contemporary Islamic societies. The civilizational paradigm has the merit of simplicity, and it seems to make sense of some important contemporary events. So why not simply send a copy of the book to every head of state, legislator, and senior government official in the West and gird our loins for the kulturkampf that lies ahead?

To fully grasp why The Clash of Civilizations should not become the blueprint for U.S. (let alone "Western") foreign policy, we must first consider what world politics was like in the past. Doing so will highlight how Huntington believes it is changing and help us to see the flaws in his argument.

DISSECTING THE THESIS

What was world politics like prior to the end of the Cold War, which Huntington identifies as the starting point for the new era of cultural competition? For the past 200 years or so, states—and especially the great powers—have been the key actors in world affairs. It was generally recognized that some of these states belonged to different civilizations, but nobody argued that these differences mattered very much for understanding international politics. Cultural differences did matter, but their main political expression took the form of nationalism. The belief that distinct cultural groups—or nations—should have their own state proved to be an extremely powerful political ideology, and it reinforced the state system that has existed since the mid-17th century.

Great-power conflict was a common occurrence throughout this period. Wars occasionally arose for essentially "cultural" (i.e., nationalist) reasons, most notably in the War of Italian Unification (1859) and the wars of German unification (1864, 1866, and 1870). For the most part, however, great-power conflict resulted from the combination of fear, greed, and stupidity that is characteristic of life in the anarchic world of international politics.

According to Huntington, great-power conflict before 1990 was largely, if not entirely, intracivilizational. In his words, "for over four hundred years, the nation-states of the West—Britain, France, Spain, Austria, Prussia, Germany, the United States, and others—constituted a multipolar international system within Western civilization and interacted, competed, and fought wars with each other." This characterization is wrong, however, because it omits the two non-Western great powers (Japan and Russia) that "interacted, competed, and fought wars" with the West (and with others) during these four centuries.

With Japan and Russia included, what does the historical record show? There have been four hegemonic conflicts since 1800 (the Napoleonic Wars, World War I, World War II, and the Cold War), all of which involved states from two or more civilizations. Moreover, most of the other wars involving great powers (including their colonial wars) were intercivilizational as well. Thus, Huntington is wrong to claim that "in the post–Cold War world, for the first time in history, global politics has become multipolar and multicivilizational."

Among other things, this error casts doubt on Huntington's claim that the end of the Cold War constitutes a radical historical watershed. It also means that he cannot use past intercivilizational wars as support for his own thesis, because these various conflicts did not arise from the cultural or "civilizational" differences that Huntington now sees as central to world politics.

At this point, one begins to suspect that Huntington has merely given a new label to an old phenomenon: Sometimes states with different cultural backgrounds fight with one another. Such a view receives support from Huntington himself, when he writes that "the sources of conflict between states and groups from different civilizations are, in large measure, those which have always generated conflict between groups: control of people, territory, wealth, and resources, and relative power." Yet he clearly believes that something is different today, or why bother to formulate a new paradigm?

The novel feature is a shift in personal identities. He still regards states as the key actors in world politics but argues that the end of the Cold War has been accompanied by a profound shift in the locus of political loyalty. In a direct challenge to the concept of nationalism, he asserts that both the elites and the masses will increasingly identify with other states in their specific cultural group and that this shift in identities will largely eliminate conflict within each civilization while exacerbating tensions between them.

It is important to recognize how fundamental and far-reaching this claim is. For the past 2,000 years or so, assorted empires, city states, tribes, and nation-states have repeatedly ignored cultural affinities in order to pursue particular selfish interests. These political units have always been willing to fight other members of their own civilization and have been equally willing to ally with groups from different civilizations when it seemed advantageous to do so. Huntington now claims that states are going to act very differently, however, and will place cultural values above all others.

Yet Huntington never explains why loyalties are shifting in the manner he depicts. He asserts that globalization and the increased contact between different cultures have made broad civilizational identities more powerful, but he provides no theory explaining why this is the case. Why are "civilizational" loyalties now trumping nationalism? Why is culture or ethnicity no longer focused on

the state, but on the broader notion of "civilization"? Huntington provides no answer to these questions.

Not only is an answer lacking, but many of his examples of increasing cultural assertiveness are not about "civilizational" consciousness at all. To support his claim that the end of the Cold War led to a global "identity crisis," for example, he notes that "questions of national identity were actively debated . . . [in] Algeria, Canada, China, Germany, Great Britain, India, Iran, Japan, Mexico, Morocco, Russia, South Africa, Syria, Tunisia, Turkey, Ukraine, and the United States." Most of these "questions of identity" arose from nationalist movements rather than from any "civilizational" affinity, however, and thus do not support his thesis.

Moreover, although The Clash of Civilizations devotes roughly 300 pages to a cultural analysis of world politics, Huntington never explains why conflict is more likely to arise between civilizations than within them. He suggests that cultural values are not easily compromised and that people "naturally distrust and see as threats those who are different and have the capability to harm them." Yet even if these propositions are correct—and I am inclined to agree with him on the last one—they do not explain why intercivilizational conflicts will shape the future world order.

Cultural differences do not cause war by themselves, just as cultural similarities do not guarantee harmony. Indeed, one could argue that cultural diversity makes conflict less likely, provided different groups are free to establish their own political and social orders. As Huntington's own analysis of "cleft states" suggests, cultural clashes are most likely not when separate groups come into contact, but when members of different cultures are forced to live in the same community. Once again, many of Huntington's more compelling examples of cultural conflict come from local settings rather than from true "civilizational" clashes. But the ways in which members of different cultures interact within a single community are quite different from the ways in which whole civilizations interact on a global scale.

Finally, the evidence in favor of Huntington's thesis is quite thin. As we have seen, past examples of intercivilizational conflict do not support his thesis, because these were simply conflicts of interest between states and not the result of "civilizational" differences. Given that Huntington sees the civilizational paradigm as relevant only for the post–Cold War period, we have roughly six years of experience with which to evaluate his claims. What does the record show thus far? Huntington supports his argument by reference to numerous examples of contemporary political leaders employing cultural or even civilizational rhetoric. Not surprisingly, he takes these statements at face value and regards them as persuasive evidence of growing civilizational affinities. But the question is not just what Lee Kuan Yew or Muammar Qadaffi say, because talk is cheap and political rhetoric serves many functions. The real issue is what these leaders (or their countries) will actually do, and how much blood and treasure they will devote to "civilizational" interests.

On this point, the record of state behavior since 1990 does not lend much support to Huntington's argument. Consider the 1991 Persian Gulf war. Huntington's paradigm predicts that conflicts between civilizations will be more frequent and intense than conflicts within them. Yet in the Gulf war, Iraq attacked a fellow Islamic state, only to be repulsed

by a coalition of Western and Islamic states, with tacit support from Israel. Huntington tries to salvage his thesis by arguing that most Islamic populations actually favored Iraq, but, even if this were true, it merely underscores the fact that state interests mattered more than loosely felt and politically impotent loyalties to a particular "civilizational" entity. In the Gulf war, in short, civilizational identities were irrelevant.

What about Bosnia, where Muslims, "Western" Croats, and "Orthodox" Serbs were at war from 1991 to 1995? Although some aspects of the Bosnian tragedy are consistent with Huntington's argument, the overall picture is a striking refutation of it. More than 50,000 U.S.-led troops were deployed to Bosnia in 1996, but they were not there to defend Western (in this case, Croatian) culture. Rather, they were there primarily to protect Muslims. Indeed, although several Islamic countries did send modest amounts of aid to the Bosnian Muslims, the Western states ultimately did far more for them than did their Islamic brethren. Similarly, Russia offered some rhetorical support to the Serbs, but it backed away from its "Orthodox" brethren when Serbian bellicosity made Belgrade an unappealing ally. Even the Western states failed to line up according to cultural criteria, with Britain and France being more sympathetic to the Serbs, Germany backing the Croats, and the United States reserving most of its support for the Muslims.

What about the Rwandan genocide and the subsequent carnage in Zaire? Huntington is not certain whether a true "African civilization" exists, but it is abundantly clear that these bloodlettings did not arise from a clash of civilizations. And, as in the earlier humanitarian mission in Somalia, outside assistance is being provided by members of other civilizations, once again irrespective of the cultural criterion Huntington now claims is paramount. Thus, conflict and cooperation do not observe the civilizational boundaries that Huntington's thesis predicts. Interestingly, The Clash of Civilizations provides decisive evidence on precisely this point. On pages 256 to 258, Huntington presents two tables on current ethnopolitical conflicts in order to demonstrate the conflictive nature of contemporary Islam. These tables also show that conflicts within civilizations are roughly 50 percent more frequent than conflicts between them. This result directly contradicts Huntington's core thesis, because the number of potential conflicts between members of different civilizations is much greater than the number of potential conflicts between members of the same civilization. For example, there are roughly 20 "Western" states with which the United States could find itself at odds, but there are more than 175 non-Western states that the United States could quarrel with as well. Even if conflict occurred on a purely random basis, we would expect most clashes to be between groups from different "civilizations." This gap should be even more pronounced if "civilizational" differences are a powerful cause of conflict, as Huntington posits, but the evidence he presents shows that exactly the opposite is occurring. This result merely underscores the fact that cultural differences are of secondary importance in explaining the origins of global conflict in the post–Cold War world.

The Clash of Civilizations is also strangely silent about Israel, which has been a central concern for U.S. foreign policy since its founding in 1948. During the Cold War, U.S. support for Israel could be justified on both ideological and strategic grounds. From a cultural perspective, however, the basis for close ties between Israel and the "West" is unclear. Israel is not a member of the West (at least not by Huntington's criteria) and is probably becoming less "Western" as religious fundamentalism becomes more salient and as the Sephardic population becomes more influential. A "civilizational" approach to U.S. foreign policy can justify close ties with Europeans (as the common descendants of Western Christendom) but not Israelis. Moreover, given that Huntington wants to avoid unnecessary clashes with rival civilizations and given that U.S. support for Israel is a source of tension with the Islamic world, his civilizational paradigm would seem to prescribe a sharp reduction in Western support for the Jewish state. I do not know whether Huntington favors such a step, but that is where the logic of his argument leads. His silence on this issue may reflect an awareness that making this conclusion explicit would not enhance the appeal of the book, or Israel may simply be an anomaly that lies outside of his framework. In either case, however, the issue reveals a further limitation of the civilizational paradigm. What has gone wrong here? As should now be apparent, Huntington's central error is his belief that personal loyalties are increasingly centered on "civilizations" rather than on the nation-state. If there is a dominant trend in the world today, however, it is not the coalescing of a half-dozen or so multinational civilizations. On the contrary, the dominant trend is the tendency for existing political communities to split into smaller units, organized primarily along ethnic or national lines. Being part of some larger "civilization" did not convince the Abkhaz, Armenians, Azeris, Chechens, Croats, Eritreans, Georgians, Kurds, Ossetians, Quebecois, Serbs, or Slovaks to abandon the quest for their own state, just as being part of the West did not slow Germany's rush to reunify. Thus, it is not civilization that is thriving in the post–Cold War world; it is nationalism.

This neglect of nationalism is the Achilles' heel of the civilizational paradigm. As Huntington himself points out, "civilizations" do not make decisions; they are an abstract cultural category rather than a concrete political agency. States, on the other hand, have defined borders, designated leaders, established decision-making procedures, and direct control over political resources. States can mobilize their citizens, collect taxes, issue threats, reward friends, and wage war; in other words, states can act. Nationalism is a tremendously powerful force precisely because it marries individual cultural affinities to an agency—the state—that can actually do something. In the future as in the past, the principal conflicts in the world will be between states—not civilizations—and between existing states and groups within them who seek to establish states of their own. Some of these conflicts will occur across cultural boundaries—as in the "fault-line" areas that Huntington correctly highlights—but cultural differences will be at best a secondary cause of conflict.

Once again, Huntington's analysis implicitly acknowledges this point. His emphasis on the "core states" within each civilization reaffirms the central role of the great powers—defined in traditional realist terms—and he admits that "the issues in [core state conflicts] are the classic ones of international politics," such as relative influence, economic and military power, and the control of territory. When it comes to the great powers, therefore, culture does not matter very much, and the concept of civilization largely drops out of his analysis.

The enduring relevance of the realist, statist paradigm is most clearly revealed at the end of the book, when Huntington lays out a possible scenario for a war between China and the West. Several details of this imagined war are striking. First, it begins with a Chinese attack on Vietnam, which by Huntington's criteria is a clash within a particular civilizational group. Thus, World War III is caused not by a clash of civilizations, but by a clash within one—precisely the sort of event that increasing cultural affinities were supposed to overcome. Second, cultural factors play virtually no role either in starting the war or in causing it to escalate; instead, it arises from a competition for oil and escalates because other states are worried about the long-term balance of power. Third, the subsequent war features a number of important intercivilizational alliances (for balance-of-power reasons), which further contradicts the claim that cultural factors are becoming decisive. In short, when he turns away from expounding his paradigm and describes what a 21st-century conflict might actually look like, Huntington largely ignores his own creation and relies on the traditional principles of realpolitik.

A CALL FOR NEW ENEMIES?

In the end, The Clash of Civilizations and the Remaking of World Order is a book replete with ironies. It is ironic that a scholar whose earlier works offered brilliant analyses of the role of the state now offers a paradigm in which states are the handmaidens of diffuse cultural groups. It is also ironic that a scholar who effectively challenged the "declinist" arguments made by Paul Kennedy and others now goes them one better: Not only is the United States declining, but so is the rest of Western civilization. And it is surely ironic that a scholar who was sounding alarm bells about Japan only four years ago is now obsessed with China and Islam and is calling for active efforts to preserve Japan's ties with the West.[1]

There may be a common theme in these ironies, however. Huntington has always been a staunch defender of Western civilization in general and the United States in particular, and he is clearly worried that the hedonistic, individualistic culture of the West is no longer up to the challenges it faces. By portraying the contemporary world as one of relentless cultural competition, therefore, he may be trying to provide us with the bogeymen we need to keep our own house in order.

He may be right, and a reaffirmation of certain "Western" values might be wholly desirable. But even if the West does need new enemies in order to hold it together, the civilizational paradigm that Huntington has offered is not a sound basis for making foreign policy. Relying upon an overly broad category like "civilization" would blind us to the differences within broad cultural groups and limit our ability to pursue a strategy of "divide and conquer." Thus, adopting Huntington's paradigm might unwittingly rob policymakers of the flexibility that has always been a cardinal diplomatic virtue. If the world is as dangerous as he seems to think, why limit our options in this way?

Moreover, if we treat all states who are part of some other "civilization" as intrinsically hostile, we are likely to create enemies that might otherwise be neutral or friendly. In fact, a civilizational approach to foreign policy is probably the surest way to get diverse foreign cultures to coordinate their actions and could even bring several civilizations together against us. The West is still the strongest civilization and will remain so for some time to come. Accordingly, a civilizational strategy could encourage two or more civilizations to gang up on us, solely out of a sense of self-preservation. In this sense, The Clash of Civilizations offers a dangerous, self-fulfilling prophecy: The more we believe it and make it the basis for action, the more likely it is to come true. Huntington would no doubt feel vindicated, but the rest of us would not be happy with the results.

NOTE

1. For his earlier views, see Samuel P. Huntington, "The U.S.—Decline or Renewal?" *Foreign Affairs* 67:2 (Winter 1988/89); "America's Changing Strategic Interests," *Survival* 33:1 (January 1991); and "Why International Primacy Matters," *International Security* 17:4 (Spring 1993).

QUESTIONS

1. What are the three most important criticisms that Walt has to offer about Huntington's Clash of Civilizations theory?

2. Why does Walt conclude that Huntington underestimates the importance of the state?

CIVILIZATIONIST PERSPECTIVE OF SEPTEMBER 11

31.   The west has won: Radical Islam can't beat democracy and capitalism. We're still at the end of history

Francis Fukuyama

This short piece by Francis Fukuyama presents his analysis of the events of September 11. He asserts that the war on terrorism does not represent a defeat for the liberal democratic west. Fukuyama says, the events of September 11 represent a backlash against modernity and the West will prevail against the reactionary forces of radical Islam.

He is the Bernard L. Schwartz Professor of International Political Economy at Johns Hopkins University. He is the author of several articles and books including his most recent publication *Our Posthuman Future: Consequences of the Biotechnology Revolution* (2002).

A stream of commentators have been asserting that the tragedy of September 11 proves that I was utterly wrong to have said more than a decade ago that we had reached the end of history. It is, on the face of it, insulting to the memory of those who died to declare that this unprecedented attack did not rise to the level of a historical event. But the way in which I used the word *history* was different: it referred to the progress over the centuries toward modernity, characterised by institutions like democracy and capitalism.

My observation, made in 1989 on the eve of the collapse of communism, was that this evolutionary process did seem to be bringing ever larger parts of the world toward modernity. And if we looked beyond liberal democracy and markets, there was nothing else towards which we could expect to evolve; hence the end of history. While there were retrograde areas that resisted that process,

it was hard to find a viable alternative civilisation that people actually wanted to live in after the discrediting of socialism, monarchy, fascism and other types of authoritarianism.

This view has been challenged by many people, and perhaps most articulately by Samuel Huntington. He argued that rather than progressing toward a single global system, the world remained mired in a "clash of civilisations" in which six or seven major cultural groups would co-exist without converging and constitute the new fracture lines of global conflict. Since the successful attack on the centre of global capitalism was evidently perpetrated by Islamic extremists unhappy with the very existence of western civilisation, observers have been handicapping the Huntington "clash" view over my own "end of history" hypothesis.

I believe that in the end I remain right: modernity is a very powerful freight train that will not be derailed by recent events, however painful. Democracy and free markets will continue to expand as the dominant organising principles for much of the world. But it is worthwhile thinking about what the true scope of the present challenge is.

Modernity has a cultural basis. Liberal democracy and free markets do not work everywhere. They work best in societies with certain values whose origins may not be entirely rational. It is not an accident that modern liberal democracy emerged first in the Christian west, since the universalism of democratic rights can be seen as a secular form of Christian universalism.

The central question raised by Huntington is whether institutions of modernity will work only in the west, or whether there is something broader in their appeal that will allow them to make headway elsewhere. I believe there is. The proof lies in the progress that democracy and free markets have made in regions such as east Asia, Latin America, orthodox Europe, south Asia and even Africa. Proof lies also in the millions of developing world immigrants who vote with their feet every year to live in western societies. The flow of people moving in the opposite direction, and the number who want to blow up what they can of the west, is by contrast negligible.

But there does seem to be something about Islam, or at least the fundamentalist versions of Islam that have been dominant in recent years, that makes Muslim societies particularly resistant to modernity. Of all contemporary cultural systems, the Islamic world has the fewest democracies (Turkey alone qualifies), and contains no countries that have made the transition to developed nation status in the manner of South Korea or Singapore.

There are plenty of non-western people who prefer the economic part of modernity and hope to have it without having to accept democracy as well. There are others who like both the economic and political versions of modernity, but just can't figure out how to make it happen. For them, transition to western-style modernity may be long and painful. But there are no insuperable cultural barriers to prevent them from getting there, and they constitute about four-fifths of the world's people.

Islam, by contrast, is the only cultural system that seems regularly to produce people like Osama bin Laden or the Taliban who reject modernity lock, stock and barrel. This raises the question of how representative such people are of the larger Muslim community, and whether this rejection is somehow inherent in Islam. For if the rejectionists are more than a lunatic fringe, then Huntington is right that we are in for a protracted conflict made dangerous by virtue of their technological empowerment.

The answer that politicians east and west have been putting out since September 11 is that those sympathetic with the terrorists are a "tiny minority" of Muslims, and that the vast majority are appalled by what happened. It is important to say this to prevent all Muslims from becoming targets of hatred. The problem is that hatred of America and what it stands for are clearly much more widespread.

Certainly the group of people willing to go on suicide missions against the US is tiny. But sympathy may be manifest in nothing more than initial feelings of schadenfreude at the sight of the collapsing towers, a sense of satisfaction that the US was getting what it deserved, to be followed by pro forma expressions of disapproval. By this standard, sympathy for the terrorists is characteristic of much more than a "tiny minority" of Muslims, extending from the middle classes in countries like Egypt to immigrants in the west.

This broader dislike and hatred would seem to represent something much deeper than mere opposition to American policies like support for Israel or the Iraq embargo, encompassing a hatred of the underlying society. After all, many people around the world, including many Americans, disagree with US policies, but this does not send them into paroxysms of anger and violence. Nor is it necessarily a matter of ignorance about the quality of life in the west. The suicide hijacker Mohamed Atta was a well-educated man from a well-to-do Egyptian family who lived and studied in the US for years. Perhaps the hatred is born out of a resentment of western success and Muslim failure.

But rather than psychologise the Muslim world, it makes more sense to ask whether radical Islam constitutes a serious alternative to western liberal democracy. (Radical Islam has virtually no appeal in the contemporary world apart from those who are culturally Islamic to begin with.) For Muslims themselves, political Islam has proved much more appealing in the abstract than in reality. After 23 years of rule by fundamentalist clerics, most Iranians, especially the young, would like to live in a far more liberal society. Afghans who have experienced Taliban rule feel much the same. Anti-American hatred does not translate into a viable political program for Muslim societies to follow.

We remain at the end of history because there is only one system that will continue to dominate world politics, that of the liberal-democratic west. This does not imply a world free from conflict, nor the disappearance of culture. But the struggle we face is not the clash of several distinct and equal cultures fighting amongst one another like the great powers of 19th-century Europe. The clash consists of a series of rearguard actions from societies whose traditional existence is indeed threatened by modernisation. The strength of the backlash reflects the severity of this threat. But time is on the side of modernity, and I see no lack of US will to prevail.

QUESTIONS

1. The author contends that radical Islam does not constitute a serious alternative to Western liberal democracy. Do you agree or disagree? Why?

2. Has the global war on terrorism weakened Fukuyama's thesis that we have reached an end of history?

32.   Beyond Jihad vs. McWorld

Benjamin R. Barber

In this reading, Benjamin Barber presents a civilizationist analysis of the events of September 11. The author contends that the realist paradigm fails to provide useful guidance for U.S. foreign policy because nonstate actors like terrorist organizations may not be rational actors. Instead, terrorists must be understood in terms of a violent backlash against modernity. The author concludes that the only lasting solution to this conflict is the expansion of democratic values and institutions.

Benjamin R. Barber is Gershon and Carol Kekst Professor of Civil Society and Wilson H. Elkins Professor of Maryland School of Public Affairs and the College of Behavioral and Social Sciences at the University of Maryland. He is the author of the international bestseller *Jihad vs. McWorld,* the theory classic *Strong Democracy,* and most recently, *The Truth of Power: Intellectual Affairs in the Clinton White House.*

The terrorist attacks of September 11 did without a doubt change the world forever, but they failed to change the ideological viewpoint of either the left or the right in any significant way. The warriors and unilateralists of the right still insist war conducted by an ever-sovereign America is the only appropriate response to terrorism, while the left continues to talk about the need for internationalism, interdependency and an approach to global markets that redresses economic imbalances and thereby reduces the appeal of extremism—if, in the climate of war patriotism, it talks a little more quietly than heretofore. The internationalist lobby has a right to grow more vociferous, however, for what has changed in the wake of September 11 is the relationship between these arguments and political realism (and its contrary, political idealism). Prior to September 11, realpolitik (though it could speak with progressive accents, as it did with Ronald Steel and E. H. Carr before him) belonged primarily to the right—which spurned talk of human rights and democracy as hopelessly utopian, the blather of romantic left-wing idealists who preferred to see the world as they wished it to be rather than as it actually was.

Following September 11, however, the realist tiger changed its stripes: "Idealistic" internationalism has become the new realism. We face not a paradigm shift but the occupation of an old paradigm by new tenants. Democratic globalists are quite abruptly the new realists while the old realism—especially in its embrace of markets—looks increasingly like a dangerous and utterly unrealistic dogma opaque to our new realities as brutally inscribed on the national consciousness by the demonic architects of September 11. The issue is not whether to pursue a military or a civic strategy, for both are clearly needed; the issue is how to pursue either one.

The historical realist doctrine was firmly grounded in an international politics of sovereign states pursuing their interests in a setting of shifting alliances where principles could only obstruct the achievement of sovereign ends that interests alone defined and served. Its mantras—the cliches of Lord Acton, Henry Morgenthau, George Kennan or, for that matter, Henry Kissinger—had it that nations have neither permanent friends nor permanent enemies but only permanent interests; that the enemies of our enemies are always our friends; that the pursuit of democratic ideals or human rights can often obfuscate our true interests; that coalitions and alliances in war or peace are tolerable only to the degree that we retain our sovereign independence in all critical decisions and policies; and that international institutions are to be embraced, ignored or discarded exclusively on the basis of how well they serve our sovereign national interests, which are entirely separable from the objectives of such institutions.

However appealing these mantras may seem, and though upon occasion they served to counter the hypocritical use of democratic arguments to disguise interests (as when true democrats attacked Woodrow Wilson's war to make the world "safe for democracy"), they can no longer be said to represent even a plausible, let alone a realistic, strategy in our current circumstances. To understand why, we need to understand how September 11 put a period once and for all at the end of the old story of American independence.

Many would say the two great world wars of the past century, even as they proved American power and resilience, were already distinct if unheeded harbingers of the passing of our sovereignty; for, though fought on foreign soil, they represented conflicts from which America could not be protected by its two oceans, struggles whose outcomes would affect an America linked to the then-nascent global system. Did anyone imagine that America could be indifferent to the victory of fascism in Europe or Japanese imperialism in Asia (or, later, of Soviet Communism in Eurasia) as it might once have been indifferent to the triumph of the British or Belgian or French empires in Africa? By the end of the twentieth century, irresistible interdependence was a leitmotif of every ecological, technological and economic event. It could hardly escape even casual observers that global warming recognizes no sovereign territory, that AIDS carries no passport, that technology renders national boundaries increasingly meaningless, that the Internet defies national regulation, that oil and cocaine addiction circle the planet like twin plagues and that financial capital and labor resources, like their anarchic cousins crime and terror, move from country to country with "wilding" abandon without regard for formal or legal arrangements—acting informally and illegally whenever traditional institutions stand in their way.

Most nations understood the significance of these changes well enough, and well before the end of the past century Europe was already on the way to forging transnational forms of integration that rendered its member nations' sovereignty dubious. Not the United States. Wrapped in its national myths of splendid isolation and blessed innocence (chronicled insightfully by Herman Melville and Henry James), it held out. How easy it was, encircled by two oceans and reinforced lately in its belief in sovereign invincibility by the novel utopia of a missile shield—technology construed as a virtual ocean to protect us from the world's turmoil and dangers—to persist in the illusion of sovereignty. The good times of the 1990s facilitated an easy acquiescence in the founding myths, for in that (suddenly remote) era of prideful narcissism, other people's troubles and the depredations that were the collateral damage of America's prosperous and productive global markets seemed little more than diverting melodramas on CNN's evening "news" soap operas.

Then came September 11. Marauders from the sky, from above and abroad but also from within and below, sleepers in our midst who somehow were leveraging our own powers of technology to overcome our might, made a mockery of our sovereignty, demonstrating that there was no longer any difference between inside and outside, between domestic and international. We still don't know authoritatively who precisely sponsored the acts of September 11 or the bioterror that followed it: What alone has become clear is that we can no longer assign culpability in the neat nineteenth-century terms of domestic and foreign. And while we may still seek sovereign sponsors for acts of terror that have none, the myth of our independence can no longer be sustained. Nonstate actors, whether they are multinational corporations or loosely knit terrorist cells, are neither domestic nor foreign, neither national nor international, neither sovereign entities nor international organizations. Going on about states that harbor terrorists (our "allies" Egypt and Saudi Arabia? Our good friend Germany? Or how about Florida and New Jersey?) simply isn't helpful in catching the bad guys. The Taliban are gone, and bin Laden will no doubt follow, but terrorism's network exists in anonymous cells we can neither identify nor capture. Declaring our independence in a world of perverse and malevolent interdependence foisted on us by people who despise us comes close to what political

science roughnecks once would have called pissing into the wind. Pakistan and Saudi Arabia still foster schools that teach hate, and suicide bombers are still lining up in Palestine for martyrdom missions in numbers that suggest an open call for a Broadway show.

The American myth of independence is not the only casualty of September 11. Traditional realist paradigms fail us today also because our adversaries are no longer motivated by "interest" in any relevant sense, and this makes the appeal to interest in the fashion of realpolitik and rational-choice theory seem merely foolish. Markets may be transnational instruments of interests, and even bin Laden has a kind of "list of demands" (American troops out of Saudi Arabia, Palestine liberated from Israeli "occupation," down with the infidel empire), but terrorists are not stubborn negotiators pursuing rational agendas. Their souls yearn for other days when certainty was unencumbered, for other worlds where paradise offered other rewards. Their fanaticism has causes and their zeal has its reasons, but market conceptions of interest will not succeed in fathoming them. Bombing Hanoi never brought the Vietcong to their knees, and they were only passionate nationalists, not messianic fundamentalists; do we think we can bomb into submission the millions who resent, fear and sometimes detest what they think America means?

Or take the realist epigram about nations having neither permanent friends nor permanent enemies. It actually turns out that America's friends, defined not by interests but by principles, are its best allies and most reliable coalition partners in the war on terrorism. Even conservative realists have acknowledged that Israel—whatever one thinks of Sharon's policies—is a formidable ally in part because it is the sole democracy in the Middle East. By the same token, we have been consistently betrayed by an odd assortment of allies born of shifting alliances that have been forged and broken in pursuit of "friendship" with the enemies of our enemies: Iraq, Iran and those onetime allies of convenience in the war against the Soviets, the Taliban. Then there are the countless Islamic tyrannies that are on our side only because their enemies have in turn been the enemies of American economic interests or threats to the flow of oil. I will leave it to others to determine how prudent our realist logic is in embracing Egypt, Saudi Arabia, Yemen or Pakistan, whose official media and state-sponsored schools often promulgate the very propaganda and lies we have joined with them to combat.

On the other hand, the key principles at stake—democracy and pluralism, a space for religion safe from state and commercial interference, and a space for government safe from sectarianism and the ambitions of theocrats—actually turn out to be prudent and useful benchmarks for collecting allies who will stand with us in the war on terrorism. In the new post–September 11 realism, it is apparent that the only true friends we have are the democracies, and they are friends because they are democracies and share our values even when they contest our interests and are made anxious by our power. In the war against terror or the war for freedom, what true realist would trade a cantankerous, preternaturally anti-American France for a diplomatic and ostentatiously pro-American Saudi Arabia?

Yet the pursuit of democracy has been a sideline in an American realist foreign policy organized around oil and trade with despots pretending to be on our side—not just in Republican but in Democratic administrations as well, where democracy was proclaimed but (remember Larry Summers) market democracy construed as market fundamentalism was practiced. In the old paradigm, democratic norms were very nice as emblems of abstract belief and utopian aspiration, or as rationalizations of conspicuous interests, but they were poor guides for a country seeking status and safety in the world. Not anymore. The cute cliche about democracies not making war on one another is suddenly a hard realist foundational principle for national security policy.

Except the truth today is not only that democracies do not make war on one another, but that democracies alone are secure from collective forms of violence and reactionary fundamentalism, whether religious or ethnic. Those Islamic nations (or nations with large Islamic populations) that have made progress toward democracy—Bangladesh, India or Turkey, for example—have been relatively free of systematic terrorism and reactionary fundamentalism as well as the export of terrorism. They may still persecute minorities, harbor racists and reflect democratic aspirations only partially, but they do not teach hate in their schools or pipe propaganda through an official press or fund terrorist training camps. Like India recently, they are the victims rather than the perpetrators of international terrorism. Making allies of the enemies of democracy because they share putative interests with us is, in other words, not realism but foolish self-deception. We have learned from the military campaign against the Taliban and Al Qaeda how, when push comes to shove (push has come to shove!), the Egyptians and the Saudis can be unreliable in sharing intelligence, interdicting the funding of terrorism or standing firm against the terrorists at their own door. Pakistan still allows thousands of fundamentalist madrassahs to operate as holy-war training schools. Yet how can these "allies" possibly be tough when, in defense of their despotic regimes, they think that coddling the terrorists outside their doors may be the price they have to pay for keeping at bay the terrorists already in their front parlors? The issue is not religion, not even fundamentalism; the issue is democracy.

Unilateralism rooted in a keen sense of the integrity of sovereign autonomy has been another keynote of realism's American trajectory and is likely to become another casualty of September 11. From the Monroe Doctrine to our refusal to join the League of Nations, from the isolationism that preceded World War II, and from which we were jarred only by Pearl Harbor, to the isolationism that followed the war and that yielded only partially to the cold war and the arms race, and from our reluctance to pay our UN dues or sign on to international treaties to our refusal to place American troops under the command of friendly NATO foreigners, the United States has persisted in reducing foreign policy to a singular formula that preaches going it alone. Despite the humiliations of the 1970s, when oil shortages, emerging ecological movements and the Iranian hostage crisis should have warned us of the limitations of unilateralism, we went on playing the Lone Ranger, the banner of sovereign independence raised high.

We often seem nearly comatose when it comes to the many small injuries and larger incursions to which American sovereignty is subjected on a daily basis by those creeping forms of interdependence that characterize modernity—technology, ecology, trade, pop culture and consumer markets. Only the blunt assault of the suicide bombers awoke the nation to the new realities and the new demands on policy imposed by interdependence. Which is why, since September 11, there has been at least a wan feint in the direction of multilateralism and coalition-building. The long-unpaid UN bills were finally closed out, the Security Council was consulted and some Republican officials even whispered the dreaded Clinton-tainted name of nation-building as a possible requirement in a postwar strategy in Afghanistan.

Yet there is a long way to go. While the Colin Powell forces do battle with the Dick Cheney forces for the heart of the President, little is being done to open a civic and political front in the campaign against terrorism. After what seemed a careful multilateral dance with President Putin on missile defense, President Bush has abruptly thrust his ballroom partner aside and waltzed off into the sunset by himself, leaving the Russians and Chinese (and our European allies) to sulk in the encroaching gloom. Even in Afghanistan, Nicholas Kristof, in his first contribution as the *New York Times*'s new crisis-of-terrorism columnist, complained that even as other nations' diplomats poured into the capital after its fall, the United States posted not a single representative to Kabul to begin nurturing a postwar political and civil strategy—a reticence it has only just now begun to remedy.

Is there anything realistic about such reluctance? On the contrary, realism here in its new democratic form suggests that America must begin to engage in the slow and sovereignty-eroding business of constructing a cooperative and benevolent interdependence in which it joins the world rather than demanding that the world join it or be consigned to the camp of the terrorists ("You are with us or you are with the terrorists," intoned the President in those first fearful days after September 11). This work recognizes that while terrorism has no justification, it does have causes. The old realism went by the old adage *tout comprendre, c'est tout pardonner* and eschewed deep explanations of the root causes of violence and terror. The new realism insists that to understand collective malice is not to pardon it but to assure that it can be addressed, interdicted and perhaps even pre-empted. "Bad seed" notions of original sin ("the evil ones") actually render perpetrators invulnerable—subject only to a manichean struggle in which the alternative to total victory is total defeat. Calling bin Laden and his associates "the evil ones" is not necessarily inaccurate, but it commits us to a dark world of jihad and counterjihad (what the President first called his crusade), in which issues of democracy, civil comity and social justice—let alone nuance, complexity and interdependence—simply vanish. It is possible to hate jihad without loving America. It is possible to condemn terror as absolutely wrong without thinking that those who are terror's targets possess absolute right.

This is the premise behind the thesis of interdependence. The context of jihadic resistance and its pathology of terrorism is a complex world in which there are causal interrelationships between the jihadic reaction to modernity and the American role in shaping it according to the peculiar logic of US technology, markets and branded pop culture (what I call McWorld). Determining connections and linkages is not the same thing as distributing blame. Power confers responsibility. The power enjoyed by the United States bestows on it obligations to address conditions it may not have itself brought into being. Jihad in this view may grow out of and reflect (among other things) a pathological metastasis of valid grievances about the effects of an arrogant secularist materialism that is the unfortunate concomitant of the spread of consumerism across the world. It may reflect a desperate and ultimately destructive concern for the integrity of indigenous cultural traditions that are ill equipped to defend themselves against aggressive markets in a free-trade world. It may reflect a struggle for justice in which Western markets appear as obstacles rather than facilitators of cultural identity.

Can Asian tea, with its religious and family "tea culture," survive the onslaught of the global merchandising of cola beverages? Can the family sit-down meal survive fast food, with its focus on individualized consumers, fuel-pit-stop eating habits and nourishment construed as snacking? Can national film cultures in Mexico, France or India survive Hollywood's juggernaut movies geared to universal teen tastes rooted in hard violence and easy sentiment? Where is the space for prayer, for common religious worship or for spiritual and cultural goods in a world in which the 24/7 merchandising of material commodities makes the global economy go round? Are the millions of American Christian families who home-school their children because they are so intimidated by the violent commercial culture awaiting the kids as soon as they leave home nothing but an American Taliban? Do even those secular cosmopolitans in America's coastal cities want nothing more than the screen diet fed them by the ubiquitous computers, TVs and multiplexes?

Terror obviously is not an answer, but the truly desperate may settle for terror as a response to our failure even to ask such questions. The issue for jihad's warriors of annihilation is of course far beyond such anxieties: It entails absolute devotion to absolute values. Yet for many who are appalled by terrorism but unimpressed by America, there may seem to be an absolutist dimension to the materialist aspirations of our markets. Our global market culture appears to us as both voluntary and wholesome; but it can appear to others as both compelling (in the sense of compulsory) and corrupt—not exactly coercive, but capable of seducing children into a willed but corrosive secular materialism. What's wrong with Disneyland or Nikes or the Whopper? We just "give people what they want." But this merchandiser's dream is a form of romanticism, the idealism of neoliberal markets, the convenient idyll that material plenty can satisfy spiritual longing so that fishing for profits can be thought of as synonymous with trolling for liberty.

It is the new democratic realist who sees that if the only choice we have is between the mullahs and the mall, between the hegemony of religious absolutism and the hegemony of market determinism, neither liberty nor the human spirit is likely to flourish. As we face up to the costs both of fundamentalist terrorism and of fighting it, must we not ask ourselves how it is that when we see religion colonize every other realm of human life we call it theocracy and turn up our noses at the odor of tyranny; and when we see politics colonize every other realm of human life we call it absolutism and tremble at the prospect of totalitarianism; but when we see market relations and commercial consumerism try to colonize every other realm of human life we call it liberty and celebrate its triumph? There are too many John Walkers who begin by seeking a refuge

from the aggressive secularist materialism of their suburban lives and end up slipping into someone else's dark conspiracy to rid the earth of materialism's infidels. If such men are impoverished and without hope as well, they become prime recruits for jihad.

The war on terrorism must be fought, but not as the war of McWorld against jihad. The only war worth winning is the struggle for democracy. What the new realism teaches is that only such a struggle is likely to defeat the radical nihilists. That is good news for progressives. For there are real options for democratic realists in search of civic strategies that address the ills of globalization and the insecurities of the millions of fundamentalist believers who are neither willing consumers of Western commercial culture nor willing advocates of jihadic terror. Well before the calamities of September 11, a significant movement in the direction of constructive and realistic interdependence was discernible, beginning with the Green and human rights movements of the 1960s and '70s, and continuing into the NGO and "anti-globalization" movements of the past few years. Jubilee 2000 managed to reduce Third World debt-service payments for some nations by up to 30 percent, while the Community of Democracies initiated by the State Department under Madeleine Albright has been embraced by the Bush Administration and will continue to sponsor meetings of democratic governments and democratic NGOs. International economic reform lobbies like the Millennium Summit's development goals project, established by the UN to provide responses to global poverty, illiteracy and disease; Inter Action, devoted to increasing foreign aid; Global Leadership, a start-up alliance of corporations and grassroots organizations;

and the Zedillo Commission, which calls on the rich countries to devote 0.7 percent of their GNP to development assistance (as compared to an average of 0.2 percent today and under 0.1 percent for the United States), are making serious economic reform an issue for governments. Moreover, and more important, they are insisting with Amartya Sen and his new disciple Jeffrey Sachs that development requires democratization first if it is to succeed.

George Soros's Open Society Institute and Civicus, the transnational umbrella organization for NGOs, continue to serve the global agenda of civil society. Even corporations are taking an interest: Hundreds are collaborating in a Global Compact, under the aegis of UN Secretary General Kofi Annan, to seek a response to issues of global governance, while the World Economic Forum plans to include fifty religious leaders in a summit at its winter meeting in New York in late January.

This is only a start, and without the explicit support of a more multilateralist and civic-minded American government, such institutions are unlikely to change the shape of global relations. Nonetheless, in closing the door on the era of sovereign independence and American security, anarchic terrorism has opened a window for those who believe that social injustice, unregulated wild capitalism and an aggressive secularism that leaves no space for religion and civil society not only create conditions on which terrorism feeds but invite violence in the name of rectification. As a consequence, we are at a seminal moment in our history—one in which trauma opens up the possibility of new forms of action. Yesterday's utopia is today's realism; yesterday's realism, a recipe for catastrophe tomorrow. If ever there was one, this is democracy's moment. Whether our government seizes it will depend not just on George Bush but on us.

QUESTIONS

1. Why does the author believe that the realist paradigm fails to provide U.S. guidance for U.S. foreign policy in the twenty-first century?

2. What does Walt mean by the phrase "the jihadic reaction to modernity"? Do you agree or disagree with this characterization of Radical Islamic?

Chapter 7

DECISION-MAKING PROCESS THEORY

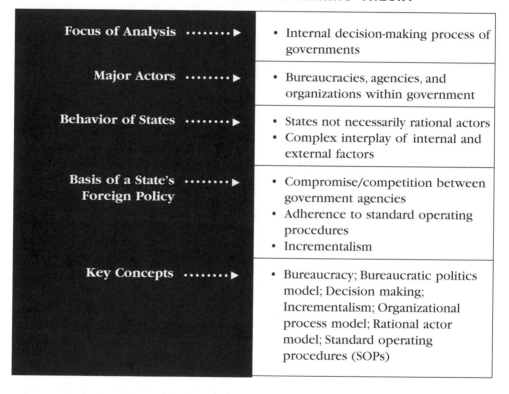

COMPONENTS OF DECISION-MAKING THEORY

Focus of Analysis ········▶	• Internal decision-making process of governments
Major Actors ········▶	• Bureaucracies, agencies, and organizations within government
Behavior of States ········▶	• States not necessarily rational actors • Complex interplay of internal and external factors
Basis of a State's Foreign Policy ········▶	• Compromise/competition between government agencies • Adherence to standard operating procedures • Incrementalism
Key Concepts ········▶	• Bureaucracy; Bureaucratic politics model; Decision making; Incrementalism; Organizational process model; Rational actor model; Standard operating procedures (SOPs)

INTRODUCTION

In the introduction to Part II, we discussed how state-level theories examine the impact of domestic factors on the course and conduct of foreign policy. This chapter focuses on decision-making process theory, a state-level theory that emphasizes the role of bureaucratic organizations and how the process of decision-making within these organizations, and within a government as a whole, can affect its foreign policy and international relations.

As this notion suggests, decision-making process theory disassembles the state bureaucratic structure, taking a targeted look at specific component parts to understand how decisions are made. The idea here is that different factions of a large bureaucracy are likely to approach problems or issues from different perspectives and with different preconceptions and priorities. These different perspectives result from the fact that each faction or department has unique responsibilities. A pattern of decision-making is established based on the priorities that stem from these individualized responsibilities. Thus, bureaucratic agencies address issues from different points of view, or, as the saying goes, "Where you stand is largely determined by where you sit." Certainly, international conditions and forces surrounding an event or crisis have an impact, but, according to decision-making process theorists, the inner workings of the bureaucracy—bargaining strategies, departmental priorities, and the like—cannot be disassociated from an assessment of foreign policy or international relations.

BUREAUCRACIES AND DECISION MAKING

Before we proceed in our discussion of decision-making process theory, it might be helpful to answer two important questions. First, what is a bureaucracy, and, second, what do we mean by decision-making? A **bureaucracy** could be defined as a network of interconnected departments and organizations designed to manage and administrate the operations of a state. Authority for different aspects of this administration and management is diffused throughout the various offices. That is, a single department generally takes the lead over a unique and specific area of policy or governance, though several departments usually have input into any given decision.

Decision-making theorists believe that the manner in which government bureaucracies arrive at these decisions is a critical part of both foreign policy and relations between states. The method that a state or bureaucracy uses to reach decisions is called **decision making.** Decision making is the process by which government officials select a policy to pursue from a range of options. A key part of this process and a defining feature of large bureaucracies is their dependence on **standard operating procedures (SOPs).** SOPs are accepted routines or patterns used by bureaucracies to organize and simplify the decision-making process. Standard operating procedures are utilized to handle problems or make decisions on a wide array of issues that confront governments on a daily basis—from internal personnel decisions to matters of international trade and diplomacy. Bureaucracies use SOPs because time, resources, and information in the decision-making process can be in short supply. Presumably, these standardized procedures simplify the decision-making process and help preserve the orderly function of government.

While standard operating procedures are aimed at making government more efficient and methodical, they have a profound impact on the type and quality of decisions made as well as on the policies adopted by governments. By relying on a set of specific procedures, a bureaucracy can limit the range and variety of policy options available to decision makers. Hence, both bureaucracies and leaders tend to depend on past policies or procedures in handling new problems. New policy decisions generally conform to those made in the past. A new, nonconforming policy would not only send a mixed message about a government's foreign policy platform and complicate the implementation process but would also disrupt the orderly workings of bureaucratic policy formulation. Therefore, if it is impossible to find a policy that is compatible with established SOPs, bureaucracies conduct a narrow search for alternatives and solutions that will require minimum change from accepted practices.

New policies, then, are often the result of what is called **incrementalism.** That is, a bureaucracy allows only incremental or marginal alterations in existing policy to prevent major changes from established norms. This "new" policy may not be the best available alternative but is, instead, a broadly palatable option resulting from bargains and compromises between competing individuals and bureaucratic organs or factions. To a certain extent, the nature of a bureaucracy—with its competing departments jostling for position—creates a measure of rivalry, territoriality, and one-up-manship among the various offices. This translates into a cautious pattern of decision making, designed to avoid risk-taking both in the process itself and with respect to the final decision or policy.

STATES AND FOREIGN POLICY

Decision-making process theorists view foreign policy and international relations largely as a by-product of these inner workings and the interaction of various state bureaucracies. The development of the decision-making approach to the study of foreign policy and international relations actually began in the 1950s as scholars became interested in applying the methodology of the traditional "hard" sciences to the study of human behavior. The "behavioralist school" of political science emerged as scholars began to rely more on the use of empirical research and quantitative analysis in developing and testing theories of international politics. Emphasizing the decision-making process of governments fit in quite well with this new, more scientific approach to the study of international relations and incorporated a number of features that had, up to that point, been largely overlooked.

The excerpt from Snyder, Bruck, and Sapin's book, *Foreign Policy Decision Making,* represents one of the first systematic approaches to the study of the decision-making process. Snyder and his colleagues developed a method for examining various components that influence the decisions taken by governments. The authors set up diagrams of "relevant factors" that might influence a state's behavior in a given situation. The premise here is that once the situation is defined, the path or policy a state chooses can be predicted by determining the factors that are relevant to the choice.

The diversity of viewpoints and responsibilities within a bureaucracy almost inevitably leads to conflict. Making a decision is not merely a progression of selecting goals, accumulating information, analyzing the various choices, and selecting a policy that most optimizes those goals. Policies are the result of diplomatic bargaining and compromise that take place within and between government agencies and bureaucracies. Also, being part of a bureaucracy can affect an individual's perceptions of the decision-making process and their role within it. The structure, purpose, and objectives or duties of these organizations can influence the decisions made by individuals working within them. These conditions tend to direct their attention away from purely international objectives and toward internal, domestic, and intra-bureaucratic concerns.

There is a subtle but crucial distinction between this notion and the premise of the theories in the following chapter that specifically address the role of individuals. It might be said, without oversimplifying the difference between these ideas, that the discussion here revolves around how bureaucratic organizations affect individuals. The next section presents theories on how individuals affect government decisions.

According to decision-making process theorists, then, there are a number of factors that influence a state's foreign policy and international relations. First, individuals operating within a large bureaucratic organization are constrained by position, loyalties, and duties within their individual departments and the bureaucracy as a whole. Second, the standard operating procedures (SOPs) used to guide the functions and decisions of the bureaucracy can limit the range of policy options. Decisions or policies are made largely to conform to existing SOPs and are often the result of compromise between various factions (usually competing) within the bureaucratic organization. Finally, as a result, policy follows a fairly pedantic, incremental course that can be predicted based on precedent and on an analysis of the decision-making mechanism itself.

One of the classic works of theory using this framework is Graham T. Allison's study of the Cuban missile crisis. In the excerpt, taken from Allison's article "Conceptual Models and the Cuban Missile Crisis," the author isolates three distinct models for explaining foreign policy decisions: the rational actor model, the organizational process model, and the bureaucratic politics model. According to the **rational actor model,** decision makers carefully define and identify foreign policy problems, gather all available information about the foreign policy options, weigh all possible alternatives, and select policies that are most likely to promote the state's national interests.

By contrast, the **organizational process model** focuses on the routines, standard patterns of behavior, and institutional perspectives of particular agencies and their impact on foreign policy decisions. It assumes that all governments generally rely on standard operating procedures, are relatively predictable, and favor only marginal changes in existing policy. The **bureaucratic politics model** emphasizes the struggle between various agencies of the government and its impact on the decision-making process. This model contends that the formulation of policy is largely the result of the competition among government agencies, representing diverse views. Such a competitive process means that foreign policy is often based more on domestic political struggles than on objective calculations of the national interest.

The point of Allison's highly regarded study is that each of the three models produce different explanations and each provides its own unique insights into the foreign policy decision-making process. While each model has particular strengths and weaknesses, Allison concludes that a complete understanding of any foreign policy situation must take into account several different institutional, political, and international factors.

A CRITIQUE OF DECISION-MAKING PROCESS THEORY

Certainly, it would be difficult to charge proponents of decision-making process theory with overlooking the details and minutiae of government that are a part of how decisions might be made. In fact, realists have criticized the inclusive approach of decision-making process theory for focusing too much on the details of the foreign policy-making process, thus losing the broader analytical and theoretical implications of history and events. By attempting to incorporate such a broad range of factors into their analysis, decision-making process theorists are often accused of describing the interaction of states, as opposed to providing a true theory of international relations—or, as the classic argument goes, not seeing the forest for the tress.

In response, Allison and other decision-making theorists challenge the realist assumption that states base their foreign policy decisions on a rational cost-benefit analysis of the relative risks and potential gains associated with particular policy options as too narrow. They argue that while the rational actor model is valuable, it is also limited on its own and fails to provide an adequate explanation of international relations.

For example, the rational actor model suggests that decision makers behave in a similar fashion, seeking to maximize strategic goals and objectives. The implication here is that governments use the best information available and select the policy that is most likely to maximize the national interests. Decision-making theory proceeds several steps farther, suggesting that all decisions must be analyzed and understood within the context of how governments really operate. Government bureaucracies function under conditions that often involve limited time, resources, and information—all of which are incompatible with the realist's rational-actor model. If we wish to understand why particular policies were selected over others, decision-making theorists insist we must first understand the process by which these choices were made. In short, process affects outcome.

Decision-making theory has also been attacked for being western-centric. Critics contend that decision-making theory is useful primarily for explaining the pluralistic foreign policy process of western democratic governments. It does not, however, present an accurate model for studying the more centralized, hierarchic decision-making process of non-western, non-democratic states. Decision-making theorists counter that every type of government, from the most rigid authoritarian regime to pluralistic democracies, have large bureaucratic structures with competing interests. Bureaucratic politics and adherence to standard operating procedures are not limited to democratic regimes but represent vital parts of the decision-making process in any type of government.

In the end, the manner in which governments make decisions about relations with other nations, particularly regarding decisions on war and peace, are basic to the study of international politics. It is critical, therefore, to understand how those decisions are reached and how they are actually implemented. In order to do this, we must examine the relationship between the process and the decisions that are produced from it. Decision-making theory focuses on the complex policy-making process and the governmental and bureaucratic settings in which those decisions are made.

KEY CONCEPTS

Bureaucracy is a network of interconnected departments and organizations designed to manage and administrate the operations of a state.

Bureaucratic politics model is one of three conceptual models devised by Graham Allison to explain and predict the foreign policy behavior of states. The bureaucratic model focuses on the struggle between various agencies of the government and its impact on the decision-making process. This model contends that the formulation of policy is largely the result of the competition among government agencies, representing diverse views. Such a competitive process means that foreign policy is often based more on domestic political struggles than on objective calculations of the national interest.

Decision making is the process of identifying problems, devising alternative policy options, and selecting which one of the alternatives to pursue.

Incrementalism is a tendency of decision makers to make only incremental or marginal alterations in existing policy in order to prevent major changes from established norms.

Organizational process model is the second of the three models devised by Graham Allison to explain and predict the foreign policy behavior of states. The organizational process model focuses on the routines, standard patterns of behavior, and institutional perspectives of particular agencies and their impact on foreign policy decisions. It assumes that all governments generally rely on standard operating procedures, are relatively predictable, and favor only marginal changes in existing policy.

Rational actor model is associated with the realist theory of decision making and the first of three models used by Graham Allison to explain and predict the foreign policy behavior of states. According to the rational actor model, decision makers carefully define and identify foreign policy problems, gather all available information about the foreign policy options, weigh all possible alternatives, and select policies that are most likely to promote the state's national interests.

Standard operating procedures (SOPs) are accepted routines or patterns used by bureaucracies to organize and simplify the decision-making process. Standard operating procedures are utilized to handle problems or make decisions on a wide array of issues that confront governments on a daily basis—from internal personnel decisions to matters of international trade and diplomacy.

33.   Foreign Policy Decision Making

Richard Snyder, H. W. Bruck, and Burton Sapin

In this except, Richard Snyder, H. W. Bruck, and Burton Sapin examine the various interrelationships between nation-states. The authors provide a typology of nations that includes "basic political organizations, range of decision-making systems, strengths and weaknesses of decision-making systems, and types of foreign policy strategies employed." This selection is from *Foreign Policy Decision Making* (1962).

Richard Snyder taught political science at Northwestern University, University of California, Irvine, and Ohio State University. His other works include *American Foreign Policy* (1948), *Theory and Research on the Causes of War* (1969), and contributions to political science journals.

Burton Sapin is a professor emeritus at George Washington University. His other major work is *The Making of U.S. Foreign Policy.*

H. W. Bruck was affiliated with the Foreign Policy Analysis Project when this article was written. He later held a position with the Department of Commerce.

DEFINITION OF INTERNATIONAL POLITICS

Definition of phenomena to be observed and explained is not, of course, identical with definition of methods of observation and explanation. Both will be spelled out as this essay proceeds. Suffice it to say here, we believe that those who study international politics are mainly concerned with the actions, reactions, and interactions among political entities called national states. Emphasis on action suggests *process* analysis, that is, the passage of time plus continuous changes in relationships—including the conditions underlying change and its consequences. Since there is a multiplicity of actions, reactions, and interactions, analysis must be concerned with a *number of processes.*

Action arises from the necessity to establish, to maintain, and to regulate sat- isfying, optional contacts between states and to exert some control over unwanted yet inescapable contacts. Action is plan- ful in the sense that it represents an at- tempt to achieve certain aims, and to prevent or minimize the achievement of the incompatible or menacing aims of other states.

The action-reaction-interaction for- mulation suggests that sequences of ac- tion and interaction are always closed or symmetrical. This may be diagrammed State A ↔ State B which implies a recip- rocal relationship. Such is clearly not always the case. Many sequences are asymmetrical, that is, State A → State B → in which case State A acts, State B reacts, but there is no immediate further action by A in response to B's action. With more than two states involved, of course, there are other possibilities—as suggested by:

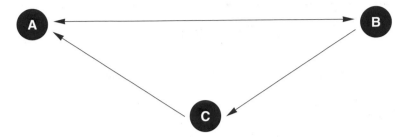

Given the fact that relationships may be symmetrical or asymmetrical and given the fact that action sequences though initiated at different times are nonetheless carried on simultaneously, there will be both the appearance and the possibility of *discontinuity* (that is, discontinuous processes) within the total set of processes which link any one state with all others. The process of state interaction is not, to repeat, always a sequence of action and *counteraction,* of attempt and frustration, of will opposing will. Nor should it be assumed that the process *necessarily* has an automatic chess-game quality or that reactions to action are necessarily immediate or self-evident. Not all national purposes are mutually incompatible, that is, it is not necessary that one nation's purposes be accomplished at the expense of another set of national purposes. One state may respond to the action of another without opposing that action per se; it may or may not be able to block that action effectively; it may or may not want to do so. The response may be in the form of inaction (calculated inaction we shall regard analytically as a form of action), or it may be in the form of action quite unrelated to the purposes of the state which actcd first. Much diplomacy consists in probing the limits of tolerance for a proposed course of action and in discovering common purposes. As action unfolds, purposes may change due to resistances or altered circumstances and hence, often, head-on conflicts are avoided or reduced in impact. For these reasons the processes of state interaction are much less orderly than—hopefully—the analysis of these processes.

State action and therefore interaction obviously takes many forms—a declaration, a formal agreement, regulation of relationships, discussion, a gift or loan, armed conflict, and so on. Reactions take the same forms only they are viewed as responses. Since we are dealing with planful actions (rather than random behavior), interaction is characterized by *patterns,* that is, recognizable *repetitions* of action and reaction. Aims *persist.* Kinds of action become *typical.* Reactions become *uniform.* Relationships become *regularized.* Further comment on the identification and characterization of patterns will be made below.

Thus far, there would probably be few disagreements except relatively minor ones on specific terminology. Now the question is: how is the political process (remembering always that this connotes multiple processes and *kinds* of processes) at the international level to be analyzed? Clearly there are *what, how,* and *why* questions with respect to state interaction. In order to be true to our previously stated philosophy, we should recognize that there is more than one possible approach, depending on the purposes of the observer and on the kinds of questions which interest him most.

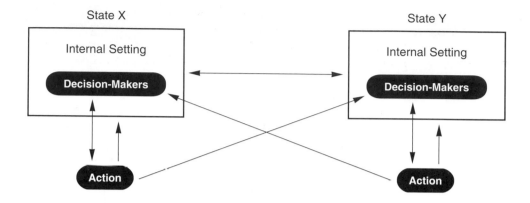

COMMENTARY

1. The first aspect of this diagrammatic presentation of an analytical scheme is the *assumption* that the most effective way to gain perspective on international politics and to find ways of grasping the complex determinants of state behavior is to pitch the analysis on the level of *any state.* An understanding of *all* states is to be founded on an understanding of *any one* state through the use of a scheme which will permit the analytical construction of properties of action which will be shared in common by all specific states. That is, the model is a fictional state whose characteristics are such as to enable us to say certain things about all real states regardless of how different they may appear to be in some ways. Therefore, if the scheme is moderately successful, we should be able to lay the foundation for analyzing the impact of cultural values on British foreign policy and on Soviet foreign policy even though the values are different in each case and produce quite different consequences. "State X," then, stands for all states or for any one state. We have rejected the assumption that two different analytical schemes are required simply because two states behave differently.

It should be added immediately that theoretical progress in the study of international politics will require eventually a *typology* of states based on basic political organization, range of decision-making systems, strengths and weaknesses of decision-making systems, and types of foreign policy strategies employed. This will facilitate comparison, of course, but it will also make it possible to take into account certain significant differences among states while at the same time analyzing the behavior of all states in essentially the same way.

2. We are also assuming that the nation-state is going to be the significant unit of political action for many years to come. Strategies of action and commitment of resources will continue to be decided at the national level. This assumption is made on grounds of analytical convenience and is not an expression of preference by the authors. Nor does it blind us to the development or existence of supranational forces and organizations. The basic question is solely how the latter are to be treated. We prefer to view the United Nations as a special mode of interaction in which the identity and policy-making capacity of individual national states are preserved but

subject to different conditioning factors. The collective action of the United Nations can hardly be explained without reference to actions in various capitals.

3. The phrase "state as actor in a situation" is designed primarily as a shorthand device to alert us to certain perspectives while still adhering to the notion of the state as a collectivity. Explicit mention must be made of our employment of action analysis and (both here and in the detailed treatment of decision-making) *of some of the vocabulary* of the now well-known Parsons-Shils scheme. We emphasize vocabulary for two reasons. First, as new schemes of social analysis are developed (mostly outside of political science), there is a great temptation to apply such schemes quickly, one result being the use of new words without comprehension of the theoretical system of which they are a part. Second, we have rejected a general application of the Parsons-Shils approach as an organizing concept—for reasons which will emerge later. At this point we may simply note that our intellectual borrowings regarding fundamental questions of method owe much more to the works of Alfred Schuetz.

Basically, action exists (analytically) when the following components can be ascertained: actor (or actors), goals, means, and situation. The situation is defined by the actor (or actors) in terms of the way the actor (or actors) relates himself to other actors, to possible goals, and to possible means, and in terms of the way means and ends are formed into strategies of action subject to relevant factors in the situation. These ways of relating himself to the situation (and thus of defining it) will depend on the nature of the actor—or his orientations. Thus, "state X" mentioned above may be regarded as a participant in an action system comprising other actors; state X is the focus of the observer's attention. State X orients to action according to the manner in which the particular situation is viewed by certain officials and according to what they want. The actions of other actors, the actor's goals and means, and the other components of the situation are related meaningfully by the actor. His action flows from his definition of the situation.

4. We need to carry the actor situation scheme one step further in an effort to rid ourselves of the troublesome abstraction "state." It is one of our basic methodological choices to define the state as its official decision-makers— those whose authoritative acts are, to all intents and purposes, the acts of the state. *State action is the action taken by those acting in the name of the state.* Hence, the state is its decision-makers. State X as *actor* is translated into its decision-makers as actors. It is also one of our basic choices to take as our prime analytical objective the re-creation of the "world" of the decision-makers as *they* view it. The manner in which *they* define situations becomes another way of saying how the state oriented to action and why. This is a quite different approach from trying to recreate the situation and interpretation of it *objectively,* that is, by the observer's judgment rather than that of the actors themselves.

To focus on the individual actors who are the state's decision-makers and to reconstruct the situation as defined by the decision-makers requires, of course, that a central place be given to the analysis of the behavior of these officials. One major significance of the diagram is that it calls attention to the sources of state action and to the essentially subjective (that is, from the standpoint of the decision-makers) nature of our perspective.

5. Now let us try to clarify a little further. We have said that the key to the explanation of why the state behaves the way it does lies in the way its decision-makers as actors define their situation. *The definition of the situation* is built around the projected action as well as the reasons for the action. Therefore, it is necessary to analyze the actors (the official decision-makers) in the following terms: (a) their *discrimination* and *relating* of objects, conditions, and other actors—various things are perceived or expected in a relational context; (b) the existence, establishment, or definition of *goals*—various things are wanted from the situation; (c) attachment of *significance* to various courses of action suggested by the situation according to some criteria of estimation; and (d) application of "*standards of acceptability*" which (1) narrow the range of perceptions, (2) narrow the range of objects wanted, and (3) narrow the number of alternatives.

Three features of all orientations emerge: *perception, choice,* and *expectation.*

Perhaps a translation of the vocabulary of action theory will be useful. We are saying that the actors' orientations to action are reconstructed when the following kinds of questions are answered: what did the decision-makers think was relevant in a particular situation? how did they determine this? how were the relevant factors related to each other—what connections did the decision-makers see between diverse elements in the situation? how did they establish the connections? what wants and needs were deemed involved in or affected by the situation? what were the sources of these wants and needs? how were they related to the situation? what specific or general goals were considered and selected? what courses of action were

deemed fitting and effective? how were fitness and effectiveness decided?

6. We have defined international politics as processes of state interaction at the governmental level. However, there are nongovernmental factors and relationships which must be taken into account by any system of analysis, and there are obviously nongovernmental effects of state action. Domestic politics, the non-human environment, cross-cultural and social relationships are important in this connection. We have chosen to group such factors under the concept of *setting.* This is an analytic term which reminds us that the decision-makers act upon and respond to conditions and factors which exist outside themselves and the governmental organization of which they are a part. Setting has two aspects: *external* and *internal.* We have deliberately chosen setting instead of environment because the latter term is either too inclusive or has a technical meaning in other sciences. Setting is really a set of categories of *potentially relevant factors and conditions* which may affect the action of any state.

External setting refers, in general, to such factors and conditions beyond the territorial boundaries of the state—the actions and reactions of other states (their decision-makers), the societies for which they act, and the physical world. Relevance of particular factors and conditions *in general* and *in particular situations* will depend on the attitudes, perceptions, judgments, and purpose of state X's decision-makers, that is, on how they react to various stimuli. It should be noted that our conception of setting does *not* exclude certain so-called environmental limitations such as the state of technology, morbidity ratio, and so on, which *may* limit the achievement of objectives or which *may* otherwise become part of the conditions of action *irrespective* of *whether* and *how* the decision-makers perceive them. However—and this is important—this does not in our scheme imply the substitution of an omniscient observer's judgment for that of the decision-maker. Setting is an analytical device to suggest certain enduring kinds of relevances and to limit the number of non-governmental factors with which the student of international politics must be concerned. The external setting is constantly changing and will be composed of *what the decision-makers decide is important.* This "deciding" can mean simply that certain lacks—such as minerals or guns—not imposed on them, that is, must be *accepted.* A serious native revolt in South Africa in 1900 was not a feature

of the external setting of United States decision-makers; it would be in 1963. Compare, too, the relatively minor impact of Soviet foreign activities on the United States decision-makers in the period of 1927 to 1933 with the present impact.

Usually the factors and conditions referred to by the term *internal setting* are loosely labeled "domestic politics," "public opinion," or "geographical position." A somewhat more adequate formulation might be: some clues to the way any state behaves toward the world must be sought in the way its society is organized and functions, in the character and behavior of its people, and in its physical habitat. The list of categories under B [see diagram, below] may be

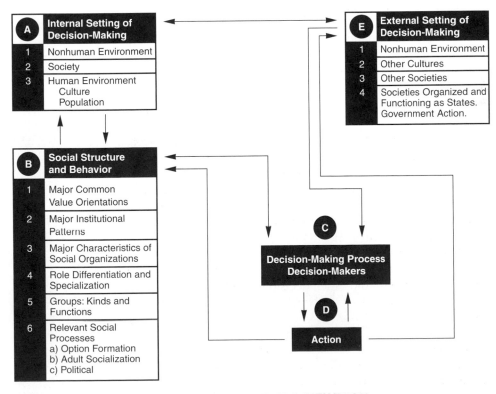

STATE "X" AS ACTOR IN A SITUATION

(SITUATION IS COMPRISED OF A COMBINATION OF SELECTIVELY RELEVANT FACTORS IN THE EXTERNAL AND INTERNAL SETTING AS INTERPRETED BY THE DECISION-MAKERS.)

somewhat unfamiliar. There are two reasons for insisting that the analysis of the society for which state X acts be pushed to this fundamental level. First, the list invites attention to a much wider range of potentially relevant factors than the more familiar terms like morale, attitudes, national power, party politics, and so on. For example, the problem of vulnerability to subversive attack is rarely discussed by political scientists in terms of the basic social structure of a particular nation, that is, in terms of B3. Nor is recruitment of manpower often connected with the way the roles of the sexes are differentiated in a society. Second, if one is interested in the fundamental "why" of state behavior, the search for reliable answers must go beyond the *derived* conditions and factors (morale, pressure groups, production, attitudes, and so on) which are normally the focus of attention.

7. The diagram suggests another important point. Line BC is a two-way arrow connoting rightly an interaction between social organization and behavior on the one hand and decision-making on the other. Among other things this arrow represents the impact of domestic social forces on the formulation and execution of foreign policy. BC implies that the influence of conditions and factors in the society is felt through the decision-making process. But line DB is also important because it indicates that a nation experiences its own external actions. State action is designed primarily to alter factors and behavior or to otherwise affect conditions in the external setting, yet it may have equally serious consequences for the society itself. We need only suggest the range of possibilities here. Extensive foreign relations may enhance the power of the

central government relative to other regulatory institutions. Particular programs may contribute to the redistribution of resources, income, and social power. For example, the outpouring of billions in foreign aid by the United States since 1945 has contributed to the increased power and influence of scientists, military leaders, engineers, and the managerial group. The people of a state experience foreign policy in other ways—they may feel satisfaction, alarm, guilt, exhilaration, or doubt about it. There will be nongovernmental *interpretations*—perhaps several major ones—shared by various members or groups of the society. Such interpretations may or may not be identical with the prevailing official interpretation. There will also be nongovernmental expectations concerning state action which, again, may or may not correspond to official expectations. Discrepancies between nongovernmental and governmental interpretations and expectations may have important ramifications. For one thing, public support and confidence may be undermined if state action produces consequences which fundamentally violate public expectations.

The point to be made here is that the diagrammatic expression of our scheme shows that the impact of domestic social factors (line BCD) must be viewed also as a part of a larger feedback process as indicated by line BCDBC.

8. Another significant set of relationships emerges from the diagram in line ABE. The external and internal settings are related to each other. Among others, two implications may be stressed here. First, because we have defined international politics as interaction process at the governmental level, it may appear that we are making the focus unduly

narrow, thus ignoring a whole host of private, nongovernmental interactions. Nothing could be further from the truth. Societies interact with each other in a wide range of ways through an intricate network of communications—trade, family ties, professional associations, shared values, cultural exchanges, travel, mass media, and migration. While all of these patterns may be subject to governmental regulation (in some form), they *may* have very little to do with the origins and forms of state action. At any rate, the question of the political significance of intersocietal, intercultural, nongovernmental interactions requires an analytical scheme which will make possible some understanding of how such interactions condition official action. This in turn requires a much more systematic description of inter-actions than we now have, plus a way of accounting for their connection with state action.

One can, however, study the interactions connoted by line ABE for their own sake with only a slight interest in their political aspects. In this case, it seems proper to say that the focus is international relations rather than international politics.

Nongovernmental international relations do not enter the analysis of state behavior *unless* it can be shown that the behavior of the decision-makers is in some manner determined by or directed toward such relations. For example, assume a bitter, hostile campaign against a foreign government by powerful United States newspapers and assume the campaign is well publicized in the other nation. By itself this would constitute an asymmetrical interaction between two societies. It would not become a matter of state interaction unless or until the following happened: (a) an official

protest to the U.S. State Department by the foreign government; (b) retaliation against United States citizens in the foreign country; (c) disturbance of negotiations between the two governments on quite another issue; (d) arousal of public opinion in the foreign country to the point where the effectiveness of United States policies toward that country was seriously affected; (e) the pressure generated by the campaign in the United States caused the decision-makers to modify their actions and reactions vis-à-vis the other state; (f) the United States government officially repudiated the criticism and apologized to the other government. This same *kind* of argument would hold for all types of nongovernmental relations except that there would be varying degrees of directness (that is, change in intersocietal relations → change in state action) and indirectness (that is, change in intersocietal relations → change in social organization and behavior → derived condition or factor → change in state action) and therefore different time-sequences.

Second, while the most obvious consequences of state action are to be looked for in the reactions of other states along the lines CDE4C in the diagram, changes in the external setting can influence state action along the lines CDE3A3BC, that is, indirectly through changes in nongovernmental relations which ultimately are recognized and taken into account by the decision-makers.

9. To get back to the center of the diagram, it should be noted that CD is a two-way arrow. The rest of this essay is concerned with the nature of decision-making, but it can be said here that in addition to the feedback relationships CDBC and CDE3A3, DC connotes a direct feedback from an awareness by the

decision-makers of their own action and from assessments of the progress of action. This is to say that state action has an impact on decision-making apart from subsequent reactions of other states and apart from effects mediated through the state's social organization and behavior.

10. So far as this diagram is concerned, most attention in the field of international politics is paid to interactions CDE4CD. CD represents action(s); DE (particularly DE4) represents consequences for, or impact upon, the external setting; EC represents new conditions or stimuli—reactions or new actions (E4C). Therefore, CDECD represents the action-reaction-interaction sequence.

Obviously these lines stand for a wide range of relationships and kinds of action. What should be emphasized here is that interactions can be really understood fully only in terms of the decision-making responses of states to situations, problems, and the actions of other states. The combination of interaction and decision-making can be diagrammed as shown on page 455.

Naturally if one thinks of all the separate actions and reactions, and all the combinations involved in the governmental relationships between one state and all others, it seems unrealistic and somewhat absurd to let a few lines on a diagram represent so much. Indeed, all would be lost unless one could speak of *patterns* and *systems*. Patterns refer to *uniformities* and *persistence* of actions and sets of relationships. "Nationalism," "imperialism," "internationalism," "aggression," "isolationism," "peace," "war," "conflict," and "cooperation" are familiar ways of characterizing kinds of actions and reactions as well as patterned relationships among states. These terms are, of course, both descriptive and judgmental—they are shorthand expressions covering complicated phenomena and also may imply approval or disapproval, goodness or badness.

System in this context refers to the modes, rules, and nature of reciprocal influence which structure the interaction between states. Five kinds of system—there are others—may be mentioned: *coalitions* (temporary and permanent); *supranational organization; bilateral; multilateral* (unorganized); and *ordination-subordination* (imperial relationships and satellites). Once again, the way these interactions and relationships arise and the particular form or substance they take would seem to be explainable in terms of the way the decision-makers in the participating political organisms "define their situation." As we have said elsewhere, there seem to be only two ways of scientifically studying international politics: (1) the description and measurement of interaction; and (2) decision-making—the formulation and execution of policy. Interaction patterns can be studied by themselves without reference to decision-making except that the "why" of the patterns cannot be answered.

SUMMARY

To conclude this brief commentary, it may be said that the diagram presented . . . is designed in the first instance to portray graphically the basic perspectives of our frame of reference: *any* state as a way of saying something about *all* states; the central position of the decision-making focus; and the integration of a wide range of factors which may explain state action, reaction, and interaction.

The lines of the diagram carry *two* suggestive functions. First, they alert the observer to possible (known and hypothetical) relationships among empirical factors. Thus, the diagram simultaneously invites attention to three interrelated, intersecting empirical processes—state interaction (CDEC) at the governmental level, intersocietal interaction (ABE) at the nongovernmental level, and intrasocietal interaction (BCDB) at both the governmental and nongovernmental level. These processes arise, to put the matter another way, from decision-makers interacting with factors which constitute the dual setting, from state interaction as normally conceived, and from the factors which constitute internal and external settings acting upon each other.

Second, the diagram is intended to suggest possible analytic and theoretical relationships as well. The boxes indicate ways of specifying the relevant factors in state behavior through the employment of certain concepts—decision-making, action, setting, situation, society, culture, and so on—which provide, if they are successfully developed, criteria of relevance and ways of handling the empirical phenomena and their interrelationships. There are in existence a large number of tested and untested hypotheses, general and "middle range" theories, applicable

within each of the categories comprising the diagram. The central concept of decision-making may provide a basis for linking a group of theories which hitherto have been applicable only to a segment of international politics or have not been susceptible of application at all. We may cite two examples. The concept of culture is clearly suggested by A2, B2, and E2 which specify empirical phenomena branded analytically as cultural in the technical sense. Based on this important social science concept is the derived concept of National Character—typical behavior patterns uniquely (or allegedly so) characteristic of one nation. Suggestive as national character analysis has been, it has been thus far impossible to bridge the analytic gap between behavior patterns at the cultural level and state action on the governmental level. Communication theory (really a cluster of related theories) has been applied almost exclusively to mass media (B6) and to techniques of state action (D). Only recently has an attempt been made to apply recent developments in communication theory to intersocietal interaction and to decision-making.

QUESTIONS

1. Describe the various interrelationships that affect decision-making by the nation-state.

2. What conclusions can be drawn from this regarding foreign policy decision making?

34.   Essence of Decision

Graham T. Allison

In this article, Graham T. Allison provides three models of the decision-making process in foreign affairs. The rational actor model is the traditional realist paradigm. The organizational process and bureaucratic politics models are also examined in this essay. This study provides important questions about the coherency of the rational actor model (realism) to explain foreign policy decision making and assesses the strength and weaknesses of the three models. This selection is from the *American Political Science Review* (1967).

Graham T. Allison is Douglas Dillon Professor of Government at Harvard's John F. Kennedy School of Government and author of many books and articles on American foreign policy and the decision-making process.

The Cuban missile crisis is a seminal event. For thirteen days of October 1962, there was a higher probability that more human lives would end suddenly than ever before in history. Had the worst occurred, the death of 100 million Americans, over 100 million Russians, and millions of Europeans as well would make previous natural calamities and inhumanities appear insignificant. Given the probability of disaster—which President Kennedy estimated as "between 1 out of 3 and even"—our escape seems awesome.[1] This event symbolizes a central, if only partially thinkable, fact about our existence. That such consequences could follow from the choices and actions of national governments obliges students of government as well as participants in governance to think hard about these problems.

Improved understanding of this crisis depends in part on more information and more probing analyses of available evidence. To contribute to these efforts is part of the purpose of this study. But here the missile crisis serves primarily as grist for a more general investigation.

This study proceeds from the premise that marked improvement in our understanding of such events depends critically on more self-consciousness about what observers bring to the analysis. What each analyst sees and judges to be important is a function not only of the evidence about what happened but also of the "conceptual lenses" through which he looks at the evidence. The principal purpose of this essay is to explore some of the fundamental assumptions and categories employed by analysts in thinking about problems of governmental behavior, especially in foreign and military affairs.

The general argument can be summarized in three propositions:

1. Analysts think about problems of foreign and military policy in terms of largely implicit conceptual models that have significant consequences for the content of their thought.[2]

Though the present product of foreign policy analysis is neither systematic nor powerful, if one carefully examines explanations produced by analysts, a number of fundamental similarities emerge. Explanations produced by particular analysts display quite regular, predictable features. This predictability suggests a substructure. These regularities reflect an analyst's assumptions about the character of puzzles, the categories in which problems should be considered, the types of evidence that are relevant, and the determinants of occurrences. The first proposition is that clusters of such related assumptions constitute basic frames of reference or conceptual models in terms of which analysts both ask and answer the questions: What happened? Why did the event happen? What will happen?[3] Such assumptions are central to the activities of explanation and prediction, for in attempting to explain a particular event, the analyst cannot simply describe the full state of the world leading up to that event. The logic of explanation requires that he single out the relevant, important determinants of the occurrence.[4] Moreover, as the logic of prediction underscores, the analyst must summarize the various determinants as they bear on the event in question. Conceptual models both fix the mesh of the nets that the analyst drags through the material in order to explain a particular action or decision and direct him to cast his net in select ponds, at certain depths, in order to catch the fish he is after.

2. Most analysts explain (and predict) the behavior of national governments in terms of various forms of one basic conceptual model, here entitled the Rational Policy Model (Model I).[5]

In terms of this conceptual model, analysts attempt to understand happenings as the more or less purposive acts of unified national governments. For these analysts, the point of an explanation is to show how the nation or government could have chosen the action in question, given the strategic problem that it faced. For example, in confronting the problem posed by the Soviet installation of missiles in Cuba, rational policy model analysts attempt to show how this was a reasonable act from the point of view of the Soviet Union, given Soviet strategic objectives.

3. Two "alternative" conceptual models, here labeled an Organizational Process Model (Model II) and a Bureaucratic Politics Model (Model III) provide a base for improved explanation and prediction. . . .

MODEL I: RATIONAL POLICY

Rational Policy Model Illustrated

Where is the pinch of the puzzle raised by the *New York Times* over Soviet deployment of an antiballistic missile system?[6] The question, as the *Times* states it, concerns the Soviet Union's objective in allocating such large sums of money for this weapon system while at the same time seeming to pursue a policy of increasing détente. In former President Johnson's words, "the paradox is that this [Soviet deployment of an antiballistic missile system] should be happening at a time when there is abundant evidence that our mutual antagonism is beginning to ease."[7] This question troubles people primarily because Soviet antiballistic missile deployment, and evidence of Soviet actions towards détente, when juxtaposed in our implicit model, produce a question. With reference to what objective could the Soviet government have rationally chosen the simultaneous pursuit of these two courses of actions? This question arises only when the analyst attempts to structure events as purposive choices of consistent actors. . . .

How do analysts attempt to explain the Soviet emplacement of missiles in Cuba? The most widely cited explanation of this occurrence has been produced by two RAND Sovietologists, Arnold Horelick and Myron Rush.[8] They conclude that "the introduction of strategic missiles into Cuba was motivated chiefly by the Soviet leaders' desire to overcome . . . the existing large margin of U.S. strategic superiority."[9] How do they reach this conclusion? In Sherlock Holmes style, they seize several salient characteristics of this action and use these features as criteria against which to test alternative hypotheses about Soviet objectives. For example, the size of the Soviet deployment, and the simultaneous emplacement of more expensive, more visible intermediate range missiles as well as medium range missiles, it is argued, exclude an explanation of the action in terms of Cuban defense—since that objective could have been secured with a much smaller number of medium range missiles alone. Their explanation presents an argument for one objective that permits interpretation of the details of Soviet behavior as a value-maximizing choice.

How do analysts account for the coming of the First World War? According to Hans Morgenthau, "the first World War had its origin exclusively in the fear of a disturbance of the European balance of power.[10] In the period preceding World War I, the Triple Alliance precariously balanced the Triple Entente. If either power combination could gain a decisive advantage in the Balkans, it would achieve a decisive advantage in the balance of power. "It was this fear," Morgenthau asserts, "that motivated Austria in July 1914 to settle its accounts with Serbia once and for all, and that induced Germany to support Austria un-

conditionally. It was the same fear that brought Russia to the support of Serbia, and France to the support of Russia."[11] How is Morgenthau able to resolve this problem so confidently? By imposing on the data a "rational outline."[12] The value of this method, according to Morgenthau, is that "it provides for rational discipline in action and creates astounding continuity in foreign policy which makes American, British, or Russian foreign policy appear as an intelligent, rational continuum . . . re-gardless of the different motives, preferences, and intellectual and moral qualities of successive statesmen."[13] . . .

Most contemporary analysts (as well as laymen) proceed predominantly—albeit most often implicitly—in terms of this model when attempting to explain happenings in foreign affairs. Indeed, that occurrences in foreign affairs are the *acts* of *nations* seems so fundamental to thinking about such problems that this underlying model has rarely been recognized: to explain an occurrence in foreign policy simply means to show how the government could have rationally chosen that action.[14] These brief examples illustrate five uses of the model. To prove that most analysts think largely in terms of the rational policy model is not possible. In this limited space it is not even possible to illustrate the range of employment of the framework. Rather, my purpose is to convey to the reader a grasp of the model and a challenge: let the reader examine the literature with which he is most familiar and make his judgment.

The general characterization can be sharpened by articulating the rational policy model as an "analytic paradigm" in the technical sense developed by Robert K. Merton for sociological analyses.[15] Systematic statement of basic assumptions, concepts, and propositions employed by Model I analysts highlights the distinctive thrust of this style of analysis. To articulate a largely implicit framework is of necessity to caricature. But caricature can be instructive.

Rational Policy Paradigm

I. Basic Unit of Analysis: Policy as National Choice

Happenings in foreign affairs are conceived as actions chosen by the nation or national government.[16] Governments select the action that will maximize strategic goals and objectives. These "solutions" to strategic problems are the fundamental categories in terms of which the analyst perceives what is to be explained.

II. Organizing Concepts

A. *National Actor.* The nation or government, conceived as a rational, unitary decision-maker, is the agent. This actor has one set of specified goals (the equivalent of a consistent utility function), one set of perceived options, and a single estimate of the consequences that follow from each alternative.

B. *The Problem.* Action is chosen in response to the strategic problem which the nation faces. Threats and opportunities arising in the "international strategic market place" move the nation to act.

C. *Static Selection.* The sum of activity of representatives of the government relevant to a problem constitutes what the nation has chosen as its "solution." Thus the action is conceived as a steady-state choice among alternative outcomes (rather than, for example, a large number of partial choices in a dynamic stream).

D. *Action as Rational Choice.* The components include:

1. *Goals and Objectives.* National security and national interests are the principal categories in which strategic goals are conceived. Nations seek security and a range of further objectives. (Analysts rarely translate strategic goals and objectives into an explicit utility function; nevertheless, analysts do focus on major goals and objectives and trade off side effects in an intuitive fashion.)

2. *Options.* Various courses of action relevant to a strategic problem provide the spectrum of options.

3. *Consequences.* Enactment of each alternative course of action will produce a series of consequences. The relevant consequences constitute benefits and costs in terms of strategic goals and objectives.

4. *Choice.* Rational choice is value-maximizing. The rational agent selects the alternative whose consequences rank highest in terms of his goals and objectives.

III. Dominant Inference Pattern

This paradigm leads analysts to rely on the following pattern of inference: if a nation performed a particular action, that nation must have had ends towards which the action constituted an optimal means. The rational policy model's explanatory power stems from this inference pattern. Puzzlement is relieved by revealing the purposive pattern within which the occurrence can be located as a value-maximizing means.

IV. General Propositions

The disgrace of political science is the infrequency with which propositions of any generality are formulated and tested. "Paradigmatic analysis" argues for explicitness about the terms in which analysis proceeds, and seriousness about the logic of explanation. Simply to illustrate the kind of propositions on which analysts who employ this model rely, the formulation includes several.

The basic assumption of value-maximizing behavior produces propositions central to most explanations. The general principle can be formulated as follows: the likelihood of any particular action results from a combination of the nation's (1) relevant values and objectives, (2) perceived alternative courses of action, (3) estimates of various sets of consequences (which will follow from each alternative), and (4) net valuation of each set of consequences. This yields two propositions.

1. An increase in the cost of an alternative, i.e., a reduction in the value of the set of consequences which will follow from that action, or a reduction in the probability of attaining fixed consequences, reduces the likelihood of that alternative being chosen.

2. A decrease in the costs of an alternative, i.e., an increase in the value of the set of consequences which will follow from that alternative, or an increase in the probability of attaining fixed consequences, increases the likelihood of that action being chosen.[17]

V. Specific Propositions

A. *Deterrence.* The likelihood of any particular attack results from the factors specified in the general proposition. Combined with factual assertions, this general proposition yields the propositions of the sub-theory of deterrence.

1. A stable nuclear balance reduces the likelihood of nuclear attack. This proposition is derived from the general proposition plus the asserted fact that a second-strike capability affects the potential attacker's calculations by increasing the likelihood and the costs of one particular set of consequences which might follow from attack—namely, retaliation.

2. A stable nuclear balance increases the probability of limited war. This proposition is derived from the general proposition plus the asserted fact that though increasing the costs of a nuclear exchange, a stable nuclear balance nevertheless produces a more significant reduction in the probability that such consequences would be chosen in response to a limited war. Thus this set of consequences weighs less heavily in the calculus.

B. *Soviet Force Posture.* The Soviet Union chooses its force posture (i.e., its weapons and their deployment) as a value-maximizing means of implementing Soviet strategic objectives and military doctrine. A proposition of this sort underlies Secretary of Defense Laird's inference from the fact of 200 SS-9s (large intercontinental missiles) to the assertion that, "the Soviets are going for a first-strike capability, and there's no question about it."[18]

Variants of the Rational Policy Model

This paradigm exhibits the characteristics of the most refined version of the rational model. The modern literature of strategy employs a model of this sort. Problems and pressures in the "international strategic marketplace" yield probabilities of occurrence. The international actor, which could be any national actor, is simply a value-maximizing mechanism for getting from the strategic problem to the logical solution. But the explanations and predictions produced by most analysts of foreign affairs depend primarily on variants of this "pure" model. The point of each is the same: to place the action within a value-maximizing framework, given certain constraints. Nevertheless, it may be helpful to identify several variants, each of which might be exhibited similarly as a paradigm. The first focuses upon the national actor and his choice in a particular situation, leading analysts to further constrain the goals, alternatives, and consequences considered. Thus, (1) national propensities or personality traits reflected in an "operational code," (2) concern with certain objectives, or (3) special principles of action, narrow the "goals" or "alternatives" or "consequences" of the paradigm. For example, the Soviet deployment of ABMs is sometimes explained by reference to the Soviet's "defense-mindedness." Or a particular Soviet action is explained as an instance of a special rule of action in the Bolshevik operational code.[19] A second, related, cluster of variants focuses on the individual leader or leadership group as the actor whose preference function is maximized and whose personal (or group) characteristics are allowed to modify the alternatives, consequences, and rules of choice. Explanations of the U.S. involvement in Vietnam as a natural consequence of the Kennedy-Johnson Administration's axioms of foreign policy rely on this variant. A third, more complex variant of the basic model recognizes the existence of several actors within a government, for example, Hawks and Doves or military and civilians, but attempts to explain (or predict) an occurrence by reference to the objectives of the victorious actor. Thus, for example, some revisionist histories of the Cold War recognize the forces of light and the forces of darkness within the U.S. government, but explain American actions as a result of goals and perceptions of the victorious forces of darkness.

Each of these forms of the basic paradigm constitutes a formalization of what analysts typically rely upon implicitly. In the transition from implicit conceptual model to explicit paradigm much of the richness of the best employments of this model has been lost. But the purpose in raising loose, implicit conceptual models to an explicit level is to reveal the basic logic of analysts' activity. Perhaps some of the remaining artificiality that surrounds the statement of the paradigm can be erased by noting a number of the standard additions and modifications employed by analysts who proceed *predominantly* within the rational policy model. First, in the course of a document, analysts shift from one variant of the basic model to another, occasionally appropriating in an *ad hoc* fashion aspects of a situation which are logically incompatible with the basic model. Second, in the course of explaining a number of occurrences, analysts sometimes pause over a particular event about which they have a great deal of information and unfold it in such detail that an impression of randomness is created. Third, having employed other assumptions and categories in deriving an explanation or prediction, analysts will present their product in a neat, convincing rational policy model package. (This accommodation is a favorite of members of the intelligence community whose association with the details of a process is considerable, but who feel that by putting an occurrence in a larger rational framework, it will be more comprehensible to their audience.) Fourth, in attempting to offer an explanation—particularly in cases where a prediction derived from the basic model has failed—the notion of a "mistake" is invoked.

Thus, the failure in the prediction of a "missile gap" is written off as a Soviet mistake in not taking advantage of their opportunity. Both these and other modifications permit Model I analysts considerably more variety than the paradigm might suggest. But such accommodations are essentially appendages to the basic logic of these analyses. . . .

MODEL II: ORGANIZATIONAL PROCESS

For some purposes, governmental behavior can be usefully summarized as action chosen by a unitary, rational decision-maker: centrally controlled, completely informed, and value maximizing. But this simplification must not be allowed to conceal the fact that a "government" consists of a conglomerate of semi-feudal, loosely allied organizations, each with a substantial life of its own. Government leaders do sit formally, and to some extent in fact, on top of this conglomerate. But governments perceive problems through organizational sensors. Governments define alternatives and estimate consequences as organizations process information. Governments act as these organizations enact routines. Government behavior can therefore be understood according to a second conceptual model, less as deliberate choices of leaders and more as *outputs* of large organizations functioning according to standard patterns of behavior.

To be responsive to a broad spectrum of problems, governments consist of large organizations among which primary responsibility for particular areas is divided. Each organization attends to a special set of problems and acts in quasi-independence on these problems.

But few important problems fall exclusively within the domain of a single organization. Thus government behavior relevant to any important problem reflects the independent output of several organizations, partially coordinated by government leaders. Government leaders can substantially disturb, but not substantially control, the behavior of these organizations.

To perform complex routines, the behavior of large numbers of individuals must be coordinated. Coordination requires standard operating procedures: rules according to which things are done. Assured capability for reliable performance of action that depends upon the behavior of hundreds of persons requires established "programs." Indeed, if the eleven members of a football team are to perform adequately on any particular down, each player must not "do what he thinks needs to be done" or "do what the quarterback tells him to do." Rather, each player must perform the maneuvers specified by a previously established play which the quarterback has simply called in this situation.

At any given time, a government consists of *existing* organizations, each with a *fixed* set of standard operating procedures and programs. The behavior of these organizations—and consequently of the government—relevant to an issue in any particular instance is, therefore, determined primarily by routines established in these organizations prior to that instance. But organizations do change. Learning occurs gradually, over time. Dramatic organizational change occurs in response to major crises. Both learning and change are influenced by existing organizational capabilities.

Borrowed from studies of organizations, these loosely formulated propositions amount simply to *tendencies.* Each must be hedged by modifiers like "other things being equal" and "under certain conditions." In particular instances, tendencies hold—more or less. In specific situations, the relevant question is: more or less? But this is as it should be. For, on the one hand, "organizations" are no more homogeneous a class than "solids." When scientists tried to generalize about "solids," they achieved similar results. Solids tend to expand when heated, but some do and some don't. More adequate categorization of the various elements now lumped under the rubric "organizations" is thus required. On the other hand, the behavior of particular organizations seems considerably more complex than the behavior of solids. Additional information about a particular organization is required for further specification of the tendency statements. In spite of these two caveats, the characterization of government action as organizational output differs distinctly from Model I. Attempts to understand problems of foreign affairs in terms of this frame of reference should produce quite different explanations.[20]

Organizational Process Paradigm[21]

I. Basic Unit of Analysis: Policy as Organizational Output

The happenings of international politics are, in three critical senses, outputs of organizational processes. First, the actual occurrences are organizational outputs. For example, Chinese entry into the Korean War—that is, the fact that Chinese soldiers were firing at U.N. soldiers south of the Yalu in 1950—is an organizational action: the action of men who are soldiers in platoons which are in companies, which in turn are in armies, re-

sponding as privates to lieutenants who are responsible to captains and so on to the commander, moving into Korea, advancing against enemy troops, and firing according to fixed routines of the Chinese Army. Government leaders' decisions trigger organizational routines. Government leaders can trim the edges of this output and exercise some choice in combining outputs. But the mass of behavior is determined by previously established procedures. Second, existing organizational routines for employing present physical capabilities constitute the effective options open to government leaders confronted with any problem. Only the existence of men, equipped and trained as armies and capable of being transported to North Korea, made entry into the Korean War a live option for the Chinese leaders. The fact that fixed programs (equipment, men, and routines which exist at the particular time) exhaust the range of buttons that leaders can push is not always perceived by these leaders. But in every case it is critical for an understanding of what is actually done. Third, organizational outputs structure the situation within the narrow constraints of which leaders must contribute their "decision" concerning an issue. Outputs raise the problem, provide the information, and make the initial moves that color the face of the issue that is turned to the leaders. As Theodore Sorensen has observed: "Presidents rarely, if ever, make decisions—particularly in foreign affairs—in the sense of writing their conclusions on a clean slate. . . . The basic decisions, which confine their choices, have all too often been previously made."[22] If one understands the structure of the situation and the face of the issue—which are determined by the organizational outputs—the formal choice of the leaders is frequently anti-climactic.

II. Organizing Concepts

A. *Organizational Actors.* The actor is not a monolithic "nation" or "government" but rather a constellation of loosely allied organizations on top of which government leaders sit: This constellation acts only as component organizations perform routines.[23]

B. *Factored Problems and Fractionated Power.* Surveillance of the multiple facets of foreign affairs requires that problems be cut up and parcelled out to various organizations. To avoid paralysis, primary power must accompany primary responsibility. But if organizations are permitted to do anything, a large part of what they do will be determined within the organization. Thus each organization perceives problems,processes information, and performs a range of actions in quasi-independence (within broad guidelines of national policy).Factored problems and fractionated power are two edges of the same sword. Factoring permits more specialized attention to particular facets of problems than would be possible if government leaders tried to cope with these problems by themselves. But this additional attention must be paid for in the coin of discretion for *what* an organization attends to, and *how* organizational responses are programmed.

C. *Parochial Priorities, Perceptions, and Issues.* Primary responsibility for a narrow set of problems encourages organizational parochialism. These tendencies are enhanced by a number of additional factors: (1) selective information available to the organization, (2) recruitment of personnel into the organization, (3) tenure of individuals in the organization, (4) small group pressures within the organization, and (5) distribution of rewards by the organization. Clients (e.g., interest groups), government allies (e.g., Congressional committees), and extranational counterparts (e.g., the British Ministry of Defense for the Department of Defense, ISA, or the British Foreign Office for the Department of State, EUR) galvanize this parochialism. Thus organizations develop relatively stable propensities concerning operational priorities, perceptions, and issues.

D. *Action as Organizational Output.* The preeminent feature of organizational activity is its programmed character: the extent to which behavior in any particular case is an enactment of pre-established routines. In producing outputs, the activity of each organization is characterized by:

1. *Goals: Constraints Defining Acceptable Performance.* The operational goals of an organization are seldom revealed by formal mandates. Rather, each organization's operational goals emerge as a set of constraints defining acceptable performance. Central among these constraints is organizational health, defined usually in terms of bodies assigned and dollars appropriated. The set of constraints emerges from a mix of expectations and demands of other organizations in the government, statutory authority, demands from citizens and special interest groups, and bargaining within the organization. These constraints represent a quasi-resolution of conflict—the constraints are relatively stable, so there is some resolution. But conflict among alternative goals is always latent; hence, it is a quasi-resolution. Typically, the constraints are formulated as imperatives to avoid roughly specified discomforts and disasters.[24]

2. *Sequential Attention to Goals.* The existence of conflict among operational constraints is resolved by the device of sequential attention. As a problem arises, the subunits of the organization most concerned with that problem deal with it in terms of the constraints they take to be most important. When the next problem arises, another cluster of subunits deals with it, focusing on a different set of constraints.

3. *Standard Operating Procedures.* Organizations perform their "higher" functions, such as attending to problem areas, monitoring information, and preparing relevant responses for likely contingencies, by doing "lower" tasks, for example, preparing budgets, producing reports, and developing hardware. Reliable performance of these tasks requires standard operating procedures (hereafter SOPs). Since procedures are "standard" they do not change quickly or easily. Without these standard procedures, itwould not be possible to perform certain concerted tasks. But because of standard procedures, organizational behavior in particular instances often appears unduly formalized, sluggish, or inappropriate.

4. *Programs and Repertoires.* Organizations must be capable of performing actions in which the behavior of large numbers of individuals is carefully coordinated. Assured performance requires clusters of rehearsed SOPs for producing specific actions, e.g., fighting enemy units or answering an embassy's cable. Each cluster comprises a "program" (in the terms both of drama and computers) which the organization has available for dealing with a situation. The list of programs relevant to a type of activity, e.g., fighting, constitutes an organizational repertoire. The number of programs in a repertoire is always quite limited. When properly triggered, organizations execute programs; programs cannot be substantially changed in a particular situation. The more complex the action and the greater the number of individuals involved, the more important are programs and repertoires as determinants of organizational behavior.

5. *Uncertainty Avoidance.* Organizations do not attempt to estimate the probability distribution of future occurrences. Rather, organizations avoid uncertainty. By arranging a *negotiated environment,* organizations regularize the reactions of other actors with whom they have to deal. The primary environment, relations with other organizations that comprise the government, is stabilized by such arrangements as agreed budgetary splits, accepted areas of responsibility, and established conventional practices. The secondary environment, relations with the international world, is stabilized between allies by the establishment of contracts (alliances) and "club relations" (U.S. State and U.K. Foreign Office or U.S. Treasury and U.K. Treasury). Between enemies, contracts and accepted conventional practices perform a similar function, for example, the rules of the "precarious status quo" which President Kennedy referred to in the missile crisis. Where the international environment cannot be negotiated, organizations deal with remaining uncertainties by establishing a set of *standard scenarios* that constitute the contingencies for which they prepare. For example, the standard scenario for Tactical Air Command of the U.S. Air Force involves combat with enemy aircraft. Planes are designed and pilots trained to meet this problem. That these preparations are less relevant to more probable contingencies, e.g., provision of close-in ground support in limited wars like Vietnam, has had little impact on the scenario.

6. *Problem-directed Search.* Where situations cannot be construed as standard, organizations engage in search. The style of search and the solution are largely determined by existing routines. Organizational search for alternative courses of action is problem-oriented: it focuses on the atypical discomfort that must be avoided. It is simple-minded: the neighborhood of the symptom is searched first; then, the neighborhood of the current alternative. Patterns of search reveal biases which in turn reflect such factors as specialized training or experience and patterns of communication.

7. *Organizational Learning and Change.* The parameters of organizational behavior mostly persist. In response to non-standard problems, organizations search and routines evolve, assimilating new situations. Thus learning and change follow in large part from existing procedures. But marked changes in organizations do sometimes occur. Conditions in which dramatic changes are more likely include: (1) Periods of budgetary feast. Typically, organizations devour budgetary feasts by purchasing additional items on the existing shopping list. Nevertheless, if committed to change, leaders who control the budget can use extra funds to effect changes. (2) Periods of prolonged budgetary famine. Though a single year's famine typically results in few changes in organizational structure but a loss of effectiveness in performing some programs, prolonged famine forces major retrench-

ment. (3) Dramatic performance failures. Dramatic change occurs (mostly) in response to major disasters. Confronted with an undeniable failure of procedures and repertoires, authorities outside the organization demand change, existing personnel are less resistant to change, and critical members of the organization are replaced by individuals committed to change.

E. *Central Coordination and Control.* Action requires decentralization of responsibility and power. But problems lap over the jurisdictions of several organizations. Thus the necessity for decentralization runs headlong into the requirement for coordination. (Advocates of one horn or the other of this dilemma—responsive action entails decentralized power vs. coordinated action requires central control—account for a considerable part of the persistent demand for government reorganization.) Both the necessity for coordination and the centrality of foreign policy to national welfare guarantee the involvement of government leaders in the procedures of the organizations among which problems are divided and power shared. Each organization's propensities and routines can be disturbed by government leaders' intervention. Central direction and persistent control of organizational activity, however, is not possible. The relation among organizations, and between organizations and the government leaders, depends critically on a number of structural variables including: (1) the nature of the job, (2) the measures and information available to government leaders, (3) the system of rewards and punishments for organizational members, and (4) the procedures by which human and material resources get committed. For example, to the extent that rewards and punishments for the members of an organization are distributed by higher authorities, these authorities can exercise some control by specifying criteria in terms of which organizational output is to be evaluated. These criteria become constraints within which organizational activity proceeds. But constraint is a crude instrument of control.

Intervention by government leaders does sometimes change the activity of an organization in an intended direction. But instances are fewer than might be expected. As Franklin Roosevelt, the master manipulator of government organizations, remarked:

> The Treasury is so large and far-flung and ingrained in its practices that I find it is almost impossible to get the action and results I want. . . . But the Treasury is not to be compared with the State Department. You should go through the experience of trying to get any changes in the thinking, policy, and action of the career diplomats and then you'd know what a real problem was. But the Treasury and the State Department put together are nothing compared with the Na-a-vy . . . To change anything in the Na-a-vy is like punching a feather bed. You punch it with your right and you punch it with your left until you are finally exhausted, and then you find the damn bed just as it was before you started punching.[25]

John Kennedy's experience seems to have been similar: "The State Department," he asserted, "is a bowl full of jelly."[26] And lest the McNamara revolution in the Defense Department seem too striking a counter-example, the Navy's recent rejection of McNamara's major intervention in Naval weapons procurement, the F-111B, should be studied as an antidote.

F. *Decisions of Government Leaders.* Organizational persistence does not exclude shifts in governmental behavior.

For government leaders sit atop the conglomerate of organizations. Many important issues of governmental action require that these leaders decide what organizations will play out which programs where. Thus stability in the parochialisms and SOPs of individual organizations is consistent with some important shifts in the behavior of governments. The range of these shifts is defined by existing organizational programs.

III. Dominant Inference Pattern

If a nation performs an action of this type today, its organizational components must yesterday have been performing (or have had established routines for performing) an action only marginally different from this action. At any specific point in time, a government consists of an established conglomerate of organizations, each with existing goals, programs, and repertoires. The characteristics of a government's action in any instance follows from those established routines, and from the choice of government leaders—on the basis of information and estimates provided by existing routines—among existing programs. The best explanation of an organization's behavior at t is $t-1$; the prediction of $t+1$ is t. Model II's explanatory power is achieved by uncovering the organizational routines and repertoires that produced the outputs that comprise the puzzling occurrence.

IV. General Propositions

A number of general propositions have been stated above. In order to illustrate clearly the type of proposition employed by Model II analysts, this section formulates several more precisely.

A. *Organizational Action.* Activity according to SOPs and programs does not constitute far-sighted, flexible adaptation to "the issue" (as it is conceived by the analyst). Detail and nuance of actions by organizations are determined predominantly by organizational routines, not government leaders' directions.

1. SOPs constitute routines for dealing with *standard* situations. Routines allow large numbers of ordinary individuals to deal with numerous instances, day after day, without considerable thought, by responding to basic stimuli. But this regularized capability for adequate performance is purchased at the price of standardization. If the SOPs are appropriate, average performance, i.e., performance averaged over the range of cases, is better than it would be if each instance were approached individually (given fixed talent, timing, and resource constraints). But specific instances, particularly critical instances that typically do not have "standard" characteristics, are often handled sluggishly or inappropriately.

2. A program, i.e., a complex action chosen from a short list of programs in a repertoire, is rarely tailored to the specific situation in which it is executed. Rather, the program is (at best) the most appropriate of the programs in a previously developed repertoire.

3. Since repertoires are developed by parochial organizations for standard scenarios defined by that organization, programs available for dealing with a particular situation are often ill-suited.

B. *Limited Flexibility and Incremental Change.* Major lines of organizational action are straight, i.e., behavior at one time is marginally different from that behavior at $t - 1$. Simpleminded predictions work best: Behavior at $t + 1$ will be marginally different from behavior at the present time.

1. Organizational budgets change incrementally—both with respect to totals and with respect to intra-organizational splits. Though organizations could divide the money available each year by carving up the pie anew (in the light of changes in objectives or environment), in practice, organizations take last year's budget as a base and adjust incrementally. Predictions that require large budgetary shifts in a single year between organizations or between units within an organization should be hedged.

2. Once undertaken, an organizational investment is not dropped at the point where "objective" costs outweigh benefits. Organizational stakes in adopted projects carry them quite beyond the loss point.

C. *Administrative Feasibility.* Adequate explanation, analysis, and prediction must include administrative feasibility as a major dimension. A considerable gap separates what leaders choose (or might rationally have chosen) and what organizations implement.

1. Organizations are blunt instruments. Projects that require several organizations to act with high degrees of precision and coordination are not likely to succeed.

2. Projects that demand that existing organizational units depart from their accustomed functions and perform previously unprogrammed tasks are rarely accomplished in their designed form.

3. Government leaders can expect that each organization will do its "part" in terms of what the organization knows how to do.

4. Government leaders can expect incomplete and distorted information from each organization concerning its part of the problem.

5. Where an assigned piece of a problem is contrary to the existing goals of an organization, resistance to implementation of that piece will be encountered.

V. Specific Propositions

1. *Deterrence.* The probability of nuclear attack is less sensitive to balance and imbalance, or stability and instability (as these concepts are employed by Model I strategists) than it is to a number of organizational factors. Except for the special case in which the Soviet Union acquires a credible capability to destroy the U.S. with a disarming blow, U.S. superiority or inferiority affects the probability of a nuclear attack less than do a number of organizational factors.

First, if a nuclear attack occurs, it will result from organizational activity: the firing of rockets by members of a missile group. The enemy's *control system,* i.e., physical mechanisms and standard procedures which determine who can launch rockets when, is critical. Second, the enemy's programs for bringing his strategic forces to *alert status* determine probabilities of accidental firing and momentum. At the outbreak of World War I, if the Russian Tsar had understood the organizational processes which his order of full mobilization triggered, he would have realized that he had chosen war. Third, organizational repertoires fix the range of effective choice open to enemy leaders. The menu available to Tsar Nicholas in 1914 has two entrees: full mobilization and no mobilization. Partial mobilization was not an organizational option.

Fourth, since organizational routines set the chessboard, the training and deployment of troops and nuclear weapons is crucial. Given that the outbreak of hostilities in Berlin is more probable than most scenarios for nuclear war, facts about deployment, training, and tactical nuclear equipment of Soviet troops stationed in East Germany—which will influence the face of the issue seen by Soviet leaders at the outbreak of hostilities and the manner in which choice is implemented—are as critical as the question of "balance."

2. *Soviet Force Posture.* Soviet force posture, i.e., the fact that certain weapons rather than others are procured and deployed, is determined by organizational factors such as the goals and procedures of existing military services and the goals and processes of research and design labs, within budgetary constraints that emerge from the government leader's choices. The frailty of the Soviet Air Force within the Soviet military establishment seems to have been a crucial element in the Soviet failure to acquire a large bomber force in the 1950s (thereby faulting American intelligence predictions of a "bomber gap"). The fact that missiles were controlled until 1960 in the Soviet Union by the Soviet Ground Forces, whose goals and procedures reflected no interest in an intercontinental mission, was not irrelevant to the slow Soviet buildup of ICBMs (thereby faulting U.S. intelligence predictions of a "missile gap"). These organizational factors (Soviet Ground Forces' control of missiles and that service's fixation with European scenarios) make the Soviet deployment of so many MRBMs that European targets could be destroyed three times over, more understandable. Recent weapon developments, e.g., the testing of a Fractional Orbital Bombardment System (FOBS) and multiple warheads for the SS-9, very likely reflect the activity and interests of a cluster of Soviet research and development organizations, rather than a decision by Soviet leaders to acquire a first strike weapon system. Careful attention to the organizational components of the Soviet military establishment (Strategic Rocket Forces, Navy, Air Force, Ground Forces, and National Air Defense), the missions and weapons systems to which each component is wedded (an independent weapon system assists survival as an independent service), and existing budgetary splits (which probably are relatively stable in the Soviet Union as they tend to be everywhere) offer potential improvements in medium and longer term predictions. . . .

Model III: Bureaucratic Politics

The leaders who sit on top of organizations are not a monolithic group. Rather, each is, in his own right, a player in a central, competitive game. The name of the game is bureaucratic politics: bargaining along regularized channels among players positioned hierarchically within the government. Government behavior can thus be understood according to a third conceptual model not as organizational outputs, but as outcomes of bargaining games. In contrast with Model I, the bureaucratic politics model sees no unitary actor but rather many actors as players, who focus not on a single strategic issue but on many diverse intranational problems as well, in terms of no consistent set of strategic objectives but rather according to various conceptions of national, organizational, and personal goals, making government decisions not by rational choice but by the pulling and hauling that is politics.

The apparatus of each national government constitutes a complex arena for the intra-national game. Political leaders at the top of this apparatus plus the men who occupy positions on top of the critical organizations form the circle of central players. Ascendancy to this circle assures some independent standing. The necessary decentralization of decisions required for action on the broad range of foreign policy problems guarantees that each player has considerable discretion. Thus power is shared.

The nature of problems of foreign policy permits fundamental disagreement among reasonable men concerning what ought to be done. Analyses yield conflicting recommendations. Separate responsibilities laid on the shoulders of individual personalities encourage differences in perceptions and priorities. But the issues are of first order importance. What the nation does really matters. A wrong choice could mean irreparable damage. Thus responsible men are obliged to fight for what they are convinced is right.

Men share power. Men differ concerning what must be done. The differences matter. This milieu necessitates that policy be resolved by politics. What the nation does is sometimes the result of the triumph of one group over others. More often, however, different groups pulling in different directions yield a resultant distinct from what anyone intended. What moves the chess pieces is not simply the reasons which support a course of action, nor the routines of organizations which enact an alternative, but the power and skill of proponents and opponents of the action in question.

This characterization captures the thrust of the bureaucratic politics orientation. If problems of foreign policy arose as discreet issues, and decisions were determined one game at a time, this account would suffice. But most "issues," e.g., Vietnam or the proliferation of nuclear weapons, emerge piecemeal, over time, one lump in one context, a second in another. Hundreds of issues compete for players' attention every day. Each player is forced to fix upon his issues for that day, fight them on their own terms, and rush on to the next. Thus the character of emerging issues and the pace at which the game is played converge to yield government "decisions" and "actions" as collages. Choices by one player, outcomes of minor games, outcomes of central games, and "foul-ups"—these pieces, when stuck to the same canvas, constitute government behavior relevant to an issue.

The concept of national security policy as political outcome contradicts both public imagery and academic orthodoxy. Issues vital to national security, it is said, are too important to be settled by political games. They must be "above" politics. To accuse someone of "playing politics with national security" is a most serious charge. What public conviction demands, the academic penchant for intellectual elegance reinforces. Internal politics is messy; moreover, according to prevailing doctrine, politicking lacks intellectual content. As such, it constitutes gossip for journalists rather than a subject for serious investigation. Occasional memoirs, anecdotes in historical accounts, and several detailed case studies to the contrary, most of the literature of foreign policy avoids bureaucratic pol-

itics. The gap between academic literature and the experience of participants in government is nowhere wider than at this point.

Bureaucratic Politics Paradigm[27]

I. Basic Unit of Analysis: Policy as Political Outcome

The decisions and actions of governments are essentially intra-national political outcomes: outcomes in the sense that what happens is not chosen as a solution to a problem but rather results from compromise, coalition, competition, and confusion among government officials who see different faces of an issue; political in the sense that the activity from which the outcomes emerge is best characterized as bargaining. Following Wittgenstein's use of the concept of a "game," national behavior in international affairs can be conceived as outcomes of intricate and subtle, simultaneous, overlapping games among players located in positions, the hierarchical arrangement of which constitutes the government.[28] These games proceed neither at random nor at leisure. Regular channels structure the game. Deadlines force issues to the attention of busy players. The moves in the chess game are thus to be explained in terms of the bargaining among players with separate and unequal power over particular pieces and with separable objectives in distinguishable subgames.

II. Organizing Concepts

A. *Players in Positions.* The actor is neither a unitary nation, nor a conglomerate of organizations, but rather a number of individual players.

C. *Interests, Stakes, and Power.* Games are played to determine outcomes.

But outcomes advance and impede each player's conception of the national interest, specific programs to which he is committed, the welfare of his friends, and his personal interests. These overlapping interests constitute the stakes for which games are played. Each player's ability to play successfully depends upon his power. Power, i.e., effective influence on policy outcomes, is an elusive blend of at least three elements: bargaining advantages (drawn from formal authority and obligations, institutional backing, constituents, expertise, and status), skill and will in using bargaining advantages, and other players' perceptions of the first two ingredients. Power wisely invested yields an enhanced reputation for effectiveness. Unsuccessful investment depletes both the stock of capital and the reputation. Thus each player must pick the issues on which he can play with a reasonable probability of success. But no player's power is sufficient to guarantee satisfactory outcomes. Each player's needs and fears run to many other players. What ensues is the most intricate and subtle of games known to man.

D. *The Problem and the Problems.* "Solutions" to strategic problems are not derived by detached analysts focusing coolly on *the* problem. Instead, deadlines and events raise issues in games, and demand decisions of busy players in contexts that influence the face the issue wears. The problems for the players are both narrower and broader than *the* strategic problem. For each player focuses not on the total strategic problem but rather on the decision that must be made now. But each decision has critical consequences not only for the strategic problem but for each player's organizational, reputational, and personal stakes. Thus the gap between the problems the player was solving and the problem upon which the analyst focuses is often very wide.

E. *Action-Channels.* Bargaining games do not proceed randomly. Action-channels, i.e., regularized ways of producing action concerning types of issues, structure the game by pre-selecting the major players, determining their points of entrance into the game, and distributing particular advantages and disadvantages for each game. Most critically, channels determine "who's got the action," that is, which department's Indians actually do whatever is chosen. Weapon procurement decisions are made within the annual budgeting process; embassies' demands for action cables are answered according to routines of consultation and clearance from State to Defense and White House; requests for instructions from military groups (concerning assistance all the time, concerning operations during war) are composed by the military in consultation with the Office of the Secretary of Defense, State, and White House; crisis responses are debated among White House, State, Defense, CIA, and Ad Hoc players; major political speeches, especially by the President but also by other Chiefs, are cleared through established channels.

F. *Action as Politics.* Government decisions are made and government actions emerge neither as the calculated choice of a unified group, nor as a formal summary of leaders' preferences. Rather, the context of shared power but separate judgments concerning important choices determines that politics is the mechanism of choice. Note the *environment* in which the game is played: inordinate uncertainty about what must be done, the necessity that something be done, and crucial consequences of whatever is done. These features force responsible men to become active players. The *pace of the game*—hundreds of issues, numerous games, and multiple channels—compels players to fight to "get other's attention," to make them "see the facts," to assure that they "take the time to think seriously about the broader issue." The *structure of the game*—power shared by individuals with separate responsibilities—validates each player's feeling that "others don't see my problem," and "others must be persuaded to look at the issue from a less parochial perspective." The *rules of the game*—he who hesitates loses his chance to play at that point, and he who is uncertain about his recommendation is overpowered by others who are sure—pressures players to come down on one side of a 51–49 issue and play. The *rewards of the game*—effectiveness, i.e., impact on outcomes, as the immediate measure of performance—encourages hard play. Thus, most players come to fight to "make the government do what is right." The strategies and tactics employed are quite similar to those formalized by theorists of international relations.

G. *Streams of Outcomes.* Important government decisions or actions emerge as collages composed of individual acts, outcomes of minor and major games, and foul-ups. Outcomes which could never have been chosen by an actor and would never have emerged from bargaining in a single game over the issue are fabricated piece by piece. Understanding of the outcome requires that it be disaggregated.

III. Dominant Inference Pattern

If a nation performed an action, that action was the *outcome* of bargaining among individuals and groups within the government. That outcome included *results* achieved by groups committed to a decision or action, *resultants* which emerged from bargaining among groups with quite different positions and *foul-*

ups. Model III's explanatory power is achieved by revealing the pulling and hauling of various players, with different perceptions and priorities, focusing on separate problems, which yielded the outcomes that constitute the action in question.

IV. General Propositions

1. *Action and Intention.* Action does not presuppose intention. The sum of behavior of representatives of a government relevant to an issue was rarely intended by any individual or group. Rather separate individuals with different intentions contributed pieces which compose an outcome distinct from what anyone would have chosen.

2. *Where You Stand Depends on Where You Sit.*[29] Horizontally, the diverse demands upon each player shape his priorities, perceptions, and issues. For large classes of issues, e.g., budgets and procurement decisions, the stance of a particular player can be predicted with high reliability, from information concerning his seat. In the notorious B-36 controversy, no one was surprised by Admiral Radford's testimony that "the B-36 under any theory of war, is a bad gamble with national security," as opposed to Air Force Secretary Symington's claim that "a B-36 with an A-bomb can destroy distant objectives which might require ground armies years to take."[30]

3. *Chiefs and Indians.* The aphorism "where you stand depends on where you sit" has vertical as well as horizontal application. Vertically, the demands upon the President, Chiefs, Staffers, and Indians are quite distinct.

The foreign policy issues with which the President can deal are limited primarily by his crowded schedule: the necessity of dealing first with what comes next. His problem is to probe the special face worn by issues that come to his attention, to preserve his leeway until time has clarified the uncertainties, and to assess the relevant risks.

Foreign policy Chiefs deal most often with the hottest issue *de jour,* though they can get the attention of the President and other members of the government for other issues which they judge important. What they cannot guarantee is that "the President will pay the price" or that "the others will get on board." They must build a coalition of the relevant powers that be. They must "give the President confidence" in the right course of action.

Most problems are framed, alternatives specified, and proposals pushed, however, by Indians. Indians fight with Indians of other departments; for example, struggles between International Security Affairs of the Department of Defense and Political-Military of the State Department are a microcosm of the action at higher levels. But the Indian's major problem is how to get the *attention* of Chiefs, how to get an issue decided how to get the government "to do what is right."

In policy making then, the issue looking *down* is options: how to preserve my leeway until time clarifies uncertainties. The issue looking *sideways* is commitment: how to get others committed to my coalition. The issue looking *upwards* is confidence: how to give the boss confidence in doing what must be done. To paraphrase one of Neustadt's assertions which can be applied down the length of the ladder, the essence of a responsible official's task is to induce others to see that what needs to be done is what their own appraisal of their own responsibilities requires them to do in their own interests.

V. Specific Propositions

1. *Deterrence.* The probability of nuclear attack depends primarily on the probability of attack emerging as an outcome of the bureaucratic politics of the attacking government. First, which players can decide to launch an attack? Whether the effective power over action is controlled by an individual, a minor game, or the central game is critical. Second, though Model I's confidence in nuclear deterrence stems from an assertion that, in the end, governments will not commit suicide, Model III recalls historical precedents. Admiral Yamamoto, who designed the Japanese attack on Pearl Harbor, estimated accurately: "In the first six months to a year of war against the U.S. and England I will run wild, and I will show you an uninterrupted succession of victories; I must also tell you that, should the war be prolonged for two or three years, I have no confidence in our ultimate victory."[31] But Japan attacked. Thus, three questions might be considered. One: could any member of the government solve his problem by attack? What patterns of bargaining could yield attack as an outcome? The major difference between a stable balance of terror and a questionable balance may simply be that in the first case most members of the government appreciate fully the consequences of attack and are thus on guard against the emergence of this outcome. Two: what stream of outcomes might lead to an attack? At what point in the stream is the potential attacker's politics? If members of the U.S. government had been sensitive to the stream of decisions from which the Japanese attack on Pearl Harbor emerged, they would have been aware of a considerable probability of that attack. Three: how might miscalculation and confusion generate foul-ups that yield attack as an outcome? For example, in a crisis or after the beginning of conventional war, what happens to the information available to, and the effective power of, members of the central game. . . .

CONCLUSION

This essay has obviously bitten off more than it has chewed. For further developments and synthesis of these arguments the reader is referred to the larger study.[32] In spite of the limits of space, however, it would be inappropriate to stop without spelling out several implications of the argument and addressing the question of relations among the models and extensions of them to activity beyond explanation.

At a minimum, the intended implications of the argument presented here are four. First, formulation of alternative frames of reference and demonstration that different analysts, relying predominantly on different models, produce quite different explanations should encourage the analyst's self-consciousness about the nets he employs. The effect of these "spectacles" in sensitizing him to particular aspects of what is going on—framing the puzzle in one way rather than another, encouraging him to examine the problem in terms of certain categories rather than others, directing him to particular kinds of evidence, and relieving puzzlement by one procedure rather than another—must be recognized and explored.

Second, the argument implies a position on the problem of "the state of the art." While accepting the commonplace characterization of the present condition of foreign policy analysis—personalistic, non-cumulative, and sometimes insightful—this essay rejects both the counsel of despair's justification of this condition as a consequence of the character of the enterprise, and the "new frontiersmen's" demand for *a priori* theorizing on the frontiers and *ad hoc* appropriation of "new techniques."[33] What is required as a first step is non-casual examination of the present product: inspection of existing explanations, articulation of the conceptual models employed in producing them, formulation of the propositions relied upon, specification of the logic of the various intellectual enterprises, and reflection on the questions being asked. Though it is difficult to overemphasize the need for more systematic processing of more data, these preliminary matters of formulating questions with clarity and sensitivity to categories and assumptions so that fruitful acquisition of large quantities of data is possible are still a major hurdle in considering most important problems.

Third, the preliminary, partial paradigms presented here provide a basis for serious reexamination of many problems of foreign and military policy. Model II and Model III cuts at problems typically treated in Model I terms can permit significant improvements in explanation and prediction.[34] Full Model II and III analyses require large amounts of information. But even in cases where the information base is severely limited, improvements are possible. Consider the problem of predicting Soviet strategic forces. In the mid-1950s, Model I style calculations led to predictions that the Soviets would rapidly deploy large numbers of long-range bombers. From a Model II perspective, both the frailty of the Air Force within the Soviet military establishment and the budgetary implications of such a buildup would have led analysts to hedge this prediction. Moreover, Model II would have pointed to a sure, visible indicator of such a buildup: noisy struggles among the Services over major budgetary shifts. In the late 1950s and early 1960s, Model I calculations led to the prediction of immediate, massive Soviet deployment of ICBMs. Again, a Model II cut would have reduced this number because, in the earlier period, strategic rockets were controlled by the Soviet Ground Forces rather than an independent Service, and in the later period, this would have necessitated massive shifts in budgetary splits. Today, Model I considerations lead many analysts both to recommend that an agreement not to deploy ABMs be a major American objective in upcoming strategic negotiations with the USSR, and to predict success. From a Model II vantage point, the existence of an ongoing Soviet ABM program, the strength of the organization (National Air Defense) that controls ABMs, and the fact that an agreement to stop ABM deployment would force the virtual dismantling of this organization, make a viable agreement of this sort much less likely. A Model III cut suggests that (a) there must be significant differences among perceptions and priorities of Soviet leaders over strategic negotiations, (b) any agreement will affect some players' power bases, and (c) agreements that do not require extensive cuts in the sources of some major players' power will prove easier to negotiate and more viable.

Fourth, the present formulation of paradigms is simply an initial step. As such it leaves a long list of critical questions unanswered. Given any action, an imaginative analyst should always be able to construct some rationale for the government's choice. By imposing, and relaxing, constraints on the parameters of rational choice (as in variants of Model I) analysts can construct a large number of accounts of any act as a rational choice. But does a statement of reasons why a rational actor would choose an action constitute an explanation of the *occurrence* of that action? How can Model I analysis be forced to make more systematic contributions to the question of the determinants of occurrences? Model II's explanation of t in terms of $t-1$ is explanation. The world is contiguous. But governments sometimes make sharp departures. Can an organizational process model be modified to suggest where change is likely? Attention to organizational change should afford greater understanding of why particular programs and SOPs are maintained by identifiable types of organizations and also how a manager can improve organizational performance. Model III tells a fascinating "story." But its complexity is enormous, the information requirements are often overwhelming, and many of the details of the bargaining may be superfluous. How can such a model be made parsimonious? The three models are obviously not exclusive alternatives. Indeed, the paradigms highlight the partial emphasis of the framework—what each emphasizes and what it leaves out. Each concentrates on one class of variables, in effect, relegating other important factors to a *ceteris parabus* clause. Model I concentrates on "market factors:" pressures and incentives created by the "international strategic marketplace." Models II and III focus on the internal mechanism of the government that chooses in this environment. But can these relations be more fully specified? Adequate synthesis would require a typology of decisions and actions, some of which are more amenable to treatment in terms of one model and some to another. Government behavior is but one cluster of factors relevant to occurrences in foreign affairs. Most students of foreign policy adopt this focus (at least when explaining and predicting). Nevertheless, the dimensions of the chess board, the character of the pieces, and the rules of the game—factors considered by international systems theorists—constitute the context in which the pieces are moved. Can the major variables in the full function of determinants of foreign policy outcomes be identified?

Both the outline of a partial, *ad hoc* working synthesis of the models, and a sketch of their uses in activities other than explanation can be suggested by generating predictions in terms of each. Strategic surrender is an important problem of international relations and diplomatic history. War termination is a new, developing area of the strategic literature. Both of these interests lead scholars to address a central question: *Why* do nations surrender *when?* Whether implicit in explanations or more explicit in analysis, diplomatic historians and strategists rely upon propositions which can be turned forward to produce predictions. Thus at the risk of being timely—and in error—the present situation (August, 1968) offers an interesting test case: Why will North Vietnam surrender when?[35]

In a nutshell, analysis according to Model I asserts: nations quit when costs outweigh the benefits. North Vietnam will surrender when she realizes "that continued fighting can only generate additional costs without hope of compensating gains, this expectation being largely the consequence of the previous application of force by the dominant side."[36] U.S. actions can increase or decrease Hanoi's strategic costs. Bombing North Vietnam increases the pain and thus increases the probability of surrender. This proposition and prediction are not without meaning. That—"other things being equal"—nations are more likely to surrender when the strategic cost-benefit balance is negative, is true. Nations rarely surrender when they are winning. The proposition specifies a range within which nations surrender. But over this broad range, the relevant question is: why do nations surrender?

Models II and III focus upon the government machine through which this fact about the international strategic marketplace must be filtered to produce a surrender. These analysts are considerably less sanguine about the possibility of surrender *at the point* that the cost-benefit calculus turns negative. Never in history (i.e., in none of the five cases I have examined) have nations surrendered at that point. Surrender occurs sometime thereafter. *When* depends on process of organizations and politics of players within these governments—as they are affected by the opposing government. Moreover, the effects of the victorious power's action upon the surrendering nation cannot be adequately summarized as increasing or decreasing strategic costs. Imposing additional costs by bombing a nation may increase the probability of surrender. But it also may reduce it. An appreciation of the impact of the acts of one nation upon another thus requires some understanding of the machine which is being influenced. For more precise prediction, Models II and III require considerably more information about the organizations and politics of North Vietnam than is publicly available. On the basis of the limited public information, however, these models can be suggestive.

Model II examines two subproblems. First, to have lost is not sufficient. The government must know that the strategic cost-benefit calculus is negative. But neither the categories, nor the indicators, of strategic costs and benefits are clear. And the sources of information about both are organizations whose parochial priorities and perceptions do not facilitate accurate information or estimation. Military evaluation of military performance, military estimates of factors like "enemy morale," and military predictions concerning when "the tide will turn" or "the corner will have been turned" are typically distorted. In cases of highly decentralized guerrilla operations, like Vietnam, these problems are exacerbated. Thus strategic costs will be underestimated. Only highly *visible* costs can have direct impact on leaders without being filtered through organizational channels. Second, since organizations define the details of options and execute actions, surrender (and negotiation) is likely to entail considerable bungling in the early stages. No organization can define options or prepare programs for this treasonous act. Thus, early overtures will be uncoordinated with the acts of other organizations, e.g., the fighting forces, creating contradictory "signals" to the victor.

Model III suggests that surrender will not come at the point that strategic costs outweigh benefits, but that it will not wait until the leadership group concludes that the war is lost. Rather the problem is better understood in terms of four additional propositions. First, strong advocates of the war effort, whose careers are closely identified with the war, rarely come to the conclusion that costs outweigh benefits. Second, quite often from the outset of a war, a number of members of the government (particularly those whose responsibilities sensitize them to problems other than war, e.g., economic planners or intelligence experts) are convinced that the war effort is futile. Third, surrender is likely to come as the result of a political shift that enhances the effective power of the latter group (and adds swing members to it). Fourth, the course of the war, particularly actions of the victor, can influence the advantages and disadvantages of players in the loser's government. Thus, North Vietnam will surrender not when its leaders have a change of heart, but when Hanoi has a change of leaders (or a change of effective power within the central circle). How U.S. bombing (or pause), threats, promises, or action in the South affect the game in Hanoi is subtle but nonetheless crucial.

That these three models could be applied to the surrender of governments other than North Vietnam should be obvious. But that exercise is left for the reader.

NOTES

1. Theodore Sorensen, *Kennedy* (New York, 1965), p. 705.
2. In attempting to understand problems of foreign affairs, analysts engage in a number of related, but logically separable enterprises: (a) description, (b) explanation, (c) prediction, (d) evaluation, and (e) recommendation. This essay focuses primarily on explanation (and by implication, prediction).
3. In arguing that explanations proceed in terms of implicit conceptual models, this essay makes no claim that foreign policy analysts have developed any satisfactory, empirically tested theory. In this essay, the use of the term "model" without qualifiers should be read "conceptual scheme."
4. For the purpose of this argument we shall accept Carl G. Hempel's characterization

of the logic of explanation: an explanation "answers the question, '*Why* did the explanadum-phenomenon occur?' by showing that the phenomenon resulted from particular circumstances, specified in $C_1, C_2, \ldots C_k$, in accordance with laws $L_1, L_2, \ldots L_r$. By pointing this out, the argument shows that, given the particular circumstances and the laws in question, the occurrence of the phenomenon was to be *expected;* and it is in this sense that the explanation enables us to understand why the phenomenon occurred." *Aspects of Scientific Explanation* (New York, 1965), p. 337. While various patterns of explanation can be distinguished, *viz.,* Ernest Nagel, *The Structure of Science: Problems in the Logic of Scientific Explanation,* New York, 1961), satisfactory scientific explanations exhibit this basic logic. Consequently prediction is the converse of explanation.

5. Earlier drafts of this argument have aroused heated arguments concerning proper names for these models. To choose names from ordinary language is to court confusion, as well as familiarity. Perhaps it is best to think of these models as I, II, and III.

6. *New York Times,* February 18, 1967.

7. *Ibid.*

8. Arnold Horelick and Myron Rush, *Strategic Power and Soviet Foreign Policy* (Chicago, 1965). Based on A. Horelick, "The Cuban Missile Crisis: An Analysis of Soviet Calculations and Behavior," *World Politics* (April, 1964).

9. Horelick and Rush, *Strategic Power and Soviet Foreign Policy,* p. 154.

10. Hans Morgenthau, *Politics Among Nations* (3rd ed.; New York, 1960), p. 191.

11. *Ibid.,* p. 192.

12. *Ibid.,* p. 5.

13. *Ibid.,* pp. 5-6.

14. The larger study examines several exceptions to this generalization. Sidney Verba's excellent essay "Assumptions of Rationality and Non-Rationality in Models of the International System" is less an exception than it is an approach to a somewhat different problem. Verba focuses upon models of rationality and irrationality of *individual* statesmen: in Knorr and Verba, *The International System.*

15. Robert K. Merton, *Social Theory and Social Structures* (Revised and Enlarged Edition; New York, 1957), pp. 12-16. Considerably weaker than a satisfactory theoretical model, paradigms nevertheless represent a short step in that direction from looser, implicit conceptual models. Neither the concepts nor the relations among the variables are sufficiently specified to yield propositions deductively. "Paradigmatic Analysis" nevertheless has considerable promise for clarifying and codifying styles of analysis in political science. Each of the paradigms stated here can be represented rigorously in mathematical terms. For example, Model I lends itself to mathematical formulation along the lines of Herbert Simon's "Behavioral Theory of Rationality," *Models of Man* (New York, 1957). But this does not solve the most difficult problem of "measurement and estimation."

16. Though a variant of this model could easily be stochastic, this paradigm is stated in non-probabilistic terms. In contemporary strategy, a stochastic version of this model is sometimes used for predictions; but it is almost impossible to find an explanation of an occurrence in foreign affairs that is consistently probabilistic.

   Analogies between Model I and the concept of explanation developed by R. G. Collingwood, William Dray, and other "revisionists" among philosophers concerned with the critical philosophy of history are not accidental. For a summary of the "revisionist position" see Maurice Mandelbaum, "Historical Explanation: The Problem of Covering Laws," *History and Theory* (1960).

17. This model is an analogue of the theory of the rational entrepreneur which has been developed extensively in economic

theories of the firm and the consumer. These two propositions specify the "substitution effect." Refinement of this model and specification of additional general propositions by translating from the economic theory is straight-forward.

18. *New York Times,* March 22, 1969.

19. See Nathan Leites, *A Study of Bolshevism* (Glencoe, Illinois, 1953).

20. The influence of organizational studies upon the present literature of foreign affairs is minimal. Specialists in international politics are not students of organization theory. Organization theory has only recently begun to study organizations as decision-makers and has not yet produced behavioral studies of national security organizations from a decision-making perspective. It seems unlikely, however, that these gaps will remain unfilled much longer. Considerable progress has been made in the study of the business firm as an organization. Scholars have begun applying these insights to government organizations, and interest in an organizational perspective is spreading among institutions and individuals concerned with actual government operations. The "decisionmaking" approach represented by Richard Snyder, R. Bruck, and B. Sapin, *Foreign Policy Decision-Making* (Glencoe, Illinois, 1962), incorporates a number of insights from organization theory.

21. The formulation of this paradigm is indebted both to the orientation and insights of Herbert Simon and to the behavioral model of the firm stated by Richard Cyert and James March, *A Behavioral Theory of the Firm* (Englewood Cliffs, 1963). Here, however, one is forced to grapple with the less routine, less quantified functions of the less differentiated elements in government organizations.

22. Theodore Sorensen, "You Get to Walk to Work," *New York Times Magazine,* March 19, 1967.

23. Organizations are not monolithic. The proper level of disaggregation depends upon the objectives of a piece of analysis. This paradigm is formulated with reference to the major organizations that constitute the U.S. government. Generalization to the major components of each department and agency should be relatively straightforward.

24. The stability of these constraints is dependent on such factors as rules for promotion and reward budgeting and accounting procedures, and mundane operating procedures.

25. Marriner Eccles, *Beckoning Frontiers* (New York, 1951), p. 336.

26. Arthur Schlesinger, *A Thousand Days* (Boston, 1965), p. 406.

27. This paradigm relies upon the small group of analysts who have begun to fill the gap. My primary source is the model implicit in the work of Richard E. Neustadt, though his concentration on presidential action has been generalized to a concern with policy as the outcome of political bargaining among a number of independent players, the President amounting to no more than a "superpower" among many lesser but considerable powers. As Warner Schilling argues, the substantive problems are of such inordinate difficulty that uncertainties and differences with regard to goals, alternatives, and consequences are inevitable. This necessitates what Roger Hilsman describes as the process of conflict and consensus building. The techniques employed in this process often resemble those used in legislative assemblies, though Samuel Huntington's characterization of the process as "legislative" overemphasizes the equality of participants as opposed to the hierarchy which structures the game. Moreover, whereas for Huntington, foreign policy (in contrast to military policy) is set by the executive, this paradigm maintains that the activities which he describes as legislative are characteristic of the process by which foreign policy is made.

28. The theatrical metaphor of stage, roles, and actors is more common than this metaphor of games, positions, and play-

ers. Nevertheless, the rigidity connotated by the concept of "role" both in the theatrical sense of actors reciting fixed lines and in the sociological sense of fixed responses to specified social situations makes the concept of games, positions, and players more useful for this analysis of active participants in the determination of national policy. Objections to the terminology on the grounds that "game" connotes non-serious play overlook the concept's application to most serious problems both in Wittgenstein's philosophy and in contemporary game theory. Game theory typically treats more precisely structured games, but Wittgenstein's examination of the "language game" wherein men use words to communicate is quite analogous to this analysis of the less specified game of bureaucratic politics. See Ludwig Wittgenstein, *Philosophical Investigations,* and Thomas Schelling, "What is Game Theory?" in James Charlesworth, *Contemporary Political Analysis.*

29. This aphorism was stated first, I think, by Don K. Price.

30. Paul Y. Hammond, "Super Carriers and B-36 Bombers," in Harold Stein (ed.), *American Civil-Military Decisions* (Birmingham, 1963).

31. Roberta Wohlstetter, *Pearl Harbor* (Stanford, 1962), p. 350.

32. *Bureaucracy and Policy.*

33. Thus my position is quite distinct from both poles in the recent "great debate" about international relations. While many "traditionalists" of the sort Kaplan attacks adopt the first posture and many "scientists" of the sort attacked by Bull adopt the second, this third posture is relatively neutral with respect to whatever is in substantive dispute. See Hedly Bull, "International Theory: The Case for a Classical Approach," *World Politics* (April, 1966); and Morton Kaplan, "The New Great Debate: Traditionalism vs. Science in International Relations," *World Politics* (October, 1966).

34. A number of problems are now being examined in these terms both in the Bureaucracy Study Group on Bureaucracy and Policy of the Institute of Politics at Harvard University and at the Rand Corporation.

35. In response to several readers' recommendations, what follows is reproduced *verbatim* from the paper delivered at the September, 1968 Association meetings (Rand P-3919). The discussion is heavily indebted to Ernest R. May.

36. Richard Snyder, *Deterrence and Defense* (Princeton, 1961), p. 11. For a more general presentation of this position see Paul Kecskemeti, *Strategic Surrender* (New York, 1964).

QUESTIONS

1. Compare and contrast the organizational process model and the bureaucratic politics model.

2. How do these models differ from realism?

Individual Level International Relations Theories

We have now reached the third and final of our levels of analysis for international relations theory: the individual level. This section includes theorists who view the foreign policy and interaction of states as a result of the nature, characteristics, and values of either people in general or individuals in leadership roles. Proponents of these theories emphasize that systems, countries, and governments don't necessarily dictate the behavior of states—people do.

Each theory differs significantly, however, in its approach to the role of the individual. The first theory presented in this section, human nature theory, and the last, peace studies theory, both focus on the broad characteristics of humans as a race, but from vastly different perspectives. Human nature theorists view the more violent tendencies of the human race as unavoidable and, therefore, an essential and integral part of our relationships with one another. Scholars dedicated to the theory of peace studies suggest that people can overcome this kind of aggression and learn to live and work together peacefully.

If we look at the individual level of analysis as a spectrum, with human nature theory and peace studies theory at one end emphasizing a broad, all-encompassing look at the human race in general, then the second theory presented in this section, cognitive theory, stands at the opposite end of that spectrum. Cognitive theorists believe that the personalities of specific leaders and the personality traits characteristic of those who hold leadership positions often have a significant impact on the course and implementation of a state's foreign policy. Certainly in the first instance, Adolf Hitler played a key role in the rise of Nazi Germany and is often used as a glaring historic example of the power of one individual to dictate, quite literally, the policies of a nation. In the second instance, we might view the pursuit and attainment of leadership positions as somewhat self-selecting. For example, not everyone wants to be president, and those individuals who aspire to that level usually have certain personality traits in common: drive, ambition, willingness to lead, ability to compromise, and so on. Whether the topic is a specific person or simply "a leader," cognitive theorists argue that when it comes to making a decision that could affect the course of a nation and the course of history, the key component in the equation is the man or woman facing that decision.

So, we see that the individual level of analysis looks at the distinctive characteristics of people within our society to specific individuals. We will begin with the fairly pessimistic view of human nature theorists, then take a look at cognitive perspectives, and end with perhaps a more optimistic analysis by the proponents of peace studies.

Chapter 8

HUMAN NATURE THEORY

INTRODUCTION

In looking at the individual level of international relations theory, we begin with the fairly broad interpretation of "individual" that actually encompasses all of humanity—human nature theory. **Human nature** refers to the qualities and traits shared by all people, regardless of ethnicity, gender, culture, and so forth. Human nature theorists assert that the behavior of states is fundamentally patterned after the behavior of humans themselves. Human nature, then, can provide clues about when and why states might behave in a particular fashion.

Human nature theorists argue that, on a basic level, human nature—and, indeed, the nature of other species as well—is often guided by instinct. **Instinct** could be defined as an innate impulse that is prompted in response to specific environmental conditions. It is almost as if humans and other species are preprogrammed to respond in a certain manner when confronted with a particular set of circumstances. Just as the antelope of the African plains have an instinctive fear of lions and other predators, these scholars suggest it is basic human nature that makes states fearful of a neighboring country's perceived military strength and defensive of their territorial rights.

In the excerpt by the Greek scholar and philosopher Aristotle, it is indicated that the nature of man is essentially divided into two parts (good and evil) and, therefore, life and the relations between people are also divided. That is, one cannot know or understand the bounty and tranquillity of peace without having experienced the hardship and terror of war. Although the human race can, according to Aristotle, emphasize one facet over the other (presumably peace over war), this exercise does not negate the presence of the less desirable side of existence. He also extends this theory of human nature to the nature of governments formed by humans, asserting that the government of "freemen" is nobler than that of authoritarian rule. Here we might go so far as to say that what is good for individuals (citizenry) is also good for the state.

In the excerpt taken from Thomas Hobbes' classic work *Leviathan,* the author asks us to imagine the wretchedness of human existence in a "**state of nature**" when there was no central government able to control the baser instincts of humans and to provide order. Hobbes points to three specific causes of conflict that are endemic to human nature: competition, diffidence, and glory. It is important to understand the context in which he uses these terms. **Competition,** as Hobbes views it, represents the perpetual struggle between humans for resources, power, or anything else that might represent some sort of gain. We might presume that at some point relative parity is achieved between individuals or that a person could be content with the fruits of his or her individual labors in a civilized world.

This path, however, leads to diffidence in Hobbes' estimation. **Diffidence** arises from a perception of equality or a sense of self-satisfaction that occurs when individuals attain a particular set of goals or ends. Hobbes suggests conflict arises from the need to protect these gains from other humans who, because of their very nature, cannot help but try to subdue, conquer, and master another's holdings. So, whether you look at the individual attempting to seize another's possessions or the individual protecting his or her assets, both will likely be moved to violent means.

The quest for glory in human nature is the third portion of Hobbes' trilogy about the unavoidable violence of existence. He defines **glory** as the quest for and preservation of honor, respect, or reputation as it refers to the individual or, indeed, as it reflects on the family, friends, name, and so forth, associated with that individual. Under these conditions, Hobbes appears far less certain than Aristotle of man's capacity to avoid conflict. It is, in essence, impossible for an individual to be a pacifist, content with the status quo, because others will strive to change this balance. Humans seek to master others who present, may present, or are perceived as presenting a threat. It is not surprising, given this overall perception of human nature, that Hobbes declares that, in the state of nature, the "life of man was solitary, poore, nasty, brutish, and short." Later in his book, Hobbes concludes that life becomes bearable only when humans subjugate themselves to the control of a strong central authority that can enforce law and order.

Though we might hypothesize that these base traits are inevitably passed from the nature of humans to the nature of the states and other institutions that humans create, the last article by twentieth-century psychologist Sigmund Freud suggests otherwise. Freud argues that the natural violence of the human animal can actually be "overcome by the transference of power to a larger unity" or group. The group comes together and is linked by the emotional ties (belief in democracy and freedom, protection from a common threat, etc.) of its members. In his letter to Albert Einstein addressing the scientist's query about how future wars could be avoided, Freud states that transferring power to a central authority mitigates the possibility of violence. He suggests further that although humans have an instinct for hatred and destruction, this is only half of the essential dichotomy of human instincts. In pairings of seemingly opposite characteristics, humans also have instincts for love and cooperation, which might be promoted and enhanced by such an overarching group authority.

Despite this more hopeful acknowledgment, the enduring theme linking the three articles in this section is that humans are by nature—and can generally be counted upon to be—violent and aggressive. Human nature theorists suggest that these traits, so instinctive to men and women, are thereby carried over to our relations on an international level. Just as the saying suggests that an apple doesn't fall far from the tree, the behavior of states does not stray far from the behavior of the people within them.

A CRITIQUE OF HUMAN NATURE THEORY

The use of psychology and examination of human behavioral patterns that characterize human nature theory have made some insightful contributions to the study of states and international relations. Classical realist theory is itself based in part on the assumption that man is inherently aggressive, and, as we noted earlier, represents a popular and widely accepted theory among contemporary scholars.

The critics of human nature theory argue, however, that it does not delve deeply enough into the driving forces of foreign policy and global politics. Proceeding on the assumption that the human animal is by nature competitive and prone to violence leads to a number of questions. First, does human nature theory provide a sufficient explanation of the complex character of international relations? We might also wonder whether this theory has the analytic depth necessary to understand international relations in our world today. The disintegration of the Soviet Union and its communist ideology, the integrated world economic structure, and the ever-expanding global communications network are just three of the many significant events and processes that have changed and are changing our planet. Can we assume that human beings' natural aggression and lust for power or even Aristotle's notion of the conflict between good and evil in individuals, represent the driving forces behind not only the behavior of states but behind all of these other events, as well?

It appears that human nature theory alone does not offer a sufficiently detailed framework to address these issues. Certainly, however, proponents of this theory can point to a number of instances throughout history where human instincts toward aggression and domination affected the course of international relations. Nazi Germany of the 1930s and 1940s, Iraq's invasion of Kuwait in 1990, and the rampage of the Mongols across the Asian continent in the thirteenth century are examples that come readily to mind. But, staying with an individual-level perspective in our examination of the behavior of states, is the driving force actually human nature as we have defined it here? Or should we take a closer look at individual leaders, their particular features, and unique ambitions?

KEY CONCEPTS

Competition   is a term used to represent the perpetual struggle between humans for resources, power, or anything else that might represent some sort of gain. According to Thomas Hobbes, competition is one of the three specific causes of conflict that are endemic to human nature. The other two causes are diffidence and glory.

Diffidence   is one of the three causes of conflict, according to Thomas Hobbes, that are endemic to human nature. Diffidence arises from a human's perception of equality or a sense of self-satisfaction and occurs when individuals attain a particular set of goals or ends.

Glory   is defined by Thomas Hobbes as the quest for and preservation of honor, respect, or reputation as it refers to the individual or as it reflects on the family, friends, name, and so forth, associated with that individual. According to Hobbes, glory is one of the three causes of conflict that are endemic to human nature.

Human nature   refers to the qualities and traits shared by all people, regardless of ethnicity, gender, culture, etc. Human nature theorists assert that the behavior of states is fundamentally patterned after the behavior of humans themselves. Human nature, then, can provide clues about when and why states might behave in a particular fashion.

Instinct   is an innate pattern of behavior characteristic of species, including humans. To varying degrees, humans and other species are preprogrammed to respond in a certain manner when confronted with a particular set of circumstances.

State of nature   refers to Thomas Hobbes' pessimistic view of life prior to the creation of a central government or authority to control the baser instincts of humans and provide order. Under these conditions the life of humans would be "solitary, poore, nasty, brutish, and short."

35.   The Politics

Aristotle

In this except, Aristotle suggests that states reflect the nature of the individuals living within them. Thus, just as some individuals are more prone to violence than others, some nations are more inclined to peace and others more inclined to war. Aristotle argues that people conditioned exclusively for war will never enjoy the virtues and values of peace. This selection is from *The Politics.*

Aristotle (*c.* 384–322 B.C.) was a Greek philosopher and teacher who studied under Plato and later tutored Alexander the Great. Although he laid out many empirical formulations in the study of the natural sciences, his greatest work was in the field of philosophy. Aristotle's other writings include *Nichomachean Ethics* and *On Philosophy,* each of which analyzes the use of logic in the field.

Now the soul of man is divided into two parts, one of which has a rational principle in itself, and the other, not having a rational principle in itself, is able to obey such a principle. And we call a man in any way good because he has the excellences of these two parts. In which of them the end is more likely to be found is no matter of doubt to those who adopt our division; for in the world both of nature and of art the inferior always exists for the sake of the superior, and the superior is that which has a rational principle. This principle, too, in our ordinary way of making the division, is divided into two kinds, for there is a practical and a speculative principle. This part, then, must evidently be similarly divided. And there must be a corresponding division of actions; the actions of the naturally better part are to be preferred by those who have it in their power to attain to two out of the three or to all, for that is always to everyone the most desirable which is the highest attainable by him. The whole of life is further divided into two parts, business and leisure, war and peace, and of ac-

tions some aim at what is necessary and useful, and some at what is honorable. And the preference given to one or the other class of actions must necessarily be like the preference given to one or other part of the soul and its actions over the other; there must be war for the sake of peace, business for the sake of leisure, things useful and necessary for the sake of things honourable. All these points the statesman should keep in view when he frames his laws; he should consider the parts of the soul and their functions, and above all the better and the end; he should also remember the diversities of human lives and actions. For men must be able to engage in business and to go to war, but leisure and peace are better; they must do what is necessary and indeed what is useful, but what is honourable is better. On such principles children and persons of every age which requires education should be trained. Whereas even the Greeks of the present day who are reputed to be best governed, and the legislators who gave them their constitutions, do not appear to have framed their governments with a regard to the best end, or to have given them laws and education with a view to all the excellences, but in a vulgar spirit have fallen back on those which promised to be more useful and profitable. Many modern writers have taken a similar view: they commend the Lacedaemonian constitution, and praise the legislator for making conquest and war his sole aim, a doctrine which may be refuted by argument and has long ago been refuted by facts. For most men desire empire in the hope of accumulating the goods of fortune; and on this ground Thibron and all those who have written about the Lacedaemonian constitution have praised their legislator, because the Lacedaemonians, by being trained to meet dangers, gained great power. But surely they are not a happy people now that their empire has passed away, nor was their legislator right. How ridiculous is the result, if, while they are continuing in the observance of his laws and no one interferes with them, they have lost the better part of life! These writers further err about the sort of government which the legislator should approve, for the government of freemen is nobler and implies more excellence than despotic government. Neither is a city to be deemed happy or a legislator to be praised because he trains his citizens to conquer and obtain dominion over their neighbours, for there is great harm in this. On a similar principle any citizen who could, should obviously try to obtain the power in his own state—the crime which the Lacedaemonians accuse king Pausanias of attempting, although he had such great honour already. No such principle and no law having this object is either statesmanlike or useful or right. For the same things are best both for individuals and for states, and these are

the things which the legislator ought to implant in the minds of his citizens. Neither should men study war with a view to the enslavement of those who do not deserve to be enslaved; but first of all they should provide against their own enslavement, and in the second place obtain empire for the good of the governed, and not for the sake of exercising a general despotism, and in the third place they should seek to be masters only over those who deserve to be the slaves. Facts, as well as arguments, prove that the legislator should direct all his military and other measures to the provision of leisure and the establishment of peace. For most of these military states are safe only while they are at war, but fall when they have acquired their empire; like unused iron they lose their edge in time of peace. And for this the legislator is to blame, he never having taught them how to lead the life of peace.

Since the end of individuals and of states is the same, the end of the best man and of the best constitution must also be the same; it is therefore evident that there ought to exist in both of them the excellences of leisure; for peace, as has been often repeated, is the end of war, and leisure of toil. But leisure and cultivation may be promoted not only by those excellences which are practised in leisure, but also by some of those which are useful to business. For many necessaries of life have to be supplied before we can have leisure. Therefore a city must be temperate and brave, and able to endure: for truly, as the proverb says, 'There is no leisure for slaves,' and those who cannot face danger like men are the slaves of any invader. Courage and endurance are required for business and philosophy for leisure, temperance and justice for both, and more especially in times of peace and leisure, for war compels men to be just and temperate, whereas the enjoyment of good fortune and the leisure which comes with peace tend to make them insolent. Those then who seem to be the best-off and to be in the possession of every good, have special need of justice and temperance—for example, those (if such there be, as the poets say) who dwell in the Islands of the Blest; they above all will need philosophy and temperance and justice, and all the more the more leisure they have, living in the midst of abundance. There is no difficulty in seeing why the state that would be happy and good ought to have these excellences. If it is disgraceful in men not to be able to use the goods of life, it is peculiarly dis-graceful not to be able to use them in time of leisure—to show excellent qualities in action and war, and when they have peace and leisure to be no better than slaves. That is why we should not practise excellence after the manner of the Lacedaemonians. For they, while agreeing with other men in their conception of the highest goods, differ from the rest of mankind in thinking that they are to be obtained by the practice of a single excellence. And since these goods and the enjoyment of them are greater than the enjoyment derived from the excellences ... and that for its own sake, is evident from what has been said; we must now consider how and by what means it is to be attained.

QUESTIONS

1. How does Aristotle view war? Does he recognize the need for war?

2. What is Aristotle's view of human nature and does this affect his view of politics?

36.   Leviathan

Thomas Hobbes

In this excerpt, Thomas Hobbes presents a pessimistic view of human nature. He suggests that human existence, without benefit of a strong central authority to en-force order, can be characterized as "solitary, poore, nasty, brutish, and short." Hobbes argues that this darker side of human nature guides not only individuals but nations and relations between states as well. This selection is from *Leviathan* (1651).

Thomas Hobbes (1588-1679) began his writing career in 1628 with a translation of Thucydides. One of the leading English political philosophers of the seventeenth century, his other writings include *The Elements of Law, Natural and Politic* (1640), and *De Cive* (1642).

Nature hath made men so equall, in the faculties of body, and mind; as that though there bee found one man sometimes manifestly stronger in body, or of quicker mind then another; yet when all is reckoned together, the difference between man, and man, is not so considerable, as that one man can thereupon claim to himselfe any benefit, to which another may not pretend, as well as he. For as to the strength of body, the weakest has strength enough to kill the strongest, either by secret machination, or by confederacy with others, that are in the same danger with himselfe.

And as to the faculties of the mind, (setting aside the arts grounded upon words, and especially that skill of proceeding upon generall, and infallible rules, called Science; which very few have, and but in few things; as being not a native faculty, born with us; nor attained, (as Prudence,) while we look after somewhat els,) I find yet a greater equality amongst men, than that of strength. For Prudence, is but Experience; which equall time, equally bestowes on all men, in those things they equally apply themselves unto. That which may perhaps make such equality incredible, is but a vain conceipt of ones owne wisdome, which almost all men think they have in a greater degree, than the Vulgar; that is, than all men but themselves, and a few others, whom by Fame, or for concurring with themselves, they approve. For such is the nature of men, that howsoever they may acknowledge many others to be more witty, or more eloquent, or more learned; Yet they will hardly believe there be many so wise as themselves: For they see their own wit at hand, and other mens at a distance. But this proveth rather than men are in that point equall, than unequall. For there is not ordinarily a greater signe of the equall distribution of any thing, than that every man is contented with his share.

From this equality of ability, ariseth equality of hope in the attaining of our Ends. And therefore if any two men desire the same thing, which neverthelesse they cannot both enjoy, they become enemies; and in the way to their End, (which is principally their owne conservation, and sometimes their delectation only,) endeavour to destroy, or subdue one an other. And from hence it comes to passe, that where an Invader hath no more to feare, than an other mans single power; if one plant, sow, build, or possesse a convenient Seat, others may probably be expected to come prepared with forces united, to dispossesse, and deprive him, not only of the fruit of his labour, but also of his life, or liberty. And the Invader again is in the like danger of another.

And from this diffidence of one another, there is no way for any man to secure himselfe, so reasonable, as Anticipation; that is, by force, or wiles, to master the persons of all men he can, so long, till he see no other power great enough to endanger him: And this is no more than his own conservation requireth, and is generally allowed. Also because there be some, that taking pleasure in contemplating their own power in the acts of conquest, which they pursue farther than their security requires; if others, that otherwise would be glad to be at ease within modest bounds, should not by invasion increase their power, they would not be able, long time, by standing only on their defence, to subsist. And by consequence, such augmentation of dominion over men, being necessary to a mans conservation, it ought to be allowed him.

Againe, men have no pleasure, (but on the contrary a great deale of griefe) in keeping company, where there is no power able to over-awe them all. For every man looketh that his companion should value him, at the same rate he sets upon himself: And upon all signes of contempt, or undervaluing, naturally endeavours, as far as he dares (which amongst them that have no common power to keep them in quiet, is far enough to make them destroy each other,) to extort a greater value from his contemners, by dommage; and from others, by the example.

So that in the nature of man, we find three principall causes of quarrell. First, Competition; Secondly, Diffidence; Thirdly, Glory.

The first, maketh men invade for Gain; the second, for Safety; and the third, for Reputation. The first use Violence, to make themselves Masters of other mens persons, wives, children, and cattell; the second, to defend them; the third, for trifles, as a word, a smile, a different opinion, and any other signe of undervalue, either direct in their Persons, or by reflexion in their Kindred, their Friends, their Nation, their Profession, or their Name.

Hereby it is manifest, that during the time men live without a common Power to keep them all in awe, they are in that condition which is called Warre; and such a warre, as is of every man, against every man. For WARRE, consisteth not in Battell onely, or the act of fighting; but in a tract of time, wherein the Will to contend by Battell is sufficiently known: and therefore the notion of *Time,* is to be considered in the nature of Warre; as it is in the nature of Weather. For as the nature of Foule weather, lyeth not in a showre or two of rain; but in an inclination thereto of many dayes together: So the nature of War, consisteth not in actuall fighting; but in the known disposition thereto, during all the time there is no assurance to the contrary. All other time is PEACE.

Whatsoever therefore is consequent to a time of Warre, where every man is Enemy to every man; the same is consequent to the time, wherein men live without other security, than what their own strength, and their own invention shall furnish them withall. In such condition, there is no place for Industry; because the fruit thereof is uncertain: and consequently no Culture of the Earth; no Navigation, nor use of the commodities that may be imported by Sea; no commodious Building; no Instruments of moving, and removing such things as require much force; no Knowledge of the face of the Earth; no account of Time; no Arts; no Letters; no Society; and which is worst of all, continuall feare, and danger of violent death; And the life of man, solitary, poore, nasty, brutish, and short.

It may seem strange to some man, that has not well weighed these things; that Nature should thus dissociate, and render men apt to invade, and destroy one another: and he may therefore, not trusting to this Inference, made from the Passions, desire perhaps to have the same confirmed by Experience. Let him therefore consider with himselfe, when taking a journey, he armes himselfe, and seeks to go well accompanied; when going to sleep, he locks his dores; when even in his house he locks his chests; and this when he knowes there bee Lawes, and publike Officers, armed, to revenge all injuries shall bee done him; what opinion he has of his fellow subjects, when he rides armed; of his fellow Citizens, when he locks his dores; and of his children, and servants, when he locks his chests. Does he not there as much accuse mankind by his actions, as I do by my words? But neither of us accuse mans nature in it. The Desires, and other Passions of man, are in themselves no Sin. No more are the Actions, that proceed from those Passions, till they know a Law that forbids them: which till Lawes be made they cannot know: nor can any Law be made, till they have agreed upon the Person that shall make it.

It may peradventure be thought, there was never such a time, nor condition of warre as this; and I believe it was never generally so, over all the world: but there are many places, where they live so now. For the savage people in many places of *America,* except the government of small Families, the concord whereof dependeth on naturall lust, have no government at all; and live at this day in that brutish manner, as I said before. Howsoever, it may be perceived what manner of life there would be, where there were no common Power to feare; by the manner of life, which men that have formerly lived under a peaceful government, use to degenerate into, in a civil Warre.

But though there had never been any time, wherein particular men were in a condition of warre one against another; yet in all times, Kings, and Persons of Soveraigne authority, because of their Independency, are in continuall jealousies, and in the state and posture of Gladiators; having their weapons pointing, and their eyes fixed on one another; that is, their Forts, Garrisons, and Guns upon the Frontiers of their Kingdomes; and continuall Spyes upon their neighbours, which is a posture of War. But because they uphold thereby, the Industry of their Subjects; there does not follow from it, that misery, which accompanies the Liberty of particular men.

To this warre of every man against every man, this also is consequent; that nothing can be Unjust. The notions of Right and Wrong, Justice and Injustice have there no place. Where there is no common Power, there is no Law: where no Law, no Injustice. Force, and Fraud, are in warre the two Cardinall vertues. Justice, and Injustice are none of the Faculties neither of the Body, nor Mind. If they were, they might be in a man that were alone in the world, as well as his Senses, and Passions. They are Qualities, that relate to men in Society, not in Solitude. It is consequent also to the same condition, that there be no Propriety, no Dominion, no *Mine* and *Thine* distinct; but onely that to be every mans, that he can get; and for so long, as he can keep it. And thus much for the ill condition, which man by meer Nature is actually placed in; though with a possibility to come out of it, consisting partly in the Passions, partly in his Reason.

The Passions that encline men to Peace, are Feare of Death; Desire of such things as are necessary to commodious living; and a Hope by their Industry to obtain them. And Reason suggesteth convenient Articles of Peace, upon which men may be drawn to agreement. These Articles, are they, which otherwise are called the Lawes of Nature. . . .

QUESTIONS

1. What are the conditions of humans in the state of nature described by Hobbes? Do you agree with his characterization? Explain.

2. According to Hobbes, why do individuals sacrifice their liberty to the Leviathan?

37.   Why War?[1]

Sigmund Freud

In this letter, a response to Albert Einstein, Sigmund Freud examines why war exists and concludes that humans have a tendency toward violence. He argues that people have propensities for both war and peace, and suggests that war may be a natural part of human existence. This excerpt was part of a debate with Albert Einstein on the future of the League of Nations (1932).

Sigmund Freud (1856–1939), considered the father of modern psychoanalysis, wrote many books on human psychology.

VIENNA, *September,* 1932.

DEAR PROFESSOR EINSTEIN,

When I heard that you intended to invite me to an exchange of views on some subject that interested you and that seemed to deserve the interest of others besides yourself, I readily agreed. I expected you to choose a problem on the frontiers of what is knowable to-day, a problem to which each of us, a physicist and a psychologist, might have our own particular angle of approach and where we might come together from different directions upon the same ground. You have taken me by surprise, however, by posing the question of what can be done to protect mankind from the curse of war. . . .

You begin with the relation between Right and Might.[2] There can be no doubt that that is the correct starting-point for our investigation. But may I replace the word "might" by the balder and harsher word "violence"? To-day right and violence appear to us as antitheses. It can easily be shown, however, that the one has developed out of the other; and if we go back to the earliest beginnings and see how that first came about, the problem is easily solved. . . .

It is a general principle, then, that conflicts of interest between men are settled by the use of violence. This is true of the whole animal kingdom, from which men have no business to exclude themselves. In the case of men, no doubt, conflicts of *opinion* occur as well which may reach the highest pitch of abstraction and which seem to demand some other technique for their settlement. That, however, is a later complication. To begin with, in a small human horde,[3] it was superior muscular strength which decided who owned things or whose will should prevail. Muscular strength was soon supplemented and replaced by the use of tools: the winner was the one who had the better weapons or who used them the more skilfully. From the moment at which weapons were introduced, intellectual superiority already began to replace brute muscular strength; but the final purpose of the fight remained the same—one side or the other was to be compelled to abandon his claim or his objection by the damage inflicted on him and by the crippling of his strength. That purpose was most completely achieved if the victor's violence eliminated his opponent permanently, that is to say, killed him. This had two advantages: he could not renew his opposition and his fate deterred others from following his example. In addition to this, killing an enemy satisfied an instinctual inclination which I shall have to mention later. The intention to kill might be countered by a reflection that the enemy could be employed in performing useful services if he were left alive in an intimidated condition. In that case the victor's violence was content to subjugate him instead of killing him. This was a first beginning of the idea of sparing an enemy's life, but thereafter the victor had to reckon with his defeated opponent's lurking thirst for revenge and sacrificed some of his own security.

Such, then, was the original state of things: domination by whoever had the greater might—domination by brute violence or by violence supported by intellect. As we know, this régime was altered in the course of evolution. There was a path that led from violence to right or law. What was that path? It is my belief that there was only one: the path which led by way of the fact that the superior strength of a single individual could be rivalled by the union of several weak ones. 'L'union fait la force.' Violence could be broken by union, and the power of those who were united now represented law in contrast to the violence of the single individual. Thus we see that right is the might of a community. It is still violence, ready to be directed against any individual who resists it; it works by the same methods and follows the same purposes. The only real difference lies in the fact that what prevails is no longer the violence of an individual but that of a community. But in order that the transition from violence to this new right or justice may be effected, one psychological condition must be fulfilled. The union of the majority must be a stable and lasting one. If it were only brought about for

the purpose of combating a single domineering individual and were dissolved after his defeat, nothing would have been accomplished. The next person who found himself superior in strength would once more seek to set up a dominion by violence and the game would be repeated *ad infinitum*. The community must be maintained permanently, must be organized, must draw up regulations to anticipate the risk of rebellion and must institute authorities to see that those regulations—the laws—are respected and to superintend the execution of legal acts of violence. The recognition of a community of interests such as these leads to the growth of emotional ties between the members of a united group of people—feelings of unity which are the true source of its strength.

Here, I believe, we already have all the essentials: violence overcome by the transference of power to a larger unity, which is held together by emotional ties between its members. What remains to be said is no more than an expansion and a repetition of this.

The situation is simple so long as the community consists only of a number of equally strong individuals. The laws of such an association will determine the extent to which, if the security of communal life is to be guaranteed, each individual must surrender his personal liberty to turn his strength to violent uses. But a state of rest of that kind is only theoretically conceivable. In actuality the position is complicated by the fact that from its very beginning the community comprises elements of unequal strength—men and women, parents and children—and soon, as a result of war and conquest, it also comes to include victors and vanquished, who turn into masters and slaves. The justice of the community then becomes an expression of the unequal degrees of power obtaining within it; the laws are made by and for the ruling members and find little room for the rights of those in subjection. From that time forward there are two factors at work in the community which are sources of unrest over matters of law but tend at the same time to a further growth of law. First, attempts are made by certain of the rulers to set themselves above the prohibitions which apply to everyone—they seek, that is, to go back from a dominion of law to a dominion of violence. Secondly, the oppressed members of the group make constant efforts to obtain more power and to have any changes that are brought about in that direction recognized in the laws—they press forward, that is, from unequal justice to equal justice for all. This second tendency becomes especially important if a real shift of power occurs within a community, as may happen as a result of a number of historical factors. In that case right may gradually adapt itself to the new distribution of power or, as is more frequent, the ruling class is unwilling to recognize the change, and rebellion and civil war follow, with a temporary suspension of law and new attempts at a solution by violence, ending in the establishment of a fresh rule of law. There is yet another source from which modifications of law may arise, and one of which the expression is invariably peaceful; it lies in the cultural transformation of the members of the community. This, however, belongs properly in another connection and must be considered later.

Thus we see that the violent solution of conflicts of interest is not avoided even inside a community. But the everyday necessities and common concerns that are inevitable where people live together in one place tend to bring such struggles to a swift conclusion and under such conditions there is an increasing probability that a peaceful solution will be found. But a glance at the history of the human race reveals an endless series of conflicts between one community and another or several others, between larger and smaller units—between cities, provinces, races, nations, empires—which have almost always been settled by force of arms. Wars of this kind end either in the spoliation or in the complete overthrow and conquest of one of the parties. It is impossible to make any sweeping judgement upon wars of conquest. Some, such as those waged by the Mongols and Turks, have brought nothing but evil. Others, on the contrary, have contributed to the transformation of violence into law by establishing larger units within which the use of violence was made impossible and in which a fresh system of law led to the solution of conflicts. In this way the conquests of the Romans gave the countries round the Mediterranean the priceless *pax Romana,* and the greed of the French kings to extend their dominions created a peacefully united and flourishing France. Paradoxical as it may sound, it must be admitted that war might be a far from inappropriate means of establishing the eagerly desired reign of 'everlasting' peace, since it is in a position to create the large units within which a powerful central government makes further wars impossible. Nevertheless it fails in this purpose, for the results of conquest are as a rule short-lived: the newly created units fall apart once again, usually owing to a lack of cohesion between the portions that have been united by violence. Hitherto, moreover, the unifications created by conquest, though of considerable extent, have only been *partial,* and the conflicts between these have cried out for violent solution. Thus the result of all these warlike efforts has only been that the human race has exchanged numerous, and indeed unending, minor wars for wars on a grand scale that are rare but all the more destructive.

If we turn to our own times, we arrive at the same conclusion which you have reached by a shorter path. Wars will only be prevented with certainty if mankind unites in setting up a central authority to which the right of giving judgement upon all conflicts of interest shall be handed over. There are clearly two separate requirements involved in this: the creation of a supreme authority and its endowment with the necessary power. One without the other would be useless. The League of Nations is designed as an authority of this kind, but the second condition has not been fulfilled: the League of Nations has no power of its own and can only acquire it if the members of the new union, the separate States, are ready to resign it. And at the moment there seems very little prospect of this. The institution of the League of Nations would, however, be wholly unintelligible if one ignored the fact that here was a bold attempt such as has seldom (perhaps, indeed, never on such a scale) been made before. It is an attempt to base upon an appeal to certain idealistic attitudes of mind the authority (that is, the coercive influence) which otherwise rests on the possession of power. We have heard that a community is held together by two things: the compelling force of violence and the emotional ties (identifications is the technical name) between its members. If one of the factors is absent, the community may possibly be held together by the other. The ideas that are appealed to can, of course, only have any significance if they give expression to important concerns that are common to the members, and the question arises of how much strength they can exert. . . . Indeed it is all too clear that the national ideals by which nations are at present swayed operate in a contrary direction. Some people are inclined to prophesy that it will not be possible to make an end of war until Communist ways of thinking have found universal acceptance. But that aim is in any case a very remote one to-day, and perhaps it could only be reached after the most fearful civil wars. Thus the attempt to replace actual force by the force of ideas seems at present to be doomed to failure. We shall be making a false calculation if we disregard the fact that law was originally brute violence and that even to-day it cannot do without the support of violence.

I can now proceed to add a gloss to another of your remarks. You express astonishment at the fact that it is so easy to make men enthusiastic about a war and add your suspicion that there is something at work in them—an instinct for hatred and destruction—which goes halfway to meet the efforts of the war-mongers. Once again, I can only express my entire agreement. We believe in the existence of an instinct of that kind and have in fact been occupied during the last few years in studying its manifestations. Will you allow me to take this opportunity of putting before you a portion of the theory of the instincts which, after much tentative groping and many fluctuations of opinion, has been reached by workers in the field of psycho-analysis?

According to our hypothesis human instincts are of only two kinds: those which seek to preserve and unite—which we call "erotic," exactly in the sense in which Plato uses the word 'Eros' in his *Symposium,* or "sexual," with a deliberate extension of the popular conception of 'sexuality'—and those which seek to destroy and kill and which we class together as the aggressive or destructive instinct. As you see, this is in fact no more than a theoretical clarification of the universally familiar opposition between Love and Hate which may perhaps have some fundamental relation to the polarity of attraction and repulsion that plays a part in your own field of knowledge. We must not be too hasty in introducing ethical judgements of good and evil. Neither of these instincts is any less essential than the other; the phenomena of life arise from the operation of both together, whether acting in concert or in opposition. It seems as though an instinct of the one sort can scarcely ever operate in isolation; it is always accompanied—or, as we say, alloyed—with an element from the other side, which modifies its aim or is, in some cases, what enables it to achieve that aim. Thus, for instance, the instinct of self-preservation is certainly of an erotic kind, but it must nevertheless have aggressiveness at its disposal if it is to fulfil its purpose. So, too, the instinct of love, when it is directed towards an object, stands in need of some contribution from the instinct of mastery if it is in any way to possess that object. The difficulty of isolating the two classes of instinct in their actual manifestations is indeed what has so long prevented us from recognizing them.

If you will follow me a little further, you will see that human actions are subject to another complication of a different kind. It is very rarely that an action is the work of a *single* instinctual impulse (which must in itself be compounded of Eros and destructiveness). In order to make an action possible there must be as a rule a *combination* of such compounded motives. . . . So that when human beings are incited to war they may have a whole number of motives for assenting—some noble and some base, some of which they speak openly and others on which they are silent. There is no need to enumerate them all. A lust for aggression and destruction is certainly among them: the countless cruelties in history and in our everyday lives vouch for its existence and its strength. The gratification of these destructive impulses is of course facilitated by their admixture with others of an erotic and idealistic kind. When we read of the atrocities of the past, it sometimes seems as though the idealistic motives served only as an excuse for the destructive appetites; and sometimes—in the case, for instance, of the cruelties of the Inquisition—it seems as though the idealistic motives had pushed themselves forward in consciousness, while the destructive ones lent them an unconscious reinforcement. Both may be true.

I fear I may be abusing your interest, which is after all concerned with the prevention of war and not with our theories. Nevertheless I should like to linger for a moment over our destructive instinct, whose popularity is by no means equal to its importance. As a result of a little speculation, we have come to suppose that this instinct is at work in every living being and is striving to bring it to ruin and to reduce life to its original condition of inanimate matter. Thus it quite seriously deserves to be called a death instinct, while the erotic instincts represent the effort to live. The death instinct turns into the destructive instinct if, with the help of special organs, it is directed outwards, on to objects. The living creature preserves its own life, so to say, by destroying an extraneous one. Some portion of the death instinct, however, remains operative *within* the living being, and we have sought to trace quite a number of normal and pathological phenomena to this internalization of the destructive instinct. We have even been guilty of the heresy of attributing the origin of conscience to this diversion inwards of aggressiveness. You will notice that it is by no means a trivial matter if this process is carried too far: it is positively unhealthy. On the other hand if these forces are turned to destruction in the external world, the living creature will be relieved and the effect must be beneficial. This would serve as a biological justification for all the ugly and dangerous impulses against which we are struggling. It must be admitted that they stand nearer to Nature than does our resistance to them, for which an explanation also needs to be found. It may perhaps seem to you as though our theories are a kind of mythology and, in the present case, not even an agreeable one. But does not every science come in the end to a kind of mythology like this? Cannot the same be said to-day of your own Physics?

For our immediate purpose then, this much follows from what has been said: there is no use in trying to get rid of men's aggressive inclinations. We are told that in certain happy regions of the earth, where nature provides in abundance everything that man requires, there are races whose life is passed in tranquillity and who know neither compulsion nor aggressiveness. I can scarcely believe it and I should be glad to hear more of these fortunate beings. The Russian Communists, too, hope to be able to

cause human aggressiveness to disappear by guaranteeing the satisfaction of all material needs and by establishing equality in other respects among all the members of the community. That, in my opinion, is an illusion. They themselves are armed to-day with the most scrupulous care and not the least important of the methods by which they keep their supporters together is hatred of everyone beyond their frontiers. In any case, as you yourself have remarked, there is no question of getting rid entirely of human aggressive impulses; it is enough to try to divert them to such an extent that they need not find expression in war.

Our mythological theory of instincts makes it easy for us to find a formula for *indirect* methods of combating war. If willingness to engage in war is an effect of the destructive instinct, the most obvious plan will be to bring Eros, its antagonist, into play against it. Anything that encourages the growth of emotional ties between men must operate against war. These ties may be of two kinds. In the first place they may be relations resembling those towards a loved object, though without having a sexual aim. There is no need for psycho-analysis to be ashamed to speak of love in this connection, for religion itself uses the same words: 'Thou shalt love thy neighbour as thyself.' This, however, is more easily said than done. The second kind of emotional tie is by means of identification. Whatever leads men to share important interests produces this community of feeling, these identifications. And the structure of human society is to a large extent based on them.

A complaint which you make about the abuse of authority brings me to another suggestion for the indirect combating of the propensity to war. One instance of the innate and ineradicable inequality of men is their tendency to fall into the two classes of leaders and followers. The latter constitute the vast majority; they stand in need of an authority which will make decisions for them and to which they for the most part offer an unqualified submission. This suggests that more care should be taken than hitherto to educate an upper stratum of men with independent minds, not open to intimidation and eager in the pursuit of truth, whose business it would be to give direction to the dependent masses. It goes without saying that the encroachments made by the executive power of the State and the prohibition laid by the Church upon freedom of thought are far from propitious for the production of a class of this kind. The ideal condition of things would of course be a community of men who had subordinated their instinctual life to the dictatorship of reason. Nothing else could unite men so completely and so tenaciously, even if there were no emotional ties between them. But in all probability that is a Utopian expectation. No doubt the other indirect methods of preventing war are more practicable, though they promise no rapid success. An unpleasant picture comes to one's mind of mills that grind so slowly that people may starve before they get their flour.

The result, as you see, is not very fruitful when an unworldly theoretician is called in to advise on an urgent practical problem. It is a better plan to devote oncsclf in cvcry particular casc to meeting the danger with whatever weapons lie to hand. I should like, however, to discuss one more question, which you do not mention in your letter but which specially interests me. Why do you and I and so many other people rebel so violently against war? Why do we not accept it as another of the many painful calamities of life? After all, it seems quite a natural thing, no doubt it has a good biological basis and in practice it is scarcely avoidable. There is no need to be shocked at my raising this question. For the purpose of an investigation such as this, one may perhaps be allowed to wear a mask of assumed detachment. The answer to my question will be that we react to war in this way because everyone has a right to his own life, because war puts an end to human lives that are full of hope, because it brings individual men into humiliating situations, because it compels them against their will to murder other men, and because it destroys precious material objects which have been produced by the labours of humanity. Other reasons besides might be given, such as that in its present-day form war is no longer an opportunity for achieving the old ideals of heroism and that owing to the perfection of instruments of destruction a future war might involve the extermination of one or perhaps both of the antagonists. All this is true, and so incontestably true that one can only feel astonished that the waging of war has not yet been unanimously repudiated. No doubt debate is possible upon one or two of these points. It may be questioned whether a community ought not to have a right to dispose of individual lives; every war is not open to condemnation to an equal degree; so long as there exist countries and nations that are prepared for the ruthless destruction of others, those others must be armed for war. But I will not linger over any of these issues; they are not what you want to discuss with me, and I have something different in mind. It is my opinion that the main reason why we rebel against war is that we cannot help doing so. We are pacifists because we are obliged to be for organic reasons. And we then find no difficulty in producing arguments to justify our attitude.

No doubt this requires some explanation. My belief is this. For incalculable ages mankind has been passing through a process of evolution of culture. (Some people, I know, prefer to use the term "civilization.") We owe to that process the best of what we have become, as well as a good part of what we suffer from. Though its causes and beginnings are obscure and its outcome uncertain, some of its characteristics are easy to perceive. It may perhaps be leading to the extinction of the human race, for in more than one way it impairs the sexual function; uncultivated races and backward strata of the population are already multiplying more rapidly than highly cultivated ones. The process is perhaps comparable to the domestication of certain species of animals and it is undoubtedly accompanied by physical alterations; but we are still unfamiliar with the notion that the evolution of culture is an organic process of this kind. The psychical modifications that go along with the cultural process are striking and unambiguous. They consist in a progressive displacement of instinctual aims and a restriction of instinctual impulses. Sensations which were pleasurable to our ancestors have become indifferent or even intolerable to ourselves; there are organic grounds for the changes in our ethical and aesthetic ideals. Of the psychological characteristics of culture two appear to be the most important: a strengthening of the intellect, which is beginning to govern instinctual life, and an internalization of the aggressive impulses, with all its consequent advantages and perils. Now war is in the crassest opposition to the psychical attitude imposed on us by the cultural process, and for that reason we are bound to rebel against it; we simply cannot any longer put up with it. This is not merely an intellectual and emotional repudiation; we pacifists have a constitutional intolerance of war, an idiosyncracy magnified, as it were, to the highest degree. It seems, indeed, as though the lowering of aesthetic standards in war plays a scarcely smaller part in our rebellion than do its cruelties.

And how long shall we have to wait before the rest of mankind become pacifists too? There is no telling. But it may not be Utopian to hope that these two factors, the cultural attitude and the justified dread of the consequences of a future war, may result within a measurable time in putting an end to the waging of war. By what paths or by what sidetracks this will come about we cannot guess. But one thing we *can* say: whatever fosters the growth of culture works at the same time against war.

I trust you will forgive me if what I have said has disappointed you, and I remain, with kindest regards,
Yours sincerely,
Sigm. Freud

NOTES

1. *Warum Krieg?* was the title of an interchange of open letters between Professor Albert Einstein and Freud. This formed one of a series of similar interchanges arranged by the International Institute of Intellectual Co-operation under the auspices of the League of Nations, and was first published simultaneously in German, French, and English in Paris in 1933. Freud's letter was reprinted *Ges. Schr.*, 12, 347, and *Ges. W.*, 16. Professor Einstein's, which preceded it, was a short one setting out the problems to be discussed. Present translation by James Strachey.

2. In the original the words *Recht* and *Macht* are used throughout the essay. It has unfortunately been necessary to sacrifice this stylistic unity in the translation. *Recht* has been rendered indifferently by "right," "law" and "justice"; and *Macht* by "might," "force" and "power."

3. Freud uses the word "horde" to denote a comparatively small group.

QUESTIONS

1. How does Freud explain the existence of war and peace?

2. According to Freud, what factor that might prevent war is absent in the structure of the League of Nations?

Chapter 9

COGNITIVE THEORY

COMPONENTS OF COGNITIVE THEORY

Focus of Analysis ········▶	• Personality and cognitive experience of leaders
Major Actors ········▶	• Individual
Behavior of States ········▶	• Guided by experience, preconceptions, background, and personality of leader(s)
Basis of a State's Foreign Policy ········▶	• Driven by operational reality of elites
Key Concepts ········▶	• Cognition; Independent leader; Operational reality; Participatory leader; Personality

INTRODUCTION

In the course of growing up and learning to live with others, we have all probably heard the phrase, "Imagine how dull the world would be if everyone were the same." Dull, certainly, but such uniformity would make it easier for political scientists to predict people's behavior and put together theories of international relations. Doubtless, however, even most political scientists would thankfully acknowledge—along with the rest of us—that we are all unique individuals, with different personalities, beliefs, ambitions, skills, and so on. The theory presented in this chapter, which we will call cognitive theory, suggests that a leader's specific personality guides not only his or her own actions but the destiny of the state and its relations with other countries.

We can define the term **personality** as the package of behavior, temperament, and other individualistic qualities that uniquely identifies each of us. Cognition is one element of this personality package. **Cognition** is what an individual comes to know as a result of learning and reasoning or, on a more instinctual level, intuition and perception. All of these components combine to form a person's cognitive facility. In our daily lives, we are perhaps more familiar with the term *recognize*. When you recognize a person or place, for example, you identify him, her, or it using accumulated knowledge or experience.

Cognitive theorists believe that the personality traits of leaders can often define both the agenda and specific features of a state's foreign policy. In his article "World Politics and Personal Insecurity," Harold Lasswell suggests that, unconsciously, leaders actually superimpose their own sense of self over that of the state. That is, the line separating the leader from the state becomes blurred, with the personality of the leader—complete with flaws and insecurities—shaping the policy and perceptions of the state.

A leader's individual perception of reality is naturally conditioned by emotional attachments and aversions that he or she formed in life. In putting together a worldview, Lasswell asserts, people tend to displace emotions of those close to us onto symbols that are more removed, such as nations, classes, and rulers. For example, the frustration of a peasant in pre-revolutionary France was not solely directed at a single aristocrat, but at the entire aristocracy. Or, a neighbor's dispute with one who is from a foreign country might prejudice his view toward that country as a whole. According to Lasswell, in political personalities, these associations—however loose—are likely to have some conditioning effect on performance and, hence, policy.

Margaret Hermann provides a structure for analyzing the individual traits that might affect a leader's decisions and policy making. In "Explaining Foreign Policy Behavior Using the Personal Characteristics of Political Leaders," Hermann isolates four broad types of personal characteristics: beliefs, motives, decision style, and interpersonal style. Although other factors do come into play (interest in foreign affairs, diplomatic and foreign policy training), these can be combined with an assessment of a leader's basic characteristics to form a fairly complete profile.

From her analysis, Hermann concludes that leaders generally have one of two orientations toward foreign affairs: independent or participatory. An **independent leader** tends to be aggressive, with a limited capacity to consider different alternatives, and, not surprisingly, is willing to be the first to take action over a perceived threat. In regard to foreign policy, independent leaders seek to preserve a state's individual identity and tend to be somewhat isolationist, viewing contact with other nations as a slippery slope toward dependence and practicable only under their own specific terms or conditions.

By contrast, Hermann defines a **participatory leader** as generally conciliatory, with an inclusive nature that encourages relationships with other countries, considers various alternatives in problem solving, and rarely seeks to initiate action. Participatory leaders also have a different approach to foreign policy. They promote contact and ventures with other nations and are likely to be quite sensitive and responsive to the international environment.

Whether independent or participatory, cognitive theorists view leaders' perceptions of other states and other heads of state as key components of foreign policy. Robert Jervis' well-respected work, *Perception and Misperception in International Politics,* discusses how decision makers perceive others' behavior and form judgments about their intentions. He actually focuses on several vital misperceptions that are common among people and often lead to disputes or even war. These misperceptions might be compared to the stereotypical images of "good guys" versus "bad guys" in an old Hollywood western. First, we tend to view the people of other nations as more hostile than we are. That is, we might represent ourselves as the peace-loving townspeople and the other side as a band of aggressive marauders. Second, we also view other countries as organized and integrated, behaving according to a coherent strategic plan. Returning to our old western movie analogy, the "bad guys" always seemed to operate within an accepted and rigid hierarchy and to have some sort of a plan to get what they wanted, whether it was robbing the town bank, getting control of the town, or capturing rights to the local water supply.

Finally, just as it is difficult to envision the gentle townspeople in this image intimidating the fierce band of marauders, we too find it difficult to believe that others might be afraid of or intimidated by us. But it is these kinds of misperceptions that can foster errors in judgment about the motives and aims behind the actions of other countries. We see, then, that the perceptions (and misperceptions) of leaders could affect the foreign policy of states and the international system as a whole.

If we accept that leaders are, in fact, conditioned by the unique features of their own personality, cognitive theorists would argue that we must also acknowledge that a leader's perception of policy, the state, and the system will be conditioned by these same features. **Operational reality** refers to the picture of the environment held by an individual (usually a leader) as it is modified by his or her personality, perceptions, and misperceptions. Essentially, we all live and work within our own operational reality, but a leader's view of reality has an impact on policies and decisions that influence millions of people and could well affect the course of history.

At this point, we need to acknowledge that often these policies and decisions are made by an influential collective or group. Although this chapter and the other chapters in this section focus on individual level of analysis theories, we might expand the image somewhat to include such groups of like-minded individuals. These individuals' beliefs about, ideology of, and approach to foreign policy fall within sufficiently narrow confines as to be considered a single voice.

Cognitive theory is really about individual personalities and perceptions and how they can affect the behavior of states in the international system. These unique qualities are based on both a person's innate, instinctive reactions and learned or reasoned patterns that come from knowledge and experience. Cognitive theorists suggest that a leader's personality conditions how he or she makes decisions, implements those decisions, and judges the outcome within a global context. It would seem that the distinctions that make us who we are would quite likely have an impact on how we try to shape or control the world around us. But, should personality be the defining feature in an analysis of international relations?

A CRITIQUE OF COGNITIVE THEORY

The notion that individuals make foreign policy and can shape the international system in which they exist is the most important contribution of the individual level of

> ## KEY CONCEPTS
>
> **Cognition** is an individual's knowing as a result of learning and reasoning or, on a more instinctual level, intuiting and perceiving. All of these components combine to form a person's cognitive facility.
>
> **Independent leader** is one of the two major orientations of leaders according to Margaret Hermann. Independent leaders tend to be aggressive, have a limited capacity to consider different alternatives, and are willing to be the first to take action over a perceived threat. Independent leaders seek to preserve a state's individual identity and tend to be somewhat isolationist, viewing contact with other nations as a slippery slope toward dependence and practicable only under their own specific terms or conditions.
>
> **Operational reality** refers to the picture of the environment held by an individual as it is modified by his or her personality, perceptions, and misperceptions.
>
> **Participatory leader** is a term used by Margaret Hermann to characterize a type of leader who is generally conciliatory and encourages relationships with other countries, considers various alternatives in problem solving, and rarely seeks to initiate action. Participatory leaders are likely to be quite sensitive and responsive to the international environment.
>
> **Personality** is the package of behavior, temperament, and other individualistic qualities that uniquely identifies each of us. Cognition is one element of this personality package.

analysis. Cognitive theory, with its emphasis on studying the values, beliefs, and personal characteristics of leaders, forces us to recognize that all explanations of political behavior must take into account the role of the individual. Only by narrowing our focus to the level of the individual can we understand fully the actions of states.

Critics of cognitive theory might argue that focusing on personality profiles of individual leaders to determine an analytical framework for studying international relations is, indeed, limiting. In addition, one's assessment of any leader should be based on a sophisticated and complete psychoanalysis. Such a scenario is improbable, at best, since most leaders have not subjected and would not subject themselves to this type of scrutiny. Thus, it is left to the scholar to examine the background and behavior patterns of leaders or potential leaders, which would tend to produce both vague and problematic results.

Other criticisms of cognitive theory revolve around its limited scope. The emphasis of the theory (personality/cognition) is so narrow that it seems inappropriate to attempt a broad, all-encompassing application to international relations as a whole. The price of focusing on specific individuals is the danger of getting bogged down in a detailed analysis of the subject's idiosyncractic characteristics and losing sight of the broader picture. In addition, the principles of cognitive theory might lead us to believe that all wars are simply the result of misperceptions or misunderstandings between individual leaders. Cognitive theorists ignore the fact that wars often result from fundamental conflicting interests between states on larger issues, such as national security, competition over scarce resources, or dozens of other factors that affect global politics.

One final comment is similar to the critique used against human nature theory: Can cognitive theory provide a framework substantial enough to analyze contemporary issues of foreign policy in a contemporary context? Do personality, perceptions, and beliefs hold the key to understanding international monetary policy, the formation of interdependent trading blocs, or the changing nature of collective security? We would have to say under these circumstances that cognitive theory—though important and useful in understanding how and in what way individual leaders do play a role in the formulation and conduct of foreign policy—may not offer a complete understanding of the patterns and process for international relations today and in the future.

38.   World Politics and Personal Insecurity

Harold D. Lasswell

In this exerpt, Harold Lasswell analyzes the impact of the "ego symbol" and "collective emblem" on the foreign policy of a nation-state. He argues that a leader will use these tools when confronted by pressure from the international community. Lasswell also investigates the use of symbols to enhance a leader's personal ambitions. This selection is from *World Politics and Personal Insecurity* (1965).

Harold Lasswell (1902–1978) was best known for his use of psychological theory in political study. Another of is books, *Politics: Who Gets What, When, How* (1936), was accepted first by psychiatrists and only later, in the 1950s, by political scientists.

Owing to the assumption of violence in international and interclass relations, collective symbols are presented at the focus of attention under circumstances which are particularly prone to precipitate all manner of anxiety reactions. The meaning of these symbols is a function of the total personalities in which they occur, and they necessarily derive much of their significance from deeper and earlier sources than those connected with the immediate political situation.

Insecurities which are induced by threats of loss may be abated by direct acts of counterassertion. But in a world of limited opportunities the impulses toward boundless counteraggression which are elicited under such circumstances must submit to incessant chastening. Impulsive counterassertions are rarely consummated, and the most direct means by which the underlying anxieties may be removed are therefore unavailable. The continuing necessity of suppressing hostility, or of giving it indirect expression, means that a substantial measure of anxiety remains related to the secondary symbols. There are many ways of disposing of accumulated insecurities in relation to political symbols without directly implicating political symbols. Hence anxieties which arise from the rumors of foreign conspiracies may be effectively abolished by displacing hostilities upon wives, secretaries, or chauffeurs; or by orgiastic and diffuse release in orgasm, alcoholism, or pugilism. The routes to release are very numerous; they may be classified into acts which involve object orientations, reflective thinking, autism (moods and irrelevant fantasies), and somatic reactions (headaches and other bodily changes in which functional factors are important). Despite the rich variety of insecurity-abolishing alternatives, several circumstances conspire to connect world political symbols with anxiety reactions. The expectation of violence sustains an organization of communication which pays attention to what the various key participants in the balancing process are doing. Their names are continually before the population as targets for affective displacements of all kinds, and they are reported in connection with many events which directly expose the local symbol to the possibility of losing its independence, its material claims, or its prestige. Vested interests arise in connection with the special function of transmitting symbols in the press and elsewhere; and many of these vested interests extract direct advantages from emphasizing the threatening aspects of the world situation.

Although insecurities arising within the personality in its political aspects may be removed by nonpolitical acts, many of the reactions to insecurity are immediately relevant to politics. We have seen how the suppression of vigorous counterassertion in a world of many limitations sustains insecurities arising from the balancing process. Some of the aggressions which are mobilized and denied direct expression against the foreign environment are directed against the self. This is one of the most important dynamisms of our intrapsychic life, displaying itself in extreme form as suicide.

One of the chief immediate results of subjecting an ego symbol to external danger and of inhibiting counteraggression is thus the preoccupation of the ego with its own relations to the world. This represents a partial withdrawal of libido (affective interest) from the symbols of the surrounding environment. This growing absorption in the more central self-symbols reactivates the earlier, more primitive, less disciplined attitudes of the personality. The result is the elaboration of narcissistically gratifying fantasies of the self. A personality so reacting may create symbols to which he exposes others, boasting of the high moral worth and ultimate omnipotence of the collective symbol; or in the absence of autonomous elaboration, he may respond positively to such symbols when they are supplied by others in conversation or in print. A particular value is attached to acts of ceremonial deference to the collective emblem, since to personalities in such a condition each small detail seems to involve the fate of the whole collective symbol, and of national or class or race "honor.". . .

The ego symbol of any selected personality within a class or nation is a highly complicated structure which includes symbols of all degrees of differentiation. The ego sentiments which are organized with reference to brothers, sisters, friends, professional associates, and neighbors are much fuller of nuance than those which refer to such secondary objects as nations or classes. The personality-in-relation-to-partner is controlled by many reflective considerations, since there is much tested knowledge available about the capacities and proclivities of the partner.

That part of the ego symbol which is organized in relation to the ambiguous "we" called our nation, or class, or race, is in most instances but slightly modified by knowledge. In view of the undeveloped character of such a "we" symbol, it may properly be called a *rudimentary* sentiment or symbol. The ambiguity of reference of these secondary terms and the residues of early emotional attachments and aversions combine to minimize the "reality critique." The resulting instability of judgment is displayed in the ease with which uncorrected swings occur between extremes of hostility and of admiration in relation to secondary symbols. A study by E. S. Bogardus of the attitudes of Californians toward various national and racial groups showed that it was not the Japanese who were the most hated nation, but the Turks, whom the subjects had never seen.[1] The absence of information about Belgium made it easier to build up a vast idealization of the Belgian people than of the British or the Germans.

It should be explicitly stated that persons who are well integrated in their immediate personal relationships may be poorly developed toward remote objects and, reversely, that people who are poorly organized toward primary situations may have acquired the special knowledge which chastens reactions in dealing with remote objects. Indeed one of the principal functions of symbols of remote objects, like nations and classes, is to serve as targets for the relief of many of the tensions which might discharge disastrously in face-to-face relations. The hatred of the physical father may be displaced upon the symbol of the monarch, enabling the person to keep on good terms with the person toward whom the early animosities were mainly directed.

From this analysis it follows that the rudimentary self-symbols which are related to world politics may function in loose association with other aspects of the personality and, like all partly dissociated systems, may predominate in shaping overt conduct in situations which call them up.

The elaboration of regressive and fantastic processes in connection with the rudimentary self-symbols of world politics is favored by the weak superego formations which arise in consequence of the comparative absence of world mores. The assumption that the resort to violence is the ultimate appeal in world politics indicates the weakness of moral imperatives in this sphere of human re-

lations. Impulses are permitted to discharge in elementary form owing to the fragmentary nature of world culture.

Strictly speaking, it is not legitimate to refer to rudimentary self-symbols as pathological expressions of the individual. Nor is it correct to oppose a sick society to a basically healthy person. Pathology is neither social in contrast with individual, nor individual in contrast with social; pathology is configurational. If the word is used at all, it may be defined as referring to events destructive of certain patterns defined as "normal" or "supernormal."

We have seen that one of the principal consequences of the expectation of violence in world politics is to build up insecurities which arise from the curbing of counteraggressive tendencies which are initially elicited by the dangers connected with the we-symbol in the balancing process. This prolonged indulgence of the reality-testing, cautious, self-controlling features of culture and personality favors the drastic redefinition of the situation in directions gratifying to the underindulged, unreflecting, incautious, and spontaneous patterns of culture and personality.

NOTE

1. See the articles on "Social Distance" by E.S. Bogardus in the *Journal of Applied Sociology* since 1925.

QUESTIONS

1. What role does the "ego" identified by Lasswell play in shaping a nation's actions in the international system?

2. Provide an example in which a leader promoted the use of symbolism to achieve particular international aims.

39.   Explaining Foreign Policy Behavior Using the Personal Characteristics of Political Leaders

Margaret G. Hermann

In this article, Margaret G. Hermann studies the impact of personality on foreign policy. Hermann examines whether the characteristics of individual heads of state can influence the behavior of that state in the international system. Dividing individual interests into two broad foreign policy orientations, the author uses a number of examples in her analysis.

Margaret G. Hermann is a professor with the Mershon Center at Ohio State University. She has written extensively on the impact of personality and ideology on American foreign policy.

INTRODUCTION

Parties to the continuing debate concerning whether the personal characteristics of political leaders can affect policy have increasingly turned to empirical research to seek resolution to the controversy. . . . Emerging from this research are portraits of national political leaders who influence their governments toward aggressive or toward conciliatory relations with other nations. The data suggest that aggressive leaders are high in need for power, low in conceptual complexity, distrustful of others, nationalistic, and likely to believe that they have some control over the events in which they are involved. In contrast, the data suggest that conciliatory leaders are high in need for affiliation, high in conceptual complexity, trusting of others, low in nationalism, and likely to exhibit little belief in their own ability to control the events in which they are involved.

The present article has as its purpose a further examination of how these 6 personal characteristics relate to foreign policy behavior for some 45 heads of government. The study is unique in several ways. (1) To date, researchers have not examined all 6 characteristics in the same study. (2) A conceptual scheme is presented to link these characteristics to foreign policy behavior. (3) An attempt is made to broaden the foreign policy behaviors that are examined beyond specifically aggressive (i.e., entry into war, arms increases) and conciliatory (i.e., entry into international agreements) behaviors.

CONCEPTUAL SCHEME[1]

The six personal characteristics we are examining in this research were selected because they have been found to relate to foreign policy behavior in several studies. The characteristics represent four broad types of personal characteristics that journalists and scholars alike suggest have an impact on the content as well as the means of making political decisions. These four types of personal characteristics are beliefs, motives, decision style, and interpersonal style.

International Studies Quarterly.

Beliefs refer to a political leader's fundamental assumptions about the world. Are events predictable, is conflict basic to human interaction, can one have some control over events, is the maintenance of national sovereignty and superiority the most important objective of a nation? Answers to questions such as these suggest some of a political leader's beliefs. Beliefs are proposed by many (e.g., Axelrod, 1976; DeRivera, 1968; Frank, 1968; Holsti, 1967; Jervis, 1976; Verba, 1969) to affect a political leader's interpretation of his environment and, in turn, the strategies that the leader employs. Two of the personal characteristics examined in the present study fall under the category of beliefs—nationalism and belief in one's own ability to control events. Nationalism is often used by journalists and policy makers as a reason for a specific political leader's actions, particularly in discussions of leaders of Third World countries. Ascertaining a political leader's belief in the controllability of events is thought to be fundamental in developing his/her operational code—the way a political leader defines the basic rules that govern political behavior (see George, 1969; Holsti, 1977).

It is hard to find journalistic political analysis that does not consider at some point the reasons why a political leader is doing what he/she is doing—in effect, the political leader's motives. Need for power is probably the most discussed motive with reference to political leaders. But others, such as need for affiliation and need for approval, also appear regularly in such writings. Motives appear to affect political leaders' interpretations of their environment and the strategies they use (see Barber, 1965; Hermann, 1977, 1978). In the present research we will look at need for power and need for affiliation. . . . These two motives appeared to influence the type of foreign behavior the presidents urged on their governments.

By decision style is meant preferred methods of making decisions. How does the political leader go about making decisions? Are there certain ways of approaching a policy-making task which characterize the leader? Possible components of decision style are openness to new information, preference for certain levels of risk, complexity in structuring and processing information, and ability to tolerate ambiguity. . . .

The last type of personal characteristic—interpersonal style—deals with the characteristic ways in which a policy maker deals with other policy makers. Two interpersonal style characteristics—paranoia (excessive suspiciousness) and Machiavellianism (unscrupulous, manipulative behavior)—are often noted as particularly pronounced in political leaders (see Christie and Geis, 1970; Guterman, 1970; Hofstadter, 1965; Rutherford, 1966). Tucker (1965) has proposed that these two traits are related in a type of political leader having a "warfare personality," for example, Stalin and Hitler. The political behavior of such a leader is combative in nature. Suspiciousness or distrust of others is the interpersonal style variable examined in the present research.

These four types of personal characteristics are expected to affect both the style and content of foreign policy. Because beliefs and motives suggest ways of interpreting the environment, political leaders are likely to urge their governments to act in ways consistent with such images. Specifically, political leaders' beliefs and motives provide them with a map for charting their course. . . .

With regard to decision style and interpersonal style, we make an assumption that a political leader will generally engage in similar stylistic behavior regardless of arena. Thus, political leaders' preferred methods of making personal decisions and interacting with others will carry over to their political behavior. Style is probably one of the first differences, for example, noted when heads of government change as the new leader tries to make himself comfortable in his role. One head of state may focus foreign policy-making within his own office, while his predecessor may have been willing to let the bureaucracy handle all but problems of crisis proportions. One head of state may be given to rhetoric in the foreign policy arena; his predecessor may have wanted action. Moreover, the bureaucracy tends to adjust to changes in style from one chief executive to the next hoping to minimize differences between itself and the chief executive. The result may be to accentuate the stylistic predilections of high level decision makers. In turn, the policy begins to reflect the stylistic preferences of these high level policy makers.

Given this description of the types of personal characteristics that will affect foreign policy and how they will affect it, what kinds of foreign policy would we expect from political leaders with the six characteristics under study here? In addition to aggressive and conciliatory behavior, what foreign policy behaviors will such leaders urge that their governments consider? If we examine the dynamics of the traits associated with the aggressive leader, we find a need to manipulate and control others, little ability to consider a range of alternatives, suspiciousness of others' motives, a high interest in maintaining national identity and sovereignty, and a distinct willingness to initiate action. Extrapolating from

these dynamics to foreign policy behavior, the characteristics are suggestive of a foreign policy which is independent in style and content. Such leaders will seek to maintain their nation's individuality, to keep their nations as much as possible apart from the other nations in the international system, since extensive contact with other nations may lead to dependence on these nations. They will urge their governments to be suspicious of the motives of leaders of other nations. When interaction is necessary, they expect it to be on their nations' terms.

Contrast the personal dynamics for the aggressive leader with those for the leader who has been found to be generally conciliatory. The personal characteristics of the conciliatory leader indicate a need to establish and maintain friendly relationships with others, an ability to consider a wide range of alternatives, little suspiciousness of others' motives, no overriding concern with the maintenance of national identity and sovereignty, and little interest in initiating action. These dynamics suggest a more participatory foreign policy. Such leaders are likely to be interested in having their nations interact with other nations, in learning what other nations have of value for their nation and find valuable about their nation, and in seeking a wide range of alternative solutions to problems jointly plaguing their nation and other nations. They will probably keep attuned to what is going on in international relations, being sensitive and responsive to this environment. In effect, these leaders will attempt to facilitate their nations' participation in the international system.

What we are suggesting by this discussion is that the personal characteristics under study interrelate to form a personal orientation to behavior or a general way of responding to one's environment. This personal orientation is transformed by the head of government into a general orientation to foreign affairs. By knowing a head of government's orientation to foreign affairs, one knows his predispositions when faced with a foreign policy-making task—how he will define the situation and the style of behavior he will be likely to emphasize. Heads of government with the personal characteristics in the present study are thought to be predisposed toward either an independent or participatory orientation to foreign affairs depending on how the characteristics interrelate. Traits that have characterized the aggressive political leader in previous research are expected to interrelate to form an independent orientation to foreign affairs and to lead to foreign policy behaviors which emphasize an independent foreign policy in style and content. On the other hand, traits that have characterized the conciliatory political leader in previous research are expected to interrelate to form a participatory orientation to foreign affairs and to lead to foreign policy behaviors which emphasize participation with other governments in style and content.

As the writer has proposed elsewhere (Hermann, 1976, 1978, 1979; Hermann and Hermann, 1979), the personal characteristics and orientations of heads of government examined in this research are likely to have more impact on a government's foreign policy under some circumstances than under others. We will explore two such conditions in this study—one that is hypothesized to enhance the effect of leader personality on foreign policy behavior and one that is thought to diminish such effects. The two variables we will study here are interest in foreign affairs and training in foreign affairs. Interest in foreign affairs will enhance the effect of a political leader's characteristics on government policy, whereas training in foreign affairs will diminish such an effect.

Interest in foreign affairs acts as a motivating force. An important consequence of interest in foreign policy will be increased participation in the making of foreign policy. The head of government will want to be consulted on decisions and to be kept informed about what is happening in foreign affairs. Moreover, the reasons behind a head of government's interest in foreign policy— he places value on good external relations, he fears an enemy takeover, he sees it as a way of gaining re-election—may predetermine the course of action he will seek to implement. With little interest in foreign affairs, the head of government is likely to delegate authority to other people, negating the effect of his personality on the resultant policy except as his spokesman's personality is similar to his own.

With regard to training in foreign affairs, the head of government with little or no training has no expertise on which to call. He has no previous experience to suggest possible alternatives or plans of action. As a result, his natural predispositions come into play. The head of government with training, on the other hand, has some knowledge about what will succeed and fail in the international arena. As a consequence of his experience, he has very likely developed certain styles and strategies for dealing with a foreign policy situation that are particular to the issue and/or target nation involved. There is less dependence on his underlying predispositions.

MEASUREMENT OF PERSONAL CHARACTERISTICS . . .

Determining Orientations to Foreign Affairs

In the conceptual scheme presented earlier, we hypothesized that . . . personal characteristics . . . interrelate to form two orientations to foreign affairs that affect the content and style of foreign policy behavior. To test this hypothesis most directly, two composite measures were created. The first, which we call characteristic of the independent leader, consisted of being high in nationalism, high in belief in one's own ability to control events, high in need for power, low in conceptual complexity, and high in distrust of others. The second, which is characteristic of the participatory leader, consisted of being low in nationalism, low in belief in one's own ability to control events, high in need for affiliation, high in conceptual complexity, and low in distrust of others.[2] To determine these two composites, the heads of governments' scores on each of the six personal characteristics were ranked. For the independent composite, ranks for nationalism, belief in one's own ability to control events, need for power, conceptual complexity, and distrust in others were summed. For the participatory composite, ranks for nationalism, belief in one's own ability to control events, need for affiliation, conceptual complexity, and distrust in others were summed. . . .

Interest in Foreign Affairs

Interest in foreign affairs refers to the amount of concern or attention which a head of government directs toward foreign policy-making. Is foreign policy a "passion"? Or does the head of government only become a participant in foreign policy-making on specific issues? Perhaps the head of government only deals with foreign affairs when forced to by circumstances.

Interest in foreign affairs was operationalized in this study by noting the percentage of foreign policy events in which a head of government participated while in office. Higher interest was indicated by a higher rate of participation. One of the variables in the CREON foreign policy events data set on which each event is coded notes if the head of government participated in the event or if his/her approval was probably needed for the action to take place (see Hermann et al., 1973: 102). The number of foreign policy events falling into these two categories for each head of government during his/her tenure in office formed the numerator for calculating rate of participation. Total number of foreign policy events during a head of government's term in office was the denominator. For most of the analyses in which we will examine interest, the variable will be dichotomized at the median denoting heads of government with high and low interest in foreign affairs.

Training in Foreign Affairs

By training in foreign affairs is meant having held some political or governmental position that would give one knowledge about foreign affairs and foreign policy-making. To determine amount of training for the heads of government in the present sample, a search was made of reference sources such as *Statesman's Year-Book* as well as autobiographies and biographies. All past political and governmental positions were noted. From this biographical record on the heads of government, the number of years each had held positions involving foreign affairs (e.g., foreign or defense minister, ambassador, in foreign ordefense ministry, representative to UNESCO or the Common Market) was determined. The number of years the head of government had held his/her present office was also counted in the measure of training on the assumption that such a position was a good training ground in foreign affairs. A training score was calculated by finding what percentage of the years a head of government had been in politics involved positions inforeign affairs and foreign policy-making. . . .

Relationships among Personal Characteristics, Orientations, Interest, and Training

. . . The correlations . . . indicate that the two orientations are significantly inversely related as would be expected from the nature of their construction. All five of the personal characteristics that were used in determining the independent orientation are significantly related to this composite measure in the directions suggested by the conceptual framework. Such is not the case for the participatory orientation. Nationalism, belief in one's own ability to control events, and distrust of others contribute more to this orientation than conceptual complexity and need for affiliation. The reason why conceptual complexity and need for affiliation make a smaller contribution may lie in the significant inverse relationship between these two personal characteristics, contrary to the conceptual framework.

Several other correlations among the personal characteristics included in the orientations are noteworthy. Nationalism, need for power, and distrust of others are all three significantly interrelated. At least for this sample of heads of government, the nationalist appears to be high in need for power and distrust of others.

. . . The significant correlations with the interest variable suggest that the head of government with an independent orientation was more interested in foreign affairs than the head of government with the participatory orientation. Moreover, the more conceptually complex the leader was, the lower his interest in foreign affairs. For training, only the correlation with belief in one's own ability to control events is significant. The more highly trained the head of government was, the lower his/her belief in the ability to control events. Experience may lead to a realization of the range of variables which affect foreign policy over which one can have little control.

RELATIONSHIPS BETWEEN PERSONAL CHARACTERISTICS AND FOREIGN POLICY BEHAVIOR

Having suggested how the personal characteristics are expected to affect foreign policy behavior and having operationalized the personal characteristics employed in this research, let us examine how the personal characteristics do, in fact, relate to foreign policy behavior. The specific foreign policy behaviors included in this study are professed orientation to change, independence/interdependence of action, commitment, affect, and environmental feedback. . . . In what follows, we will focus on each foreign policy behavior by itself, further explicating conceptually how the personal characteristics are expected to affect it and showing the relationships between it and the personal characteristics that were found.

Professed Orientation to Change

By professed orientation to change we mean a government's public posture regarding the need for change in the international environment. Do the policy-makers of a nation express little or no need for change in the international arena, or do they argue that short-term and/or long-term changes are in order? Professed orientation to change is measured by noting what percentage of the time goal statements are present in the foreign policy events of a nation during a head of government's tenure in office. Goal refers here to a desired future condition. If goal statements are generally absent, the policy-makers of a nation are considered as professing little or no need for change in the international environment, i.e., as affirming the status quo. If goal statements are generally present, the policy-makers of a nation are viewed as professing a need for change in the international environment.

How is professed orientation to change probably affected by the independent and participatory orientations to foreign affairs examined in the present study? In describing the independent orientation, we noted the importance of maintaining the status quo, that is, the importance of maintaining national individuality and the power base the head of government now has. Change is anathema to such leaders, since there is always the chance of losing what has already been gained in power and position. In some sense, heads of government with independent orientations are present or "now" oriented rather than future-oriented. They are concerned with the realities of day-to-day politics as opposed to future states or conditions. Moreover, independent leaders are secretive. Such leaders cannot be held to

what they have not stated publicly; they maintain a certain maneuverability because their positions are not a matter of public record. Thus, heads of government with independent orientations are unlikely to urge their governments publicly to propose changes in the international arena.

On the other hand, heads of government with participatory orientations are likely publicly to advocate change in the international environment. One way for such heads of government to participate in the international arena is to make public their goals. Through such public goal statements, they can solicit support from and initiate relations with other nations. In effect, they signal the direction in which they are moving and their intentions to other nations through public goal statements. . . .

The correlations . . . are in the predicted direction for the participatory orientation for all but heads of government with much training. For the independent orientation, the correlations are only in the predicted direction for heads of government with low interest and heads of government with little training. The correlations are significant for both orientations for heads of government with little training. For the independent orientation, the correlation for heads of government with much training is significant but in the reverse direction from that predicted. In effect, the results . . . suggest support for the hypotheses for heads of government with little training in foreign affairs and the opposite of the hypotheses for heads of government with much training in foreign affairs. Training may afford the heads of government with a participatory orientation a wider variety of ways of signaling intent than the use of goal statements; it may teach the heads of government with an independent orientation ways of suggesting change that do not necessarily commit them publicly to a particular policy (e.g., by proposing the need for change in other nations than their own).

Looking at the individual characteristics, we note support for the hypotheses for nationalism, need for power, and need for affiliation under various of the interest and training conditions. For nationalism and need for power, the correlations are significant and in the predicted direction for heads of government with low interest and for heads of government with little training. On the contrary, for need for affiliation, the correlations are significant and in the predicted direction for heads of government with high interest and for heads of government with much training. Conceptual complexity was related in the opposite direction from that predicted foreach group of heads of government. High conceptual complexity was related to little professed need for change.

Independence/Interdependence of Action

Independence/interdependence of action is concerned with the amount of autonomy that a nation maintains in its foreign policy actions. At issue are whether foreign policy actions are taken alone or in concert with other nations, and whether such actions are initiated by a nation or in response to a prior stimulus directed at the nation. Actions taken alone and initiated by the nation are considered to denote independence of action, while actions taken in concert with other nations and in response to a prior direct stimulus denote interdependence of action. . . .

In some sense, this foreign policy behavior gets at the essence of the con-

ceptual difference between the independent and participatory orientations toward foreign affairs. Heads of government with the independent orientation are likely to want to act alone and to initiate behavior on their own terms. They will seek to maintain autonomy, that is, to control their own national behavior. Such leaders believe that they can have some effect on events. Moreover, they distrust the leaders of other nations. These two traits coupled with a desire to maintain their own and their nation's position and power base suggest an emphasis on independence of action. Heads of government with a participatory orientation, on the other hand, are probably willing to relinquish some autonomy or control over their own behavior. An individual (or nation) can benefit from working with rather than against others. Building on their low level of distrust in others, heads of government with a participatory orientation perceive little harm in acting in consort with others if by doing so they can achieve an objective. Moreover, such leaders are likely to be sensitive to stimulation from the environment, picking up on behaviors directed toward them. . . .

The relationships for the participatory orientation may be low, because the emphasis for such heads of government is less on elicited behavior than on acting with other nations. In other words, heads of government with a participatory orientation may be interested in initiating behavior but prefer to include other nations in their activity. . . . The percentage of such actions during a head of government's tenure in office was the dependent variable. Examining these relationships, we note that one for the participatory orientation is significant and two approach significance. These correlations occur for the sample of heads of government as a whole, for the heads of government with low interest, and for the heads of government with little training. Moreover, all five of the individual personal characteristics involved in the participatory composite have correlations with initiative-multilateral actions that are significant or that approach significance.

Commitment

A commitment is a behavior which limits a government's future capacity to act either because it uses up physical resources, involves pledges of resources in the future, or involves a statement of intent to use resources for a specific purpose. In other words, commitments reduce the pool of available resources fordealing with other problems or generate expectations that limit future behavior. . . .

By limiting future behavior, commitments reduce the independence and maneuverability of a government's policy makers. They are no longer completely in charge of their nation's behavior. As such, commitments are seen as inappropriate foreign policy behavior by heads of government with an independent orientation. Reducing control over one's resources and putting constraints on one's ability to act, particularly if it involves trusting leaders in other nations—this is anathema to independent heads of government. They are interested in increasing their power and maintaining their nations' separateness, not limiting their power and reducing their nation's separateness. On the other hand, the heads of government with a participatory orientation are willing to commit their nations' resources, expecting to gain resources from others that are beneficial to their nations in return. They have no predisposition to distrust the leaders of other nations, figuring cooperation may increase their gain in the longrun. Moreover, heads of government with a participatory orientation are less concerned about maintaining their nations' separateness; they are willing to become somewhat dependent on other nations, if such dependencies are built on supportive relationships. . . .

One of the individual personal characteristics, distrust of others, is significantly related to commitment for the same three groups of heads of government as the independent orientation. As expected, the more distrusting these heads of government were of others, the fewer commitments their nations made. Need for affiliation changes the direction of the relationship with commitment depending on which group of heads of government is analyzed. Need for affiliation is positively related—the predicted direction—when the head of government's interest is low and when training is limited, negatively related when the head of government's interest is high and when there is much training. Interest and training may provide the head of government whose need for affiliation is high with less extreme strategies than commitment for maintaining positive relations with other nations.

Affect

Affect denotes the feelings ranging from friendliness to hostility which policymakers of one nation express toward the policies, actions, or government of another nation. . . .

Direction and intensity of affect are expected to relate to scores on the independent and participatory orientations in the following manner. Because heads of government with an independent orientation to foreign affairs are interested in emphasizing the differences between their nation and other nations and because they generally distrust the leaders of other nations, they are likely to express negative affect toward other nations, being fairly intense in the expression of such affect. By using such techniques, heads of government with an independent orientation accentuate their separateness and the fact that they maintain control over their own behavior. They move on their own terms; they are their own bosses. Heads of government with a participatory orientation, on the contrary, have as a basic premise of their world-view a desire to maintain friendly relations with others. Moreover, they do not distrust others nor are they overly concerned with the differences between their nation and other nations. Such heads of government are likely to emphasize the positive in their relations with other nations and to not "rock the boat" by being too intense in the expression of their affect. They perceive that consistent, positive reinforcement to others enables them to participate freely in the international environment. A "low, positive profile" keeps channels and opinions open.

. . . The results suggest support for the hypotheses for both orientations. For all groups of heads of government, the correlations are in the predicted direction. Moreover, sixteen of the twenty correlations for the orientations are significant or approach significance. With regard to the individual characteristics, all but belief in one's own ability to control events have correlations in the predicted direction that are significant or approach significance with these two affect variables.

The largest number of significant or near significant correlations occur for nationalism and distrust of others.

Feedback from the Environment

How do other nations respond to the foreign policy behavior of a specific nation, i.e., what is the nature of their feedback? Is it favorable or unfavorable, accepting or rejecting? . . .

Our hypotheses for feedback follow from the previous hypotheses on affect. Heads of government with an independent orientation to foreign affairs are prone to actions that are negative in tone and fairly intense. Such behavior is likely to elicit mirror image behavior from other nations if they bother to respond at all. Because more independent heads of government do not develop relations with other nations and seek to maintain an independent status in the international arena, it may be easy to reject their behavior. There are fewer strings attached and probably fewer repercussions to such a rejection than would be the case with a more involved nation. Turning this rationale around, we expect more positive feedback for heads of government with a participatory orientation. Such heads of government tend to be positive toward other nations, eliciting positive behavior in return. Moreover, heads of government with a participatory orientation actively involve their nations in the international system so that a rejection of their nation's behavior may have repercussions not desired by the responding nation. If any feedback is to be given, positive feedback is probably safest.

. . . For all the groups of heads of government except those with high interest in foreign affairs, the correlations were in the predicted direction for the independent and participatory orientations. Of those eight relations in the predicted direction, one was significant and four approached significance. The significant correlation occurred for heads of government with low interest in foreign affairs.

Only need for affiliation in the individual characteristics does not have a correlation with feedback that is significant or approaches significance. For nationalism, need for power, and distrust of others, the correlations are reversed in sign for heads of government with low and high interest and for heads of government with little and much training. The correlations are all negative, as hypothesized, for heads of government with low interest and for heads of government with little training, but they are positive for heads of government with high interest and for heads of government with much training. Interest and training may increase the foreign policy stature of heads of government with these characteristics and/or make them more adept in foreign policy-making so that positive rather than negative feedback is directed toward their nations.

CONCLUSIONS

The research reported in this article has examined how six personal characteristics of heads of government interact to form two orientations to foreign affairs. Based on a set of premises about the ways heads of government with these two orientations will urge their governments to act, we have related the two orientations to six foreign policy behaviors. . . .

The results suggest the need to reconceptualize the impact of interest in foreign affairs on the relationship between personal characteristics and for-

eign policy behavior. Much like the lack of training in foreign affairs, low interest appears to provide heads of government with little to tap but their predispositions when they must make a foreign policy decision. With high interest in foreign affairs, the heads of government have probably read about, discussed, and formulated positions on foreign policy issues before taking office, and, after taking office, have kept themselves informed on problems in the foreign policy arena. They have developed some basis on which to make a decision other than their predispositions. Interest, like training, appears to increase the range of activities which heads of government can consider in dealing with foreign affairs. Instead of relying on strategies and styles dictated by their personal orientations, interested heads of government have a choice of several ways of acting and some knowledge of the probable outcomes when these alternative strategies and styles are used. Interested heads of government have a broader repertoire of possible behaviors.

Before leaving this discussion of interest and training, we should note that we learned as much about the particular foreign policy variables examined in this research by focusing on the sample of heads of government as a whole as from looking at the effects of interest and training in foreign affairs. The numbers of correlations with $p < 10$ are virtually the same for the whole sample as for those heads of government with little interest or with little training. In other words, the relationships between these personal characteristics and foreign policy behaviors tend to show up without taking such mediating variables as training or interest in foreign affairs into account. However, a closer examination of the correlations indicates that they are stronger—the personal characteristics account for a larger percentage of the variance in the foreign policy behaviors—for heads of government with little interest or with little training in foreign affairs than for the whole sample of heads of government. . . . Specifying the conditions under which personal characteristics can affect foreign policy behavior appears to enhance the explanatory power of the personal characteristics.

We have examined in this study the direct effects of leaders' personal characteristics on their governments' foreign policy behavior and several conditions that appear to enhance this direct effect. Many other conditioning variables can be posited (see Hermann, 1976, 1978; Hermann and Hermann, 1979). Some other possible enhancing conditions involve being a predominant as opposed to nonpredominant leader (i.e., having a disproportionately large amount of power in the government), being part of a cohesive as opposed to a fragmented regime, facing an ambiguous as opposed to a structured situation, and having to deal with a small as opposed to a large bureaucracy. An important objective of the CREON Project, of which this study is a part, is the building of integrative links among these types of variables in explaining governments' foreign policy be-

havior. We are interested in developing models showing how national attributes, regime factors, decision structures and processes, situational variables, and external relationships interrelate in affecting foreign policy activities (see Salmore et al., 1978). The present study suggests that the personal characteristics and orientations to foreign affairs of political leaders are worth including in this integrative effort. It is, however, only a first step in the process of trying to explain why governments do certain things in the foreign policy arena.

NOTES

1. The conceptual scheme sketched here appears in a more detailed form in Hermann (1978).
2. The reader will note that although we are examining six personal characteristics, each of the orientations is composed of five characteristics. The orientations differ in motivating forces. Need for power is included in the independent orientation but not in the participatory orientation; need for affiliation is included in the participatory orientation but not in the independent orientation. It was unclear conceptually that need for affiliation was relevant to an independent orientation or that need for power was relevant to a participatory orientation; thus, both motives were not included in each orientation.

REFERENCES

Atkinson, J. W. (1958) *Motives in Fantasy, Action, and Society.* New York: Litton.
Axelrod, R. (1976) *Structure of Decision: The Cognitive Maps of Political Elites.* Princeton, NJ: Princeton Univ. Press.
Barber, J. D. (1972) *The Presidential Character.* Englewood Cliffs, NJ: Prentice-Hall.
——— (1965) *The Lawmakers.* New Haven, CT: Yale Univ. Press.
Callahan, P., L. P. Brady, and M. G. Hermann (1981) *Events, Behaviors, and Policies: Measuring the Foreign Activities of National Governments.* Columbus: Ohio State Univ. Press.
Christie, R. and F. L. Geis (1970) *Studies in Machiavellianism.* New York: Academic.

Crow, W. J. and R. C. Noel (1977) "An experiment in simulated historical decision making," pp. 385–405 in M. G. Hermann (ed.), *A Psychological Examination of Political Leaders.* New York: Free Press.

De Rivera, J. H. (1968) *The Psychological Dimension of Foreign Policy.* Columbus, OH: Merrill.

Driver, M. J. (1977) "Individual differences as determinants of aggression in the Internation Simulation," pp. 337–353 in M. G. Hermann (ed.), *A Psychological Examination of Political Leaders.* New York: Free Press.

Eckhardt, W. and R. K. White (1967) "A test of the mirror-image hypothesis: Kennedy and Khrushchev." *J. of Conflict Resolution* 11: 325–332.

Falkowski, L. (1978) *Presidents, Secretaries of State, and Crises in U.S. Foreign Relations: A Model and Predictive Analysis.* Boulder, CO: Westview.

Frank, J. D. (1968) *Sanity and Survival.* New York: Random House.

George, A. L. (1969) "The 'operational code': a neglected approach to the study of political leaders and decision-making." *Int. Studies* Q. 13: 190–222.

Guterman, S. S. (1970) *The Machiavellians.* Lincoln: Univ. of Nebraska Press.

Hermann, C. F., M. A. East, M. G. Hermann, B. G. Salmore, and S. A. Salmore (1973) "CREON: A foreign events data set." *Sage Professional Papers in International Studies* Vol. 2, No. 02-024. Beverly Hills, CA: Sage.

Hermann, M. G. (1979) "Who becomes a political leader? Some societal and regime influences on selection of a head of state," in L. Falkowski (ed.), *Psychological Models in International Politics.* Boulder, CO: Westview.

—— (1978) "Effects of personal characteristics of leaders on foreign policy," pp. 49–68 in M. A. East, S. A. Salmore, and C. F. Hermann (eds.), *Why Nations Act.* Beverly Hills, CA: Sage.

—— (1977) "Some personal characteristics related to foreign aid voting of congressmen," pp. 313–334 in M. G. Hermann (ed.), *A Psychological Examination of Political Leaders.* New York: Free Press.

—— (1976) "Circumstances under which leader personality will affect foreign policy: some propositions," pp. 326–333 in J. N. Rosenau (ed.), *In Search of Global Patterns.* New York: Free Press.

—— (1974) "Leader personality and foreign policy behavior," pp. 201–234 in J. N. Rosenau (ed.), *Comparing Foreign Policies: Theories, Findings, and Methods.* New York: Sage-Halsted.

—— and C. F. Hermann (1979) "The interaction of situations, political regimes, decision configurations, and leader personalities in interpreting foreign policy: leader effects when controlling for selected variables." Presented at the Moscow International Political Science Association Congress, August 12–18.

Hofstadter, R. (1965) *The Paranoid Style in American Politics and Other Essays.* New York: Knopf.

Holsti, O. R. (1977) "The 'operational code' as an approach to the analysis of belief systems." Report to the National Science Foundation.

—— (1967) "Cognitive dynamics and images of the enemy." *J. of Int. Affairs* 21: 16–39.

Jervis, R. (1976) *Perception and Misperception in International Politics.* Princeton, NJ: Princeton Univ. Press.

Johnson, I. (1977) "The operational code of Senator Frank Church," pp. 82–119 in M. G. Hermann (ed.), *A Psychological Examination of Political Leaders.* New York: Free Press.

Levine, R. A. (1966) *Dreams and Deeds: Achievement Motivation in Nigeria.* Chicago: Univ. of Chicago Press.

Osgood, C. E., and L. Anderson (1957) "Certain relations among experienced contingencies, associative structure, and contingencies in encoded messages." *Amer. J. of Psychology* 70: 411–420.

Rutherford, B. M. (1966) "Psychopathology, decision-making, and political involvement." *J. of Conflict Resolution* 10: 387–407.

Salmore, S. A., M. G. Hermann, C. F. Hermann, and B. G. Salmore (1978) "Conclusion: toward integrating the perspectives," pp. 191–210 in M. A. East, S. A. Salmore, and C. F. Hermann (eds.), *Why Nations Act.* Beverly Hills, CA: Sage Publications.

Shneidman, E. S. (1963) "The logic of politics," pp. 177–199 in L. Arons and M. A. May (eds.), *Television and Human Behavior.* Englewood Cliffs, NJ: Prentice-Hall.

Thordarson, B. (1972) *Trudeau and Foreign Policy: A Study in Decision-Making.* Toronto: Oxford Univ. Press.

Tucker, R. C. (1965) "The dictator and totalitarianism." *World Politics* 17: 55–83.

Verba, S. (1969) "Assumptions of rationality and non-rationality in models of the international system," pp. 217–231 in J. N. Rosenau (ed.), *International Politics and Foreign Policy.* New York: Free Press.

Winter, D. G. (1973) *The Power Motive.* New York: Free Press.

—— and A. J. Stewart (1977) "Content analysis as a technique for assessing political leaders," pp. 28–61 in M. G. Hermann (ed.), *A Psychological Examination of Political Leaders.* New York: Free Press.

QUESTIONS

1. According to Hermann, what impact does training (or the lack of training) have on the foreign policy behavior of a leader?

2. What evidence does Hermann provide to support her contention that the personal characteristics of leaders affect their governments' foreign policy behavior?

40.   Perception and Misperception in International Politics

Robert Jervis

In this introductory chapter to his book *Perception and Misperception in International Politics* (1976), Robert Jervis examines each of the generally accepted levels of analysis for decision making—the international system, the state system, the bureaucracy, and the individual. (In this textbook, we use only three levels of analysis.) He argues that scholars have ignored the influence that perception and image have on each of these levels, especially that of the individual leader. In addition, Jervis critiques each of the levels of analysis and concludes that the perception of the individual leader needs to be examined further.

Robert Jervis is the Adlai E. Stevenson professor of political science and a member of the Institute of War and Peace Studies at Columbia University. His other works include *The Illogic of American Nuclear Strategy* (1984), as well as numerous contributions to various political science journals.

Do Perceptions Matter?

Before discussing the causes and consequences of the ways in which decision-makers draw inferences from the world, we must ask a preliminary question: do the decision-makers' perceptions matter? This is an empirical question. Logic permits us to distinguish between the "psychological milieu" (the world as the actor sees it) and the "operational milieu" (the world in which the policy will be carried out) and to argue that policies and decisions must be mediated by statesmen's goals, calculations, and perceptions.[1] But it does not follow from this that we must deal with these intervening variables in order to understand and predict behavior. This is not an uncommon claim:

> One may describe particular events, conditions, and interactions between states without necessarily probing the nature and outcome of the processes through which state action evolves. However, and the qualification is crucial, if one wishes to probe the "why" questions underlying the events, conditions, and interaction patterns which rest upon state action, then decision-making analysis is certainly necessary. We would go so far as to say *that the "why" questions cannot be answered without analysis of decision-making.*[2]

But theory and explanation need not fill in all the links between cause and effect. Indeed, this is impossible. One can always ask for the links between the links. High density theories have no privileged status; they are not automatically illuminating or fruitful.[3] It is true that re-creating a decision-maker's goals, calculations, and perceptions is a satisfying method of explaining his behavior because the scholar, sharing as he does the decision-maker's characteristics of being a thinking, goal-seeking person, can easily say: "If that is the way the statesman saw the situation, it is no wonder that he acted as he did." But the comfort we feel with this form of explanation should not blind us to the fact that, unless there are significant variations in the ways people see the world that affect how they act, we need not explore decision-making in order to explain foreign policy. Most case studies assume that the details presented significantly affected the outcomes. This may not be true, however. "Pleikus are streetcars," McGeorge Bundy said in explaining that the Viet Cong attack on the American installation in February 1965 had affected only the timing of the American bombing of North Vietnam.[4] If you are waiting for one, it will come along. The specifics of the triggering event cannot explain the outcome because so many probable events could have substituted for it. To understand the American policy of bombing the North we should not examine the attack on Pleiku. Had it not occurred, something else would have happened that would have permitted the same response. Logic alone cannot tell us that a similar claim about the decision-making process is invalid: the way people perceive others and make decisions only marginally influences outcomes. So we must seek empirical evidence on the question: do the important explanatory variables in international relations involve decision-making? In terms of perceptions this can be separated into two subsidiary questions:"are important differences in policy preferences traceable to differences in decision-makers' perceptions of their environments?" and "are there important differences between reality and shared or common perceptions?"[5] Detailed affirmative answers to these questions will emerge in this book, but a brief general discussion is in order here.

These questions raise the familiar level of analysis problem. Although it has been much debated, agreement is lacking not only on the substantive dispute but even on the number of levels. Arnold Wolfers proposes two, Kenneth Waltz three, and James Rosenau five.[6] To fill in the sequence, we will discuss four. One is the level of decision-making, the second is the level of the bureaucracy, the third is that of the nature of the state and the workings of domestic politics, and the fourth focuses on the international environment.[7] Which level one focuses on is not arbitrary and is not a matter of taste—it is the product of beliefs (or often hunches) about the nature of the variables that influence the phenomena that concern one. To restate the first question in terms of the level of analysis problem, we need not adopt a decision-making approach if all states behave the same way in the same objective situation, if all states of the same kind (i.e. with the same internal characteristics and politics) behave the same way in the same objective situation, or if state behavior is determined by bureaucratic routines and interests.

Although the empirical questions are central here, we should also note that the level of analysis problem has important moral implications. When all people would respond the same way to a given situation, it is hard to praise or blame the decision-maker. Thus, those accused of war crimes will argue that their behavior did not differ from others who found themselves in the same circumstances. And the prosecution will charge, as it did against Tojo and his colleagues, that, "These defendants were not automatons; they were not replaceable cogs in a machine. . . . It was theirs to choose whether their nation would lead an honored life . . . or . . . would become a symbol of evil throughout the world. They made their choice. For this choice they must bear the guilt." Similarly, if all nations follow similar courses of action, one cannot argue that some deserve to be branded as immorally aggressive. Thus in 1918 Bethmann-Hollweg rebutted those who blamed Germany for the war by pointing to the "general disposition towards war in the world . . . how else explain the senseless and impassioned zeal which allowed countries like Italy, Rumania and even America, not originally involved in the war, no rest until they too had immersed themselves in the bloodbath?"[8]

The three non-decision-making levels assert the importance of various aspects of the objective situation or the actor's role.[9] They say that if we know enough about the setting—international, national, or bureaucratic—we can explain and predict the actor's behavior. An interesting sidelight is that if other actors believed that the setting is crucial they would not need to scrutinize the details of the state's recent behavior or try to understand the goals and beliefs held by the state's decision-makers.[10] It would be fruitless and pointless to ask what the state's intentions are if its behavior is determined by the situation in which it finds itself. Instead, observers would try to predict how the context will change because this will tell them what the state's response will be. Decision-makers could then freely employ their powers of vicarious identification and simply ask themselves how they would act if they were in the other's shoes. They would not have to worry about the possibility that the other might have values and beliefs that differed from theirs. It is interesting, although not decisive, to note that decision-makers rarely feel confident about using this method. They usually believe both that others may not behave as they would and that the decision-makers within the other state differ among themselves. So they generally seek a great deal of information about the views of each significant person in the other country.

Of course it is unlikely that there is a single answer to the question of which level is most important. Rather than one level containing the variables that are most significant for all problems, the importance of each level may vary from one issue area to another.[11] Furthermore, which level of analysis is the most important may be determined by how rich and detailed an answer we are seeking. The environment may influence the general outline of the state's policy but not its specific responses. Thus it can be argued that, while decision-making analysis is needed to explain why World War I broke out in August 1914, the external situation would have led the states to fight sooner or later. Or the importance of variables at each level may vary with the stages of a decision. For example, domestic politics may dictate that a given event be made the occasion for a change in policy; bargaining within the bureaucracy may explain what options are presented to the national leaders; the decision-maker's predisposition

could account for the choice that was made; and the interests and routines of the bureaucracies could explain the way the decision was implemented. And the same variable may have different effects at different stages of the decision-making process—for example, conflicts among subordinates may increase the variety of information and the number of opportunities for decision that the top decision-maker gets, but may simultaneously decrease his ability to see that his decisions are faithfully implemented.

The importance of variables at one level can also vary with the state of variables at other levels. Rosenau suggests that the international environment is more important in determining the policy of small states than it is of large ones, and Stanley Hoffmann argues that nuclear weapons and bipolarity have reversed this relationship.[12] More generally, the importance of the other levels decreases if the variables in one level are in extreme states.[13] Thus, maneuvering within the bureaucracy may be more important when the top decision-makers are inexperienced or preoccupied with other matters.[14] And Wolfers argues that states tend to behave the same way when they are faced with extreme danger or extreme opportunity, but that when environmental constraints are less severe there will be differences in behavior that must be explained at the decision-making level. More complex interactions among the levels are also possible. For example, the effect of internal instability on expansionism could vary with the opportunities for success in war. Unstable states may be more prone to aggression than stable ones when the chances of victory are high but might be more cautious than others when their leaders perceive a significant probability of defeat or even of temporary setback. Or the stability of the regime might influence its propensity for aggression, but the nature of the regime (e.g. whether it is democratic or dictatorial) might be more important in explaining how it makes peace.

To deal with all these questions would require another book. Here all I will try to do is to outline the kinds of evidence necessary to establish the validity of simple propositions about the importance of the various levels. In doing so, I will sketch the most extreme arguments for the importance of each level. It is obvious that the questions and arguments could be rephrased in more subtle terms but since I am concerned with the kinds of evidence that the propositions call for the gain in analytical clarity is worth the sacrifice involved in ignoring more complete explanations that combine a multitude of variables at many levels.

The International Environment

To argue that the international environment determines a state's behavior is to assert that all states react similarly to the same objective external situation. Changes in a state's domestic regime, its bureaucratic structure, and the personalities and opinions of its leaders do not lead to changes of policies. Changes in the external situation, however, do alter behavior, even when variables on the other levels remain constant. To test these claims, we would need good measures of all the variables, especially the nature of the objective situation and the state's policies.[15] Even if we had such indicators, we would have to cope with the paucity of the most desired kinds of comparisons. This is easily understood

by glancing at the similar issue in the study of individual behavior—the debate over the relative importance of situation and role versus idiosyncratic variables in determining individual behavior.[16] Because so many people of widely differing backgrounds, personalities, and opinions fill the same role and because the same person fills many different roles, we can try to determine the relative impact of situational and idiosyncratic variables by examining how a person's behavior varies as his role changes and how people of widely differing characteristics perform in similar situations.

It is much harder to make the analogous comparisons in international relations. In only a few international systems do we find many cases in which states play, either simultaneously or consecutively, several roles and in which each role is filled by states that are otherwise quite different. This would occur in a long-lasting system where there were frequent changes in the relations among the actors. Thus each state might at one time be a neutral, a "holder of the balance," a state with aggressive designs, a defender faced by a state whose intentions are difficult to determine, and so on. To a limited degree this test is possible in a balance-of-power system. But it is not available for most other systems, for example the one prevailing since World War II. Most nations have not changed roles, and indeed cannot do so because of such permanent factors as size and geography. The United States can never play the role of a second-ranking state caught between two blocs of greater powers. France can never be the leader of one of two dominant blocs. And while the United States and France may have played roles similar to these in the past, the extensive differences in the situation mean that any differences in response that might be found would not show that roles are unimportant.

COMPULSION IN EXTREME CIRCUMSTANCES?

It is worthwhile to look at cases of the kind that are supposed to show most strongly the influence of external conditions. If there are differences of behavior here, the argument for not ignoring the other levels of analysis will apply a fortiori to a wider domain of cases. Arnold Wolfers argues that, the greater the external compulsion, the greater the homogeneity of behavior and therefore the less the need to study decision-making. In a well-known passage he says: "Imagine a number of individuals, varying widely in their predispositions, who find themselves inside a house on fire. It would be perfectly realistic to expect that these individuals, with rare exceptions, would feel compelled to run toward the exits. . . . Surely, therefore, for an explanation of the rush for the exits, there is no need to analyze the individual decisions that produced it."[17]

But the case is not as clear as this analogy suggests. If a situation were so compelling that all people would act alike, decision-makers would not hesitate nor feel torn among several alternative policies, nor would there be significant debates within the decision-making elite. In fact, key decisions that are easily reached, such as those involving the Truman Doctrine and Marshall Plan, stand out because they are so rare. For despite the implication of Wolfers' proposition that we know when we are faced by extreme danger, just as we can tell when the house is on fire, in fact this question is often bitterly contested. (To say that once decision-makers perceive the fire

they will head for the exits leads us back to decision-making analysis.) For Churchill, the house was burning soon after Hitler took power in Germany; for Chamberlain, this was the case only after March 1939; and for others there never was a fire at all. To some decision-makers, the Soviet Union is a threat to which the United States is compelled to respond. To others the threat passed years ago. Again, to a growing number of scholars it never existed. Similarly, American statesmen see a much greater threat from communism in both Europe and Southeast Asia than do the leaders of our allies. Decision-makers may even agree that their state's existence is threatened but disagree about the source of the threat. This was true, for example, in the United States around the turn of the nineteenth century, when the Federalists believed France so much a menace that they favored war with her. At the same time, the Republicans believed England an equal menace. (It should be noted that this disagreement was rooted as much in differences in values and interests as in divergent empirical analyses of the situation.)

In extreme cases we can specify with some certainty an indicator of the "fire" that all decision-makers will recognize—for example a large armed attack—and we can be relatively certain that the state will react. But even then the objective situation will not determine all aspects of the state's response. There are apt to be several exits from the burning house. Will the state limit the extent of its involvement? What will its war aims be? While the United States may have had no choice but to declare war on Japan after Pearl Harbor, the major decisions that followed were less compelled and require further explanation. For example: the United States decided not to concentrate its energies on the country that had attacked it but to fight Germany first; the war was to be fought with few considerations for the shape of the postwar world; and no compromise with the enemies would be accepted (had the Japanese realized this would be the case, they almost certainly would not have attacked).

Even if all states and all statesmen responded similarly to similar high threats, we have to explain how the threat arose— i.e. why the adversary was so aggressive. In some cases we may be able to do this by reference to the other's objective situation, for example by focusing on the anarchic nature of the international system and the resulting security dilemma . . . . But when this analysis is insufficient, the state (and later scholars) must examine variables at other levels of analysis to establish some of the most important facts about the objective situation that the state faces.

Finally, one cannot prove that the external environment determines the response by simply showing that the decision-makers believed this to be the case. It is not enough to say with Kecskemeti that "In tense war situations, the decision-maker is likely to feel that he is acting from necessity rather than from deliberate choice." Nor is it sufficient to cite Holsti's finding that the decision-makers on both sides in July 1914 felt that they had no choice but to make the decisions they did, or to show that when "Mr. Acheson was advised not to favor the production of the first thermonuclear bomb, he is reported to have declared that its production was a matter of necessity and not of choice: in other words, that he was experiencing 'compulsion.' "[18] The subjective feeling of determinacy is interesting and may lead decision-makers unnecessarily to

restrict their search for alternatives, but it does not show that other decision-makers in the same situation would have felt the same compulsion and acted in the same way. Indeed the theory of cognitive dissonance and other theories of irrational cognitive consistency lead us to expect that decision-makers may avoid psychological conflict by thinking that they had no choice but to act as they did. This also means that, when scholars claim that a situation permitted no policy other than the one that was adopted, it may be that at least part of the reason why the circumstances appear overwhelming in retrospect is that they were claimed to be so by the decision-makers.

These arguments are, of course, far from conclusive. The necessary comparisons have merely been mentioned, not made. But, as we have seen, there are many points at which people can disagree about what the objective situation is or what policies will best cope with it, and there is little evidence for the existence of the homogeneity of behavior that would allow us to ignore everything except the international setting.

DOMESTIC DETERMINANTS

Even if all states do not behave similarly in similar situations, the details of decision-making and images may not be significant. Instead, the state may be the appropriate level of analysis—i.e. variations in decision-makers' policies may be accounted for by variations in social and economic structure and domestic politics of the states they are serving. Wilsonian and Marxist theories are examples of this position. Other theories at this level of analysis argue for the importance of a state's geographical position, its traditions, its national style, or the consequences, often unintended, of domestic conflicts. Extreme formulations hold that the state's internal system determines its foreign policy, while weaker versions claim that foreign policies are a product of both domestic politics and international circumstances.

The forms of the assertions correspond to those discussed in the previous section. States with the same critical internal attributes behave the same way in similar situations—and often behave the same way in the face of significant variations in the environment—and this behavior is different from that displayed by other states with different attributes even when the setting is the same. The latter claim denies the overriding importance of the international environment. Thus while Cold War revisionists stress the importance of America's domestic political and economic needs, others reply that American actions were heavily influenced by external constraints and that her behavior was not peculiarly American or peculiarly capitalist but rather was typical of any great power in such a situation.[19] Because we are concerned with examining the importance of decision-making, we will not treat this part of the argument that deals with conflicts between claims for two other levels of analysis.

If states of the same type behave in the same way, then changes in a state's leadership will not produce significant changes in foreign policy, and we need not examine the images, values, and calculations of individual decision-makers. Unfortunately, claims about continuity in a state's foreign policy are notoriously difficult to judge. We might try to see whether we could deduce changes in the identities of the state's decision-makers from the course of its foreign policy. Could we tell when Democrats replaced Republicans or Conservatives replaced

Labour governments? Scholars used to agree that Stalin's death led to major foreign policy changes, but now even this is in doubt.[20] Before taking office, decision-makers often claim they will introduce new policies. But these promises are often neglected. Eisenhower's foreign policy more closely resembled that of his predecessor than it did his campaign rhetoric. Gladstone pledged himself to avoid immoral and wasteful imperialism, and, although he successfully extricated Britain from some entanglements, he was eventually drawn into commitments similar to those made by Disraeli. And while in 1937 Clement Atlee said that "the foreign policy of a Government is the reflection of its internal policy," when his party took power the foreign secretary declared that "Revolutions do not change geography, and revolutions do not change geographical needs."[21]

Many arguments about the wisdom of policies can be understood in terms of claims about the autonomy of the decision-making level. Those who praise Bismarck's diplomacy claim that, had he continued in office, he would have been able to maintain German security by avoiding the errors of severing Germany's ties to Russia, being forced to rely on Austria, and recklessly antagonizing several powerful countries. The rejoinder is that the dynamics of German domestic society and of the international system would have destroyed Bismarck's handiwork no matter who was in power. The glittering skill of Bismarck's diplomacy could not alter the underlying forces at work. Debates about the origins of the Cold War must deal with the similar question of whether Roosevelt's death changed American policy. Most traditional accounts argue that F.D.R. was coming to an anti-Soviet position and would have acted much as Truman did.

This view is shared by those revisionists who look to the American political and economic system for the roots of foreign policy but is disputed by those who see the Cold War as avoidable. Similarly, those who defend President Kennedy but opposed the war in Vietnam argue that he would not have acted as Johnson did. Those who either favored the war or opposed not only it but also most recent American foreign policies argue that the policies of these—and other—presidents were consistent. While those who supported the war see the determinants as international and those who criticize the general lines of America's postwar policy see the causes as domestic, both argue that few significant differences can be traced to the identity of the president.

These questions are so difficult to resolve partly because the situation facing the new government always differs from that which confronted the old. Kennedy was never forced to choose between defeat in Vietnam and fighting a major war. F.D.R. did not live to see Russia consolidate her hold over East Europe. The questions must then be hypothetical, and the comparisons that underlie our judgments are often strained. This problem can be avoided by using alternative comparisons—by examining the views of members of the elite to see whether they favor the policy that was adopted.[22] Of course disagreement with a policy does not prove that a person would have acted on his views were he in office. His opposition might be rooted in his role in the government, lack of information, freedom from the pressures that accompany holding power, or the belief that opposition is politically expedient. But when these explanations are not satisfactory, internal elite disagreement reveals the limits of the impact of both domestic politics and the international situation.

The Bureaucracy

Even if state behavior cannot be explained by the state's internal politics and external environment, we still may not need to examine the perceptions and calculations of the top decision-makers. The workings of the bureaucracy may determine policy. It is not enough for proponents of this position to show that the state's course of action appears inconsistent and lacks value integration. Such inadequacies can be the product of individual decision-making. As we will show later, normal human behavior often does not fit even a loose definition of rationality. Individuals as well as organizations fail to coordinate their actions and to develop carefully designed strategies. The fact that people must reach decisions in the face of the burdens of multiple goals and highly ambiguous information means that policies are often contradictory, incoherent, and badly suited to the information at hand. Unless we understand this, puzzling state behavior will automatically be seen as the product of either internal bargaining or the autonomous operation of different parts of the government. Thus if we did not know better it would be tempting to argue that the contradictory and erratic behavior displayed by Richard Nixon in Watergate and related matters shows that "Nixon" is not a single individual at all, but rather a title for the set of behaviors that are produced by the interaction of conflicting entities, each pursuing its own narrow interests in ignorance of or indifference to any wider goal of the "general Nixon interest." Similarly, if we were to insist that theories of individual behavior apply only when the actor is following a coherent path guided by his self-interest, we would have to say that Spiro Agnew was an uncoordinated bureaucracy rather than a person because he simultaneously accepted kickbacks and sought the presidency.

Because incoherent policy is insufficient evidence for the importance of bureaucracies, the "pure" theories of this type must make two basic assertions. First, bureaucrats' policy preferences are determined by their positions in the government: "Where you stand is determined by where you sit." The external environment and the nature of the state and domestic politics have only limited and indirect impact on these preferences. Of course if the concept of bureaucratic interest is to be more useful than the concept of national interest, we must be able to specify in advance what the bureaucratic position will be.[23] Even if we cannot do this, it would still be significant if everyone in each unit of the government had the same position on a given issue. If, on the other hand, there is a good deal of disagreement within the organization about the goals to be sought or the means that are appropriate, then we would have to apply decision-making analysis to the bureaucratic level, and so this approach would lose much of its distinctiveness. More importantly, if people in different units share the same policy preferences or if preferences are distributed at random throughout the government, then the first assertion would be undermined.

The second basic claim of theories on this level of analysis is that the state's policies are formed by bureaucratic bargains and routines. Bureaucratic actions either determine the statesman's decision or else implement it in a way that renders the decision largely irrelevant to what is actually done. This point is vital

because, even if bureaucrats' policy preferences were linked to their positions within the government, this would be relatively unimportant unless these preferences explain policy outcomes.[24] But we should note at the start that even if this were true we would have to explore the sources of power of parts of the bureaucracy. If we find, for example, that the military often prevails in conflicts with the organization in charge of arms control, this may be because over a period of years the state's leaders have supported the former more than the latter. Sometimes we can go back some years to find a decisive action that set the guidelines for both the policy and the distribution of power within the bureaucracy. In less dramatic cases the relative strengths of interests represent the standing decision of the decision-makers—and often of wider publics—and their choices among competing policies and values. To the extent that this distribution of power is both important and accounted for by factors outside the bureaucracy, an explanation of specific outcomes in terms of bureaucratic maneuvering will be superficial at best.

Are policy preferences determined by one's role within the government? With the important exception of questions of military hardware and doctrine, the evidence is limited and ambiguous. It is not hard to find examples of units taking consistent and unified stands and political appointees adopting their units' views and thus expressing different opinions depending upon their positions in the government. "General Marshall, while Chief of Staff, opposed the State Department's idea of using aid to promote reforms in the Chinese government. Then, when he became Secretary of State, he defended this very idea against challenges voiced by the new chiefs of Staff." In

"1910, Winston Churchill, as Home Secretary, led the attack upon the demand of McKenna, First Lord of the Admiralty, for more ships; by 1913 they had exchanged offices and each, with equal conviction, maintained the opposite view." When Samuel Hoare was secretary of state for air, he strongly fought against naval control of the Fleet Air Arm; when he later served as first lord of the Admiralty he took the opposite position. When Théophile Delcassé was the minister of colonies in France before the turn of the century, he supported an expedition to the Nile that would give France a lever to use against Britain. As foreign secretary, he sought to recall the adventure.[25]

But not all policy disagreements are traceable to roles. Organizational perspectives and loyalties are less important when issues are unusual rather than routine, necessitate relatively quick decisions, and involve important and generally shared values. Beliefs about the most important issues of foreign policy—those involving war and peace—are usually unrelated to roles. When we look at the major decisions of American foreign policy—those that set the terms for future debates and established the general framework within which policy was then conducted—it does not seem to be true, at least for the top decision-makers, that "where you sit determines where you stand."

In several important cases what is most striking is the degree of unanimity. In the spring of 1947 there was general agreement within the government that massive aid for Europe was needed. Three years later most officials felt that foreign policy considerations argued for large-scale rearmament, although there was a disagreement—which was not tightly connected with bureaucratic interests—over whether domestic political and economic constraints made such a policy feasible. Once the Korean War removed this opposition, government officials were again in general agreement. In other important cases there are basic disputes, but the key to them is not divergent bureaucratic interests. Doves and hawks on Vietnam were to be found in all parts of the American government. Views on whether to take a hard line toward Japan before World War II, and specifically on the crucial issue of embargoing oil and other vital raw materials, were only loosely related to organizational affiliations. The advice that Truman received at the start of the Berlin blockade and the Korean War and most of the differences that emerged in the discussions during the Cuban missile crisis were not predictable by the participants' roles.

In the missile crisis none of the leading officials espoused views that were linked to his position within the government. The Republican secretary of the treasury was concerned about the effects of a "soft" response on the fortunes of the Democratic party in the coming elections; the secretary of defense at first argued that the missiles did not present a major military threat; the secretary of state did not take a strong position and did not pay special attention to the political consequences of various moves; and the attorney general opposed an air strike. (It should also be noted that his view carried great weight not because of his governmental position or independent political resources, but because he was thought to speak for the president.)

The other claim—that policies can be explained by bureaucratic maneuvering—could be supported in either of two ways. First, it could be shown that different parts of the government carry out, or fail to carry out, policies in ways that are consistent with their preferences and routines rather than with the decisions of the national leaders. But the other possible linkage in the second point—the argument that authoritative decisions can be explained by the interaction of bureaucratic stands—raises difficulties that go deeper than the temporary absence of evidence. To verify this claim we must be able to specify the expected relationship between the variety of bureaucratic positions on the one hand and policy outcomes on the other. It is not enough to show that the outcome can be seen as a compromise among views that have been advocated by various parts of the government. Almost any decision could fit this description. The theory must provide generalizations that tell us more exactly what the outcome will be. If the goals of different parts of the bureaucracy are complementary, then presumably each agency will give up its position on the part of the program it cares least about in order to gain a larger voice on those issues that are more important to it. Presumably the success of an organization in conflicts with others is related to its strength (determined independently of outcomes), although as we noted this raises further questions. Still another likely pattern is that the symbols will be given to one side in a bureaucratic conflict and the substance to the other. But much more detail is needed. Furthermore, these generalizations must not involve the values and beliefs that vary with the identity of the top decision-makers, and they must be able to explain how policies change. The latter task poses great problems since bureaucratic structures and interests often remain constant over periods in which policies shift.

Although the paucity of research on this level makes conclusions especially tentative, it is hard to see how any of the major decisions of American foreign policy in recent years could meet this test. The Marshall Plan, the establishment of NATO, the crucial decisions in Korea, the rearmament that followed, the decision to integrate West Germany into West Europe, the New Look in defense, American policy in the Suez crisis, Kennedy's attempt to increase conventional forces in Europe, the major decisions to fight and later withdraw from Vietnam, and crucial choices in the Cuban missile crisis cannot be explained as the outcome of intrabureaucratic conflict. That these decisions combined major elements of positions held within the bureaucracy is hardly surprising because different parts of the bureaucracy serve and represent divergent values that the president seeks to further. Thus what seems to be a clash of bureaucratic interests and stands can often be more fruitfully viewed as a clash among values that are widely held in both the society and the decision-makers' own minds. What embarrasses the theories under consideration here is that, while the decisions listed above did embody some of the preferences that had been articulated by parts of the bureaucracy, they did not combine them in a way that can be predicted by rules of bureaucratic politics. Or, to put the argument more exactly, until we have a theory that specifies how policy is formed out of conflicting bureaucratic perspectives and preferences, we cannot tell whether any given outcome can be explained by this level of analysis. As things stand now, there is no way to explore the extent to which bureaucratic factors cause the outcome because we have no grounds for claiming that a different constellation of bureaucratic interests and forces would have produced a different result or that the outcome would have been different were there no bureaucracies at all.

PERCEPTIONS, REALITY, AND A TWO-STEP MODEL

Our discussion thus far leads to the conclusion that it is often impossible to explain crucial decisions and policies without reference to the decision-makers' beliefs about the world and their images of others. That is to say, these cognitions are part of the proximate cause of the relevant behavior and other levels of analysis cannot immediately tell us what they will be. And even if we found that people in the same situation—be it international, domestic, or bureaucratic—behave in the same way, it is useful to examine decision-making if there are constant differences between the decision-makers' perceptions and reality. In this case all people might react in the same way to the same situation, but this behavior would puzzle an observer because it was self-defeating, based on incorrect beliefs about the world, or generally lacking in a high degree of rationality.[26] Many of the propositions advanced in this book fit in this category: they are generalizations about how decision-makers perceive others' behavior and form judgments about their intentions. These patterns are explained by the general ways in which people draw inferences from ambiguous evidence and, in turn, help explain many seemingly incomprehensible policies. They show how, why, and when highly intelligent and conscientious statesmen misperceive their environments in specified ways and reach inappropriate decisions.

Other propositions in this book deal with cases in which an analysis of decision-making is necessary because people in the same situations behave differently. This is often the case because people differ in their perceptions of the world in general and of other actors in particular. Sometimes it will be useful to ask who, if anyone, was right; but often it will be more fruitful to ask why people differed and how they came to see the world as they did.

The exploration of the images actors hold and the development of the two kinds of propositions discussed above should be seen in the context of a mediated or two-step model.[27] Rather than trying to explain foreign policies as the direct consequence of variables at the three levels of analysis previously discussed, we will examine the actor's perceptions as one of the immediate causes of his behavior. Thus Britain and France felt that their security was endangered by Germany before both world wars. They may have been mistaken in the first case and correct in the second, but both cases can be grouped together in discussing the immediate causes of their responses.

Our understanding of the actor's images and beliefs affects the further question that we ask about that event and the behavior that we expect of the actor in other cases. For example, when it was believed that most American decision-makers had thought that escalation would bring a quick victory in Vietnam, the interesting questions concerned the reasons for this error and the ways by which successive small steps increased the stakes of the conflict. If the decision-makers believed that victory was cheap, it is not surprising that they acted as they did. But by revealing that the decision-makers had a relatively accurate view of the chances of success, the Pentagon Papers and related commentaries have shown that the crucial question is why saving Vietnam was considered important enough to justify the high expected price. This then leads us to look at this and other American actions in terms of beliefs about "domino effects" rather than directing our attention to commitments that develop inadvertently and "quagmires" that trap unwary statesmen. Similarly, the question about Russian behavior raised by the Cuban missile crisis probably is not "What Soviet calculus and risk-taking propensity could explain this bold and dangerous step?" but rather "How could they have so badly misestimated the probable American response?"[28] And previous Soviet behavior can be re-examined to see if it could be explained by similar misperceptions. . . . Actors as well as scholars must engage in these kinds of analyses.

Of course perceptions, and more specifically perceptions of other actors, are not the only decision-making variables that are important. That two actors have the same perceptions does not guarantee that they will adopt the same response. But their responses will often be the same, and, when they are not, it is usually relatively easy to find the causes of the differences. Although people with different images of an adversary may agree on the appropriate response, just as people may favor the same policy for different reasons, this agreement is apt to be short-lived. . . . The roots of many important disputes about policies lie in differing perceptions. And in the frequent cases when the actors do not realize this, they will misunderstand their disagreement and engage in a debate that is unenlightening.

Images, however, are not first causes, and so we will try to find the causes both of common misperceptions and of differences in perceptions. Thus the second step in the model involves relating the images held, if not to reality, then at least to the information available to the actor. How, for example, do statesmen come to develop their images of other actors? What evidence do they pay most attention to? What makes them perceive threat? Under what conditions do they think that the other, although hostile, has only limited objectives? What differentiates legitimate inducements from bribes? What kinds of behavior are most apt to change an established image?

This is not to claim that we will be able to explain nearly all state behavior. As we will discuss in the context of learning from history, propositions about both the causes and the effects of images can only be probabilistic. There are too many variables at work to claim more. In the cases in which we are interested, decision-makers are faced with a large number of competing values, highly complex situations, and very ambiguous information. The possibilities and reasons for misperceptions and disagreements are legion. For these reasons, generalizations in this area are difficult to develop, exceptions are common, and in many instances the outcomes will be influenced by factors that, from the standpoint of most theories, must be considered accidental. Important perceptual predispositions can be discovered, but often they will not be controlling.

NOTES

1. See especially the following works by Harold and Margaret Sprout: *Man-Milieu Relationship Hypotheses in the Context of International Politics* (Princeton, N.J.:

Center of International Studies, 1956); *The Ecological Perspective on Human Affairs* (Princeton, N.J.: Princeton University Press, 1965); and *An Ecological Paradigm for the Study of International Politics* (Princeton, N.J.: Center of International Studies, Princeton University, Research Monograph No. 30, March 1968).

2. "Decision-Making as an Approach to the Study of International Politics," in Richard Snyder, H. W. Bruck, and Burton Sapin, eds., *Foreign Policy Decision-Making* (New York: Free Press, 1962), p. 33. For a similar argument see Fred Greenstein, "The Impact of Personality on Politics: An Attempt to Clear Away Underbrush," *American Political Science Review* 61 (September 1967), 631–33. This is related to the debate about the significance of developmental sequences. For differing views on this question see Herbert Hyman, *Survey Design and Analysis* (Glencoe, Ill.: Free Press, 1955), pp. 254–63, and Travis Hirschi and Hanan Selvin, *Delinquency Research* (New York: Free Press, 1967), pp. 82–85. (The latter book [republished in paperback as *Principles of Survey Analysis*] has much broader relevance than its title indicates and is extremely valuable not only for its explanation of the use of survey research data but for its treatment of general questions of theory, causation, and evidence.) This issue is also related to the broader debate between what Maurice Natanson has called the "Two distinctively opposed philosophic attitudes . . . underlying the social sciences: . . . [the] 'objective' and 'subjective' *Weltanschauungen.*" ("Foreword" in Natanson, ed., *Philosophy of the Social Sciences* [New York: Random House, 1963], p. viii.) This reader is a good introduction to the arguments.

3. Hirschi and Selvin, *Delinquency Research*, p. 38. As Abraham Kaplan puts it, "I would not wish to say that something has been explained only when we have traced the microconnections with their antecedents, or even only when we can believe that such conditions exist." ("Non-causal Explanation," in Daniel Lerner, ed., *Cause and Effect* [New York: Free Press, 1965], p. 146.)

4. Quoted in Townsend Hoopes, *The Limits of Intervention* (New York: McKay, 1969), p. 30.

5. The question of the existence and nature of reality need not be treated here in its profound sense. For our purposes the consensus of later observers usually provides an adequate operational definition of reality.

6. Arnold Wolfers, "The Actors in International Politics," in *Discord and Collaboration* (Baltimore, Md.: Johns Hopkins Press, 1962), pp. 3–24; Kenneth Waltz, *Man, the State, and War* (New York: Columbia University Press, 1959); James Rosenau, "Pre-Theories and Theories of Foreign Policy," in R. Barry Farrell, ed., *Approaches to Comparative and International Politics.* (Evanston, Ill.: Northwestern University Press, 1966), pp. 29–92.

7. We refer to the international environment rather than the international system because we are not dealing with systems theories. Our concern is with explaining specific foreign policies rather than finding general patterns of interaction.

8. Quoted in Robert Butow, *Tojo and the Coming of the War.* (Princeton, N.J.: Princeton University Press, 1961), p. 506; quoted in Egmont Zechlin, "Cabinet versus Economic Warfare in Germany," in H. W. Koch, ed., *The Origins of the First World War* (London: Macmillan & Co., 1972), p. 165.

9. See K. J. Holsti, "National Role Conceptions in the Study of Foreign Policy," *International Studies Quarterly* 14 (September 1970), 233–309.

10. It is interesting to note that in interpersonal perception people tend to overestimate the degree to which the other's behavior is determined by his personality and underestimate the impact of the external situation. See, for example, Gustav Ichheiser, *Appearances and Realities* (San Francisco: Jossey-Bass, 1970),

pp. 49–59. But when the person explains his own behavior, he will attribute his actions to the requirements of the situation, not to his own predispositions. See Edward Jones and Richard Nisbett, *The Actor and the Observer: Divergent Perceptions of the Causes of Behavior* (New York: General Learning Press, 1971).

11. Two recent articles explore the utility of the concept of issue areas in foreign-policy research, but they are not concerned with the level of analysis problem. See Thomas Brewer, "Issue and Context Variations in Foreign Policy," *Journal of Conflict Resolution* 17 (March 1973), 89–114, and William Zimmerman, "Issue Area and Foreign-Policy Process," *American Political Science Review* 67 (December 1973), 1204–12.

12. James Rosenau, "Pre-Theories and Theories of Foreign Policy," pp. 47–48; Stanley Hoffmann, "Restraints and Choices in American Foreign Policy," *Daedalus* (Fall 1962), 692–94.

13. Most of the propositions in Greenstein, "The Impact of Personality on Politics," about the conditions under which personality is most important can be subsumed under this heading.

14. Thus the famous remark by a cabinet officer that you only have to obey the president when he repeats an order for the third time.

15. An excellent discussion of the evidence on this point derived from quantitative studies is Dina Zinnes, "Some Evidence Relevant to the Man-Milieu Hypothesis," in James Rosenau, Vincent Davis, and Maurice East, eds., *The Analysis of International Politics* (New York: Free Press, 1972), pp. 209–51. But these studies have limited utility for the questions being asked here because they do not provide adequate measures of the similarity of the objective situation and the similarity of the state's responses. This is also true for the growing body of literature that examines these questions using event-scaling techniques. For a study that copes

with these problems relatively well and finds that differences in perceptions among decision-makers decrease as tension increases, see Ole Holsti, "Individual Differences in 'Definition of the situation,'" *Journal of Conflict Resolution* 14 (September 1970), 303–10.

16. For a general discussion, see Herbert Blumer, "Society as Symbolic Interaction," in Arnold Rose, ed., *Human Behavior and Social Processes* (Boston: Houghton Mifflin, 1962), pp. 180–91. For an inventory of findings see Kenneth Terhune, "Personality in Cooperation and Conflict," in Paul Swingle, ed., *The Structure of Conflict* (New York: Academic Press, 1970), pp. 193–234. This subject has received much attention from psychologists in the past few years. For a review of the literature and an excellent argument, see Daryl Bem and Andrea Allen, "On Predicting Some of the People Some of the Time," *Psychological Review* 81 (1974), 506–20.

17. Wolfers, *Discord and Collaboration,* p. 13.

18. Paul Kecskemeti, *Strategic Surrender* (New York: Atheneum, 1964), pp. 19–20; Ole Holsti, "The 1914 Case," *The American Political Science Review* 59 (June 1965), 365–78; Wolfers, *Discord and Collaboration,* p. 14.

19. See, for example, Charles Maier, "Revisionism and the Interpretation of Cold War Origins," *Perspectives in American History* 4 (1970), 313–47; Robert Tucker, *The Radical Left and American Foreign Policy* (Baltimore, Md.: Johns Hopkins Press, 1971); James Richardson, "Cold-War Revisionism: A Critique," *World Politics* 24 (July 1972), 579–612; and Ole Holsti, "The Study of International Politics Makes Strange Bedfellows: Theories of the Radical Right and the Radical Left," *American Political Science Review* 68 (March 1974), 217–42. Comparisons with the reactions of European statesmen would also shed light on the question of whether there was anything

peculiarly American in the United States' perceptions.

20. Marshall Shulman, *Stalin's Foreign Policy Reappraised* (Cambridge, Mass.: Harvard University Press, 1963).

21. Michael Gordon, *Conflict and Consensus in Labour's Foreign Policy, 1914–1965* (Stanford: Stanford University Press, 1969), p. 6; M. A. Fitzsimons, *The Foreign Policy of the British Labour Government, 1945–1951* (Notre Dame, Ind.: University of Notre Dame Press, 1953), p.26.

22. In this group we include potential leaders who could come to power without drastic changes in the state's internal political system. Dissent from those outside this group does not undermine the arguments for the importance of the nature of the state, and, indeed, if such people have been rejected as possible power-holders because of their foreign policy views, this would demonstrate the importance of this level of analysis rather than showing the autonomy of the decision-making level.

23. Most light is shed on this subject by the writings of Philip Selznick. See his *TVA and the Grassroots* (Berkeley and Los Angeles: University of California Press, 1947) and *Leadership in Administration* (Evanston, Ill.: Row, Peterson, 1957). Also see Morton Halperin, "Why Bureaucrats Play Games," *Foreign Policy* No. 2 (Spring 1971), 74–88, and *Bureaucratic Politics and Foreign Policy* (Washington: Brookings Institution, 1974), pp. 26–62.

24. During the Second World War the British set up an intelligence section to try to recreate the German perspective. They did well at predicting the positions taken by various parts of the German bureaucracy but could never adequately predict when Hitler would side with a particular faction or impose his own solution. (Donald McLachlan, *Room 39* [New York: Atheneum, 1968], pp 252–58.)

25. Ernest May, "The Development of Political-Military Consultation in the United States," in Aaron Wildavsky, ed., *The Presidency* (Boston: Little, Brown, 1969), p. 668; Patrick Gordon Walker, *The Cabinet* (New York: Basic Books, 1970), p. 67; W. J. Reader, *Architect of Airpower: The Life of the First Viscount Weir* (London: Collins, 1968), p. 270; Roger Brown, *Fashoda Reconsidered* (Baltimore, Md.: Johns Hopkins Press, 1970), pp. 24–32, 85.

26. The knowledge gained by studying how people view the world and process incoming information can lead to the discovery of patterns in state behavior that would not be apparent to an observer who had ignored decision-making. We may be able to say, for example, that two kinds of situations, although not seeming alike to later scholars, will appear to be similar to contemporary decision-makers and will be seen to call for similar responses. Thus, once we have examined a number of cases, detected common deviations, and isolated their causes, we could apply this knowledge to theories that do not call for intensive analysis of decision-making.

27. See Charles Osgood, "Behavior Theory and the Social Sciences," in Roland Young, ed., *Approaches to the Study of Politics* (Evanston, Ill.: Northwestern University Press, 1958), pp. 217–44. For a recent discussion and application, see Richard Jessor and Shirley Jessor, "The Perceived Environment in Behavioral Science," *American Behavioral Scientist* 16 (July/August 1973), 801–27. In an interesting critique, Robert Gorman asks "Must we look into the perception of the decision-maker at the time the decision was being made by centering our political analysis on the decision-maker himself? Or, should we concentrate on the social organization of which the decision-maker is a part and the social environment in which both the organization and the individual function? If we accept the first choice, then social factors assume a secondary,

instrumental purpose. If we choose the second framework, the perceptions of the decision-maker would seem to be *logically* dependent on external rules, and investigation into the nature of individual perception would be absurd. If we combine the two, as the decision-making theorists seem to have done, we are left with a theory in which each premise is negated by the existence of the other, and the general theory itself is left to flounder in a formalistic but meaningless syncretism." ("On the Inadequacies of Non-Philosophical Political Science: A Critical Analysis of Decision-Making Theory," *International Studies Quarterly* 14 [December 1970], 408.) The use of a two-step model avoids this contradiction.

28. Daniel Ellsberg, "The Quagmire Myth and the Stalemate Machine," in *Papers on the War* (New York: Simon and Schuster, 1972), pp. 42–135; Leslie Gelb, "Vietnam: The System Worked," *Foreign Policy* No. 3 (Summer 1971), 140–67; Klaus Knorr, "Failures in National Intelligence Estimates: The Case of the Cuban Missiles," *World Politics* 16 (April 1967), 455–67. Theodore Draper fails to see the significance of these kinds of questions in explaining the American intervention in the Dominican Republic. ("The Dominican Intervention Reconsidered," *Political Science Quarterly* 86 [March 1971], 26–28.) To take an example from another field, the fact that young people in less politicized homes share fewer of their parents' political views than do those in more highly politicized families is not to be explained by the former group having less desire to adopt their parents' beliefs, but by their lack of knowledge about what their parents believe. (Richard Niemi, *How Family Members Perceive Each Other* [New Haven: Yale University Press, 1974], pp. 200–201.)

QUESTIONS

1. What are the inherent problems of the levels of analysis in explaining the influence of perception?

2. What are the two propositions that Jervis identifies regarding his perceptions model?

Chapter 10

PEACE STUDIES THEORY

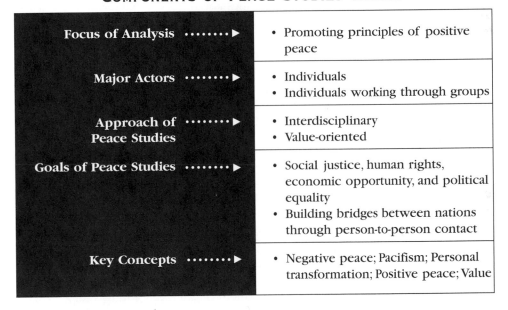

COMPONENTS OF PEACE STUDIES THEORY

Focus of Analysis ········▶	• Promoting principles of positive peace
Major Actors ········▶	• Individuals • Individuals working through groups
Approach of Peace Studies ········▶	• Interdisciplinary • Value-oriented
Goals of Peace Studies ········▶	• Social justice, human rights, economic opportunity, and political equality • Building bridges between nations through person-to-person contact
Key Concepts ········▶	• Negative peace; Pacifism; Personal transformation; Positive peace; Value

INTRODUCTION

We complete our look at the individual level of analysis with an examination of peace studies theory. Peace studies is a relatively new approach to the study of international relations and pushes boldly past many of the guiding principles that commonly characterize the study of foreign policy and the behavior of states. That is, peace studies theorists argue that the study of international affairs should reach beyond the more traditional evaluations and measurements of power, balance of power, and national security. Particularly in our increasingly interconnected world, issues such as poverty, social injustice, and environmental destruction, to name only a few, reach to the heart of our security as human beings. We might say that peace studies suggests there can be no national security in the traditional sense until there is social, economic, and political justice on a global scale.

These elements come together to form a foundation for a theory emphasizing nonviolence, equality, and working—both independently and together—for the collective good. As the name implies, peace studies involves the study of peace and ways to promote peace within the international community. Though proponents aspire to this global cause, we have included peace studies in our look at the individual level of analysis. The reason behind this classification is, as we will discuss in greater detail later, that profound change on an international level begins with personal transformation. **Personal transformation,** in this sense, is a change or shift in an individual's outlook, habits, or worldview in a way that makes that individual more socially conscious of the global effect of his or her actions. The implication is that each of us, working as individuals, can have a positive influence on a much larger, even global, scale—a positive energy "ripple effect," if you will. In this way, peace studies opens up some new possibilities about how we might view the world and our own role within the global community.

Any discussion of peace studies theory must begin with a brief examination of the impact of Mahatma Mohandas K. Gandhi. Gandhi remains the preeminent contemporary example of the nonviolent approach to resolving conflict. Gandhi was born in Western India in 1869. As a young man, his family sent him to study law in London. After he began practicing law, Gandhi moved to South Africa where he worked ceaselessly to improve the rights of immigrant Indians living in that country. It was there that he developed his creed of passive resistance against injustice. Mahatma Gandhi was a pacifist who sought political change through non-violent means. **Pacifism** is the rejection of the use of force for dealing with domestic or international conflicts. Gandhi's philosophy is encapsulated in his famous statement, "Nonviolence is the greatest force at the disposal of mankind. It is mightier than the mightiest weapon of destruction devised by the ingenuity of man." Staying true to his philosophy, Gandhi organized and led a passive resistance movement in South Africa. He was frequently jailed as a result of the peaceful protests that he led. Eventually, the South African authorities agreed to reform many of their laws and practices resulting in dramatically improved conditions for Indians living in South Africa.

Back in India, it was not long before Gandhi began leading India's long struggle for independence from Great Britain. From 1919 to 1947 Gandhi worked tirelessly to promote his strategy of nonviolent resistance to British rule. He never wavered in his unshakable belief in nonviolent protest and religious tolerance. When Indian Muslims and Hindus committed acts of violence he fasted until the fighting stopped. Mahatma Gandhi's unyielding commitment to nonviolent resistance represented a triumph of human will over violence and military might. The selection by Gandhi contains an outline of his nonviolent approach to resolving conflict.

PEACE STUDIES: AN INTERDISCIPLINARY APPROACH TO INTERNATIONAL RELATIONS THEORY

Though the study of international relations, with its theories and levels of analysis, generally falls in the realm of political science, peace studies is actually an interdisciplinary field. It incorporates information, analyses, and discourse from not only political science but also the traditional hard sciences (such as physics and mathematics), psychology, anthropology, sociology, and areas of the humanities (such as literature and linguistics). This intellectual crossover is one of several key characteristics that distinguish peace studies theory from other paradigms found in the study of international affairs. Using this broad base of information, the theory can examine a full range of human activities and behavior—from peaceful to violent—and can analyze these activities from hard science and social science perspectives.

Another inclusive characteristic of peace studies as a theory and method for studying international relations is its broad historical look at human interaction. The historical reach of peace studies extends farther back than most other fields in examining the patterns and traditions in our relationships with one another. It also projects various scenarios for future world orders. These projected scenarios are based on alternatives to the traditional nation-state structure commonly used as a standard for analysis by other theorists in the international relations field. This means that links between individuals or groups might be based not simply on territorial boundaries or geographic proximity (states or blocs of states within a region), but on common interests, ideas, beliefs, or goals (religion, environmental concerns, etc.).

In addition to the inclusive approach of peace studies theory, this paradigm is also a prescriptive, rather than simply descriptive, paradigm. A prescriptive theory is a set of principles and guidelines that contain overt value judgments about how the world ought to be, rather than how the world actually is. A prescriptive theory actually contains specific recommendations with regard to foreign policy and the conduct of international relations. Consequently, peace studies offers policies, political agendas, and other criteria and conditions designed to promote nonviolence and achieve peace. Thus, just as a physician prescribes medicine to cure an illness, these theorists prescribe a particular course of action to attain a particular end.

Peace studies also evaluates existing policies made and actions taken by governments with an eye to their impact—both direct and indirect—on society. By assessing actions and motives in this way, peace studies is considered a value-based theory. A **value** is an ideal or principle that people generally consider worthwhile and desirable. Peace studies assigns value to the actions, policies, activities, and methods of governments and individuals based on their benefit or harm to society. We might say that rather than the end justifying the means, both the means *and* the end are judged with respect to values and moral appropriateness.

And the ideal end for proponents of peace studies is not simply peace but positive peace. **Positive peace** is the absence of war in combination with the establishment of broader, worldwide forms of social justice, economic prosperity, and political power-sharing. This notion is contrasted with what some peace studies theorists call "negative peace." **Negative peace** is defined only as the absence of war, a condition in which direct forms of organized violence are absent but the underlying reasons for war, such as social injustice and economic exploitation, are left unresolved. Peace studies theorists would point to the period just after World War I as an example of negative peace. Although military operations and violence had ended, broader social violence (widespread homelessness and hunger, for example), as well as political and economic retribution on the part of the victors continued, helping to sow the seeds for World War II. True peace, positive peace, could not be achieved under such conditions, according to the principles of peace studies.

It is important to point out here that advocates of peace studies differentiate between violence and conflict. Even in a situation of positive peace, peace is not necessarily the absence of conflict. Conflict—as opposed to violence—is viewed by peace studies theorists as healthy debate, disagreement, or dialogue and an integral part of life and growth in human existence. The key, according to some theorists, is to manage and resolve conflict and prevent an escalation to violence, while preserving justice and freedom within society.

Part of prevention, according to peace studies theorists, is to look at the tools of violence. Here, we see the crossover between various fields of study that was discussed earlier. In peace studies, scientists and researchers are asked to look at the consequences (environmental, social, economic) of their work. The invention of the atomic bomb, chemical weaponry, and other such devices cannot be disassociated from their violent purpose. Peace studies encourages scientists, scholars, and social activists from all fields to work together in assessing the potential political, social, and environmental ramifications of these instruments, as well as future technologies and innovations. In short, the variety of work under the rubric of peace studies seeks not only to understand the many causes of war and conflict but also to go beyond them in its quest for possibilities of peace building.

As Robin J. Crews points out in her article "A Values-Based Approach to Peace Studies," the search for complete knowledge or "truth" cannot be conducted in separate inquiries among divergent parts of the scientific community. An interconnected inquiry is the only way to reach this goal. Crews emphasizes that epistemological issues—issues dealing with the nature and roots of knowledge—need to be addressed as part of reducing society's violent tendencies. Learning changes our experience as humans in numerous ways, and peace studies, as part of that process, is geared to help channel an individual's search for knowledge, enlightenment, and "truth" in positive directions. She suggests that we need to instill love in our search for truth, make appropriate changes in the curricula of our schools and universities, and take social responsibility for what knowledge brings to, and can do, in our lives. We can begin this process by analyzing current values, norms, standards, and practices within society in order to understand how and what must be done to improve our future.

As we touched on earlier, this kind of global improvement begins with the person's potential for growth and deeper understanding. The next article, "The Individual and Global Peace-Building: A Transformational Perspective," by Arthur Stein, focuses on the transformational approach to peace studies. The transformational, or transformative, approach examines the relationship between thought and deed, and seeks to reconcile the two. For example, concern for the preservation of our environment and natural resources must be accompanied by actions that promote this goal. One might begin by recycling on an individual basis, then take action to help develop a comprehensive town or county program. Besides ecological awareness, Stein highlights several key areas as targets for personal transformation, including human rights, civic responsibilities, shared economic well-being, and nonviolent social change. He illustrates the potential of each individual not only to change himself or herself but, through example, to make a positive contribution in transforming family, friends, neighborhoods, states, and the international community. Stein emphasizes the importance of the qualities of inclusiveness, civility, and empathy to the development of truly participatory democracies.

The final reading, "A Nonviolent Approach to the Intifada," by Raed Abusahlia is an excellent example of the application of the philosophy and principles promoted by peace studies. The author, a Palestinian priest and Chancellor of the Latin Patriarchate of Jerusalem, wrote this article in an attempt to persuade Palestinians to adopt a strategy of nonviolence in their struggle to achieve statehood for Palestine.

Certainly, the transformational perspective of peace studies—or peace building—theory clearly shows the proactive nature of this paradigm. Peace studies theorists are not content simply to describe the behavior of states and its impact on the international system. They begin by ascribing value to this behavior and proceed to make recommendations on how it might be improved. There is, as we have seen, a significant amount of thought, effort, and research behind such an innovative approach to international relations. We must now ask where peace studies theory excels and where it might fall short.

A Critique of Peace Studies Theory

Peace studies outlines specific goals and offers underlying principles and, in some instances, courses of action designed to fulfill them. The prescriptive, interdisciplinary, value-oriented nature of this theory is actually one of its primary strengths.

The goals are noble and broad-based: social justice, human rights, building positive peace, and changing the fundamental way we view the world and ourselves. Peace studies theorists suggest promoting these goals by creating a more communitarian, global ethic in which the fundamental causes of violence might be overcome by better understanding human nature. Such understanding can be enhanced by person-to-person contact that crosses boundaries and builds bridges of knowledge and communication on an individual level, yet in a global context.

Another goal of peace studies looks for balance within these new relationships. That is, we should strive for global equilibrium between the powerful and the powerless, the wealthy and the poor. Personal and community security, which then translates to global security, can be achieved by providing food and shelter to those in need, justice to those who are persecuted, and a voice to those who have been politically silenced.

It may appear somewhat like bursting the proverbial bubble to point out that a critique of peace studies can legitimately question its idealistic worldview, which some might even call utopian. Peace studies theorists, indeed, have developed such an optimistic outlook that some critics argue it could be potentially dangerous in real-world situations. Though noble in intent, the policies fostered by peace studies could subtly weaken the resolve of people and states to resist or combat a nation bent on extending its power or influence through aggressive actions.

On a theoretical level, peace studies has been similarly criticized for underestimating the inherent conflict between nation-states. Certainly, a realist would describe the international environment as anarchic and characterized by the violence of an ongoing struggle for power between states. Under this scenario, peace studies

---

KEY CONCEPTS

Negative Peace   is the absence of war. Direct forms of organized violence are absent, but the underlying reasons for war, such as social injustice and economic exploitation, are left unresolved. This term is contrasted with what peace studies theorists refer to as positive peace.

Pacifism   is the rejection of the use of force for dealing with domestic or international conflicts.

Personal Transformation   is a change or shift in an individual's nature, outlook, habits, or worldview in a way that makes that individual more socially conscious of the global effect of his or her actions.

Positive Peace   is the absence of war in combination with the establishment of broader, worldwide forms of social justice, economic prosperity, and political power-sharing. This notion is contrasted with what peace studies theorists call negative peace.

Value   is an ideal or principle that people generally consider worthwhile and desirable. Peace studies assigns value to the actions, policies, activities, and methods of governments and individuals based on their benefit or harm to society.

---

falls short in explaining present conditions and projecting future behavior. As a theoretical construct, critics consider it disjointed and lacking a coherent framework for analyzing international relations.

Peace studies theorists respond to these arguments by stating that the only way to change the international environment is to build bridges (through both person-to-person and government contacts), which, in turn, will reduce the fear and insecurity that lead to war. They recognize that this kind of change comes about incrementally but believe it is a logical, productive course of action. By focusing on disparities of wealth and power, individuals, communities, nongovernmental organizations, and governments can formulate effective policies to redress these imbalances and create greater stability within the system. If these global disparities continue in a world of growing environmental, economic, and political instability, even powerful nations will no longer be safe.

The peace studies path to this kind of change is long and gradual. Proponents suggest, though, that the prescriptive nature of the approach and the transformational aspects may offer the only realistic route for long-term, positive change in our world. This transformational process generally proceeds upwards, from individuals to states to the global system, and relies on the idea that people's attitudes and actions can affect international relations. Within its value-based, moral context, peace studies theory emphasizes positive change, social justice, and greater balance between the weak and the powerful.

We might question, however, how successful such a social contract might be. The goals of peace studies contain what are many traditional leftist elements: to more equitably redistribute wealth, to empower the poor and powerless, and to equalize the distribution of power. At a time when we see more and more developing nations turn to capitalism and a free-market system, peace studies theory could face some significant challenges. Then again, peace studies theorists might suggest that we can change the world only by changing ourselves, and that effort begins with one individual at a time.

41.   Nonviolence: The Greatest Force

Mohandas K. Gandhi

This excerpt from Mahatma Gandhi outlines his view that nonviolence is the most powerful approach to resolving conflict.

Nonviolence is the greatest force humanity has been endowed with. Truth is the only goal we have. For God is none other than Truth. But Truth cannot be, never will be reached except through nonviolence.

That which distinguishes us from all other animals is our capacity to be nonviolent. And we fulfill our mission only to the extent that we are nonviolent and no more. We have no doubt many other gifts. But if they do not serve the main purpose—the development of the spirit of nonviolence in us—they but drag us down lower than the brute, a status from which we have only just emerged.

The cry for peace will be a cry in the wilderness, so long as the spirit of nonviolence does not dominate millions of men and women.

An armed conflict between nations horrifies us. But the economic war is no better than an armed conflict. This is like a surgical operation. An economic war is prolonged torture. And its ravages are no less terrible than those depicted in the literature on war properly so called. We think nothing of the other because we are used to its deadly effects.

Many of us in India shudder to see blood spilled. Many of us resent cow slaughter, but we think nothing of the slow torture through which by our greed we put our people and cattle. But because we are used to this lingering death, we think no more about it.

The movement against war is sound. I pray for its success. But I cannot help the gnawing fear that the movement will fail if it does not touch the root of all evil—human greed.

Will America, England, and the other great nations of the West continue to exploit the so-called weaker or uncivilized races and hope to attain peace that the whole world is pining for? Or will Americans continue to prey upon one another, have commercial rivalries, and yet expect to dictate peace to the world?

Not till the spirit is changed can the form be altered. The form is merely an expression of the spirit within. We may succeed in seemingly altering the form, but the alteration will be a mere make-believe if the spirit within remains unalterable. A whited sepulcher still conceals beneath it the rotting flesh and bone.

Far be it from me to discount or underrate the great effort that is being made in the West to kill the war spirit. Mine is merely a word of caution as from a fellow seeker who has been striving in his own humble manner after the same thing, maybe in a different way, no doubt on a much smaller scale. But if the experiment demonstrably succeeds on the smaller field and, if those who are working on the larger field have not overtaken me, it will at least pave the way for a similar experiment on a large field.

I observe, in the limited field in which I find myself, that unless I can reach the hearts of men and women, I am able to do nothing. I observe further that so long as the spirit of hate persists in some shape or other, it is impossible to establish peace or to gain our freedom by peaceful effort. We cannot love one another if we hate Englishmen. We cannot love the Japanese and hate Englishmen. We must either let the law of love rule us through and through or not at all. Love among ourselves based on hatred of others breaks down under the slightest pressure. The fact is, such love is never real love. It is an armed peace. And so it will be in this great movement in the West against war. War will only be stopped when the conscience of humankind has become sufficiently elevated to recognize the undisputed supremacy of the Law of Love in all the walks of life. Some say this will never come to pass. I shall retain the faith till the end of my earthly existence that it shall come to pass.

QUESTIONS

1. Under what conditions would the nonviolent approach to resolving conflict be most likely to succeed and most likely to fail?

2. Do you agree or disagree with Gandhi's assertion that economic war is no better than armed conflict?

---

42. A Values-Based Approach to Peace Studies

Robin J. Crews

In this excerpt, Robin J. Crews describes the goals of peace studies as including, among other things, the pursuit of knowledge about peace and its development. She reminds the reader that approaches to the study of peace are as varied as approaches to the pursuit of knowledge. Finally, she develops an approach to the study of peace that is informed by sociological analysis, principles of Gandhian nonviolence, and notions of epistemology. This selection is from *Peace and World Order Studies: A Curriculum Guide* (1989).

At the time of this writing, Robin J. Crews was the director of the Peace Studies Association.

The goals of peace studies include, among other things, the pursuit of knowledge about peace and its development. Approaches to the study of peace are as varied as approaches to the pursuit of knowledge in general. In this essay, I develop an approach to the study of peace that is informed by sociological analysis, principles of Gandhian nonviolence, and notions of epistemology.

THE ROLE OF PEACE STUDIES IN THE UNIVERSITY

It is sometimes assumed that there is such a thing as purely theoretical learning—learning wherein one investigates reality at the level of theory without affecting reality itself. This assumption (which is closely associated with the Cartesian delineation between mind and matter, and which underlies the belief that learning should not be involved with the application of knowledge, i.e., with social change) contradicts the fact that our familiarity with reality is based upon our perceptions of it. As we comprehend existing symbols or create new theoretical constructs to help explain the world around us, that world changes because our perceptions of it are no longer the same. When a student understands relativity theory in physics, the physical world has changed for that student forever.

Thus all learning contributes in essential ways—some enormous, some minute—to a restructuring of the human experience. Peace studies specifically and intentionally constitutes such learning. It is generally accepted that at the heart of the undergraduate educational process is the goal of learning about the world in which we live. In this way the formal training of the university experience contributes to the universal and ultimate human quest for meaning.

Fundamentally, the role of peace studies in the university is to assist in the human quest for meaning—and to do so in such a way that the world benefits from this search in the process. This quest has many manifestations, including the empirical pursuit of physical "truth" entailing the scientific measurement and interpretation of sensate perceptions; the pursuit of metaphysical "truth" through faith; the search for social linkage by belonging to a community of others; and the elemental process of growth by choosing among alternative futures, both immediate and distant. A key aspect of peace studies is the examination of these images—an enterprise that the field approaches in many diverse ways.

Examining and Challenging Values

Underlying the search for modes of learning that lead to constructive social change and a more peaceful world is a consensus about the inadequacy of present directions—a shared belief that we will not achieve a peaceful world in the future if we continue down the road we are on now. Because the future reality that humanity will create depends upon our *image* of that reality, we must develop new, more humane visions of the future. And because those visions depend upon our culture, a fundamental task for peace studies is the critical examination of our values, beliefs, and assumptions as well as of our hopes and fears, our rituals and our traditions.

The objectives of this examination are liberation from those parochial ideologies and provincial dogmas of the past that prevent us from envisioning and creating a peaceful world, and the development, in their place, of those value constellations that contribute to the full potential of peaceful coexistence in life. The controversial questions about what we leave behind and what we take with us from the past into the future are difficult to formulate and often more difficult to articulate. They are at the heart of peace studies.

Human values—and the methods by which they are shaped—are central to our quest for meaning. We teach them through actions and words, through role modeling, through traditions and rituals. As noted earlier, they underlie our images of meaning, which include, among others, our images of truth, belonging, and choosing.

Images of Truth

In Western scientific culture, we have historically chosen to pursue knowledge about physical reality through the use of scientific methods. This knowledge has often been equated with immutable "Truth." We have also pursued metaphysical dimensions of truth through faith. Both avenues of understanding have contributed much to our larger pursuit of truth. Yet the assumption that these are the only two avenues available to us, and that they are intrinsically antithetical and mutually exclusive of each other, has contributed to a competition for ideological primacy between them—a competition that has persistently hindered the search for truth.

Truth Through Science

The assumptions that objectivity is an achievable goal, that the pursuit of knowledge is a priori beneficial, that value-neutrality is possible, that "Truth" can be discovered through the scientific pursuit of knowledge in the physical world, that scientific inquiry can exist in a vacuum apart from social reality, that increased material well-being is an inevitable result of economic and technological growth, and that it is inherently useful and appropriate to seek technological solutions to social problems—these are all tenets of the social institution of science that contemporary society has come to accept and demand as it waits passively for its scientists to solve the problems that loom ever larger on our ecological and economic horizons.

These assumptions of the Newtonian, mechanistic world view are in part responsible for the unthinkable massacres that transpired on August 6 and 9, 1945. And it is these assumptions that contribute to the current research, development, testing, and deployment of space weapons and chemical munitions that threaten to rival existing technologies of mass destruction. It is these values that allow young scientists at Livermore and Los Alamos, and in weapons development firms in all industrial societies, to rationalize that their work on weapons is a noble and humane endeavor.

To alter fundamentally the course of the arms race requires a willingness to examine the values that underlie our society's pursuit of truth. After centuries of perceiving and defining reality almost exclusively in terms of the sensate world, we are finally coming to understand that science and empiricism are social institutions based upon historically and culturally specific social values.

In the teaching of Mohandas Gandhi, we are told that truth cannot be attained without love—truth, or the overcoming of injustice, is not possible unless we transform our adversaries through loving nonviolence. Indeed, for Gandhi, nonviolence is the pursuit of truth through love. Quite to the contrary, Western scientific culture has sought to separate truth and love through science. Not only does this result in a cultural acceptance and fascination with the implements of mass destruction, but it has also created an intellectual framework that has paralyzed alternative modes of seeking truth and conducting international relations. This framework has denied the legitimacy of viewing peace as the pursuit of truth through love. Many people accept our current prostitution of science as its only identity and as an historical inevitability. However, as science is a social institution—something we create—it is also something we can transform.

The challenge, then, is to critique the ethical and logical dimensions of science, to contribute to the rebirth of sciences that pursue truth through love, rather than through the design of weapons of mass destruction. The task is to reintegrate ethics and other critically essential social values into new ways of teaching science; to alter our own images of truth so as to include other ways of knowing; to assume responsibility for the development of technology in society; and to be more selective and humane in those technologies that we do elect to design and build. In other words, the role of peace studies is to comprehend more fully this empowering knowledge and to assist in the transformation of scientific approaches to truth.

In order to treat the empirical pursuit of truth through science appropriately, peace studies faculty should inject as much natural and physical science as is possible into the curriculum—and not just in "nuclear war" courses. Courses should be designed and team-taught by natural and physical scientists as often as teaching schedules allow. Peace studies faculty outside the "hard" sciences should also seek to be included in the teaching of science courses.

An understanding of scientific methods and competency in analytical problem-solving are essential if peace studies is to maintain intellectual rigor and to progress at a sufficient rate and in the appropriate directions for it to make a difference in the world of tomorrow. Therefore, scientific research methods and theory construction should be taught and used in peace studies courses as well as in physical science courses. Once introduced, logic and analytical approaches to understanding can then be employed in examinations of the assumptions of science; in other words, the methods and rules of science can be used in an examination of science itself.

Although some of this agenda must wait for students at the upper division and graduate levels, introductory courses can and should include units on science that introduce it as a social institution, and that identify it as one of *a number of* legitimate approaches to perceiving and understanding the world (rather than as the only legitimate approach). To succeed in this task, teachers should demystify images of science and technology that reinforce the "leave it to the expert" syndrome regarding policy choices, examine how the compartmentalization of science obscures social and ecological consequences, and explore the nature of "pure" versus "applied" science, including the development of civilian and military technologies.

It is important that science not be perceived as a target at which faculty in the social sciences and humanities can direct unwarranted criticism. We must examine fully the contributions of science to war (especially the history of the Manhattan Project and the resulting arms race up until the present), but such critiques should be balanced with an appreciation of the constructive uses of modern science. Finally, students should gain an understanding of the difficulty in making choices about science and technology, of the problems involved in applying ethical and moral criteria to those choices, and of the absolute necessity of doing so.

Truth Through Faith

Another way that humanity has pursued truth is through faith. In its more organized forms, this search has taken place through the development and maintenance of religious ideologies. Our religious images are based upon values taught to us through the process of inculcation as we are socialized into the world in which we live. Nothing else explains the fact that Jews produce children with an understanding of Jewish ritual and tradition, while Catholics somehow have children that understand Catholic ritual and tradition; nothing else explains the fact that Mennonites perceive an image of god significantly different from that of Muslims.

Despite the fact that few of us are specifically capable of completely and comprehensively describing our images of the divine, these images are somehow communicated to the young and then shared throughout a lifetime with others of their faith. Somehow we know how to create an image of god in our children, yet we cannot put that image into words. Clearly, these images are incredibly powerful.

However, we do use words to convey what we mean when talking about god; and the words we use to generate images of our god are often quite limit-

ing—that is, exclusive of others' images. If this is indeed the case, then our faiths—even though they are fundamentally important and constructive for us—stand between us and a peaceful world. It is a cliche, but also a truism, that more blood has been shed in the name of god than for any other reason. This is so because our images of god are so powerful, so primary in our belief systems. And so long as some peoples' images of god exclude the viability of other people's images of god, then we will continue to live in a world beset by bloody and intractable conflicts between Protestants and Catholics, Jews and Muslims, and Sikhs and Hindus, to mention a few.

Peace will remain a fantasy as well as a slogan for the initiation of combat so long as our images of god do not allow for others to have their images of god, and so long as the agenda is social conformity and missionary conversion rather than tolerance of diverse images. Accordingly, one role of peace studies is to identify and examine beliefs that contribute either to exclusiveness or inclusiveness. This does not mean that we need to abandon our images of god. It only means that we need to transform them into images that benefit from the knowledge that peace is predicated on tolerance, not on its antithesis. We will achieve peace when our religious ideologies and dogmas allow us to value diversity and to accept the sanctity of other people's spiritual paths.

Peace studies curricula can improve their treatment of the pursuit of metaphysical truth by examining the nature of "truth" as such. Here, secularly oriented programs need to balance their agendas by incorporating units on religious contributions to peacemaking. On the other hand, programs predicated on primarily theological world views should seek as ecumenical a perspective on religion as possible. In so doing, such programs must examine the assumptions and values of religious belief systems, describe the many images of god, assess the implications of these values, assumptions, and images for the production and management of conflict in the world, and address the issues of inclusiveness, diversity, and tolerance.

Images of Belonging

There are many different types of human communities, some less voluntary than others. All of them contribute to a sense of belonging in the world; many, however, foster a desire to exclude the rest of the world. In this way, most communities offer the benefits of relationship, as well as the potential for exclusiveness, intergroup competition, ethnocentricity, xenophobia, intolerance, discrimination, and unnecessary conflict. This is true of prisons and the military as well as of gender, family, ethnicity, and the nation-state. Put differently, the obverse of belonging has many faces and regularly contributes to the violent conflict and structural violence we see in the world today. The dynamics and ideologies of "us" versus "them" (as expressed, for instance, in nationalism and excessive patriotism, gender-based chauvinism, religious self-righteousness, and racial prejudice) are antithetical to the development of peace. Thus an important role of peace studies is to explore new ways of creating community that value uniqueness while minimizing exclusiveness and unnecessary competition.

Peace studies has already progressed far in this dimension. Robert Jay Lifton's (1987) seminal research into the concept of a "species self" is a major recent contribution in the field of psychology to the evolution of a global identity. Elise Boulding's new book, *Building a Global Civic Culture* (1988), is a profoundly important treatise on the creative and cooperative work involved in learning about species identity, in discovering our commonalities, and in building a shared global community. Boulding's book is essential reading for everyone in the field, because it comprehensively addresses so many aspects of the role of peace studies. Hence, in this area, we in the field of peace studies are challenged with the exciting task of building upon the work of Lifton, Boulding, and others.

College and university curricula can address problems inherent in the more traditional images of belonging in at least three basic ways: (1) by helping students identify their own images of belonging (an endeavor that includes assessments of the origins of identities, and expectations of and responsibilities to the communities involved); (2) by presenting information about communities of belonging not familiar to most students (e.g., public interest groups, the various agencies of the United Nations, peace organizations and their national and local chapters, cultural exchange programs, and so on); and (3) by jointly (with students) developing or "mapping" new constellations of communities (from local to global) that allow for overlap and mutual identification without exclusiveness or inherent competition for primacy.

Images of Choosing

"Images of choosing" is a metaphor for the ways in which we exist in the present and create our future out of it. Within the systemic limitations of genetics and history, we—as individuals and as a society—*choose* our future. The amount of freedom available for choice varies considerably with individuals and social groups, but even the poorest of the poor make choices.

Images of choosing are important to the field of peace studies because they allow for an examination of the degree of human empowerment that competes with systemic limitations. Apathy, monolithic power models, belief in technological determinism or in salvation through armageddon, and ideologies which proclaim that violence is the outcome of instinctual human characteristics all share a denial or devaluation of the element of human choice and human potential. Peace studies can and should explore the ways in which we create the future, and how we might expand that potential for creation over time. This field of inquiry involves the subject of our choices, as well as our means and structures of choosing, the role of creativity and cooperation in choice, and the consequences of refusing to acknowledge that choices exist.

Specifically, we need to ask questions about how we make these choices now, within our political and economic systems. What is democracy? How closely does our current system approach this ideal? How does this system work? Does it require participation? What form of socioeconomic organization of society is most compatible with democracy? Is the use of military force to coerce others into organizing their societies in certain ways congruous with the basic tenets of democracy? Is the possession of thermonuclear weapons of mass destruction—or the threat to use them to protect that which we choose to define as our national interests—in accordance with the principles and purposes of democracy? We also need to ask similar sorts of questions about other political systems and about the international system as a whole.

At the same time, peace studies should develop methods for *imaging the future*—that is, it should encourage students to visualize multiple world futures that incorporate new and visionary modes of social and political organization. In developing such techniques we can draw on Elise Boulding's "Imaging a World Without Weapons" workshops, which encourage a multiplicity of alternative futures and allow for new visions of practical, peaceful worlds to be created "outside" the realm of today's dominant world views.

There are many ways for images of choosing to be incorporated into peace studies curricula.

First, the apathy and alienation that appear as normative aspects of our culture, and that result in large part from the "psychic numbing" produced by our inability to deal with the ever-present risk of nuclear holocaust as well as from the compartmentalization of our complex and technical society, must be named and confronted. Connections to, and responsibility for, our lives and the world of which they are part have to be re-identified and rediscovered as important individual and social values.

Second, students must be given the opportunity to entertain the notion that social reality is constructed, and that many of the limits to what is possible that were previously assumed to be valid are in fact arbitrary and outmoded; in other words, they are the products of dogma and ideology, rather than of "truth." Here, curricula need to incorporate experiential learning through "imaging the future" exercises.

Third, the learning process needs to examine the dynamics of action. Clearly, the relationship between means and ends is an essential theme that relates in important ways to our processes of choosing. Simple slogans such as "peace through strength" should be examined logically and their influence on society assessed. At the same time, curricula need to include units on our knowledge of conflict and its resolution, and to provide training in specific skills for conflict resolution, negotiation, and mediation.

Finally, curricula need to be designed in such a way that students are empowered as they learn about the complex problems we face in the world today, rather than frightened into acquiescence—indeed, into careers with ostrich-like characteristics.

THE PEDAGOGICAL IMPORTANCE OF VALUES

It is neither useful nor appropriate to ask whether values should be taught. In one way or another they are taught or shaped in every social interaction and institution, including those whose goal is formal learning (i.e., schools). The disciplines we emphasize, the curricula we select, the authors we choose for our students to read and analyze—all of these choices impart values. The more appropriate question is to ask *how* we can teach about values in a positive, pluralistic, and empowering way. In this regard, the most important single thing we can do is to train students to ask critical epistemological questions, rather than to accept dominant ideas as "given," as "the truth," or as "the way the world is."

In this context, peace studies is especially challenged to teach about values ethically and honestly. We can do so by incorporating into our curricula the rigorous examination of competing normative positions, with an eye toward understanding how they underlie all policies and world views. When students learn to challenge and examine values successfully, at least three essential pedagogical transformations will have transpired. First, they will have learned to critically examine ideas and values, and to evaluate them on their own merit. Second, they will have come to appreciate the existence of relationships between ideas and values. Finally, and perhaps most important, they will be better prepared to select from among the examined values and ideas for themselves—better prepared to shape a philosophy of life that reflects sound ethical and logical inquiry.

To teach values by examining and challenging them is critical because the values assumed by each new generation are the essential ingredients of our common future. Drawing on metahistory and deconstructionism, we are now learning that much of the power of those who perpetuate the arms race may be hidden in the cognitive and emotive images of discourse. We must be willing to unravel those images if we wish to create new thought-worlds.[1] At the heart of old and new thought-worlds are values.

Of course, peace studies curricula must be designed so that those entering the field do not seek to exploit it as a forum for political, ideological, or religious proselytizing. When abused as such, peace studies invites criticism and loses legitimacy in the eyes of its students. Value formation and selection on the part of students should come from an examination of various ideologies about the pursuit of truth, not from their inculcation *as* truth.

PRACTICING A NEW PROCESS

In addition to analyzing the relationship between cultural content (as it exists today or as we envision it in the future) and truth, peace studies has the potential to offer a profoundly alternative view of the search for truth. Not only does this view require further definition and articulation, but its validity is predicated upon *practice*. To identify cooperation, tolerance, holistic analysis, interdisciplinary examination, and metacultural critique as elements of the search is not sufficient: Those in the field must challenge themselves with the experience of actually *practicing* the processes they seek to institutionalize in the future. What matters here is neither content nor rhetoric about process, but *process itself.* Getting beyond the dogmas of Western scientific culture that have allowed for the illogical separation of means and ends can be accomplished only by perceiving and practicing the means as ends-in-process.

The success of peace studies is dependent upon the ability of faculty in the field to (1) become cooperative in their shared endeavors; (2) minimize competition among disciplines, ideologies, and affiliations; (3) learn enough of the language, theories, and methods of other disciplines to apply interdisciplinary approaches in their own teaching and research; (4) respect different perspectives and others in the field; and (5) seek multiple alternatives rather than singular prescriptions.

Ultimately, faculty are charged with the task of learning to get beyond ideological labels in order to respect, if not to love, others. For those researching the phenomenon of nonviolence, this means interaction with arms control analysts; for devotees of international relations, it means identification with those focusing on themes of justice, gender, or environmental respect; for theologically inspired faculty, it means active listening to secular colleagues (and vice versa).

The practicing of process also may entail renaming the concepts of "negative" and "positive" peace, so as to avoid denigrating those who focus on the former, while retaining the substantive distinction between peace as the absence of war and militarism (i.e., "negative peace") and peace as the presence of justice (or "positive peace"). Whether individuals in the field choose to focus their inquiry and their curricula on ways to reduce violence in the international system, or on the conditions and characteristics of peace, all perspectives are valid and constructive, and must be pursued through cooperative interaction.

Another challenge to the field of peace studies is to fulfill the potential of its interdisciplinary character. Although some progress has been made here, that quality is still predominantly latent. Most research and teaching in peace studies is conducted within one discipline or another, or it is conducted in a superficially interdisciplinary fashion—that is, the sociologist contributes a sociological perspective in tandem with the psychologist who offers a psychological one, and so on. To the extent that it is humanly and professionally possible, individuals in the field must seek to develop their own interdisciplinary competencies and perspectives while still enhancing their specific areas of expertise and interest.

The practicing of process also suggests that those in the field focus on the development of means suitable to the development of peace. Pedagogically, the emphasis on means implies imparting healthy modes of seeking knowledge, rather than inculcating specific values or ideas as content. Intellectually, it denotes the search for a balanced relationship between traditional academic teaching styles and new experiential modes of learning. Beyond these manifestations of an emphasis on means, the practicing of process ultimately means creating learning structures that contribute to seeking truth through love and exposing those which separate the means from the end.

Seeing the world from as many vantage points as possible is a fundamental task of peacemakers. Therefore, the practicing of process also means developing the ability to engage in what might be called "transperceptual learning"—that is, the learning that comes from perceiving reality from the perspectives of others to the degree possible. Ultimately, the best solutions to our common challenges are the product of joint visualization and cooperative response. This is so because good solutions represent the truth we collectively seek, which in turn is the result of our ability to visualize the perceptions, identify the needs, and respect the rights of others. The sorts of solutions we seek are those that result from cooperative interaction, and that honor the perceptions and needs of others. Transperceptual learning, then, is the dynamic process that comes on the heels of love and precedes the discovery of truth through love.

CONCLUSION

Relationships between means, ends, meaning, truth, and values inform this approach to the construction of peace studies curricula and to the formulation of their role in the Academy. This perspective is only one of many. Peace studies invites the participation of all those whose vision affirms peace as a positive goal and as a concrete process requiring the development of specific social and technical knowledge. The field is open to all who are willing to challenge and transform outdated world views through the creation of new visions of what is necessary, desirable, and possible.

NOTE

1. "Thought-world" was a metaphor used by Pam Solo in a talk given at a conference on "The New Security Debate: Challenges and Strategies for the Peace Movement" sponsored by the Institute for Peace and International Security in Cambridge, Massachusetts in January 1987.

REFERENCES

Boulding, Elise (1988). *Building a Global Civic Culture: Education for an Interdependent World.* New York: Teachers College Press.

Lifton, Robert Jay (1987). *The Future of Immortality: And Other Essays for a Nuclear Age.* New York: Basic Books.

QUESTIONS

1. What does the author mean by the phrase "images of truth"?

2. What are the fundamental values associated with peace studies?

43. The Individual and Global Peace Building: A Transformational Perspective

Arthur Stein

In this article, Arthur Stein contends that the potential role of the individual is underestimated in humanity's quest for a more just and peaceful world order. Stein believes that the possibility of significant positive change is based on the premise that people increasingly understand the benefits of living within safe and sustainable environments and over time will commit themselves to working toward these goals. As more people take part in this process, relations among nations will improve.

Arthur Stein is a professor of political science at the University of Rhode Island. A long-time student of international relations, he has written extensively and worked personally in the field of peace building. His most recent books include *Seeds of the Seventies: Values, Work and Commitment in America*, and *Heart of Compassion*.

Some contemporary scholars of international relations, following in the footsteps of Hans Morgenthau, doubt whether humankind is innately capable of eliminating war and organized violence. These scholars point to the undeniable fact that conflicts between peoples have been occurring in one place or another from the beginning of recorded history. Sometimes the widespread occurrence of systemic violence is seen as being as natural as an earthquake or hurricane.

By contrast, other theorists contend that organized violence is not inevitable, and that humanity has the capacity to eliminate, or greatly reduce, the incidence of war. I find this contention to be more convincing and believe the cumulative evidence of historical experience shows that humans are capable of a wide range of behaviors and that "human nature" per se can be quite malleable. The very thought of international wars in the nuclear age is appalling to many people. War, then, is not inevitable.

Indeed, there are indications of a new global awakening that could bring the peoples of the world together in unprecedented and cooperative ways.

This trend presents a great challenge, for the weapons of destructiveness are too great, and the ecological crises too pressing for global "business" to continue on "as usual." Creative, non-violent ways need to be developed to prevent potentially explosive conflict situations from developing and to defuse those which do exist. Humankind is being challenged to stretch its collective imagination to envision itself as a planetary family living in peace and with social justice. An "end of history" is not at hand, but an end is required to many of the old ways of doing things. In this, the potential transformative role of the individual person is critical.

As we discuss the role of the individual in the process of peacebuilding, a number of questions arise. Each question will be addressed by looking at historical theoretical patterns, as well as contemporary events. First, do humans have the capacity to change?

THE HUMAN NATURE DEBATE

There persists the age-old question: Are we perpetually victims of our biology and our history? Socio-biologist E. O. Wilson has observed that, from their origins, homo sapiens genetically have a potential both for peaceful and for aggressive behavior. And aggression does not have to manifest in violence. This premise leaves open a number of possibilities, depending on the circumstances in which we find ourselves and those we create. Wilson concludes that violent behavior itself is learned, not inborn.[1]

Beliefs about human nature can become self-fulfilling prophesies. If you believe that human beings are naturally violent or bad, you may be persuaded that it is "realistic" to be that way yourself. In short, humans have both the capacity for good and negative thoughts, words, and actions. Our behavior is rarely all black or white. There are numerous areas of grey in between. As individuals, we only have to look closely at our daily ups and downs to ascertain this.

THE KEY ROLE OF THE INDIVIDUAL IN TRANSFORMATIVE CHANGE[2]

In order to respond to the challenges of our rapidly changing age, we need to develop fresh perspectives. One emerging approach, which can be called transformative or transformational, asserts that more is required than to call for needed reforms or restructuring of political institutions. This approach stresses the need to examine the existential question of what it is to be fully human and the relationship between our psyches and social behaviors. Implicit in this notion is the belief that humans do have the capacity to develop a level of self-understanding that will enable us to deal more effectively with violence and other social disfunctions.

Writing from a transformationist perspective, political scientist Louis Rene Beres, in *People, State and World Order,* emphasizes that it is necessary to balance a person's individual needs and aspirations with the needs of society as a whole. "The core of a good world order inheres originally in each individual person." Beres contends that humans are born into a world of unconsciousness with respect to understanding the evolutionary potential and prospects of the human race. He adds, though, that "we are capable of upward development of consciousness and ascent into reaches where personal growth easily harmonizes with the good of the whole."[3]

In this scenario, the role of the individual person is central. The possibility of meaningful societal change is based on the premise that enough people want to have a good quality of life for themselves and their families and to live in a world that is peaceful and life sustaining. These people would, therefore, commit themselves to working toward these goals. In short, those individuals who discover new feelings of kinship, unity, and creativity within themselves will begin to help shape social orders more hospitable to human imagination, growth, and cooperation.

The individual, then, is the key to peace building and other transformative changes. However, "no man [or woman] is an island." Through cooperative activity utilizing the principle of synergy, creative ideas, feelings, and emotions can then be shared and further developed by the interaction with others.

Looking at the history of social change in the United States as an example, virtually all major social or political changes—whether they be anti-slavery or civil-libertarian, working class rights, feminist, or anti-war—started with an individual or small group of concerned citizens. Sometimes the person with a new approach might be, in the name of I.F. Stone's newsletter of the 1960s–70s, *A Minority of One.* These concerns expanded outward, invoking more people and gaining momentum until they were gradually accepted (or co-opted) into the mainstream political process or social fabric. These ideas were not always popular, especially in the earlier years of struggle, but if individuals persevere in their perceptions of truth and justice, the ideas will ultimately be heard. It may not happen in the person's lifetime, but seeing oneself in a long tradition of peacemakers often provides the impetus to "carry-it-on."

It is encouraging to hear the views of those who see the positive aspects of human possibility. Affirmative vision sometimes gets reduced to simplistic clichés, however, and there are no ready-made blueprints for a "New Age." As poet-futurist David Spangler aptly put it, "When it comes to the evolution of a new culture there are no experts, but we can figure it out together and build as we go along. [It] is something that must be lived into beingness. It is not a product to be manufactured like a new car."[4]

The real energy crisis is within the human psyche. An abundance of human energy can be generated by working together in common cause, bringing the principle of synergy into play. This principle was employed by Buckminster Fuller in the construction of his geodesic domes. In essence it holds that the sum is greater than the total of its component parts. The concept is also applicable to efforts involving human interaction. If each member of a group puts forth his or her best efforts, the result will be greater than the mere sum of individual inputs. Also, the synergy, "shared energy," that the collective effort has produced will return more than the original investment of time, efforts, or resources to the participating individuals.

Often programs that encourage person-to-person interaction can expand knowledge of other cultures and further the cause of global goodwill. During the Cold War years, reciprocal exchanges of thousands of students, researchers, artists, and factory workers helped to break down the barriers that ideological differences had created. Other forms of citizen diplomacy also take place when people volunteer to serve in another country. Those who have participated in the Peace Corps, World Friends Service Committee, Oxfam, or similar organizations generally feel that they have provided some useful service to the host countries. Almost universally, however, these individuals acknowledge receiving even more from the experience than they have given. Those who serve in poor areas of their own countries report a similar experience.

PEACEBUILDING, NON-VIOLENCE AND PEACE EDUCATION

Peace, both within oneself and within the world, is probably the most common human desire. Peace on earth must begin within the hearts and minds of individuals. This is something that has been understood by enlightened teachers through the ages. In the 6th century B.C., Lao Tse said, "Force is not the Tao or Way for human beings to follow." Jesus of Nazareth, in his message of peace and non-violence spoke: "My peace I give unto you, a peace which passes all understanding."

The yearning for peace can also be found in the languages of many cultures. Both the Hebrew greeting *shalom* and the Arabic *salaam* embrace peace and well-being not only for oneself but for everyone. The Chinese word *ping* implies harmony, the emergence of unity out of diversity. The Russian word for peace, *mir*, also means world—suggesting the notion, perhaps, of a world at peace. Peace obviously is far more than the absence of war. The period between World War I and II, for example, were hardly years of peace, for the seeds of the next international conflict were being sown.

What we will describe as "peace" has certain positive qualities that are built through transformative processes. American peace activist A. J. Muste often said, "There is no way to peace. Peace is the way." For him, "to fight for peace" was an oxymoron. Muste believed that the key to peace within communities, nations, and, ultimately, the world is the development of peace-full individuals.[5] The Vietnamese teacher Thich Nhat Hanh provides an eastern perspective suggesting that it is not enough to talk about peace; we have to learn to be peace. A prerequisite for inner peace is the development of a harmonious balance between one's mind, body, and spirit.[6]

Indian scientist and spiritual teacher Sant Rajinder Singh describes the potential multiplier effect that truly peaceful individuals can have: "Transformed individuals can transform families, transformed families can transform communities, transformed communities can transform nations, and transformed nations will transform the world."[7]

The principle of non-violence is the primary component of peace building.

For India's Mohandas Gandhi, *ahimsa* (non-violence) was not a philosophy of passivity but was an active and principled response based on a profound respect to all life forms. He set forth *ahimsa* as the central principle to freeing India from colonial rule, and *satyagraha* (which means "grasping on to truth") as the basis for his non-violent campaigns. The means were (and are) as important as the ends to be accomplished. If the means were distorted, so would be the goal. Success was not measured in terms of just achieving immediate goals, but in terms of how those goals were obtained.[8] Gandhi once told his followers that if India could not rid itself of its debilitating caste system, and if Hindu, Moslem, and Sikh could not reconcile their differences peacefully, then India did not deserve to gain its independence. These words remain relevant today not only for the Indian subcontinent but for the world.

Dr. Martin Luther King brought the philosophy of non-violence to the Afro-American's struggle for civil rights. King emphasized: "Nonviolence is the answer to the crucial political and moral questions of time. . . . Man must evolve for all human conflict a method which rejects revenge, aggression and retaliation. The foundation of such a method is love."

Freedom and racial harmony were also part of the message espoused by the first two Africans to receive the Nobel Peace Prize, Chief Luthuli and Bishop Desmond Tutu.[9] Both men are South Africans who opposed apartheid and sought a free and racially harmonious society. The words of Bishop Tutu reinforce those uttered by Dr. King almost three decades ago, "We know that darkness can overcome evil, that light overcomes darkness, and love can overcome hatred."

Peace building and world order studies are the focus of many new courses and programs at the university level. Sometimes Peace and Global Security are linked together in the titles, because until people and nations experience a sense of security from the fear of aggressive behavior by others, there will not be any real possibility for a peaceful new world order. Professor David Barash explores some facets of this new discipline in his book *Introduction to Peace Studies.* While acknowledging there are no simple solutions to the problems of war and violence, he suggests that humankind has the potential to move toward a more cooperative, just, and sustainable world.

There is reason for hope, not just as an article of faith but based on the premise that once human beings can understand the larger situation and recognize their own best interests, they can behave rationally, creatively, and with compassion. Positive steps can be taken that will diminish humanity's reliance on organized violence to settle conflicts.[10]

Johan Galtung, one of the pioneers of Peace Studies, established the world's first Peace Research Institute in 1959 in Oslo, Norway. He is an advocate of "positive peace building" in which the basic systemic causes of war and violence are eliminated. In a condition of "positive peace," the exploitation of one person or society by another would be minimized or eliminated. There would be no overt violence nor, in a more subtle form, structural violence.[11]

Admittedly, these are difficult goals, not easily achieved. It is the ideals, however, that these scholars believe are worth pursuing, studying, and codifying. The pursuit of peace and justice in society cannot be considered utopian idealism. From a theoritical standpoint, it is up to mankind to build personal, national, and systemic frameworks for peace.

On a practical level, there are three basic approaches to teaching peace stud-

ies: reformist, reconstructionist, and transformational. Betty Riordan of Columbia University considers the transformational approach the most comprehensive. She writes:

> It espouses as its overarching goal nothing short of profound social change. This approach puts equal emphasis on behavioral and structural change but it views as the most essential development a transformation of consciousness, asserting that the fundamental causes of war, violence and oppression lie in the way we think. Only through fundamental changes in values and modes of thinking, this approach posits, can we achieve a comprehensive global peace that rejects all forms of violence and coercive authority in favor of a social order held together by communal values and consensual politics.[12]

Because we often fail to grasp the full complexity of the problems that produce war and violence, we tend to focus on the symptoms, rather than the root causes. With the goal of creating new understanding, the transformational approach emphasizes "transdisciplinary, synthesizing, extending scholarly methods and where necessary inventing new ones. The method integrates fields such as macro-history, feminist scholarship, human ecology, process theology and action research in developing its content," and encourages integrative and holistic learning by the students.

The transformational approach is basically a normative one and deals with the often neglected areas of personal and societal values. Professional associations of scholars, such as the International Political Psychology Society, are just now beginning to advance studies in this field. There are four general areas of focus: human rights, ecological wholeness, economic well-being, and non-violent social change.

In 1947, the United Nations adopted its Universal Declaration of Human Rights, championed in the United States by Eleanor Roosevelt. The Declaration spells out specific inalienable human rights. Individuals have the right to be involved in making the basic decisions that affect their lives, and the right to security for themselves and their families. There is also the inherent right to freedom of conscience, self-expression and assembly, and freedom from want and fear.

In 1988, a Declaration of Human Responsibilities was drawn up by an international conference meeting at the University for Peace. The Declaration spells out the linkages between human rights and responsibilities. The document calls for strong commitments by individuals as well as governmental authorities because the signators recognize that meaningful change begins within individuals and communities. The more advantaged have a responsibility to share their resources with others to advance these goals.[13]

The Declaration of Human Responsibilities issued a strong challenge. But to what extent are we willing in fact to take responsibility to secure the rights of others? What will be our ability to respond, individually and collectively to the urgent challenges of our era? But who will take the responsibilities to fulfill these rights? What will be our ability to respect, individually and collectively, to the urgent challenges of our era?

Peace implies a state of personal tranquility and satisfaction, but it is very hard to be calm when denied basic such needs as food, clothing, shelter, education, and medical care. To put it bluntly, a hungry person is more often than not

an angry person. New models for "third-world" development are needed, involving widespread participation by the people who are themselves most directly affected—involving grass-roots decentralized programs.

In 1993, John K. Galbraith warned, "If we don't address the needs of the have-nots, the have-nots will address the haves—there's no question about it." Globally, we have to provide a more level playing field. The problems of poverty and economic scarcity are not insoluble. Solutions do exist, invoking various redistribution strategies, development programs, family planning, etc. As we have seen, these solutions can begin with the concern and commitment of a single individual. New programs and fields of study in peacebuilding can make that beginning possible.

EXEMPLARY PEOPLE AND VOICES OF HOPE

The development of a new awareness by humankind involves the participation of individuals throughout the world. Indeed, a positive view of human potential is necessary if widespread change is to be achieved.

This perspective energizes a practical visionary like Robert Muller, who served as United Nations Undersecretary General, coordinating the thirty-two U.N. specialized agencies for three decades. Born in Alsace-Lorraine, long a focal point for German-French armed conflicts, Muller became a strong advocate of European unity. Among his colleagues at the United Nations, he was known as the "philosopher of hope." In *New Genesis: Shaping a Global Spirituality*, Muller foresaw the dawning of a global age and the development of a sense of community among all people.[14] Despite the international conflicts currently facing the United Nations, Muller sees nations slowly overcoming their divisiveness, as well as a re-formed U.N. helping humanity to realize the goal of peace. As incipient signs of an emerging worldwide consciousness, he points to global conferences on disarmament, ecology, the aged, the malnourished, AIDS, and "the year of the child." Muller had a major role in preparing the groundwork for many of these conferences. Now in his seventies, Muller is the pro bono Chancellor of the University for Peace in Costa Rica, and is committed to the notion that "everything depends upon personal commitment."

Muller is supportive of groups and programs that seek to realize the inherent potential of the United Nations, such as the series of annual international Conferences for a More Democratic U.N. (CAMDUN). These conferences have been co-sponsored by over two hundred Non-Governmental Organizations (NGOs) and have produced scores of ideas for U.N. reform. Their recommendations include the development of new conflict resolution mechanisms, especially preventative diplomacy to reduce international tensions before violence occurs.

The year 1995 will mark the fiftieth year of the United Nations. CAMDUN will put forth a detailed proposal for the creation of a new bicameral legislature for the U.N. consisting of the present general assembly (representing national governments) and a newly-created peoples assembly. The peoples assembly would have elected delegates from all the world's regions directly representing the diversity of peoples and cultures and their non-governmental organizations.[15]

There are many people internationally whose work is not widely known, but who offer practical and hopeful approaches to resolving problems of resource depletion, environmental degradation, and societal injustice. In 1980, Jakob von Uexkull, a Swedish-German writer and philatelic expert, set up The Right Livelihood Awards to honor those working on practical and exemplary solutions to the real problems facing humankind, locally and globally. The foundation recognizes activists, researchers, scientists, and social movements for their work. In its first decade, forty-four people and organizations (out of over 250 nominees from fifty countries) received these awards, presented annually in the Swedish Parliament in Stockholm on the day before the Nobel Prize presentations.[16]

In 1979, Mildred and Glen Leet, who had worked for many years as international civil servants, decided to do something worthwhile with part of their retirement pension. They started the Trickle Up Program as an "independent nonprofit organization dedicated to creating new opportunities for employment and economic and social well-being among the low income populations of the world." In the early 1980s, Trickle Up opposed the tide of "trickle down" development projects and "trickle down" economics. The "experts" scoffed at the concept that poor people in Africa, Asia, and Latin America could create small business enterprises and solve their own problems. Trickle Up provides small loans of $50 or $100 as start-up funds for self-sufficiency projects to families or small groups. For example, five women from Guatemala, who had lost their husbands during the civil violence, started up a local business raising baby chicks. A family in Nepal, which had long aspired to own a small bakery, received start-up funds to bake and market their own special rotis (breads).

The recipients of the loans are linked up with volunteer field coordinators who understand the local infrastructures and who can help with the initial paper work.

Accounts are kept on the operation, on a computer in New York. As of the end of 1992, 29,000 businesses and close to 200,000 small entrepreneurs in ninety-eight countries had taken advantage of the Trickle Up Program, and repayment of the initial loans was at over ninety percent.

Today, even the larger development agencies such as the World Bank (whose failure rate in its large development projects has been acknowledged at over eighty percent) have accepted people-oriented trickle-up development as an effective and efficient way to create purposeful change—and are seeking the organization's advice. The concept of involving people in creating their own solutions is becoming more universally accepted. World political, social, and economic thinking is gradually shifting, and the trickle-up process is used by many as an example that proves the practicality of empowering people at the grass roots level.

In Africa, Asia, and Latin America, Trickle Up is promoting cooking and water purification with solar energy. Workshops in over a dozen countries have provided an opportunity for the indigenous poor to learn how to produce, use, and market Solar Box cookers in a cost effective way. Women are usually the actual users of the technology.

In a project with women in rural Nigeria, local coordinator Christopher Ugwu wrote, "With our women's groups we are emphasizing local action for maintaining bio-diversity. . . . No environmental crusade has even the slightest chance of succeeding without women being pivotal in the execution."

Even in circumstances of natural or man-made disasters, Trickle Up works effectively with indigenous organizations. In the Philippines, victims of volcanic eruptions have been helped to rebuild their lives and restart their own businesses. Indigenous-run organizations in war-torn Sudan and Haiti are helping people to create their own income and jobs amid political upheaval.[17] With their small but effective program, John and Mildred Leet illustrate how individuals can make a difference in the movement toward global transformation.

ENVIRONMENTAL AWARENESS

Scholars and activists in many parts of the world are advocating the idea of sustainable development.[18] This notion is similar to the Native American ideal that each individual and society should assess the impact of its actions not only on one's own generation but for seven generations to come.

Conservation and environmental protection are growing trends in global politics. Many organizations—Greenpeace, the Friends of the Earth, the Sierra Club, The Nature Conservancy, and green political parties—have sprung up in many countries.[19] Since there is so much to be done, international agreements on the ozone layer and on the protection of biodiversity have been steps in the right direction. There are signs of hope as governments and citizenry alike attempt to find appropriate responses to uniquely global problems.[20] At the UNCED Conference held in Rio de Janeiro in 1992, economists, environmentalists, and the world's national leaders got together in large numbers for the first time to try to find a common language and to work together cooperatively for the rehabilitation of Mother Earth and her inhabitants.

Increased amounts of information on the condition of the world's environment, natural resources, and peoples is increasingly accessible through the publications of the Worldwatch Institute and other sources.[21] Each of us can continue to educate ourselves on how to be better stewards of our planet, learning new information, and sharing it with others.

The word "ecology" derives from the Greek word *oikos,* meaning "house."[22] Broadly defined, it refers to the relationship between living things and their environment. As a newly emerging global society we have to get our common home in order, and to do so we have to get our priorities straight.

The search for ecological "wholeness" leads to a recognition that there is an underlying unity between all life forms. Scientists such as the late David Bohm of Oxford, England, developed holographic models to help visualize the notion of an "implicate order" linking and embracing all of reality. He hypothesized that ultimately each person is connected to the totality of the life force in the universe, and believed that people will soon come to better comprehend this linkage.[23] Our new ecological and environmental understanding is teaching us that everyone and everything on the planet is linked together in an interconnected web of life. Part of the new transformative movement toward peace on the planet is this focus on environmental education, especially for the young people.

Courage is a word derived from the French *coeur,* meaning "heart." We are indebted to courageous people throughout the world, such as Russian physicist Andrei Sakharov and the American chemist Linus Pauling, who in 1963 convinced their nations' leaders of the necessity for a ban on nuclear testing in the atmosphere. Further activism on nuclear education over the years was carried out by such groups as the International Physicians for Social Responsibility, the Union of Concerned Scientists, and by individuals like Australia's Dr. Helen Caldicott. Internationally, we acknowledge the exemplary courage of people like Cesar Chavez of the United Farm Workers, the Mothers of the Missing (in Argentina and Chile), and the young people who confronted the tanks in Peking's Tienamman Square. It takes a certain fortitude to "buck the system" and make it work, as PIRG organizer and educator Ralph Nader can testify. Another person who exemplifies working with great effectiveness within the system is civil rights trial lawyer Morris Dees, co-founder of the Southern Poverty Law Center. Dees has used the legal system to successfully bring lawsuits against the Ku Klux Klan, and has made the Teaching Tolerance program available to tens of thousands of schoolchildren.

Education, in its many forms, is the most essential ingredient in the long-term quest for a peaceful world. Peace education, mediation training, and conflict resolution are necessary at all levels. The following are a number of organizations designed to further this endeavor: The Fellowship of Reconciliation, based in Nyack, New York, has pioneered conflict resolution workshops for public schools, peace activists, and the general public. On the college campus, sociologists Elise and Kenneth Boulding and activist-writer Joanna Macy are among those who have linked academic and community peace-building concerns. Professors Richard Falk and Saul Mendlovich focus on the role of international law and institutions in the ongoing search for a just, new world order. Peace conversion work was pioneered by economist Seymour

Melman. The Carter Center of Emory University provides mediation assistance in global and civil conflicts.[24] And centers like the United States Institute of Peace, based in Washington, D.C., provide a needed link between academic research, the government, and the public.

The Harvard University group headed by Dr. Roger Fisher, through its books, *Getting to Yes* and *Getting Together,* has made conflict resolution techniques, in politics, business, and daily living, accessible to millions. Fisher and his colleagues have also applied their "win-win" approach by themselves serving as mediators in various international crisis situations.[25]

Another kind of conflict is addressed by psycho-linguist Deborah Tannen in her insightful study, *You Just Don't Understand,* in which she addresses the different communication styles of men and women. In some respects, males and females have grown up in separate subcultures. In today's world, the traditional "battle of the sexes" has intensified, and better levels of communication and understanding between the genders are necessary if our species is to have domestic tranquility, let alone global community.[26]

ROLE OF RELIGION

One area that the discipline of international relations does not sufficiently address is the complex role of religion in the contemporary world. Organized religions, throughout history, have alternately been "part of the problem and part of the solution."

The Parliament of the World's Religions, held in Chicago in August, 1993, was probably the largest and most inclusive gathering of world religious and spiritual leaders, lay people, and scholars in history. Christians, Zoroastrians, Buddhists, Native Americans and other indigenous peoples, Jains, Taoists, Hindus, and practically every other tradition met for eight days and shared ideas and fellowship. They sought to identify the shared values that are at the core of all religions and to respect the diversity of human spiritual experience.

It was encouraging at the Parliament to witness Moslems and Jews getting to know each other's traditions better and listening to the other's concerns. Such interfaith dialogues will help to build the welcome breakthrough between Israel and the PLO into a just and lasting peace.

Things have come a long way since the original Parliament in 1893 in which American Indians, for example, were not even recognized as having a legitimate spiritual tradition. Still, the organized religions that have given so much to what is valued in human culture are still the source of much intolerance and discord. In many of 50 major conflicts around the globe, from Northern Ireland to the former Yugoslavia to the Indian subcontinent, ethnic and religious differences often fuel the fires of misunderstanding and hatred.

Two important aspects of the Parliament of Religions received little media coverage. The first was the active participation of the secularly-oriented Council for the 21st Century, which focused on the linkages between religion in its broader sense and the economic, social, and ecological issues confronting humanity. In a document prepared by the Council, "Global 2000 Revisited: The Critical Issues for the 21st Century," Dr. Gerald Barney challenged the religious leaders to respond creatively to the crises and new opportunities facing the planet.

Thirteen years earlier, Barney directed the Global 2000 Report upon the request of then President Jimmy Carter. At that time, he did not see the role of the religious community as important in peacebuilding. But in 1993, Barney was convinced that without active participation and cooperation of religious and spiritual groups, it would be impossible for political leaders to muster the vision and leadership to move forward successfully into the next century.

Another significant aspect of the conference was the adoption of a "Declaration of a Global Ethic" by the great majority of the religious leaders there. The document, prepared by German reformist theologian Dr. Hans Kung, provides a declaration of responsibility for the leaders to work for interfaith understanding, for just and peaceful resolution of conflicts throughout the world, and for the healing of Mother Earth.

The Global Ethic provides a touchstone of accountability, declaring that "Any form of aggression or hatred in the name of God or religion is soundly condemned." The denunciation of genocide and ethnic cleansing, for example, is directly applicable to the Bosnian tragedy. As the Da'lai Lama of Tibet put it, the declaration can provide a focal point where world religious and spiritual communities and concerned individuals everywhere can find a united voice to help prevent future Bosnias.

On the last evening of the Parliament, an African-American woman of the Ba'hai faith read the Preamble to the Global Ethic to the assemblage: "We make a commitment to respect life and dignity, individuality and diversity, so that every person is treated humanely, without exception. . . . We consider humankind our family. We commit ourselves to a culture of non-violence, mutual respect, justice and peace. Each person on earth, whether of a religious inclination or not, is invited to join in the commitment to nurturing these basic ethical values."

The Council of the Parliament plans to cooperate with other groups in fostering activities at the global, regional, and local levels. In the Chicago area, the Parliament's positive example has spurred representatives of 130 religious and other organizations to establish an organization to facilitate interfaith dialogue and community action programs. This is the kind of response that the Parliament would like to stimulate world-wide, putting the ideals expressed in the new Global Ethic into practice.

Some of the themes concerning peace making discussed at the World Parliament were further developed at the World Fellowship of Religions Conference held in Delhi, India, in February, 1994. One practical result, put in the form of a formal request to the Secretary-General of the United Nations calls, for the creation of a U.N. Center for Nonviolent Conflict Prevention and Resolution, with a full-time staff of trained personnel.

The proposal for the new U.N. center points out that "the Cold War was characterized by a cycle of fear where armaments bred insecurity and insecurity bred more armaments. We believe it is time to create a new cycle of life where trust, confidence, and non-violent preventative diplomacy" can become the new norm. The permanent center at the U.N. (and regional centers elsewhere) would utilize all available means of mediation, negotiation, conciliation, and conflict resolution techniques known to humankind. Since this center could not be most effectively created by the U.N. alone, non-governmental organizations, academic institutions, parliamentarians, business and professional communities, and media and the public at large all need to be involved. "The faith-based communities also need to be included, since so much conflict has roots in ethnic and religious misunderstanding." Offering to be of service themselves, the signatories of the proposal point out that some within the religious communities already have had experience with mediation techniques that can be utilized in conflict resolution and preventative diplomacy. The request closed: "This is the time and the opportunity to bring into action the deepest intentions for peace which are at the heart of humankind."

AMERICA'S ROLE

Virtually all the world's racial, religious, ethnic, and cultural traditions are found in the United States. In this sense, the United States is a microcosm of the world's peoples, and is an ongoing experimental workshop in the evolution of democratic theory and practice.

America today is at a crossroads. Without discernment, the American dream at times can easily fade into a nightmare, leading on the personal level to a desire for excessive wealth and power, and on the societal level to a nation with little purpose or direction.

At its best, though, the American dream could be more accurately described as a vision. Unlike an ordinary dream, a vision connotes a deeper level of truth. This vision is of a society that allows each person—regardless of race, religion, creed or class—the opportunity to fulfill his or her unique aspirations. It is of a land where people care for and help one another, where children can grow up safely and realize their full potential as human beings. This view of America is one in which each person has the inalienable right to live without fear or want. To paraphrase Mahatma Gandhi, the world has enough to meet each person's need, but not enough to meet anyone's greed. The same principle applies to the United States.[27]

The U.S. plays a pre-eminent political, economic, and military role in the world. As a nation that proclaims high principles, the United States is often judged critically when it fails to live up to its own ideals or others' expectations. We are challenged to develop more fully the humility and compassion that are evidences of a mature people.

There are a number of qualities that might promote and enhance positive social change.

1) Develop a life pattern based more on voluntary simplicity so that America uses its resources more wisely and is less of a drain on the rest of the world. This would improve the quality of our individual lives, create fewer antagonisms, and lessen the divisions between haves and have-nots at home and abroad.

2) Learn to work together in human-scaled groups to hone the skills of participatory democracy. Get involved in organizations that emphasize ethical standards, cooperation and inclusiveness, those which will help lay the groundwork for a more egalitarian, non-sexist and non-racist society.

3) Recognize the importance of life-affirming practices to help save and restore the environment, from urban centers to the wilderness.

4) Be willing to help others and promote human dignity.

5) Be open, appreciative of life, and remember to maintain a sense of humor. Become centered, more fully integrated human beings with a greater sense of purpose.

6) Recognize that education is a lifelong process. Listen with empathy, learn about other cultural traditions, and realize that there is something to be learned from everyone and from every situation in which we find ourselves.

7) When discouraged, remember the words of anthropologist Margaret Mead: "Never doubt that a small group of thoughtful committed citizens can change the world. Indeed it is the only thing that ever has."

Those who will lay the groundwork for positive change at home and abroad include educators who encourage in their students the spark of honest inquiry, students who are responsive and exercise their own creative capacities; public servants who practice the art of politics with integrity; those in the healing arts who take a holistic and people-oriented approach toward their profession; and creative writers and musicians who help sensitize us to the human condition and awaken our shared humanity. Each person's input is significant in that oft-elusive pursuit of finding our common ground.

WHERE DO WE GO FROM HERE?

In 1776 Thomas Paine wrote that "we have the power to begin the world again." But what we are talking about today, more than 200 years after the American Revolution, is something far more complex than gaining political independence.

It is a struggle that cannot be won with bullets and barricades, neither in America nor elsewhere in the world. It involves a different kind of revolution— the working through of a process, and not just a final climactic political act. Revolution in the full sense, literally a complete turning around, appears necessary if we are not only to survive but to become more humane in the process.

What is most needed is an opening of the heart, a deepening of insights, and a willingness to listen with empathy to others. Such a "turning" by a substantial portion of the population would be truly revolutionary.

Sant Darshan Singh of India insightfully writes that the greatest revolutionary change can only be brought about by a change of attitude within the human heart: "We are witnessing the dawn of a spiritual revolution. By definition, such a revolution, unlike political, social or economic ones, cannot be enforced from without. It is an inner revolution which centers on a change of consciousness. We cannot convert others, we can only convert ourselves."[28]

Thoughtful people from many backgrounds and disciplines have suggested ways to attain a more peaceful world. Unfortunately, articulation of our goals and even of the methods to attain them are not enough to bring about substantive change. What is required additionally is a re-visioning of our values and developing a clearer understanding that we are all linked together as members of the human family. In short, what we need additionally, individually and collectively, is a change of perspective.

Just as the breakthroughs in the discoveries of quantum physics brought about a paradigm shift in understanding the physical world so a paradigm shift may well be necessary in the social sciences for us to better understand the human psyche and social evolution in our complex times. A greatly accelerated understanding of our physical universe also necessitates a parallel growth in the metaphysical (philosophical) realm. Just as scientific inquiry has led to exciting discoveries both in subatomic matter and in outer space, humanity is now recognizing the need to probe more deeply into the far reaches of the frontiers of inner space.[29]

Global change will begin with personal transformation that will help us to become more integrated human beings. But the transformation of individuals is itself predicated on a fundamental shift in that which we value in our lives. What we seek in our search for personal happiness needs to be expanded to include the well-fare of all.

This transformation of the human spirit has been experienced and spoken of in the esoteric teachings of virtually all the world's religious and spiritual traditions. The process by which a person "taps within," recognizes and develops spiritually oriented values, and then puts these values into action within families, communities, nations, and, transnationally, can contribute to the development of an enriched political democracy in which the human spirit will prevail.[30]

The great majority of countries today say they wish to implement political democracy. But without a reawakening of the human spirit that we can experience for ourselves, acknowledging that our lives and fate are inextricably linked together, there can be no true political democracy. Nor will there be the impetus and motivation to create truly participatory systems that respect cultural differences and promote societal equity.

As we approach the year 2000 A.D., questions are often raised about the future of humankind. In what basic direction is our world heading? What might our lives be like in the years to come? Can we continue to keep "muddling along," pursuing business as usual?

Among the responses to these fundamental questions two increasingly polarized points of view have emerged. In broad terms, one viewpoint holds that great ecological disasters and social chaos lie ahead; the other contends that transformative responses are emerging to meet the challenges of our era and that somehow humankind can learn to resolve its differences and live sensibly.

Both positions can muster "evidence" to support their views. Those with a more optimistic vision adhere to the belief that the forces of life will yet prevail, that over the next several decades, humanity will become increasingly aware of, and will act on the necessity to lay the groundwork for, a peaceful planetary order. This perspective is less visible to the general public and receives less media attention. It draws ultimately on the innate human capacity to care for and cooperate with one another and is evidenced by the goodwill that many people extend daily.

Should we become discouraged at times, our spirits are renewed when we witness an unexpected handshake between Yasser Arafat and Yitzak Rabin on the front lawn of the White House, bringing new hope to the Middle East, or the Mandela-deKlerk accords ending the scourge of apartheid in South Africa. And there are the countless daily acts of random kindness by people everywhere who choose to lend a helping hand, or share the warmth of a smile with friend or stranger.

A growing number of people in all parts of the world are developing a "one-humanity" consciousness and sharing what they have learned with others. The practice of "thinking globally, acting locally," is beginning to take root. This involves working within one's own community and simultaneously being aware of the planetary implications of one's actions.

Sanity and human dignity can yet prevail.

NOTES

1. Edward O. Wilson, *On Human Nature* (Harvard University Press: Cambridge, 1978). Also see a succinct discussion on "Violence and Human Nature" in Howard Zinn, *Declarations of Independence: Cross-Examining American Ideology.* (Harper-Collins: San Francisco, 1990) 32–47.

2. One definition given to the word "transform" in *Webster's Dictionary of the English Language* (1987) is "to change the character or nature of radically."

   Transformational change in our time needs to be radical in the etymological sense of getting to the roots (or the heart) of a situation, but not in the way that the word is often used to describe political radicalism.

3. Louis Beres, *People, States and World Order* (S. E. Peacock: Itasca, IL, 1981) 139–140. Also see Richard Falk, *Explorations on the Edge of Time: The Prospects for the World Order,* Philadelphia PA.: Temple University Press, 1992.

4. David Spangler, "On the New Humanity," a transcribed talk at the Omega Institute's 1979 summer conference held at Bennington College, Vermont.

   See in David Barash, *Introduction to Peace Studies* (Wadsworth: Belmont, CA, 1991), the sections on Eastern and Judeo-Christian Concepts, 6–7, and Ethical and Religious Perspectives, 439–457.

5. See the chapter on A. J. Muste in Charles DeBenedetti (Ed.), *Peace Heroes In Twentieth Century America* (Indiana University Press: Bloomington, 1986) 149–167.

6. Thich Nhat Hanh is a Buddhist teacher who advocated a "middle-way" approach to resolving the Vietnam Conflict. Harassed by both sides, he escaped to France where he founded the Plum Village community. He has led the resettlement movement for refugee Vietnamese boat people in the United States and France, and has brought together groups of former American servicemen and Vietnamese citizens in order to bring about healing and reconciliation. Among his most recent books is *Peace Is Every Step: The Path of Mindfulness in Everyday Life* (Bantam Books: New York City, 1991).

7. Quoted from Rajinder Singh's "Peace Begins Within You: A Message to the 1993 Parliament of the World's Religions" held in Chicago in August–September.

8. M. K. Gandhi, *Non-Violent Resistance* (Schocken Books: New York, 1951). For a book of interviews with a dozen remarkable people, Western and Eastern, whose life philosophies and work have been influenced by Gandhi, see Catherine Ingram, *In The Footsteps of Gandhi: Conversations With Spiritual Social Activists* (Parallax Press: New York, 1990).

9. An insightful portrait of the life and work of Desmond Tutu is included in Leonard S. Kenworthy, *Twelve Trailblazers of World Community,* Kenneth Square, PA.: The Friendly Press, 1988. pp. 210–231.

10. David Barash, op. cit. 4.

11. See e.g., Johan Galtung, *The True Worlds: A Transnational Perspective.* (Free Press: New York, 1980).

12. Betty Riordan, "Pedagological Approaches to Peace Studies," in Daniel Thomas and Michael Klare (Eds), *Peace and World Order Studies (5th edition)* (Westview Press: Boulder, CO, 1989).

13. Arthur Stein and Eileen Borris, "Towards a More Peaceful Planet," *Peacehaven*

Winter, 1990, 18–21. See also Abelardo Brenes-Castro (ed.), *Seeking the True Meaning of Peace,* San Jose, Costa Rica: University for Peace Press, 1991.

14. Robert Muller, *New Genesis: Shaping A Global Spirituality* (Doubleday: New York, 1982). His most recent book is *The Birth of a Global Civilization* (World Happiness and Cooperation: Anacorter, WA, 1991).

15. The CCCUN Newsletter, published by the Communications Coordinating Committee of the United Nations, provides a comprehensive source of information about CAMDUN and other areas of work being done by the several hundred NGOs functioning to assist the work of the United Nations. Also see the *United Nations Observer.*

16. Paul Ekins, *A New World Order: Grassroots Movements for Global Change* (Routledge: London, 1992). Right Livelihood Awards were given, for example, for converting the Kenyan ecological debate into mass action for reforestation (1984), for organizing to protect rights of the Indians in the Amazon Basin (1986), and for reversing economic decline in rural areas of Finland (1992).

17. See *Trickle Up Program: The Second Decade* (Trickle Up Program Inc.: New York, September 1, 1993).

18. See Jeremy Seabrook, *Pioneers of Change* (New Society: Philadelphia, 1993).

19. John Rensenbrink, *The Greens and the Politics of Transformation* (R. & E. Miles: San Pedro, CA, 1992). Magazines containing articles with transformative perspectives include: *The Futurist, Peacework, Transpersonal Perspective, Re-Vision, Utne Reader, Common Cause,* and *Fellowship in Prayer.*

20. As a follow-up three years after the publication of *Our Common Future,* the report of the World Commission on Environment headed by Norway's Gro Harlem Brundtland, the Center for Our Common Future published Linda Starke, *Signs of Hope: Working Towards Our Common Future* (Oxford University Press: New York, 1990).

21. Beginning in 1984, under the leadership of Lester Brown, the Worldwatch Institute has published annually the *State of the World.* The 1993 edition was published in twenty-seven languages worldwide. For the first time, teachers and students, government officials and environmentalists, and others from many parts of the globe at the same time can be reading and discussing the same planetary issues, and can have access to comprehensible statistics from a variety of sources. Worldwatch also facilitated the ten-part television series "Race to Save the Planet."

22. To enhance our understanding, such books are available as Thomas Berry, *Dream of the Earth* (Sierra Club Books: San Francisco, 1990) and David Ehrenfeld, *Beginning Again: People and Nature in the New Millennenium* (Oxford University Press: New York, 1993).

23. David Bohm, *Wholeness and the Implicate Order* (Kegan Paul: Boston, 1980).

24. Former President Jimmy Carter remains active in his role of senior statesman. His civic concerns and energies are seen is his hands-on work with Habitat for Humanity and in such books as *Talking Peace: A Vision for the Next Generation* (Dutton Children's Books: New York, 1993).

25. Roger Fisher and Scott Brown, *Getting Together: Building a Relationship That Gets To Yes* (Houghton Mifflin Co.: Boston, 1988).

26. Deborah Tannen, *You Just Don't Understand* (William Morrow: New York, 1990).

27. See Arthur Stein, *Seeds of the Seventies: Values, Work and Commitment in Post-Vietnam America* (University of New England Press: Hanover, NH, 1985).

28. Darshan Singh, *Spiritual Awakening* (S. K. Publications: Bowling Green, VA, 1982) p. 7.

29. For a dialogue exploring the frontiers of science, society, and spirituality, see

Fritjof Capra and David Stendl-Rast, *Belonging to the Universe* (Harper: San Francisco, 1991).

30. Arthur Stein and Daniel Campbell, "Personal Transformation, Spiritual Democracy and Global Change," in *General Systems Approaches to Alternative Economics and Values*. Proceedings of the 36th Annual Conference of the International Society for the Systems Sciences (1992), vol. 2, 818–828.

QUESTIONS

1. According to the author, what role can the individual play in the peace-building process?

2. Compare and contrast Stein's conception of human nature with those of Sigmund Freud and Thomas Hobbes.

PEACE STUDIES PERSPECTIVE OF SEPTEMBER 11

44.   A Nonviolent Approach to the Intifada

Raed Abusahlia

This excerpt is an excellent example of the application of the philosophy and principles promoted by peace studies. The author, a Palestinian priest and Chancellor of the Latin Patriarchate of Jerusalem, wrote this article in an attempt to convince Palestinians to adopt a strategy of nonviolence in their struggle to achieve statehood for Palestine.

The myth says that a giant sent a letter threatening another competing giant in a neighboring land. When the latter received the message, he tore it up, cursed the sender, and rushed for revenge, the ground shaking under his feet. When the sender heard those footsteps, he was scared to death. His wife cooled him down and advised him to lie down in bed and hide. She would handle the matter using brain rather than muscle. She then covered him with a blanket, leaving out his huge feet. When the furious, roaring giant approached, she expressed her regret at the absence of her husband and begged the giant not to raise his voice so that her "son" would not wake up. When the giant looked and saw the

From *Fellowship,* 68, 1–2, 1/2.

protruding feet, he said to himself, "If this is the son, what must the father look like!" Frightened, he ran away.

I have not narrated this story at the outset with the intention of foiling the extraordinary efforts being exerted in resisting the occupation—although it is true that we are fighting a giant boasting of his strength. I have narrated it so as to put forward a new idea: that success is not based on the strength of muscles but on the strength of the brain and the strength of truth derived from rightfulness and UN resolutions. I will call this alternative approach "nonviolence." Nonviolence attempts to seek civil, nonviolent defensive means that enable the people to organize real resistance for averting any aggression instead of doubling condemnations that, experience has taught us, are useless and ineffective.

I call upon my Palestinian brothers and sisters to adopt the nonviolence strategy. It is based on the following clear principle: The Palestinian people, possessing the force of truth and UN resolutions, is stronger with stones than with arms, and still stronger with olive branches than with stones. Consequently it is essential to summon historical courage, lay down arms and stones, and raise again the olive branch that President Arafat raised in his famous speech in the United Nations in 1974 when he said, "I have come here carrying an olive branch in one hand and a gun in the other. Do not let the olive branch fall from my hand." Yes, the olive branch alone will be victorious!

I am very much convinced, for the following valid reasons, that this period necessitates choosing the olive branch strategy.

1. We adopted all violent means of resistance before the creation of Israel, during its creation, and after it, and until the present day. We have proved our courage and recorded a history of heroic acts. Unfortunately, we have lost all our battles. And the world has called us terrorists because we did not know how to convince it, in a civilized way, that we have rights to be acknowledged, that we are not the oppressors but the oppressed, and that we are not the executioner but the victim.

2. The world, despite a growing awareness, knowledge, and recognition of our rights, still does not support us enough. This is due to Israeli propaganda that distorts the image of the Arabs in the mass media, and due to the world's sensitivity to any violent act we commit. The exaggerated violence practiced by Israel is condoned and acceptable, but resistance on our side is always rejected, condemned, and labeled as terror. We must use a new language that is understood by the whole world: the language of nonviolence. Think of the original force of the daily pictures carried by the press of children throwing stones at soldiers, and soldiers shooting at them. Now even pictures of shelling and detonations have become normal, while simple people daily pay a heavy price in terms of their lives and nerves.

3. The cycle of resistance and violence, and the corresponding exaggerated violence on the Israeli side, is a continuing and escalating vicious circle that cannot be stopped. It must be broken. The stubborn enemy does not understand that the sacrifices of a whole people for its freedom and independence are not terrorist acts. And the enemy will not give in because of its pride: it considers itself a superpower that cannot be defeated by children's stones. So there must be an outlet from this stalemate. The purpose is not to spare the enemy from embarrassment,

but to embarrass it with new techniques. We must not give it the justifications or pretexts to respond violently, since it cares about its image before the world. By proceeding this way, we will drive away occupation and preserve our dignity, as well.

4. The strongest and most important reason for a strategic turn to nonviolence is that the energy inherent in the crowds of people must be expressed somehow. Without employment it will procure more violence and escalation, and will thus become explosive and outrageous and difficult to be controlled. And its results cannot be predicted, because it is built on spontaneous individual or group emotions.

5. Finally, all sectors of society are affected by, suffer from, and participate in the Intifada activities. The participation of the vast majority is passive because it suffers silently and grumbles. But through the new peaceful way, everybody could be mobilized to participate actively in the efforts undertaken. The neighboring Arab and Islamic countries might be affected as well. I am positive that many foreigners and friends all over the world, even Israelis from peace movements who sympathize with our just cause, will be mobilized and will come to our rescue and will dare to actively participate in our activities without being labeled as terrorists.

I call upon the political, religious, and popular leadership to study this idea and develop it as soon as possible. It will be advisable to consult local and international specialists in this field, especially academics who have conducted relevant researches.

I end with a verse from the Bible: "Love your enemies and pray for those who hate you." For loving our enemies does not mean submission and weakness or relinquishment of our rights, but rather claiming those rights with the force of love.

I know very well that these strategic ideas require knowledge and understanding, education and preparation, time and leadership. But I also know that it is good to start now before it is too late and before more blood is shed.

QUESTIONS

1. According to the author, how can nonviolent protest achieve a just political resolution to the conflict between Palestinians and Israelis?

2. The author offers five reasons why nonviolence is a more effective approach for achieving Palestinian statehood. Which ones are most compelling and why?

CREDITS

Abusahlia, Raed, *A Nonviolent Approach to the Intifada.* From *Fellowship,* 68, 1-2, 1/2.

Allison, Graham T., *Essence of Decision.* Reprinted by permission of the author.

Aristotle, *The Politics.* From *The Complete Works of Aristotle.* Reprinted by permission of Princeton University Press.

Barber, Benjamin R. *Beyond Jihad vs. McWorld.* Reprinted by permission of The University of Maryland.

Bull, Hedley, *The Anarchical Society.* From *The Anarchical Society,* pp. 23-27, 38-52, © 1977. Reprinted with permission of Columbia University Press.

Chomsky, Noam, *The New War Against Terror.* Reprinted by permission of the author.

Crews, Robin J., *A Values-Based Approach to Peace Studies.* © 1989 Westview Press.

Freud, Sigmond, *Why War?*

Fukuyama, Francis, *The End of History?* Reprinted by permission of the publisher.

Fukuyama, Francis, *The west has won: Radical Islam can't beat democracy and capitalism. We're still at the end of history.* Reprinted by permission of the author.

Gandhi, Mohandas K., *Nonviolence: The Greatest Force.*

Gilpin, Robert, *War and Change in World Politics.* From *War and Change in World Politics* pp. 1-15, 39-44. Reprinted with permission of Cambridge University Press.

Grotius, Hugo, *On the Law of War and Peace.*

Halliday, Fred, *A Singular Collapse: The Soviet Union, Market Pressure, and Inter-State Competition.* Reprinted by permission of the publisher from *Contention,* Vol. I, No. 2, pp. 121-139, Fall 1991.

Hermann, Margaret, *Explaining Foreign Policy Behavior Using the Personal Characteristics of Political Leaders. International Studies Quarterly.*

Hobbes, Thomas, *Leviathan.* Reprinted by permission of Cambridge University Press.

Huntington, Samuel, *The Clash of Civilizations.* From *Foreign Affairs,* 72, 3, Summer 1993.

Jervis, Robert, *Perception and Misperception in International Politics.* © 1976, © renewed 2004 by Princeton University Press. Reprinted by permission of the publisher.

Kennan, George, *The Sources of Soviet Conduct.* From *Foreign Affairs Review,* pp. 566-582, Index Volume 25, Nos. 1-4, 1946.

Keohane, Robert O., *Beyond Dichotomy: Conversations Between International Relations and Feminist Theory.* From *International Studies Quarterly* (1998), Vol. 42(1) pp. 194-199. Reprinted by permission of Blackwell Publishers.

Keohane, Robert O., *Cooperation and International Regimes.* © 1984 by Princeton University Press. Reprinted by permission of the publisher.

Keohane, Robert O., *The Globalization of Informal Violence, Theories of World Politics, and "The Liberalism of Fear."* Reprinted by permission of the author.

Khattak, Saba Gul, *The U.S. Bombing of Afghanistan: A Women-Centered Perspective.* From the Social Science Research Council, New York, NY.

Kissinger, Henry, *Foreign Policy in the Age of Terrorism.* From the Center for Policy Studies, Lecture at Rattenberg, October 31, 2001.

Lapid, Yosef. *The Third Debate: On the Prospects of International Theory in a Post-Positivist Era.* From *International Studies Quarterly* (1989), 33, 235-251.

Lasswell, Harold D., *World Politics and Personal Insecurity.* Reprinted with the permission of The Free Press, a division of Simon & Schuster Adult Publishing Group, from *World Politics and Personal Insecurity* by Harold